Greenhill Books

1812
THE MARCH ON MOSCOW

'It's for posterity to judge whether I made a mistake in going to Moscow.'

Napoleon, at St Helena

'When I read history, which is a subject for everyone, I've made a habit of taking into account who the writer is. When they are soldiers, one looks to matters concerning their profession and, more especially, to descriptions of actions in which they have themselves taken part.'

Montaigne: *Essaies*

'Reading modern history is generally the most tormenting employment a man can have: one is plagued with the actions of a detestable set of men called conquerors, heroes, and great generals, and we wade through pages loaded with military detail...'

Arthur Young (1741-1820)

'I always prefer an eye-witness to a line of reasoning.'

Baron Fain: *Mémoires*

1812
THE MARCH ON MOSCOW

PAUL BRITTEN AUSTIN
Foreword by David G. Chandler

GREENHILL BOOKS, LONDON
STACKPOLE BOOKS, PENNYSYLVANIA

This edition of *1812: The March on Moscow*
first published 1993 by
Greenhill Books, Lionel Leventhal Limited, Park House,
1 Russell Gardens, London NW11 9NN
and
Stackpole Books, 5067 Ritter Road,
Mechanicsburg, PA 17055, USA.

British Library Cataloguing in Publication Data
Austin, Paul Britten
1812: March on Moscow
I. Title
940.27
ISBN 1-85367-154-1

Designed and edited by DAG Publications Ltd.
Designed by David Gibbons; edited by Michael Boxall.
Printed and bound in Great Britain by Biddles Limited,
Guildford and King's Lynn.

Note:
First references to the eyewitnesses
whose accounts make up this 'documentary'
of Napoleon's invasion of Russia appear in
italic.

CONTENTS

To my son THOM
and my grandson BENNY
without whose patient encouragement
and computer expertise this work
would never have been possible.

FOREWORD

BY DAVID G. CHANDLER,

M.A. (OXON.), D.LITT., F.R.HIST.S., F.R.G.S
HEAD, DEPARTMENT OF WAR STUDIES, R.M.A. SANDHURST

Of all the many campaigns of war throughout History from the onset of the age of gunpowder down to the opening of the 20th century, Napoleon's invasion of Tsarist Russia in 1812 is probably the best known throughout the world – and for good reason. In terms of scale, both of man-power engaged and of geographical extent, the only applicable word is epic. Well over half a million of Napoleon's soldiers were involved, and eventually almost as many warriors of Alexander I. From Berlin to Moscow is one thousand miles, and for the French and their allies seven hundred of these, once the River Niemen had been crossed, were through hostile and mainly barren expanses of forest and plains. For Napoleon the Niemen was to prove his Rubicon: fateful and irreversible results were to follow – leading to his twin downfalls – first in April 1814, then (after the episode of exile in Elba) the ultimate cataclysm of Waterloo in 1815. The scale of operations in 1812 almost beggar belief, and the casualties – military and civilian, French invaders and Russian defenders – cause a shudder even today, despite the horrendously greater losses of two successive World Wars in the 20th century. But it must be remembered that populations were far smaller in 1812 than in either 1914 or 1939 – so proportionately there is less differentiation than at first appears to be the case.

The famous Prussian soldier-philosopher-historian, Carl von Clausewitz, once called warfare 'a passionate drama'. So it is to be sure – and one major attribute of this new treatment of an old subject by Paul Britten Austin is his use of the words, recollections and, occasionally incorrect, memories – for the passage of time can play the strangest tricks with human memory, as every historian who has ever attempted to debrief or question old soldiers will be only too well aware – of one hundred and more survivors who participated in the dramatic events of one hundred and eighty-one years ago in eastern Europe. The bare historical events have been recounted time and again – there have been four notable treatments in the last five years alone – but there has never been one quite like this before or on such a scale.

For it is the story of 1812 as seen by eye-witnesses – French, Russian, Ukrainian, Germans of many kinds and Italians prominent amongst them – of many ranks and military as well as civilian avocations – that forms the main focus of this new treatment; in other words, the human angle. War, when all is said and done, is about human beings under the combined stresses in multi-variant proportions of discomfort, hunger, homesickness, boredom and danger, with occasional brief minutes of sheer elation or absolute terror thrown in to add a little 'spice' as it were.

To borrow a proposition from Euclid, the Ancient Alexandrian geometrician, 'a whole is the sum of all of its parts'. On both sides, over a million armed men – including some women fighting in Davydov's irregular partisan bands – and perhaps three more million civilians, became directly involved in one way or another in Napoleon's invasion of Russia and the subsequent cataclysm that overwhelmed his army. Over 650,000 Frenchmen and their allies entered Russia (to include reserves); only an estimated 110,000 lived to pass back over the River Niemen (to include the forces on the flanks and retiring ahead of the main army group) – and probably as many as 75% of the survivors were suffering from starvation, frost-bite, wounds and illnesses from which they soon died or remained crippled by for the rest of their lives. The armies and inhabitants of Holy Russia certainly fared even worse, although they had the solace of ultimate victory over a foreign enemy led by one of the two greatest military geniuses of all History. More we shall never know.

Of the active and literate participants, Paul Britten Austin has woven together the stories of 100 human beings – or one ten thousandth part of the men who shared in this campaign, a mere 0.1%, a tenth of a tenth of a tenth part. He has needed all of 400 pages to bring us from the unopposed crossing of the River Niemen on 21 June with barely a foe in sight to the French occupation of a deserted Moscow just 85 days later. Martial events both great and small crowd his canvas – ranging from huge set-piece battles such as Borodino or Smolensk to tiny skirmishes and outpost actions that never received a name. But what lay beyond Moscow? We know the bare historical facts, to be sure: Napoleon's lingering for a month in Moscow hoping for peace-overtures from Tsar Alexander which never came: the start of the long retreat in fine autumnal weather; the unnecessary check at Malojaroslavetz; the fatally redesignated line of retreat past Borodino to Smolensk as the weather changed for the worst; battles of all shapes and sizes with the harrying and pursuing Russians under command of Kutusov at such places as Krasnoe and Orsha; the huge drama of the crossing of the River Beresina under close enemy fire; the fate of the straggling thousands; the breakdown of formation cohesion and individual discipline as the survivors – deserted by their Emperor from 5 December as he headed back for Paris to quell rumours of his supposed death, to crush conspiracies, and above all to start building a new army ready to meet the advancing Allied hordes of the Sixth Coalition – limped back through rapidly deteriorating weather conditions, the temperature plummeting to minus 30 degrees on some occasions and the casualty figures from exposure to the elements rather than the foe soaring; and then, the very last man of all to leave the soil of Holy Mother Russia – the totally unrecognizable Marshal Ney, already dubbed the 'bravest of the brave' by his master – on his rag-wrapped feet, unshaven and unwashed after ten days of desperate actions in command of the rearguard, a private-soldier's musket carried in the crook of his left arm: all this has still to come in an eagerly-awaited second volume.

Here is all the drama of Ancient Greek tragedy within the bounds of a single campaign. Great aspirations, fatal miscalculations, heroic and intrepid contenders, immense but ultimately flawed achievements, and, towards the end, the 'twilight of the gods' leading inexorably on to the nemesis of cataclysmic failure: and, last but not least, the founding of a new legend to beguile, fascinate and horrify successive generations of mankind. It all represents a new Heroic Age with a vengeance.

Little wonder that the great novelist Tolstoi made this story the second half of the greatest historical novel of all time – *War and Peace*. Nor that this great book has fascinated successive generations of film-makers. Many will remember Aubrey Hepburn and Henry Fonda starring in the American *Paramount Films* version (1966), with Herbert Lom as Napoleon, to be followed – and indeed surpassed – by Sergei Bondarchuk's definitive seven-and-a-half hour masterpiece, *Voina I Mir*, made between 1963 and 1967, employing over 20,000 Soviet soldiers as battle-extras. Then there came BBC Television's first great colour multipart epic in 20 episodes (1972) by David Conroy and John Davis working to Jack Pulman's scripts (which used a cast of famous British actors headed by Morag Hood, Tony (now Sir Anthony) Hopkins and Alan Dobie in the key roles, not to forget the services of 2,500 Yugoslav territorial soldiers for the great battle-scene shot in two main locations near the Danube and the city of Novi Sad (the ancient Peterwardein). And now, most recently of all, Cromwell Production's one hour home-video, *The Road to Moscow* (1992), in the *Campaigns in History* series. The writer of this introduction has had the great good fortune to be actively involved as a military adviser for both the last two projects.

So much for the media treatments; far more significantly, many notable military historians have produced some memorable works of scholarship on the 1812 Campaign. One thinks of General Jackson's *Seven Roads to Moscow* (1958), Antony Brett-James's anthology, *1812: Eyewitness Accounts of Napoleon's Defeat in Russia* (1966), Alan Palmer's *With Napoleon in Russia* (1967), C. Vossler's *With Napoleon in Russia* (1969), Christopher Duffy's *Borodino: Napoleon against Russia* (1972), Curtis Cate's *The War of the Two Emperors* (1985), John Nicholson's *Napoleon, 1812* (1986), George Nafziger's *Napoleon's Invasion of Russia* (1988), and Richard Riehn's *1812: Napoleon's Russian Campaign* (1990) – and even my own small in-house offering for British Army officers studying for the Junior Command and Staff Course (Part Four, Correspondence Course), *Napoleon's Campaign in Russia 1812* (1986) (which unexpectedly led directly to the inauguration of the *Osprey Campaign Series*) – is to mention but nine since 1958. Thus there has been no lack of recent treatments of this theme.

One day in 1973 a concept took root in the publisher Lionel Leventhal's office to create a wholly different on-the-ground account of 1812. Then, in 1979, (the original) Arms and Armour Press republished the *Memoirs of Sergeant Bougogne*, mainly covering the terrible retreat. The present volume has taken almost 20 years to reach fruition, and a second is already on the way, a project which has taken up perhaps a quarter of its author's productive life. In style it comes nearest to Antony Brett-James's

1966 offering. But whereas Brett-James was a professional linguist and military historian of the 'Sandhurst school', Paul Britten Austin is first and foremost a writer on cultural subjects and a professional translator, whose hitherto most celebrated work is his study of the extraordinary 18th-century Swedish poet *Carl Michael Bellman*, and his congenial translations, so much admired by W. H. Auden, of Bellman's immortal songs. Among other books he has also written *The Organ-Maker's Wife*, a dramatic novel of Reformation days, it too a unique verbal – albeit fictional – reconstruction of a past age. The author calls the present work 'a word-film shot by over 100 of the survivors'. Very few indeed have been translated into English before, and he interweaves their accounts to constitute an unforgettable historical tapestry. Incidentally, always abstaining from comment or innuendo, it is also a probing study of the perils of omnipotence, or anyway of Napoleon's near absolute power. There are indeed many levels in this remarkable *jeu d'esprit*, which is also a *tour de force*.

Not that Paul Britten Austin is a stranger to military history. He is the son of F. Britten Austin, the celebrated historical short-story writer of the 1930s, who also wrote those two fascinating historical novels that Wavell recommended as essential reading for all aspiring military men: *The Road to Glory* (1936), treating of the young Bonaparte's First Italian Campaign, and *Forty Centuries Look Down*, which deals with Napoleon in Egypt. They were to have been the first two volumes in a series devoted to Napoleon's complete career; but alas death intervened and only two were ever written. Indeed even they might never have seen the light of day but for Paul, aged 10. One day, walking with his father to visit the Invalides ("as a boy I was dotty about Napoleon") he piped up and asked the great man why he didn't write Napoleon's life as a novel. We can be grateful for those two remarkable books in the 1930s, but also for this new and very different project seeing the light of day over 60 years later.

It is indeed a vast project – but one which has been brilliantly brought off. In sum, to cite what the French historian Octave Aubrey wrote of Napoleon himself, which to my mind is equally apt as a description of this scholarly yet vibrantly alive enterprise: As the historian Hudson wrote of Napoleon himself: 'This is his distinction, and if necessary, his excuse. When an achievement lasts so long and bears such fruit, it produces its own justification.'

1812: The March on Moscow, provides brilliant insight into men at war. The book is almost as epic as the campaign.

David G. Chandler
Hindford and RMA Sandhurst

PREFACE

Of the third of a million men with whom Napoleon, on Midsummer Day 1812, invaded Russia, few ever got back. The ghastly story of the retreat has been often told; the story of the advance less frequently. Yet it's no less dramatic – in some ways more so.

This book is a word-film, shot by more than 100 of the survivors. My 'cameramen' came from almost every country in Europe – Frenchmen, Dutchmen, Germans, Swiss, Italians... Most reliable of course are the diaries. Lejeune says that his was

'smaller than my hand, and I carried it against my heart. It's all torn, all soaked by storms and sweat caused by Russia's extreme heats...'

The always critical Labaume – whose account was the first to appear in print only two years later, while Napoleon was temporarily away on Elba[1] – says that his, too, was based on just such a diary:

'Reduced, like all my companions in arms, to struggling for the ultimate needs, pierced with cold, tormented by hunger, prey to all kinds of sufferings, unsure at each rising of the sun whether I'd see its last rays that evening, doubting in the evening whether I'd see a new day, all my feelings focused in this one desire: to live to preserve the memory of what I was seeing. Every night, seated in front of a wretched campfire in a temperature of 20-25 degrees below freezing,[2] surrounded by dead and dying, I'd retrace the day's events. The same knife I used for cutting up horsemeat was used for sharpening crows' feathers. A pinch of gunpowder diluted in the hollow of my hand with melted snow served me for ink, and a cannon for a writing desk! It was by the light of Moscow in flames I've described the sack of that city. It was on the banks of the Berezina I've traced my account of that fatal crossing...'

Glory-seeking Césare de Laugier, too, scribbled his down 'with a piece of charcoal by the light of some house or village in flames, on certain days below 28 degrees of frost'. Even Sergeant Bourgogne's immortal classic, written to exorcize terrible memories, may have been based on a diary. So certainly are the memoirs of Caulaincourt, Napoleon's loyal but always critical Boswell:

'My notes were made everywhere, at my desk and in camp every day and at all times of day; they are the work of every moment, I have touched up nothing, because although there were moments when the man showed himself, it was the demigod one mostly recognized. More than once the thought occurred to me that this journal, written under the Emperor's very eyes, might fall into his hands; but that reflection didn't check my pen. No doubt truth chilled his goodwill,

11

but his strong and lofty character raised him above all criticism made in good faith.'

How many hundreds, perhaps thousands, of other diaries perished with their writers? For a generation afterwards Europe echoed with the reminiscences of old soldiers recounting their tales in every language. Little Coignet, the smallest grenadier in the Imperial Guard, wrote his down at the age of 70 in intervals of playing endless games of manille and piquet in a cafe at Auxerre; and when he died left 600 francs for his surviving comrades to drink his health after his funeral and sing a song that went to the tune of Béranger's *Le Vieux Sergeant.* Amazingly, we've a *photograph* of him, taken in old age. So it didn't happen all that long ago!

Always it's the details that fascinate! To edit even a small part of these thousands of kilometres of 'film' into a comprehensible dramatic pattern has been no small labour.

For reasons of space I have *not*:

(a) tried to see events from the Russian side. War, unless one is taken prisoner, is always a one-sided experience;

(b) entered into tactical intricacies – the war-gamer is referred to George F. Nafziger's *Napoleon in Russia* (Presidio Press, Novato CA, 1988), which also contains an admirable précis of Franco-Russian relations 1806-12, as well as a great deal of statistical information. For an overall view of the 1812 drama Curtis Cate's *The War of the Two Emperors* (Random House, NY, 1985) cannot be bettered; nor for information on Napoleon's armies in general, can John R. Elting's *Swords Around a Throne* (The Free Press, New York, 1988). For a strategic overview I've followed David Chandler's classic *Campaigns of Napoleon* (Macmillan, New York, 1966);

(c) for reasons of space been able to follow other corps than those making up the 'Moscow army'. Even II and VI Corps' operations have had to be skimped;

(d) ascribed to my protagonists thoughts or feelings they have not themselves put on record;

(e) tried to evaluate, except occasionally in the notes, the accuracy of my eye-witnesses' memories, or how much is hindsight. On the whole, anyone ploughing through all these memoirs will gain the impression that the writers are mostly telling very exactly what they experienced, whether in the present (diaries) or past (memoirs). Sometimes, but rarely, they catch one another out telling fibs or exaggerating their own exploits. Ségur's masterpiece is particularly inaccurate, as Gourgaud long ago pointed out, and I've only drawn on it very little.

A word about my translation method. However vivid in themselves, my eye-witnesses' nineteenth-century prose is slower, more fraught with subordinate clauses and therefore heavier than ours; and to have rendered their sentences in all their syntactical intricacy would often have been to lose much of their contemporary speed and impact. I have therefore taken certain liberties with punctuation, syntax and even tense. Even the exact order of phrases, sentences and paragraphs may not tally. But the sense does, always. When omitting and abbreviating I have also skipped the customary '...'. Most of the originals can in any case be consulted in the Bibliothèque National, Paris, or elsewhere. In a word, I've tried to render my authors' prose as if they'd used typewriters or word-processors, not goose quills. Or, in Labaume's case, crows' feathers.

Paul Britten Austin
Dawlish, Devon

ACKNOWLEDGEMENTS

My grateful thoughts go to the late Antony Brett-James who, having travelled this ground before me, generously lent me many a rare volume (now in the Staff College Library). Also to David Chandler, for his unfailing encouragement and suggestions, and giving me the benefit of his unparalleled expertise. I am also especially grateful to my sister-in-law, Else Fisher-Bergman, for indefatigably writing into my computer hundreds of semi-illegible fragments of text, scribbled down in various libraries. And lastly to Mr Peter Harrington, Librarian of the Anne S. K. Military Collection, Brown University, Providence, Rhode Island, USA, for generously waiving copyright fees on many of the illustrations; likewise to the Royal Library, Stockholm, for free access to its wonderfully sharp edition of Faber du Faur's engravings. Last but not least, my wife, the Swedish novelist Margareta Bergman, deserves a special accolade for allowing endless breakfast-table monologues about the doings of these long-dead heroes to disturb her own much more profound reflections.

CHAPTER 1

OVERTURE TO 1812

'Half-way between Bedlam and the Pantheon!' – a new war with Russia? – Colonel Ponthon goes down on his knees – Napoleon's nightmare – economics – the Master of the Horse is naïve – Polish quagmires – 'without transport all is useless' – Sergeant Coignet fills cartridges – Lieutenant Bourgoing shuffles his recruits – seven armies march north – 'he arrived like the Prince of Darkness' – fireworks at Dresden – Narbonne's fruitless errand – Turkey and Russia make peace – 'Alexander the Great marched on India'

One early March night in 1812, young Villemain, secretary to General Count Louis de Narbonne,[1] aide-de-camp to the Emperor Napoleon, was sitting in his master's carriage in the courtyard of the palace at St-Cloud, reading Chateaubriand's newly published *Journey to Jerusalem*, when

'suddenly there was a noise, as of servants. The horses, more bored than I, pricked up their ears. The carriage moved forward several paces; and the general, flinging himself briskly into it, ordered the coachman to drive to Foreign Minister Maret's house, in Paris.'

Reputedly an illegitimate son of the dissolute and effete Louis XV, the 57-year-old but already white-haired Narbonne 'admired Napoleon personally, but didn't like his absolute and military empire, and thought it doomed to perish if it didn't mend its ways'. But according to what he'd tell his temperamental First Ordnance Officer *Gaspard Gourgaud* on St Helena, Napoleon didn't give a damn for what others thought or felt; only for what they said and did. And he enjoyed Narbonne's intelligent and cultivated conversation and was glad to have this scion of the *ancien régime* about his own imperial but thoroughly bourgeois person. As his coach rolled swiftly out of the courtyards – Villemain goes on – Narbonne

'put his hand to his bald forehead, as if passing in review all he'd just heard. And said in a low voice: "What a man! What stupendous ideas! What dreams! Where find a fireguard against such a genius? It staggers belief! We're half-way between Bedlam and the Pantheon. Each time I see him I'm worried sick. His specious reasonings, his optimistic sophisms, his gigantic illusions, are all engraved in his mind, and in a tête-à-tête come out as ineffaceable axioms."'

What the two men have been discussing is a new war with Russia. In 1807 Tsar Alexander had bound his defeated country, under the Treaty of Tilsit, to exclude British goods from her ports. The Continental System was the one great stranglehold Napoleon had on his arch-enemy. Only Russia's total defeat could have led to such a result, for she needed British industrial products and colonial goods as much as the British market needed bar iron from Russia's rapidly expanding iron industry. But soon economics had spoken louder than politics. By 1811 the rouble, which in

1807 had stood at 2.90 francs, had fallen as low as 1.50 francs. In vain Napoleon had first remonstrated, then fulminated against the import licences Alexander – imitating his own example – had begun to grant for goods delivered in neutral, namely American, vessels. And by 1810 both empires had begun to prepare for a new war.

It was a prospect which filled at least one of Napoleon's officers with dread. Engineer-Colonel Ponthon had been attached as an observer to the Russian Army after Tilsit; and his reports had been so detailed and well-written that Napoleon had afterwards brought him into his war cabinet. But Ponthon, it seems, was also a man of moral courage. One day he'd literally gone down on his knees and begged Napoleon 'in the name of France's happiness and your own glory' to abstain from invading Russia:

"The peoples under your yoke, Sire, will never be true allies. Your army will find neither food nor forage. The first rains will make the terrain impassable. And if the campaign drags on into winter, how will the troops stand up to temperatures of minus 20 to 30 degrees?"

Staring sternly at Ponthon, Napoleon had let him have his say. It seems his words had even had some effect. For several days afterwards the Grand Equerry General *Armand de Caulaincourt* noticed Napoleon had looked troubled – but then overcome his doubts by telling everyone 'this is going to be a short war, over in two months'. Even, if all went well, within a fortnight.

But the man who is trying hardest of all to avert this new war is Caulaincourt himself. Having been the French Ambassador at Petersburg during four years of mounting tension, he too realizes what an invasion of Russia must entail. Indeed in early 1811 he'd found his mission impossible and asked to be recalled, on grounds that the climate was 'ruining his health'.[3] Caulaincourt had been replaced by General Lauriston, a soldier of tougher fibre.

Before he'd left, the Tsar had given him a singular token of his friendship. It's the secret grief of Caulaincourt's life that in 1800 Napoleon, then First Consul of the French Republic, had implicated him in the arrest – if not the actual execution – of the young Duke of Enghien. In the eyes of all supporters of the *ancien régime* this judicial murder of a member of the Bourbon family, by which the First Consul had once and for all alienated the reaction, was an unforgivable crime. But as it happened Tsar Alexander, too, was under suspicion of having connived at another assassination: that of his own father Tsar Paul. And before parting with Caulaincourt he'd given him a certificate to the effect that he'd never believed him guilty of Enghien's death, and added to it the prestigious Order of St Andrew and his own miniature, signed on the back 'a present from a friend'. Although Napoleon liked to see familiar faces around him, such amiable sentiments on the eve of a new and, as he hoped, decisive war didn't please him. And for a while the Master of the Horse had been under a cloud. The government-controlled theatres had been allowed to lampoon him as a sentimental dove, forever extolling the virtues of eternal peace. And at court, where he'd resumed his normal duties, Napoleon had kept twitting him with his having let himself be 'seduced' by the Tsar's 'wily and Asiatic' character. Not perhaps that he really has anything against their friendship. This 'purely political' war once over and the Tsar of all the Russias again brought to heel, it can come in handy when it's a question of signing a new peace. And by and by Caulaincourt had been taken back into favour.

During their several long conversations in that spring of 1812 he claims he never minced his words. One day the talk turned to Poland, partitioned between Austria, Prussia and Russia in 1794 and in 1807 erected by Napoleon into a Grand Duchy, its territory aggrandized with parts of East Prussia. Although the thousands of patriotic Poles serving with the French armies are longing to see their ancient kingdom restored *in toto,* Napoleon says he has no intention of doing any such thing. In that case, Caulaincourt ripostes, he doesn't understand why he has sacrificed his alliance with Russia.

'Napoleon smiled and pinched my ear: "Are you really so fond of Alexander?" – "No Sire, but I'm fond of peace."'

There lay the difference. In vain Caulaincourt stresses the dangers of another war in the far north, with 220,000 soldiers already tied up in Spain fighting Wellington and the guerrillas. Napoleon simply turns a deaf ear. And when Caulaincourt tries to disabuse him of his notion that Russian aristocrats are no different from their western European counterparts and after 'a good battle... fearing for their palaces' will force the Tsar to make peace, Napoleon simply won't believe him:

"I don't want war, and I don't want Poland."

The Poles, he'd told Narbonne, with whom he'd also discussed the matter, were 'a trivial nation'. Why were they always divided among themselves?

'I love the Poles on the field of battle. They're a valiant race. As for their free veto, their diets-on-horseback with drawn sabres, I want none of all that! I've thought the matter over very carefully. In Poland I want a camp, not a forum. The war I'm going to wage on Alexander will be a courteous one, with 2,000 pieces of artillery and 500,000 soldiers, but without any insurrection. It's not for me to reestablish a breeding-ground of republicanism in the heart of Europe. No, my dear Narbonne, all I want out of Poland is a disciplined force, to furnish a battlefield. That's the whole question: how excite the spirit of national liberation in Poland, without re-exciting the fibre of liberalism? And where would I find a king for Poland? I haven't got one in my own family, and it'd be dangerous to take one from somewhere else.'

The difficulty with this new war, he'd gone on, was wholly of a moral order:

'Whilst using the material force accrued from the Revolution, it's necessary to unleash no passions, to raise Poland without emancipating it, and assure the independence of western Europe without reanimating any republican ferment. There you've the whole problem in a nutshell.'

It was the Russian government which, by systematically evading the terms of the Tilsit treaty, was forcing on a new war. And when Caulaincourt contradicts him and says 'it's not the Russian government, Sire, which wants a war, but your own, which is losing no opportunity of hastening it on,' Napoleon merely smiles the seductive smile which – all eye-witnesses agree – neither friend nor foe could resist,[4] pinches Caulaincourt's ear and tells him he's naïve and 'doesn't understand politics'. Whereupon the Master of the Horse takes out his notebook, in which, before leaving Petersburg, he has taken the precaution of jotting down the Tsar's exact words: 'If the Emperor Napoleon makes war on me,' Alexander had said,

'it's possible, even probable, we'll be defeated – that is, assuming we fight. The Spaniards have often been defeated, yet they aren't beaten. And they're not so far from Paris! We shall take no risks. We've plenty of elbow room. I shan't be the first to draw the sword; but I'll be the last to sheath it. If the fighting goes against me I'll retire to Kamtchatka [in Siberia]. Our climate, our winter, will fight on our side.'

Napoleon, who has listened with closest attention, 'even with some astonishment', remains silent awhile:

'The harder he found it to persuade me, the more art and persistence he deployed to reach his ends. From his calculated wiles and the language he employed anyone would have thought I was one of the great powers he was so concerned to win over. That was how he acted toward anyone he wished to persuade – and he was always trying to persuade someone. "When I need anyone," he said, "I don't put too fine a point upon it. I'll kiss his arse."'

Narbonne's assessment of Napoleon's character as he rides into Paris, talking to his young secretary, coincides exactly with Narbonne's:

'He's naturally fond of truth. His pride is immense. Yet he's patient, attentive. Though he's an excellent conversationalist, one must be able to stand firm when contradicting him. And that's hard, faced with so much power and genius! One ends up by letting oneself be convinced. You put your hands over your eyes, doubt, and ask yourself whether even so such a man's logic isn't the truth, and his ambition a presentiment of the future?'

If Napoleon possessed the art of fascinating everyone, Caulaincourt goes on,

'it was because he'd already fascinated himself. He spared no pains, no trouble to gain his ends, in small matters as in great. One could say he gave himself wholly over to his ends. Always he developed all possible means, all his faculties, and all his attention, and directed them to whatever matter was just then in hand. Never was there a man more fascinating when he chose to be! Woe to him who admitted a single modification... it led from concession to concession, to the end *he* had in view! You had to stick to the question as it appeared to you, and above all not follow the Emperor in his digressions; for as soon as he ran into opposition he unfailingly shifted the centre of argument.'

As for Alexander's repeated assurances that he'll fight to the death, he dismisses them as verbiage. So the two men wrangle on hour after hour, Napoleon always manoeuvring for position. When Caulaincourt says his mobilization against Russia is

'"either for a political end or to gratify his fondest passion". Napoleon asks laughing: "What passion is that?" "War, Sire." Protesting weakly it wasn't so, he tweaked my ear and said jokingly; "You certainly don't mince your words. It's time to go to dinner."'

Not all critics, however, are being fobbed off with such amiable banter. For many years the French consul-general in Petersburg, de Lesseps, a man 'deeply familiar with Russian life and affairs', has been

'looking after the interests of French shipping better than his own. This honest man was in as bad odour as myself, for not providing trumped up evidence conducive to a new war. Beyond all suspicion of bribery, his thirty years of service, his probity, his well-known trustworthiness, all went for nothing. With his own hand Napoleon had cancelled his annual expense account, and he was faced with being deprived of all means of earning a living.'

As yet, however, few Western Europeans know much about Russian life. And those who do are too valuable to be spared. Before the year is out de Lesseps, much to his own reluctance, will find himself civil governor of a Moscow in ashes.

'The detractors of this great epoch,' Caulaincourt assures us, 'may say what they like; never was a sovereign surrounded by more capable men. Honest, full of zeal and devotion, we remained moderate, and above all good Frenchmen. Never was the truth so dinned into a sovereign's ears, but alas to no effect.'

As early as at his last frustrating meeting with Alexander, at Erfurt four years earlier, Napoleon's more intuitive self had been warned of the true state of their apparently cordial relationship. On a raft moored in the middle of the Niemen at Tilsit, each had tried to out-charm the other – and Napoleon, undoubtedly, had come off best. But by 1810, privily encouraged by Talleyrand's murmurs that 'the giant has feet of clay', it had been the Tsar who'd begun to call the tune. And one night Napoleon's First Valet *Constant Wairy*,[5] asleep as usual in the next room, had been awakened by 'dull and plaintive cries, as of someone being strangled'. Jumping out of bed, 'with such precautions as my alarm permitted' he'd opened the door:

'Going over to the bed, I saw His Majesty lying across it in a convulsive posture, his sheets and bedcover thrown off and all his person in a terrible state of nervous constriction. Inarticulate sounds were coming from his open mouth, his chest seemed deeply oppressed, and he was pressing one fist against the hollow of his stomach. Terrified to see him like this, I speak to him. When he doesn't reply, I shake him lightly. At this the Emperor wakes up with a loud cry and says: "What is it? What is it?" [And then, interrupting Constant's apologies] "You've done quite right, my dear Constant. Ah! my friend, what a horrible nightmare! A bear was ripping open my chest and tearing my heart out." Whereupon the Emperor got up and walked to and fro in the room while I was rearranging his bedclothes. He was obliged to change his shirt, the one he had on being drenched in sweat. The memory of this dream followed him a very long while. He often spoke of it, each time trying to extract different deductions from it and relate it to circumstances.'

That Napoleon has forseen the coming campaign's exceptional difficulties, at least in part, there is no question. None of his others have called for such meticulous planning. Or for so huge a mobilization of men and resources. 'Without transport,' he'd written in 1811 to his stepson Eugène de Beauharnais, Viceroy of Italy, 'all is useless'. And as early as June that year his 'geometrical mind' had begun wrestling with the problem.

Unprecedented mobility had always been a condition of Napoleonic blitzkrieg. And therefore the French armies had always lived off the rich lands they had conquered. But the far north was a different matter, as Sergeant *Jean-Roch Coignet*, the 2nd Guard Grenadiers' little drill instructor, all too vividly remembers. In Poland's sandy quagmires in 1806

'we'd had to tie on our shoes with string under the insteps. Sometimes, when the bits of string broke and our shoes got left behind in the mud, we had to take hold of our hind leg and pull it out like a carrot, lift it forward, and then go back and look for the other one. The same manoeuvre over and over, for two days on end.'

Neither were Lithuanian roads – insofar as they existed – like western European ones. 'In this part of the world,' the Prussian lieutenant *H.A. Vossler* of Prince Louis' Hussars will soon be discovering, 'all heavy transportation normally goes by sledge in winter. Roads aren't as important as in more southerly climes.'

Although the French army has a Supply Train, it consists of only 3,500 men and 891 vehicles, certainly not enough to maintain an invasion force of at least a third of a million men. For that's what's in question. One day, taking aside his War Minister Clarke on the terraces of St-Cloud, Napoleon had confided to him: 'I'm planning a great expedition. The men I shall get easily enough. The difficulty is to prepare transport.'

Huge quantities of rice, flour and biscuit will have to be assembled and paid for. Well there's gold and enough for that! The gold millions extorted from Prussia as reparations for her attack on him in 1806 and, in 1805 and 1810, from Austria, are lying in the Tuileries cellars, to which only Napoleon himself and his infinitely hard-working, enormously capable Intendant-General *Pierre Daru*[6] have keys. By March 1812 he's hoping to have 270,000 quintals of wheat, 12,000 of rice, 2,000,000 bushels of oats, equivalent to 20 million rations of bread and rice – enough for 400,000 men and 50,000 horses for 50 days. Since armies are also apt to be thirsty and brandy is also needed for amputations, on 29 December he has already ordered the Minister of Administration of the Army to buy at Bordeaux '28 million bottles of wine, 2 million bottles of brandy', i.e., 200 days' rations of wine and 130 of brandy for 300,000 men.

But the transport question remains. On such terrain will the existing 1,500 large-wheeled battalion wagons, each drawn by eight horses and capable of carrying 10,000 rations, suffice to feed the army for 25 days, the time needed for his swift campaign? Although really too heavy, h'd at first assumed that they would. But next day he had thought the matter over. If such a wagon is

"'loaded with biscuit, it has to be in barrels, otherwise the biscuit crumbles, and the men complain. Nor is it suitable for grain, flour, oats, bales of hay, or barrels of wine or brandy. So each battalion must keep its wagon for its normal needs. All others must be replaced by good carriers' wagons with big wheels, each drawn by eight horses and driven by four men, or, if need be, by three,"

all of them, preferably, foreigners. On 4 July 1811, writing to the head of his supply corps, he'd come to the conclusion that a wholly new, much lighter kind of cart must also be invented, "normally designed to carry 4,000 rations, or if necessary 6,000, and driven by two men and four horses'. Since even these can't be counted on to cope with the terrain at its worst, an even lighter type of cart must be designed, drawn by a single horse, used to walking nose to tail, "so that only one man will be needed for several carts". Oxen, too, will be useful. Even when prodded on by conscripts not used to wielding a goad, they can at least eat grass by the wayside before themselves being eaten.

How long will the biggest army in the history of European warfare be able to sustain itself amid Lithuania's conifer forests? Long enough, at least, Napoleon has calculated, to roll up and annihilate its enemy.

To defend their vast country the Russians, he knows, have two armies, plus a third, currently engaged fighting the Turks in Moldavia. The First West Army is commanded by Barclay de Tolly, a Lithuanian of Scottish descent who, remarkably, had once served in the ranks and who since the Friedland disaster, as Minister for War, has modernized the Russian army on French lines. It's being concentrated around Vilna (Vilnius). The Second West Army, commanded by the fiery and temperamental Georgian Prince Bagration, is cantoned further south around Grodno, 75 miles further up the Niemen. By driving a wedge between Barclay and

Bagration in a surprise attack of the kind he has so often launched before, Napoleon, with the reputation of his own invincibility and no fewer than ten army corps and three 'reserve' cavalry corps at his disposal, is planning to defeat them in detail. And if all goes well the campaign will indeed be over within a couple of weeks.

But how, on a given day in the summer of 1812, concentrate the Grand Army, with its 150,000 horses and 1,000 guns, on the banks of the Niemen – frontier between Poland and Russian Lithuania? That's the immense logistic problem he has set himself. And on which day? Neither too early – summer comes late to the North and the corn must be ripe for fodder. Nor too late; with autumn coming on in mid-August that would be to risk the very winter campaign so feared by Colonel Ponthon. Midsummer Day should be about right.

All over Europe units are being reinforced. Regiments normally four battalions strong are being increased to five. In its Courbevoie barracks outside Paris the infantry regiments of the Imperial Guard – an entire crack army corps 50,000 strong – are being brought up to scratch. Two whole companies of oldsters, 'only too happy to be assigned such pleasant duties', are being weeded out from the 2nd Grenadiers and replaced by 'superb men who keep arriving daily' from the Line, for which Guard NCOs are in turn being trained to take commissions. While teaching a squad of officer cadets their new command duties Sergeant Coignet is having them teach *him* his ABC, while the adjutants-major train them in theory. Such is the system, and

> 'Napoleon himself checked up on the results. For fifteen days a hundred men, presided over by the adjutants-major, were making up cartridges. To avoid any danger of an explosion they had to wear shoes without hobnails, taken off and inspected every two hours. We made up 100,000 packets. The moment this harvest was in – major manoeuvres in the plain of St-Denis, and reviews at the Tuileries, together with sizeable artillery parks, wagons and ambulances! The Emperor had them opened and himself climbed up on a wheel to make sure they were full.'

The regiments of the Young Guard, too, are hurriedly being brought up to strength. Its officers, taken from the Old Guard, will still draw their higher pay; but otherwise its regiments are really no different from those of the Line. Now it's to consist of thirteen regiments of tirailleurs, thirteen of voltigeurs, one of fusilier-grenadiers, one of fusilier-chasseurs, one of flankers, one of éclaireurs, and one of national guards – 'ten distinct denominations for infantry units armed in exactly the same way and all carrying the same model of standard-issue musket'. Paul de Bourgoing, a well-educated young lieutenant of the 5th Tirailleurs just back from fighting in Spain, is present as the new recruits come in,

> 'fifteen hundred young men in blouses, waistcoats, village costumes,
> or citizens of various provinces of the vast French Empire, traipsing

over the vast barrack square to the rattle of sixteen drums. The drummers had almost all been taken from the Pupils of the Guard [a regiment consisting wholly of soldiers' sons]. Almost all were Dutchmen. Some, from Amsterdam and Frisia, were only fifteen. Great care had been taken not to let any one company contain too many nationals of any one country: "That won't be good either for discipline or for warfare," my major told me. "Shuffle them together like a pack of cards! Choose the twelve men who seem to have the thickest beards, or are likely to grow them. Above all, don't take any blondes or redheads; only men with black beards, whom you'll place out in front.'"

Carrying axes and wearing tall bearskins and white leather aprons, these are to be sappers and march at the head of the regimental column:

'So I passed these 1,500 two-year-old chins in review as swiftly as possible. Most were still beardless. Scarcely 25 or 30 of them were destined ever to see their maternal hearths again.'

On the Elbe, meanwhile, an Army of Observation, soon to become I Corps, is being drilled to a degree of efficiency 'almost equalling the Imperial Guard' under its fearsomely disciplinarian commander, Marshal Davout, Prince of Eckmühl. One of its strongest infantry regiments, the 85th Line, has spent the winter in the strongly fortified town of Glogau, 'as in a besieged city'. Its 1st battalion's portly 2nd major *C.F.M. Le Roy*[6] is a staunch democrat who regards all blue-blooded persons with contempt, Napoleon as 'an enterprising genius' and the Russians as barbarians. After 'deciding to be born in the midst of a nation execrated by all others', he'd begun his military career 'by chance' as a conscript in 1795 but 'continued it by taste'. During that winter of 1811/12 he has been amused to see how at the Grand Casino the wives of the local nobility, 'without fear of besmirching their sixteen quarterings of nobility' have been happy to gamble and dance with the young officers; and, not least, how 'more than one felt an impulse to fall into [the] Line – and enjoyed doing so'.

In Southern Germany, too, the various principalities of the French-dominated Confederation of the Rhine are reluctantly supplying fresh contingents to General Vandamme's VIII Corps. Meanwhile Jerome Bonaparte, King of Westphalia, Napoleon's troublesome youngest brother, though destitute of military experience, is no less reluctantly preparing himself to assume overall command both of it, as well as Prince Poniatowski's V (Polish) Corps and General Reynier's Saxons (VII). None of these sacrifices, though unwelcome, are novel. In 1806 the little duchy of Saxe-Coburg had been overrun by the bluecoats; and only ten months have gone by since the kind-hearted Duchess Augusta[7] was pained to see

'the fragments of our poor little contingent return from Spain – eighteen men out of 250! Most of the losses haven't been due to actual fighting, but mainly to disease, scarcity and neglect, added to the hardships caused by the Spanish climate. Half the town turned out to meet the survivors,' she'd noted in her diary. Now she's depressed to see a fresh contingent march out,[8] this time northwards.[9]

What is their destination? Coignet, in Paris, may not know; but all these tens of thousands of conscripted Germans certainly do. Writing home to his family for some pocket money for this new campaign, one of Davout's corporals hears it's going to be India, a country evidently populated by monkeys ['*aux Singes*' = *aux Indes*]. Which way? Via Russia, of course, whose emperor is, for the third time, to be 'taught a lesson'.

This new Grand Army is certainly not only made up of willing soldiers. Far from it. All over Europe – even from faraway Naples where Napoleon's glamorous brother-in-law *Joachim Murat* is putting his *lazzaroni* and released convicts into exceptionally colourful uniforms – all unmarried 18-year-olds who haven't been able to afford to pay for a substitute to go and get killed for them[10] and who've drawn the recruiting sergeant's shortest straw – all, that is, who haven't fled to the hills and become 'bandits' – are being accompanied to the outskirts of their towns or villages by weeping relatives who never expect to see them again. As usual, desertion en route for the depots is wholesale. Most of the reluctant peasants whom Lieutenant *Heinrich von Brandt*[11] is seeing co-opted into the 2nd Vistula Regiment at Posen have never in their lives worn boots or slept in a bed and 'only knew of white bread and coffee by hearsay' and are having to be kept to the colours by a combination of good food and lodgings and, for deserters ('almost all were caught') 50 to 60 strokes of the cane on their backsides. After fetching a whole route-regiment of deserters from the Ile de Ré to Lübeck *Joseph Guitard*[12] a tall chestnut-haired captain in Coignet's regiment, is having to go back into Prussia and fetch another. The equivalent of a whole division of the Grand Army consists of such would-be deserters.

Napoleon, of course, knows perfectly well what he's about, and whose interests he's serving. The French nation's of course. But who are the 'nation'? The middle classes, of course, as opposed to *le peuple*, whom he one day boasts to Narbonne that he has "pacified by arming it". Adding as a corollary: "In my hands war has become the antidote to anarchy." As for the old aristocracy, those of them who've rallied to the cause of an upstart throne "borne up", as Napoleon himself realized, "on the bayonets of the Imperial Guard, all sons of self-owning peasants", some are really devoted to his cause, if not always, like Caulaincourt and Narbonne, to his policies. Others, perhaps most, are decidedly ambivalent: "A blue is always a blue, a white always a white," he'll ruefully tell his First Ordnance Officer Gaspard Gourgaud one day on St Helena.

Among aristocratic officers wholeheartedly devoted to his cause is General Count *Philippe de Ségur*. One day during the Consulate this son of a distinguished father, both bitter enemies of the Revolution, had been loitering outside the Tuileries gates in a state of such deep depression that he was contemplating suicide, when a troop of Chasseurs of the Consular Guard had come trotting out. On this scion of France's ancient military caste the sight of their brilliant green and red uniforms and other accou-trements had had an effect only comparable to that of St Paul's vision en route for Damascus. Throwing in his lot with the new Caesar, the young Philippe de Ségur had gone and joined up; and like his fellow aristocrat *Montesquiou Fézensac* had of course been swiftly promoted. After various exploits he is now an officer at Imperial Headquarters, where his special task as Assistant Prefect of the Palace is to supervise the pack mules which, on campaign, transport the imperial gold dinner service and other domestic chattels. If half of de Ségur's mind is deep in military matters, the other is no less deep in classical literature; and it's by no means impos-sible that he's already contemplating a great historical work – not that either he or anyone else, in this spring of 1812, can envisage what it will be. Filled with what will turn out to be a passionate, if, in the event – in Gourgaud's eyes – altogether too ambivalent admiration for his idol, he is already well aware that of all the allies being pressed into service in this gigantic expedition 'only the Italians and Poles were really enthusiastic for our cause'.

Of none of the Grand Army's officers is this truer than of a certain Elban officer, by name *Césare de Laugier* (or Loggia). Setting out from Milan in February with the rest of Prince Eugène's IV Corps, the adjutant-major of the Guards of Honour of the Kingdom of Italy, each company of which comes from a different North Italian city and has a dif-ferent-hued facing to its green-and-white uniform, has crossed the Alps and gone into cantonments in Southern Germany, where he's sure the inhabitants 'love' them. Inside its new-fangled Grecian-style helmet, whose huge plumed and combed crest culminates in an agressively beaked, rapa-cious and gilded eagle's head, Césare de Laugier's head is full of notions of antique military exploits. Not a little naïve himself, he paints a touch-ing picture of his compatriots' mentality:

'They know no other divinity than their sovereign. No other reason but force. No other passion but glory. All is levelled out in discipline and passive obedience, the soldier's prime virtue. Ignorant of what's in store for them, they're so convinced of the justice of their cause that they never try to find out which country it is they're being sent to. Having heard it said at each war's commencement that they're destined to deal the final blow to the Englishmen's tottering power, they end up by confusing all existing powers with England. They assess the distance separating them from it by the number of marches they, for several years now, have been making from one side of Europe to the other, without ever reaching that country which, goal of all their efforts, vanishes before their eyes.'

Reviewed on 14 May on the esplanade at Glogau outside that town's forti-fications, the adjutant-major will write in his diary:

'The whole of IV Corps is under arms. The Viceroy got here yester-day. The Royal Guard, occupying as of right the right of the front line, which is very long, finds itself situated in the town cemetery.

Only the graves interrupt our regular alignment. Some superstitious minds are trying to extract a sinister presage from this circumstance, and are complaining of our being put here. The Roman legions would certainly have sacrificed to their gods to exorcize such sinister auguries.'

But evidently Prince Eugène, a somewhat stolid but very capable soldier, is above such fears; and, in an order of the day expressess his satisfaction with IV Corps' turnout. Nothing could make the Guardia d'Onore's adjutant-major feel more ecstatic.

As ever, there are political complications. Some, unlike the domestic ones,[13] can't be ironed out by imperial edict. For some time now the French and British embassies in Constantinople have been outvying each other in the art of bribing Turkish officials. The French to keep Turkey at war with Russia; the British to get them to make peace. And since the Turks have recently been getting the worst of it there's a distinct danger of British gold weighing heavier than French, thus freeing General Tormassov's Army of Moldavia to march northwards and threaten the Grand Army's southern flank. An eventuality Napoleon hopes he has guarded himself against by forcing his new-found father-in-law, the Emperor Francis, to provide him with 30,000 Austrians under Prince Schwarzenberg. Well, not exactly forcing, because there has been a price for it: that he guarantee his fellow-emperor the quiet possession of his ill-gotten Polish dominions in Galicia, wrested from the Poles in 1794. Here's an insoluble clash of claims: the Poles' that he shall reintegrate Galicia in their dreamed of kingdom. The Austrians' that he shan't.

Sweden, resoundingly defeated by Russia in 1809, is another problem. At that all-time ebb in her affairs, with Finland and even the Åland islands lost, her parliament, its elbow jogged by an independently minded young subaltern who'd happened to be in Paris at the time, had elected Napoleon's one-time rival Marshal Bernadotte to be that country's Crown Prince. One of the first things he'd found out on arriving in Stockholm was that his adoptive country's all-important iron industry was no less dependent than Russia's on the British market. And Franco-Swedish relations had rapidly gone from bad to worse. Finally Berndotte had declared himself neutral in the great power struggle; and in May 1810 Count Lagerbielke, the Swedish Ambassador in Paris, had been received in audience at the Tuileries:

'I'd never seen the Emperor so utterly furious, it exceeded anything one can imagine. He declared angrily that he hadn't slept one hour all night because of his Swedish business. "You could let me get some rest, I need it! British prisoners of war have been returned without compensation, isn't that so, Monsieur de Cadore?" (The Minister, all a-tremble, didn't fail to answer this question, like all others, in the affirmative.)'

For an hour and a quarter Napoleon had talked and shouted, so often repeating himself and interrupting his own line of thought that Lagerbielke would afterwards have some difficulty in clearly recalling all he'd said. He'd spared Sweden at the end of the 1807 war, he'd shouted, but had been 'deceived' by Lagerbielke:

'Neutrality no longer exists. Britain doesn't recognize it, neither can I. You're suffering? Don't you think I suffer, that France, Bordeaux, Holland and Germany are suffering? That's why there must be an end to it. Peace on the seas must be sought, no matter what the cost.' (Here the Emperor became terrifyingly angry.) 'Well, Sweden alone is responsible for the crisis I find myself in! Sweden has done me more harm than all five Coalitions put together. Open war, or else reliable friendship. Choose now. There's my last word. Farewell. May I see you again under happier circumstances.'[14]

With these words the Corsican Tyrant had walked out of the room,[15] leaving the Swede amazed to find the antechamber deserted 'even by the duty officer... whether in obedience to orders or out of voluntary politeness, the Emperor on several occasions having raised his voice to such a degree of loudness it was impossible not to hear him in the next room.' And early in 1812, while Narbonne and Napoleon were having their fascinating conversations at St-Cloud, Davout had been ordered to occupy Swedish Pomerania by a *ruse de guerre*, seize all Swedish shipping in its ports and have the Swedish garrisons sent back to France as prisoners of war.

This, for the Swedes, had been the last straw. Bernadotte had declared Sweden neutral, made peace with Britain, and opened secret negotiations with the Tsar.

Prussia is yet another problem, albeit apparently not too serious a one. Stripped of almost half her land area, and still seething with resentment after the stupendous war indemnities still being paid since 1806, she, as an 'ally' of France, has been ordered to provide the Grand Army with a 30,000-man contingent to protect its left wing, in the same way as the Austrians are to protect its right. This has caused the Berlin court to put out secret feelers to Vienna – feelers which, after three no less ruinous defeats, have fallen on deaf ears. Even so, just to make sure there are no misunderstandings, Marshal Oudinot is ordered to occupy Berlin with his 30,000-strong II Corps, while Narbonne at the same time is sent there to exercise his old-style diplomacy on a traumatized Prussian court.

All through the spring and early summer of 1812 Europe's roads resound to the tramp of marching boots as no fewer than seven armies march northwards. Each division sets out after the one ahead of it at two-day intervals. With a distance of 100 paces (70m) between battalions, its regiments march 'in two files sharing the road whose crown they leave free'. Halting for 'five minutes in every hour and at three-quarters of the day's march for half an hour' and with a day's rest every fifth, they tramp on northwards at an average speed of 25 miles a day. Every second day they pick up rations, provided along the route by Count Daru's[16] administration. 'The step of the NCO who marches at the head of the regiment,' explains that amusing raconteur Captain *Elzéar Blaze* (who is himself lucky enough not to be sent to Russia),

'must be short and regular; for if the right advances at a regular pace, the left will have to gallop. The least obstacle on the road, even if it's only a runnel to cross, and if the first man to encounter the obstacle pauses for even half a second, the men in the last battalion will have to run for a quarter of an hour to catch up. All this an experienced officer sees at a glance; orders a brief halt; and everything resumes its wonted course. After we've marched an hour there's a five-minute halt, to light our pipes. This is known as *la halte des pipes*. The soldier must never be deprived of any of his pleasures. Everyone dines on what he has in his pack, and then off we go again, breaking each league with five-minute halts.'

Looking out of his window in Dresden, capital of the kingdom of Saxony, a nine-year-old boy, *Wilhelm von Kügelgen*, watches them go by:

'The long dark columns of the Old Guard with their proud eagles, tall bearskins, and martial faces hovering like gloomy dream-pictures. The warlike sound of drums and pipes; then the ghostly figures of the pioneers with glinting axes and long black beards, and behind them the endless transport columns. Day after day they passed under our window, man by man, brigade after brigade. I saw almost all the arms of the Grand Army: the tall carabiniers with plumed helmets and gilded cuirasses; the light chasseurs, hussars, voltigeurs; all types of infantry and artillery with good horse-drawn vehicles. And, lastly, long columns of pontoon-bridging and other military equipment.'

It's at Dresden, namely, that the new Charlemagne has ordered the kings and princes of a conquered Europe to come and do him homage. Since few if any – the King of Saxony apart – are sincerely attached to his cause, perhaps a festive display of political and military might will impress on everyone the futility of stirring up trouble behind his back? His father-in-law the Emperor of Austria is to be guest of honour and his young daughter, Marie-Louise, Empress of the French, leading lady – Prussia's king and queen have to beg to be allowed in and even then are only grudgingly admitted.

What, one wonders, are the 47-year-old upstart emperor's thoughts as, with his young blonde empress seated at his side, the imperial cortège leaves Paris at 5.30 a.m. on 9 May, for 'the supreme effort, the most difficult task of all?' – namely, by crushing Russia to crush Britain and secure for himself and for France the domination of the world? Is he perhaps even hoping the Dresden event may, in itself, suffice to bring the Tsar to heel? Otherwise what was the meaning of his rueful aside to his police prefect, just before leaving:

'Well, one must finish what one has started!'

No previous campaign, as far as we know, had been preluded by such a remark.

Von Kügelgen goes on:

'One stormy night when the torches would hardly burn he arrived like the Prince of Darkness. Flashes of lightning lit the sky, and peals of thunder mingled with the populace's half-hearted cheers and the ghostly ringing of churchbells. There was a good deal to be seen in Dresden at this time. The presence of so many armies filled the town with martial pomp. Bells pealed and cannons boomed to welcome the princes. Grand parades and manoeuvres entertained them. At night the town shone under the magical glare of a thousand lamps. A broad rainbow of gay paper lanterns arched the sky high above the Elbe, which reflected every colour of the spectrum, the prettiest light-effect one could possibly imagine. Fireworks crackled in the air. Every house was filled to the brim with soldiers who talked, laughed and swore in almost every European language.'

The romantic poet Heinrich Heine, too, sees him

'high on horseback, the eternal eyes set in the marble of that imperial visage, looking on, calm as destiny, at his guards as they march past. He was sending them to Russia, and the old grenadiers glanced up at him with so anxious a devotion, such sympathy, such earnestness and lethal pride: *Ave Caesar, morituri te salutant!*

Among the princelings who are anxiously waiting here to placate him, two of Duchess Augusta's sons have every reason to be worried. For a third brother has been so imprudent as to take a commission in the Russian army, causing Napoleon, like an angry landlord, to threaten to 'chase' their father out of his duchy. But at the festivities what impresses them most is

'the contrast between the very human Emperor Franz, with his friendly courteous bearing,[17] and Napoleon, decidedly curt and rude, though possibly not intentionally so, merely over-elated by his extraordinary luck and cleverness. The adulation and sickening flattery with which he's everywhere received further increase the contemptuous, harsh attitude peculiar to him.'

An assessment certainly not shared by Napoleon's First Secretary, Baron *Claude-François Méneval*[18] has

'many opportunities to observe these august assemblies. In the vast apartments of the Dresden palace I contemplated the procession headed by Napoleon. The Empress of Austria's health being too feeble for her to stand the fatigue of walking through all these apartments, the Emperor walked ahead of her, hat in one hand, the other resting on the door of her sedan chair, as he talked gaily to her. All who witnessed these social events agreed that by his affability, intellect and seductive manners he exerted an irresistible ascendancy over his noble guests. He was the most amiable and charming man in the world when he wanted to be.'

Napoleon may be invincible, the Duchess concedes in her diary: but at what cost in human blood and suffering?

The Tsar meanwhile has left Petersburg for Vilna, in a last-minute attempt to enlist the support of his more influential Lithuanian subjects. And when Lauriston follows and applies for an audience, refuses to receive him. So Narbonne, at Berlin, gets new instructions. He too is to go to Vilna, ostensibly to try and save the peace, actually to sniff out all he can about Russo-Swedish and Russo-Turkish relations and, in the event of the Russian army crossing the Niemen, try to negotiate a truce "to give His Majesty time to reach the front".

Narbonne is more welcome than Lauriston. Invited to dinner, he delivers Napoleon's personal message:

"In the last analysis, there's only one, but very important, issue between us and Russia: of neutral nations and of English trade. Compared with this, Poland doesn't matter. His Majesty has only French interests at heart."

To this Alexander, who also has the knack of being all things to all men, replies that he'll neither be the aggressor, nor will he

"sign a peace dictated on Russian territory. The Russian nation doesn't recoil in the face of danger. All Europe's bayonets on my frontier won't make me alter my language."

Deeply impressed by so firm and dignified a stance, no sooner is Narbonne back at his lodgings than three high Russian officials come knocking at his door. His carriage, they tell him, is already harnessed up and ready to leave. The Tsar has even been so considerate as to have it provisioned out of his own kitchen with food for the journey. Reaching Dresden on 24 May at the height of the festivities, Narbonne brings his master four items of information. One is correct. The others not. The Russians won't break the peace, he tells him, nor will they cross the Niemen. But if he, Napoleon, does so, then he "has the impression they'll immediately give battle. And Russia will at once ally herself with Britain." As for the Swedes, though it's true their Crown Prince seems to be siding with Alexander, there's still no pact between them. Neither is there any prospect of a Russo-Turkish peace.

(Actually, unknown both to Napoleon and his envoy but loyal to the interests of his adoptive country, Bernadotte has already assured the Tsar that Sweden will remain neutral until the moment comes for her to show her hand. At the same time he has urged Alexander to stand fast. As for Turkey, only two days earlier, on 22 May, a certain one-eyed General Kutusov, who had come off very much second best at Austerlitz in 1804, has met the Grand Vizir at Budapest and signed a peace treaty between

Russia and Turkey. Two events in the light of which Napoleon will say on St Helena that his invasion of Russia was a mistake.)

Paying scant heed to his envoy's report, Napoleon launches out into another rhetorical flight of the kind that had so worried Narbonne at St-Cloud:

"Very well, then! Let destiny be accomplished, and Russia be crushed under my hatred of England! At the head of four hundred thousand men, paid and equipped on a hitherto unexampled scale, with reserves on our flanks, with a Lithuanian corps of the same blood as some of the populations we'll be passing through, I don't fear this long road fringed with deserts. After all, my dear fellow,' he went on as if in an exalted dream, 'this long road is the road to India. Alexander the Great set out to reach the Ganges from a distance no less great than from Moscow. Imagine Moscow taken – Russia crushed – the Tsar reconciled or dead in some palace conspiracy – a new and dependent throne, perhaps. And tell me whether we a great army of Frenchmen and auxiliaries from Tiflis would have to do more than touch the Ganges with a French sword for the whole scaffolding of Britain's mercantile greatness to collapse. It'd be a gigantic expedition, I admit; but possible in the nineteenth century. At a blow, France will have conquered the independence of the West and the freedom of the seas."

Five days later he'll leave for the army.

In one of Davout's baggage wagons is a map of India. Just in case.[19]

CHAPTER 2

THE RAPE OF POLAND

A Dutch diplomat turns soldier – a heavily laden army – pillage and violence – `Napoleono magni Caesari' – miserable villages, splendid châteaux – Brandt visits his parents – a campaign for men only – cantinières – `this child should be with his mother' – Napoleon dictates in a terrible voice – a priest with his wits about him – `terror and desolation are let loose in Poland'

On 11 June, writes *Dedem van der Gelder*, the army was set in motion. A dapper little man, more suited for the profession his father had put him into than for the military life he'd always hankered after, Dedem had been a Dutch diplomat. But after the incorporation of his country into France in 1810 he'd gone to Fontainebleau and offered his services. Napoleon had wanted to give him a military governorship in the Netherlands. But 'not wanting to begin by shooting my compatriots' Dedem had asked for a post on active service; whereupon Napoleon, who was increasingly short of educated officers, had promoted him *général de brigade* and sent him to Davout at Hamburg, where the Iron Marshal – surprisingly in view of Dedem's lack of military experience – had entrusted him with the command of 2nd Infantry Brigade, under his brother-in-law Friant. And it had been in that capacity Dedem had taken part in the treacherous occupation of Swedish Pomerania, an operation he, having been Dutch Ambassador in Stockholm and still having many friends there, found utterly distasteful.[1]

The whole army is maximally burdened. Each infantryman, at least in I Corps, is carrying on his back bread and flour for 20 days – Dedem says a bag containing ten pounds of flour and another with ten pounds of rice. It's just as well. For three days on end little *Jean-Marc Bussy*, a voltigeur of the 3rd Swiss Regiment, sees 'not a village, not a house'. Besides his musket (ten pounds), he's carrying *inside* his pack:

2 shirts,
1 pair of thick linen trousers,
1 pair of thick black linen half-gaiters,
1 brush-bag,
1 bandage and lint, and
2, or perhaps 3, pairs of shoes [right and left foot identical], together with spare hobnails and soles.

On either side of his pack:

4 'biscuits' (large slices of twice-baked bread, each weighing sixteen ounces).

Under his pack is slung a canvas bag containing five pounds of flour. Thereto in a canvas bandoleer, two loaves of bread, each weighing three pounds, i.e., bread for four days, biscuit for four more, and flour for seven, the whole weighing 58 pounds (25.5kg), enough for him to live on for fifteen days. Passing through Warsaw with VIII Corps, another voltigeur, lance-corporal *William Heinemann* of the Brunswick Chasseurs – though an old campaigner[2] he'd made made an abortive attempt to escape in Germany – swaps his extra pairs of shoes for 'forty eggs and some bunches of radishes'. Such initiatives might perhaps pass muster in Vandamme's corps: not under Davout's fiercely disciplined regiments. Upon some young soldiers of Dedem's brigade throwing away their sacks of flour, the colonel of the 127th, reviewing them, had ordered the empty sacks to be filled with sand. The guilty men were to carry them until further notice. This, says Caulaincourt, did the trick, 'the more so as the time for filling them with flour never came'.

Nor is it only the infantry which is so heavily burdened. The 2nd ('Red') Lancers of the Guard are a new élite regiment. Although their uniform emulates that of the famous 1st (Polish) Guard Lancers, albeit with reversed colours – scarlet with dark-blue facings and yellow trimmings – the unit consists mostly of Dutchmen. Originally Napoleon had intended it to be a cuirassier regiment for the Guard; but in the end, for lack of sufficiently powerful horses, has equipped it with lances. And a great deal else besides. At Koenigsberg its farriers – one per company – have been issued with a big axe 'for felling forests or butchery', and each troop's brigadier with eight little hatchets, for sharpening stakes to tether their horses and build shacks and bivouacs. Finally, besides lance, carbine, ammunition, and other regulation equipment, each trooper has to find room for a sickle, fastened on his horse's rump on top of his cylindrical portmanteau, for cutting standing crops and grass. All these extras, on top of the lancers' heavy harness, are already proving too much for their mounts:

'In the long run all the regiment's companies had some horses hurt. Since most of these sores appeared on the right side, it was their withers which were wrung, and we assumed this was due to the combined weight of lance and carbine. We tried to remedy this in every thinkable way: by shifting the lance from right to left, and then by having the carbine carried on the hook of the bandoleer. But we soon saw that this latter measure had the drawback of more or less causing the trooper to lean forward under its weight and thus cause fresh sores.'

If this is the state of affairs in a 'light' cavalry regiment, what, one wonders, can it be like for massively weighted cuirassiers and carabiniers, wearing their plumed and maned brass helmets and 16lb steel cuirasses?

But though the rank and file are burdened to the last ounce, some of the supply wagons obviously aren't. Arriving at Gumbinnen on the Polish-Prussian border on 21 June, Napoleon dictates an angry letter to Berthier:

'The wagons of the select headquarters have left here only halfloaded. Send an express courier forthwith, with an order to assemble the whole load on 20 wagons, and for the 20 empty ones to be sent to Insterburg to reload. Tell the supply officer I'm displeased with him for going forward in this way with his wagons empty. I've sometimes seen nonchalant administrators, but never any more stupid.'

Each officer and soldier, Dedem goes on, has been

'summarily ordered to relieve his Prussian hosts of ten days' rations. The countryside was stripped of horses and vehicles to carry forage, and even of straw. Altogther 90,000 horses were officially requisitioned from the Prussians, who [although nominally allies] were treated at very least as a conquered people. In other words, the order about 10 days' rations had been nothing but an authorization of pillage and violence.'

Pillage and violence, indeed, are the real order of the day. On Napoleon's arrival at Gumbinnen the civil authorities complain to him that a local landowner, whose château has been taken over by the Guard, has been found at the bottom of a well, whether having committed suicide or been thrown down no one knows. But though Napoleon orders an immediate 'very serious' joint investigation by themselves and the Guard's commanders, nothing is done about it.

Official manifestations staged by a cowed administration are not the less spectacular for all these distresses. At Posen on 29 May, Lieutenant *Heinrich von Brandt* of the Vistula Legion[3] has seen the Emperor

'eloquently received under a triumphal arch bearing the words "Heroi invincibli". The town hall's five big windows were decorated with a transparency of the civic arms, alternating with the initials of Napoleon, the Empress Marie Louise,[4] the French eagle and the escutcheon of the Grand Duchy. On the church tower, which the Emperor could see from his windows, the illuminations showed a gigantic crown of laurels surmounting this motto: "Napoleoni magno Caesari et victori". A vast crowd from the surrounding countryside was bivouacked in all the squares, notably in the one called Place Napoleon, and which, before the year was out, would resume the name of Frederick William! Only the old 'grumblers' (for we Poles had some among us) remained rather aloof amid the general hubbub. They maintained that the enthusiasm was partly artificial and stimulated by the authorities, who wanted to throw dust in the Emperor's eyes.'

But though the Poles, according both to Ségur and Brandt, really are enthusiastic for the French cause, they're finding themselves no less roughly handled than the unwilling and resentful Prussians. The troops, for their part, are appalled by the extreme and appalling poverty of their villages. 'What a contrast', exclaims Le Roy, 'between the beautiful German villages, which had yielded us all we needed, and these little Polish towns where we only found miserable Israelites, rife with vermine and the scab.' Colonel *Lubin Griois* of the Guard Horse Artillery – a great lover of Italian opera and, not least, Italian women (though he doesn't despise the Germans, despite their resistance to being seduced and their eventual capitulation) – agrees wholeheartedly:

'Thinly populated, the villages lie far apart, and the towns are almost
wholly occupied by Jews. They are as wretched as their inhabitants.
All peasants are the property of their lords, whose magnificent
châteaux contrast sharply with the poverty of the shacks, and whose
superb gardens and numerous servants offer a luxury and splendour
unknown in France. That part of the countryside which wasn't forest
was covered as far as the eye could see with fields of rye, promising
the richest of harvests. But soon these fields were devastated in order
to nourish our horses, for which we had the greatest difficulty in
finding any dry forage.'

Colonel *St-Chamans*, riding along at the head of his 7th Chasseurs, is finding it repugnant to obey orders

'to take away all the grain, brandy and cattle we could find between
the Vistula and the Niemen. I must admit it was very cruel of us,
after spending a few days in the home of the lord of some village or
of some farmer who'd received us well, and often better, than we
were in France, to thank them on leaving by carrying off their carriages, grain and cattle. These unhappy people begged us with
groans to modify the rigour of an order which, from their having
been well off, plunged them into poverty. I fancy all the officers tried
to soften their fate. But even with such concessions we still did them
a lot of harm.'

Even crueller, it is, if one is oneself Polish. Passing through Strzelnow,
between Posen and Thorn, Brandt pays a brief visit to his parents:

'It was this part of old Poland which had suffered worst. The evils of
the 1807 war had been followed without pause by the miseries of the
Continental Blockade, by epidemics among humans and animals,
and now by the continual troop movements. My parents, once
well-off proprietors, had had the costly honour of first putting up
Marshal Ney, then the Prince of Württemberg. All their forage had
been taken away by the artillery trains, and the daily and nightly req-
uisitions had taken their horses. In a word, everything was happening exactly as in an enemy country, apart from the government
vouchers, repayable only after a long period. For me the forty-eight
hours I spent in my father's house were as many hours of torture.'

No woman, whatever her social rank, is to be allowed to cross the Niemen.
So among all these thousands of marching men there can be only very
few, apart from the formidable breed of Mutter Courages, the sutleresses,
or *cantinières*. 'It was a fine profession, the cantinière's,' writes Elzéar
Blaze:

'These ladies had usually begun by following a soldier who'd
inspired them with tender sentiments. At first one saw them making
their way on foot with a barrel of brandy slung over one shoulder.
Eight days later they were comfortably seated on a horse they'd

found. To right, to left, in front, behind, barrels and saveloy sausages, cleverly disposed, balanced each other. The month was never out without a two-horse wagon, filled with provisions of all kinds, being there as evidence of the growing prosperity of their trade. An officer knew no greater pleasure than to lend them money. They were much less afraid of the Cossacks and the bands of stragglers who would sometimes strip them of their crowns than that some of their insolent debtors might get killed. In camp the cantinière's tent is the company's sitting room, bar, café.'

Many of course have children, usually by a succession of fathers, many of whom have slain their predecessor in a duel. Some of the boys are destined to become drummer-boys. But one of General Friant's surgeons, by name Déchy, who left Paris 'by the light of the immense tail of that year's comet' has brought his 13-year-old son. At Mecklenburg they find the 2nd Division 'encamped around the town, within sight of the British cruisers we could see from the coast'. From there they go on via Thorn to Insterberg, where an immense artillery park has been set up:

'At 9 a.m., June 22, a great rumour arose in the town. Soldiers with a martial air the like of which had never been seen and covered in dust, were drawing up in battle array on the public square. It was the Foot Grenadiers of the Guard. The whole population stood around,'

young Déchy among them. Once again it's Napoleon who's approaching. Since he's rumoured to be less than two hours away, the boy runs to tell his father, who promptly dons his sombre uniform – blue with yellow trimmings – and his fore-and-aft hat, and goes out beyond the suburbs to meet the Emperor. At a crossroads, one kilometre outside town,

'we saw in the plain a whirl of dust. It was the Emperor's carriage. Drawn by six little local horses driven by three peasants, with a mameluke on the box and only escorted by a few horse-gunners, it was making slow progress along the sandy road. To the Emperor's left we saw a sleeping man, whose head, knocking against the panel, fell back on His Majesty's shoulder.'

Déchy's father immediately recognizes the sleeper as Marshal Berthier, Prince of Neuchâtel, Napoleon's chief-of-staff and the army's major-general:

'As the carriage turned a corner its wheels sank deep into the sand and brought it to a standstill. By a natural movement the Emperor stuck his head out of the window, looked at us, and signed to my father to come closer.'

Seeing he's the doctor in charge of the Isterberg hospital, Napoleon wants to know whether its patients' health is satisfactory. The last artilleryman, Dr Déchy replies proudly, has just been given a clean bill of health. 'The Emperor took this news with pleasure. Then he asked my father who this child was he was holding by the hand.' On being told it was his son,

'the Emperor's face took on a stern impression. And he said: "Monsieur, this child ought to be at school or with his mother, not here. When orders are given for no women to follow the army, such orders should a fortiori be extended to include children." To excuse himself my father risked this answer: That when he'd taken me with him he hadn't expected to find himself so far from France. "Monsieur, anyone who belongs to the army in any capacity whatsoever must be prepared for anything."

A brief encounter which will be decisive for the boy's whole life.

And now it's sunset, 22 June. And this time it's the turn of the inhabitants of the little town of Wilkowiszki, about a day's march from the Niemen, to see

'a cloud of dust approaching along the road and hear trumpets heralding the Emperor's approach. A few moments later he appeared, seated alone in his carriage. Five trumpeters rode ahead, and he had an escort of officers and NCOs. He made straight for the castle, where a lodging had been prepared for him.'

His study, the local priest Butkevicius goes on, had been installed in

'a rustic pavilion surrounded by poplars. Numerous maps were spread out on his desk. Although the weather was very hot, Napoleon kept his dark greatcoat on and his little hat which he wore while talking to his generals and marshals, who all stood uncovered to listen. Through its coating of dust the Emperor's features showed signs of fatigue, annoyance and displeasure caused by the news he'd received on the way. His ill humour turned to anger when he was told that not only the army, but even the Guard, was short of provisions. Throughout his stay he was certainly in a very bad mood, because he dictated letters in a terrible voice. He didn't sleep that night, and everywhere people were organizing ovens to bake bread.'

Doubtless it's in the same 'terrible voice' he now dictates his declaration of war. Dated Wilkowiszki 22 June 1812, it's in the form of a proclamation to the army:

"Soldiers! The second Polish war has begun. The first ended at Friedland and Tilsit. At Tilsit Russia swore to be an eternal ally of France and to make war on Britain. Today she is violating these oaths. She refuses any explanation of her strange behaviour, so that the French eagles have been unable to recross the Rhine, which would be to leave our allies at her mercy. Russia is being swept away by her fate, her destinies must be accomplished. Does she think we are degenerates? Aren't we still the soldiers of Austerlitz? She makes us choose between dishonour and war. The choice cannot be in doubt. So let us march on, across the Niemen, and carry the war on to her territory. The second Polish war will be as glorious as the first, but the peace we shall conclude will carry its own guarantee. It will put an end to the baneful influence Russia for fifty years has been exercising on the affairs of Europe. – Napoleon."

The Reverend Butkevicius, at least, has his wits about him. Next day he invites Brandt to dinner, shows him a bed Napoleon has allegedly just done him the honour of sleeping in, likewise the table on which he'd signed his declaration of war. And in return for being allowed to keep 'at least one bull' offers Brandt 'two bottles of the imperial liqueurs and a glass of schnapps for each officer'. The bottles are afterwards found to contain... water, and cause Brandt to reflect that good nature is seldom rewarded, least of all in wartime. Before leaving Wilkowiski he has to requisition

'a whole herd of 50 cows, watched over by a very pretty girl. In despair at seeing us grab her herd, this Amaryllis weeps, wrings her hands, and finally throws herself at my feet, begging me to leave her at least two cows for her parents. Which I did without exacting any kind of ransom, though she seemed resigned to make great sacrifices to soften my heart.'

Catching up next day, a subaltern, left behind to escort the regimental baggage, tells Brandt of the

'disorders being committed and the confusion and indiscipline already prevailing in this immense army. "Everyone", he said, "is doing whatever he likes, taking from wherever he can. Frenchmen, Italians, Württembergers, Badeners, Bavarians, even Poles, are sacking the country just as they like. If this goes on much longer we'll be eating each other, like starving rats. The Emperor must be blind to such excesses."

In fact he isn't. Only, as usual, overestimating the power and range of his authority. From Thorn he'd written to Berthier to tell Davout that

'when you gave him orders to procure food for twenty days you assumed this would be done under regular forms and without stripping the countryside; that terror and desolation are let loose in Poland; and that he shall take the promptest measures to prevent the country from being devastated, otherwise we'll find ourselves in the same situation as we were in Portugal.'

By and by they will, and worse. Even so, riding on at a brisk 15 miles per hour through the immense forest of Pilkowiski, '25-miles broad by 37-mile long', Caulaincourt sees his master has no reason to be dissatisfied with the results of Davout's efforts:

'The troops marching along the road were superb, and received the Emperor with real enthusiasm. The men of I Corps were noticeable for their fine uniforms and general smartness. They could rival the Guard. All this mass of youth was full of ardour and good health.'

With certain exceptions. In the forest another eye-witness overtakes 'a fat major on a horse driving on stragglers with a long cane, who were answering him with loud shouts of abuse'.

CHAPTER 3

MIDSUMMER AT THE NIEMEN

'At present we must give back what doesn't belong to us' – 'his air was gay, even mischievous' – Major Le Roy's cookpot goes missing – Dumonceau stumbles on I Corps – a sunshade of pine branches – a staggering spectacle – birds of paradise – effectives – the Imperial Guard – the cavalry – the veterans – three classes of officers – recruits at Posen – too young an army – an immense baggage train – 'what a crowd of protégés!' – Napoleon falls off his horse – 'a military promenade to Petersburg and Moscow'

On Midsummer's Eve, 1812, the patriotic Polish count *Roman Soltyk* is resting in his bivouac not far from the Niemen's 'sluggish yellow waves' and probably swatting the mosquitoes which are so numerous in those latitudes at that time of year, when

'a travelling coach drawn by six swift coursers arrived at a brisk trot by the Königsberg road and stopped abruptly in the middle of our camp. It was only escorted by a few Chasseurs of the Guard, whose horses were exhausted and out of breath.'

Soltyk is an artillery officer. His friend *Josef Grabowski* calls him 'a handsome man but a bit of a boaster, who always made a good impression on the French by speaking their language with all its refinements. Above all he was remarkable for his knowledge of the theory and practice of gunnery'. Judge Soltyk's excitement when

'the carriage door opened, and we saw Napoleon get vivaciously out. He was wearing his uniform of a chasseur of the Guard and was accompanied by Berthier. None of his aides-de-camp put in an appearance. Shortly afterwards General Bruyères arrived, alone, at a gallop. The Emperor, apparently much wearied by his journey, wore a preoccupied air.'

Soltyk and some other officers run over:

'Taking several quick steps toward our major, Napoleon asked where the regiment's commanding officer was. Untroubled by the colonel's absence – he was still resting – Major Suchorzewski replies that he's standing in for him, and was at his orders. Whereupon the Emperor asked which road led to the Niemen, where our outposts were, and various other questions as to the Russians' whereabouts. While interrogating us in this way he said he wanted to change his coat, asking for a Polish uniform.[1] It had been agreed, or rather ordered, that no French soldier should be visible to the Muscovites. So he took off his coat, and the Prince of Neuchâtel, Suchorzewski, myself and Colonel Pagowski, who'd just come running up, likewise. Also General Bruyères.'

So now there they are

'five or six of us, standing around the Emperor in our shirtsleeves, in the middle of our bivouac, holding our uniforms in our hands. A singular sight! Of all our uniforms Colonel Pagowski's greatcoat and forage cap fitted the Emperor best. At first we'd offered him a lancer officer's chapka [flared helmet], but he declined, saying it was too heavy. All this took only a few minutes. Berthier, too, donned a Polish uniform. The colonel's two horses were quickly brought up. Napoleon mounted one, and Berthier the other. Since Lieutenant Zrelski's company was doing outpost duty that day, he was detailed off to accompany the Emperor as guide.'

The party proceed to the hamlet of Alexota, three miles downstream, 'opposite and only a cannonshot distant from the little walled town of Kovno'. Three days earlier Soltyk had, from this point, drawn a map of the Niemen's eastern shore. Here

'the Emperor dismounted in the courtyard of a doctor's house whose windows overlooked the Niemen and gave him a good view of the surroundings. Without showing himself, and with his horses carefully hidden in the courtyard, he reconnoitred the country perfectly. Back at our bivouac he wants to have details of the enemy's positions. More particularly he asks me where the main Muscovite bodies were, whether on Vilia's left or right bank? Doubtless he wanted to know whether the route to Vilna was open.'

A glance at the map shows the sense of Napoleon's question. It's at Kaunas – known in those days as Kovno – that the Vilia, after winding westwards from Vilna, flows into the Niemen. As usual he has taken his enemy on the hop.[2] Barclay de Tolly's First West Army is 75 miles away, concentrated around Vilna. Bagration's Second West Army is 75 miles further up the Niemen, at Grodno. Will his enemies never learn? His plan is to defeat them in detail, just as he'd done during his very first campaign back in 1796. And this time he has overwhelming numbers to do it with.

Flanked along the Vilia's north-western bank by Oudinot's II Corps and headed by Murat's immense command (I, II, III and IV 'reserve' Cavalry Corps), a main striking force, Davout's mostly French I Corps and Ney's Württembergers (III Corps), backed up by the Imperial Guard, will make a beeline for Vilna. While Oudinot fends off Wittgenstein's Finnish corps northwards towards Petersburg, farther down the Niemen at Tilsit Macdonald's (mostly Prussian) X Corps will drive northwards and besiege Riga, on the Baltic. Meanwhile farther upstream, at Grodno, three more army corps – Poniatowski's Poles (V), Reynier's (Saxons) (VII) and Vandamme's Westphalians (VIII) – advancing from Warsaw, will strike at Bagration, who at the same time will be prevented from liaising with Barclay by being stricken in flank by Eugène's (mostly Italian) IV Corps, supported by Saint-Cyr's Bavarians (VI), who are to cross the Niemen midway between Kovno and Grodno, at Piloni, and thus safeguard the main force's right flank as it advances swiftly on Vilna. First Barclay, then

Bagration, will be caught between overwhelming forces; and the war will be over in its allotted two or three weeks. Such is Napoleon's perfectly designed plan, and there's no reason in the world why it shouldn't succeed.

All possible contingencies having been taken care of, the Poles return to their bivouac. And as they do so Soltyk notices

'a visible change in the Emperor's face. His air was gay, even mischievous. No doubt he relished the idea of the surprise he was preparing for the Muscovites for the morrow, and whose results he'd calculated in advance. We brought him some refreshments, which he ate on the main road in our midst. He seemed to take pleasure in his change of costume and twice asked us whether the Polish uniform didn't suit him. Having breakfasted, he said laughingly: "At present we must give back what doesn't belong to us." Taking off his borrowed garments, he resumed his uniform of a Chasseur of the Guard, climbed back into his carriage and, accompanied by Berthier, left abruptly.'

Not far away from Soltyk's bivouac but evidently out of sight of it, 'in a vast plain of standing corn', there's another, whose men, though they're wearing Polish-style uniforms, aren't Poles but Dutchmen. It's the 2nd ('Red') Lancers of the Imperial Guard. The Belgian Captain *François Dumonceau* is in command of its 2nd squadron's 6th troop. In the oppressive heat – the temperature is up in the 30s – he has just had all the trouble in the world to clear a way through the immense masses of men on the only highroad through the Pilkowisky forest. Now his regiment is on a war footing, with loaded carbines. And though no one is allowed to unsaddle, their sickles have come into use and are harvesting the half-ripe corn. Fortunately their bivouac is close to a small stream. As for victuals,

'a wise providence had just brought three oxen on to the scene to supplement what was left of our provisions issued to us the day before yesterday. Unfortunately we lacked firewood for our camp fires, and were having to go a long way to get some. At about 7 p.m., just as we were settling in, a violent storm passed over us and for more than half an hour drenched us in torrents of rain.'

As yet the 85th Line's five battalions are still trudging on through the forest; and when a tremendous thunderstorm breaks out and the rain comes lashing down, Major Le Roy, his friend Lieutenant Jacquet and his ever resourceful 'philistine' (servant) Guillaume are instantly soaked through. All around them the storm is bringing pines and spruces crashing down and great lightning flashes, striking the tallest pines, have started a forest fire which Dumonceau, looking back over his shoulder, assumes is a smokescreen 'lit deliberately to conceal the army's concentration'.

Of none of the thousands of officers approaching the Niemen that day could it be more truly said that armies march on their stomachs than of Le Roy. A good portly man i'sooth, his diary is nothing so much as a record of how he gets his dinner each day and what it consists of. Alas, no sooner has his battalion emerged at long last from the endless forest and begun to bivouac in another soaking cornfield, than Guillaume is horrified to find that the major's iron cookpot, his most treasured possession, has gone missing – and with it their rice rations! 'But only since we've left the forest,' says the ever-optimistic Guillaume. 'Quite right,' rejoins Le Roy. 'And since you're wet through anyway you can take the same road back again. You'll be sure to find it. Run along now and fetch us back our wet-nurse.'

Said and done. The cookpot is found by the roadside, as well as – amazingly – the rice stowed inside it. Not far away is another of I Corps' regiments, the 57th Line. And one of its lieutenants, the 21-year-old *Aubin Dutheillet*, is watching his men

'slaughter such cows or other animals following in the wake of each unit as we had need of, making broth of our flour and cooking pancakes amid the embers of our campfires.'

Not all units are as well supplied. And despite all the elaborate arrangements – the company of bricklayers and bakers Davout has sent on ahead to build ovens at the river bank, the 'enormous flocks and herds and immense parks of wagons laden with food each regiment was dragging behind it to the Niemen', etc., – other units, belonging to less strictly disciplined corps, are already beginning to feel hungry.

An unusually observant man, all the 22-year-old Dumonceau can see from his 'solitary spot' is

'a few stragglers or isolated wagons searching about for their units in this vast plain. Only to our left, in the neighbourhood of Nougardisky, could we make out a little group of white tents, which we took to be the Emperor's. Seized by a desire to witness the passage of the Niemen, which we assumed was just then going on,'

he requests permission to go and take a look. Gets it. Mounts. And rides off. The horse he's riding is 'an excellent Polish cross-bred mare, a dark 5-year-old bay, well built and full of vigour and liveliness' called Liesje. When he'd bought her in East Prussia her tangled mane had hung down to her knees and her previous owner had begged him 'with tears in his eyes not to disentangle it, as the animal's life depended on it'. But Liesje has had to submit to comb, shears and bit, and of Dumonceau's three horses she's already his favourite:[3]

'Penetrating the curtain of woods bounding our horizon, I reach the end of the plateau. There, through the gaps in the dense foliage, I discover the river. Its yellowish waters, flowing along a river bed about 50 metres wide, washed the foot of our high ground, circumventing a kind of promontory on the opposite bank, and presenting a low unbroken plain, sandy and deserted, about three miles long and perhaps three-quarters wide. The only object to be seen anywhere was a little shack, flanked by two arid pines like parasols.'

But no sign of an enemy, or even inhabitants:

'No bridge had yet been established, nor was there any sign of any preparations to construct one. Everywhere reigned only a profound silence. But furthest away to my left, opposite the promontory, I thought I could make out some troops. Going in that direction, I encounter an artillery column, coming down by a very narrow hollow road. Following in its tracks, I reach a kind of hollow, three-quarters of a mile wide, surrounded by high ground, opposite the elbow formed by the river bank. At the centre of this basin a little hillock, shaped like a truncated cone, rose abruptly to a height of six or seven metres. Since it was sloped at its rear, two guns had been hauled up. Screened by bushes, I saw they were trained on the opposite bank. At the base of the mound was a big farm.'

And in the same instant, behind the farm, Dumonceau sees

'an imposing mass of infantry drawn up in close order, on several very extensive lines. Several similar lines of artillery and cavalry stood behind them, and out in front a mass of pontoons, loaded on their drays. It was Marshal Davout's army corps, resting silently under arms! I tried to bypass them and get closer to the river bank. But a sentry placed at its approaches stopped me, saying it was forbidden to reveal oneself. They were waiting for nightfall and definitive orders to start the crossing.'

Napoleon's reconnaissance in Polish uniform, Caulaincourt notes in his diary, had been made during the morning:

'Arrived at Naugaraidski at 1 a.m. Mounted Gonzalon. Wore a Polish cloak, black silk cap, with General Haxo, the Prince of Neuchâtel and the Master of the Horse to reconnoitre the Niemen. Followed the river bank along the left bank from below Kovno to a league and half above it. Returned to Naugaraidski at 3 p.m. Went into his tent.'

On another hillock, some 300 paces from the river bank and a few yards from his blue-and-white striped tents, Guard sappers have improvised a sunshade of pine branches. And he evidently spends some part of the sultry afternoon under it, watching the divisions debouch from the Pilkowski forest and drawing up on the sloping plain. Marshal Oudinot's remarkable factotum 'Grenadier' *François Pils*[4] finds a moment to open his watercolour box and sketch the scene. Besides Napoleon himself, only his Armenian bodyguard *Roustam Raza*[5] can be made out with any certainty as he stands there holding one of the Emperor's six Arab greys.

When, at about midday, Berthier's ADCs turn up, one of them, the future painter of ballet-like battle scenes, Baron *Louis-François Lejeune*[6] finds the scene from the imperial hillock

'the most extraordinary, the most pompous, the most inspiring spectacle imaginable – of all sights the one which, by exaggerating the extent of his power, both material and moral, is most capable of inebriating a conqueror. Under our gaze, around the culminating point we occupied, were seven reigning princes, King Murat prancing about in his theatrical costume at the head of the cavalry, all

Europe's most handsome men in parade uniforms, and all its finest horses. In the distance the massed battalions covered the plain with their sparkling bayonets and emulated the blazing sun, whose flashing mirage was reflected in the river waters and in lakes ruffled by a light breeze. The salutes of thousands of trumpets and drums – the enthusiastic shouts acclaiming the Emperor whenever he appeared – so much devotion and discipline, shortly to set in motion this multitude whose immensity lost itself on the horizon where its weapons still twinkled like so many stars – all this exalted everyone's confidence in the chief who was leading us.'

All day division after division debouches from the forest; until by the time the 2nd Cuirassiers, in Nansouty's I Cavalry Corps, emerges on to the plateau, Sergeant-major *Auguste Thirion*[7] finds

'the ground so thick with men and horses we could hardly find a spot to bivouac on. No anthill is more agitated. And the variety of uniforms, moving in all directions, the noise arising from this multitude, and the incessant uproar of drums, trumpets and bands – all made the moment solemn and the scene a curious one.'

Another of the shadowy figures up there on the imperial hillock may well be *Planat de la Faye*[8]. A lieutenant in the Artillery Train, to his own great surprise, he has been appointed ADC to General Lariboisière, once Lieutenant Napoleone Buonaparte's messmate, but now commanding all the Grand Army's artillery. Unexampled though it is for a mere lieutenant of the Train to be offered such a position, Planat, faced with the choice between 1,800 and 2,500 francs a year and the prospect of further brilliant advancement on Lariboisière's staff, has naturally jumped at this chance, which among other things will enable him to send home more pay to his two impecunious brothers, especially as 'on campaign one spends almost nothing, and the habitual distractions of military men weren't to my taste'. Planat is a close friend of Lariboisière's son Honoré who is his fellow-ADC:

'Nothing was commoner than to see generals' sons situated like this. It was supposed to vaccinate them with the germs of the most brilliant military qualities. But the sternest general is almost always the feeblest and most indulgent father.'

Though enhanced with silver aiguillettes – the emblem of a staff officer – Planat's iron-grey uniform is admittedly nothing like as spectacular as the one Lejeune has designed for himself and his aristocratic colleagues on Berthier's staff:

'Scarlet tight-fitting trousers, with two gold stripes down the sides, a sky-blue pélisse trimmed with white fox-fur and, across the chest, gold brandenburger lacings, crossed transversely by a broad scarlet shoulder-strap. The tall new-style black-peaked hussar helmet, likewise scarlet, sported an inverted gold chevron on either side and around the top a gold lace band. The dangling scarlet schabraque, too, was fringed with gold lace and had a gold eagle in the centre,' a painting to which Secretary Fain adds some finishing touches. The shako, he says, was

'ornamented with a white aigrette of heron's plumes and the uniform's effect still further heightened by gilt cordings and a mass of gold tassles and buttons. A superb silk and gold sash, a little cartridge case, a sabretache and a damascened sword completed their outfit. Their parade horses were Arab greys with long fluttering silky manes and hussar-style bits with braidings and gold tufts.'

So magnificent a horseman in the full pride and vigour of his youth can of course sit on nothing less than 'a gold and scarlet festooned panther skin', likewise edged with gold and sporting scarlet tassles. One of Lejeune's colleagues has even gone so far as to fit his pélisse with *diamond* buttons.[9]

How many men are assembled that day at the Niemen? How many horses? How many guns? The most authentic – if not necessarily the most accurate – assessment is on a slip of paper afterwards preserved by Napoleon's ambitious, jealous and fiery-tempered First Ordnance Officer, the 28-year-old Gaspard Gourgaud.[10] 'Scribbled all over in the Emperor's handwriting' it gives a total of 350,000 combatants, whereof 155,000 Frenchmen (but that would include Dutchmen), 162,000 allies, and 984 guns.

Crème de la crème is of course the Imperial Guard. An army corps in itself, with its own infantry, engineer, cavalry and artillery regiments, officers and rankers alike have been skimmed off from Line. At the Courbevoie barracks Coignet had seen them come in. Each had served for five years, done at least two campaigns, and would now draw pay a rank above what they'd have got in the Line. The Guard Artillery was superb. Major *Jean-François Boulart*, a man who in odd moments likes to play the flute, has brought one of the Guard's three artillery columns all the way from its depot at La Fère, outside Paris. In their tall plaqueless bearskins and dark-blue red-trimmed uniforms, he says, his gunners were

'a magnificent object of general admiration. On 5 June the Emperor had come and reviewed my artillery. He wasn't a man to make compliments, but he found it handsome. He had the goodness to spend a lot of time in my company.'

The Guard is a law unto itself. Outside its own hierarchy it is absolutely no respecter of persons. Sarcastically known as 'The Immortals' because its infantry units, at least, practically never fight, its function is to give the knockout blow in battle and in the unimaginable eventuality of a retreat ('a word unknown in the French army') provide a kind of marching bastion. It also gets all the pickings. If not the largest of all the corps (Davout's numbered 70,000), the Guard, 43,000 strong plus the 8,300 Poles of Claparède's Vistula Legion and the Hessian Royal Guard, is certainly the most formidable.

Many of the other cavalry regiments are especially magnificent. Major *Marcelline Marbot's*[11] 23rd Chasseurs, serving with Oudinot's II Corps and numbering – quite exceptionally – 2,000 mounted men, was as fine a regiment as that beau sabreur says he'd ever seen, or ever would:

'Not that it comprised out-of-the-way individuals of transcendent merit; but there was no one who wasn't up to his duties. Everyone marched in step, both in point of bravery and zeal. All the officers, intelligent and sufficiently educated, lived as true brothers-in-arms. So also with the NCOs. And since the troopers followed this good example, they lived in perfect harmony. Almost all being old veterans of Austerlitz, Iéna, Friedland and Wagram, most sported the triple or double stripe. General Bourcier, whose task it had been to find mounts for these vast masses of cavalry, had given the 23rd Chasseurs the tallest and finest horses he could find. So this regiment was known as the carabiniers of the light cavalry.'

Jean-Michel Chevalier, a long-serving lieutenant of the Chasseurs of the Imperial Guard, its senior cavalry regiment, may think the Saxon Guard Cuirassiers 'not very elegant, with cast iron cuirasses weighing 30 pounds and more, and a Roman-style helmet'; but some of the Italian Guard regiments, it's generally agreed, are superb. For Murat's Neapolitan Guard, resplendent in sky-blue or yellow uniforms, 'the Marquis of Livorno had formed one of the most beautiful regiments you could hope to see. He'd summoned old French and German military men and himself set them an example of enterprise and strict discipline.' The Guardia d'Onore of the Kingdom of Italy – of which Césare de Laugier is adjutant, too, is

'composed of young men of the best Italian families, each being supported by his family with 1,200 frs a year [a Line lieutenant's pay]. It drew attention to itself by its handsome turnout and good discipline.'

Cuirassier Sergeant-major Thirion is rhapsodic:

'Never had more beautiful cavalry been seen! Never had the regiments reached such high effectives. And never had cavalry been so well mounted. Our regiments were so numerous that three had been adjudged enough for a division.'

At the same time he's critical of the way it's organized and commanded:

'Each regiment formed a brigade in itself, with a brigadier-general commanding it: a vicious organization, however, because a regiment isn't a proper command for a general, and it tended to annihilate its colonel's authority.'

All the Line infantry regiments, too, have a backbone of veterans – men like Captain *Charles François* of the 36th Line, nicknamed 'the Dromedary of Egypt' because he'd fought at the Pyramids and once been a Turkish slave. Ségur says such old-timers could easily be recognized

'by their martial air. Nothing could shake them. They had no other memories, no other future, except warfare. They never spoke of anything else. Their officers were either worthy of them or became it.'

For to exert one's rank over such men one had to be able to show them one's wounds and cite oneself as an example.'

De Laugier – still trudging across Poland in the heats toward Poloni – is noticing how his Italian veterans, men who'd fought in Spain at the sieges of Saragossa and Gerona,

'are stimulating the new arrivals with their warlike tales, so that the conscripts brighten up. The continual marching is giving them a military bearing. By so often exaggerating their own feats of arms, the veterans oblige themselves to authenticate by their conduct what they've led others to believe of them.'

If many of these 'old' campaigners, men of thirty or forty, have never been promoted, it's usually because they can't read or write. Another of Berthier's brilliant aides, Major *Montesquiou de Fézensac*, a scion of one of France's most ancient military families, who'd joined up as a ranker at the time of the Boulogne Camp, divides the army's officers at this time into three categories:

'The first class, made up of graduates recently out of military school, zealous, trained, but inexperienced and little developed physically, were from the outset unable to stand up to the campaign's excessive fatigues. The second class, quite the contrary, consisted of ex-NCOs whose total lack of education should have blocked their further promotion, but who'd been commissioned so as to keep up the spirit of emulation and replace the enormous losses caused by such murderous campaigns; excellent soldiers, for the rest, hardened to fatigues and from long habit knowing everything war can teach in the lower ranks. The third class, halfway between, was made up of educated officers in the prime of life, formed by experience, and all inspired with a noble ambition to distinguish themselves and carve out a career. Unfortunately these were the least numerous.'

Into which class would he have put sergeant – soon to become sous-lieutenant – Jean-Roch Coignet? Certainly the second. A guardsmen had to be at last 5 feet 7 inches tall. And the 2nd Grenadiers' little drill sergeant had only been smuggled in by padding out the soles of his boots with a pack of cards. As we've seen, he'd only recently learnt his alphabet, certainly with an eye to the infinitely desirable commission which 'on campaign could make all the difference between life and death' especially if one had the misfortune – as both Le Roy and Fézensac had in 1807 – to be taken prisoner. Yet that hot day at the Niemen, Coignet is responsible for part of the Imperial Treasure.[12]

If the regiments drawn up on the river bank that blazing afternoon have a fault it is that they contain altogether too many young soldiers. No regiment in I Corps is stronger than the 85th Line. Yet when Le Roy had joined it in East Prussia he'd found his battalion 'consisted entirely of young soldiers needing a lot of care; not,' he adds, 'that this would save them from being subjected to the same demands as our veterans, or from having the same marches exacted of them'. And already, after the three-day march across Poland, only four-fifths have even reached the Niemen. The average age of Bourgoing's fellow-subalterns in the 5th Tirailleurs is hardly over twenty.

Although troopers take much longer to train, the cavalry, too, is full of striplings. General Count Dejean, who'd raised 40,000 new troopers in Alsace, had confessed to Napoleon at the Tuileries that 'half of them hadn't the necessary vigour to wield a sabre. "If it hadn't been for Your Majesty's express orders I'd have sent them back to the depots." – "You'd have done very ill if you had," Napoleon had replied tartly. And explained that sheer numbers "combined with the supposed quality of my regiments of already known worth," exaggerated in the newspapers and passing from mouth to mouth, had the result that "on the day I open a campaign I'm preceded by a moral power that makes up for the real effectives I haven't been able to obtain." Which no doubt is why, though at Hanover they'd been given 'very beautiful horses,' Colonel *St-Chamans*' young recruits for the 7th Chasseurs

'who'd left the depots in France without even having learnt to sit a horse or any of a trooper's duties on the march or on campaign, if the truth be told didn't know how to use them, and wouldn't be able to turn them against the old and tried cavalry to be opposed to us.'

Results which had shocked Napoleon himself. Appearing suddenly on horseback at the 2nd Vistula Regiment's march-past at Insterberg, he'd said 'in the curt strident voice he used on his bad days "I find these young men too young. What I need is people who can stand fatigues. Men who're too young only fill the hospitals."'

But what is striking everybody most of all as the army debouches on the wooded slopes on that blazing afternoon is the immense, the unprecedented numbers of vehicles. Never has Captain *Girod de l'Ain*, ADC to General Dessaix, commanding a division of I Corps, or anyone else

'seen such immense preparations. The Emperor had assembled all the forces of Europe for this expedition; and each one of us had followed his example and brought with him everything he possessed. Each officer had at least one carriage, and the generals several. The number of horses and servants was prodigious.'

An officer's 'philistine' cooks, launders and, on occasion, marauds for him. Even subalterns such as Paul de Bourgoing have brought one: a plucky little 13-year-old Parisian street urchin, by name Victor, who'd done his damnedest to join the 5th Tirailleurs as a drummer-boy, but been turned down because of his tender age and puny physique, and whom Bourgoing has taken on out of sheer compassion.

The host of domestics is partly explained by the strict rule which forbids any officer to employ a ranker as batman. In the Imperial Guard it is

'forbidden, under pain of dismissal, for a chasseur or a grenadier to tend an officer's horse, or even hold it by the bridle. So we took old fife-players who had served out their time, soldiers' children or retired veterans.'

Gone too are the republican days when any officer under the rank of major had had to hoof it with his men. For the top brass alone the famous Parisian coachbuilder Gros-Jean has built no fewer than 300 carriages, specially for the campaign.[13] Colonel Count *François Roguet* of the 1st Grenadiers, who has just covered 1,200 miles in sixteen weeks in his own travelling carriage to take command of the Guard's 2nd Division, has brought with him six servants, twelve horses and two wagons filled with his personal effects, among them books and a great many maps. Girod de l'Ain goes on:

'Much of the baggage train, it's true, was made up of vehicles stocked up with provisions while crossing Prussia and Poland. But add the trains of the big artillery parks, the pontoon bridges, the ambulances, etc., and you can judge what such an army looked like.'

Least competent – and certainly least popular – of all branches of the service is the Administration. By no means all the war commissaries and intendants responsible for all these thousands of transports can be prevailed upon to emulate their chief, the indefatigable Daru, an administrator of utmost probity and energy. 'What a mob of fellows wearing collars of every hue!' exclaims Artillery Inspector *Paixhans*:

'What a brilliant crowd of youthful protégés! Their holy persons filled with self-importance but oblivious of their functions, not even knowing what their duties consisted in, with an arrogance only equalled by their ineptitude, they regarded themselves as our superiors. In their wake, what a dirty sombre swarm of subordinate agents, a cloaque of ineptitude, baseness and rapacity!'

Colonel St-Chamans, too, is discovering to his dismay that compared with the Army of Andalusia, which he has just left, the Grand Army's administration is

'full of types who'd never seen war, and who were saying out loud they'd only come on this campaign to make their fortunes'.

A certain pudgy and no little conceited captain of dragoons, by name *Henri Beyle*,[14] one day to become one of France's greatest novelists, is in it mostly for the experience. A younger cousin of Daru's, he has secured himself a job as a war commissary by paying court to Daru's wife.

As for the horses, their numbers, either at the Niemen or still in the rear, are almost beyond belief. Over and above the cavalry's 80,000 mounts there are 50,000 draft horses and more than 10,000 officers' mounts – in all 140,000.

And now it's afternoon. Friant's crack infantry division, which is to spearhead the advance, has turned up late. And to get his orders Dedem, too, has to mount the imperial hillock. Meanwhile the rest of the division stands waiting in column at its base. The scene may be spectacular; but Dedem finds the mood up there strangely sombre:

'I went up to the group of generals in Napoleon's entourage. A grim silence, almost a feeling of consternation, reigned among them. Upon my allowing myself a little gaiety, General Auguste de Caulaincourt (the Governor of the Pages and brother to the Master of the Horse) signed to me, and said in a low voice: "No one here is laughing. It's a historic occasion [une journée]." He gestured toward the other bank, as if to add: "There's our tomb!"'

Hindsight? Or foresight? Caulaincourt says his brother was always in pain from his old wounds and 'often longed for death'. Has he a premonition of his own death in battle six weeks later? Or has he perhaps been influenced by his elder brother's outspoken antipathy to this new war? Or is it the complete lack of news. Where, exactly, are the Russians? Quartermaster-General *Anatole de Montesquiou* is noticing how 'Davout, the staff, everyone,' is complaining that

'none of their spies are coming back. The only sign of life on the opposite shore was an occasional patrol of Cossacks. The corps on our right knew no more about the enemy's movements than we did. A major got the idea of crossing the river, alone, to find out what was happening on the opposite bank. Not a sentry, not a soldier did he find. Proceeding further, he interrogated some inhabitants, who told him the enemy had retired, and he came back to inform the Emperor. This was certainly to render an important service; yet being improvised and outside the hierarchy it lacked legality. And the Emperor's righteous anger was extreme.'

At 6 p.m., Caulaincourt goes on, Napoleon

'mounted Friedland, inspected the pontoon train on the Kovno road, reconnoitred towards Marienpol. Returned at 8 p.m. At 9 p.m. mounted the same horse and rode over the high ground and the river banks from the point opposite Kovno to where the pontoons had been thrown across. After spending two hours dictating orders he decided to make a moonlight reconnaissance, closer to the river, to decide exactly where to cross. To avoid attracting attention from any Russian outposts he left everybody, without exception, at a distance. Accompanied only by General Haxo of the Engineers, he rode to and fro along the bank, before rejoining his staff.'

It is now that an incident occurs that in any other circumstance would go unheeded, but which strikes both Berthier and Caulaincourt as ominous. By no means a good horseman, only an indefatigable one,[15] Napoleon rode, says Odenleben,

'like a butcher. Without moving his legs, holding the reins loosely in his right hand, the left hanging down, he looked as if he'd been hung up in his saddle. At a gallop his torso swayed forwards and sideways with the horse's movements.'

And this summer he has also put on a lot of weight. 'His Majesty,' Captain Count *Boniface de Castellane,* an orderly officer who's seeing him daily at close quarters at IHQ, writes in his diary, 'has put on a good deal of weight, and rides with more difficulty than before. The Grand Equerry has to give him a hand up when he mounts.' That evening, Napoleon is riding through a wheatfield in the moonlight, followed by Caulaincourt and Berthier, when

'a hare, starting up between his horse's legs, caused it to swerve slightly.[16] The Emperor, who hadn't a good seat, rolled to the ground; but got up again so quickly that he was on his feet again before I could reach him to lend him a hand. He mounted again without saying a word. The ground was very soft, and he suffered only a slight bruise on his hip.'

In spite of themselves, says Caulaincourt, men are superstitious on the eve of great events: 'Instantly the reflection occurred to me that it was a bad augury. Nor was I the only one to think so, for the Prince of Neuchâtel seized my hand and said: "We'd better not cross the Niemen. This is a bad omen!"'

At first Napoleon says nothing; but

'by and by he began to joke with Berthier and me about his fall. Yet his bad temper and forebodings were obvious, no matter how he tried to conceal them. In other circumstances he'd have blamed the charger which had caused this silly accident, and wouldn't have spared the Master of the Horse. As it was, he affected the utmost serenity, and did all he could to banish the gloomy doubts no one could help feeling.'

Gossip is general:

'Some of the headquarters staff observed that the Romans wouldn't have crossed the Niemen. All that day the Emperor, usually so cheerful and active when his troops were carrying out extensive operations, was very serious and preoccupied.'

At dinner that evening he asks Caulaincourt whether his fall has given rise to much talk? What are Russian peasants like? Are they likely to form guerrilla bands, as the Spaniards have done? Barclay, he suspects, is concentrating his forces around the little town of Novo-Troki, a dozen or so miles on this side of Vilna. Surely his ex-ambassador to Petersburg doesn't think his 'brother Alexander' will give up the Lithuanian capital without a fight?

Between hasty mouthfuls – dinner never takes more than fifteen minutes – Caulaincourt opines with his usual candour[17] that, in a campaign where the theatre of war is so vast, he 'doesn't much believe in pitched battles'. Hasn't the Tsar himself told him that if the fighting should go against him he'll retire to Siberia? Barclay can afford to yield a lot of ground, 'if only to lead you a long way from your base and oblige you to divide your forces'.

'"Then I've got Poland!" retorts Napoleon briskly. "And in the eyes of the Poles Alexander will have earned everlasting shame by giving it up without a fight. To give me Vilna is to lose Poland."'

But didn't he tell Caulaincourt at the Tuileries that he doesn't want Poland anyway?

The Grand Army's self-confidence, General Count *Philippe de Ségur* assures us, was boundless:[18]

'It was going to be a military promenade to Petersburg and Moscow. One last effort, and maybe everything would be achieved. This being the last opportunity that would present itself, we were loth to let it slip out of our hands. We should have been embarrassed by the glorious stories others would have to tell of it.'

Of course there are sceptics. And one or another of our writers even claims to have foreseen the disaster. One of Boulart's immediate subordinates is a certain Captain *Pion des Loches*. A more than unusually inveterate grumbler, he claims that he

'foresaw clearly that this campaign would bring about the Emperor's ruin; and though I loved neither his person nor his government, the prospect of his fall terrified me, on account of the consequences it would have'.

But such seers must have been few.[19] And certainly no one, that Midsummer's Eve, could have forseen that of this vast and glittering host at most some 20,000 ragged, stunned, starving, stinking, frostbitten men, a handful of women and almost none of its 140,000 horses would recross the frozen river six months later. Young Déchy was among the most impressed: 'What men! What an epoch!' he'd exclaim, long afterwards. 'Alas,' sighs that man of steel, cuirassier Sergeant-major Thirion,

'how many of the personages in this picture are still alive to tell the tale today! What became of these conquerors of Europe? With few exceptions all died – some the beautiful death of a soldier on the field of battle; others of misery and hunger.'

CHAPTER 4

'GET INTO VILNA!'

A tremendous thunderstorm – 'A desert' – a lethal diet for horses – an abandoned countryside – pillage – quagmires – Captain Fivaz writes his will – Lyautey listens to the band – a military promenade – Napoleon leaves Kovno – desperate looters – a carriageful of commanders – Murat – Davout – Berthier – strategic considerations – 'I sow dissension among my generals' – a serious mistake – where's Barclay? – Dumonceau flanks the army – Montbrun loses his temper – a skirmish – into Vilna – Ségur's brother taken prisoner

Three bridges are to be thrown, at 100-metre intervals. And at 10 p.m. Eblé's engineers begin launching the pontoons from their 12-horse drays. To cover the operation, three companies of the 13th Light cross silently in skiffs, land on the opposite bank and lie down in the sand, 'hiding behind the little escarpment formed by the river bank'. By now the night sky is full of glimmering stars.[1]

Soltyk, whose fluent French has meanwhile attached him to Imperial Headquarters' topographical department, is perhaps the very first staff officer to cross, with orders to bring Napoleon some villagers:[2]

'It was so dark we didn't know whether we had any enemy in front of us or not. As far as we could see, no patrol, no scout appeared at any point. Only after about 100 men had established themselves on the right bank did we hear a distant sound of galloping horses, and a strong troop of Muscovite hussars halted at about a hundred paces from our weak advance guard. Dark though it was, we recognized them by their white plumes.[3] Coming toward us, the officer in command shouts out in French: *"Qui vive?"* "France!" our men reply quietly. "What are you doing here? F... off!" "You'll soon see!" our skirmishers reply resolutely. Whereon the officer goes back to his men and orders them to fire their carbines. None of ours reply. And the enemy hussars disappear at a gallop.'

Ségur, with his literary turn of mind, thinks he hears *three* shots – like *les trois coups* in a French theatre – 'and this irritated Napoleon'. Even though the Russian army is 75 miles away.

At 3 a.m. Dumonceau is roused by his regiment's silver trumpets 'joyously sounding the reveille and, immediately afterwards, the saddle-up'. The Red Lancers not being scheduled to move down to the river until well into the forenoon, General Count Colbert, its commanding officer, 'formed us up in square. After a flourish of trumpets had prepared us for it, Adjutant Fallot, in a resounding voice, read out the Emperor's proclamation.' So also in all the other regiments. To Captain *Pierre Auvray* of the 23rd Dragoons it seems that the army reacts with 'unparalleled enthusiasm. Its sentiments were shared by everyone around Napoleon, whether Frenchmen or foreigners.' So also Ségur:

'The word Niemen inflamed our imagination. Everybody was on fire to get across it – a desire the more natural as the miserable conditions in Poland had been daily augmenting our privations. To put an end to our complaints we were made to see the enemy's country as a promised land.'

At 4 a.m. the sun rises over the plains of Lithuania beyond the bridges; and Planat de la Faye, watching from the top of the imperial hillock, sees how

'the army, in parade uniforms, begins defiling in good order on to the three bridges. At its head each regiment had its band playing fanfares, mingled with the shouts of "Vive l'Empereur!". It all seemed like one vast military parade.'

Major Boulart of the Guard Artillery, too, is impressed:

'Unit after unit came and took up its position on the heights, ready when its turn came to cross the bridges. Arriving from all sides, they seemed to be springing up out of the ground. These 200,000 men, assembled in a small space, pressing incessantly on to the bridges then rallying on the vast plain on the right bank and going off in various directions, were a magnificent spectacle, perhaps unique in history.'

His colleague Colonel *Lubin Griois* – that great lover of the good things of life, and more particularly of Italian music and women – will always remember how the sun 'flashed on the arms and cuirasses of the innumerable troops of all nations as they poured uninterruptedly over the three bridges. All these troops rivalled each other in ardour and covered both banks to a great distance.' And to Lieutenant Chevalier of the Guard Chasseurs – who sincerely believes Napoleon has 'done everything in his power to avoid this war' – it all seems positively supernatural, 'as if the earth were producing armed men instead of harvests'.

By now, after exhausting forced marches of 35 miles a day, Ney's III Corps too has turned up; and as it emerges from the Pilkowiski forest one of its Württemberg artillery officers, Major *Faber du Faur*, sketches the scene, showing some Württemberg grenadiers in the foreground and, in the distance, a glimpse of columns crossing the three pontoon bridges. 'As soon as the first division was established on the far bank,' Ségur goes on,

'the Emperor, seized with sudden impatience, galloped cross-country as fast as his horse could go to the forest bordering the river. In his haste he seemed to be wanting to reach the enemy all on his own.'

Pure literary imagination, explodes Gourgaud. 'Has the Assistant Prefect of the Palace taken his characters from the madhouse?' On this occasion, however, Ségur seems to be right, even if his manner of expressing himself is melodramatic. To Caulaincourt, riding a few paces behind him with a map of the district dangling on a leather thong from his left buttonhole, Napoleon seems to be 'amazed to learn that the Russian army had retreated. Several reports had to be given him and various people brought before him before he'd believe the news. He followed the advance guard's movements for more than five miles, pressing the whole army forward and questioning all the country folk he could find, yet without obtaining any positive news. Poles were sent out in all directions to collect information.'

No enemy being in sight – or 'only an occasional Cossack lance flashing on the horizon' – Napoleon returns to his headquarters on the left bank. And at about 1 p.m. makes a second, more ceremonious entry into Lithuania, this time at the head of the Imperial Guard, which 'crossed the river to the sound of its bands'.[5]

The crossing is proceeding so smoothly and swiftly that as the Red Lancers ride down to join the rest of the Guard cavalry Dumonceau is wondering where all the scores of regiments have gone to. Already Davout's I Corps, making a bee-line for Vilna, has completely 'disappeared into the vast plains beyond'. Debouching from the bridges together with the Guard's four other cavalry regiments (Chasseurs, Grenadiers, Dragoons, and 1st (Polish) Lancers) the Red Lancers turn left and 'at a steady trot' follow 'a broad sandy road' downstream.

By and by Kovno comes into sight. 'A well-built little town set in an amphitheatre of pinewoods', it puts Lieutenant Vossler of Prince Louis' Hussars in mind of an Italian city. No enemy is defending its walls. And to Colonel St-Chamans, riding quickly through the streets at the head of his 7th Chasseurs, most of the inhabitants still seem to be there. 'They received us in a friendly fashion and no one did them any harm.'

Dumonceau's Dutchmen are still pushing their way along the sandy road 'amid a crush of all kinds of vehicles in the stifling almost insupportable heat', when

'the sky became charged with electricity which rumbled horribly in clouds that came rolling up at a speed we'd never seen the like of. At about 3 p.m. the lightning struck, close at hand. It killed two men and three horses.'

Back at the bridges the storm breaks so suddenly that the 2nd Cuirassiers, leading unit of Montbrun's II Cavalry Corps, hardly have time to unbuckle their white capes and

'the 6th Troop was still on the bridge, when a clap of thunder burst with such violence that all our heads, as if in a drill movement, jerked down on to our horses' necks. I've seen many storms in my life, but never any to approach that thunderclap on the Niemen! The cloudburst had flung its thunderbolt at the pontoon bridge which 6th Company were just then crossing. It fell in little stones, some of which struck against our cuirasses. One of them hit M. Henri Vandendrier on the cheek. Either the thunderclap or the rattling of the hailstones so terrified the colour-sergeant's horse that it leapt into the river and reached the shore swimming. All we saw above the water during his voyage was the poor bather's head and the pole of the standard attached to his saddle! Never have I received such a waterspout on my body!'

There the storm is violent but brief – by the time Thirion's men have drawn up to the right of the bridges in line with the 1st Lancers it has already gone over. But at Kovno, only a couple of miles away, where the 'burning torrential rain' drenches Dumonceau for two hours, it has also flooded the Vilia, whose only bridge has been burnt by the Russian rearguard. And the swollen waters are holding up the French pursuit. By and by Napoleon himself turns up on the scene and orders young Colonel Géheneuc[5] of the 6th Light Infantry to take some Polish lancers and find a ford. Said and done. Accompanied by two other resolute swimmers, Géheneuc swims his horse over to the far bank. But returning to his regiment, sees a Polish lancer being swept away by the current, and leaps

'fully clothed into the river to save him. This action, praiseworthy enough in itself, the Emperor considered unbecoming in a colonel at the head of his regiment in the presence of the enemy and told him so.'[9]

Heroics are all very well. What's wanted is some pontoons. And Napoleon orders Lariboisière to lend Haxo the battalion of military labourers of the so-called Navy of the Danube. To Lejeune's painterly eye the scene as they get down to work is positively Raphaelesque:

'The Emperor, though drenched through like the rest of us, was present at the rebuilding of the bridge. He impressed an extraordinary activity on all who were working at it, including two hundred of General Haxo's engineers [*sic*], stripped naked.'

The Russians have also destroyed the permanent timber bridge over the Niemen. But it's soon restored, and other units are streaming across. Ordering Haxo to throw a fourth pontoon bridge, plus two more on piles, Napoleon leaves the scene at about 8 p.m. and makes for his new headquarters in a convent, about half a mile outside the town.

Normally it should be the duty of the Prefect of the Palace, *Louis-François Joseph de Bausset* – a man so corpulent that Spanish chairs have a way of collapsing under his bulk – to select a building for IHQ. But Bausset is still in Paris, and according to Gourgaud the task is falling on Ségur, his first assistant. Which among other things means it's unlikely he witnessed the scene at the Vilia. Yet evidently it's in some such semi-mythical version as he'll afterwards give that the incident, passing through the army and being steadily improved as it goes, reaches Dumonceau. Just as he's settling into his wet bivouac outside the town walls he hears from some comrades 'who'd gone into town to do some shopping' an even more melodramatic version. It had been the Emperor himself, they tell him, who, 'supported by two troopers', had risked his life trying to cross the swollen stream!

'Seeing us arrive in the dishevelled state inflicted by the storm on our faces and clothes,' Lejeune goes on, 'the little town's inhabitants and its many monasteries' religious brought us abundant refreshments. It was their habitual luxury to drink iced honey-water and a beer of their own admirable brew. But this sudden transition to iced liquors, avidly gulped down by men drenched in rain and sweat, instantly made many of us ill.'

Dedem's infantry brigade has been one of the first to cross the Niemen, and by now must be miles down the Vilna road; so he too can only be reporting by hearsay when he says that the first units to enter Kovno had harmed neither the town nor its inhabitants:

'We found any amount of supplies; but soon an order comes to place sentries at the doors and allow neither soldiers, officers nor generals to enter. Everything is reserved for the Imperial Guard. It alone is allowed into town. The other corps, including the advance guard, marched round outside its walls. The inhabitants fled, spreading consternation far and wide.'

And by the time Lieutenant *Carl von Martens* of III Cavalry Corps passes through, everything in Kovno has been smashed up:

'Camp fires were still smoking in the market place, the furniture had been taken out of the houses and the windows shattered. At most a Jew was to be seen here and there. One glance was enough. Kovno was a totally plundered town.'

The 'liberation' of Lithuania has begun.

For Dumonceau's Dutchmen, grilling their meat rations at a stick's end outside Kovno town walls, their first brief summer night on Lithuanian soil is dank and chill. Sergeant-major Thirion, too, is shivering and so are all the other steel-clad men whom I Cavalry Corps' kindly and philosophical senior veterinary surgeon Dr *Raymond Faure* sees

'wrapped in their big white mantles, seeming as much by their heroic bearing as by their nigh colossal forms to be the very embodiments of a force everything must yield to'.

Thirion's horse, a magnificent Hanoverian, can hardly lift its hoofs and 'tottered like a drunken man. I walked him up and down in front of my company to warm him and get the blood circulating.' Such a damp chilly night is unexpectedly disastrous. When dawn breaks over the wet trampled rye fields, Thirion realizes

'this night had cost us as dearly as a battle. Everyone has told of the numbers of horses lost that night. No one how many men! But what was the loss of mere men? Horses cost money; the army's ranks repopulated themselves by decree, one more felling in the human forest.'

Fortunately, Dr Faure goes on,

'a gentle dawn refreshed the air and seemed just what was needed to reanimate the forces of vegetation, always busily reproducing while men seemed only to meditate destruction'.

The French high command has assumed that Lithuania's wide fields, stretching away to the sombre spruce forests, will be ripe for harvesting and yield plenty of fodder. They aren't. The northern summer has come two weeks late and green crops of rye and barley are a lethal diet for the horses. Dumonceau and his colleagues have to be

'exceedingly careful not to feed them the barley until after the green corn; and even then only very little at a time. But above all not to let them drink for a long while afterwards. Otherwise the barley, suddenly swelling inside the stomach, caused violent cholics, such as almost invariably led to sudden death.'

Already he has blotted his copybook by emulating his general's habit, famous throughout the army, of smoking a meerschaum on the march. Now something more serious happens. One of his troopers ignores the order and his horse drops dead. And Dumonceau gets a swingeing reprimand. 'Two other captains were in like case as myself.'

The Red Lancers and the rest of the Guard cavalry spend that day in what seems a senseless exercise of the kind endemic in military life:

'In the morning, unexpectedly, the trumpets on all sides sound "To horse!", as if we've been surprised by the enemy. In a jiffy the various regiments assemble. Coming and placing himself at our head and preceded by an advance guard, the Duke of Istria [Marshal Bessières, commanding the Guard Cavalry] leads us by column of troops along the same road we'd taken yesterday to get here. Then he turns off to the left, into the road being followed by the King of Naples' and Marshal Davout's columns.'

Since the Imperial Guard always has absolute right of way, its cavalry's irruption into the chaos prevailing around the bridgeheads – the crossing will go on for three days – can hardly have diminished it, or helped Generals Guilleminot and *Jomini* in their vain efforts to control it. No matter. The six proud cavalry regiments continue their promenade. For that's what it turns out to be. Towards evening

'with the left, i.e., the Horse Grenadiers, at our head, we finally retrace our steps along a fine paved highway through an immense sombre forest, out of which, to our vast amazement, we emerge in front of our bivouac of that same morning, which we immediately re-occupy.'

Davout's infantry divisions had cheered as they passed under Napoleon's all-seeing eye: if many commanding officers have so far managed to maintain strict discipline it's been by telling the ranker 'once we're on Russian territory we'll take anything we like'. But no sooner have Dedem's men debouched on to the Niemen's right bank than he's horrified to hear them

'burst out into joyful shouts, horrible to hear, as if to say: "At last, we're on enemy territory! Now our officers won't punish us when we make the bourgeois[6] wait on us!'

Otherwise the whole army is a bit frightened at the sight of so sparsely populated and poverty-stricken a countryside. Dedem finds himself in 'a desert'. What kind of a land is this they've come to 'liberate'? 'Not a soul in sight, not an inhabitant in the villages we were passing through.' Even men who've served in Spain – and there are many – soon begin to feel depressed by its sombre aspect. Captain *Karl von Suckow* of the Württemberg Cavalry and his men are 'all struck by the absence of any birds flying up at our approach'. And in Dr Faure the 'countryside's repulsive appearance' is 'giving rise to serious reflections'.

Certainly the Lithuanian peasants aren't welcoming their liberators. After two failed harvests the abandoned barns have been stripped to the last grain of corn, and the patriotic Soltyk is grieved to see how

'the terrified people who cultivated this land, all but for a few poor people who came to our bivouacs to beg for bread, were fleeing to the woods, uttering dolorous cries and invoking the divine pity'.

Grenadier-Captain *Guillaume Bonnet* of the 18th Line, Ney's III Corps, following the Vilia's serpentine left bank, is shocked to see how the peasants' clothing consists of only

'a shirt, a pair of coarse cloth trousers, a hooded cloak of sheepskin and some kind of a fur cap. The women's dress is virtually the same. The head is wrapped in bad linen, the face pale, and the skin blackened by smoke.'

As for their villages, they're even more squalid than the Polish ones. Spending his first night in Lithuania in a hamlet whose name he hasn't been able to identify, the commander of the (Polish) Vistula Legion, the newly married General Claparède, writes home[7] to his young bride:

'The inhabitants and their houses are very ugly and extremely dirty, and the latter only differ from the peasants' log cabins in possessing a chimney or two. When the weather is fine, I sleep under a shelter of branches and manage very well; or else, when it's bad, in my carriage.'

The serfs' dwellings, writes Captain *Abraham Rosselet* of the 1st Swiss,

'are built of pieces of timber laid on top of each other without any framework. The chinks are blocked up with moss. To let in some daylight people cut out a sort of porthole, opened and closed by means of slots or grooves. One finds no furniture and seldom a bed, however wretched. There's only one room, a sort of stable, big enough to accommodate the family and animals. A quarter of it is taken up by a big stove which also serves as a bed. Here mother, father, daughter and son-in-law sleep together on straw and everything goes on much as in a rabbit warren.'

Although General Compans, commanding Davout's crack 5th Division, is finding the countryside 'quite attractive', he refuses even to set foot inside such hovels. And though all are deserted, many aren't available for a second occupation, since the first-comers have a way of lighting so rousing a fire in the primitive stove that first the chimney, then the cottage itself goes up in flames and not infrequently cremates its exhausted occupants.

Although the harvest isn't ripe, Major Faber du Faur advancing with Ney's heavy artillery, sees

'the fields being devastated by foragers. As sole traces of our brief visit we left behind us empty huts, fields stripped and forests thinned out.' – 'Crops trampled down, ancient trees felled, hamlets, entire timber villages of thatched houses devastated, thrown down and almost vanished – thatch, doors, shutters, furniture – all was being carried off to the bivouacs, the terrible and inevitable effect of warfare, above all when waged with such huge masses of men.'

All this is only justifiable, the patriotic Soltyk consoles himself, as being incidental to a war of national liberation.

The Supply Train takes no priority over anyone, and in no time the marching columns have pushed its 'heavy wagons and smaller carts' off the roads. Every battalion has such a wagon; but even these either turn up late at the bivouacs, where they find the exhausted men fast asleep, or else after they've already left again; or perhaps not at all. German officers such as Lieutenant Vossler are infuriated that their

'laboriously and often humiliatingly acquired provisions fall a prey to the French commissariat. Many of the regiments had no more than three days' supply of rations. Because of the countryside's total devastation, we had to subsist on the flesh of exhausted starving cattle, of which each regiment dragged at least one herd with it.'

Some of these herds, lackadaisically goaded onwards by their 'fearsomely unqualified drivers', have come from as far afield as Hungary or Italy. And they too soon fall behind:

'From the very first day the ranker found himself very badly fed. For lack of bread, and often of vegetables, he ate too much meat, which was plentiful. This rapid movement without supplies exhausted and destroyed all the resources and houses along the way. The advance guard,'

complains Dedem, whose brigade is marching in its wake, 'lived quite well, but the rest of the army was dying of hunger.'

The 18-year-olds, particularly, are finding it impossible to keep up. Marching ever onwards in the steadily falling rain, Claparède's veterans from Spain see 'the Young Guard, marching immediately ahead of us, sowing stragglers behind it. Each instant we came upon them, stretched out beside the roadside and sometimes across it, pell-mell with dead horses.' Von Suckow, too, is distressed to see how

'these exceptional marches were thinning our ranks to an exceptional degree. Within no time thousands of men had disappeared.'

'Our drink', Dedem goes on,

'consisted of a brackish liquid scooped from stinking wells and putrid ponds. Under these circumstances it isn't surprising if, within two or three days of crossing the Niemen, the army, and in particular the infantry, was being ravaged by diseases, particularly dysentery,[8] ague and typhus.'

Sous-lieutenant Dutheillet of the 57th Line is seeing how at the hourly *halte des pipes* the generals are having 'to station sentries, so that the men shan't pull down their trousers almost in the column's very ranks'. Then the drums beat again. The cornets shrill, ordering the light infantrymen back into the ranks. The trumpets blare 'To horse!'. And the troops stagger on, some marchers actually asleep as they march, 'only kept on their feet by two limp arms flung round the necks of two sturdier comrades'. Staff officers are distinguishable by a red armband tied in a bow. And now and then one, carrying an order, comes cantering along the edge of the road.

Napoleon, says Caulaincourt, 'would gladly have given wings to the army'. But the Lithuanian roads are militating against it. Lieutenant Vossler sees that

'most of the road from the Niemen to Vilna is either so sandy or so marshy that even in the most favourable weather conditions it presents great problems to the passage of heavy wagons and matériel. These difficulties were multiplied almost beyond endurance on the short but correspondingly steep slopes of the many ravines which intersect the road at right angles.'

Certain stretches are paved with transversely laid pine trunks. But since they're often decayed, there are gaps as lethal to a horse's legs as the green rye is to its belly. Elsewhere are quagmires. 'The roads were bottomless, unviable,' writes General *Jean Rapp*, Napoleon's favourite ADC:

'We drowned in mud or collapsed from weakness or hunger. Ten thousand horses had died within a distance we travelled in two days.'

Really that many? Murat's chief-of-staff, General *Augustin-Daniel Belliard*, puts the figure at 8,000. Some think only 5,000. And Captain *Franz Roeder*,[9] following on a few days later with the Hessian Footguards, will count '3,000 horses lying dead by the roadside, together with other rotting corpses which at this season of the year made a hideous stench'. He'll also see 'hundreds of dismounted cavalry trekking away westwards in the hope of finding remounts'. A general, says the Flemish war-commissary *Bellot de Kergorre*, had already been detailed off to get all these stinking cadavers buried. The weather, too,

'seemed to be doing its best to contribute to our discomforture. Before crossing the Niemen we'd been thoroughly parched by the persistent oppressive heats. Thereafter we endured three days of continuous and torrential rain, followed by alternating periods of unbearable heat and downpours whose like I've never known. Under skies now unbearably hot, now pouring forth freezing rain, we were either smothered in sand or knee-deep in mud.'

Despite his privileged position at imperial headquarters Ségur is finding midday 'the moment of greatest discouragement. Then the heat became intolerable. Then the sky, heavy with thick clouds, seemed almost to press on the ground, oppressing us with all their weight.'

Taking blocks of ice from the peasants' outdoor ice cellars, the 3rd Württemberg Chasseurs pass them 'from hand to hand until they were either consumed or melted away'.

From the very first days there are suicides:

'Hundreds of men, feeling they could no longer endure such hardships, killed themselves. Every day we heard isolated shots ring out in the woods near the road. Patrols, sent to investigate, always came back to report: "It's a cuirassier, a hussar, an infantryman, a Frenchman or an ally, who's just taken his own life..."'

In these sombre circumstances even a hardened veteran such as the Swiss Captain *François Fivaz*,[10] who has fought in all the wars of the Consulate and Empire, even though as yet he is 'hardly embarked upon this accursed war which can lead to no good', feels he's had enough. Staggering into his bivouac in the evening of 26 June, he sits down to write his will:

'In the name of God, amen! – Having given mature reflection to the inconveniences of the military estate and its few advantages, I feel it is my fatherly duty to forbid any of my sons to embrace this profession. I recommend my wife and my children to God and to our relatives, who are to be consulted on everything, and that she shall have exclusive charge of our children's education. She is full of good sense. Had I consulted her I should never have left my own country.'

What has happened to the romance of war? *Hubert de Lyautey*, a young lieutenant in the Guard artillery, may be 'enchanted by the bivouacs besides the shores of lakes, where in the warm evenings the bands play one after another in the dusk, and by the spectacle of these long lines of campfires on which the moon sometimes came and shed its light'. Few can be sharing his lyrical feelings.

Most of Napoleon's campaigns had started in similar fashion. None quite like this.

'When the army was carrying out major manoeuvres at great distances,' writes Gourgaud,

'he remained at his headquarters, attending to the interior administration of France and replying to the reports sent him daily by his ministers in Paris, until the marching corps were almost in the positions he had indicated. To economize with his time, he calculated his moment of departure so as to be at the head of his corps in the same moment as his presence there became necessary. Then he travelled swiftly by carriage. Yet even during such a transit he wasn't idle. He busied himself reading despatches and immediately sent off replies. Sometimes the mail brought by the Paris courier arrived at the same time.'

Not until dawn on 26 June does he leave the Kovno monastery. And once again it's presumably Ségur's task to go on ahead and make arrangements for the next headquarters. In this case they're to be in a handsome white-pillared manor-house near the village of Jejwe (or Ewë), half-way to Vilna.[11] It seems Napoleon has set out on horseback; for he's riding along, followed by his glittering staff, when he's stopped

'by the supplications and cries of a venerable old man, M. Prozov, an ex-soldier and a good patriot. Surrounded by his family he was flee-ing from his home, only a musket shot's distance from the main road. Stragglers had invaded it and were devastating it from top to bottom. He begged Napoleon's justice and protection. Moved by the poor old man's straits and indignant at the soldiers' behaviour, the Emperor grants him a safeguard, and orders me to take some men of the escort, surround Prozov's house and seize those responsible. I'm to take them to the provost-marshal and tell him to have them shot.'

Shocked by the pillage, but even more appalled at the rigour of his orders, Soltyk has

'Prozov's house surrounded by some lancers. Many of the marauders were making off in all directions. Thirteen were seized and brought before me. Finding myself their judge and master, with power of life and death, I at least wanted to know what their crime was. So I inter-rogated each in turn and had my lancers search them. They replied that they had had no food and had vainly asked their commander for some. Unable to distribute any rations, he'd authorized them to get whatever they could, wherever they could. And indeed nothing was found on them except the food they'd taken – admittedly by force – in M. Prozov's house.'

Letting them off with a reprimand which he knows can only be futile, Soltyk catches up with IHQ, wondering anxiously what to say. But no ques-tions are asked. The whole incident has already been forgotten. Soon the Emperor exchanges his horse for a 'light travelling carriage or droshki'. As Dedem's brigade slogs on through a pine forest it comes bouncing by, and he catches a glimpse of its occupants. Besides Napoleon himself they are: the army's major-general and Napoleon's chief-of-staff, Alexandre Berthier; the commander of its four 'reserve' cavalry corps, Joachim Murat, King of Naples; and Davout, Prince of Eckmühl.

No three commanders could be more different, or more mutually antipathetic.

Well over six feet tall, immensely handsome and vain, Murat speaks in a husky voice with a strong Gascon accent and has what in a woman would be called bedroom eyes. One of his many baggage wagons is filled with perfumes, and each morning he appears in a new and highly theatrical get-up of his own devising. Not a little peeved to have been the only reign-ing prince excluded from the Dresden *son et lumière*, he has nothing to gain from this new campaign which is taking him away from his Neapolitan kingdom and his adored children. On morosely reporting for duty at Danzig, he'd been promptly bawled out for his wife's intrigues with the Austrian government and told he looked 'sickly'. Whereafter his imperial brother-in-law, after cowing him with talk of 'pitiless punishments', had softened his tone and appealed to him, as an old comrade-in-arms. 'I took turn and turn about with anger and sentimentality,' he'd told Duroc, Berthier, Caulaincourt and Bessières cynically at dinner that evening,

'because that's all that's needed with this Italian pantalone. At bottom he has a good heart. He loves me even more than he does his lazzaroni. He only has to set eyes on me to be my man. But far away from me, anyone can flatter and approach him, like all people without character.'

And Murat of course had come to heel, protesting his sincere devotion. 'There were not, I believe,' Napoleon will say at St. Helena,

'two such officers in the world as Murat for the cavalry, and Drouot for the artillery. Murat was a most singular character. Twenty-four years earlier, when he was only a captain, I'd made him my aide-de-camp, and thereafter raised him to be what he became. He loved, I may rather say, adored me. In my presence he was as it were awe-stricken, ready to fall at my feet. With me, he was my right arm. Order Murat to attack and destroy four or five thousand men in such or such a direction, it was done in a flash. But left to himself he was an imbecile, without judgement. It's more than I can understand how so brave a man could be so cowardly.'

The carriage's second occupant is a man of totally different stamp. Bald and bespectacled, with a head bearing a striking resemblance to Seneca's, Davout, Prince of Eckmühl, is in all points Murat's exact opposite. An extreme disciplinarian, at Mecklenburg he'd placed General Dalton, one of Dedem's fellow-brigadiers, under arrest and cited him in the order of the day for spending more than regulations permitted on his table. But Davout is a brilliant administrator and a first-class corps commander. If Murat has little tactical and less strategic sense, Davout has both in eminent degree, treating his staff as he does everyone else, with icy detachment and no consideration whatever for their creature comforts. Biot describes him as 'the most slovenly of men' and 'incontrovertibly the least polite of our marshals'. He's utterly unpopular with everyone. General *François Roguet*, commanding the 2nd Guard Grenadiers, complains of his always 'interfering in everything, trying to do everything himself, and forever scolding and fulminating'. Only Dedem has a good word to put in for him:

'If ever I have to make war again, it's under Marshal Davout I'd wish to do so. The Prince of Eckmühl is the man who best knows how to obey, and thereby has learnt to command. There was never a chief more severe in point of discipline, juster, or who occupied himself more with the welfare of the ranker, his instruction and his needs; and no sovereign ever had a more faithful or devoted servant.'

While conceding that Davout had 'twice laid a heavy iron hand on Prussia and each time showed a hardness outrageous to humanity', Dedem acquits him of all self-seeking:

'His hands were as pure as gold. He never took anything for himself. He was always the father of his army. He liked people to think he was more ill-natured than he really was. Those he ordered to be shot[12] had fully merited it under the military laws of all countries, and the number was small compared with that of the guilty.'

If Napoleon is just now treating Davout with a certain coolness, it's perhaps because he, like the whole army, is well aware that his dour but efficient marshal is aspiring to the throne of Poland. And anyway Davout's loyalty, unlike Murat's, is unshakeable.

Such are the two commanders whose corps are spearheading the main striking force. Their mutual detestation is only equalled by the 'terrible hatred' prevailing between Davout and the carriage's fourth occupant: Napoleon's all-seeing, all-fixing, all-remembering – yet little understanding chief-of-staff, Marshal Alexandre Berthier, Prince of Neuchâtel:

'No one ever saw greater exactitude, a more entire submission, a more absolute devotion. Busy all day, it was by writing at night he rested from the day's fatigues. Often he'd be summoned in the middle of his sleep to change all his work of yesterday, and sometimes his only reward was unjust or, at very least, severe reprimands. Yet nothing slowed down his zeal.'

Berthier and Davout haven't seen each other for several years, but on their having recently done so at Hamburg the occasion had been marked by a blazing row. Having no talent whatever for independent command, Berthier has never forgiven Davout for rescuing an army he'd put gravely at risk. Berthier too is a slovenly man. He speaks in a nasal voice and usually keeps his hands in his pockets – that is, when he hasn't got one finger in his nose. His badly cut clothes hang on him like a sack:

'Short, ill-grown without actually being deformed, he had a head slightly too large for his body, hair rather tousled than curly, neither dark nor fair; hands, ugly by nature, made still uglier by forever biting his nails, so that his fingers were almost always bleeding. Add to this a rather severe stammer and the grimaces he made – well, if not exactly grimaces, then odd jerky movements – to anyone who wasn't directly impressed by his elevated status he seemed to cut a very comical figure.'

Unlike Davout, he's extremely decent to his staff, treating them with

'that blend of kindness and brusqerie which made up his character. Often he seemed to pay no heed to us. But we were sure on occasion to gain his whole attention, and during his long military career he never failed to advance any of the officers employed under his orders.'

Though exercising none of the functions of a modern chief-of-staff, Berthier's grasp of each unit's strength, its whereabouts and march route have for many years always been immaculate. 'I count for nothing in the Army,' he once wrote to Marshal Soult. 'I receive the marshals' orders on His Majesty's behalf, and I sign his orders for him. But personally I am nothing.' And again: 'The Emperor needs neither advice nor to have his plans drawn up for him. No one knows his thoughts, and it's our duty simply to obey.' When taking Napoleon's orders, which he writes down in a green notebook, Berthier like everyone else always stands hat in hand – a hat of the same Swiss civilian cut as his master's and which it is his unique privilege to wear.[13]

Nor is Berthier, in this summer of 1815? quite the man he has been, as those in daily contact with him will shortly be noticing. 'Unfortunately,' Dedem sees, Berthier is ' already beginning to be the old man. All that shop was badly run. Few talents and much presumption.' And Ségur agrees:

'Berthier's mental forces were declining. Since 1805 he'd hated every war. His talent resided above all in his meticulousness and memory. At any hour of the day or night whatsoever he was able to go through the most numerous news and orders.'

Even First Secretary Méneval, though deeply respecting Berthier's 'loyalty of character and sense of responsibility', feels forced to admit that

'I shouldn't be telling the truth if I didn't also say that in proportion to the honours and wealth which had come Berthier's way, his serious and real qualities had declined. Several times during the 1812 campaign the Emperor reproached him in my presence for his carelessness. "Berthier," he told him, "I'd give my right arm for you to be back at Grosbois. Not merely are you no use to me at all, you're harming me." After these altercations Berthier sulked and wouldn't come to dinner. Then the Emperor would send for him, and himself wouldn't sit down to table before he was there. Putting his arm round his neck, he'd tell him they were inseparable, etc., tease him about Mme. Visconti,[14] and finally sit down at table facing him.'

Of his doggily faithful, endlessly painstaking chief-of-staff Napoleon once said candidly:

'Truly, I can't understand how a relationship which looks like friendship can have arisen between Berthier and myself. Useless sentiments don't amuse me, and Berthier is so mediocre. Yet at bottom, when nothing turns me against him, I do believe I'm not without a certain penchant for him.'

And again: 'Out of this goose I've made an eagle.'

One would think a command structure compounded at top level of such mutual antipathies and jealousies can hardly be making for good collaboration. Yet far from discouraging them, Napoleon confessedly fosters them. 'You see,' he'd told the Tsar in the days of their friendship (words the Tsar will soon be repeating to Napoleon's arch-enemy Madame *Germaine de Staël*, she too just then on her way to Moscow)'

'I always try to sow dissension among my generals so that each shall discover the others' shortcomings. By my way of treating people around me I keep all their jealousies alive. One day one of them imagines himself preferred; the next, another. So no one can be sure of being in my good books.'

In this summer of 1812 Napoleon is nearly 43, Davout 42, Murat 45, and Berthier 59. Like Murat, Berthier only has three more years to live.

Seeing the open carriage go bouncing along the sandy road it seems to Dedem that its four occupants looked 'astonished, maybe terrified' to see neither inhabitants nor foe. Terrified is hardly a word to use of four such war-hardened commanders. Worried they certainly are. Although three days have gone by, the first of all strategic desiderata – knowledge of the enemy's whereabouts and movements – still hasn't been met.

And what is Jerome doing?

The danger with outflanking movements is that they can themselves be outflanked; and Eugène's march across Poland, which is to guard against the eventuality of Bagration taking the main striking force in flank, has been seriously delayed. And Napoleon, by crossing the Niemen on 24 June rather than next day as originally planned, has left his right flank in the air. Here's a delaying factor which, unlike the weather, the appalling roads or lack of food, can't be ignored. Already Napoleon has had to curb Murat's headlong gallopings in pursuit of the foe: "There can be no question of your actually marching into Vilna," he writes to Davout some time after leaving the droshky, to warn him of the danger of Wittgenstein, eluding both Oudinot, on the Vilia's right bank, and Ney on its left, taking him in flank.

But most important of all, will Barclay stand and fight? And if so, where? Surely Davout's I Corps, with its 60 cannon, should long ago have made contact with the enemy somewhere near the little town of Novo-Troki? 'To prevent any minor Russian success at the campaign's outset,' says Dedem,

'Napoleon had ordered even the least reconnaissance to be made at brigade strength. The result was to exhaust the horses and men by useless gallopings after foes who refused to cross sabres with them.'

At most some Poles, 'sent up to some high ground, reported seeing an enemy rearguard afar off retiring toward Vilna. And only a few very keen-sighted officers claimed to have spotted Cossacks in the distance.'

That night the heavens open again. And all along the Vilna road the rain comes pelting down, forcing Major Boulart to spend the night in one of his artillery wagons. In a freezing wet dawn, somewhere beyond Ewë, he climbs out to see in front of him 'a quarter of my horses lying on the ground, some dead or almost, the others shivering'. Harnessing up the survivors, he orders men and horses to march – not so much because there's any great hurry, 'but to restore their circulation'. The 2nd

Company of the 9th Artillery Regiment, too, is losing its Frisians at an alarming rate. 'Exposed to this rain as long as it lasted, and after living for several days off barley and other standing crops,' Lieutenant *N. J. Sauvage* sees in the morning

'two or three of these beasts in their death-throes or laid out lifeless in front of each ammunition wagon. At their side we saw our gunners and soldiers of the Train standing in a gloomy silence, tears in their eyes, trying to avert their gaze from this afflicting scene. Troops of horned cattle, driven by detachments from the various units, were wandering about as their drivers tried to get out of the terrible weather.'

Away to the left Captain *Pierre Pelleport* is following the twists and turns of the Vilia, a river, he notices, which 'flows slowly and isn't very deep. Its course is embarrassed by rocks and it never stops winding'. In the hot weather his men have been 'throwing away their waistcoats'. But now, his fellow-captain Bonnet writes in his diary on 27 June,

'we've ceased hugging the riverline to continue our way over the hills which follow its left bank at a distance. A violent storm has frozen and drenched us, penetrating us to our very bones. At 1 a.m. we arrived in much diminished numbers at... From Kalwary to here we've made a wide circuit, doubtless a manoeuvre. The countryside is densely covered with vegetation. The few cultivated fields are sown with extraordinarily tall rye, the forests extremely thick.'

All Colbert's lancers, seconded to Murat's advance guard, and detailed off to cover its sensitive right flank, scour a 'beautiful undulating countryside' but meet no living soul. Dumonceau notices how his regiment's thousand Dutchmen, as if troubled by finding themselves alone amidst so much emptiness,[16] keep inclining insensibly to their left, in towards Novo-Troki. By and by their three Polish lancer interpreters elicit scraps of information from some peasants. The Russian army is 'retiring towards the interior under General Toutchkoff'.

By now the great masses of Nansouty's and Grouchy's cavalry corps are only some fifteen miles from Vilna. And still there's no sign of a general engagement! Next day (27 June) the 30th Line are tramping onwards through the steadily falling rain when Voltigeur-captain François sees

'the Emperor sitting on the steps of an inn. He watched us go by in the very best order. After our division had marched past he left like lightning on horseback for the outposts.'

At long last some Russians have been intercepted; and they have told Napoleon that the Tsar is still at Vilna, where Bagration has been ordered to join him. The Lithuanian capital lies in a crescent of hills, with its back to the Vilia, and any attempt by the Russians to defend it with less than equal forces will only be to invite another disaster of the kind they'd suffered at Friedland in 1807. Hearing that the information he'd received is false, and afraid that Barclay will give him the slip, Napoleon now sends orders to General Montbrun, commander of II Cavalry Corps, to get into

Vilna with all speed. Above all he must save the immense grain stores assembled there by the Russian commissariat.

After Murat, the 42-year-old Montbrun is the most prestigious and popular of all the Grand Army's cavalry commanders, and is certainly not a man to sleep on the job. Dedem calls him 'a fine warrior, brilliant with glory, an officer of talent, but too ardent'. On the other hand, if what Staff-captain *Hubert Biot* says is true, he's ill-served by his four ADCs:

'Squadron-leader Martin, in charge of his carriages, who never appeared under fire; Squadron-leader Hubert, who had altogether too high an opinion of himself and only deigned to budge on grand occasions; and Captain Caillot, colder than cold, a mere nothing. Remained only young Linz, an officer full of goodwill, bravery and dash.'

Vossler, the only officer in Prince Louis' hussars who can speak even halting French, has much the same opinion. He has spent the last few days of

'very cold drizzling rain, either in Montbrun's retinue or else riding both myself and my horses to a standstill delivering messages and orders. The first night had found me in pouring rain by a dying campfire, without food or drink, silently cursing my French comrades, who had plenty of both but were in no mood to share it. The second had passed in delivering a message to the King of Naples, at whose headquarters I was at least served a decent meal.'

Ill-served or not, Montbrun now becomes the victim of a muddle. Seize Vilna? That's an exploit Murat wants to reserve for himself! Finding Montbrun's corps mounted at an earlier hour than he'd ordered, he asks him why. In obedience to the Emperor's direct orders, Montbrun replies.

'What order?'

'To get into Vilna before the Russians can leave it.'

'No need. I'll deal with that myself!'

'But I've the Emperor's personal orders!'

'What the hell does that matter, providing the thing's done?' says Murat in his husky Gascon voice, and orders Montbrun to follow on behind Nansouty's I Cavalry Corps. Whereupon the whole cumbersome cavalry mass, with Bruyère's light brigade scouting ahead, moves on – evidently at no great speed – towards Vilna.

At that moment Napoleon himself, who only a few moments ago has left Captain François (Morand's division) trudging on through the drizzle, appears on the scene. Seeing Montbrun riding at the head of his corps but in the tail of the operation, he gallops furiously up to him and, livid with rage, threatens to exile him to the rear for such incompetence. Montbrun tries to excuse himself.

'Shut up!' shouts Napoleon.

'But, Sire.'

'Will you be quiet?'

Napoleon's threats and reprimands become more and more angry. Montbrun appeals with a glance to Murat. But seeing him tongue-tied, loses his temper. Draws his sword and – grasping it by its point – flings it over his shoulder. With a shout of "Go to hell, the whole lot of you!" he puts spurs to his horse, leaving the weapon quivering in the soggy ground more than forty paces away. Napoleon, pale with fury and surprise, stands stock-still. Then he too, without another word, plies spurs to his horse, leaving the spectators dumbfounded.

Surely Montbrun will be court-martialled, sent to a fortress, or at very least dismissed the army?

Nothing of the sort. That evening Murat receives a cold inquiry: "His Majesty wishes to know why General Montbrun didn't reach Novo-Troki until midday?" No doubt Murat plucks up enough courage to explain. For nothing more is heard of that matter, either. On the other hand no small conciliatory gesture follows, of the kind Napoleon is in the habit of making towards objects of his wrath, deserved or undeserved. Montbrun is left in command of his divisions. But will remain under a cloud.[17]

'Nothing resembles the view as one surveys Vilna from the hills all around,' Oudinot's courageous young duchess will think, reaching the brow of Ponari Hill when she gets there, four months later, to nurse her wounded husband. 'Although the Vilia vainly wends its way through a countryside it seems unable to fertilize, a multitude of domes and church towers rise brilliantly above the thirty-six convents.' But now, from this vantage point, Dumonceau at about 2 or 3. p.m. on 18 June sees 'that vast city swathed in thick smoke, whose cause we didn't know'.

It's coming from the burning grain stores.

To save the honour of Russian arms and give the fires time to do their work the Russian rearguard are making a token stand on the southern heights. Ordered to take the town by assault, General Wathier de St-Alphonse, however, only sends 'a strong detachment of élite companies, under the 11th Chasseurs' colonel'. Captain *Tomas-Joseph Aubry* is ordered to support it with 100 men of the 12th Chasseurs:

'I'd hardly got to the point indicated, loaded my men's firearms and drawn them up in line of battle, than what do I suddenly hear but a troop coming at the gallop down this main road I'm guarding. It's its colonel, returning flat out with his troopers, a very superior force he's bumped into at his heels. Never did I see a man more relieved than when he saw my squadron coming to his aid! He'd been utterly routed. My chasseurs caught a number of the riderless horses that came after him. At the sight of my squadron drawn up in line, the enemy ceased his pursuit. I didn't have to fire so much as a pistol shot.'

Is it signs of this affray that Dumonceau, approaching the town with the rest of the Guard cavalry, sees 'at the entrance to a defile, where the ground was violently churned up on all sides by numerous cavalry, which seemed to bear witness to a sharp engagement'? There he sees his first enemy corpse. Stretched out at the corner of a hedge, the dead man is 'clad in a bizarre greyish-brown costume, which only seemed military because of its regularity, and which we supposed to belong to a Russian militiaman'.

Soltyk claims that it's the 6th Polish Lancers, led by Major Suchorzewski, who are the first unit to enter Vilna, at 8 a.m. on 28 June; but their exploit 'not being authorized from above, gained no official mention, was even regarded as reprehensible'. What they do get is a delirious welcome:
> 'Our entry was a triumph. Streets and public places were full of peo-
> ple. All the windows were adorned with wildly enthusiastic ladies.
> Valuable carpets hung on the façades of several houses. Every hand
> seemed to be waving a handkerchief, and shouts of joy kept ringing
> out.'

One patriotic Lithuanian lady – like everyone else she's wearing the national colours, white and crimson – sees the Poles come 'galloping in, full-tilt, sabres drawn yet laughing, waving their pennons, also in the national colours'. Captain *Victor Dupuy's* 7th Hussars, too, are welcomed
> 'with the most joyous acclamations. The ladies in their party dresses
> were throwing down flowers and biscuits to us from the windows – a
> kindly forethought useless to us as we were unable to dismount and
> pick them up.'

Everywhere in the streets Ségur sees people
> 'embracing and congratulating each other. Old men appeared again
> in their former costume, with its memories of honour and indepen-
> dence. They wept with joy at the sight of the national banners being
> followed by innumerable crowds.'

Galloping straight through the town and across the half-burned Vilia bridge, the Polish lancers fling themselves at the Russian rearguard, cap-turing 'five hundred prisoners and a good deal of baggage'. So far so good. But nine miles beyond the town Soltyk sees the red-and-green uni-formed 8th Hussars run into serious resistance. Although the Cossack irregulars scatter at their approach, the scarlet-clad Cossacks of the Russian Imperial Guard stand all too firm:
> 'Only a few hundred yards from us Captain Ségur fell in the midst of
> a party of the enemy who took him prisoner. He was the brother of
> the one who has written the history of this unhappy campaign.' – At
> 'the same moment I arrived at Vilna, Duroc, the Grand Marshal of
> the Palace, called me over, squeezed my hand, and told me that two
> leagues beyond the city my brother, flung imprudently into a wood
> by his general, had just run into three regiments of the Russian
> Guard while mounting a hillside. His company had been crushed;
> and he himself had disappeared! At this news, I hurried to my
> brother's hussars. Those that were left were still drawn up in line of
> battle in front of the scene of their defeat.'

They tell Ségur[18] how his brother had

'several times tried to cut his way out, but been felled by a
lance-thrust, and then, while struggling to get up from the ground,
by several more. Some Russian officers had dragged him away into
the forest. One of the hussars gestured toward a conifer forest and
the sandy slope of the broad highway which went into it.
Bloodstained shreds of uniforms lay scattered in the middle of the
road. In each I trembled to recognize my brother, particularly when
the faces were hidden in the sand and their hair was black and their
stature great. What anguish when the hussar who accompanied me,
seizing these heads by their hair and brusquely turning them round,
showed me their features!'

But none is his brother. So Ségur, 'defying the order forbidding all communications with the enemy', quickly gets hold of a trumpeter and scribbles some hasty words to his brother. Then, equipping his servant with a
purse of money, accompanies him and the trumpeter into the wood.
'Only after I'd left it again did I catch sight of the first Russian scouts.
Soon the servant and the trumpeter were among them. An hour of anxiety followed, the cruellest in my whole life.'

Dusk falls. What's become of his emissaries? The Russians know he's a
high-ranking officer at IHQ. Will they try to capture him too? No. Here,
at last, comes the trumpeter – dead drunk:

'The Russians had received him so cordially he was unable to speak.
But he brought me some lines written by a generous hand. My
brother's wounds, though serious, weren't mortal. His name and
courage assured him a gentle and honourable captivity. I breathed
again.'

In Paris Napoleon had told Caulaincourt he'd wage a 'polite war' against
Alexander; and that, for officers of Ségur's status, is what it still is. Hardly
for others. Riding sadly back into Vilna, he hears a shot ring out, 'followed
by an unusual murmur'. A French infantryman who's just blown his
brains out is lying in the middle of the road. His comrades are staring
down at him in consternation when a second shot is heard. Everyone runs
over. Another suicide. The spectators, Ségur says, 'exclaimed with their
usual exaggeration that if this went on, the whole army would go the same
way'.

According to another of Pajol's ADCs, Captain *Jean-Pierre Dellard*, the
8th Hussars' setback 'wouldn't have happened if General Wathier de
St-Alphonse, who was to have debouched on the enemy's left by the
Wacha and Novo-Troki roads, hadn't turned up too late'. And in fact he's
relieved of his commmand. It's taken over by General Sébastiani – who
won't do much better. But Captain Aubry and his chasseurs are deeply
affected by their ex-commander's disgrace. None of them will be either
decorated or promoted.

By now Murat has ridden in at the head of Bruyère's division, and Vilna's
narrow streets are packed with men and horses. Even before entering the

city, Napoleon's photographic memory has recalled – no doubt in connection with a large donation he'd made to its university in 1810 – the name of a certain Professor Sniadecky, its aged rector. Sent off to fetch him, Soltyk finds the old man

'wearing the Academy uniform. He wanted to put on silk stockings instead of his boots. I told him my mission admitted of no delay. When he insisted, I said: "Rector, it's of no consequence. The Emperor attaches no importance to externals which only impress the vulgar. Science is the garb of the wise. Let's be off." And he acquiesced with good grace.'

Next day old Sniadecky will find himself co-opted willy-nilly into a provisional government, together with six other notables who haven't left with the Russians.

But what has happened to the first-comers' delirious welcome? Either it must have subsided remarkably quickly, or else Caulaincourt is projecting his own pessimistic frame of mind on to the situation:

'The Emperor passed through Vilna without making himself known. The town seemed deserted. Not a face showed at a single window, not a sign of enthusiasm or even curiosity. Everything was gloomy. Passing straight through the town, he inspected the burnt Vilia bridge, the terrain beyond the city, and the magazines the enemy had set fire to and which were still burning. Hastening on the repairs to the bridges, he gave orders for defensive outworks, and then returned and went to the palace.'

In this case 'the palace', as IHQ is always called on campaign, is in the palace of the Archbishop of Vilna, vacated only two days ago by the Tsar. 'Although his return was made public,' Caulaincourt goes on,

'and the Household, the Headquarters, the Guard and all the paraphernalia indicating his presence had been established there, the population didn't show the slightest interest. The Emperor was struck by this. Entering his study, he remarked: "The Poles hereabouts aren't like the ones at Warsaw. They're cooler than Poles and much more reticent."'

He's right. They're Lithuanians. Since 1807 the Tsar has made great efforts to win over the wealthier segment of the population, and now it's divided between pro-French and pro-Russian factions. And in fact many of the town's leading families have left with the Russian army. Near the town gate Dumonceau, riding in earlier that morning, has noticed

'a kind of cloister with a chapel. Its bell tower was a parti-coloured striped ball, the first bizarre Russian bell tower we'd seen. Its walls were placarded all over with lengthy proclamations in Russian we'd have liked to decipher.'

Not all, however, are in Russian, for Labaume says 'everyone could read them'. It's Alexander's dignified if wordy reply to Napoleon's declaration of war:

"We have long noticed on the part of the Emperor of the French proceedings hostile to Russia, but have always hoped to avert them by concilatory and pacific means. Finally, seeing the continual renewal of obvious offences and despite our desire to preserve the peace, we have been constrained to complete and assemble our armies. However, we still flatter ourselves we shall reach a reconciliation by remaining on the frontiers of our empire... ready only to defend ourselves..."

By 'suddenly attacking our army at Kovno' Napoleon has become the aggressor:

"Seeing, therefore, that nothing can make him accessible to our desire to keep the peace, it only remains for us, while invoking the Almighty, witness and defender of the truth, to succour us, to oppose our forces to the enemy's. We do not need to remind corps and unit commanders and the soldiers of their duty and their courage. The blood of the valorous Slavs runs in their veins. Warriors! You are defending religion, the country and freedom! I am with you. God is against the aggressor. – Alexander"

Looking up at the ancient ruined citadel, Dumonceau has also seen flying on its summit an 'immense white and sky-blue flag, said to be the colours of the Jagallons, ancient sovereigns of Lithuania'.[19] As his lancers walk their horses through the streets past 'the wreckage of military stores that were smoking and even still in flames' they see here and there 'soldiers rifling them to extract a few remains of victuals'. So he leaves behind some of his men, duly provided with sacks, to 'gather up some oats, of which we saw some half-burnt morsels'. Oats are all that have been saved, but so smoked the horses won't eat them. All the corn has been consumed by the flames.

Just as Planat de la Faye and the artillery staff are installing themselves in town, the weather suddenly changes. 'A gale, followed by a cold rain, lasted for almost two days.' Out on the Kovno road the long continuous cloudburst overtakes Sergeant Coignet that evening just as his little convoy of two treasury wagons is reaching a village near Vilna, causing him hurriedly to take shelter inside one them. But Dumonceau's men find themselves locked up inside a walled monastery garden, where they have no shelter at all and where they're having to make do with the most meagre of rations, sent them by a municipality which is already at its wits' end in suddenly having to feed all these thousands of men and horses.

'The rain was coming down in bucketsful, accompanied by a glacial cold which we felt the more keenly for its following immediately on the overwhelming heats. Soon the soil of the garden, churned up and drowning in water, was nothing but a vast swamp of mud. We stood knee-deep in it, having neither straw to lie down on nor any shelter, and without wood to light a fire. And then, to cap it all, came a terrible hurricane. Finding it equally hard to stand up or lie down, we squatted dozing on our mantles in the mud; and awoke only to find the rain still pouring down and the hurricane growing steadily more furious. Chimneys and tiles were coming down all around us. Equally tormented whether lying down or standing up, all we could do was crouch there under our capes. Arms and equipment were lying in the mud. Our dismal fires had gone out. Our horses were shivering at least as violently as ourselves. Several succumbed during the night or else died next day, destroyed by cold and misery.'

All this the new Guard regiment resents so much the more because 'rightly or wrongly we supposed the other Guard cavalry regiments were lodged with the inhabitants and that this was a mere caprice of General Colbert, and that we were being treated as illegitimates, pariahs. We observed between ourselves that not one of our superior officers, nice and snug in the neighbouring houses, put his nose out into the wind to enquire after our sufferings.'

Not until the evening of the following day (29 June) will adjutants arrive, order the trumpeters to sound the fall-in, and distribute billets. Next morning, when Coignet peers out of his treasury wagon, it's to find

'the ground in the nearby cavalry bivouac covered with horses, dead from cold. Climbing out, I saw three of mine had perished. I immediately distributed the survivors among my four wagons. The poor beasts were trembling so violently that no sooner were they harnessed up than they smashed everything, throwing themselves about wildly in their halters. They were mad, prancing about with rage. On reaching the road we found some dead soldiers who hadn't been able to stand up to this appalling storm, and this demoralized a great many of our men.'

Far away to the south-west, too, a Lieutenant *Sauvage*, struggling on eastwards through the same rainstorm with one of Jerome's artillery parks, sees his young drivers shedding tears over their dead teams.

It's 'heartbreaking' for Napoleon, Caulaincourt sees, to have been cheated of his 'good battle'. But supposing there'd been one? In Lieutenant Brandt's view

'it could only have been indecisive; the ground was so thoroughly soggy, neither artillery, cavalry, nor even infantry could have budged except with extreme difficulty'.

As for the Russians' withdrawal, it strikes the French as extremely well-planned and orderly. And will continue to do so.

CHAPTER 5

BAGRATION GIVES DAVOUT THE SLIP

A disappointing conquest – a letter from the Tsar – Sergeant Bertrand gatecrashes a supper party – sudden departures – the trap is sprung – a heart-rending spectacle – the Tsar's emissary – where's Jerome? – Caulaincourt is upset – the Italian army crosses the Niemen – frustrations at Novo-Troki – impossibilities at Grodno – 'tell him it's impossible to manoeuvre in worse fashion' – Dumonceau meets the Iron Marshal – forced marches – a disgraceful scene

Vilna may not be the 'fine city of 40,000 souls' Napoleon writes of in his letter to Marie Louise – actually it has only half as many – nor is it politically any great capture. Few people in western Europe can even have heard of it. Yet it forms a forward base from which the main army, like a two-headed snake, can strike either at Barclay, retreating north-eastwards towards the River Dwina and the Drissa Camp, or at Bagration, coming up from Grodno; or, should they make junction, at both. Hardly less important, the vast stocks of food and other supplies assembled at Danzig and Königsberg can be brought up by barge along the Vilia; the thousands of stragglers and would-be deserters can be netted in; and a Lithuanian army raised for the 'national' cause. But is there one? Ségur says Napoleon has been

> 'counting on four million Lithuanians. Only a few thousand supported him. The inhabitants seemed little disposed to respond to appeals made to their patriotism. Moreover the Russians weren't far away, and no decisive action had yet been fought.'

And that's the crux of the matter.

On the morning of 29 July he's dealing with these and a myriad other urgent matters when a despatch arrives from Davout. A certain Count Balashoff, the Tsar's police minister, has presented himself at the outposts with a personal letter from Alexander, asking to be taken to Murat. Receiving him politely, Murat has told him that he, for his part, 'most earnestly hopes our two emperors will come to an understanding, and that this war, begun against all my inclinations, will be over as soon as possible.' Which is true. All he wants is to get back to Naples.

Relieving Balashoff of the Tsar's letter, Davout, not so politely, has sent it on to Napoleon, with a request for further orders. Opening the letter in the presence of Duroc, Berthier, Bessières and Caulaincourt, Napoleon finds that it is in fact in the Tsar's handwriting and asks why 'in times of deepest peace and without any preliminary declaration of war' the Emperor of the French has invaded Russian territory. The letter proposes that he withdraw behind the Niemen, pending negotiations.

This is too much:

'Alexander's laughing at me!' Napoleon exclaims. 'Does he imagine I've come to Vilna to negotiate trade treaties? I've come to finish off the barbarian colossus of the North, once and for all. They must be thrust back into their snow and ice, so that for a quarter of a century at least they won't be able to interfere with civilized Europe. The sword is drawn. The Tsar sees his army has been cut in two. He wants to come to terms. The acquisition of Finland has turned his head. If he must have victims, let him defeat the Persians; but don't let him meddle in Europe's affairs. My manoeuvres have disconcerted the Russians. Before a month has passed they'll be on their knees to me.' Not, he adds hastily, that he has any personal grievance against Alexander. He'll treat his emissary well. But since a police minister presumably has his eyes and ears about him, Balashoff is to be brought to Vilna by 'another route' so as not to have a chance to see the frightful wreckage of men, horses and *matériel* lining the Kovno road. Anyway the whole thing's just a gambit to gain time...

By no means everyone has had a roof over his head this drenching night. The 85th Line have bivouacked outside the town under pine trees. And together with the rest of Gudin's 3rd division of I Corps, the 7th Light, 'up to its ankles in water and mud took up its position in a hollow, en masse and by divisions.[1] But just as Carabinier-sergeant *Bertrand* is expecting, as so often before, to pass the night standing 'with musket grounded in this morass', he has a stroke of luck. The adjutant comes and tells him he's been selected for orderly duty at Davout's headquarters, which he finds is in a house between The Palace and Murat's, in the next best house in town. There NCO orderlies 'from all arms' are crammed together in a single room. All have but one longing – to go off and find something to eat; but are only being allowed to do so one by one. Looking about him for somewhere to lie down, Bertrand opens some double doors and is surprised to see in the next room

'two townsmen and two other persons in turbans seated around a well-lit table, on which was a good dinner. Valets dressed in the Emperor's livery were waiting on them. Stupefied, I didn't know whether to advance or retreat. But not yet knowing how to beat a retreat, I go in, raising my hand to my shako. "What do you want?" says one of my two turbans. "A corner where I can get some rest. But I see this isn't the place, please excuse me." – "If there's only you," replies the turban whom I'd recognized as Roustam, the Emperor's mameluke, "come in. Your division has been in the advance guard all day. You must be dead beat." Amazed at my lucky windfall, I valiantly plant my fork in a chicken wing, followed by an iced ham, the whole washed down with the finest vintages. The second turban, Murat's mameluke,[2] orders up a square-shaped bottle wrapped in straw, and we drink the healths of the Emperor, of his worthy spouse, of the Prince Imperial, of King Murat.'

Since his hosts' generosity is at the expense of *their* hosts it knows no bounds. But just as they're stuffing his pack with provisions Bertrand hears someone shouting for 'the sentry from the 7th Light'. Profusely thanking the two mamelukes, he hurries off – with urgent orders to General Gudin. What orders? We'll see in a moment.

And indeed Sergeant Bertrand is by no means alone in having to go out again into the wind and pelting rain. At the 2nd Lancers' monastery Dumonceau and his fellow-captain Post are just turning in for what they hope is going to be the campaign's first comfortable night when 'to our annoyance, the sound of the trumpets was heard under our windows'. Resisting the temptation to pretend they're deaf, they get back into their saturated uniforms and go downstairs. And there, in the terrible wind and rain, they stand holding their horses' reins:

> 'Our trumpeters kept reiterating their calls, but the regiment responded only very slowly. And when, toward midnight, the time came to leave, it still lacked over a hundred men and two officers.'[3]

Yet another officer who's had to spend a most uncomfortable night encamped in the mud outside the town is Grouchy's artillery commander, Colonel Griois. As morning comes he's just limbering up his batteries and wondering how he'll ever get them some food and forage, when counter-orders arrive – to unlimber again and wait until all the teams and guns he's had to leave behind on the Kovno road have caught up. Never in all his military career has his colleague Major Boulart known the Guard artillery to suffer such losses – most, he's sure, avoidable if only he'd been given the oats ration Napoleon had promised him during their pleasant chat together at Thorn. How can he report them to 'Old Thunderer', General Sorbier, the Guard artillery's commander? Only yesterday he'd been complimented by him on the excellent state of

> 'the teams of 20 vehicles, 90 train horses and 70 peasant ponies. I expected Sorbier to be stupefied. But he'd already been informed of the other divisions' losses, and listened without apparent emotion to mine.'

Now Boulart is to stay outside Vilna until they've been made good. But his colleague Griois is to leave,

> 'bringing with me such guns and ammunition wagons as I could harness up to healthy horses, and leave the rest of our artillery at Vilna, together with the lame horses and useless men'.

So saying, Grouchy had ridden off, 'indicating roughly which direction I should follow to rejoin him'. Even so, not until 4 p.m. (29 June) is Griois able to get going, 'with about two-thirds of what I'd brought this far, escorted by 50 dragoons from the dragoon division Grouchy had left behind.'

There's a reason for these hasty departures.

Early in the course of that drenching night of 28/9 June Napoleon has at last got what he takes to be reliable news of Bagration, said to be march-

ing toward Svetsianya, due east of Vilna. And has instantly sent off orders
to Murat, Ney and Oudinot not to press Barclay too hard, but, on the contrary, let him get as far as possible from what is now to be the real scene of
action. And at 2 a.m. another staff officer had galloped off with equally
urgent orders to Davout, who's already gone on ahead in the direction of
Ochmiana. To his extreme chagrin his corps has already been lopped of
three of its finest infantry divisions.[4] Instead of marching under his command, Friant, Gudin and Morand are to provide a powerful striking force
to support Murat's cavalry, while the rest of I Corps, plus Nansouty's (I)
and Grouchy's (II) Cavalry Corps, marching in three columns, is to inter-
pose itself between the two Russian armies. Nansouty, to the left, is to circumvent Bagration's advance guard. Davout will attack his centre. And the
right-hand column (Grouchy's corps, with its cuirassier division, headed
by Griois' horse artillery) is to pin down his rearguard – all on the
assumption that Bagration is by now being hard-pressed by Jerome's
55,000 infantry and cavalry, coming up from Grodno. That is to say, four
whole army corps, to be backed up – as soon as they've crossed the
Niemen – by Eugène (IV) and Saint-Cyr (VI), are to envelop Bagration
from all sides – 110,000 men against a mere 45,000, and annihilate him.
After which it will be Barclay's turn.

Riding out of the town gate at midnight, the Red Lancers take the
Smorgoni road 'in the direction of Miednicky' to protect Nansouty, on
Davout's left flank, against any attempt by Barclay to intervene in the
great enveloping movement. Dumonceau is happy to see that the
Lithuanian peasants, 'in return for promises to respect their homes', are
hastily consenting to supply his men with food and forage. At Smorgoni,
which turns out to be a small town almost wholly made up of wooden
houses,[6] his men can at last snatch 'two hours' happy sleep in its town
square and cemetery'. Then the trumpets sound again. The lancers
fall-in. And after five or six more hours' march they catch up with the rest
of I Corps at the small town of Ochmiana. From time to time Dumonceau
hears shots still being fired, Barclay's rearguard having only been dislodged that afternoon. But fails to catch even a glimpse of what's going
on. The long summer day drawing to a close and 'the smoke from the
campfires beginning to mingle with everything', he bivouacs and waters
his horses.

The situation being what it is – or at any rate what on 30 June it seems to
be – it's with a certain glee that Napoleon prepares to receive the Tsar's
emissary. Duly brought to Vilna by the 'roundabout route', Balashoff has
slept the night at Berthier's headquarters. And after breakfast is fetched
by the one-eyed chamberlain Count Turenne. Conducted upstairs to 'the
selfsame room from which, five days ago, Alexander had despatched me
on my errand', he finds himself in the presence of Napoleon. The interview's twists and turns, its seemingly erratic leaps and angry outbursts, its

cat-and-mouse tirades interspersed with sudden bouts of *faux bonhomie*, all bear the authentic Napoleonic hallmark. After some preliminary remarks ('I've seized one of his fairest provinces without firing a shot, and here we are, neither he nor I knowing what we're fighting for...') Napoleon declares Alexander has insulted him by demanding he withdraw behind the Niemen:

> 'At this moment, the gale blew a window open. Napoleon went over to it (we were both pacing the room) and quickly shut it. And upon its again blowing open – by now he was no little agitated – he didn't bother to shut it again, but tore it from its frame and flung it out into the street.'

So little has it been his intention to attack Russia, Napoleon goes on, he has even sent his personal carriages to Spain, where he'd really wanted to go. 'I know a war between France and Russia is no trifling matter, either for Russia or France. I've made extensive preparations, and my forces are three times as big as yours. I know the size of your armies as well as you do, perhaps better.' (Which he does. Upon the editor of *The Lithuanian Courier* setting the Russian effectives at 300,000, Napoleon had sardonically shown him a torn and crumpled despatch, intercepted from Barclay's chief-of-staff, which showed they at most added up to 185,000.)

Accusing Alexander of having connived at the assassination of his father, Tsar Paul, in 1802, he goes on to inveigh against Alexander's foreign associates, whose relatives, he says, he'll 'chase out of Europe'. Nor does he conceal his annoyance at Barclay's having refused battle in front of Vilna. 'I don't know Barclay de Tolly, but to judge from his first moves he hasn't much military talent.' A lecture follows on the folly of assembling stores, only to burn them: 'Did you think I'd just have a look at the Niemen and not cross it? Aren't you ashamed? With all Europe behind me, how can you resist me?'

'We shall do our best, Sire.'

Immediately Napoleon (who a moment before has been boasting of the Poles' unshakeable loyalty to himself) begins blandly talking about a settlement under which Alexander should 'in due course get the Duchy of Warsaw'.

And invites Balashoff to dinner.[6]

Even worse nourished and over-marched than the main body, Jerome's leading divisionss have only been making eighteen miles a day across Poland in the blazing heat. Only that morning have they, after immense efforts and sufferings,[7] entered an abandoned Grodno. A 24-year-old Westphalian lieutenant *Friedrich Giesse*, who'd not had a bite to eat for five successive nights, has seen his men die of thirst after drinking muddy river water. Another subaltern, *Eduard Ruppel*, seeing his 2nd Westphalian Hussars sprinkle their horsemeat with gunpowder for lack of salt, had trembled to think that this, so far from being the last stages of a campaign, was only its outset. Then the rains had come down; and the

Westphalians' and Saxons' horses, too, had begun to die. Now, struggling into Grodno without even having made contact with the enemy, Jerome receives a peremptory order from Vilna. He's to

> "unleash the Poles, put the advance guard under Poniatowski's orders. Give him all your light troops and yourself be always ready to support him. Don't be afraid to put your troops at risk. Bagration has plenty else to think about besides turning back to fight and manoeuvre. All he's trying to do is to get clear away out into the countryside. So harass the Russians. Delay their march if they advance. Bar their way if they retire."

All of which is good tactics, but, in the circumstances, very much easier said than done. Everyone in Jerome's three corps, from general to drummer boy, is dead beat. Even Vandamme, one of Napoleon's very toughest generals, and Maison, Jerome's no less capable chief-of-staff, realize the troops must rest up. And when Jerome tries to enforce the imperial order to march, Vandamme protests. Whereupon a piqued Jerome, playing the emperor,[8] promptly dismisses him.

This is bad enough. But to make matters worse Jerome finds the worst possible replacement to command VIII Corps. Namely the youthful Bonaparte's one-time comrade-in-arms General Junot. A choice which will turn out to be perhaps the campaign's single most damaging act.[9] Foreseeing disaster, Vandamme appeals to Napoleon. Receives no reply. And goes home.

That same morning too Eugène's Italians and Saint-Cyr's Bavarians have at last arrived at the Niemen. Crossing Poland, the Elban officer Cesare de Laugier has written in his diary:

> 'Our very swift march and the sandy terrain are putting more and more distance between us and the wagons carrying the food that's been assembled. But it would be unjust to accuse the head of the army of improvidence. For the time being we must subsist as best we can, aim at the main goal, i.e., make contact with the enemy; fall on him with a colossal mass of men; win a decisive victory; and conclude a glorious peace!'

Now, after literally stumbling on the Niemen at Piloni, the Italian Royal Guard 'find the Viceroy, the Duke of Abrantès (Junot) and the staff surveying the construction of a bridge'. One of the regiments which cross it as soon as it's ready – the (mostly Swiss) 35th Line – has in its ranks a Genevan shepherd, *Pierre-Louis Mayer*. Although his professional know-how has come in handy when driving flocks of requisitioned sheep across Poland, he's finding it a 'sad forboding of having to steal to live'. And now, at the pontoon bridge, he sees

> 'incomparable torments and weeping. A commandant of engineers, supervising four sentries, was only allowing one cantinière per battalion to cross. All unauthorized persons, and those unhappy women who'd followed their lovers in the capacity of vivandières and laundresses, were being stopped.'

Most of these women, he fancies (rightly, as it will turn out) will nevertheless rejoin by and by. But the 36 horses he also sees lying there dead from hunger are gone for good. In the afternoon, Cesare de Laugier again scribbles in his diary:

'the first divisions have crossed over in the greatest order and silence. Since the Viceroy believes the enemy to be nearby, he has forbidden us to light fires.'

At Vilna, meanwhile, Napoleon is dining with his Russian guest. That afternoon in his office his second secretary, Baron *A-J-F. Fain*,[10] has heard him,

'while walking rapidly to and fro, mutter to himself: "Return behind the Niemen...?" Containing himself, he meditates his reply. Soon, ignoring this condition [that he should return behind the Niemen], so hurtful to his feelings, he returns to the main point at issue. "Those fellows only want a few days' respite. They're laughing at all that's most sacred and all they're thinking of is how to save Bagration. Very well then, let's busy ourselves solely with what's been begun so well."'

Also present at that dinner are Marshals Duroc, Berthier and Bessières, and Caulaincourt. In the last four years Jomini's *Treatise on Great Operations in Warfare* have had almost as great an influence on Russian military thinking as Barclay's army reforms. And Napoleon's opening shot is an allusion to the Tsar's underhand efforts to recruit the services of this Swiss writer, whose highest ambition – year after year frustrated by Berthier – is to become his chief-of-staff:

'"Your generals imagine they can resist me because they've read Jomini. But knowing the principles isn't everything."

BALASHOFF (according to himself): "The Russians, like the French, say all roads lead to Rome. The road to Moscow is a matter of choice. Charles XII went via Poltava."

NAPOLEON: "I've no intention of making the same blunder." And then, by way of a joke: "My brother Alexander has turned Caulaincourt into a proper Russian."

CAULAINCOURT: "Sire, I'm a very good Frenchman. The marks of kindness the Tsar Alexander has so often honoured me with were in reality addressed to Your Majesty. As your faithful servant, Sire, I'll never forget them."'

But Napoleon, who's having a good time, takes Caulaincourt's irritation in good part: 'I hear the Emperor Alexander wants to take command himself. Why? It'd be to assume responsibility for a defeat. War is my profession. I'm used to it. But he isn't. He's an emperor by birth. He should rule, and appoint a general to command the army. If the general does his job well, he can reward him. If not, he can punish and discharge him.'[11]

And so the conversation goes on. By now they must have come to the coffee, for Napoleon, pacing the room, goes up to Caulaincourt and taps him lightly on the neck: "Well, you old St Petersburg courtier, why don't you say something? Are the general's horses ready for him? Give him some of mine. He's got a long journey ahead of him."

Seeing Balashoff off, Caulaincourt asks to be kindly remembered to the Tsar. Then, returning to the dining room, tells Napoleon 'in a trembling voice' (Ségur) he's 'a better Frenchman than those who've cried up this war'. And asks to resign – or be given a commission in Spain, with permission to set out tomorrow.

'NAPOLEON: "I was only joking. You know perfectly well I esteem you. Just now you're talking foolishly and I shan't reply to what you're saying."'

'Bessières tugged at one of my coattails, and Berthier at the other. Between them they drew me aside and begged me to cease my retorts. Seeing I was beyond listening to reason, Napoleon, who, I'm bound to admit, kept his patience and spoke with the same kindness, retired to his study. I'd lost my head completely.'

Next morning, when Caulaincourt doesn't appear at the levée,

'first Berthier then Duroc came and remonstrated with me. Seeing I didn't appear, the Emperor, having taken some turns about the town and after halting by the bridge, gave orders for me to be sought for and fetched. Unable to refuse obedience, I joined him while he was inspecting the outworks in front of Vilna.'

Napoleon pinches his ear: '"Are you mad, wanting to leave me?" With these words he galloped off, reined in his horse; and soon afterwards began talking of other matters.'

And that was that.

After the pontoon bridge at Piloni has been crossed by the Italian Royal Guard 'under the Viceroy's eyes' they're followed by the 35,000 men of Pino's division who, says Cesare de Laugier,

'broke out into spontaneous acclamations. The movement has been carried out with the same order, the same discipline, the same turnout and the same brio as if it had been a parade movement on some festive occasion in front of the prince's palace in Milan.'

But no sooner are they on the right bank than, out of a clear sky, comes an ominous rumble. Cannon fire? Every one strains his ears. General Roguet is sure they're about to be attacked; and Eugène, despite his instructions to advance with all speed to plug the gap between the main force and Jerome at Grodno, sends off a Colonel Battaglia to Vilna for orders. After which the Italians pile arms. Their first bivouac on Lithuanian soil, like the main army's before them, looks like being cold, dank and misty. But then, suddenly,

'a furious gust of wind upsets our stacked muskets and flings disorder into the camp. The horizon is covered with black clouds. Soon we're enveloped in a cloud of dust, drenched by torrents of rain which have now been falling with unheard of violence for thirty-six hours. Roads and fields are swamped; the heat we've been enduring

for several days has changed into a very keen cold. The horses are
dying like flies. Many of them have perished during the night and we
must expect many more to do so.'
In a pallid dawn, after a night when no campfire would stay alight,
'pierced through to the bone with cold, half-asleep and at our wits'
end, we look like phantoms or shipwrecked men saved from the .
waters. A lack of food is aggravating our situation.'
Quitting their 'accursed bivouac', the Italians find the little town of
Kronie deserted down to its last inhabitant. All it can offer is some very
welcome brandy. While they're gulping it down, here comes Colonel
Battaglia, back from Vilna with a flea in his ear. The two corps' halt at
Piloni, the irate Emperor has written scathingly to his stepson, is
'ridiculous. General Roguet has no common sense. These delays are
turning all IV Corps' fatigues into pure losses. His Majesty wants to
hear undelayedly from that officer the reasons for such an idiotic
supposition.'
So that day (2 July) the Army of Italy, bedraggled and hungry and with its
horses too 'falling by the hundreds', makes tracks for Vilna. 'All along the
road we met with nothing but dead horses, overturned vehicles and scattered baggage. And here we are, exposed to cold, rain and famine – in
July!' Next day the Viceroy instals his headquarters in 'a château near the
miserable village of Rouicontouï, very near the fork in the road leading to
Novo-Troki'. Novo-Troki itself, despite 'an impressive abbey and a picturesque castle on an islet', turns out to be only
'a little town of about 300 houses, every single one of which has been
stripped bare by its owner. Entering the town, the Viceroy has found
himself surrounded by a swarm of Jews, each dirtier than the others,
followed by a long line of women, old men and children, who pros-
trate themselves before him, howling and weeping and begging him
to protect them against the men's rapacity. They're scattering through
the town and pillaging everything. Nowhere have we found any straw
to lie on, and to get forage for the horses we've had to go nearly
seven miles.'
Though hardened to warfare in Catalonia, the Guardia d'Onore's adjutant-major is horrified by the pillage. But can do nothing to prevent it.
'Discipline, temperance, military honour, the superior officers' wise foresight, all are collapsing,' his diary laments. In vain Eugène sends urgent
messages to Vilna, begging for food. 'The help we've been given from
there is so meagre it hardly suffices for one day.' All IV Corps finds at
Novo-Troki to fill its 30,000 empty stomachs are great quantities of linden
honey. Gobbling it down, many men instantly fall victim to 'dysentery'.
  By now the Italians are longing for only one thing – to get to Vilna.
Judge their disappointment next day when orders arrive to stay where
they are:
'Everyone cried out with vexation, saying our corps is doomed.
They've tried to console us by saying we'll be going to Witebsk and

Smolensk, and that those two towns will make us forget all about Vilna.'
- obviously they've no idea of how many versts[12] they'll have to march to get there. Newspapers arriving from Vilna tell how Napoleon has 'set up some kind of provisional government of Lithuania, whose first concern has been to create five regiments of infantry and five of cavalry'. The flower of the young Vilna nobility, Laugier notes with something of his earlier enthusiasm, is forming a guard of honour under the command of Prince Oginski:

'Many young men of good family and 300 students from the university have enrolled, and are providing themselves with uniforms at their own expense. What a contrast to the abandonment of these houses and the flight of the population!'

Less encouragingly, the Vilna hospitals are reported as being choked with the sick.

That day the former Swiss shepherd Mayer confesses to a small but horrible murder:

'I saw a calf grazing peacefully in a garden around a hut. I go up to him and the poor beast lets me take him. I attack him, throw him down, and half cut his throat with my knife. As long as I live I'll recall the effect produced on me by this kind of murder. I said to myself: "What kind of a soul can assassins have who commit such a crime on their own kind?" But we've got to eat.'

Next day he makes up for it by saving a Russian landlord's daughter from being raped by a Pole.

So three days pass. Then IV Corps sets off for fresh fields and new tribulations.

Jerome's reply to his order to 'unleash the Poles' has thrown Napoleon into a rage less certainly feigned than his diplomatic ones. None of his cavalry probes in the direction of Ochmiana, his brother has written, have found Bagration's army. The fateful import is obvious. Somehow or other Bagration is managing to slip away, probably in the direction of Minsk. And the danger of this happening and the entire grand strategy being set at nought mmake him send a furious answer galloping off to Grodno:

"To the Prince of Neuchâtel, Major-general: *Mon Cousin.* Tell him [Jerome] it would be impossible to manoeuvre in worse fashion. I am severely displeased at his failure to place all the light troops at Poniatowski's disposal and so harass Bagration. Tell him he has robbed me of the fruit of my manoeuvres and of the best opportunity ever offered in war – all because of his extraordinary failure to grasp the first principles of warfare."

Nor is Napoleon's mood improved by a letter from Poniatowski to Berthier. Although his officers have accepted a 33 per cent cut in salary, Poniatowski has written, they've actually received no pay at all and can't even buy food. One of the secretaries[13] scribbles a letter to Berthier. He's to tell Poniatowski that

'His Majesty is most displeased that you should speak to him of pay and bread when it's a question of pursuing the enemy. The Emperor could not but be pained to see that Poles are such bad soldiers. His Majesty hopes to hear no more such talk.'

Stung by this reprimand, the Poles make a new and convulsive effort. And on 5 July, near the little town of Mir, their advance guard at last makes contact with Platov's retiring rearguard. Without waiting to be supported by artillery or infantry which are anyway a whole day's march to their rear, they fling themselves at the Cossacks – and get a bloody nose. Next day an entire cavalry division – 3,000 lancers, this time reinforced by infantry – is flung in. And is no less badly mauled.

Meanwhile the 85th Line, Le Roy's regiment, is spearheading Davout's corps as it probes for signs of Bagration's army. On 1 July the regiment had turned off 'sharply to the right, parallel with the Grodno road near Surviliski, to link up with the Westphalian army, which was to our right but in arrears'. And indeed is still at Grodno. Next day, failing of course to make any such junction, the 85th had taken 'the Minsk road, via Volokzin and Rahow'. Bumping into what he takes for Bagration's advance guard, Captain Biot, riding on south-eastwards with Pajol's cavalry, finds it's only a convoy Bagration has sent to Barclay.

Who will get to Minsk first – Davout or Bagration?

On 3 July the sun comes out again and is greeted with cheers by the men of the Vistula Legion; sent off from Vilna as an afterthought and to make up for Davout's loss of Friant's, Gudin's and Morand's divisions, they're marching down the Minsk road to catch up with I Corps and bring its nominal strength up to 50,000 men.

Next day at dawn Dumonceau, provided with a Polish interpreter, is ordered to probe the countryside toward Zabrès, on the Berezina, 'a name which as yet meant nothing to us'. Although his two troops of lancers run into Barclay's rearguard, they find the bridge over the Vilia's upper reaches still intact. Rejoining his fellow-officers at dinner, Dumonceau overeats, and is smitten with a cruel fit of indigestion; but next day in the afternoon (5 July) he's sent out again, this time under the regiment's veteran commandant Coti, to save the bridge by a night attack. Although the cool night air dissipates his dyspepsia, by the time the detachment gets there

'the bridge had just been burnt. Only a few half-consumed piles remained, still more or less in flames above the water. A cavalry trooper posted on the far side fired a shot at us and then cleared off.'

Nine miles further on, after finding a 'a deep and uncertain ford', they reach Zabrès at daybreak, to find it's just been evacuated by the Russian cavalry. Although the Dutchmen's sudden appearance at their town gate throws the locals into confusion, they're generous with useful information. I Corps, they say, is only five or six miles away to the right. So Coti sends off Dumonceau, 'accompanied by six of our best lancers and a mounted guide', to tell Davout he's at Zabrès. It's a dangerous mission. His guide is

'a kind of country gentleman of ferocious appearance, bearded, a black bearskin on his head, dressed in a Polish tunic, armed with a sabre and two pistols at his waist – in a word, got up like a comic-opera brigand and evidently very much exalted'.

But since Dumonceau knows no Polish and the Pole no French, the latter's patriotic eloquence is as lost on everyone as it is on the unending pine trees. Just as all this incomprehensible talk is showing signs of ebbing away, the party, deep in the forest solitudes, catch sight of some villagers who are furiously driving away 'some horsemen armed with long perches in guise of lances'. "Cossacks! Cossacks!," shouts the bellicose guide, eager to join in the fray. But that's none of Dumonceau's business and, to his guide's disgust, he refuses.

Reaching the town of Volagin, he finds I Corps bivouacked. Asks for Davout's headquarters and finds him at dinner in the local château, 'a great seigneurial building, with vast dependencies'. Dry and severe, and wearing his bifocal spectacles, Davout notes what Dumonceau has to say; bids him curtly sit down beside him at table with the rest of his staff. Pays him no more attention. As it happens, Dumonceau has met the Prince of Eckmühl before he had been made a prince, on the eve of Austerlitz. Shall he remind him of it? Dumonceau finds he lacks the courage. The meal over, Davout gets up from table and, saying he'll have some orders for him to take back to Colbert, leaves the room:

'Everyone made haste to follow him, except one little elderly senior officer, seated at the table's end, who muttered something about there surely not being all that hurry. The marshal heard and snapped back a few words as he left the room. Then I saw him address the lady of the manor with infinite courtesy, hoping he was disturbing her as little as possible. After which he went out and, with some of his aides packed around him, took his place on the lengthwise seat of a char-à-banc that stood waiting at the base of the peristyle.'

After a well-deserved nap Dumonceau tries to obtain his orders; but gets no help from Davout's disgruntled staff, who keep bitching about their chief's 'brusqueries, his haughty character and excessive severity'. Hadn't he only yesterday 'pitilessly had an unfortunate grenadier shot for pillaging?'[14] By and by Davout 'collarless, in his shirtsleeves on account of the heat, emerges from his office, severely reprimanding a grey-headed senior officer who's coming out backwards, resolutely but deferentially excusing himself'. Seeing Dumonceau standing there, the Iron Marshal calms down and calls him into the office, the whole of the middle of which is taken up by a huge table covered with maps and papers. At a card table by the window an officer whose acquaintance Dumonceau has made in Holland is sitting writing. And it's to him Davout dictates Colbert's orders. That very evening he's to force the inhabitants of Zabrès, 'on pain of military execution', to start rebuilding the burnt bridge. More importantly, Dumonceau is to tell him – verbally, if his despatches should be at risk – that I Corps' destination is Minsk. Colbert himself is to make for Veleika, to protect its rear.

'"You remember those place names, I suppose? Minsk and Veleika?"

"Yes yes, M. le Maréchal. But I'll jot them down in my notebook anyway."

"Quite right, get going." And with a slight inclination of his head the marshal dismissed me.'

And it's at Veleika, on 7 July, the Red Lancers have their first real clash with the enemy:

'We carried the bridge over the Vilia by a brisk attack before they could burn it. We seized a considerable convoy of camp equipment, a military pay chest and various baggage, among them a sutler's store of rice, oatmeal, salt, coffee, tea, sugar and such haberdasheries as thread, cordage, ribbons, buttons, clasps, etc., of which my servant took in an ample stock. The convoy's escort managed to make off into the woods after firing a few shots at us.'

The weather is again blazing. Even in this new crack lancer regiment men and horses are falling sick; and before leaving the captured stores (for the Italians to lay famished hands on) Colbert has to evacuate a second big batch of sick Dutchmen back to Vilna.

For three days 'at an even more rapid pace than before', through 'an agreeable countryside, covered with rich cornfields and fine forests where there are plenty of bees' I Corps makes forced marches for Minsk. Once again it's leaving in its wake hundreds, if not thousands of 'starving stragglers, marauders, and sick and exhausted men'. Until, on 8 July, Biot, General Pajol's ADC, with 200 men of the 6th Hussars and 200 of the 2nd Chasseurs, enters the capital of White Russia:

'I was ignorant of the marshal's order forbidding anyone to enter the town. When I got near it, I ordered my troop to a canter, passed through Minsk, and went and took up a position on the far side. We'd arrived in the nick of time. A Russian colonel, ADC to Bagration, was already in the town hall, busy collecting victuals for his army corps. He'd had to jump on his horse and make off as fast as he could go.'

Proud of his achievement, Biot reports back to Pajol; who sends him to Davout. Who, to Biot's dismay, flies into a rage: '"What! You've flouted my express orders, and entered Minsk? I'll have you shot!" Fortunately, I didn't lose my head; and replied bravely: "I didn't go *into* Minsk, M. le Maréchal. I went round it." – "In that case how do you know about that

Russian staff colonel?"' From an aged Russian official, Biot says. Dressed in full uniform, with stars and decorations and attended by footmen and lackeys, fulsomely declaring himself an old friend of France, he'd come in an open carriage drawn by four magnificent greys to present his compliments to the head of the French army. Davout doesn't believe a word of it: 'Odd, that bit about the old fellow being smothered in Russian decorations!'

Compared to Vilna, Minsk, with its mere 3,000 inhabitants, and though 'fortified, with its two citadels', turns out to be only a small town. 'This little town's streets', Lieutenant *Jacquemot*[21] of the 5th Artillery Regiment will write when he reaches it three months later, 'are dark and dirty. Though there are any number of churches and convents, the Jews are in a majority, disgusting, doing all the business and above all the money-lending.' But its great military stores – 3,600 quintals of flour, 22,000 bushels of oats, 6,000 quintals of hay, and 200 firkins of brandy – are intact, and their preservation is 'the greatest service its inhabitants could render the French army. Though united to Russia', Brandt notes proudly, 'they were still Polish at heart.'

Le Roy, of course, is particularly happy to be able to replenish his larder. Seeking out a Polish count whose guest he'd been as a prisoner of war in 1807, the Lucullan major finds his benefactor is ill and

'his house full of administrative officers of the kind who, for a few services they do us, without in any way participating in its victories, often disturb an army's march and are the only ones to profit by them'.

But Davout lets him station two NCOs to protect his friend's property against these parasites.

Pierre Auvray, arriving at Minsk four days later with the 21st Dragoons on 12 July just as the 85th are leaving, will be less lucky. His unit is sent straight through the town to the outposts beyond:

'No rations were distributed. Severe orders were at once issued against marauding, though we'd lived on nothing else since we'd entered Lithuania. In this unhappy situation we were glad the town's Jews brought us food for our money. Brandy and beer were cheap.'

'We'd stayed there for three days,' Le Roy goes on, 'during which we'd been given every sort of victuals and were made to erect great huts, as if we were going to establish ourselves there for a long time to come.'

All Davout's marching has been in vain. Bagration has eluded him. Making tracks by forced marches for the lower reaches of the Berezina, he's aiming to join up with Barclay in the interior.[15]

The realization that this is so throws Davout into an icy rage. And a scapegoat is needed. All the regiments have left innumerable stragglers. The 57th Line has left 1,400 men behind, and the 25th almost 1,700. Each company of Brandt's 2nd Vistula Regiment, for instance, is lacking 'on an average 15 to 20 men', 800 out of its nominal strength of 2,400 having been left 'lying on the roads, in the fields and marshes, some dead, others lacking strength to keep up with us. Other regiments, with nominal strengths of 4,000, have suffered proportionately'. But the 33rd Line, it too consisting largely of Dutchmen, is in specially sorry case.[16]

The 11th of July being a Sunday, a grand parade is ordered in the town square. Follows a scene the like of which no one has ever witnessed before. 'When the Prince of Eckmühl lost his temper he was like Vesuvius in eruption,' writes Sergeant *Henri-Pierre Everts*:

'Having attended Mass,[17] His Excellency, surrounded by several generals and a numerous staff, appears at the parade. Hardly is he there than he comes galloping toward our élite companies, yelling at us in a voice of thunder and losing his temper in an utterly brutal manner. Reaching our fusilier companies, he again begins cursing us in a monstrous manner on account of our stragglers, threatening to have every tenth man present shot. Our divisional and brigade generals, like our colonel, also get a terrible bawling out.'

By and by Davout calms down:

'Our unit isn't to have the honour of marching past him with the others, but shall instantly return to its bivouac.'

Turning to one of his ADCs, Davout asks him what punishment is suitable. The ADC suggests the regiment shall be made to march past with reversed arms, 'musket butts in the air'. Said and done. The band of 57th Line, says Lieutenant Dutheillet,

'was ordered to play during this shameful execution. General Barbangère and many of his officers refused to be associated with the disgraceful event, and quit the ranks under the eyes of the Marshal, who couldn't force them to stay there. But the mass of the regiment marched past under the officers still on parade; and I was there.'[18]

Everyone is utterly indignant. But although General Dessaix immediately goes out into the plain to the 33rd's bivouac and orders the men to fall in just as they are, without greatcoats or muskets, and explains that it isn't they, who've stayed with the colours, but the stragglers His Most Serene Highness the Prince of Eckmühl is so angry with, it does nothing to dispel the baneful impression. 'I'd never heard of such a thing,' Everts concludes indignantly. Nor has anyone else.

More horrible, if less 'disgraceful' scenes are to follow. When Le Roy and the 85th and the rest of I Corps march out of Minsk on 12 July to make for the Berezina in further pursuit of Bagration, the 33rd, except for its 3rd Battalion, is left behind. It is occupy Minsk, which 'certainly couldn't be left without troops, since the Russians were still occupying the fortified town of Bobruisk, on our right and another force of 15,000 men, under General Ertel, was at Moziev, in our rear. Furthermore, Napoleon is intending to turn Minsk into a base and a great storehouse for the army.

First and foremost Davout's thousands of stragglers are to be rounded up and brought back to their duties. Everts goes on:

'The governor of Minsk, a Polish general who had a name very hard to pronounce, which I've forgotten, and whose signature I could never read, staked everything on preventing the countryside from being devastated in this way.'

Flying columns are being sent out daily, and

'each day numbers of these disbanded men were brought back into town; many of them were condemned by court-martial and immediately shot. But this did not suffice, for the governor kept receiving complaints from landlords of the intolerable way in which they were being maltreated, they and their peasants.'

One day when Everts is at table with His Excellency just such a complaint comes in:

'He ordered me to go out with a column of infantry and cavalry (Polish lancers), about 1,000 men strong, and punish on the spot all who didn't submit or follow me. I asked for one of his ADCs who also spoke French, and was willingly granted one.'

On the second day out of Minsk he sends back some 500 stragglers and marauders 'whom I'd disarmed. To prevent more trouble I had all their muskets, whose barrels I'd removed, placed on carts.' His prisoners are twice as many as their escort, and 'to my great regret I was obliged and materially constrained to have two men from an Illyrian regiment shot who with blows of their muskets had struck and killed a sergeant-major of my cavalry, whom I had at my side.' Thanks to the governor's Polish ADC he can explain to all his men and their prisoners, drawn up in line, the reasons for this sentence.

'I ordered a corporal and four men to step out of the ranks and shoot these rebels. I was the more obliged to take such rigorous measures as a violent and mutinous spirit was very openly manifesting itself among those who had belonged to these bands of furious men. I consecrated eight days to this disagreeable and wearisome mission, daily arresting some hundreds of stragglers and sending them into town. But the rumour of my presence seemed to have spread terror, and at Minsk a military commission was in permanent session. One needs oneself to have witnessed all the numbers of pillaged and devastated houses I saw, and their unfortunate inhabitants, fully to grasp the barbarity and the horror of the spectacle.'

Yet Everts is well aware that it's the excessive speed of Davout's advance that has caused them:

'It was without precedent and exceeded human strength. Often after a march of almost 40 leagues (160 versts) [120 miles], the troops were hardly allowed to rest for a mere couple of hours. So they weren't able to use the few victuals they still had on them. The horses of superior officers, though only walking, came to a halt between their riders' legs and collapsed on the ground. No one bothered. In this campaign neither men nor beasts had a right to rest or nourishment if they were to keep up with the rapidity of our operations.'

CHAPTER 6

PROBLEMS AT VILNA

'The Emperor's incredible activity' – 'I could wish that carriage to the devil' – Planat learns the hard way – why no prisoners? – General Tayrayre is worried – how get on without maps? – 'we had to hunt for life's barest necessities' – the pillage of Lithuania – 'under the Law of 21 Brumaire' – IHQ on parade – Coignet gets his epaulette – Fézensac has a nice time – the diplomatic corps – the Polish question – 'how many leagues is it to Moscow?' – 'our fatuous and unlimited confidence in Napoleon's genius' – Sébastiani surprised – two incompatible governors

Jomini would afterwards call Napoleon's two weeks at Vilna 'a fatal mistake'. But where else could he have been? So long as the outcome of the enveloping movement is uncertain he can pursue neither Bagration nor Barclay.

Certainly he's not idle. 'During his stay at Vilna', Caulaincourt assures us, 'the Emperor showed incredible activity. ADCs, orderlies and staff officers were forever on the roads. He waited with insatiable impatience for reports from the corps on the march.'

Baron Pierre-Paul Denniée, an inspector of reviews in Berthier's cabinet, sees how 'the Emperor alone set everything in motion. He alone gave directions inside all departments of the General Staff.' His quarters in the archbishop's palace consists as always of three rooms *en suite*. The innermost, his bedroom, contains one of his three folding iron green-curtained campaign beds. The middlemost, his office, has a big map table in the centre of it and in each corner a chair and a small table, for the four secretaries. The outermost room, lastly, is for the duty adjutants. Although Berthier has his own headquarters in the third best building available in town, there's also a room for him, and it is there that he spends most of his days and nights.

The pace is hectic. To his secretaries' ever-scratching quills – and sometimes to all four at once, or if no secretary is available, then to anyone who is – the Emperor dictates, always at breakneck speed, an endless stream of detailed orders. No one is exempt. Everyone, says First Secretary Méneval, has to sit down and do their stint:

'So fast did the Emperor dictate, no one but the person who'd written it down could have transcribed a clean copy. As soon as his idea has matured he begins walking slowly to and fro in the room. Then, in a serious, sharply emphatic tone of voice and with never a pause, he begins dictating. As inspiration comes to him, it finds expression in a livelier tone of voice and a kind of jerky movements of his right arm, whose sleeve he begins plucking at. He has no difficulty in formulating his thoughts. Sometimes the form is incorrect. Yet this very lack of correctness sets its lively stamp on his language, always admirably depicting what he wants to say.'

Everything proceeds swiftly and methodically. "Tomorrow! Night brings good advice," Méneval hears him say sometimes. At other moments, often, he'll joke and laugh with his secretaries, and at such times his usually mild thoughtful air breaks into a 'gentle caressing smile'. His terrifying rages pass over quickly, and his threats, though drastic, are almost never implemented.

All orders are addressed to Berthier, who passes them on to Colonel Salomon, his chief assistant, to copy into the order book before despatch. This is always done in duplicate, sent by two separate adjutants, and Napoleon is notified of the times of their departures. Nor does he ever send a new order to the same recipient without first consulting the order book. Secrecy is absolute, confined to himself, to his chief topographer, little Colonel *Bacler d'Albe*,[2] and 'perhaps to Berthier'.

'A little dark fellow, handsome, amiable, highly educated, talented and a clever draughtsman', Bacler d'Albe is Napoleon's most intimate collaborator. As chief cartographer it's his business to see to it that the maps are 'corrected and the various units' marches and lines of operation worked out'. Also to summarize, immediately on receipt, any important despatch. For seventeen years d'Albe has hardly had a moment to himself. One of the orderly officers, Captain Castellane, who doesn't like him, calls him scathingly 'the topographer par excellence, the great topographer, who has no excess of intelligence'. But Napoleon thinks otherwise[2] – always his first words on returning to his maps are "Fetch d'Albe!" And there are moments when Méneval sees the two of them lying flat on the big map table and hears them 'let out loud cries as their heads bumped together'.

No one ever knows from moment to moment what Napoleon's next move will be. After dictating his last word he exclaims: "To horse! My carriage!" And everyone has to scramble for it:
'This he called "keeping my people in good breath". As soon as he has formed a plan, he rings. Abruptly, the office door opens. An usher of the household comes forward and shouts in a loud voice: "The Emperor!" – a shout repeated by the grenadiers on sentry duty at the various doors, who present arms. At the same moment a carriage or a saddle-horse is brought round to the exit,'
and Caulaincourt emerges, carrying the imperial riding-whip, followed by Napoleon himself, 'walking quickly. He mounted. And left like a flash of lighting'. Well, not quite. On 7 July Captain Castellane confides to his diary:
'When I'm on duty I follow the Emperor when he rides out. We go the whole way at a walk. When the Emperor travels, he does most of the journey by carriage. This is very tiring for the officers who have to follow, because His Majesty, having rested up when the time comes for him to mount, assumes that the rest of us, who've covered the distance on horseback, are also. And behaves accordingly. Sometimes I could wish this confounded carriage to the devil. When His

Majesty's on the move there's not a moment of rest to be expected the clock round.'

Not a few of the innumerable orders pouring out from Napoleon's office are being passed on by Salomon to Lariboisière, head of the artillery. Which in effect means to Lieutenant Planat de la Faye, who forwards them to his assistants. These assistants, who are his seniors in rank, are six arrogant but badly educated artillery captains:

'I give them my minutes to copy, and sometimes, when their copies aren't sufficiently legible, make them begin all over again. The Emperor wants to be informed of the state of affairs, both matériel and personnel, at all his reserve depots, from Metz to Vilna. He's writing letter after letter to hasten on the arrival of everything in the rear; and each letter from him means I'm having to write at least twenty.'[3]

All this pen-pushing on a starved stomach – for there's a terrible shortage of food – is causing the six artillery captains to dub him sarcastically their 'man of letters'. Poor Planat! He's learning the hard way that

'in war one shouldn't make oneself too indispensable. Almost always one ends up by becoming the dupe or victim of such devotedness, in which vanity plays so large a part. It's precisely those officers who spare themselves most and sin least by excess of zeal who get on best. A little worldly-wise charlatanism and boasting goes much further.'

A lesson also being learnt by Sergeant-major Thirion. After taking him into his confidence, the commander of his cuirassier brigade, 'General Bruno, of Metz, an excellent man who liked to tell tall stories, and whom I really ought to be annoyed with, overwhelmed me with missions and rides, while my companions took it easy.'

After only two days at Vilna even the artillery staff, 'exhausted by marching and working', have no bread, indeed nothing to eat apart from what they've been able to steal from the villages en route. And after four even Caulaincourt is finding it has 'become necessary to search for life's barest necessities'. Many of the inhabitants are already reduced to 'living on berries'.

Small wonder then if, as at Minsk, thousands of starving deserters are pillaging the countryside. Marshal Mortier, the Young Guard's jovial giant of a commander, is setting their number at 30,000, equivalent of a whole army corps. The Lithuanian gentry are appalled at this side-effect of their supererogatory liberation. Heinrich von Brandt talks to 'a Lithuanian gentleman, an old soldier, who'd come to offer his services to the French Army, but found he must leave again in all haste to defend his property against the pillagers'. And when another, Eismont by name, makes so bold as to remind some French officers how Pharaoh's host, though innumerable, had all been drowned in the Red Sea, his frankness almost costs him his life:

'One of these madcaps drew a 3-foot dagger and ran at me, shouting: "Die, thou unbeliever in the earthly god and his inscrutable order of things!" After that, I've learnt to hold my tongue. A third Lithuanian landowner arrived on the steps of the Palace in rags, after soldiers had killed his serfs and driven his wife and daughter mad.'

Nor are the Lithuanians the only sufferers. Back at Novo-Troki, Césare de Laugier sees the newly appointed French sub-prefect turn up on foot, after being pillaged by stragglers. Whereupon his escort had eaten his provisions and made off with his horses; so that he when he'd got to Novo-Troki, Fézensac says, he was 'almost naked. Everyone took this man, who was to be our chief administrator, for a spy.'

Normally, says Ségur, Napoleon winked at pillage. But obviously things are going too far; and already on 2 July he has signed an order that all marauders 'if found guilty' are to be court-martialled and shot. And two days later he signs another, for the "despatch of cavalry detachments under staff officers to catch the stragglers, of whom many are committing crimes and end up by falling into the hands of the Cossacks". Immediately three flying columns, each consisting of 100 men and subdivided into ten patrols of ten men apiece (30 gendarmes, 30 Dragoons of the Guard, 30 lancers and ten local mounted guards) under a superior officer, have set out from Vilna with orders to go wherever 'they might be invited by the inhabitants'. Marauders convicted of crimes by the provost-court are to be 'executed within 24 hours, conformably with the Law of 21 Brumaire, Year V'. But though Coignet soon sees 'gendarmes everywhere, picking up stragglers', what can 300 men do against 30,000? Although 'military commissions and the making of several examples frightened a number of stragglers into returning to their duty, order was only indifferently restored,' says Caulaincourt.

Where, in this vast shortage of everything, are the immense supplies of foodstuffs, assembled at Danzig? Despite the heavy rains the Vilia, a shallow river at the best of times, has in places almost dried out. And it isn't until 9 July that Napoleon personally supervises the arrival of the first barges.[3]

Every day new units are arriving and wanting rations. All are reviewed by Napoleon with his usual close attention to detail. On Monday, 8 July it's the turn of the Old and Young Guard. On the Tuesday, of the ambulances, 'lightly equipped to follow the army on the battlefields'. And on 10 July Fézensac has 'an opportunity of observing in every detail the way the General Staff is made up:

'The Administration, directed by the Intendant-General Count Dumas, was subdivided into an administrative service proper; ordonnateurs, inspectors of reviews and war commissaries; the health service; doctors, surgeons and pharmacists; the victualling service in its various branches, and all kinds of employees.'

Berthier's aristocratic ADC doesn't know whether to be more impressed or dismayed by the

'great number of officers of all grades, commanded by General Mouthon. At a distance one would have thought they were troops drawn up in battle order. Just imagine the entire headquarters staff assembled at one spot. Imagine the prodigious numbers of domestics, of lead-horses, of baggage of all kinds which it had to drag along in its wake, and you'll have some notion of the spectacle offered by the headquarters.'

Since Vilna's market place isn't big enough to contain it, the extraordinary parade takes place in a plain beyond the town, where Dr *René Bourgeois* is also among the witnesses. Unfortunately, he sees, looking up at the sky, a storm was brewing.

'Thunder was heard grumbling in the distance. The sky got darker and darker. Finally, at the very moment when Napoleon emerged from the town, thick blue-black clouds let fly a deluge of rain. The Emperor refused to be deterred. But soon lightning flashes, cracks of thunder and an impetuous wind, raising whirlwinds, forced him to dismount, so as not to be carried away. In all haste he took refuge behind an ammunition wagon. Whereon everyone dispersed in the darkness to find shelter. The review couldn't take place and Napoleon went back into the town drenched to the skin. Likewise his suite.'

But why are there no prisoners? All officers arriving at IHQ from the various corps are immediately asked how many have been taken. 'The Emperor was anxious to get some trophies, so as to encourage the Poles. But no one gave him any.' This doesn't prevent him from making provision for them:

'As soon as there are 1,200 of them, they are to be divided up into twelve companies of 100 men apiece and marched in four days to Kovno, under a strong detachment commanded by a major and escorted by a Baden company of 100 men, 40 mounted Prussians, and a squad of five gendarmes.'

The returning Niemen barges, he thinks, will serve admirably to transport the prisoners – after they've taken a day's rest locked up in a church at Kovno – downstream to Tilsit, 'if it presents no difficulties, at the bottom of the holds and strictly supervised'. Should navigation prove difficult, or water transport take longer than land transport, then, issued with four days' bread rations, they're to be marched along the Niemen's left bank to Königsberg and thence to Pilau 'where they're to be shut up in a prison'. From there the officers and NCOs are to be sent on to Danzig, where 'vast localities are to be prepared to hold 10,000 prisoners'.

All this is very well, or would be if there were any. But Captain Franz Roeder, arriving at Kovno on 15 July to join the Hessian Footguards, only sees 850, 'mostly hospital orderlies, stragglers or officials'. His friend

General Tayrayre, the town's military governor ('one of the most modest Frenchmen I've ever met, as well as being a sympathetic and extremely honest man') has 'counted on finding all needful equipment, but been horrified to find neither tents, bandages nor blankets, and no prospects of getting any'. Inviting Roeder to dinner, he asks him to become his ADC, – a post the fiery-tempered captain would gladly accept 'if I could have gone with him to headquarters, but it's precisely there he won't be needing an adjutant of my stamp, and a German to boot'. High administrative officials, Tayrayre tells him, are obviously in no hurry to reach Lithuania and take up their duties: 'God knows what'll happen when the Grand Army is extended over such immeasurable distances and advancing at speed.'

Hasn't everything been thought of?

Everything, it seems, except maps.

Even while still en route for Vilna, General Compans had realized the sketchy nature of the campaign map. 'Everyday', he'd written home to his young bride,

'I'm becoming aware of the inadequacy of the maps we have; so I've bought a compass to guide me. Although I'm not used to this instrument I'm not unhopeful that it'll enable me to find St Petersburg or Moscow.'

Poring over the campaign map, specially engraved and printed on an enormous and unwieldy roll of paper, even the usually admiring Soltyk is beginning to realize that

'the geographical notions of the Muscovite empire entertained in Napoleon's office were about as imperfect as could be, and likewise of its topography. At all hours Napoleon kept interrogating the Polish General Soholnicki about such matters. On my offering to rectify the place names' orthography, I was ordered to write them in on the map, so that Napoleon could have a better idea of his whereabouts.'

As for the outlandish place names, the locals have never so much as heard of them. And since all the verst-posts have been removed by the Russians it's hardly surprising if smaller fry, who've no maps at all, are going astray; or if a half-witted psychopath like Roeder's irascible Colonel Follenius (Roeder himself, oddly enough, seems to have had some kind of a map) manages to lose his way and yet stumble on his destination a day too early! Even Davout has only been issued with *six* copies of the campaign map – one for himself, and one for each of his divisional commanders,

'but none for the generals commanding the artillery or engineers, for the generals commanding the light cavalry, nor for any of the army's generals of brigade. I therefore implore Your Highness to send me a dozen copies, which I shall distribute to the army corps, and which will be most usefully employed,

he'd written to Berthier before leaving Vilna on 30 June.

All of which points to a gross over-centralization of command. In

Napoleon's office little Baron Fain, who's sure everything's going well, notes in his journal that his master

'is only telling each of the participants about the bit that concerns him. The whole remains in his thoughts. Like writings in invisible ink which only fire can bring out, his military combinations will remain unperceived until revealed on the field of battle.'

And Tayrayre, at Kovno, is perfectly right in his apprehensions. Already the theatre of war is fanning out dangerously. For several days Oudinot has marched in pursuit of Wittgenstein without so much as catching up with his rearguard. Then, on 28 June, while he and his staff were taking breakfast in a farmhouse, a Polish lancer of his escort had found a Russian straggler asleep under a bush; and Marbot's light cavalry advance guard ('any army's eyes and ears') had seen Wittgenstein's corps drawn up in front of the little market town of Winkowo. Oudinot, says Marbot who affects to despise his talents as a corps commander, had amiably refused to believe his reports – until, proceeding to the edge of the forest, he and his staff had had to jump ditches to elude bouncing Russian roundshot. A small but full-scale battle had followed. The Russians had been driven out of Winkowo. And Oudinot had sent off a report of his victory to Vilna. But the distance between him and IHQ was now so great that it had taken three days before he received an acknowledgement.

Neither to Fain nor to Napoleon does it seem to occur that a system that leaves little or nothing to the corps commanders' initiative, when applied over such great and ever-growing distances, must in the end come unstuck.

Although victuals are so hard to come by, Fézensac's fortnight at Vilna, at least, is passing pleasantly enough. Nor is it the first time he's been here. As a pampered prisoner of war in 1807, captured while carrying Ney's despatches, this scion of the old French aristocracy had made many acquaintances in the town. This time too

'there was nothing burdensome about our duties. Assemblies, balls, concerts succeeded one another uninterruptedly. We found it hard to recognize the capital of a country ravaged by two hostile armies, and whose inhabitants were being reduced to indigence and despair.'

In Berthier's *salon de service*, where they aren't 'even allowed to read or write', the 'heart-breakers' preserve 'a profound silence' as they take turn and turn about, two at a time, one to receive, the other to despatch messages. But since these are normally carried by

'other staff officers, our turn only came every fourth or fifth day, when none of us was out on mission, something that happened only rarely. As Berthier himself always lodged physically close to the Emperor, his own lodgings belonged to his aides. It was most agreeable, in the midst of war and without having to take the least trouble, to find oneself better lodged and fed than anyone else in the army. At times it was as if we were in Paris.'

It's also at Vilna that the ambassadors of Austria, Prussia and the – still neutral – United States of America have foregathered, nothing doubting the outcome. Their opposite number is the former journalist, now Napoleon's minister of foreign affairs, *Hugues Bernard Maret*, Duke of Bassano.[5] A rare survivor of the pre-revolutionary diplomatic service, though certainly not the peer of his formidable but devious forerunner Talleyrand,

'M. Maret distinguished himself by the elegance of his manners, as much as by the solidity and pleasantness of his mind. His devotion to Napoleon arose from the conviction he'd gained from day to day of this great man's superiority.'

Secretary Fain notes his singular gift of wholeheartedly supporting policies of which he personally disapproved. His ducal title, he says, had been 'acquired by the most legitimate means, for it was the price of hard work and the most honourable services'. Maret is in effect Napoleon's prime minister 'and under any other man would have been so by right'. But just now Napoleon is not particularly pleased with the efforts of his diplomatic service. Relationships with Turkey, Sweden and the USA are all extremely sensitive. One day Fain sees Napoleon

'vivaciously drop his reading of the English newspaper to open despatches announced from the USA. They're of greater interest. The Americans are at war with the British. He exclaimed: "If this rupture had occurred earlier it might perhaps have contributed to keep Alexander inside the Continental System!"'

And in fact an American army will shortly – if not very successfully – be invading Canada. News from Spain, on the other hand, isn't so good. After starving out Masséna's army, Wellington has left his impregnable position among the hills round Torres Vedras and is steadily driving it back into Spain. As for the Turks, Napoleon still doesn't know a peace has been signed between them and the Russians. Nor is Sweden's neutrality to be taken for granted.

Lastly, and most urgently, there's the Polish question.

Ambivalent attitudes yield ambiguous choices. Abbé *Pradt*,[6] Bishop of Malines, the man Napoleon has chosen as his ambassador-extraordinary to the Grand Duchy of Warsaw, has immediately shown himself unequal to his task. Two days before the Niemen crossings the Warsaw Diet had assembled and in a fever of excitement declared the Kingdom of Poland re-established. And all that's needed now to trigger off a national uprising which can provide the Grand Army with thousands of 'Polish Cossacks' is a word from Napoleon, confirming the decision.

A word he's determined not to utter. After all, there's his father-in-law the Emperor Francis to consider, and his guaranteed claim on Polish Galicia; as a quid pro quo for Schwarzenberg's 30,000 Austrians, fending off a potential threat to the Grand Army's southernmost flank from the Russian Army of Moldavia.

On 5 July Napoleon hears that Pradt, after three days of high-flown rhetoric in the Diet, instead of skilfully directing its patriotic fervour, has quite simply dissolved it. For a moment, utterly furious, he thinks of replacing Pradt with the strongly pro-Polish Narbonne. But reflecting no doubt that this could be equally disastrous in the opposite direction, refrains from doing so. Finally, on 11 July, an eight-man delegation gets to Vilna – but only after being seriously molested en route by marauders. Roman Soltyk's father is one of the delegates. At a solemn Te Deum in the cathedral Captain *Fantin des Odoards* of the 2nd Guard Grenadiers (Coignet's regiment) watches them renew their oath of fidelity to a united Poland in front of the high altar:

'The tremendous enthusiasm of all present was particularly notice-able among the women. All wore on their bosoms a large rosette in the Lithuanian colours, crimson and blue.'

Afterwards, in the archbishop's palace, Maret solemnly receives the dele-gates' petition and presents it, no less ceremoniously, to his all-puissant master who, Fézensac sees, receives it 'with benevolence'. Whereupon the delegation's francophile spokesman, the aged Wybicki, steps forward and appeals pathetically: 'Sire, say but the word, say Poland exists. For the world your decree will be the equivalent of reality!'

Will it? Solemn oaths and ceremonies are one thing. Power politics quite another. Napoleon's reply is at once candid and evasive:

'I love your nation. For sixteen years now I've seen your soldiers beside me on the battlefields of Italy and Spain. I applaud all you've done. But in lands so distant and far-flung you must above all place your hopes in the efforts of the local population. Let me add that having guaranteed the Emperor of Austria the integrity of his domains I cannot sanction any moves or manoeuvres that might trouble his peaceful possession of his remaining Polish provinces.'

Hasn't he already hinted to Balashoff that he's reserving 'Polish' Lithuania as an important pawn in his future peace negotiations with Alexander?

Faces fall. There'll be no Polish uprising. But at the ball that follows, Fantin des Odoards has

'a better opportunity of judging the fair sex of Vilna, of whose charms I'd formed a favourable opinion at the religious service. This time I was filled with quite another sort of admiration when I saw them animated by dancing, pleasure and patriotism and noticed how white and rounded were the objects rising and falling under the national colours during the gentle embraces of the waltz.'

Dedem, the ex-diplomat, says he'd often seen his colleagues neglect to take Napoleon at his word when he'd told them the plain truth about his intentions. So now. After dinner that evening he takes one of the delgates aside and tells him confidentially: "I see you aren't well off. I advise you not to compromise yourself vis-à-vis the Emperor of Russia. I may make peace with him at any moment."

On one of those days in Vilna Berthier presents the Line regiments' needs for new subalterns. As usual they're to be picked from among Guard NCOs. And little Coignet, much to his dismay, finds he's among the candidates:

'Since the Foot Chasseurs had left, all these promotions fell on us. We had to be in our places at two o'clock to be presented to the Emperor. At midday I was in the public square with my packet of letters under my arm, to distribute them. Taking me by the arm, Major Belcourt squeezed it hard and said: "Mon brave! Today you're going to be promoted lieutenant in the Line!" – "Thank you, but I don't want to go back to the Line." – "And I tell you today you'll be wearing a lieutenant's epaulette. If the Emperor sends you to the Line, I give you my word I'll bring you back into the Guard. So, don't answer back! Two o'clock, on the square, without fail!"'

And at two o'clock sharp they're there, all twenty-two of them

'all in one row. The Emperor arrives to review us. Beginning at the right, looking these handsome NCOs up and down from head to foot, he says: "These'll make fine regimental officers!" Coming to me, he sees I'm the smallest. The major says to him: "He's our instructor, and doesn't want to be sent to the Line." – "What's that? You don't want to go to the Line?" – "No, Sire. I want to stay in your Guard." -"Very well, then, I appoint you to my select staff." – How happy I was to be able to stay close to the Emperor!'

sighs Coignet. But adds: 'I didn't guess I was leaving paradise to fall into hell. That same evening my comrades shot my pack.' And next day, presenting himself for his new duties, he's

'graciously received by the general, whose face showed he loved old soldiers. "Well, so you'll be on duty close to the Emperor. If you don't mind, you'll do me the kindness of cutting off your long moustaches. The Emperor doesn't like moustaches at his headquarters. So you'll have to sacrifice them."'

For a few hours Coignet, stripped of his sergeant's stripes and his moustache, feels 'like a demoted NCO' – a loss made up for that evening by a large sabre, an officer's fore-and-aft hat and a gold epaulette from the quartermaster's store. All these new accoutrements have been paid for personally by General Monthyon, who even offers him a horse from his own stable. As it happens some soldiers of the Train – remarkably in view of the present acute dearth of horsepower – have already made him a present of 'a fine horse, together with its saddle and portmanteau'. Thus equipped, he presents himself for his first task as a commissioned officer. It will be extremely exacting.

Even as late as 14 July IHQ is still in the dark as to Barclay's plans. The Russian commander has four options. Either (a) to withdraw northwards and defend Petersburg; in which case Napoleon will attack him with an overpowering concentration, consisting of Murat's cavalry, Oudinot's II, Ney's III, Eugène's IV, St-Cyr's VI Corps and the Imperial Guard. Or (b) he can shut himself up in the Drissa Camp – in which case the invaders' vastly superior forces will quite simply outflank it and take him from the rear. Or again (c) he can stand and fight on the River Dwina near the little town of Kamen. Or lastly, (d) he can try to make junction with Bagration by retiring on to the important city of Witebsk.

Whichever of these courses Barclay opts for, Glubokoïë, a small town 90 miles east of Vilna on the Witebsk road, 24 miles due south of the Drissa Camp, commands a central position. And already on 7 July the Guard has been ordered to leave for there. For its three-day march it's to carry on its backs 90,000 bread rations, sufficient for ten days.

'The bridging equipment, the engineer units, the artillery, and everyone who leaves must take with them half-rations for six days, and three-quarters of a pound or a pound of meat per man.'

Four more days' bread rations,

'loaded on the headquarters auxiliary vehicles, must be assured by two convoys leaving on 11 and 12 July and on those vehicles replacing the 2nd, 9th, 10th and 11th Battalions and on such others as may yet arrive, so that during 10 and 11 July 11,000 quintals of flour shall have followed the Guard, which makes 360,000 bread rations or ten days of victuals assured for the Guard and headquarters; which, added to the ten days' rations the Guard will carry, will make bread for ten days.'

Whoever else is going to go hungry, the Guard isn't:

'If the army doesn't march, other convoys will arrive. If it does, it'll find resources in the towns. But I cannot be tranquil until the Guard and headquarters have 20 days' rations assured, since the Guard, marching last, should set an example of discipline. In this account the biscuits and brandy, etc., contained in the headquarters' 40 wagons should not be included, these being a last resource.'

(How the Guard, marching last, can set an example isn't clear.)

All these preparations have been made and all these orders given when, on 14 July, some mortifying news comes in. An entire cavalry brigade of General Sébastiani's advance guard, commanded by General St-Gèniez, has been surprised, driven into a swamp and forced to surrender. This is distressing enough. But does it portend a Russian counter-offensive? Immediately Napoleon decides to advance his headquarters to Glubokoïë.

Before he can leave Vilna, however, two appointments must be made. Lithuania must have a governor; and so must Vilna. To the first post he has already appointed a Dutch general *Dirk van Hogendorp*. A stiff and stuffy but in his own eyes irreproachable officer whom Napoleon had honoured by making him his ADC but 'laughed at because I hadn't even asked for the Cross of the Legion of Honour,' but whom he esteemed, Hogendorp claims, because he'd flouted his orders to burn down a Prussian town, is already on his way to take up his duties. For the second post, as military governor of Vilna, Napoleon selects a man of completely different, not to say incompatible, character.

If Napoleon had needed a chief-of-staff with ideas of his own, the Swiss General Jomini, author of *The Grand Operations of Warfare*, the greatest military work of the age, would have been his man. But he has no such need.[8] And in the end an exasperated Jomini, aware of his own status as the recognized theorist *par excellence* of modern warfare, had begun to listen to siren tones from Petersburg, steadily upping his price until the secret negotiations, which Napoleon of course had known about all along, had fallen through; or rather, at the critical moment, had been scotched, on the one hand by threats against which Jomini's status as a Swiss citizen availed nothing, on the other by giving him a post at IHQ – as official historian of the forthcoming campaign. So far, however, his only task has been to police the Niemen bridges.

But now, on the eve of the Emperor's departure, he's invited to dinner. Also present are two members of the Polish delegation:

"How many leagues is it from Vilna to Moscow, M. Vibicki?" Napoleon asks, by way of making table talk. And before the other can answer: "Two hundred and fifty, I believe? Hardly forty days' march of six leagues apiece!"

"Oh certainly, Your Majesty can easily be in Moscow in forty days!"

"You see how easy it is to skip distances by movements on maps! I prefer to take two years. If the Russian gentlemen fancy I'm going to run after them they're mistaken. We'll go as far as to Smolensk, and enter into cantonments on the Dwina. I'll resume my headquarters here, send for the Théâtre Français, and finish the job off next spring. Isn't that wise, *Monsieur le tacticien?*"

"Very wise," Jomini (says he) replied. "But even wiser to make peace without going any further."

"Ah, that's quite another matter!"

Dinner over, Napoleon takes him aside and says: "Any amount of guns and wagons are being left here. I'm expecting convoys of oxen from Hungary and Galicia. You'll manufacture as many yokes as are needed. From Danzig and Kovno you'll bring up convoys of flour, which can only get here by the Vilia. You'll construct the necessary barges. The town must be defended against any surprise assault, so you'll dig such trenches around it as are requisite.'

Jomini is also to rope in all the stragglers, victual the reserve corps, organize hospitals, bury several thousand dead horses, and, in general, teach the Lithuanians their new duties. It'll be for Hogendorp and his colleague General *Roch Godart* to raise a Lithuanian army. Nor is this all.

Next day Jomini is dismayed to receive a 16-page memorandum, listing a host of other tasks.

Napoleon, true to his divide-and-rule tactics, couldn't have chosen two more mutually antipathetic fellow-governors.

How had that ignominious surrender of an entire cavalry brigade come about? Captain Zalusky of the Polish Guard Lancers – he who'd so narrowly escaped drowning at Kovno – has virtually foreseen it.

It is Napoleon's habit on the eve of an important departure to send out his light travelling carriages

'in various directions, partly because he didn't really know where he'd make contact with the Russians, and partly to deceive his enemies as to his real intentions'.

And it's with one of these *calèches* Zalusky, with his 1st Squadron of the Polish Guard Lancers, has been sent ahead to Murat's headquarters at a place called Belmont. During their three-day march they talk en route to an intelligent Russian prisoner,

'an elderly NCO from Docturov's corps. When we asked him why they were abandoning so many towns and terrain without standing and fighting, he, neither frightened nor boastful, replied that their plan was to draw us as far as they could into the interior, where we'd gradually grow weaker: and then surround us and stifle us.[9] However, our fatuity and limitless confidence in Napoleon's genius made light of these auguries. We could have been asked to conquer the moon, and we'd have responded with "Forward, march!"'

And just now Zalusky is anyway less interested in the campaign's outcome than in what may be happening – with the Russians only a couple of miles away – on one of his mother's estates at Druï, on the Dwina. Belmont turns out to be a palatial residence owned by an Italian, who's much more concerned for his herd of prize cattle than for the Polish pennons surrounding his house. Zalusky seeks permission to visit Montbrun and Sébastiani near Druï; and gets it, on condition that he bring back some provisions for his squadron 'and notably for its officer corps', who are 'suffering from a complete dearth of everything'. Reaching Druï with a corporal and four lancers, he's just in time to participate in a scuffle with some Cossacks, in which 'Sébastiani, with the impetuosity typical of the French generals, personally fought among the Uminski Hussars'. Then the Cossacks withdraw to the other side of the river. Behind the Dominican monastery 'which had done so much good in the town,' Zalusky goes on,

'there was an island in the Dvina which could facilitate any attack from that quarter. It was a spot which called for great vigilance. I was afraid the French cavalry's advance guard, made up of two chasseur regiments under General St-Gèniez – who also commanded the Uminski Regiment – might be attacked on this side. Next day I left, feeling dissatisfied – a feeling which grew considerably when, arriving at Sébastiani's headquarters, I found him clad only in his shirt, resting on a camp-bed in the middle of a room in an inn, under a tent of green cloth, rubbing his shins! Stupefied at this sight, I began to fear seriously for his advance guards, and for him personally.'

Despite his military dash, Sébastiani, a relative of the Bonapartes, is more diplomat than soldier. Dedem describes him as

'intelligent, of a rare impudence and immorality. Though short of stature, he had a pleasant appearance and knew how to insinuate himself and captivate others.'

After General Wathier de St-Alphonse's dismissal for his inertia outside Vilna, command of his advance guard has fallen on General St-Gèniez. When Sébastiani asks Zalusky what he's seen, he replies:

'"a corps of 40,000 men with numerous artillery whose guns one could count gleaming in the sunshine, all commanded by Wittgenstein!" At this name he exclaimed: "Wittgenstein's a bungler who doesn't know his job!" More and more I began to fear such vain self-assurance would be punished."[10]

At lunch Zalusky is no less dazzled by his host's table silver than by his knowledge of Polish affairs. Sent back to Murat with an account of the state of affairs at Druï, he's received by the King of Naples, who in a long tête-à-tête, extols the Polish ladies' charms, saying he's bored with the throne of Naples and would much prefer to command 100,000 Polish cavalrymen. Finally Zalusky, 'enchanted to have discovered a candidate for the Polish crown, but absolutely sceptical about the pretender's political worth', withdraws. And next day, sure enough, comes

'the nastiest news – viz. that the Russian general Kulmiew had crossed the Dwina with 5,000 cavalry and infantry, and having thrown a bridge over the island without being seen, had fallen on Colonel Uminski's advance guard, crushed it, rounded on St-Gèniez' brigade and taken it prisoner – a defeat the more painful for its being our first, and for a French general being captured in it.'

But Barclay has served notice that his withdrawal won't lack teeth.

CHAPTER 7

WITH THE ADVANCING COLUMNS

Barclay's options – a swift leap – how to make 700 deserters march – 'God, what a scene!' – Jerome quits – 'we felt our hearts beating faster' – Major Rossetti seizes his chance – a tragic execution – the long road to Glubokoië – a solitary adjutant-major – Italians in distress – marauding and pillaging – an intellectual commander – 'Tell General Jomini' – 'He gave himself over to the greatest gaiety'

At 11 p.m. on 18 July the imperial cortège, preceded at a regulation 50 paces by twelve light cavalry troopers and followed by the four escort squadrons,[1] rolls out of the town gate and at a brisk eighteen miles per hour sets off down the Sventsiany road. Napoleon's own carriage is
'a very simple yellow coupé, in which he could shut himself up as in a berline. There was a mattress to sleep on, paper, pens, ink, a little travelling library and a nécessaire; numerous drawers offered all the resources of a house on wheels.'
Flanked by ADCs and ordnance officers riding at its doors, it's preceded by Caulaincourt's carriage and followed by two more, for Berthier and the interpreter Hyde d'Ideville, and a servant, with a spyglass on a thong and a leather case holding writing materials and a pair of compasses. After these four vehicles comes a lighter 'calèche which served to transport the Emperor from one army corps to another, or to cover in a few hours a road for which the troops needed a whole day'. A 'brigade' of thirteen saddle-horses brings up the rear. Relays of the same strength have been placed out by Caulaincourt's office at 10 to 15-mile intervals. Since all the rest of headquarters staff have either, like Fézensac, gone on ahead or will follow after, 'the Emperor made this leap very quickly. He took with him only a very small number of officers.'
   At about midnight, travelling on through the light summer night, the party comes on a bivouac at a crossroads. In command and all alone except for a single drummer-boy *Sous-lieutenant* Coignet is already regretting his sergeant's stripes. His column, which all day has been marching to tap of drum, consists of 700 Spanish deserters from Dedem's brigade.[2] After they'd been inspected by Napoleon in a compound at Vilna, they'd trekked out eastwards:
   'Soon we found ourselves engulfed by forests. Leaving my place at the head of the battalion I'd placed my little musician on the right, to mark step, and gone to the rear to make all the stragglers follow on. At nightfall I'd seen my deserters slipping away into the forest, and could do nothing to bring them back. It's too dark. It's enough to make one chew one's horse's reins with mortification! What to do with such soldiers? I tell myself: "The whole lot are going to desert!"'
But now, after only two hours, the head of his reluctant column has halted at this crossroads, in open country:

'By the time the rear turned up, the camp fires had already been lit. Judge my surprise. "What are you fellows doing here? Why aren't you marching?" – "We've marched far enough, we need to rest and eat." The fires were made up, and the pots had been put on. At midnight, here's the Emperor passing, with his escort. Seeing my bivouac all lit up, he orders a halt and calls me over to the door of his carriage. "What are you doing here?" – "But, Majesty, it's not I who am giving the orders, it's them. I've been bringing up the rear, and found the head of the battalion encamped with their fires alight. Lots of my deserters have already gone back to Vilna. What can I do, alone, with seven hundred stragglers?" – "Do what you can, I'll give orders to have them arrested."'

The escort drives on, leaving Coignet in ever-deepening trouble. At dawn he has

'the fall-in beaten; and at daybreak away we go. I tell them the Emperor's going to have all deserters arrested. I march until midday. Emerging from the forest, I see a herd of cows grazing in a meadow. And there are my soldiers going off with their panikins to milk the cows! What can I do but wait? Again and again they find some cows, and we have to stop. That evening they again camp before nightfall. Not much fun for me! At last I reach some woods, very remote from any towns. Away to my right I see a forest fire is spreading, and I catch sight of my troops making off into the burnt woods. I gallop off to compel them to come back to the road. Judge my surprise when I see these soldiers about-face and firing at me! I'm forced to let go my grip. These soldiers of Joseph Napoleon were in a plot. There were 133 of them. Not one Frenchman had mingled with these brigands. Back at my detachment, I form them up in a circle around me, and tell them: "I shall be obliged to make my report. Be Frenchmen, and follow me! I've had enough of bringing up the rear. That's your business. By the right, march!"'

Apparently many of them obey; because by evening Coignet reaches a village where some cavalry are guarding a fork in the road, to direct passing troops. And he makes his report to its colonel, who orders the battalion to camp:

'On the basis of the directions I give him he summons his Jews and an interpreter. Guessing my deserters' whereabouts, he sends off 50 mounted chasseurs, with Jews to guide them. Half-way there, they meet with some oppressed peasants seeking help. Getting there at midnight, they surround the village and surprise the Spaniards in their sleep. Seize them. Disarm them. Throw their muskets into a cart. The men, too, are put into little carts, with a strong escort. At 8 a.m. the 133 Spaniards arrive and have their hobbles removed. Lining them up in a single rank, the colonel tells them: "You've behaved badly, I'm going to form you up in squads. Are there any sergeants or corporals among you, to form your units?" And here are two sergeants, showing their stripes, hidden under their greatcoats. "Stand over there. Any corporals?" – Three corporals make themselves known. "Stand over there! No more? Good! Now, you others draw lots." Anyone who drew a white ticket was put on one side, and anyone who drew a black one on the other. When they'd all done it, he tells them: "You've stolen. You've set fire to property. You've fired on your officers. The law condemns you to death. You shall suffer your sentence... I could have you all shot; I spare half of you. Let it be a lesson to the others. Commander, load your battalion's firearms! My adjutant will give the order to fire." We shot sixty-five of them. God, what a scene! Distraught at heart, I set off at once. But the Jews were content.'

Before leaving Vilna Napoleon has written to Bessières that if the supposed Russian counter-offensive should develop, his intention is

'to move against the enemy from all sides. If, on my arrival at Sventsiany tomorrow, I discover it's been a false alarm, I shall resume the move to Glubokoïe.'

Evidently it is. For after reaching Sventsiany at 10 a.m. on 19 July and spending the day there, he reaches his destination at 1 or 2 p.m. next day. Dominated by a huge Carthusian monastery where general headquarters has already installed itself, Glubokoïe turns out to be quite an exceptionally big town, whose 'closely huddled timber houses, twelve to fifteen feet high but looking like primitive huts', spread out for half a mile in all directions. Opinions about the surroundings differ – in Caulaincourt's eyes it's 'a stretch of very beautiful countryside', which Fezensac, for his part finds to be 'of sad and savage appearance'. While Dr René Bourgeois feels he's 'in Lapland'.

Entering the Carthusian monastery – or possibly he's already heard about it en route – Napoleon gets a second piece of news, even more mortifying than the loss of St-Gèniez's brigade. While still hoping to trap Bagration he has secretly instructed Davout, on making junction with Jerome, to take over his three corps, thus uniting the army's right wing. But Davout isn't the most tactful of men at the best of times, and hasn't waited so long. When Jerome had appeared on the scene he'd informed him by despatch from Minsk that he was now his superior. For Jerome, who hadn't wanted any part in this war anyway, this had been the last straw.[4] After being reprimanded for not achieving the impossible he, the King of Westphalia, is to subordinate himself to a mere prince! Without even confiding his orders to his chief-of-staff, General Maison, he has quite simply gone off home to Cassel, taking his white-uniformed Royal Westphalian Guard with him.

Napoleon, all eye-witnesses agree, has a singular faculty of being able to control himself in difficult situations. And all he says is: 'What a silly prank!' After which, Fain notices, 'the Emperor shut up this grievance in his heart and said no more about it'. Even so he can't wholly contain his annoyance. And Davout is sharply reprimanded for disclosing his secret orders 'before the two armies were on the field of battle and would have needed a single commander'.

Or perhaps it's a bit of good news from another quarter that has soothed his irritation? For the last two years several thousand Russians have been busy throwing up an immense system of earthworks on the Dwina, the so-called Drissa Camp. Consisting of three concentric galleries, defended by a 36-foot deep trench, its 600 guns ensconced behind a 360-foot glacis were to command a murderous field of fire whose sandy terrain had been cleared of every tree, shrub and bush for 3,000 yards in all directions. It's in this formidable earthwork fortress that, if the Tsar's Prussian adviser's plan is followed, Barclay's retiring First West Army is to shut itself up and be besieged by Napoleon, who will, if all goes well, passively sit down and let himself be assailed in the rear by Bagration – and annihilated.

On the eve of Napoleon's departure from Vilna (17 July) the van of Montbrun's cavalry corps had approached the Drissa Camp's fortifications in the most gingerly fashion. Dr von Roos and many of his comrades in the the 3rd Württemberg Chasseurs had

'felt our hearts beating quicker as we came nearer. The great redoubt, which was of an unusual height, was provided with numerous gunports. The closer we came, the deeper became the silence. Not the least clink of arms was heard. The men didn't cough. The horses didn't neigh. Expecting at each instant to be received by cannonfire, we continued our soundless approach.'

But then, suddenly, the silence is broken by

'formidable bursts of laughter. In the gigantic redoubt there was neither a man nor a gun left! Its sole occupant was a little peasant, whom we'd first taken for a sentry. He'd been taking a stroll along the top.'

There must have been some poor communications between Murat's headquarters and Montbrun's; for on the previous day one of Murat's Neapolitan staff officers had already discovered that the camp had been abandoned. Sent there under a white flag of truce, 'ostensibly with 200 louis for General St-Gèniez, captured on the 15th', Major *Marie-Joseph Rossetti*'s

'true instructions had been to observe what enemy forces were entrenched in the Drissa Camp. General Sébastiani had given me a select escort of twelve hussars and ordered St-Gèniez's brother, who was also his ADC, to accompany me with the general's carriage and servants. One hour before midnight I'd come within musket shot of the entrance to the camp, preceded by a trumpeter who every three minutes sounded calls announcing a bearer of a flag of truce. But what was my surprise to find the camp abandoned and all the fortifications stripped of their guns!'

Rossetti had entered one of the redoubts, notified Sébastiani, and drawn up a plan 'of these works which had cost such enormous sums and two years' labour'. Although his immediate trumpetings had gone unanswered, next day, farther along the river, he's courteously received by the Russian General Bagawout who invites him to lunch and gives his hussars any amount of victuals – no doubt to impress on them how well supplied the Russian army is compared with the French. St-Gèniez's carriage is shipped to him across the river. And now Murat has sent Rossetti to take the news to Napoleon, who at first

'seemed not to believe me. But having read the King of Naples' despatches and found in them the sketches I'd made of this camp, he couldn't contain himself for joy. Pacing quickly to and fro, he said to the Prince of Neuchâtel: "You see! The Russians don't know how to make either war or peace! They give up their 'palladium' without firing a shot! Come along! One more real effort on our part and my brother will repent of having taken my enemies' advice. – Well, Monsieur le Napolitain, come back in two hours and I'll have despatches for you to take to your King."'

But Rossetti, who isn't a Neapolitan for nothing, replies:

'"Sire, ever since I've been in the service I've always fought in the French ranks and for France, and I'll never exchange my title of Frenchman for that of Neapolitan or of any other nation." The Emperor replied: "That's good, and that's how I see the matter." And turning to the Prince of Neuchâtel: "Appoint him colonel. Make a note of it."'[4]

Not everyone is so fortunate. For at least one good-natured man the Drissa Camp has been the ignominious end of life's long road. If the fortifications had been abandoned, the more remote approaches had been hotly contested. For the 7th Light the affair had been a

'general, hot and protracted affair. In front of the scene of the fighting was a rich chapel, attached to a big abbey two leagues further on. On the hillock crowned by this chapel the Russians had placed a battery, which was captured after a fierce resistance. In the course of this action the chapel was sacked. As soon as we were masters of the position, companies were placed to safeguard it, in conformity with the Emperor's severe orders on the point.'

No doubt impressed by his unfortunate experiences in Spain, Ney carries out his orders to the letter. 'To rid themselves of the stolen objects,' Carabinier-sergeant Bertrand goes on,

'those who'd committed this impious sacrilege had turned to a chasseur in my regiment. Known as the rag-and-bone man, he made a habit of buying and selling. All regiments had such men, so-called Jews. This chasseur had been my bedmate. He was good-natured, willing, loved and esteemed by us all. But the poor fellow had been weak enough to buy two sacred vessels off these looters. The marshal having received some complaints, he orders our regiment's packs to be searched. The four battalions are at once formed up in open ranks, arms and packs lying open on the ground. In each company one of its three officers inspects one rank. My poor comrade is revealed as at very least a receiver of stolen goods. We're ordered to take up our packs, pick up our arms, and close ranks. The battalions form square. The unfortunate chasseur is brought out, judged, condemned to death, and shot by the men of his own company. The whole affair didn't last an hour.'

Before setting out again, Bertrand and his heart-broken comrades hardly have time

'to dig a ditch at the foot of a big oak, where the old soldier from Iéna, Eylau, Friedland and Wagram, who'd only a moment ago still been fighting bravely, slept his last sleep. A victim of military duty, his cries of despair went on ringing a long time in my ears. We left this place of sorrow and mourning and marched for Witebsk.'

IHQ's saddle-horses may have made the 90 miles from Svenziany to Glubokoië 'in eighteen hours without one of them falling sick'. The Old Guard, carrying on its backs 90,000 bread rations and 'three-quarters of a pound or a pound of meat per man' and followed by 11,000 quintals of flour, have taken three; and the Young Guard – those who've got so far – five. Many don't reach Glubokoië at all. Overtaking it en route, Fézensac had been particularly grieved to see the dust-caked green-uniformed corpses of the Regiment of Flankers, 'made up of very young men', littering the roadside:

'Since leaving St-Denis this regiment had only enjoyed one day's rest at Mayence, and one at Marienwerder on the Vistula. Even on those days when they marched, they were still being drilled when they got to their destination, the Emperor having found them insufficently trained. Thus this regiment was the first to be destroyed.'

Although no less young, the 5th Tirailleurs of the Young Guard seem to be doing somewhat better, perhaps because of the stern care being taken of them by their colonel. As they march day after day across 'the feeble undulations of Russia's verdant terrain, the long avenues of immense silver birches, that graceful tree of the North with its lightsome foliage' Lieutenant Paul de Bourgoing hears his mostly beardless conscripts

'going through the whole repertoire of songs which the soldiers and officers could remember. Each nation made its contribution. A song only had to be sung once or twice for it to soon be known by the whole group. Usually one or two verses were sung solo and then repeated in unison by the rest of the column. In our unit songs from Languedoc, Provence, or Picardy alternated with those from Paris, Piedmont or other parts of the Empire. In our ranks we had Frenchmen from Genoa, Amsterdam, Mainz and Erfurt; so we sang in every language and dialect. Here's one specially composed for our unit. I give only the chorus:

Les tirailleurs sans souci,
Où sont-ils...? Les voici.
Où sont-ils...? Les voici.

Repeated in unison after being sung by the best tenor in the leading company, this question, posed in a strong voice by the best singer and answered twice far down the battalion's long column, had a gaiety all its own.'

Yet even in the Tirailleurs the mood is far from 'carefree':

'In our young soldiers the solitudes of Russia, their monotony, produced a deep sadness, having all the qualities of homesickness; and several cases of suicide occurred in our new regiments. Yet the weather was fine, we were at the height of summer. In these latitudes and at this season the days last until half-past eleven in the evening or until midnight, and it's impossible to say whether one owes this veiled but persistant light, reigning over the countryside, to dawn or sunset.'

Unfortunately, since Paul de Bourgoing speaks German and a smattering of Polish, Colonel Hennequin, 'a man of iron authority who only laughed when he was burning himself up, otherwise irreproachable and of uncontested merit, but also of an inflexibility recalling the heads of Ancient Rome's legions', has appointed him regimental adjutant-major – 'an officer attached to no company, and who has neither captain nor soldier under him'. As such, Bourgoing is finding he's keenly missing

'the mutual assistance, the solidarity of the bivouac, the daily convivialities of simple wartime meals, where each man contributes his ration of victuals and in nearby copses helps cut the silver birch or pine branches which, put together to form a shelter, cover the earth we're to rest on'.

Although each evening as the Young Guard halts 'the roofs of interlaced branches' are forming 'a straight line as far as the eye could see and enlivening the scene when the fires were lit', Bourgoing can only turn sadly to his colonel. But Colonel Baron Hennequin is,

'giving much more thought to what orders he should give me than to my 20-year-old appetite. Returning from missions made on foot so as to save my horse a double day's work, I often found the fire out and the supper eaten.'

Not that his little Parisian street urchin Victor isn't doing his utmost to feed his lieutenant:

'One evening, a few days' march from Vilna, all he can find upon my return from my round of the outposts at 11 p.m. is two fistfuls of dried peas, gathered with great difficulty. He'd had to climb up one of those big wooden walls or latticeworks, 30 foot high, which the Polish and Lithuanian peasants erect behind their barns to dry their winter vegetables on. I recommend to no one my supper menu of July 16, 1812.'

But officer and servant share the peas.

IV Corps' wretched Italians are in even worse case. Smarting no doubt from his rebuke for the day 'ridiculously' lost at the Niemen, the normally stolid Eugène is forcing the pace as he moves up from Novo-Troki to plug the gap left by Davout's march on Minsk. Having divided IV corps into two columns, he himself is leading the first towards Ochmiana at so fast a trot that 'the horses of the Queen's Dragoons escorting him kept falling one by one'. The other, consisting of Pino's 15th Division which at Glogau, in May, had consisted of 'more than 13,000 men, so accustomed to warfare that General Pino, though captain-in-chief of the Royal Guard, thought it an honour to command them' – is

'having to protect its artillery on a very bad road rendered impracticable by the passage of cavalry. Overtaken by darkness and the least movement being extremely dangerous, it's had to remain all night in this bog. Add to all this a horrible gale and rain coming down in bucketsful,'

and at dawn Pino has to turn back, his guide having utterly lost his way. All day, in broiling heat, Pino's division 'wanders about for ages'. And when, after 'crossing immense forests without finding food or water, and making interminable detours', it at last, after forty-eight hours, rejoins the other column, Césare de Laugier shudders to think what's to become of

'its sick, the soldiers exhausted by dysentery and those who've strayed from their units and who, despite all Pino's, his generals' and his subalterns' precautions, it's had to leave behind'.

In these dire predicaments *Albrecht Adam*, a painter of battle scenes who started out in life as a cakemaker and has accompanied Eugène's staff to Russia in search of them, is beginning to lose heart. Even so, riding through 'a long dense wood' he can't help smiling to see how

'out of sheer exhaustion many riders fell asleep on horseback and kept banging their heads against trees, so that helmets fell off, or were only held on lopsidedly by the chinstraps. A few troopers slithered to the ground,'

a ridiculous contretemps that Césare de Laugier is too proud of his regiment's superb Grecian-style helmets even to mention. But, the ex-cakemaker goes on remorselessly,

'the Italian Guardia d'Onore, with their exceptionally tall helmets, fared particularly ill. The weary horses often stumbled and fell. Whole columns of hundreds of these poor beasts were in the most pitiful state; with sores on their withers or backs, stopped up with tow and discharging a stream of pus, they had to be led by the bridle. Having lost weight until their ribs stood out, they looked a very picture of abject misery.' 'Two whole months on the march,' he'll write to his wife three days later, 'and to what purpose? It distresses me to have to waste God-given time so wretchedly. War – a terrible word. It means no regard for the well-being or destruction of whole nations, and woe betide anyone who makes this termagent's acquaintance and has a heart that still beats for humanity!'

In all the advancing columns of men, horses, wagons, carriages, artillery parks and guns, relations between the French and their so-called allies have already become unendurably strained. None of the dangers and hardships is so irksome to an anonymous artillery lieutenant in III Corps as the serious daily quarrels that keep breaking out:

'If anything broke on a wagon or a gun, or if an exhausted horse had to be unharnessed, the vehicle, cut off by the troops coming on behind, very likely couldn't rejoin its battery until evening. The French infantry were so unpleasant and brutal that more often than not their officers, to prevent some unfortunate godforsaken gun from even travelling near – let alone ahead of – them would order bayonets to be levelled at its lead-horses, and strike the men of the Train – behaviour that aroused our intense hatred and bitterest resentment. Again and again our battery, after spending half a day with utmost difficulty following the brigade along appalling tracks, had to turn back and search for the road being followed by the infantry. Yet when we got to it no one would let us into the column, and we had to try and secure ourselves a tiny place on the road either by dint of asking pleasantly, but sometimes with oaths and insults, and often at sword-point. As I was the only French-speaking officer it always fell to me to conduct these wrangles.'

Few of the villages along the way can boast even twenty cottages, and only rarely do these even stand beside the main roads. On the other hand there's usually an inn -

'but what an inn! All it offers is small beer, bad brandy, and a kind of dough they call bread. These houses resemble their occupants – distressingly dirty! They're run exclusively by Jews, who do everything – are innkeepers, merchants, tailors, cobblers, almost every profession.'

A despised blessing, for the Lithuanian Jews are the only people in this godforsaken country the troops, or at any rate their officers, can converse with, either in Low German or a smattering of Latin. Almost always they've got something to sell to a famished soldier. Particularly in demand are the little rough-haired Polish ponies known as *konyas*, which are even being used to help pull the artillery. Paixhans sees how impossible a task it is for them alone: 'Twelve such little horses produce no more effect when harnessed up to the shaft of a heavy wagon than two teams of six on a light vehicle. Yet we'd still enough big horses to harness them up last.' Heinrich von Brandt is shocked to see

'these unfortunate little animals being wasted in their thousands. Knowing what a hard life they were used to, we exacted a lot of work from them, yet took no care of them at all. They perished in masses and were then replaced. Some drew the artillery, foodstuffs, baggage, etc. All the stragglers rode on them and dragged them along with them. Without them it's certain we could never have marched at all.'

When the poor little beasts are exhausted, his men just unharness them and leave them

'standing or lying there. Then the cannon and wagons rolled over them and their steaming guts got entangled in the wheels. No one cared – what with human beings hardly being treated any better.'

But by no means everything is being paid for or obtained under official forms. On the contrary, everyone is grabbing anything he can lay his hands on, not only from the peasants and the manor-houses along the way, but also from other units. One day Pion des Loches' company of Guard artillery finds its few remaining provisions have been stolen out of its wagon by some Bavarians – and next day itself promptly pillages a manor-house. Vital to each unit's survival is the

'mounted rabble or – to give it its proper name – robber band which was swarming around it, to left and right, in front and in the rear, using as its base the regiment as it marched in good order along the highroad. All carried large and small haversacks and bottles to hide their plunder in, and were armed with swords, pistols, even carbines. Roaming far and boldly on the flank, if ever they got back again they brought supplies for the troops. The work was dangerous, and many lost their lives – in agony, if they fell into the clutches of the infuriated peasants.'

On the other hand, they are providing the advancing columns with a kind of flank patrol, 'because if ever they bumped into enemy detachments they came flying back in a hurry, uttering loud cries'.

Obviously absurd though it is to forbid starving men to pillage, many are being shot for doing so. Three or four days out of Vilna, Dr von Roos sees

'a division of cuirassiers formed up in square. In the middle four soldiers were digging up the earth. We were told a court-martial had condemned them to death for flouting orders. They were going to be shot; but first had to dig their own graves. Had these four unfortunates known what they were missing out on',

he'll reflect afterwards, 'they might have counted themselves lucky.'

Between individual pillage and organized marauding there lies, namely, a fine but crucial distinction. All units except the Imperial Guard trudging along under its supplies of flour and biscuit, are sending out detachments to relieve the locals of their 'superfluous' grain, horses and cattle. Always commanded by an officer – 'the most intelligent ones', Roeder adds – their prime objectives are the manor-houses, where

'you find more or less everything needed for man as a social being, even a library and politeness. It's the nobleman who in his house has everything needed for keeping body and soul together.'

Many of these lie at a considerable distance from the five or six-mile front spanned by each corps as it advances. Usually their proprietors have fled, leaving them under the authority of a steward who may speak French, or again, may not. After being relieved of its 'superfluous' assets, each such estate is provided with a 'safeguard', a signed document exempting it from further contributions, and a picket to enforce it. One day Lance-corporal *Wilhelm Heinemann*[5] is being wined and dined by a Russian landlord and his party of Brunswick Chasseurs are busy rummaging about upstairs when suddenly a footman enters:

'Pale as a corpse, he said some words in Russian to his master, words I didn't understand. The count, too, blenched. Jumping up, he begged me in French to be a good fellow and stop my comrades doing whatever it was they were up to. Though of no use to them, it would be a catastrophe for himself.'

Coming across a lead-lined trunk in the count's bedroom, the voltigeurs have opened it with an axe.

'Inside, it was divided up into numerous compartments, in each of which were little bits of shiny paper oddly printed in all colours, red, white, blue, yellow, green. So elegant and neat were their colours they seemed to be a lot of playthings.'

It's the count's entire cash fortune the Brunswickers have taken for playing cards and are helping themselves to the prettiest, offering Heinemann several fistfuls. His host assures him they're coupons he has to issue against deliveries of goods within his administrative district – 'worthless to the soldiers but vital to himself'. But Heinemann has already seen paper currency in Austria,[6] and smiles at this fib, replying in French – which his men don't understand – 'Least of all these 500-rouble notes!' Upon his convincing them that the 'toys' really are worthless, of one them flings a bundle of white banknotes 'worth at least 50,000 roubles' back into the chest. And the count, overjoyed, is only too happy to accept his apologies for all the cartloads of farm produce he's being obliged to requisition; entertains him to the best his house can produce; and they part as friends for life. 'Where life has so little value, money has even less; and I didn't have the heart to take my part of this rich booty.'

One day *Thomas Legler*, too, an officer in the 1st Swiss Regiment, marching eastwards with II Corps after Wittgenstein, is ordered, like two other lieutenants, to go out marauding. Each is allocated a sergeant, a corporal, and twelve grenadiers. But... how proceed in such totally unknown countryside? Perhaps it's best to follow in the tracks of the French? On the other hand they'll have no use for estates which have already been given safeguards. After much discussion the three Swiss lieutenants decide to go off in different directions. And soon Legler's party sight a manor-house:

'The baron who owned it was in the drawing-room, surrounded by his servants. Addressing him in French, I gave him to understand I needed food. He replied, also in French, assuring me that the French had already taken all he owned.'

Really? Legler, sceptical, orders his men to ransack the house. 'This threat led to us being given a little bread and boiled meat with schnapps. Meanwhile my grenadiers had found twelve sacks of grain in the barn.' Even this won't go very far for the hungry 1st Swiss. Seizing the manor's cook as a guide, Legler forces the baron to tell him the whereabouts of the nearest manor. Tying the cook's hands with a rope's end, Legler tells his men, in loud clear French, that if he isn't back by 6 p.m., they're to put a bullet through the baron. 'These words, uttered in a tone of command, brought out beads of sweat on the baron's forehead. Running over to his cook, he spoke to him at length – probably begging him to make sure we got back safely!' At first the cook had tried to run away. But now he calms down,

'assuring the baron he hoped we'd be back, fully pleased and contented. This order of mine may strike the reader as inhuman. But he should consider my situation. I didn't know where the enemy was, or whether I'd even be able to find my way back to our camp. But I secretly told the sergeant to let the baron go free as soon as we were out of sight.'

After an hour and a quarter of 'following side roads and long stretches of forest where we didn't meet a soul', the guide brings them to the next manor. 'In several spots we saw horses and horned cattle and on our way the grenadiers captured a well-grown horse.' Approaching this second manor with all due caution, Legler enters and interrogates its proprietor as to the Russian army's whereabouts. This second 'baron' is so 'very amiable and accommodating' as to station four lookouts, throw open all his doors, give the Swiss some bread, brandy and dinner, and

'made his servants help us pack and load: with the result that by about 3 o'clock I'd already 20 one-horse carts fully laden with foodstuffs. On my showing him my horse lacked a saddle, he immediately provided it with an English saddle and harness.'

Even dinner is served. Legler advises his host to hide his valuables in a place of safety,

'for soon the French would be there, and they wouldn't be content merely with food. Handing him back his silver spoons and forks, I advised him to hide them away as quickly as possible. We Swiss desired nothing but food. At first the good baron wants to make me a present of his table silver; but when he sees I set no value on it he pats my shoulder and says: "honest fellow!"'

Just as Legler is about to leave, one of his grenadiers comes running, shouting: 'The French are coming!' Quite right. Here's a chasseur officer, with four troopers:

'Seeing my neatly laden carts, he gives a start. And more particularly takes a fancy to my saddled horse. "That belongs to us, and so do all those oats you've got there!" says one of his chasseurs, trying to grab the horse. But the grenadier holding it threatens to shoot him down.'

On the French officer threatening to report him, Legler tells him to go to the devil – or if he doesn't like it, he can get down off his horse and they'll settle the matter between them. 'But it went no further than French sabre-rattling. And suddenly the Frenchman and his four chasseurs dashed off, followed by Swiss curses.'[7]

Alas, this has only been the beginning of the poor landowner's misfortunes:

'Hardly has the last cart gone forty paces from the manor-house than we catch sight of a strong detachment of French light infantry approaching it. A quarter of an hour later, thick smoke billows up behind us, out of which we soon see flames rising. It seemed very likely the French, embittered at finding nothing to seize, had set fire to it – a revenge often taken by troops reaching a farm that had already been plundered.'

On their way back Legler's party come across other units, driving a lot of cattle before them. 'In the woods, chance brought into my hands first a few, then more, then finally 60 head of cattle; and I didn't hesitate to drive them in front of us.' At dusk Legler is back at camp. But what about the other two detachments? All – except one grenadier – have been captured by the Russians. 'I thanked God for my good luck in escaping.' Bread, butter, cheese, ham, brandy, honey and salt Legler has aplenty – 'brandy and flour for several days for the rank and file, and corn and oats for the regiment's horses. This,' he concludes, 'was the first and last time I went out on a marauding expedition.'

Disputes over such booty can be furious. Upon Pino's division turning up at Veleika at the same time as a French one, and finding the biscuit stores which had been captured by the Red Lancers,

'the French, being the first comers, have possessed themselves of them. We Italians, arriving at their heels, lay claim to our share. We've shared the sufferings, are dying of hunger, and have equal rights. The general makes representations to that effect to Prince Eugène.'

But the Viceroy just shrugs his shoulders and says it's a case of first-come-first-served. Isn't possession nine points of the law? Pino, who has several officers with him, waxes eloquent about his division's urgent needs. But all Eugène says is:

"Well, gentlemen, you can f— off! You're asking for something impossible. And if you don't like it you can go back to Italy. I don't give a damn for you. Let me tell you I'm no more afraid of your swords than I am of your stilettos!"

Hitherto, Laugier goes on indignantly,

'the Italians' affection for the Viceroy had never been in question. His youth, the care he was taking of the rank and file, his status as the Emperor's adoptive son, all had contributed to making him loved. But this injurious phrase, escaping him in a moment of anger, keenly wounded our Italian hearts.'[8]

The delegation is just leaving the château when they see thick smoke coming from it. It's on fire, and already partly in ashes. The Royal Guard comes running and at the orders of the very officers who'd just been told to f— off make every effort to demolish everything adjacent to the Viceroy's quarters. But this only leads to another altercation between the Viceroy and General Pino, who says 'with utmost firmness: "Very well, since Your Highness won't render the Italians the justice they deserve, I'll get it from the Emperor." And lays his sword on Eugène's table. Which forces him to try to calm him. 'Today,' the Guardia d'Onore's adjutant-major notes, 'for the first time, Italy has been reminded that Prince Eugène isn't an Italian.' And by now even he's beginning to feel despondent:

'All these factors are contributing to deprive a unit of the brio of its first days. From day to day it becomes steadily more exhausted, dwindles away. The state of weakness it finds itself reduced to inevitably diminishes the numbers of the detachments sent out to look for victuals. And so there we are! Out of the need to survive, out of humanity, out of compassion, out of sheer necessity, we have to tolerate these regrettable pillagings we'd so like to prevent. And off the men go. Sometimes they come back. At others, not. When they do, it's little they bring back with them. The bivouacs, the fastings, the forced marches are thinning our files. Numerous soldiers who possess a deep and inflexible sense of honour prefer to die of inanition rather than support a life which has become horrible to them. Though up to now they've carried their packs and their arms with an imperturbable fortitude and truly heroic firmness, they fall exhausted, measure their length on the ground. Alas! few dare linger behind to succour them. Nor have they the means to do so, and the fear of getting lost in these immense solitudes, coupled with our fear of vengeful peasants, prevails over the compassion we feel for them.'[9]

When the Bavarian infantry of General *Gouvion St-Cyr*'s VI Corps had arrived at Vilna it had been in such splendid trim, and his cavalry so impressive that, despite his protests, Napoleon had hived off the cavalry to strengthen IV Corps. As for the infantry, it had been given only twelve rations of bad bread per man for eight days' marching; and now, as it turns up at Glubokoïe it's in such an appalling state that Napoleon refuses even to review it. 'I was reprimanded', writes St-Cyr,

'for not making my troops march fast enough. In Napoleon's eyes fatigue, sicknesses and lack of victuals weren't legitimate excuses for a delay of a few hours, even though when VI Corps had left each bivouac the manor-houses had immediately been turned into hospitals and each day it had left behind the equivalent of a battalion.'[10]

St-Cyr is an intellectual and a convinced republican who has never fallen under the imperial spell. And Napoleon, who has a genius for coping with anyone who can be cajoled, flattered, intimidated, fooled or bribed, is apt to be suspicious, not to say caustic, towards men of independent judgement and principles. Which is why this is St-Cyr's first high command. But whether Napoleon now feels he has gone too far, or because he wishes to

to exert his charms and genius upon him, the imperial reprimand is followed by the usual gesture of conciliation. At their interview he
'wore an air of putting on a great deal of spontaneity, and passed in review most of the various French generals, living or dead, who'd gained reputations in the revolutionary wars'.
And not only them, 'but also his marshals' – i.e., St-Cyr's superiors, 'distributing praise or blame. The art of war, he said, was of all arts the hardest. A general needed intelligence; but what was rarer, great character. He'd sent Marmont into Spain. "He has plenty of intelligence, I still can't gauge his draught, but I'll soon be able to judge, for today he's on his own."'[11]
If Napoleon possessed the art of fascinating everyone, says Caulaincourt, 'it was because he'd already fascinated himself. In small matters as well as great, he spared no pains to gain his ends. One could say he gave himself wholly over to them. Always he developed all possible means, all his faculties, and all his attention, and directed them to whatever matter was just then in hand. Never was there a man more fascinating when he chose to be!'
In his youth, St-Cyr had been an actor, and if there's one thing he detests and can see through it's theatricality. This makes him perhaps of all the Grand Army's corps commanders the one who's just now best able to weigh up its commander-in-chief:
'He disclosed his plan of campaign, and gave all his excellent reasons for it. It was dictated by foresight and genius. By following it, all past errors could still easily be corrected.'[12]
After his reprimand St-Cyr has been feeling gloomy. But now, either flattered or genuinely impressed – or both – he feels his hopes rising again.[12]
And indeed, whether it's because he's beginning to feel he hasn't quite got the situation under control or for some other reason, the Emperor is dealing out reprimands left and right. Even Lariboisière, his old mess-mate from college days, gets his share:
"His Majesty is being told there are 600 wagons at Vilna, 40,000 artillery rounds, and a great quantity of infantry cartridges, so there is no need to transport ammunition to Vilna. We are going to have a battle which will consume an enormous quantity of ammunition. The Emperor asks what is to be done to replace them. Should empty artillery wagons be sent back to Vilna? In that case, at least a month or six weeks will be needed for them to rejoin. All possible means must be used to bring the biggest quantity of infantry and artillery ammunition wagons up to the army."
In the same way, Grouchy, instead of being congratulated when his cavalry corps, in the van of Davout's army, manages to grab huge stores of flour at the important town of Orsha, is curtly asked why he hasn't sent the flour to Glubokoïe "where the centre is assembling and where we're in direst need?"

Nor is it the moment for Jomini's lucid expositions – which are reaching Napoleon almost daily – of why he can't do all the things he's been told to. And on the eve of leaving Berthier is ordered:

"Inform Geneneral Jomini it's absurd his saying there's no bread when he receives 500 quintals of flour every day; that instead of complaining, he should get up at four every morning and go in person to the mill and commissariat and see to it that 30,000 bread rations are prepared; and that he'll achieve nothing by merely sleeping and moaning. Tell him the Emperor himself, busy though he is, visits the commissariat every day; that I don't see why he criticizes the Lithuanian government for having put all the prisoners into a single regiment; that this kind of thing indicates a critical spirit which can only harm the development of events, whereas he should be encouraging the government and helping it. Write to General Jomini to have all the muskets in the hospitals collected, and that in this way he'll find some that can be used."

Even on 22 July Napoleon is still uncertain of Barclay's movements. Is he withdrawing toward Polotsk or Witebsk? But that day he and St-Cyr are at supper when some crucial information comes in. Gleaned from a Polish deserter, it shows clearly that it's Witebsk – on the Moscow road.

'Having calculated he'd be able to catch up with Barclay, he gave himself over to the greatest gaiety. Even though the French army no longer enjoyed the numerical superiority it had enjoyed at the Niemen, he believed he could bring him to a battle, which, if it occurred, would be greatly to our advantage.'

One of Oudinot's ADCs happening just then to be at Glubokoië, Berthier is told to send him back with orders for II Corps to move toward Sebeje, thus forcing Wittgenstein to cover the Petersburg road and place still greater distance between himself and Barclay:

"Since Wittgenstein hasn't even 10,000 infantry, the Duke of Reggio can march straight at him. We're marching on Witebsk. Tell him to sweep the right bank of the Dwina and push back Wittgenstein at the sword's point. Even so, he should leave a small garrison at Polotsk in case he [Wittgenstein] throws himself to the left. When I get to Witebsk I'll direct a corps to the Newel, which will communicate with him."

Having dictated these orders, Napoleon climbs into his carriage and – at long last – sets out for the front.

CHAPTER 8

FIRST CLASHES

Polotsk – how Murat wasted the cavalry – putrid hay bundles – the most dangerous moment – an extraordinary costume – 'they never say anything to me!' – Napoleon wounds Italian sensibilities – psychological warfare – d'Hautpoul's orders – two ladies get wet – chaos at Beschenkowiczi – von Muraldt reconnoitres in only one boot

Sick at heart at the thought of the moment, if it ever comes, when he'll get back to Toulouse and have to tell the rag-and-bone man's parents of their son's ignominious end, Sergeant Bertrand has marched with III Corps, not for Witebsk, but for Polotsk. 'At least Polotsk looks like a city,' he sighs into his diary on 24 July, seeing its green onion spires slowly come up the horizon. 'It boasts seven or eight church towers and two big monasteries.'[1] Chasseur Lieutenant *Maurice Tascher*,[2] a nephew of ex-empress Josephine, serving in Montbrun's corps, calls it less enthusiastically 'a town sprung up in the heart of a village'. Lying astride the Petersburg and Riga roads, Polotsk is destined to become the pivot of II Corps' operations.

Murat's cavalry, leading this advance, is wasting away at an alarming rate. Already only three-quarters of the troopers who'd crossed the Niemen are still with the colours. Of the light cavalry, only half. And everyone is agreeing that this is due, not to enemy action as such, but to its disgraceful mismanagement. 'The King of Naples', a nameless officer of the 16th Chasseurs writes home,

'is personally very brave, but has few military talents. He knows very well how to use cavalry in front of the enemy, but is ignorant of the art of preserving it. At high noon the horses are dropping from weariness and want.'

The chief cause of the cavalry's destruction,' Victor Dupuy agrees, is

'the scant care taken of it. Having fought all day, we were made to bivouack in windmills, on high arid ground, bare of all resources. Only with the greatest difficulty did we manage to obtain some bad forage.' – 'We marched all day. We made hourly – often two-hourly – halts, during which we could have refreshed some of the horses. But no. Strict orders not to unbridle. Death struck. We had to bivouack in the middle of forests, without making sure whether there was any forage or water nearby. Next day we had to march and fight as if we'd lacked for nothing.'

For all the light cavalry regiments the first glimmer of dawn is the most dangerous moment:

'In the French army the outposts were habitually under arms one hour before sunrise. This was called 'doing the dawn'.[3] Usually we assembled without any signal. It all took place in a deathly silence.

Then the infantry rested under arms and the cavalry remained dismounted, holding our horses by their bridles. In this fashion we waited, sometimes for three or four hours on end, for any detachments sent out on patrol or reconnaissance to come in. If we weren't to leave we went back to our bivouac, feeling safe. One of the squadrons unsaddled to rub down its horses. Each of the others followed suit, turn and turn about. Thus the horses were perpetually saddled up and laden day and night, the men always dressed and armed, ready to fight at any instant.'

All, no doubt, a model of military efficiency and in the ordinary way of things Dumonceau would have approved. But persisted in day after day, week after week, it's proving disastrous. Each morning it's the light cavalry, joined by Murat in person, that opens the march, the hussar and chasseur regiments being followed by the dragoons and lancers, escorting the cuirassiers.

Day after day the Russian rearguard carries out the same manoeuvre. By pretending to make a stand, it lures Murat into mounting a full-scale attack – and then melts away into the forests. Towards midday the heat becomes intolerable; and the chasseurs and hussars,

'seeing the Russians dismount, unbridle their horses and give them something to eat. Yet General St- Germain kept us standing in battle array, bridle on arm, at our horses' heads.'

Old St-Germain, commanding 11th Heavy Cavalry Division, is

'a swordsman who owed his promotion to his bravery and dash. On entering Russia, he'd ordered that each trooper should make up an 8 to 12-lb truss of hay, well twisted and uniformly rolled, and set it on top of his mantle strapped to his portmanteau, with the wallet of food and oats, thus raising the load behind our backs to shoulder level. Constantly exposed to rain, sun and dust, the hay ended up by being not merely inedible, but got heavier and heavier and more and more unhealthy.'

Finally Thirion's colonel lets him go and speak to the other two colonels. Wouldn't they, too, like to get rid of their rotten trusses?

'Being ADC to the Emperor, Colonel Doudenarde of the 3rd Cuirassiers, a man of most imperious character, didn't give a damn for General St-Germain, and hastened to accept. As for Colonel Murra of the 9th, he'd never have taken such an initiative himself. But backed up by his two colleagues, he too consents. Returning to my regiment, I give the order to chuck away the bales. A hurrah of joy goes up from all down the line. In a jiffy the bundles are untwisted, scattered to the wind. When the division mounts, the general flies into a terrible rage. But what's done is done! And the crude words that made up General St-Germain's vocabulary went the same way as the putrid hay.'

Each night, Thirion goes on,

'the light cavalry ahead of us bivouacked on a line parallel to ours, with 50 men on outpost duty. We, behind them, had 150. And yet our scouts were placed, pistol in hand, only 100 metres from the first line! Protected as we were by the eight light cavalry regiments ahead of us, we'd no need to fear a surprise attack. A simple colour-guard to the regiment's right, near the colonel's bivouac, would have sufficed. Those 150 horses had carried their riders on their backs all day and on the morrow would have to set out on another 12-hour march.'

Without a drop of water to drink and only an occasional nibble of wayside grasses, they arrive at the next bivouac utterly spent, collapse, and have to be shot by their riders, who, adding horsemeat to a soup of uncut rye, promptly go down with diarrhoea, an affliction not conducive to brilliant exploits on horseback. The 22-year-old Prussian Lieutenant *Count von Wedel* is seeing how 'a hundred Cossacks who knew the district and its least track could, without danger to themselves, put the wind up an entire army corps'. Certainly they know how exploit Murat's mania for chasing them. 'I can still see that marvellous officer's outlandish costume,' Karl von Suckow of the Württembergers will write long afterwards:

'On his long black curly hair he wore a Renaissance-style hat, adorned with large white plumes waving in the wind and held in place by a diamond clasp. Around his bare neck an antique Spanish-style ruff over a sort of light-blue velvet tunic, all bedecked with gold embroidery and held in tight at the waist by a silk sash of the same colour as the tunic and tipped at both ends with gold fringes. White worsted breeches in huge deerskin boots of the kind fashionable during the Thirty Years War, with massive gold spurs.'

On one memorable occasion Dr von Roos, too, sees him wearing 'a red Spanish cloak. On others a green one, with boots à la hongroise, sometimes red, sometimes green, sometimes yellow'. But everyone, not least the retreating enemy, admires him:

'Herculean in strength, excessively gallant, admirably cool in the midst of danger, his daring, his elegant costume inspired an extraordinary veneration among the Cossacks.'

One day Victor Dupuy witnesses

'their almost magical respect for him. There was a swamp we had to cross, and my general had ordered me to go and reconnoitre a path through it. I was riding ahead with three troopers when I saw the King of Naples at the far end of a little wood, looking out over a narrow stretch of flat ground in front of the swamp. He was all alone. In front of him, on the other side of the flat ground, some 40 mounted Cossacks were gazing at him, leaning on their lances. Seeing us emerge from the wood, they make a move. Taking it for an attack, I shout to my men: "Hussars! Cover the King!" No sooner have we taken up our positions in front of him than the Cossacks fire several shots, one of which strikes my horse's leg. Noticing this, the King says to me, laughing: "Serves you right! What have you come here for? They never say anything to me!'"

Nor is it only the cavalry that's suffering from Murat's precipitate leadership.'If Murat didn't spare the cavalry, he spared the infantry even less.' Dedem's infantry brigade is one of those that have been detached from I Corps to support Murat, and thirty days of a campaign conducted in this headlong fashion, he realizes, have already 'cost the French and Allied cavalry more horses than ten pitched battles'. With the result that Friant's crack division, too, has dwindled to a mere two-thirds of its original strength and the commander of its 1st Infantry Brigade is bitterly regretting being separated from Davout'.

On 23 July the Italians, farther to the south, reach the village of Botscheikovo on the Oula, 'a river joined to the Berezina by the Lepel Canal and linking the Dnieper with the Dwina, the Baltic with the Mediterranean.' They are resting up 'in an immense field of rye' and the Viceroy is deep in a long discussion with his chief-of-staff General Dessoles when suddenly Napoleon's imminent arrival is announced. Instantly the order is given to don parade uniforms. And the word goes round: 'The Emperor's coming!' It's the first time IV Corps has seen him. At once everyone is all agog, and Césare de Laugier, no less excited, snatches a moment to jot down in his diary:

'The Emperor's going to reconnoitre the army's advanced positions, here, at exactly this spot where we're its advance guard! At this news, here's the entire camp in a turmoil! Officers and men, we hurriedly strip ourselves of our marching clothes, to don our finest uniforms. Everyone wallops, brushes, launders, polishes. Valises and trunks are brought into the middle of our camp. Linen and clothes are hung up to air. The comings and goings of those who're loading and unloading the vehicles, the songs, the laughter, the jokes flying to and fro – all throw our camp into a gay mood, an explosion of the gaiety natural to us Italians which lends the countryside a festive air it's never worn before and very likely never will again. In the twinkling of an eye our dusty route-coats have been replaced by clean uniforms, opulently smothered in gold and silk.'

And now here he is:

'The Emperor arrives. The troops, ranked in battle order, present to the eye a scene of utmost brilliance. But what does he do? Cross the post-road in his carriage; get out of it near the bridge, where he listens to some reports; goes and visits some positions; gives some orders; and then leaves again, to rejoin the Imperial Guard at Kamen! What a disappointment! In a vile humour we strip ourselves of our beautiful uniforms; and slowly, without a word, put on our tattered marching clothes again.'

'This man, for whom we've come so far,' the adjutant-major goes on bitterly, 'for whom we have been willing to shed our blood, and on whose account we've already put up with such fatigues, didn't even deign to throw us a glance. Curiosity at least, we tell ourselves, should have impelled him to glance at his subjects, his faithful allies, and speak to them. What has he to reproach us with? A glance, a word, a smile of complaisance costs so little! Men are so easily contented. The masses so effortlessly enchained! Instead – *"Niente, niente, niente!"* – that's what I'm hearing said all around me as, feeling melancholy, I've come back to my bivouac.'

The incident is perhaps too painful for Albrecht Adam's artistic soul. For he skips it. Altogether the ex-cakemaker is becoming disenchanted with 'this senseless war' which so far hasn't even yielded him any battle-scenes.

As for the Russians, they're literally leaving neither horse nor straggler behind them. But one day, they leave something else instead. Leaflets. Picking one up, Césare de Laugier reads:

'Italian soldiers! You're being forced to march to a new war. They're trying to convince you it's because the Russians don't set a proper value on your valour. No, comrades, we appreciate it, as you'll soon see on a day of battle. But reflect! One army will succeed to another. You're 1,200 miles from your reinforcements. Don't let yourselves be deceived by our first movements! You know us Russians too well to believe we're running away. We'll accept battle; and your retreat will be difficult. We say to you, as between comrades: "go home en masse" . Place no faith in perfidious words that you're fighting for peace. No, you're fighting for the insatiable ambition of a sovereign who simply doesn't want peace, and who makes a sport of spilling his brave men's blood. Go home to your own country; or while waiting to do so accept if you prefer it asylum in Russia, where you'll forget the very words "conscription", "levée", "the *ban*" and "the *arrière ban*"[6] and the whole of this military tyranny which never for a moment lets you evade its yoke.'

'This document', comments Eugène's always critical staff captain Labaume, 'contained such great truths that everyone was amazed it was allowed to spread.' The Guardia d'Onore, at least, is unable to grasp them. And gets busy penning ripostes,[7] which 'the least corporal is furnishing himself with before setting out for an outpost or reconnaissance, so as to pass it over to the Russian outposts'. Napoleon, too, feels such a riposte is in order. When one such leaflet is brought to him he comments: 'My brother Alexander stops at nothing!' And under the pseudonymn 'A Letter from a Grenadier' dictates a reply, to be printed in the Paris newspapers.

Instead of standing and fighting near the little town of Kamen, on the Dwina, as Napoleon has been expecting him to, Barclay is now seen to be retiring along the river's southern bank. So orders are given for the army to cross it at the small town of Beschenkowiczi.[8] And next day, after a five-hour march, the Army of Italy, still in the van, gets there to find Bruyère's and St-Germain's cavalry divisions already on the river bank. They're having trouble with some Russian sharpshooters, ensconced on the far bank, beyond the burnt bridge, while in the plain beyond some Russian cavalry are manoeuvring.

This is the first time the Italians have seen the enemy. And to protect the sappers who are to throw new bridges two guns are immediately brought to bear. 'Some sailors of the Royal Guard swim across to fetch the ferry and drive the Russians out of houses on the opposite shore.' This forces the Russians to evacuate Beschenkowiczi and 'leave us in peace to work on the bridges'.

Meanwhile, 200 yards further downstream, General Preyssing's Bavarian light cavalry (seconded to IV Corps at Vilna) have found a ford. Labaume thinks the Bavarians' 'way of marching, the precision of their drill and the sagacity of their scouting' exemplary. Troop after troop is taking the plunge, swimming the river and scrambling up the steep sandy bank opposite, Eugène sits his horse and directs the operation – all as in Adam's print. In the distance we see the Bavarians making for Beschenkowiczi's little timber houses, on the skyline. All doubtless as it was in reality. Or was it? In fact the

'tumult and confusion can hardly be conceived. Imagine, after a month of separation, all the various army corps arriving on the same day and at virtually the same hour! The infantry are levelling their bayonets at the guns, shouting and threatening to cut the artillery and cavalry wagons' traces. Drivers and troopers are cramming themselves together, refusing to let anyone through. The officers are finding it hard to prevent the men from coming to blows. The men, at their wits' end, are complaining of the staff's lack of foresight, which they see as the cause of all this indescribable muddle.'

The Italian sappers have just constructed their first bridge between 'the Dwina's high and steep banks' when, at 2 p.m., Napoleon turns up – and 'in a very dry tone of voice' criticizes its construction, 'which in truth was very defective'. As for the Emperor's and 'his staff's great activity' Albrecht Adam keeps finding his eye returns to

'a striking individual wearing a light-blue coat trimmed all over with gold braid, red trousers edged with gold, a strange hat lavishly decked with plumes. I couldn't make him out. What struck me most was that he'd so much business near the Emperor, who, like the whole of his suite, was on foot. In the end I asked an officer who was standing beside me: "Maybe you can solve an enigma. How come the Emperor has so much to do with that drum major?" Surprised, the officer looked at me and said: "What do you mean?" I explained. "My God!" he exclaimed, "but that's Murat, the King of Naples!"'

Labaume sees Napoleon, 'determined to cross over to the other side', traverse the rickety bridge on foot, mount his horse, and join the Bavarians who've halted there in the plain. Or is it an optical illusion? With the rest of IV Corps' four Bavarian chasseur regiments Lieutenant *Albrecht von Muraldt* has had to 'swim the river to cover him on this reconnaissance', and he sees Napoleon, Berthier and Murat cross in a little boat,

'to be sure of the enemy's strength there. At a loss of two men carried away by the current and drowned, we reached the other shore. After we'd drawn up in line of battle, the Emperor himself put himself at our head and personally led the reconnaissance.'

Alas, von Muraldt hasn't reckoned with the imperial tempo. Having pulled off a boot to void it of the Dwina's water, he's only wearing the other:

'The signal "Mount!" was sounded, and despite my most desperate efforts it had been more than I could do to pull my wet boot on again. So I'd had to get into the saddle with a boot on one foot but none on the other. Everyone laughed at me, which didn't improve matters. At a quick trot or canter the Emperor rode with us for two hours, but without coming upon the enemy. After which we returned to Beschenkowiczi. I was ordered to stay at the outposts, and because of the enemy's supposed proximity not dismount all night, nor light any fire. You can imagine what a long night that was for me!'

Not until he gets back to his regiment next morning will he get his 'damned boot' on again. But some Bavarian troopers, wounded by enemy fire when crossing the river, have fared much worse. IHQ having installed itself in the town's little houses, General Preyssing sends von Muraldt to its military governor to request billets for them. The governor, a French general of brigade, receives him politely in a ground-floor room where a 'tall man in a buttoned-up blue greatcoat was sitting writing' in one corner. At that moment a French general appears on horseback in the open doorway, accompanied by his two ADCs and an orderly officer. Not even bothering to dismount, he begins cursing and swearing and complaining that his lodgings aren't worthy of a 'lieutenant-general attached to General Headquarters. I demand you instantly find me something else!' Polite as ever, the commandant points out that, what with lodgings being needed for the Emperor and all the headquarters staff, there's very little choice.

'The man doesn't accept this sensible reply, but starts insulting the governor, who's standing there in the doorway. Suddenly the tall man gets up from his writing-table, pushes the governor aside, and in a voice of thunder roars up at the raging general: "If you aren't satisfied, you can f— off! D'you think we've nothing better to do than listen to your f—ing complaints?" The man on horseback only had to set eyes on the tall man to whip off his hat, bend his back in an equestrian bow, and stammer out an apology. But the tall man just tells him to go to the devil and returns to his writing-table.'

Muraldt, who has 'watched this scene open-mouthed', asks another officer who the tall man is. It's Caulaincourt. 'So I was no longer surprised at the raging general's suddenly obsequious behaviour.' But quarters are found for the Bavarian wounded; and by and by Captain Roeder and his Hessian Guards will turn up to look after them.

Nansouty's I Cavalry Corps have already crossed the Dwina farther downstream two days before, near Drissa, where the river is 'between 80 and 90 yards wide, its waters rushing between great boulders. Several attempts to bridge it were frustrated by its swift current and rocky bed.' Prince Henry of Württemberg's Hussars 'swam across in columns, but lost a fair number of riders and many more horses'. And when the turn had come for the 3rd Württemberg Chasseurs to cross, Dr von Roos had

'followed the procedure I'd recently grown used to. Accompanying the first squadron as it moved down to the river bank, I ordered two well-mounted NCOs to take me between them. They did so willingly; and into the water we went... and across. Swimming swiftly and easily, we soon reached the further bank. But from our heels up to our thighs, yes, even up to our ribs, we were as soaked as our horses. None of our men were drowned; but the next regiment didn't get over without loss.'

Safely on the other side, the Württembergers had lit their pipes, shared any brandy they'd left in their flasks, and lit their campfires:

'But the persistent rain didn't give us a chance to dry our clothes. Sorriest of all, we were, for two of the regiment's wives – the highly esteemed Frau Worth, who could always fend for herself, and the careful Frau Weiler. Sergeant-majors' wives both, they were riding little horses, so their clothes and baggage had sunk deeper than ours, and they'd no greater prospects of getting dry.'

CHAPTER 9

BATTLE AT OSTROWNO

Systematized flight of the population – IHQ hears gunfire – Murat doesn't wait for the infantry – 'we're wondering how it'll end' – an artist gets his battle – 'Murat, his wildness inflamed' – Thirion sits it out – the mortification of being overlooked -after the battle – a fatality of strategies

A splendid highway, flanked by double avenues of silver birches, leads from Beschenkowiczi to Witebsk across 'an immense plateau, full of swamps and quagmires. One only had to make a hole with one's foot or a spade to get water. The entire army was suffering severely from heat, lack of food, and bad water.'

Now the march order is Murat, Eugène, Ney, Davout's three detached infantry divisions under Lobau, and the Imperial Guard. Only at Beschenkowiczi does Napoleon tumble to a sinister fact which Caulaincourt and everyone else has 'noticed two days ago', namely that the population's wholesale flight is being organized by the Russian authorities. 'All the upper classes had fled, except the Jesuits.'

He has just finished dictating orders for Oudinot and St-Cyr[1] when there comes a rumble of distant gunfire:

'At this sound everything becomes animated. It's the first time since the campaign opened that IHQ finds itself in the vicinity of a combat. So the Russians have made up their minds to dispute Witebsk with us! We make haste to leave.' – 'All reports gave us to believe the enemy would stand and give a major battle in front of Witebsk. The regiments' ardour was extreme, and we all shared it.'

Like everyone else Fézensac is 'suffering severely from heat, lack of food and bad water'. Eugène's staff are just about to leave when an ADC arrives flat out from General Delzons, commander of 13th Division. With his usual impetuousness Murat, without waiting for Delzons' infantry to come up, has flung his light cavalry into some woods packed with Russian sharpshooters.

'The sound of the guns redoubling, His Highness at once ordered his headquarters baggage to halt, and, followed only by his principal officers, hastened on towards Ostrowno.'

Once again it's been the 8th Hussars who, together with the 9th Polish Lancers, have been suffering. Marching along the Witebsk road in column, they'd been approaching a rise in the ground which prevented them from seeing far ahead; and when they eventually saw the Russians massed in line 'with never a skirmisher out in front'[2] they'd taken them for friendly units. Sending an officer to liaise, they'd been shaken to see him cut down and taken prisoner. Whereupon the regiment, supposing itself to be supported on each side by other columns, which had in fact halted, has furiously charged the Russians ahead of them, and then to left

and right, and finally returned with some prisoners, but also losses. All
this Ségur hears about – since his brother's capture outside Vilna, he has
doubtless been keeping in personal touch with his regiment. Surgeon
Réné Bourgeois, arriving on the scene, sees

'a hussar of the 8th lying face down on the road, his cranium taken
off by a roundshot. The general in command had come and said
that if the enemy went on firing, they must charge the guns. The
shots beginning again, his soldiers had left like lightning, and soon
after had come back with eight guns and prisoners. By the time we
were told of this, both sides of the road were already littered with
wounded, either prisoners or French. We saw hussars, holding their
horses' bridle in one hand and a pistol in the other, bringing back
prisoners, making them run in front of them on foot. I dressed the
more urgent cases.'

Lieutenant *von Kalckreuth* of the 2nd Prussian Hussars, too, has been in
the thick of it:

'We were very close to the enemy and lost many men and horses
from his artillery, which our regiment, too, had to attack. We managed to pass between the Russian guns, but a violent infantry fire
from the nearby forest forced us to retire.'

Although in a second charge they'd 'sabred many of the gunners and
tried to carry off the guns', the Prussians, not getting the support they'd
counted on from the 7th French Hussars, had again had to retire with
heavy losses to a position where they're being continuously fired on with
grapeshot 'that thinned our ranks considerably'.

Meanwhile the heavy cavalry has drawn up in line behind the artillery,
and in no time the fighting has developed into a full-scale engagement.
Sergeant-major Thirion and his 2nd Cuirassiers find themselves in front
of a Russian line

'bristling with guns. On our side we'd only two divisions of cavalry,
led by King Murat. The road forms an elbow; and a few paces in
front of it Bruyères' division deployed in line to the right of the
road, with our division to its left and the road between us. The two
were standing in line on a single front, parallel to the Russian one.
Because of a wood the Russian army didn't stretch as far to the left as
we did. So all the burden of the day fell on General Bruyères' light
division and on ours, and above all on my regiment, whose right
touched the road. The enemy had placed his batteries astride it,
exactly facing us.'

When two French regiments are routed, together with the artillery supporting them, Piré's light cavalry division is flung in, and in its turn routs
three similar Russian regiments. But by now Eugène's infantry divisions
are arriving on the scene. Laugier sees his men are all on fire to

'measure ourselves against this hitherto invisible enemy. We can read
contentment on all faces. And then – it's in our hearts to avenge the
insult'

when Eugène had spurned their stilettos. And in fact Delzons' leading division drives the Russians right back into the forest. Such is the beginning of a full-scale battle that will last two days. Only at nightfall do the heavily outnumbered Russians fall back on to their second position.

Next morning, advancing across the battlefield before entering the forests, von Kalckreuth's hussars use their sabres hastily to cover 'at least with a little earth' as many as possible of their comrades who'd fallen in yesterday's charges. In a clearing in the woods six more of them are killed and five wounded by grapeshot from Russian guns they can't even see. Although the Italians are in motion at 4 a.m., 'the sun already lighting up the field of yesterday's carnage', they've no time to bury '400 corpses, almost all Russian. Weapons, broken wheels, shattered ammunition wagons, helmets and haversacks litter the ground.' Their divisions follow on at one-hour intervals, and at 6 a.m. Eugène can inspect his light infantry battalions' outposts and study the Russians' new and 'formidable position' among trees and boulders, barring the road to Witebsk – where, it's being said, the Russians have assembled huge stores.

This second position, too, is covered by a ravine or hollow way. Its right rests on the Dwina's swampy shore and its left on dense forest. For a field of battle, it has a most peculiar feature. Down its middle runs a long strip of forest, thickly garrisoned with Russian sharpshooters. Behind this island of conifers, are more dense woods, out of whose depths the Russians can see without being seen.

Again IV Corps deploys. And Laugier jots down the Italians' battle array in his diary:

'The 8th Light in line facing the enemy, thus covering the formation of the Croat Regiment to the left of the road, behind which is the 84th in column of divisions. The battalions of the 92nd Regiment, preceded by the 3rd Italian Light Infantry, are in line by échelons on the other side of the road. The 106th forms the reserve, and the cavalry is disposed to support the movement. A light brigade crosses the Dwina to cover the left of our line. The artillery and cavalry are distributed along our front.'

Now his watch shows it's 10 o'clock:

'Here and there sharpshooters are opening fire. The Russian guns have been crossing our column as we've been forming up in our assigned places. The Royal Guard's artillery is ordered forward and begins firing at the Russian batteries; by drawing their fire makes it less dangerous for us to cross the open terrain to take up our battle positions.'

Whereafter the Italians launch a general attack; but are

'resisted with the greatest intrepidity. Wishing to envelop our left, the enemy general brings a strong body of cavalry out of the wood touching the Dwina. The King of Naples has it charged by a regiment of hussars, but these are beaten and thrown back. Whereon the viceroy orders General Huard, commanding the left of Delzons' division, composed of the Croat Regiment and the 84th, to advance. The first shock is to his advantage. He crosses the ravine and everything yields to his troops' impetuosity. On the right the battalions of the 3rd Light and the 92nd, who're to penetrate the forest, form up under the Russian fire.'

But the Russians bring up their reserves and Huard's brigade is routed by sheer weight of numbers:

'Almost immediately an extraordinary disturbance, an undulation in the masses, terrible shouts, attract all our eyes to our left. A division of cuirassiers, too exposed to fire, is retiring at a trot to give place to Broussier's division, which is going to Delzons' assistance. The earth trembles under the horses' weight.'

Though Césare de Laugier can no longer see exactly what's going on, he's alarmed to realize that the two wings seem out of touch! To steady his Guards at such a frightening moment, Eugène rides across their front, says he's relying on them today. Muskets and swords are waved. Shouts of *'Avanti la Guardia!'* But still the Russians are coming on, and as they emerge from the forest to annihilate Delzons' division and seize its guns their shouts, too, can be heard. At this moment too the 'hitherto invisible' Russian sharpshooters emerge from their hiding-places. Everyone in the Guardia d'Onore 'is asking himself how this is going to end'. Impossible to bring the guns to bear without firing on Huard's routed brigade! The first line is falling back on the second, 'at grave risk of causing extreme confusion, an irreparable disorder, and of rendering resistance impossible. This state of affairs cannot last long.'

At such a moment Murat is supreme. 'Only a cavalry attack could be of any use.' Riding out in front of a line of red and white pennons which stretches from the Dwina's swamp on the right to the island of forest in the centre, he intends to harangue the Polish lancer division – but finds himself in a most awkward, not to say comical position. The Poles need no exhortation. With tremendous élan, like several thousand pig-stickers, they charge, driving the King of Naples like a wild boar before them. And Murat, unable to see or command, has no option but to 'lead' them:

'The brave Poles threw themselves on the Russian battalions. Not a man escaped. Not a prisoner was taken. Everything was killed, everything perished. Not even the forest could provide protection against the slashing sabres,'

he'll write that evening. Only thanks to his Herculean physique and the prowess of his gilded scimitar does he survive in the ensuing scrum. 'At the same moment', he goes on,

'the squares began moving up with seven-league boots. General Girard, who was leading the left-hand battalions, made a swing to the right, hastening down the highroad to fall on the enemy's rear. The troops to the right made the same movement. General Piré supported them, attacking the enemy at the head of the 8th Hussars.

This regiment was overthrown and only had the forest and hollow roads to thank for its salvation. The whole division followed the movement. The infantry advanced along the highroad. The cavalry rushed down from the higher ground. And I ordered the artillery to fire at the five or six regiments that were resisting us.'

Is it just then, or at some other moment, that Albrecht Adam sees

'the King of Naples at close quarters, his wildness inflamed by the fighting and opposition. He roared hither and thither, cursing and scolding, urging on his troops. Dashing to and fro, he seemed to fly, and his noble steed was all lathered. The noble Prince Eugène, displaying calm and prudence, presented a very strange contrast. Always he preserved his solemn, noble bearing.'

So, for that matter, does the intrepid war artist:

'My long-cherished desire to see a battle at close quarters and find myself involved in it was now at last being fulfilled. On this occasion I really heard the musketballs whine. Yet didn't let it distract me from drawing. During those two days I saw enough to provide me with material for a lifetime of painting battles! Although the Prince's officers and ADCs treated me amiably enough, before the action had commenced they hadn't been able to refrain from teasing me: "Just now our Adam is always hanging around. But once the bullets start flying we'll have to search for him!" When the first cannon-balls landed near us, an ADC, who looked rather pale, remarked: "Well, Monsieur Adam, how do you find this?" I replied rather tartly: "I find we're in a battle." Several hours later, when I was in a very tight spot, another well-intentioned officer came up and said this was no place for me, and I could go to the rear. I replied that I didn't value my own life more highly than the Prince's, and that if one wanted to paint battles one must have witnessed them.'

Such was the ex-cakemaker's baptism of fire which, true to his calling, he has been able to contemplate with true aesthetic detachment.

Sergeant-major Thirion, sitting his Turkish horse hour after hour in the scorching sun, has no such option. Roasted in his 16-pound steel cuirass (able to stop a musket ball at 45 paces but not a cannon-ball), tormented like everyone else by a burning thirst, he simply has to stay put while the Russian guns slowly decimate his regiment.

'We cuirassiers were an easy target. A few paces in front of me Commandant Dubois sat a white horse, and his position had caused him to be recognized as a superior officer.'

At one moment Murat makes the Prussian Black Lancers charge down the main road at two battalions of Russian artillery and infantry, in squares on either side of it; and from his high ground Thirion sees how

'this charge, made calmly at a trot, not proving successful, this cavalry retired as calmly as it had advanced. It was the first time I'd seen cavalry charge at that pace and come back from it without any shouting, any disorder. "By and by, cuirassiers!" shouted Murat, passing across our front, "Your turn will soon come!"

But it never does. For six solid hours the 2nd Cuirassiers, their lungs filled with the acrid smoke of battle, sit there in the blazing heat while the roundshot rips through and over them, a gleaming steely target for the Russian guns. Fortunately the Russian gunners tend to misjudge their trajectories and aim too high, so that – when it's all over – Thirion and his comrades are amazed to find only 187 of them have been killed. But of the 27 men in his own troop, only eleven have survived – and are counting themselves lucky to have done so.

Some units, perhaps many, are mortified to find their exploits have escaped official notice. To his left Thirion had seen the 7th Hussars make a brilliant charge against Russian infantry and cavalry, and only lose a few men in so doing.

'A short way away to our left', writes Dupuy, 'the 9th Polish Lancers pierced a square of Muscovite chasseurs and wiped it out.' To Thirion it had seemed

'these men had become fighting mad. How many didn't I see who, with arm or leg bandaged, returned to the scrum at a flat-out gallop, forcefully eluding those of their comrades who tried to hold them back.'

At the height of the action General Jacquinot had sent Dupuy to inform Bruyères of the 7th Hussars' exhilarating success. And on his way he'd paused a moment to tell General Bessières, once his colonel and now commanding the cuirassier brigade, all about it. Yet no one – absolutely no one – afterwards commends the 7th Hussars' brilliant charge! It's been omitted from all mention in favour of Piré's brigade, and General Jacquinot afterwards goes and complains bitterly to Murat. But all he gets for an answer is: 'My dear general, what do you expect? I don't know who's written this bulletin, nor how. But in truth I don't recognize myself in it.' Which is odd, seeing that it's based on his own report. 'This victory,' Surgeon Faure is thinking sadly,

'if that's what our success in so obstinate a fight can be called, was brilliant. But the surroundings offered no means of gathering its fruits. Ostrowno was a village of a few poor smoky houses. There was no one to pay these soldiers' courage the tribute of admiration they'd so well merited. Not even the smallest table could be laid where we could recount the day's exploits. After such actions one wants to absorb oneself wholly in one's experiences, and it's hard to think about anything less serious.'

Only next morning do he and his surgeons of I Cavalry Corps began their ministrations:

'There were still some dead on the road, but the greater number of those who'd been there had been flung into the ditches. Some trees had been damaged or cut down by roundshot. Off the road, where there'd been several cavalry charges, the greensward was churned up, and men were lying in every posture and mutilated in a variety of ways. Some had been burnt quite black by the explosion of an ammunition wagon. Others, who seemed dead, were still breathing. As we approached we heard them complaining. They lay on their back, their head sometimes resting on some comrade already dead for several hours, in a state of apathy, in a kind of sleep of pain they were loth to come out of, heeding no one around them. They asked for nothing, doubtless because they knew there was nothing to hope for; nor did they beg for the help already so many times refused. The Prussian lancers were walking about the places where they'd made charges, gloomily contemplating the remains of some hardly recognizable friends. In such a situation one accuses fate. The soldier is generous. He bears no grudge against whomever it is makes him fight, nor those he's fighting against. Here and there lay horses, broken harness, exploded ammunition wagons, twisted sabres, pistols, broken muskets. The ground was covered with débris. The brave hussars of the 8th lay in great numbers among the dead, having mingled their blood with the enemy's. A little further on we recognized the place where the Russians had attended to their wounded.'

Towards 3 p.m. Faure had seen 'the Emperor come and cast his master's eye on the scene. No emotion appeared on his face. His sensitivity had passed so many tests!' And in fact he'd played almost no part in the battle. No more, therefore, has Captain Zalusky, whose 1st Polish Lancer Squadron is one of the four (one from each Guard cavalry regiment) on escort duty,

'even though I was close to the Emperor, who examined the enemy's movements from a hillock. When the Russian cavalry appeared, we made a movement to protect the monarch if need should arise.'

In the upshot the Russians have left behind eight guns, several hundred prisoners and some 2,000 dead and wounded. Planat de la Faye, reaching the battlefield later next day, will study it for several hours, and be

'deeply pained to see some poor wounded Russians, exposed for the last three or four days to the sun's heat and the chill of the nights without help. Their misery and complaints made so much the greater impression on me as I'd learnt enough Russian in 1801 [his father had had business in Moscow] to know what they were begging for, but which I couldn't give them.'

Faure too is deeply worried. He and his fellow-surgeons are sending the wounded back to Beschenkowiczi. But what will become of them, with 'even the able-bodied hardly able to manage?' The Russians seemed to have suffered four times as much as the French. If so, Thirion thinks it's because, though the enemy had more guns, the French horse-gunners' fire had been more rapid and accurate. That morning, where his regiment had yesterday stood its ground so staunchly,

'two rows of dead horses marked the place it had occupied. As for our comrades who'd been killed, we buried them in the evening, each unit making it its duty to give burial to those of its men who had perished.'

And as the army marches on toward Witebsk surgeon Réné Faure sees 'the road covered with crests of enemy helmets'.

As soon as it was all over Albrecht Adam had got Eugène to sign some of his sketches – to prove he'd really been there.

CHAPTER 10

WHAT FEZENSAC HEARD ON MISSION

'We had to get hold of information as best we could' – a fatal game of billiards – a nervous Colbert smokes his meerschaum – 'Render unto Caesar...' – a most uncomfortable night – Le Roy commands Davout's advance guard – battle at Novo-Saltka – 'the Russians were walls which had to be demolished' – Davout steadies a regiment – forty ducats for a miniature – Girod de l'Ain is again passed over

What neither Barclay nor Napoleon know is that on 23 July Davout, at Novo-Salta, near Molihew, about 100 miles away to the south, has barred Bagration's attempt to break through northwards to effect liaison at Witebsk and that Bagration is now marching instead for Smolensk, 80 miles further east. Because of the very speed with which Napoleon has been driving a wedge between the two Russian armies, what had at best been a rhetorical idea – endless withdrawal and a war of attrition – is fast becoming a disastrous reality. Although Napoleon's communications with Davout are more direct than Barclay's with Bagration, his need for news of what is happening to I Corps is almost as urgent as Barclay's for news of the Second West Army. Who will make junction first?

At Beschenkowiczi Fézensac had shared the excitement at the sound of the guns. But he's not been at Ostrowno. He's on mission:

'On the morning of the 25th the Prince of Neuchâtel ordered me to follow the army's route as far as Molihew, where I should find the Prince of Ekhmühl. My instructions were to send back ordnance officers to inform the Emperor immediately of anything fresh I might learn. He was particularly concerned to know how the Prince of Ekhmühl was situated vis-à-vis Prince Bagration, and whether V and VIII corps were able to support him. At the first cannon shots announcing the King of Naples' attack I left. A Polish officer went with me to question the locals.'

En route Fézensac and his Pole stop off at Polish manor-houses,

'whose lords supplied us with horses. The country was quiet and no one had any news. That night we reached Kochanov, where General Grouchy was commanding a cavalry corps, whose advance guard was established at Orsha, under the orders of General Colbert.'

This is of course the Red Lancers. On 21 July two of their squadrons had been part of the pincer movement which had snatched the Russians' great flour stores at Orsha. 'Lying on the banks of the Dnieper – the Boristhenes of antiquity' – Orsha, the last major town in Lithuania, had reminded Dumonceau of Vilna and Kovno:

'It contained several big monasteries, was crossed by several broad streets, and in the centre, together with several others, was a vast market place, surrounded by a wooden balustrade painted in the Russian national colours, black, yellow and white. Here the Dnieper flows peacefully through a gorge at the end of the plateau. There was no bridge, only a ford, whence a sloping causeway on piers led straight up to the town, situated on the slopes of some high ground.'

But now Colbert, having pushed on from Orsha, is feeling nervous. Already a reconnaissance party of another of Grouchy's light cavalry regiments, the 21st Chasseurs, has been 'rudely attacked by thousands of Cossacks and driven back with lances at their backs, with a loss of 200 men'. And he realizes his own regiment is out on a limb. If he should be attacked in force, Grouchy's cavalry corps is too far to his rear to come to his aid. As for his Dutchmen, they're altogether too phlegmatic, too little on the *qui vive*.

Quite right. That day Dumounceau, who is duty captain, he has posted out one of his two lieutenants, Baron van Zuylen van Nijevekt, in the direction of Babinowiczi, 'which lies on the edge of a lake, on the far side of a stream, in a plain fringed by the vast forest of the same name'. He has taken care to place Van Zuylen's outposts in an 'advantageous position amid bushes, where he could scan the plain, the woods, and the highroad leading eastwards in the direction of Witebsk'. And all would perhaps have been well if Dumonceau, in this jittery situation, had stayed with his lieutenant. But 'after the return of his dawn patrols' van Zuylen, to get food and forage from the inhabitants and 'lulled by the assurances they lavished upon us' retires with some of his men to an inn at Babinowisky, for a game of billiards with his fellow-lieutenant Wichel. 'His troop under arms, horses still saddled up and bridled,' and ready to rush out at the least alert, he has just laid aside his sabre, when a lancer, 'flat out and his horse white with foam', comes dashing back along the road. A brigade of Uhlans of the Russian Imperial Guard, 'probably forewarned by the locals as to our detachment's habits and dispositions', has captured all but four of his men! In the same instant the Uhlans come galloping into town and surround the inn.

Grabbing up their carbines, Van Nijevekt and his men defend themselves by firing down from the inn's dormer windows. Had any help been near to hand, this should have sufficed to keep the Uhlans at bay. But there isn't. And his whole troop has to surrender.[1]

After this nasty incident Colbert has promptly withdrawn his regiment to a safer position west of Orsha – with orders that the duty squadron be changed every two hours during the night:

'At about midnight I, in my turn, was on my way to relieve the squadron posted out on the plateau, and passed the general's and his staff's bivouac – a long shelter, open in front, lit up by a big fire some distance from its centre. There I saw all our numerous staff lying stretched out on straw, deeply asleep, while the general alone kept watch, sitting in his stable-litter, peaceably smoking his meerschaum, and giving an example of vigilance.'

Next morning Fézensac turns up. And no doubt Colbert tells him about the contretemps, if only because he has since learnt that the Uhlans had been commanded by no lesser a personage than the Tsar's brother, Grand Duke Constantine.[2] It had been while probing for Bagration along the Smolensk-Orsha road that they'd bumped into Dumonceau's outposts.

What conclusion does Fézensac draw from this? Certainly that on 24 July Barclay had still been in the dark as to Bagration's whereabouts; was perhaps unaware that he'd been fended off by Davout at Novo-Salta[3] and is therefore unable to come to Barclay's assistance in front of Witebsk.

By and by Grouchy comes up to Colbert's support. His 'three divisions, seven to eight thousand men', are followed next day by VIII Corps, 'all Westphalians, arriving from Borissow'. By evening Colbert feels secure enough to receive the 6th Hussars' officers, 'whom he seemed to know of old, and offered them a glass of punch at his bivouac. But to everyone's astonishment none of our regimental officers is invited,' no doubt as a tacit reprimand for van Zuylen's ineptitude. Most of Babinowiczi's inhabitants have fled,

'fearing such reprisals by us as the event of the 24th might warrant. Those who'd stayed behind were interrogated as to the fate of our detachment. They told us some of the details I've mentioned above. Resistance at the inn had lasted half an hour.'

And indeed by the time Lieutenant Auvray of the 23rd Dragoons gets there the town is being given over to pillage. But the Red Lancers have to move on. Towards midnight

'two squadrons, one from our regiment and one from the 6th Hussars, had to get on their horses and leave to reconnoitre. I was with the party. The night was dark, the road very broad and irregular. Having hardly had as much sleep as I needed, I dozed off again on my horse. Riding on at random, I overtook our advance guard, and would have got lost if an old hussar, scouting ahead, hadn't woken me up.'

Shortly afterwards Dumonceau sights some Cossacks: 'Peasants, brought from a nearby village, told us everyone was saying the whole Russian army was concentrated around Witebsk.'

But Fézensac is on his way again:

'On the 26th at daybreak we reached Chlow, a very commercial little Jewish town; and, during the forenoon, at Molihew, where I Corps was. I had occasion to note the order and discipline which still distinguished the Prince of Eckmühl's troops.'

Davout tells him about the battle at Salta-Novka which has headed off Bagration and forced him, 'despairing of making junction with Barclay', to cross the Dnieper. Now he's retiring toward Smolensk. He himself is going to follow the Dnieper upstream as far as Orsha, 'to close the distance between himself and the rest of the army'.

It's a Sunday. And once again Davout, that convinced atheist, attends divine service. Coming out, he receives the Archimandrite and recommends to him 'that he recognize the Emperor Napoleon as his sovereign and to substitute his name in public prayers for that of the Emperor Alexander. He reminded him of the words of the Gospel: to render unto Caesar that which is Caesar's, adding that by Caesar is meant the stronger. The Archimandrite promised to conform with this instruction, but in a tone of voice which showed how little he approved of it.'

Should Fézensac that morning bump into Le Roy – which is by no means impossible, for his exploits at Salta-Novka have attached him to Davout's headquarters – there's a lot he can hear from him. One imagines Le Roy telling him how I Corps 'without even noticing it' had crossed the Berezina, 'at this time of year fordable at all points, with water only half-way up our legs' at Borissow, on the heels of Grouchy's cavalry corps. As he'd ridden over the 300m-long timber bridge Captain Auvray had noticed how

'between the fortifications and the town lies a marsh, intersected by the river bank, making the passage almost impossible without a bridge. Our arrival had prevented the Russians from burning the one that existed. They also had sixteen heavy calibre guns, meant for the fortifications. If the enemy had been able to finish his works there, Borissow would have been a fortified town.'[4]

Four more days on the march and I Corps had reached Molihew.

'The enemy had reached the Dnieper at the same moment as ourselves, but a little farther downstream. We detached a few companies of our first battalion; encountering no resistance, they took possession of the town.'

All of which Le Roy might well have followed up with his personal and, as usual, no little culinary account of the preliminaries of the fierce battle that had followed:

'At about 9 a.m. [20 July] the 3rd Chasseur Regiment, which made up the advance guard, was taken by surprise and thrown back at a run on to the infantry line, which just had time to fly to arms and face the Russian cavalry. More than 150 chasseurs and the regiment's colonel were captured or killed. Not having left my battalion, I soon had it assembled under arms. At the sound of the first shots, the Prince, seeing a battalion under arms, comes hastening up, speaks to me, and orders me to leave at once and follow the river. The army would be following my movement. My men eat their soup as they march. I realize they need to; and make for the Dnieper, to my left, by which I can gauge my position. Entangled in the plenteous ravines along the riverbank'

Le Roy realizes to his dismay that his battalion has become isolated. Worse, just as he reaches a little manor-house overlooking the river he hears a couple of shots ring out; and prepares for a desperate fight. But it's only two Cossacks. His men have killed one and taken both their horses. Beyond he sees a small town. Its 'filthy ragged Jews told me the

Russian cavalry had just pillaged it and taken away all the food'. Bad news for Le Roy. After barricading the bridge over a little muddy stream at the town entrance and posting sentries, he goes up to some high ground, to survey the town below him. Beyond the stream he sees several enemy regiments lined up in echelon between two forests on both its banks. Concluding that he has nothing to fear for the moment, he gives the order: 'Make the soup!' Then, summoning 'an elderly lieutenant I knew to be a good marauder', he sends him to visit the little manor-house in the battalion's rear. 'If inhabited, he was to ask for food; if deserted, as I presumed it was, to rifle it without breaking anything or letting his detachment take the least thing.' And come back as soon as possible.

All Le Roy can see from his observation post, to his right, is a single squadron of red-clad Cossacks. From which he infers that his own main body can't be far off:

'I went back into town. Having made sure the Russians hadn't pillaged or even exacted anything from the inhabitants, I had some bread and beer brought. As I was distributing these victuals to my men, I saw my marauder arriving with a cart filled with delicacies. There were biscuits, almonds, biscuits of all kinds, there were big fat sausages, some rice, some vermicelli, some figs, some dried dates, some raisins; in a word, we'd a complete dessert. A little barrel of spirits, which I ordered to be reduced to a temperature of seventeen degrees, sufficed for a ration to each man. For the officers the marauder had set aside a score of bottles of Bordeaux and four round loaves of rather fine bread. Hardly had the distribution been made than I heard, behind me: "Qui vive!" And "To arms!".

The battalion springs to arms. But it's only the 85th's adjutant-major, accompanied by several staff officers; and, at their heels, Davout himself, 'who told me how surprised he was to find me two whole leagues ahead of the army'. Well, Le Roy's luck has held. He's been facing the entire Russian Second West Army! 'But tomorrow', says Davout, 'I hope to have my revenge', i.e., for the damage done to the 3rd Chasseurs. That evening the Iron Marshal approves Le Roy's dispositions: and indeed is quite unusually friendly, perhaps because he knows he's heavily outnumbered:

'Unlike his usual self, he says some nice polite things to me. At that moment General Friedrichs arrives, and in a brusque military manner demands to know who'd ordered me to advance so boldly and expose myself and my battalion to being carried off. "I did," replied the Marshal. "This officer has been following my orders; and without this action, which to you seems so foolhardy, I'd have been groping about until evening. Whereas, as it is, I know for certain where the enemy is, and tomorrow I intend to have a go at him."'

Golden words Le Roy hastens to share with his men. At dawn the regiment's other battalions turn up and relieve him of his anxieties, which have been considerable, especially as he has 'no great confidence in my recruits, who as yet hadn't received their baptism of fire'.

If staff-captain *Girod de l'Ain* had also been among Fézensac's infor-
mants two days later, he too could have told him a thing or two; notably
about Davout's singular way of treating his divisional generals. On the eve
of the battle even the elderly cuirassier general Valence had had to spend
the night, soupless and strawless, on the bare floor of Davout's antechamber 'like so many orderlies'. Chairs being too few to go round, the generals and their aides had ignored them as invidious, but 'very fed up, as
you'll believe. The Marshal didn't so much as offer us a glass of water.'

After his uncomfortable night Girod de l'Ain had suggested to Dessaix
that he go off on his own and reconnoitre the Dnieper's swampy banks.
Finding no Russians, he'd returned to find Dessaix' and Compans' divisions drawn up in line in some narrow, wooded, swampy terrain. The
main road plunged into a ravine, where a wooden bridge crossed a
steep-banked muddy stream. Dessaix' division was to the right of the
bridge, Compans' to its left. To their right was some open ground. 'Four
or five houses had been loop-holed.'

Nothing had happened until about 10 a.m. Then, out of the dense forest ahead, great masses of Russians had emerged in attack columns, only
to be stopped dead in their tracks by

'lively artillery fire and musketry. For several minutes they let themselves be shot down without budging. We had a new chance to recognize that the Russians, as we said, were "walls which had to be demolished".'[5]

Le Roy takes up the tale:

'Our artillery and the enemy's pounded each other from one
plateau to the other at caseshot range. The stream's two banks were
lined with both nations' sharpshooters, who only had some willows
for cover. Each shot took its effect in the enemy masses, who were
trying to force a way through and throw us back into Molihew.'

Davout himself had not turned up until about midday. And instead of
going up to Dessaix, commanding his right centre, had approached one
of his brigadiers. Finding himself so coldly treated, Dessaix had

'dismounted and gone off, saying he'd no more orders to give, and
nothing remained for him but to hand over his command to someone else. At that moment the enemy seemed to make a new and serious effort to cross the ravine. After a long and lively fusillade, a battalion of the 108th (Colonel Achard), which was in the front line,
makes to retire, a movement noticed by the Marshal. And instantly
we see the latter go to the head of this battalion, halt it on the spot,
make it face about toward the enemy, and give it drill orders as if on
parade.'

Ignoring Achard's protests that he'd only been retiring because all his
ammunition is spent, Davout, his back to the Russians, goes on giving
parade orders, 'as if'd been a hundred leagues from the enemy'. In the
end Achard has physically to turn the short-sighted marshal around, to
convince him of their extreme proximity. Whereupon, Le Roy goes on,

'the Marshal threw forward a regiment along the road. It attacked the enemy and forced him to retreat. And as it was late we remained masters of the ground. We saw the enemy, who'd built three bridges during the fighting, placing himself between us and the river. He'd sacrificed a corps of 3,000 élite soldiers to save the rest of his army. Never in my life did I see so much damage caused by our artillery! Guns, horses, men, roadside trees, all piled on top of one another, beyond recognition. To our left we saw whole ranks of Russian cavalry carried off by the grapeshot or killed by the fusillades.'

According to Le Roy the French hadn't taken a single prisoner – which can only be a lapse of memory. For, on 7 August, Davout will write in his report to Berthier: 'The enemy left on the field upwards of 1,200 dead and more than 4,000 wounded, of whom seven or eight hundred are in our hands, as well as 152 prisoners.' But next day they'd collected six broken Russian guns, four thousand muskets and rendered a great deal of *matériel* unserviceable:

'That day a spokesman presented himself under a flag of truce to ask for the body of an artillery captain who'd been engaged to the general's daughter, and for this young lady's portrait, which the officer had been wearing round his neck. It had come into the hands of one of our voltigeurs. He got forty ducats for it. As for the body, it was buried with ours – friends and enemies, all were flung into a big hole on the bank of the stream.'

Having been lopped of Lobau's three divisions, I Corps had been too weak to pursue the Russians and spent two whole days burying the dead. Girod de l'Ain thinks the outcome would have been more decisive if it hadn't been for dissension between Davout and his divisional commanders.

Dissatisfaction is rife over rewards. All the divisional staffs have been overlooked; thus also for 'the seventh or eighth time' Girod de l'Ain, even though Davout now for the second time requests the Cross for him. All regimental claims, on the other hand, are being granted – no doubt Fézensac carries them back with him to Berthier in his scarlet and gold sabretache. For his mission is accomplished:

'That evening I left by the same road as I'd come by. The next day, approaching the [main] army, I learnt that the three days I'd been away had been filled with brilliant combats, in which the Russian army had been pushed back from one position to another, as far as the walls of Witebsk. I crossed the battlefields still covered with the debris of these three combats, and on the evening of the 26th [*sic*, he must mean 27 July] reached headquarters, where I gave an account of my mission to the Emperor and the Prince of Neuchâtel. The army was encamped in battle order opposite the Russian army. Only the Luchiesa stream separated them. The Emperor's tents had been erected on an eminence in the centre.[6] Everyone was expecting a general engagement next day.'

CHAPTER 11

AN ARMY VANISHES

The Russian army at last! – Homeric stand of some Parisian tirailleurs – a bewildering delay – 'is everyone here asleep?' – an army vanishes – the Grand Army enters Witebsk – golden dishes for a council-of-war

The invaders' joy was immense. There, at last, in full view on the far side of an undulating plain, 'deployed near the town on a big plateau dominating all the roads it can be reached by' lay the Russian army. At last the moment has come for the blow that will decide the campaign?

'Only the Luchiesa stream and our outposts at the foot of the plateau lay between us. After the 13th Division had moved up, it bore off to the right. The Viceroy, riding at the head of the 14th, which followed, passed over the low hills dominating the plateau where the enemy were encamped.'

Albrecht Adam reins in his horse and sketches the scene: in the distance the line of tirailleurs and voltigeurs – nearer, long massed lines of men – artillery teams moving up – cocked-hatted ADCs, galloping hither and thither, heeded by no one. A dead man, arms outstretched, lies in the foreground. Eugène's horse rears. An adjutant gallops up, pointing. The green-coated Italian Guard grenadiers stand packed in reserve, wearing their bearskins. Shortly afterwards, Lieutenant Kalckreuth, moving up into the first line, sees Napoleon ride up to the outposts and dismount:

'Immediately four Guard chasseurs got off their horses and, carbine in hand, formed a square around the Emperor which no one might enter without his express order. He observed the enemy for a quarter of an hour, and then left us.'

First across the Luchiesa bridge – apparently intact – are two voltigeur companies of the 9th Line, followed by 'the 16th Chasseurs à Cheval, led by General Piré'. These are followed at a gallop by Murat himself. And after him the leading battalion of the 53rd Line (Broussier's division). But then Césare de Laugier is alarmed to see

'a hidden battery of twelve guns suddenly unmasking against them! In a twinkling of an eye they find themselves surrounded by Cossacks and hussars. Seeing this, the chasseurs halt, firmly awaiting the shock; and when the Russians are only 30 paces away, fire their carbines. But the discharge doesn't suffice to check the Russian cavalry's impetus. Some of the chasseurs' files fall into disarray, and they're flung back en masse on to the French infantry.'

A very brisk fire from the 53rd, 'formed up in square and presenting an unbreakable front', receives the Russian cavalry, 'exhausting all attempts to drive it in. To get clear, the Russian cavalry swerves to its right and falls on the voltigeur companies which, with their backs to the Dwina, are facing them.'

Follows a combat of truly Homeric proportions. Caulaincourt is among the fascinated spectators, 'all the rest of the army, encamped on a low hill in the form of an amphitheatre and encouraging them with its reiterated applause'. 'These brave fellows' (Césare de Laugier seems to be noting it all down in his diary as soon ever he can),

'placed out along the stream amidst some bushes and houses on the ravine's far side, were surrounded by a cloud of cavalry, against which they kept up a steady fire in support of our feeble squadrons, emptying many saddles and doing such damage that by degrees they force the enemy off our squadrons' flank. Several times we see five or six of these light infantrymen stand back to back, some fifty paces from the enemy squadrons sweeping down on them, and hold their fire until at point-blank range, surrounded on all sides, we give them up for lost. But these brave men, by forming a compact mass and using every advantage offered by the terrain, put up such an energetic resistance that they enable the troopers of the 16th Chasseurs to rally and be reinforced by fresh cavalry, which hastens to deliver them.'

The 16th Chasseurs' repulse has caused 'a certain confusion in our ranks. But Napoleon was there, and it couldn't last'. From a slight eminence crowned by a burnt windmill, to the left of the main road, he'd been 'watching all the manoeuvres and ordered a regiment of cavalry retire, to leave the bridge free for the 13th Division. This retrograde movement spread terror in our rear, composed as it was of a mass of employees, army suppliers or sutlers, folk who easily take fright and, always afraid for their loot, do armies more harm than good.'

Following up their success, the Russian Guard Lancers even reach the hillock's foot, so that the service squadrons – which today consist of Chasseurs à Cheval and Polish Lancers – hardly have time to form square around its foot. Whereupon Murat, whose impetuosity in sending forward the 16th Chasseurs without adequate infantry support has caused the setback, beside himself with fury and supported only by his staff and personal escort, flings himself at the intruders. Astounded at this extraordinary apparition, the Russian Lancers, though 'thirty times more numerous' than his handful of 60 troopers, turn tail and flee. As for the gallant light infantrymen, Laugier goes on,

'the Emperor said to several of them who'd brought him prisoners and asked for the Cross: "You're all brave lads, and you all deserve it." They were the object of the whole army's admiration. Some were killed, many wounded; but even these, unless completely disabled, were loth to abandon their comrades. I can't say how deeply I regret having lost the names of the officers and NCOs, and even the number of this gallant regiment.'

But Labaume and many others[1] make a note of it. It's the 9th Line, 'Captains Guyard (or Guillard) and Savary. All were Parisians.'
After this contretemps the moment has come for a general deployment.

'Everyone is forming a thousand conjectures, each in his own way, most favourable to our leader. At 2 p.m. we at last see new ADCs detaching themselves from the group always surrounding the Emperor, to go to the various corps. The soldiers give vent to their joy. The drums beat. Everyone's under arms. Now the silence is only broken by the redoubled firing of the Russian guns. Enthusiastically the troops are getting under way,'

when something bewildering happens. Napoleon calls off his attack.

'All of a sudden we hear it's not a question of attacking, but of camping. The light infantry receive an order to cease firing and retire from the positions they've occupied. To the military operation succeeds the less heroic repose of the camp. We look at each other, stupefied, vexed. What! Now, when enfeebled by sufferings and hunger, after endless marches to reach this enemy, we at last see him, can almost touch him, and all the circumstances are favourable, an untimely decision, a quite pointless deferment, has snatched victory from our hands! Surprise stands written on all our faces. Silently we interrogate the faces of our superiors to divine in them the cause of this inexplicable holdup.'

What can be causing this wholly untypical delay, just now, at the campaign's critical moment? And at exactly what time has Fézensac returned with the crucial news that Bagration can't possibly turn up and reinforce Barclay's mere 75,000 men? Was it the previous evening? Or is it now, on the 27th? True, III Corps and the Imperial Guard, too, are 'only joining gradually' along the great silver-birch lined highway from Beschenkowiczi:

'Everyone's astounded at this suspension of hostilities at the very moment when the armies are standing face to face. Everyone's asking where the Emperor is and what his plans can be. Some think he's only waiting for all his forces to join before launching a serious attack. Others are sure Ney and Montbrun's cavalry, advancing along the Dwina's other bank, are going to turn the Witebsk position and thus cut off the Russians' retreat.'[1]

But in such a situation assurance has to be doubly sure – so far from home and especially when faced by the staunch Russian 'walls' which had almost spelt defeat at Eylau in 1807. Is it this that gives him pause?[2] Certainly it's neither doubt nor lethargy. Caulaincourt sees how cheerful he is

'and already beaming with pride, confident of measuring his strength with the enemy and obtaining a result that should give some colour to his already over-extended expedition. He spent the day in the saddle, reconnoitering the terrain in every direction, even to a considerable distance.'

But the battle has been deferred. And it isn't until after sunset, when 'the rays of the setting sun had been reflected in Witebsk's golden cupolas' and darkness is already falling that III Corps passes through the Italians' lines, through Friant's, Morand's and Gudin's divisions (the ones Davout could so well have done with at Novo-Saltka) and through the Imperial

Guard, and takes up its assigned position. 'It's we who are to lead the attack!' Captain Bonnet notes excitedly in his diary, no doubt by the fluttering light of a campfire. 'Up here this high ground we've occupied appears as one vast mass of light.'

For his part Fezensac is spending the evening with Berthier's other ADCs, 'talking about my mission and listening to the tale of the combats that had just taken place'; everyone else, Césare de Laugier writes in his diary, is thinking only of the morrow, which is to

'decide Russia's fate, once and for all. Everyone is determined to put an end to these endless marches and privations by a crushing victory. Hasn't he ended all his wars in this way, forced his enemies to submit to his law?'

That evening the adjutant-major of the Guardia d'Onore has seen 'various ADCs sent out of our line to the right' and even the Viceroy sent off in person in the same direction:

'Some time afterwards he has come back, all out of breath and in a sweat. The Emperor says to him, brusquely: "You were more diligent when you were only colonel of my guard!" This unexpected reprimand, made in a loud voice, is immediately being repeated.'

What's it due to? No one knows – perhaps a lingering resentment at Eugène's timidity on the banks of the Niemen which, together with Jerome's alleged irresolution in the campaign's early stages, had cost him its immediate success? At midnight, again, the vélites of the Italian Guard are bivouacked around Eugène's tent, 'not far from the banks of the Luchiesa' and their adjutant is getting some much-needed sleep, when there's

'a sound of approaching footsteps and our camp's sentinels' challenges awaken us. It's the Emperor, followed by a few officers who've come to visit the Viceroy. As he approaches the royal tent we all recognize his imperious exclamation, of a kind only he can permit himself: "Is everyone here asleep?"'

Eugène goes off with his stepfather to the front line to look at the enemy and 'from officers who've accompanied him on this tour of inspection I know he's given orders for the battle he's flattering himself he'll be able to deliver today. Then each of us has gone back to his tent.' Only very late does Napoleon, accompanied as usual by Caulaincourt, return to his, 'after himself seeing to and checking up on everything'. But already at 1.30 a.m. he's on horseback again. And still the dying glow of innumerable Russian campfires covers the plain to the east...

Even amidst all the shocks still in store for them in this bewildering campaign – in which, as one chief-of-staff puts it, 'nothing was destined to happen as it did in others' – the invaders will remember the one they get at 4 a.m. on 28 July, as Witebsk's cupolas begin to stand out against the first glimmer of dawn, as among the worst. A shaken de Laugier scribbles in his diary:

'July 28. Hardly has the very faintest appearance of dawn allowed us to scrutinize the horizon than, without uttering a word, we're all staring out across this immense plain that stretches away in front of us. Yesterday it was covered with the enemies we're so impatient to attack. Today it spreads out before our eyes, deserted, abandoned!'

Employing a device as old as war itself, and leaving its campfires burning, 'not merely has the enemy vanished. He has left no trace to show which way he's gone.' Not a man, not a wagon, not a horse, not a single piece of equipment – not even a footprint in the wind-blown sands[3] – have Barclay's men left behind them. Dedem and Laugier are by no means the only ones to be staggered at this vanishing act of an entire army 'as if by magic – and not merely the army, but even its very traces!'

For Napoleon the shock is of course immense. As the sun, rising over Witebsk, blazes from the east into all those thousands of staring eyes, can it be the Tsar's words Caulaincourt had read out to him verbatim from his notebook in Paris flit through his mind? "If the Emperor Napoleon makes war on me, it's possible, even probable, we'll be defeated – that is, assuming we fight." Ahead lie the immense expanses of a Russia whose real frontier the Grand Army still hasn't even reached...

A second disappointment follows, in its way hardly less keen or to the point. After 'examining, very closely and more than once, every part of the enemy's positions, especially their bivouacs, to estimate their exact strengths', Napoleon and his entourage ride up to the town gate. There, writes Soltyk,

> 'he'd expected to be met by locals, imploring his clemency. But the Russians had taken with them many eminent people as hostages, and we found few notables in Witebsk to form the deputation he demanded. When it appeared before the Emperor he was walking up and down on the greensward near the main road, his arms crossed on his chest and deep in thought. At first the Polish gentlemen, awe-stricken and unprepared to find themselves face to face with the great man and all out of breath after having done a couple of miles on foot, didn't know what to say. In vain I prompt them to open the conversation. They seem to be waiting for the Emperor to question them; and this evidently annoys him. After two or three questions about the enemy army, he tells them in a curt tone of voice that his army needs food and forage, and above all bread. Then, abruptly breaking off the conversation, ends it by saying: "I see there are no more Poles here. This isn't Polish country any more!"'[4]

And indeed when, at 11 a.m., he enters the town it's to find it empty. Virtually the entire population – 20,000 souls – have fled. 'Passing rapidly through the streets', the Master of the Horse is with him as

> 'he rejoins his Guard, which, like the other troops, is already marching along the Smolensk road. Flattering himself we'll catch up with the enemy rearguard, he hastens forward the movement of the van, asking the King of Naples at all costs to get hold of some prisoners and send them to him. But not even a peasant can we find, to show

us which way the enemy has gone! No inhabitants are to be seen, no prisoners to be taken, not a single straggler to be picked up, nor any spies. For some hours we have to play at being huntsmen and follow the enemy's tracks in every direction. But to what purpose? What's the use? What route have his masses of men and artillery followed? No one knows, and for some hours no one will; for in every direction there are signs of them. We're in the heart of populated Russia, yet, if I may be permitted the simile, are like a vessel without a compass in the midst of a vast ocean, knowing nothing of what's happening around us.'

Following on the heels of Murat's cavalry, the Italians, too, are 'straying hither and thither in every direction in an immense plain without being able to find any trace of his retreat: not an abandoned vehicle, not a single dead horse, not even a single straggler'. Labaume and his colleagues on Eugène's staff are 'in this state of uncertainty, perhaps unique of its kind, when Colonel Kliski, searching the countryside for a peasant, at last found a Russian soldier asleep under a bush'.

And it's not until Murat's leading hussars, floundering at times up to their horses' knees in the soft sandy soil, are eighteen miles beyond Witebsk that they at last catch up with the Russian rearguard. 'Suddenly it halts, about-faces, and waits for the hussars to attack. But they're unable to spur their horses, too dead-beat to charge.' Worse, at the little town of Lochesna, junction of the Sarowiczi and Surash roads, they fall into an ambush. And whole troops are decimated. Those who survive and make for the rear have to lead their mounts which are no longer able to carry them.

It's there, as evening falls, that Napoleon finally halts, intending to spend the night in a 'poor little cottage'; but on second thoughts orders his tents to be raised. Around them the Italian Royal Guard forms a hollow square – 'it's the first time since the campaign opened that circumstances accord us this distinction, to which we, in the absence of the Imperial Guard, are anyway entitled'. Albrecht Adam's quick pencil sketches the scene. And Césare de Laugier notices 'several of our most prominent generals entering the Emperor's tent. We conclude that they're going to decide what to do.'

And in fact, uniquely, Napoleon has summoned a council-of-war. Present are only Eugène, Murat and his chief-of-staff General Belliard, and the light cavalry General Lefèbvre-Desnouëttes.[5] Murat isn't even asked for his opinions. But Belliard, 'a bluff frank soldier, who could be counted on to relate the plain facts,' replies: "Sire, if we go on marching six more days like this we'll have no cavalry left." From Berthier, too, Napoleon hears – incredulously – how the advance guard's horses are so worn out they've not even been able to charge. After alluding to the ancient "Scythians and their scorched earth policy", he agrees to call a halt.

The council-of-war is followed however by a magnificent meal, served up as usual on a gold dinner service, on tables outside the imperial tents – with scant respect for the Italians' feelings. All they have for dinner after a six-hour march in glaring sunshine through a dense dust cloud, stumbling over the soft sandy soil, and with the thermometer at 29 degrees Réaumur, is

'a little muddy and unhealthy water. The men cannot but observe with surprise and indignation the abundance both in the dishes and the exquisite wines on the imperial household's table, whilst they are themselves in the most extreme penury. They find the contrast disgusting and humiliating.'

Laugier hopes the 'army's chiefs may find it a profitable lesson. Cato of old, and Bonaparte himself in Egypt and crossing the Alps,' he adds in a footnote,

'had marched on foot, bareheaded under the sun's rays and shared their hard bread with their men, knowing what influence such conduct had on their armies. On this occasion he, perhaps over-preoccupied, hasn't reflected what a bad impression it must be making on us to see so splendid a banquet, at which the least of his servants has a place, whilst his soldiers, who're sacrificing their lives for him, lack even bread and water.'

Yet even this doesn't lessen the Napoleonic charisma. And when, at 6 p.m., the Emperor comes out of his tent,

'the Royal Guard salute him with the usual acclamations. Napoleon is hatless, has his sword at his side. A folding chair is brought him. Sitting down on it, he puts some questions to two vélites on sentry duty at the entrance of his tent. His expressive features bear the imprint of health and vitality. Turning to an officer of the same vélites, the one closest to him, he asks him what the effectives of his regiment are, how many men have been lost on the march; whether there are many sick. The officer replies: "Sire, we have some companies which still haven't lost one man from Italy to here." Without showing any surprise, the Emperor replies: "What! They're still as strong as when they left Milan?" "Yes, Your Majesty." Then, after a brief pause: "Your regiment still hasn't measured itself against the Russians?" "No, Sire, but it's eagerly looking forward to doing so."'

Glancing at the 'old "moustaches" of Austerlitz', Napoleon reminds them that the blood of the Romans runs in their veins, and that they must never forget it. As de Laugier's comrades are listening spellbound to his every word, a senior Austrian officer, 'his simple white uniform contrasting singularly with the rich coats of the officers around the Emperor', is announced. He has brought a despatch from Schwarzenberg. So many years the whitecoats have been the Italians' enemy! 'He hands the Emperor an envelope, then follows him into his tent.' The Italians tell one another that he's come to report Schwarzenberg's junction with Reynier's Saxons and his imminent arrival on the scene.[6]

But next morning, says Caulaincourt, Napoleon returned to Witebsk 'in a deep gloom'.

As well he might.

CHAPTER 12

WORRIES AT WITEBSK

Its superb churches – a dingy headquarters – Napoleon's tetchiness – 'the army is lost' – 'why wait here for eight months?' – 'the Emperor is being deceived' – 'the heat's worse than in Paris' – Dr Mestivier is called in – 'the insolent arrogant Goliath' – Dumonceau fights off ants – a very pretty Spaniard – an Italian victory – Lejeune visits II Corps – a messenger from Schwarzenberg

Witebsk lies on the left bank of the Dwina at a point where it 'flows along a deep broad bed, two-thirds dry in summer, leaving on each side a broad sandy beach that reaches up to the foot of high vertical cliffs'. Seen from afar Witebsk pleases Captain *Berthezène* by its 'smiling appearance'. And to Captain Bonnet of the 18th Line 'its many churches and immense monasteries' had announced 'a great city with some impressive buildings, in the same style as Polotsk'. Franz Roeder, turning up a fortnight later with the Hessians, will admire

'the dusky golden darkness of the ancient church of Ivan Boheslav and the fine icons on its screen, separating nave from sanctuary, the altar, the towers, and the bells hung on both sides of the street. Also the great and very beautiful church of St Zapor, whose high altar is concealed by a screen covered in gold and wonderful paintings, and whose bells are hung deep in one of the two front towers which, being roofed with copper and golden balls, shine magnificently from a distance.'

While thinking the Jesuits' church – 'overlaid with an enormous amount of gold and ornamentation, where the simple Poles must feel themselves to be in the antechamber of the Lord God Himself' – a bit tasteless, he'll none the less be impressed by it, too. And find 'the charming new post office and the hexagonal street lamps flanking the main street' wholly to his taste; likewise the 'Vauxhall' [pleasure park] on Castle Hill, 'among avenues of silver birches, with a little wooden temple, a swing and a dance-hall'.

Otherwise Witebsk isn't much of a place. Entering it, the invaders are 'very disagreeably surprised' to find it criss-crossed by ravines. 'From the outside the houses, all higgledy-piggledy, small, low and built of wood, have the most wretched appearance' and their interiors offer Berthezène, at least, no comfort. Even the governor's palace, on the main square, is of timber. Fain, settling in, is disgusted to find that

'apart from several large rooms suited to a headquarters, hardly a few sticks of furniture are to be found in it. But we've soon made up the Emperor's lodging (a carpet of green cloth, the maps laid out, the book box, the big portfolio, the nécessaire and the little iron bed, these everywhere suffice for him). The rest of its layout offers only garrets.'

Outside its windows the main square is encumbered by 'a lot of miserable huts', and since this won't do for a parade ground they are to be imperiously demolished. But the heat is so extreme that the party of Guard sappers put on this fatigue take five days over it. An antique chapel also has to go. Constant, the First Valet, sees the inhabitants assemble

'in great numbers, loudly expressing their displeasure. But the Emperor has permitted them to take away the sacred objects and they've calmed down. We saw them with great pomp carry away some very tall wooden saints, which they deposited in other churches.'

As usual, only the Guard is being given billets. Riding through on 31 July, Dumonceau[1] sees the houses 'for as far as three miles around full of soldiers of the Young Guard. We saw them at all the open casement windows, busy sprucing themselves up and repairing their clothing, etc.' And he hopes similar lodgings have been reserved for himself. 'Witebsk has lost its inhabitants,' notes Réné Bourgeois. 'Never again will its population offer so numerous an affluence, or so brilliant!'

Brilliant perhaps. But though one of Napoleon's first measures on returning to the town has been to order the construction of 36 bakers' ovens, the food shortage is no less keen and frustrating than at Vilna. A day or two later Captain Faré of the 2nd Guard Grenadiers writes home that,

'prices are higher here than in Paris. Everything is madly expensive. The people at Imperial Headquarters are rich and pay for everything with its weight in gold. And we're obliged to pay at the same rate. A pound of butter sells at forty sous, a white loaf at thirty, and vegetables in proportion. So far we've been given no allowance, and there's no sign of us getting any.'

Fain sees his master 'with Count Mathieu Dumas calculating that each oven can yield 30,000 bread rations'. 'No one,' says Fézensac,

'concerned himself more with the army's supplies and hospitals than Napoleon did. But giving orders wasn't enough. They also had to be capable of being carried out.'

The bread rations may be sufficing for the Guard, or anyway part of it. But even Boulart's gunners, bivouacked for eight days on end in the blazing heat on the debris of the Russian army's camp and without even a tree to shade them, are getting neither bread nor meat, and he is having

'to send out marauding parties to get us cattle, sheep, wheat, oats or flour. After which we had to do our own slaughtering, grinding and cooking.'

If this is the state of affairs in the Guard artillery it is *a fortiori* worse in the Line. After a couple of days Dedem, too, is having to send out whole battalions 'to distances of 20 to 25 miles, so as not to die of starvation'. Apparently there's plenty to be obtained from such maraudings, even if few perhaps are faring as well as Captain François' company of the 30th Line, who never 'lack for anything. My men used the rights given to them,

and I often had five to nine carts full of victuals following me on the way
back.'

The Russians' vanishing act has clearly given Napoleon a shock. Rarely if
ever has anyone seen him in such a tetchy mood. Each morning he
reviews one Guard brigade on the enlarged main square. 'The Emperor
insisted on everyone turning out. In the presence of the general staff and
the assembled Guard he went into the smallest details of the army's
administration.' The detested commissaries and the medical officers are
'summoned and obliged to declare the state of their supplies'. How are
the sick being treated in the hospitals? How many dressings have been got
together for the wounded? "You don't realize how sacred your task is!" he
barks at them. "All you want to do is to sleep between white sheets! It's in
the open air, it's in the mud one must sleep! Glory doesn't lie in soft ways,
it's only found in privations!"'

This tirade makes 'a very bad impression' on at least one veteran.
General Delaborde, commanding a division of the Young Guard,[2] is a man
who 'walked with a limp, liked to crack solemn-faced jokes and was
endowed with an intrepid heart that drew all with it', tells Paul de
Bourgoing, whom he has taken over from the 5th Tirailleurs as his interpreter:

'I don't take the Emperor's bad temper this morning as a good
omen. He fulminated against his commissaries to console the fighting men who were present. But our grenadiers have feelings no less
sensitive than ours. They looked sarcastic, and soon they'll be
demanding bread of him, not words.'

But the reprimands continue. The bridge over the Dwina not being built
quickly enough, old General Chasseloup of the Engineers, too, is told
crudely: 'You engineer officers, you're never ready. When we need you,
that's fine. But when we don't need you any longer, we don't give a damn
for you.' Witnessing the scene from only a few paces away, even the usually
uncritical Soltyk finds himself reflecting that

'what rendered General Chasseloup's position sadder was that a fine
but abundant rain was falling, and this old and respectable warrior,
whose head was bald, was standing there in front of the Emperor hat
in hand, without the latter telling him to put it on again.'

But what shocks everyone most of all is the Emperor's treatment of the
army's universally loved and admired chief surgeon, Baron *Dominique
Larrey*. Although the army's medical service has been grievously neglected
and Larrey's reiterated requests for adequate supplies have been largely
ignored,[3] its indefatigable chief has seen to it that

'all the 2,300 men wounded in the fighting of 25-7 July had received
first aid on the field of battle. I myself had carried out 56 of the 100
amputations, and only eight of my patients had died,'

- a miracle of improvisation, seeing that the ambulances still haven't
caught up. 'We had to use the soldiers' linen to give first aid, and even use

our own shirts.' And now sick and wounded are lying all jumbled up on the floors of Witebsk's magnificent churches. Although they, fortunately, at least have wooden floorboards, Caulaincourt, ordered to visit these hotbeds of infection, is deeply shocked. Whereon Napoleon visits them himself – and bombards Larrey with reproaches. 'Not one of the *commissaires-ordonnateurs*, solely concerned with formalities of administration and the triplication of requisition forms, opened his mouth to defend me.' Suffocating with indignation, Larrey tries to defend himself. But already Napoleon has turned on his heel and walked out. Everyone is shaken. It's the first time he's ever had a hard word for 'the most honourable man I've ever known'.

But facts speak louder than words. Returning to his own headquarters, Larrey immediately sends in a detailed report, attaching copies of all his fruitless requests for medical supplies. And at his levée next morning Napoleon ostentatiously pushes the other generals aside, comes up to him, and takes him by both hands: 'Now I know what's been going on! I want you to know that I regard you as one of the State's best servants and as my friend.' Larrey's report is forwarded to the no less hard-working and devoted Intendant-General Mathieu Dumas, 'to know why linen has been lacking on the field of battle'.

The explanation is simple. Most of the ambulances' horses have died en route.

Mounting indiscipline is another worrying factor, particularly in the Guard. And Caulaincourt's younger brother Auguste, he who'd looked so sombre on that hillock by the Niemen, is detailed to set things to rights. Likewise two other high-ranking officers, one to discipline the cavalry, the other the infantry.

Since entering Poland the army has marched nearly 900 miles. By now only two-thirds of the effectives that 'with joyous acclamations' had crossed the Niemen are still with the eagles. Vilna, its most advanced base, lies 200 miles to its rear. At least a third of the horses have died. And even to Colonel Boulart and his Guard gunners, who have 'done 650 leagues since La Fère, this distance seemed immense; and we liked to think we could go no further'. Everywhere in the rear thousands of 'stragglers are destroying everything'. Yet even marauding, writes the *Marquis de Chambray*[4], has been

> 'unable to provide bread, flour, enough brandy. There'd been no time to turn the grain into flour. Such mills as stood by the roads, not having been protected by safeguards, were being burnt and sacked. The food convoys had lagged behind and were no longer rejoining. Great numbers of hospitals had had to be set up, but were always insufficient and badly organized, and their sick could hardly be given the basic necessities, provisions not having been calculated for so great a number of sick men and been no less delayed than anything else that depended on transport.'

In these unprecedented circumstances all too many experienced men are beginning to feel that words and facts, intentions and realities, have parted company. Fézensac sees how 'men of sagacity and experience' are

'becoming more than a little worried. They asked themselves not merely what would become of this army if it were beaten, but how it could even support further losses from more marches and more serious combats.'

Paul de Bourgoing, who's busy cutting up General Delaborde's copy of the unwieldy campaign map and glueing it on to two dozen of his chief's red-and-white check handkerchiefs, is noticing that it's 'more especially the old thinkers, those we called the 'brain-diggers' [*les songe-creux*] if they were officers, and 'the old grumblers' [*les vieux grognards*] if they were rankers, who were murmuring'. Dedem has a subordinate who falls exactly into this category. One of his three colonels, 'a distinguished and very intelligent officer, albeit of a sardonic disposition', Colonel Pouchelon, commanding the 33rd Line, had fought at Eylau. He is married to a wealthy Polish girl, and has local acquaintances. One day he takes Dedem aside and tells him frankly: 'I'm sending all my effects to the rear. The army is lost.'

As for the ex-diplomat Dedem himself, General Friant is finding him altogether too much the sea-lawyer; and says so to Napoleon. When the Dutchman dares admire the Russian retreat, he's 'told coldly that there was no such word as retreat in the French army's dictionary. Nevertheless I hoped ours would by and by be as elegant.'[5]

What to do? Advance still further? Retreat? Stay put? Witebsk hasn't even a town wall, only the endless palings we see in Chagall's paintings. Least of all will it be defensible in winter, when the Dwina will freeze and lose its strategic significance. Yet retreat is unthinkable. The political effect incalculable. So what to do? There are times when Napoleon, who in odd moments is reading the history of Charles XII,[6] seems to be seriously considering digging in at Witebsk.

'We shan't commit the same folly,' he tells Narbonne airily. 'We must stay here this year and finish the war off next spring.' In vain Caulaincourt tries to disabuse him of an idea he is venting ever more often: that 'the winter here is no worse than in Paris, only longer'. And when Caulaincourt, who has shivered through four severe winters at Petersburg, assures him it's indeed not merely much longer but very much worse, he just makes fun of him.

But the Master of the Horse sees that all talk of wintering at Witebsk is in fact only talk: 'He saw clearly that the French liked active, not defensive warfare. "Not merely does winter threaten us with its frosts. It also menaces us with diplomatic intrigues,"' Napoleon explains to his ex-ambassador. And Seceretary Fain, observing him at even closer quarters, sees how two words are now obsessing him: 'Peace', and 'Moscow':

'Why wait here for eight months when twenty days' march are enough for us to reach our goal?' he asks him rhetorically in his office. 'We must be in Moscow within the month, under pain of never entering it! In war, luck is half of everything. If one always waited for a coincidence of completely favourable conditions one would never finish anything off.' A successful battle, he assures his Second Secretary, will enable him to threaten either of Russia's two capitals:

'Peace and Moscow will accomplish and terminate my warlike expeditions. The European System will have been founded, and it'll simply be a question of organizing it. The cause of the century will have won out, and the Revolution be accomplished. No longer will it be a question of accommodating it with the one it hasn't destroyed. This enterprise is mine. I've given it long-term preparation, perhaps at the expense of my popularity. No matter. My glory will be in the success and in my equity. Back in France, in the bosom of the fatherland, great, strong and magnificent, tranquil and glorious, I shall associate my son with me as Emperor. My dictatorship will be over.'

All this is very well, but belongs to a highly speculative future. And Ségur – just at how close quarters the assistant prefect of the palace is observing him is hard to say – sees Napoleon at Witebsk as a man in the throes of an impossible choice,

'straying about his apartments, as if pursued by this dangerous temptation [to march on Moscow]. He takes up his work, drops it, and takes it up again. He walks aimlessly about, asks what time it is and, utterly preoccupied, comes to a halt. Then he begins to hum, and walks on again. In his perplexity he addresses these words to anyone he meets: "Well, what shall we do then? Shall we stay here? Shall we advance further? How halt on so glorious a course?" Not waiting for an answer, he goes on wandering about. He seems to be looking for something or someone to make up his mind for him. Finally, altogether overwhelmed by the weight of so considerable a thought, and as if overcome by such immense uncertainty, he throws himself down on one of the rest couches he's had laid out on the floors of his rooms.'

History? Or literature? Sheer romantic novel-writing, declares Gourgaud scornfully. Yet that Napoleon is an insomniac is no secret to his First Valet:

'More in this campaign than in any other the Emperor often got up at nights, put on his dressing-gown and worked in his office. Very often he suffered from bouts of insomnia he couldn't overcome. Then, his bed seeming insupportable to him, he'd suddenly get out of it, went over and picked out a book and while walking to and fro began to read. Feeling his head a bit refreshed, he went back to bed. It was rare for him to sleep straight through two nights in succession.'

And Ségur goes on drawing his pen-portrait:

'Impatience seizes on him. We see how restless he is, either weighed down by inaction or preferring danger to the boredom of waiting, or agitated by hope. The image of Moscow obsesses his mind. Already we're beginning to foresee that so ardent a genius, restless, accustomed to taking short cuts, won't wait eight months, now he feels his goal is within reach. At first he seems not to dare to admit to so great a temerity, even to himself; but little by little he's getting used to it. Then he deliberates; and this great irresolution, tormenting his spirit, takes possession of his whole person.'

At times he agrees with Caulaincourt that he's gone far enough. But then 'the thousand and one things that ought to have opened his eyes vanish before the slightest incident that can revive his hopes – a captured Russian officer who promises battle in front of Smolensk, for instance. He believes there'll be a battle because he wants one. And believes he'll win it because it's essential he shall. No amount of reasoning can enlighten him. The spectacle of his soldiers, their enthusiasm at the sight of him, the reviews and parades, and above all the King of Naples' and certain other generals' frequently coloured reports have gone to his head.'

And all the time the atmosphere in the rickety old timber palace overlooking the town square is becoming more and more tense. Even Lieutenant Bourgoing, tagging along in Delaborde's suite, notices how 'unusually careless the Emperor is in his expressions when speaking to his officers'. Poniatowski's V Corps not having caught up on time, one of the prince's ADCs is told rudely: 'Your prince is just a cunt.'

Never, says Caulaincourt, have his colleagues 'seen the Emperor in such a touchy state of mind'. He has taken a dislike to Berthier's staff, and in particular to Count Monthyon, 'its moving spirit'. Likewise to Dumas, the zealous head of the administration. Also to Paymaster-General Joinville. Poor nail-biting Berthier is being 'snapped at all day long':

'Duroc, without yielding, wrapped himself in a cloak of impassivity. Lobau became rude. As for Caulaincourt and Daru, the one turned pale and the other flushed with anger. The former impetuous and dogged, the latter dry and cold, they vehemently contradicted the Emperor's denials of the facts.'

Daru, in particular, isn't mincing his words. 'War's a game you're good at,' he tells Napoleon bluntly. 'But here we aren't fighting men, we're fighting nature.' But few make so bold or speak so to the point. If the always critical Dedem van der Gelder can 'find one excuse for Napoleon, it's the cruel way in which he was being deceived by the reports made to him'. For instance by Friant,

'a man of handsome physique, a martial air, and brave, not malicious, but whose manners when he let himself go a bit reminded one of his origins as a simple grenadier in the Royal Guard. He was a real master of manoeuvre. Otherwise "only intelligent on the field of battle", as his brother- in-law Davout agreed.'

When news comes in that the admired Dorsenne, commander of the two Guard grenadier regiments, has died in Paris, it's Friant who's publicly given the accolade and promoted to succeed him – but asked, even so, to remain with his division for the campaign:

'You'll be more useful there than at the head of these veterans who march of their own accord. Besides, I'm always close to them, and you're one of those rare men I'd like to see everywhere I'm not,' Napoleon tells him. Yet Friant isn't hesitating to flatter Napoleon's wishes by making nonsense of d'Ideville's patient statistical work. His division, Dumas tells Napoleon, has food for ten days,

> 'whereas we were already at our wits' end to get any at all. As usual, I spoke my mind plainly about our position, and had a violent altercation with Friant. He wanted me to produce a report on the 33rd Line and say it amounted to 3,200 men, whilst I knew that in reality no more than 2,500 men, at most, were left. Friant, who was under Murat's orders, said Napoleon would be angry with his chief. He preferred to introduce an error. And Colonel Pouchelon provided the mendacious report required.'

Later Dedem hears from Lobau that the army's effectives have been inflated by 35,000 men.

Likewise the food supplies – something even such veterans as Captain François instinctively understand:

> 'Despite all the care the Emperor took to get us food, his orders were only being carried out on paper. He was being fooled by the administrators' returns. These brigands led him to believe the army had been given victuals and was provisioned for a fortnight.'

Worst of all is the heat. It's terrific. Over and over again in his almost daily letters to Marie-Louise[7] Napoleon keeps mentioning 'the unbearable heat, 27 degrees [Réaumur]. It's as hot as in the South' (2 August): and on 7 August: 'The heat here is worse than in Paris, we're suffocating.'

Never before has Constant seen his master so bothered by the weight of his own clothes. Vain though he is about his hands' whiteness, the Emperor is breaking his invariable habit of wearing gloves when he goes out and is allowing his hands to get sunburnt. Nor is he sleeping well. 'The Emperor has slept two hours,' Narbonne scribbles in his diary:

> 'He has been physically very poorly [très souffrant]. He has taken some opium, prepared by Dr Méthivier:[8] "Duroc, we must march or die. An Emperor dies on his legs; and then he doesn't die at all. You're afraid of the Prussians, between Moscow and France. Remember Iéna, and rely even more on their fear than their hatred. But for that we must march, we must act."'

And again, almost illegibly: 'The Emperor has been ill again. "We must put an end to this fever of doubt".' One morning he shows Narbonne the dawn,

> 'already brightening on the horizon. "We've still almost three months of fine weather ahead of us," he told me. "I needed less than that for Austerlitz and Tilsit."'

But ill or well, nothing abates his activity. 'During night's silent hours' Fain sees him

'studying his regiments' and the various army corps' returns. He compares them with those of a fortnight ago, to know his losses in detail and how they've been compensated for. With equal attentiveness he consults the bulletin of troops on the march. In it he follows from day to day the arrival of his reinforcements, never letting a moment go by when he can give them fresh orders. In this way he contrives to know the enemy army just about as well as he knows his own.[9] Perhaps even better.'

From now on Lelorgne d'Ideville 'who understands and speaks Russian' is always to ride behind him. And the daily routine of top-speed dictations goes on unimpeded. Caulaincourt's courier service, too, is functioning impeccably. Each day the locked leather despatch cases brought by relays of couriers are arriving and leaving. 'Each day the Paris courier is being opened, read and replied to. The private correspondence with the Duke of Bassano at Vilna is no less regular.'

Newspapers, too, are arriving. Not always with good news. Here's a worrying item. The Turks have made peace with Russia "precisely at the moment when they should have made war on their traditional enemies. It's such a gross mistake I could never have foreseen it!" declares Napoleon; and fires off a reprimand to Maret at Vilna for not having out-lavished the British gold at Constantinople. Another almost equally unpleasant item throws doubt on Sweden's neutrality:

"Bernadotte is quite capable of forgetting he's a Frenchman by birth. But the Swedes are too energetic and enlightened not to revenge themselves for all the injuries done them since the days of Peter the Great,"

is Napoleon's comment. That the Tsar is in Moscow, arousing popular patriotic feeling, he knows already; also that the city's governor, a certain Count Rostopchin, is assembling men and money for its defence. But what's this? Far from thinking of calling it a day and making peace, here's his 'brother' Alexander, declaring a 'national' – not merely a 'political' – war against him; and what that can mean the French already know from Spain. And what's this? The Moscow Archimandrite, head of the Russian Orthodox Church, is calling him

'a Moloch, the insolent, arrogant Goliath from the frontiers of France, a tyrant who wants to destroy the whole earth. The religion of peace, that sling of David, shall soon bring him down and cut off the head of his bloodthirsty arrogance.'

'These expressions of hatred he had repeated to him several times,' Fain goes on:

'They astonished and disquieted him. Who had been instrumental in bringing about such a change in the Tsar's mind? His own moderation concerning the fate of Poland, which had upset and cooled the

Poles, had been partly due to his wish for a political settlement with Russia; which was now declaring him an outlaw.'

One day a rumour passes through the army that Alexander, like Tsar Paul before him, has been assassinated, on suspicion of suing for peace. And next morning at his levée Napoleon, 'with a joyous and satisfied air' announces it for a fact, only for it to turn out shortly afterwards to have been unfounded.[10]

Altogether his political position is hardly less problematic than the military one. It's no revolutionary army that is bivouacked around Witebsk, but an imperial one. And when the local gentry complain that the

'peasants in the surroundings, hearing people talk of liberty and independence, have thought themselves authorized to rise against their lords, and are indulging in the most abandoned licence,'

the usual flying columns are immediately sent out to crush them. 'It was a question of stopping a movement that could degenerate into a civil war. Some examples are made. And order is soon re-established' – obviously to Fezensac's aristocratic satisfaction. Remarkably, the local landlords are even 'authorized to have the peasants arrest marauders, disarm them and bring them in'. And Chambray is astounded to see an

'altogether extraordinary spectacle: in the midst of our successes to see Lithuanian serfs marching our disarmed soldiers. Any who had been pillaging were condemned to death. Had this order been rigorously carried out, thousands of soldiers would have had to be shot, since marauding was the sole means of survival, no distributions having been made. Those on whom pillaged objects were found were brought before military courts. As many as 80 were judged at a time and condemned to death. But only two or three of the guiltiest were executed.'

Perhaps this is why Boulart's gunners are suddenly ordered to a village five miles away, where there's a fine Polish château 'which really merited the name'. Its mistress, however, is in town and has only left her furniture there. 'As for food, it was I who offered her some. This lady', says the flute-playing major, 'had a real Polish head, remarkably exalted, and held the Russians in horror.' If Napoleon will only re-establish the Kingdom of Poland, she tells him, the whole country will rise en masse to support him.

But that's exactly what he has decided not to do.

And here's some bad news for Colonel Tschüdi of the Joseph Napoleon Regiment. Quite unexpectedly here's little Coignet turning up with his surviving Spanish deserters, like 350 bad halfpennies. Who 'immediately they take to their heels to rejoin their regiment'. Tschüdi is 'so furious with them he wants to have them all shot, too'. Only when Coignet points out that they've had their pardon and 'only the Emperor himself can reverse it' does their Swiss colonel drop the idea.

And here's another, less questionable reinforcement. Disappointed in their hopes of comfortable billets in town and bivouacked on the sandy

plain beyond the town where they're doing outpost duty 'to protect imperial headquarters on that side', the Red Lancers suddenly receive an
afflux of 200 fresh men from their Versailles depot, 'mainly former hussars of our 3rd Dutch Regiment, back from Spain. This brings the regiment's effectives, already reduced to 600 of the horses it had counted
when leaving Versailles,' up to 800, i.e., to four-fifths of its original
strength. Dumonceau, whose company now numbers 102 troopers, is

'making the best of a certain abundance of straw to build myself a
good hut with two compartments, provided with a table and a bench,
where I was perfectly at my ease from the hot sunshine and the rain.
I busied myself with my correspondence, interrupted since Königsberg. Now bread was arriving regularly from the town, which further
provided us with all sorts of stores,'

including sugar. But though Dumonceau puts his little larder under his
pillow, 'safe from gourmands', it's only to have it gobbled up by... ants.

Vélite-Sergeant *François Bourgogne* of the Young Guard's Fusiliers-
Grenadiers was very likely one of the lucky ones whom Dumonceau had
seen polishing their arms in comfortable billets when he'd first ridden
into the town. No sooner had Bourgogne settled in than he'd been visited
by 'twelve young men from my own part of the country [Condé]; ten were
drummers, one a drum-major, and the twelfth a corporal of voltigeurs.
They all wore side-arms.' Alas, he has nothing to offer them; but the
drum-major insists on his going back with them to share some 'wine, gin,
and other things that'll do you good' and which his unit has

'taken from the Russian general, together with a little cart holding
his kitchen. "We've put it all into the canteen cart with our cantinière. Florencia's a pretty Spaniard. She might be taken for my wife:
I protect her – honourably, I can tell you!" As he said this he struck
the hilt of his long rapier. "She's a good woman: ask the others – no
one dares say anything else. She took a fancy to a sergeant, who was
to have married her: but he was murdered by a Spaniard from
Bilbao, and until she's chosen someone else she must be taken care
of."

'We sat down near the cantinière's cart,' Sergeant Bourgogne goes on.
'She really was a very pretty Spaniard, and she was overjoyed to see us, as
we'd just come from her own country, and could speak her language
pretty well – the dragoon Flament best of all. So we spent the night in
drinking the Russian general's wine and talking of our own country.'

But not everything is pretty, and some things are hideous. One such
warm evening as Dedem is taking a stroll behind his brigade's line of huts
he's horrified to hear a grenadier boasting to a comrade: 'D'you remember the damned face that little bugger made when I had him on my bayonet and was putting him closer and closer to the fire, and how his mother
screamed?' Dedem says his recruits 'were tender-hearted enough, but
many old soldiers had lost all sensibility'. As for the Spaniards, they'd long

remained well-disciplined, 'but once let loose they surpassed the French in horrors and abominations'.

Lieutenant Paul de Bourgoing, for his part, is finding life much more agreeable than in the arduous days when he'd been Colonel Hennequin's factotum. Delaborde's staff consists of 'two ADCs, a surgeon and a major-domo with the irreproachable turn-out of a maître d'hôtel of one of today's fine houses'. There too are a Polish lancer called Gorski and a Prussian gunner. All are enjoying a superior standard of living. 'From that moment my depression passed over. I was surrounded by people I liked, and that's the first condition of contentment' – especially as Bourgoing's admiration for his 48-year-old general knows no bounds. One day some straw catches fire close to some ammunition wagons. Their crews and everyone else run for their lives. But Delaborde just limps over and calmly quenches the flames.

The delicate Planat de la Faye, by contrast, isn't feeling at all well. Ever since the shock of the Russians' rope-trick he's been

'so ill and so weakened by continual dysentery that I was tempted to quit the army. But the point of honour kept me there, and it's true to say that in the army, by a sort of state of grace and without ceasing to do one's job, one puts up with illnesses which in any other place would lay you out on your pallet. What's more, you recover without being missed or having a doctor.'

Some of the stores being gratefully consumed by Dumonceau may well have come from a small but welcome victory won by the Italians. 'Immediately on halting at Witebsk,' Fain had written in his private journal, 'the Emperor ordered the Viceroy to push outposts towards Nevel, by the Surash–Veleija road', chiefly to get news of II Corps' operations against Wittgenstein. On 1 August, at the junction of the rivers Carplia and Dwina and of the Moscow and Petersburg roads, General Villata's Italian brigade and a battalion of Croats had just been about to enter the Jewish town of Surash, 'the most advanced point yet reached by the French armies', and were finding it full of stores, when some men of the 2nd Italian Chasseurs reported that a weakly escorted enemy convoy was trying to cross the river to get to Veleija-Luki. Immediately Eugène had ordered his Russian-speaking ADC Colonel Bianco to take 200 picked men and grab it. After a 27-mile march they'd sighted the convoy – escorted, Césare de Laugier hears afterwards, by four infantry battalions and 300 cavalry. The cavalry tries to cover the infantry just as it's about to cross the bridge over the Dwina:

'Realizing they can't escape us, the Russian force forms square on the far side of the Dwina and entrenches itself behind its carts and vehicles. Though outnumbered, Colonel Bianco orders the charge to be sounded; the Russian cavalry are put to flight, and his own men are received with a shower of musketballs. A deep ditch protects the Russian kraal; but the remains of a causeway enable two Italians to cross it at a time. Bianco is wondering what to do. His chasseurs' shouts, demanding to be allowed to charge, tell him. Headed by Quartermaster-sergeant Grassini, five frontal charges are made, to no avail. Finally they manage to penetrate a weak spot in the impro-vised wheeled fortress and take 500 prisoners and 150 vehicles filled with food and ammunition. We lost some 40 men, killed or wound-ed, among them six officers.'

Would the Italians be allowed to keep their spoils? Certainly part of them. On the other hand Eugène must have known that Grouchy had been rep-rimanded for not sending the fruits of his Orsha coup to Glubokoië; and at Surash his Italians are

'living in a state of penury which is, in fact, a trifle too great. En-camped far from river banks, we're suffering horribly from thirst. To get at water, the men are digging down into the soil with their bayo-nets, and even if they're so happy as to find some, it's so terribly muddy it can't even be drunk until it's been filtered through their handkerchiefs.'

'Faithful to their system,' Ceesare de Laugier goes on,

'the Russians (wherever we've left them time to) have been burning almost all the stores, scattering the harvests, and destroying every-thing they haven't been able to carry off. This has thrown the various corps back on to living off their own resources and making trouble-some excursions whose only result is to destroy the bases of disci-pline, impoverish the population and exasperate it against us.'

But necessity knows no law. The Bavarian chasseurs have just rejoined IV Corps; and one day Lieutenant *Albrecht von Muraldt* is doing a little marauding on his own account when he bumps into no less a personage than General Montbrun, 'who bawled me out, even saying something about having me shot and so forth'. But taking Montbrun's 'hellfire ser-mon' for the empty threat it certainly is, he gets safely back to his bivouac 'with some brandy and bread'.

Away to the north, near Polotsk, a kind of stalemate has arisen between Oudinot and Wittgenstein, who instead of letting himself be pushed back on Petersburg is 'manoeuvring with considerable ability between II and X Corps'. On 1 August Oudinot had lured General Koulnieff across the Dwina, where he'd run headlong into a masked battery of 40 French guns. Koulnieff's force had been annihilated and he himself had been killed. Oudinot had captured fourteen guns, thirteen ammunition wagons and more than 2,000 prisoners. But the success (for which Marbot in his boastful way claims exclusive credit) hadn't been followed up, and Verdier's division had been driven back on to the French camp. 'I've seen few battlefields which offered such a picture of carnage,' Oudinot had written home. 'The ground for two miles is covered with their dead.' Thereafter both sides had retired – Oudinot into Polotsk. And on 5 August an irritated Napoleon sends off d'Hautpoul to Polotsk, with orders not to return 'until he can give an account of the Russians' defeat'. That same evening (whether conformably to the usual duplication of despatches or for some other reason Fain doesn't say) Lejeune, too, is sent off. After finding a shortcut by fording the Dwina and 'having with difficulty covered a distance of 105 miles', he reaches Polotsk after 24 hours, and is received in style by Oudinot in the Jesuits' great building, where the marshal explains to him how 'the Russians, by letting themselves be driven back, are trying to draw the French into a desert, where they'll be destroyed by hunger'. This is the sole reason – Lejeune can tell His Majesty – why, after several reverses but also such a signal success, he, Oudinot, has withdrawn to Polotsk, there 'undelayedly to issue his men with rations and put them into a state to begin anew'.

All this may be true. But Lejeune finds II Corps shockingly depleted, hardly 20,000 men. Dysentery, typhus, desertion and exhaustion have already reduced it to half-strength. 'Of the 2,000 men of the 1st Swiss who'd left Paris,' Captain *Louis Begos*[11] of the 2nd Swiss assures us, 'hardly 1,200 were in a state to fight.'

Fain explains that Napoleon's planning always allowed for reverses; and his response to Oudinot's request for reinforcements had been to send him St-Cyr's Bavarians. This should have been an adequate blood transfusion. But the Germans – all witnesses agree – didn't have the French flair for marauding and 'wanted to cook everything properly and get a full night's sleep'. Already starved of rations, VI Corps' wretched Bavarians are now suffering worse than anyone. On 6 August, after retracing many endless miles, they're seen by Franz Roeder just as he and his faithful sergeant-major Vogel are comfortably installing themselves in Beschenkowiczi castle. 'Surprised to see them so mightily cast down, and the soldiers dragging themselves so wearily along,' Roeder wonders whether there can even be two-thirds of the number that had crossed the Niemen; and concludes that it's their officers' fault for not taking better care of them. Many more will die en route, some only a mile and a half from Polotsk, where Colonel St-Chamans will see

'such a terrible epidemic raging among the Bavarians that they almost all fell sick, and died in their thousands. Men who were well yesterday, fell ill in the morning and were dead by evening. When they left the camp only 3,000 remained.'

For four days Lejeune follows Oudinot's movements as his corps again drives back the Russians, 'without anything of note happening, except the difficulty of feeding the army in this land of sands, forests and lakes. On 11 August, after working with the Duke and General Gouvion de St-Cyr, I left again for Witebsk.' But when he gets there he finds Napoleon in no mood to reckon with troublesome realities beyond his reach. In Oudinot's explanations of his inactivity he sees only excuses. By advancing on Opotscka and Novorjev he was convinced the marshal would have found the means to feed his army. So back to Polotsk goes Lejeune, this time to order Oudinot to 'keep abreast of the main army' in its advance on

Smolensk – for that, in spite of everything, is what Napoleon has in mind.

Meanwhile all important communications with the Austrians are being carried by another of Berthier's ADCs. On 2 August Colonel Flahaut, the 'best dancer and biggest ladykiller in France'[12] had left for Schwarzenberg's headquarters, followed next day, Fain says, by 'a trusty Polish officer with a duplicate of the same order'. According to Captain *Joseph Grüber,*[13] a Bavarian in the Austrian service, Schwarzenberg 'didn't dare do anything without orders from Napoleon'. And this is why he has sent Grüber with a despatch of his own, requesting instructions:

'I travelled as fast as I could by mail coach. Reaching the spot where the great Emperor, on horseback and surrounded by his marshals, was waiting for some troops to march past, I jump out, apply to an officer of his entourage, and am immediately taken to Marshal Duroc, to whom I hand my despatch. Duroc rides over to Napoleon, ordering me to follow. Napoleon takes a pinch of snuff from his waistcoat pocket – always, as I've learnt afterwards, full of tobacco – throws me a sombre glance, reads the despatch and says to me: "Do you speak French?" "Fluently, Your Majesty." "Good," the Emperor says, taking another pinch of snuff from his waistcoat pocket. And asks one of his generals, whom I was afterwards told was Berthier, for the map of Volhynia. At the same time he orders Duroc to inhibit the troops' march-past, and together with myself begins examining the map. Questioning me on the operations of Schwarzenberg's corps, he follows with the forefinger of his right hand each point I indicate to him on the map as having been the theatre of our struggles. And finally says to me: "My friend, you're well informed!" Then, turning to Berthier, he tells him that Schwartzenberg's report agrees perfectly with my exposé. Whereupon he most amiably orders me to accompany Duroc and get all necessary instructions for Schwarzenberg from the bureau of operations. "Tell your Field Marshal", the Emperor concluded, "to hurry up and turn back on his tracks and disengage General Reynier at Kowel; and get back as quickly as ever you can. It's urgent."'

After 'a plenteous *déjeuner à la fourchette* washed down with a bottle of champagne' while waiting for his instructions, Grüber leaves again by coach. And next day reports to Schwartzenberg. His mission, he claims, would prove crucial to the Austrians' and Saxons' fate. 'Had they advanced into Old Russia they too must infallibly have perished.'

CHAPTER 13

THE GREAT MANOEUVRE

A strategic masterstroke – Sébastiani routed a second time – the Grand Army concentrates at the 'Borysthenes' – Neverovski's fighting rearguard – Napoleon's 42nd birthday – Poniatowski doesn't understand politics – Coignet sent on mission – alarms and excursions at Witebsk – each army has its smell

Only one thing is more dangerous in warfare than to change one's lines of communication in the presence of the enemy, and that's to expose one's flank to him while doing so. Yet this is what Napoleon, behind all the grandiloquent talk, is now planning to do.

Between him and the two Russian armies, astride the Smolensk road, lies Murat's cavalry screen. And between all three and the Dnieper, to his right, lies a vast belt of primitive forests.[1] Each army corps being in principle able to move at any moment in any direction, Napoleon has been secretly planning to take advaantage of this forest, move I, III, IV, V, VIII Corps and the Guard crabwise, cross the Dnieper, and march swiftly on Smolensk, grab it, and – before Barclay and Bagration realize what's happening – attack them in the rear. Flung helter-skelter back on to Oudinot and St-Cyr – who it is to be hoped are advancing from Polotsk – both Russian armies will be caught in a gigantic trap and annihilated.

Orders have already been sent to the various corps to march for the river, and some have already broken camp, when on 8 August some unexpected news comes in. In pouring rain – the weather has suddenly broken – 10,000 (some say 12,000) Russian cavalry and Cossacks, supported by twelve guns, have flung themselves on Sébastiani's advance guard at Inkovo, and – for the second time in the campaign – routed it.

Vossler, Tascher, Roos and Aubry have all been in it. At first the Prussian and Polish cavalry stand firm. But then they're forced back through their own tents 'many of which were still standing, so that the guy-ropes kept tripping us up'. Lieutenant Tascher's horse is killed under him by the Russian guns and he owes his life to his sergeant-major who dismounts and gives him his own, only to be himself overwhelmed by Cossacks and taken prisoner.[2] Dr Roos too is entangled in the affray, but manages somehow or other to save all his wounded from capture. In the end the 24th Light, Sébastiani's forward infantry regiment, after putting up a staunch resistance, is forced to abandon its 'fine voltigeur battalion in a wood it couldn't get out of'. For a moment there's even a danger of a complete rout. But by and by Montbrun – some think much too tardily – comes up from Rudnia with the rest of II Cavalry Corps and its horse artillery, and saves the situation. After it's all over Vossler proudly notes in his diary that

'such a withdrawal as we carried out on this occasion can almost be regarded as a victory. Despite his immense superiority, the enemy

didn't at any time succeed in breaking our ranks.'
Which is to put a good face on it. Sébastiani has lost ten officers and 300 men; and a violent altercation breaks out between him and Montbrun who, Aubry explains, 'weren't on the best of terms, the inferior officer being in command of his superior'. Both are being widely blamed for the loss of a lot of cavalry and the voltigeur battalion.

Is this the beginning, at last, of a Russian counter-offensive? Napoleon immediately cancels his grand enveloping movement – a hesitation as to the enemy's movements reflected in those of the Red Lancers. They've just passed through Witebsk and in the afternoon of 9 August are already well on their way to the Rudnia road, and are getting ready to leave before daybreak next morning 'when urgent orders come to turn back at once towards Witebsk'. After retracing their steps for four or five hours they meet a convoy of wounded, who tell them all about the Inkowo affair and how the Cossacks' pursuit had only been halted by 'a regiment of Württemberg Chasseurs of their division, who'd formed square, thus giving I and II Cavalry Corps time to arrive and stem it'.

What's going to happen now? From what these casualties have to say it seems a new and more grave engagement is certainly imminent, though they're sure Ney's corps will be able to contain it.

Colbert thinks the matter over. Concludes that his regiment's support is no longer urgently needed. And bivouacs on a hilltop between Witbesk and Rudnia. Although the rain is still falling steadily, Dumonceau is enjoying a splendid view of the landscape, when he sees a horseman galloping towards him. It's one of Murat's ADCs 'on his way to IHQ, who tells us the enemy is definitely retreating'. Withdrawing his lancers a mile or two, Colbert grudgingly allows his captains to decide for themselves – on their own responsibility – whether to disperse their companies among nearby farms or to bivouac in the rain. Seizing this unexpected chance of a dry night, Dumonceau installs his company in

'a spacious farm with barns, less than half a mile from the one where regimental headquarters were. It was surrounded by high wooden walls, with only one exit, surmounted by a tall dovecote, whence we had a wide view out over the surroundings. I shut myself up in it, with all my unit sheltered in the barns. The entrance door was barricaded, and a sentry placed in the dovecote. It was like being in a fortress.'

But the Russians don't follow up their success.[3] And next day the grand operation across the Dnieper is resumed.

Everywhere the downpour is soaking the terrain. Liozna, on 11 August, is just a 'big village full of mud', where the artillery finds the going heavy, as do the Italians trudging through it all the long way to Liouvavitschi. There they see

'all the King of Naples' cavalry coming back from the environs of Rudnia and Inkowo – but instead of taking the Rudnia road it turned left, as before, to cross the Dnieper at a point much less far upstream than the place where we were to cross. The assembly of the entire army on the banks of this river proclaimed our overt intention of crossing it and attacking Smolensk by the left bank, to seize the town.'

And still the rain drenches down. Muddy marches and counter-marches are being made to find viable roads through a countryside almost void of inhabitants. Some have to be repaired by the sappers, who, 'better still, make a new one out of fascines, branches and earth'. Some of the corps are coming up via Orsha, others via Babinowiczi:

'This immense gathering of men at one point increased our misery and redoubled the confusion and disorder prevailing on the main roads. Lost soldiers were vainly looking for their regiments. Others carrying urgent orders could only execute them by encumbering the roads. The upshot was a frightful confusion on bridges and at defiles.'

At last, on 12 August, the rain gives over. And at dawn next day Dumonceau's men continue their march in brighter weather. The knowledge that they're approaching the 'Borysthenes' – limit of the ancient world – is setting all educated minds aquiver.[4] Aren't they the worthy descendants of ancient Greece and Rome? Who are going still farther? Césare de Laugier's glamorous reflections, however, evaporate

'when all we see is an ordinary little river flowing between narrow banks. Its waters are so steeply embanked you can hardly see the river until you actually come upon it.'

The road through the forests being blocked by Davout's corps, the Red Lancers don't reach the Dnieper until about midday. Across to Rossasna, 'a miserable-looking little town', three trestle bridges have just been thrown; and already the columns are pouring over. In the distance on the opposite bank Dumonceau sees

'III Cavalry Corps, recognizable by the 6th Hussars' red dolmans and the resplendant helmets of its dragoon division, deployed in the plain and moving towards the left in a long column. It was becoming obvious that the whole army was on the move and converging towards this point for some grand operation we'd been summoned to take part in',

and the panorama of which delights them. Dr Roos, too, sees 'crowds of infantry and huge artillery trains'. Obliged to wait until next day to cross, Dumonceau's regiment goes

'to bivouac on the left of the town in a hemp field, whose strong stalks, over six feet high, served for us to build excellent shelters. After that the entire Imperial Guard turned up successively. Ranging itself near us, it soon covered the surroundings for a distance of three miles, naturally causing a lively animation. Close by us they were raising the Emperor's tents. He was expected at any moment. This stimulated us to take particular care to make sure our camp was regularly laid out, thinking he might come and visit, or at least glance at it.'

Dumonceau is staggered by this

'mass of 170,000 men, assembled as if by magic at a given spot on the enemy's left, and dragging in its train a confused multitude of folk and carts and carriages, whose disordered mob seemed rather a migration of nomads, above all in view of a herd of cattle and sheep we saw moving to one side across the fields, escorted by a detachment of I Corps, which it belonged to.'

Although the ripe standing crops give the Guard cavalry plenty of forage for its horses, the fortnight's rations, issued at Witebsk, are already running out; and the supply wagons, as usual, haven't caught up:

'A few feeble distributions didn't at all meet our needs. The entire army marching en masse devoured the countryside's resources like a cloud of grasshoppers, without satisfying anyone's needs. Each of us had to live on any flour or grain he had with him. There was hardly any more question of bread or meat. We made soup of flour in water or biscuits baked in the ashes which now had to suffice to keep us alive.'

At about 6 or 7 p.m. on 14 August

'reiterated shouts of acclamation on all sides told us the Emperor had arrived. He didn't come to his tents at all, just went straight to join the advance guard, which we made haste to follow.'

That day Grouchy's van is riding through Liady – the easternmost town in Lithuania and 'the last where we saw any Jews' – and out along the great tree-lined highroad toward Krasnoië – the first in Russia – and the rest of Murat's cavalry and Davout's corps are coming on behind, when the whole mass suddenly and unexpectedly runs into resistance. Dumonceau's men, in their wake, are riding through Liady's

'single muddy street paved with logs, broken at various points, and going down a steep slope towards a stream whose half-broken bridge had been supplemented by two others hastily thrown on either side, and mounting the opposite bank to another similar plateau, when we hear the distant rumble of the guns, to which is added, more and more distinctly as we advance, the crackle of musketry'.

What opposition can this be? Certainly it's extremely dogged. By and by it becomes clear that Bagration has intentionally left behind a division at Krasnoië, 'at the intersection of the Constantinople-Petersburg road', precisely to guard against the eventuality of Napoleon trying to seize Smolensk by a *coup de main*. And now Neverovski's sixteen infantry battalions, four squadrons of dragoons and four of Cossacks and eight guns are stubbornly defending the threshold of Old Russia. First dividing his little army into two close columns, then forming a huge single compact 'filled' square, Neverovski, who has altogether too many raw recruits, is retreating slowly across the open plain, along the long straight Smolensk road with its double avenues of silver birches; and he's contesting every inch of the ground. Although Murat flings in wave after wave of cavalry, first Nansouty's cavalry corps, then Montbrun's cuirassiers, neither can make the least impression on this vast mass of Russian bayonets.

What's needed is grapeshot and canister.

Unfortunately, just behind Krasnoïe, Griois' guns have got bogged down in a steep and narrow defile.[5] And Murat, as usual, is altogether too impatient:

'Scarcely has the 2nd Württemberg Artillery got within the most efficient range for grapeshot, hardly has it opened fire to make a breach
in this mass of men and blast open a passage for the cavalry, than
Murat's boiling valour pushes regiment after regiment in front of
our battery and against this compact mass, several times charging it
himself, sabre in hand, without being able to break in. The gaps are
always closed up, leaving no traces.'

Even when breaches are made (Fain will note in his diary that evening) the

'very inexperience of the Russian peasants making up this force gave
them an inertia which took the place of resistance. This manoeuvre
repeated itself from each position to the next, until at last Neverovski
finds himself near a forest defile by which he escapes, having lost
2,000 men.'

Again the weather is blazing; and that evening the broad road, its silver birches hanging their silent boughs in the stupendous heat, is littered with dead and wounded. 'Such', says Dedem caustically, 'was the bloody affair of Krasnoïe, which Napoleon called a battle because he was present at it.' Although evidently he'd done his best to be. Advancing cross-country toward the sound of the guns, the Red Lancers had been overtaken by him at a gallop, 'followed by his numerous staff':

'Later we found him halted, on foot, standing by the roadside, holding a riding-whip, his left arm behind his back, in front of a fire
which had gone out and whose ashes he was absent-mindedly lashing
at, apparently heedless of the cries of Vive l'Empereur! the men were
incessantly saluting him with as they went by, more than ever because
of its being "Napoleon Day". He was alone, except for Prince Poniatowski, who in a most animated fashion seemed to be telling him
something. The staff were assembled at a certain distance.'

What were they talking about?

Ever since his V Corps, despite its immense efforts, had failed to grab Bagration by the tail, Napoleon's wrath with Jerome 'had fallen instead on Poniatowski, who had really made forced marches'. Poniatowski being liable to fits of melancholia and depression, this hadn't mended matters:

'I don't know whether it was on this solemn day his ADC Antoine
Potocki arrived at Napoleon's headquarters. But it seemed to me it
was only then we, the Polish officers of the Guard, heard how the
Polish army corps had dwindled. There were really no more than
11.000 under arms. Although we knew Dombrowski's division with a

brigade of cavalry had been detached from the main body,[6] we were overcome with sadness at the thought of Poland's military power being so feeble, above all just now, when the first real battle should shortly be taking place.'

Poniatowski has had to appeal to Davout to put in a word on his behalf. And now, standing there by the roadside as Colbert's lancers again file by, he's urging Napoleon to mobilize Poland and thus consolidate the army's rear, instead of marching on Moscow. But the Polish prince, who'd turned down the Tsar's handsome offers of advancement if he'd side with him, gets nowhere. Napoleon simply tells him he doesn't understand matters of high policy.

That evening the Italians, too, hear cannonfire; and hasten their footsteps. But the booming of the guns turns out to be only a salute, fired at Murat's orders to mark the Emperor's birthday. 'The army's commanders have gone to compliment him on the occasion,' notes Césare de Laugier, normally so concerned to put the best construction on things; but adds: 'the troops are definitely not thinking of celebrating this day as they usually do'. At the reception Fain hears Napoleon tell Murat, Ney and Eugène – what by now must be obvious – that he's going to seize Smolensk and take Barclay in the rear.[7] His commanders, by way of making up for the failure to crush Neverovski, have made him a birthday present of his eight guns, fourteen artillery wagons and 1,500 prisoners. 'While they were entertaining themselves with these hopes,' writes Major Boulart, whose gunners have had to drag away the captured Russian pieces and whose own cannon are among those firing the salute,

'the bands of the regiments were heard, and a 100-gun salute all down the line. Napoleon observed that they couldn't afford to waste gunpowder; but smiled when Murat replied that it had been captured from the Russians.'

Gourgaud says he told the Viceroy: 'Everything is preparing for a big battle. I shall win it and we'll see Moscow.' Ségur notices that Eugène makes no reply to this, but hears him observe to Mortier as he leaves the meeting: 'Moscow is going to be our downfall.' 'Duroc, the most reserved of all, was saying he couldn't foresee when we'd get home again.'

Such were Napoleon's forty-third birthday celebrations.

That day, too, Rapp has arrived from Danzig, where he has been governor, via Vilna. Planat notices that 'despite his elevated status' Rapp still has 'the lively gait of a hussar officer'. At Vilna Napoleon's favourite ADC has found both Hogendorp and Jomini a good deal more optimistic about the campaign's outcome than he himself is beginning to be: "You've come from Vilna?" Napoleon asks him. "What's Hogendorp doing? Nothing, I suppose. Has he got any woman with him?" And when Rapp says he doesn't know: "If he's got his wife with him she must go back to France or he must send her back to Germany. Berthier must write to him about it."[8] And when Rapp describes the 'sad picture' of the immense numbers of stragglers, etc., he's seen in the rear: "That's the usual result of long marches. I'll strike a lightning blow and everything will come together again."

That auspicious day it's Sous-lieutenant Coignet's turn to be on orderly duty at IHQ. Suddenly he's called for. One positively feels how the little fellow trembles with emotion as he stands there at attention in front of his idol, his new officer's hat under his arm, his single gold epaulette glittering in the sunshine on his left shoulder and his dangling gold sword-knot quivering:

"'*You*,*' says Napoleon – no longer using the familiar *tu* to an NCO, but the polite *vous*, to an officer, "you are to go immediately to Witebsk with these orders. They impose on everyone, of any arm whatever, to help you unsaddle your horses. If need be, all horses at relay posts are at your disposal – except those of the artillery! Do you possess one yourself?" "Two, Sire!" "Take them. When you've ridden one to death, take the other. I expect you back already tomorrow. It's three o'clock. Get going!"

'I mount my horse. Count Monthyon says to me: "Get moving, my dear chap. Take your other horse by its bridle and lead it behind you on the way. But saddle them both. Leave your best saddle here with my domestics; you've not got a moment to lose!" Away I go like lightning, leading my second horse by the hand. As soon as the first's legs give way under it I dismount, unsaddle and saddle up again, all in one movement, and leave my poor beast standing where he is. Ride on. Deep inside a wood, I come across some cantinières on their way to rejoin their corps. "Halt there! A horse, at once! I'll leave you mine here, together with its harness. I'm in a hurry! Unharness my horse!" "We've four fine Polish horses here," says the cantinière. "Which d'you want?" "This one. Harness it up, quick! Not a minute to lose!" Alas, that excellent horse, he carried me far. In the forest I come across a relay post, guarding the main road. Ride up to its commander, shout: "See here my orders! Quick, a horse! You can keep mine!"'

Not an hour is lost en route for Witebsk. Clattering down the main street between its two rows of octagonal lampposts, Coignet finds General Charpentier, the military governor, installed – not in the 'wretched timber palace' overlooking the main square – but in a stone building, which according to Roeder, was down by the Dnieper bridge:

'I hand over my despatches. He reads through them; says: "Give this officer his dinner, lay him down on a mattress for an hour's rest; get a good horse ready for him and a chasseur as escort. Near the forest he'll find a regiment camped. He can change horses at the relay posts in the forest."'

Witebsk being essentially indefensible, its garrison, only a few thousand infantry and fewer cavalry, is forever having the jitters. Roeder – who'll get there next day – will find all its churches and hospitals packed with sick

and wounded; and the 'French and Italians prodigiously slack in the execution of their duty. The guard and piquets sleep. The sentries are allowing anyone to enter who wants to, or at least anyone who can speak loud
enough in French.' There are constant alarms and excusions about
Cossacks in the neighbourhood. The newly arrived Hessians are just about
to parade in full uniform on the main square to celebrate *their* young
prince's name-day, when

> 'everything is suddenly thrown into a ridiculous uproar because a
> few Cossacks have been sighted, who're said to have carried off a
> forager. The entire garrison spring to arms, and when they've ridden
> out it's discovered that we're really only surrounded by a few dozen
> Cossacks dodging about hither and thither. In this way they'll be able
> to bring the whole garrison to hospital in about fourteen days with-
> out losing a single man.'

Scare over. Although still in full uniform and suffering from 'dysentery',
Roeder has to do picket duty for twenty-four hours. To keep himself
awake and set his sleepy men an example, he orders them to place a small
writing-desk out in the middle of the street, down there by the bridge.
Standing at it, he writes a long letter home to his new bride Sofie, friend
of his tragically deceased Mina, whom he'd married before again going
off to war (an attraction he can never resist) to provide a mother for their
children. When he's finished, he takes out his diary and writes in it what
amounts to another epistle – to the soul of his dead but much more pas-
sionately loved Mina. He doesn't give a fig for the immortality of the soul,
he writes, unless it means he'll be reunited with her. As for the Grand
Army, he has taken in its plight at a glance:

> 'On the march to Witebsk yesterday we met several cavalry depots of
> men who'd been sent back from regiments where either the riders
> had no horses or the horses no riders. They came, for example, from
> the fine 2nd Carabiniers, two regiments of cuirassiers and one of
> hussars, who every day are falling sick from the everlasting marching
> and bivouacking under the open sky. If the Russians want to send
> half our army to the dogs by the winter, all they have to do is to make
> us march hither and thither, with the individual units kept continu-
> ally under arms. Then if they give us a few battles we'll be in a tough
> spot, so long as they have plenty of light troops.'

But all this will be next day; and just now Coignet, the true believer, is
sleeping the sleep of the diligent on his straw mattress...

To the advancing army it seems as if the Cossacks are burning the entire
country. An illusion of course. The swath of devastation the Cossacks and
the Grand Army are together cutting in the immensities of the Russian
countryside is at most some thirty miles wide. When von Roos' troopers
are

> 'separated from the army for a few days and wandering around the
> countryside, we met neither friend nor foe, only occasional peasants

busy with the harvest. The further away from our route they were working, the less they bothered about us and the harder they went on with their labours. We crossed the Dnieper several times, likewise several smaller streams, and also main roads, from which we could see whether Russians or our own troops had passed, because we recognized the horses' hoofmarks from the way they were shod and from the wheel tracks. Troops always leave behind something by which one can ascertain their nationality. As soon as a column has passed, one notices a smell that's peculiar to each army, and which the veterans instantly recognize.'

One evening Dumonceau's Dutchmen pass through just such an abandoned Russian encampment:

'Behind it was a hollow where the men had gone to meet calls of nature. I noticed a considerable volume of heaps of excrement covering the ground and from it concluded that the enemy army must have any amount of food to eat.'

Dr Roos is drawing similar conclusions:

'Normally it's rather hard to identify the ownership of camp sites, but even here this campaign had the special feature that the excrement left by men and animals behind the Russian front indicated a good state of health, whereas behind ours we found the most obvious possible signs that the entire army, men and horses alike, must be suffering from diarrhoea.'

Every time he reaches a new bivouac Dr Roos brews peppermint or camomile tea for his troopers

'in one or two kettles hung over the fire, serving it to all who needed it. If these items weren't available, then our people drank tea made of balm-mint and elder-blossom. To any who were particularly ill I allowed tincture of opium and Hoffmann's drops [a mixture of alcohol and ether] with these drinks. In this way we managed tolerably well, as long as my supplies lasted.'

At the large village of Katyn, on the Dnieper, the Red Lancers come across another abandoned camp, this time of Cossacks:

'Our generals, not feeling they should content themselves with appearances, had the opposite bank explored by some dismounted cavalrymen, who swam the river with their sabres between their teeth. From the height of the dominating bank, occupied by ourselves, we anxiously watched the outcome of this reconnaissance, made by completely naked men. They found nothing. Only some cables and other bridging materials seemed to indicate that the Russians had planned to take the French in flank.'

After Liady the sombre Lithuanian forests come at long last to an end. Everywhere the rich harvest, which has begun to be reaped but then abandoned, is putting new flesh on the cavalry's scraggy nags. Three miles further on, at the village of Sinacki, the Italians bivouack in really idyllic scenery, and Césare de Laugier sits scribbling in his diary as he watches

the other corps go by, leaving IV Corps in reserve:
'The columns of infantry, cavalry and artillery are marching at an urgent pace and in line, at short intervals so as to be able to deploy at the first obstacle. But this military arrangement has the grave defect of trampling the corn underfoot over a distance of 300 paces on either side of the road.'
The troops may be hurrying on towards what is hopefully an undefended Smolensk; but Napoleon himself, it seems, is in no great hurry. All day he lingers at Liady until he's 'sure the bridge over the Dnieper had been destroyed' so he can't himself be suddenly taken in flank or rear.

CHAPTER 14

THE WALLS OF SMOLENSK

A four-mile wall – 'the bravest feat I've seen' – Bagration's dark masses – a chival-rous challenge – what was Murat wearing? – Barclay relieved of the supreme com-mand – 'the Emperor's staking out a battlefield' – effectives on 16 August – 'At last I've got them!' – a useful ford – fraternizing in the heat – Le Roy brings a herd of cows – an Italian idyll – a professor of swimming – Coignet returns from Witebsk – a painful episode

Smolensk, Russia's third most important city, lies on a steep reverse slope and is intersected by the Dnieper. Its older part, on the south bank, is sur-rounded by four miles of walls, 'very high, built of deep red bricks black-ened by time, and flanked by 32 large towers[1] – some polygonal, others square, others again capped with dovecot-shaped roofs'.

Emerging on to the slopes facing the Krasnoïe suburb at about 10 a.m. (16 August) III Corps sees to its left a great earthwork. Assuming he has only Neverovski's 4,000 survivors to deal with, Ney tries a *coup de main* by sending forward a single battalion of the 44th Line. Preceded by skirmish-ers, it drives the Russians out of the dry moat that everywhere covers the approaches, and is even within an ace of taking the earthwork. 'That's the bravest feat of arms I've seen since I've been making war!' Ney exclaims. And is promptly hit in the neck by a spent musketball. Only his tall collar, embroidered with gold acanthus leaves, saves him.

It also shows him that he's mistaken. Already 20,000 infantry and 72 guns of Raevsky's division, supported by 'a fair amount of cavalry', are holding the city. Arriving with Murat's advance guard, Colonel Griois' horse gunners have

> 'found the high ground all round Smolensk occupied by units of
> enemy cavalry. Our own charged them vigorously, pursuing them as
> far as the town walls, until held up by gunfire and musketry.
> Immediately I advanced my guns. Forming battery at two points,
> they opened a lively cannonade on the town, which kept continu-
> ously firing back at us.'

Griois' guns are busy banging away when he realizes that, at his side, someone is sitting a fabulously caparisoned horse:

> 'His beautiful brown hair fell down in tresses on to his shoulders. His
> harness, too, was bizarre but magnificent, and its beauty enhanced
> by the grace and deftness with which he handled his horse.'

It''s Murat, of course, who has spent the night at Ney's headquarters. Griois is too busy to note exactly what costume he's wearing.[2] Only that it's

> 'utterly theatrical. On anyone else it would have been ridiculous; but
> it seemed cut to his stature, the perfect accompaniment to an alto-
> gether brilliant valour, all his own.'

Enchanted with the vivacity and accuracy of the horse gunners' shooting, Murat keeps exclaiming in his husky voice: 'Bravo, boys! Knock that scum over. You shoot like angels!' And here come several squadrons of Russian dragoons; but the 7th French Dragoons, supported by the 23rd Line, move forward to drive them off: 'The two bodies approached each other at a gallop and the affray was intense and murderous. I've seen few cavalry charges driven home more thoroughly.' But in the end the Russians 'retire in disorder beneath the walls. And my artillery bombarded them so effectively at half-range that all our roundshot and shells fell in their midst and increased their disarray.'

But who are those 'dark masses' a keen-eyed Württemberg artillery officer has spotted in the distance, advancing at such a rate that they 'seemed to be running'[3]

'At first we took them for Junot's (VIII) corps, which we knew had gone astray. But then we saw it was the entire Russian army. Hearing of Neverovski's defeat [sic], it had woken up out of its trance and was making tracks for Smolensk, so as not to be cut off from the Moscow road.'

Since Ney's own supports are only coming up slowly, and 'upon the fortress suddenly belching troops and the fire of sixty guns', the Marshal calls off the badly mauled 44th, and waits for the situation to stabilize. Above all the Russian army mustn't be panicked into staging a further retreat.

'Taking out spyglasses at a great distance,' Captain Zalusky and his fellow-officers in the Polish Guard Lancers study 'with a certain emotion its walls, ancient witnesses to the siege they'd withstood in the days of Sigismund III'. 'Too frail to support the weight of heavy-calibre guns', Fézensac notices, they bristle with lighter pieces. He also sees that, 'though far from being built on the modern system, their great extent and height (8 metres) together with the broad ditch and covered way defending its approaches' will make the city hard to storm.

There'd been a chevalieresque prelude to all this. Approaching the 1st Guard Lancers on a grey horse, a Cossack officer

'at a distance of one hundred paces, or even less, challenged us in Polish to fight him. But Colonel Kozietulski wouldn't let anyone budge. Whereupon the Cossack shouted out: "Now you can capture me!" Got off his horse, and even started to unsaddle it. Finally, seeing he couldn't lure us out of our ranks, he remounted and went back to his own men. Their cannon fired a hundred rounds at us, without hurting anyone.'

But Griois' cannon go on firing until evening: 'Soon it had become general on all fronts as the corps batteries turned up one by one, and added their fire to ours. I had two guns dismounted and several men and horses killed.'

It had not been until late the previous evening that Napoleon had realized that the Russian high command had tumbled to his manoeuvre.

Leaving his bivouac at Koroutnia at 8 a.m., he'd crossed the intervening 20 miles at a gallop and at 1 p.m. reined in his horse above the heights above the city. 'We've just got here,' Fain jots down in his journal:

'The Emperor is staking out a field of battle between our line and the ramparts. Everything is being foreseen against the eventuality of the enemy emerging through the gates; or, if the Russian general should hesitate, of carrying the place by assault. But how believe Barclay de Tolly will hesitate? This time he's united with Bagration, and it's a question of Russia's third most important city!'

While waiting for the Russians to come out and fight, Fain hears 'a fusil-lading being kept up all along the line'. And Dumonceau, not far away, is noting how between himself and these massive walls, which 'put him in mind of what medieval cities must have looked like', there lies a ravine,

'on whose far side the enemy had had time to occupy some half-demolished houses. And about a mile away, where the Dnieper's further bank was covered with bushes, a suburb had been entrenched and its timber houses loopholed. Beyond, on the heights dominating the city, the Russian army was in position, ready to support the divisions which are going to defend Smolensk.'

As for the dry moat, or covered way, it

'supported a spacious glacis and everywhere separated it from the suburbs. There were only two gates. Access to one was covered by an arrow-shaped redoubt; to the other, by a modern terraced construction. The only other issue on the river side was by a simple passage down to the bridges.'

Again the time has come for the Grand Army to count its effectives. Fortunately for us, Fain jots down the returns:

	At the Niemen	At Smolensk
Imperial Guard	43,000	24,000
I Corps (Davout)	79,000	60,000
III Corps (Ney)	44,000	22,000
V Corps (Poniatowski)	39,000	22,000
Murat's cavalry	42,000	18,000
TOTALS	247,000	146,000
and in the rear		
IV Corps (Eugène)	52,000	30,000
VIII Corps (Junot)	18,700	14,000
GRAND TOTALS	318,000	190,800

Despite the units it has had to leave behind to garrison Minsk and Molihew (Sergeant Everts' 33rd Light, for instance), only Davout's corps is relatively intact. And the army's artillery, despite its shortage of horse-power, remarkably so. Gourgaud, whose business as First Ordnance Officer it is to get in its returns from Lariboisière – effectively, from Planat de la Faye, gives a detailed rundown:

'57×12-pounders, 267×8-pounders, 32×4-pounders, 2×3-pounders, 10×6.4 howitzers, 122×5.6 howitzers: altogether 490 pieces and 2,477 ammunition wagons, 'which makes up a total of 2,967 vehicles, the bridging equipment, forges, spare parts, wagons, etc., not included'.

The dwindling of the Guard has been due, of course, to the huge numbers of Young Guard conscripts lost en route. Many cavalry units have sunk pathetically. In III Corps, now at half-strength, von Suckow's company, 150 troopers strong when it set out from Württemberg, now has only 38.

Against Barclay's and Bagration's 115,000 behind those massive if anti-quated walls, Napoleon still has – at least nominally – 190,000. Training his spyglass on Raevsky's troops as they come pouring into the city over the Dnieper bridge, he exclaims: 'At last – I've got them!' At long last the moment has arrived for the grand Austerlitz-style battle he has envisaged from the outset. Most of the long hot day, Caulaincourt says, was devoted to getting as close to the fortifications as possible and straightening out the battle line. Meanwhile, on either side of a little stream which separates the two armies the skirmishers are dodging about among bushes, taking potshots at one another. Gradually it becomes evident to officers on both sides that nothing much is going to be expected of them today. And with 'both sides feeling the need to water our horses', Lieutenant Lyautey's battery of the Guard Artillery unharnesses half its guns:

'Going down into the ravine I accompanied the horses with a few gunners, leaving behind enough to service the guns, if need arose. The Russians drank on one bank. We on the other. Not understanding each other very well, we conversed with gestures. We offered liquor and tobacco; and in this we were the more generous. Soon afterwards these good friends of ours fired a few shots. I found an officer who spoke good French, and we exchanged a few words.'

The 9th Lancers are among the light infantry on the left wing, with Bruyères' division drawn up in three lines behind them. At midday Lieutenant Wedel witnesses even more extensive fraternization. Swarms of Russian dragoons and Cossacks have been attacking the French skirmishers then falling back 'to lure us into the bushes where some infantry were concealed and which opened fire, forcing us to beat a hasty retreat. This mutual playfulness lasted quite a while.' But now the Russian fire ceases:

'Placing out some of their light infantrymen at intervals of some 15 to 20 paces, they sheath their swords as a sign they don't want to go on fighting. We follow their example, disposing our skirmishers in similar fashion at 100 metres or so from each other, with orders not to shoot. Now a Russian dragoon officer comes forward a few paces and salutes us, making signs with a bottle. I follow suit, and place myself in front of our line of skirmishers. In this way we come to within 30 metres of one another; whereupon the Russian calls out in French:

"Mon camarade! There's no sense in tiring our horses and killing each others' men to no purpose. Let's take a drink together instead. By and by we'll have all the time in the world to fight."

We come closer and enjoy a friendly drink together, while further away other troops are still fighting. Soon several other Russian officers come forward. Upon my making to retire, my dragoon officer says:

"I promise you on my word of honour they won't do you any harm."

So I stay put, and we have a friendly chat. His rum tasted good in my mouth. Unfortunately, I couldn't offer him any in return.'

Gradually more and more officers from both sides are joining in. Likewise 'our Frau Ehmke, a pretty woman who always rode about among the light infantry with two little kegs of brandy on her horse. She poured the Russians a free drink, but made us pay dearly for ours. A young lieutenant of our regiment, Piessac by name, had a girlishly pretty face, and got a kiss from an elderly bearded Russian.'

The 9th Lancers, though nominally Polish, are a ragbag of all nationalities; and there are Poles in the Russian army too:

'Because of our Polish uniforms a Polish-born Uhlan officer took us for Poles, and wanted to make enquiries about his compatriots. Hearing that a Polish lancer regiment was standing behind us in the second line, he rode fearlessly over to it, as fast as his horse could carry him. We thought he meant to desert. But that wasn't at all his intention! He just wanted to meet his compatriots and air his embittered views about Barclay de Tolly's way of waging war. When he heard we wished for nothing better than a pitched battle that would decide the war's outcome, and how tired we were of wandering about in a country that could offer us so few resources, he replied that, if we were hoping for such a battle in front of Smolensk, we'd be disappointed. He'd bet anything we'd enter Smolensk tomorrow; and that the Russians would slip away without fighting.'

But now General Bruyère notices what's going on, and sends an ADC to put a stop to it – and capture the Uhlan. 'But he rode so slowly – doubtless on purpose – that the Pole was warned in time by another officer, and hurried off.'

Le Roy, too, is taking it easy. Arriving from Molihew with 'bread, brandy and flour, likewise a large herd of cows which I placed at the regiment's disposal', he's amazed to hear he's been promoted *chef de bataillon* – Davout hasn't forgotten his resourceful behaviour at Salta Nowka. Not that there's any battalion of the 85th for him to command – as yet. But the portly major is reckoning with getting one after tomorrow's slaughter.

As for the Italians, they're positively enjoying themselves. A couple of miles to the rear they've bivouacked beside an idyllic lake fringed by a silver birch wood, whose 'pellucid waters invite us to bathe'. Albrecht Adam's lithograph shows the scene exactly; and Césare de Laugier fills in other details -

'the Viceroy's carriages and wagons... the generals and other officers scattered throughout the wood... groups of officers and men resting with their backs against tree trunks or stretched out at full length on the ground... other groups busy making their soup. Further away a circle has been formed and a peaceful discussion is going on. Still others either going off foraging or else returning. Along the shores of the lake many of us are busy doing our washing, whilst others, out of necessity or for pleasure' (as Labaume, also struck by the scene, puts it) 'are waging war on the little flock of geese and ducks that have escaped the Cossacks'.

Carabinier-sergeant Bertrand of the 7th Light is also in for a dip, but of another kind. He's just looking forward to a quiet night, even if it's to be his last, when his battalion is ordered to reconnoitre the river bank downstream from the city:

'We were commanded by a staff colonel, and had two guns with us. After three hours' marching our little advance guard is attacked by cavalry. The two companies of voltigeurs and granadiers are thrown forward. First in square then in open order, they push the enemy cavalry in front of them. We clear the rough ground at the double, so fast our cannon can't keep up with us. Arrived at the limit of a big ravine – no more cavalry! And in front of us the Dnieper!'

The Russians having crossed it in little skiffs, the staff-colonel says they must go and fetch them from the far bank:

'Since I'm the regiment's professor of swimming, I collect my 20 pupils, plus 30 volunteers. Our weapons and effects we leave in the battalion's care. Our guns are in battery. At a given signal we throw ourselves into the water. The enemy sends us a few musketballs; but a whiff of grapeshot puts him to flight, and we're able to bring back the fifteen boats. One swimmer has been killed and disappeared under the waves. Two have been lightly wounded on the head and neck. Just as the voltigeurs are embarking, a staff officer brings an order: we're to go back to our corps. We don't have to be asked twice. Already the daylight was fading, and night operations are always troublesome.'

Coignet, too, on his way back from Witebsk, is experiencing some tense moments. His hour's rest at an end, General Charpentier had come into the room:

'"Your packet's waiting for you, my friend, get going! Unless something should hold you up en route you'll get there within twenty-four hours, including the time you'll need for unsaddling and saddling up." I leave with a good mount and my escort. In the forest I find a regiment encamped. Show its colonel my orders. Hardly giving himself time to read them, he says: "Adjutant-major, give him a horse. It's the Emperor's orders!"

'I'd counted on finding cavalry posts in the forest. No sign of any! All had fled or been taken prisoner. Now I'm on my own, without any escort. Seeing some dismounted cavalrymen in the offing, I thoughtfully slow my horse to a walk. So they shan't catch sight of me, I take a roundabout way. Cossacks, certainly, standing there, waiting. Suddenly, just as I'm slipping along the forest fringe, a peasant comes out of it. Says to me: "Cossacks!" Well, I'd already seen them. Without an instant's hesitation I dismount and grab my peasant; show him some gold in one hand and my pistol in the other. Comprehending me, he says: "Toc, toc!" Which means "that's good!" I stuff the gold back into my waistcoat pocket, and while holding the horse's reins under one arm and my cocked pistol in my left hand, I take my Russian under my right arm. When he's led me to the main road, he says: "Nien, nien cossacks!"'

Recognizing the highroad from its avenue of silver birches, he's beside himself with joy:

'I give my peasant three napoleons, promptly mount my horse. How I spurred that poor beast's flanks! The road vanishes behind me and even before my galloping horse has time to stumble I'm lucky enough to find a farm. Rush into the farmyard. There I see three young surgeons. I dismount, make a dash for the stable: "That horse, at once! I'll leave you mine. Read these orders!" Once again I mounted a good horse, who certainly knew how to get a move on. Yet to reach my goal I'd need yet another one. Night was falling, and I could no longer make out the road. Luckily I came across four well-mounted officers. Same ceremony begins all over again: "Try and read the Emperor's orders that you're to replace my horse." A fat gentleman whom I take to be a general says to the others: "Unsaddle your horse and give it to this officer. His orders are urgent. Help him!" I'm saved. Reaching the battlefield, here I am now, searching about for the Emperor. Everywhere the same reply: "I don't know."'

Darkness has fallen, so it must be at about 10 p.m. as not only Coignet but also Captain Biot are groping around amid the camp fires, searching for imperial headquarters. Though it wasn't his turn, Biot has been sent by Pajol with despatches for Montbrun and Napoleon. Coignet, for his part, almost wanders into the Russian lines:

'I push on. Catching sight of some camp fires to my left I leave the road. I'm just passing close by a battery when someone shouts out: "Qui vive?" "Orderly officer!" "Halt! You're going towards the enemy!" "Where's the Emperor?" "Follow me, I'll take you to my CO." We find him. He says: "Take him to the Emperor's tent." "Thanks." Reaching the tent, I have myself announced. General

Monthyon comes out, says: "Oh, so it's you, is it, *mon brave*! I'll present you at once to the Emperor." He thought I'd been taken prisoner. Whereon my general says to the Emperor: "Here's Your Majesty's officer, back from Witebsk." I hand him my despatches. The Emperor notices what a state I'm in: "How did you manage to get through the forest? Weren't there any Cossacks there?" "With gold, Sire! A peasant saved me by showing me a way round." "How much did you give him?" "Three napoleons." "And your horses?" "I've none left." "Monthyon, make good his travel expenses, his two horses and those sixty francs that peasant so well deserved. Give my old grumbler here time to get his breath back. For his two horses, six hundred francs and the post charges! I'm pleased with you!'"

What can it have been that was so urgent in those despatches? Perhaps Coignet's mission had partly been to test the state of communications to the rear? If so, Napoleon would also have been informed by Biot – it must have been one of Pajol's light cavalry regiments, guarding them, that Coignet had seen bivouacked in the forest– and there's certainly reason for anxiety. A couple of days later chasseur Lieutenant Maurice Tascher, will write in his diary: 'The Cossacks are on both flanks of the French army and in its rear. They're taking lots of prisoners and have cut the Liouvavitski road.'

But Sergeant Bertrand, still marching through the night, is 'only encountering a few poor isolated houses. Not until the moment when the regiment is about to leave do we rejoin it. It's been able to get some rest and have something to eat. But we ... we've sixteen hours of marching in our legs.'

While Coignet had been away there's been a painful incident in front of Napoleon's tent. Some staff officers looking through their spyglasses have thought that they could see Russian troops moving in *both* directions across the Dnieper bridge which links the city's two halves. Does this mean another midnight flit?[4] A fresh retreat? Murat (says Ségur) gloomily declares there'll be no battle, but is promptly contradicted by Davout. 'As for the Emperor, he believed what he wanted to.' This is too much for Murat. Who explodes: 'Since they won't stand and fight, to run after them is to go too far. It's time to call a halt!'

Napoleon tells him sharply not to meddle in matters he doesn't understand; and goes into his tent, followed by Murat. No one hears what follows. But when Murat comes out again he looks deeply depressed, angry and agitated:

'The word "Moscow" several times escaped his lips. Afterwards the King of Naples was heard to say he'd gone down on his knees to his brother-in-law, begged him to call a halt; but that all Napoleon could see in front of him was Moscow, declaring that honour, glory, repose

– all, for him, lay there. It was this "Moscow" that had been our undoing.'

Fact or fiction? Gourgaud says it's just another of Ségur's fables. Having 'spent part of the night in the Emperor's tent, we can assure the reader these allegations are false'. Well, perhaps: or partly. Maybe Murat didn't actually go down on his knees. But the morrow will confirm his despair. Evidently Napoleon feels challenged, for he tries to get Caulaincourt to agree with him. But Caulaincourt replies drily that, in his view, since the Russians can no longer take the offensive, they'll again retreat.

'"In that case," Napoleon burst out in the tones of a man who'd suddenly made up his mind, "by abandoning Smolensk, one of Russia's holy cities, the Russian army will have dishonoured itself in the eyes of its own nation and put me in a strong position. We'll drive them back a bit further, so they can't disturb us. I'll fortify my positions, give the troops a rest, and organize the country from our base at Witebsk – and see how Alexander likes that! I'll raise Poland in arms and later on, if necessary, decide between Moscow and Petersburg."'

In that moment Caulaincourt sees him as 'sublime, great, far-seeing, as on the day of his most brilliant victory'. And reiterates his long-standing view that it's the Russian plan to 'lure him further and further from his base, and shut him up among snow and ice. It was imperative we didn't go along with their little game. His Majesty seemed to approve of my reflections.' But when Caulaincourt hastens to report their conversation to Berthier and asks him 'to do everything in his power to support this wise decision, he seemed to doubt whether it would outlive the taking of Smolensk'.

CHAPTER 15

SMOLENSK – THE FIRST SHOCK

How thick are those walls? – Murat tries to get himself killed – seen in cinemascope – 'his face was a sickly hue and his look sombre' – Junot arrives – François is in the thick of it – a Russian hero – 'I'd gladly have hidden in a mousehole' – an immense furnace – Caulaincourt is worried – the Russians evacuate their holy city – Napoleon visits the battlefield – 'in six weeks we'll have peace' – Smolensk a charnel – 'a human face lay in the mud like a glove' – 'I felt I'd left hell behind me' – 'the gay strains of our bands' – 'they implored God's succour against us' – Le Roy revisits a distraught friend – Larrey does wonders – a ghastly wound

Again the sun rises in a cloudless sky; and the topographer-in-chief jots down in his journal:

'8 a.m. The Russians are beginning to pour out of the town. Our outposts are retiring, and the fighting which is now beginning is only for the houses in the outermost suburbs. Nor are they the same troops as yesterday. At dawn Raevski's men have left the city to liaise with Bagration. Today it's General Docturov, reinforced by Konownitzin's division, who's to defend Smolensk.'

As early as 3 a.m. Captain François has seen his division's light infantry regiment open a skirmishing fire, and I Corps begin to manoeuvre. And at 9 a.m. Sergeant Bertrand, suffering from lack of sleep after his night march, finds the 7th Light caught up in

'masses of troops of all kinds, debouching in every direction. Each takes up his proper place in the firing line. The Emperor appears. Like the generals in his suite he's covered in dust from head to foot. He rides up to the right of our division to give his orders. Near my company Marshal Ney dismounts, takes me by the arm, and leads me up to the top of a small hillock. Placing his telescope on my shoulder, he peers steadily through it for a full five minutes. After which he goes off and gives the Emperor an account of what he has seen.'

For a moment there's been another scare when 'some strong columns are seen moving off along the Moscow road'. Surely it's not going to be the same story as at Witebsk? 'No. Barclay's lines are standing motionless on the hills of the Petersburg suburb. Only Bagration is leaving.' Immediately Napoleon orders the bridge linking the old city with the new to be shelled by 30 heavy guns:

'The battery so harasses the enemy that his columns are crossing the bridge at the double. Obviously they're in full retreat. The Emperor wants to unleash an assault, and some officers decide to reconnoitre the wall, but haven't a scaling ladder.'

Nor are there any siege guns – the siege train is several hundred miles away with Macdonald's X Corps, investing Riga. But how will those red brick walls stand up to 12-pounders? How thick are they, really? The artillery staff are just passing in front of one of the town gates when a blast of grapeshot is fired at them at short range. It's Planat's baptism of fire. By a miracle no one's hurt. And Lariboisière tells his 'man of letters' to go and tell General Sorbier, commanding the Guard Artillery, to bring up a battery of 12-pounders as close as possible and try to batter a breach. Returning, Planat is 'present at the first attempt. Though a score of rounds were fired at point-blank range, they hardly managed to flake off a few fragments of bricks from the walls.' Davout, too, has brought up several such batteries. Roman Soltyk, that expert on ballistics, turns up 'at the very moment when Marshal Davout ordered his battery of 12-pounders to open fire'. It doesn't take him long to see they're just wasting ammunition, the more so as

> 'we were concentrating our fire on the wall, instead of on its flanking towers, whose lesser thickness would have enabled our artillery to bring them down. I was just returning from carrying a report to the Emperor. Halting there momentarily, I had occasion to admire our gunners' ability and Davout's courage, exposed as he was to the most murderous fire.'

Indeed all hell is let loose. The French position is completely dominated by some high ground on the other side of the Dnieper, and 40 Russian guns are replying. Amid bursting shells and rip-roaring roundshot Davout receives another visitor: Fézensac, sent by Berthier, quickly reaches the same conclusion. The walls are quite simply too thick.

But Napoleon, the gunner-emperor, feels he must see for himself. Mounting his horse he orders Captain *Chlapowsky* of the Polish Guard Lancers, whose turn it is to command the escort squadron, 'to chase away the Cossacks from the far side of the ravine'. A Russian shell bursts right in the midst of his lancers; and a moment later they're attacked by Cossacks. One of them lunges his lance at Chlapowsky, who parries the thrust with his sabre. But his horse suffers a nasty wound, from the tip of its ear to its nostril.

Nor is Davout alone in exposing himself. Nor – quite needlessly – is Murat. Leading his horse by the reins a few paces behind the King, his Neapolitan ADC sees

> 'the gunners, crushed by the battery dominating us, falling beside their guns. The gun carriages were being smashed, the guns overthrown. Ignited by the enemy shells, ammunition wagons keep exploding with a terrific crash. It was at that moment one such wagon blew up, only ten paces away from us, throwing me to the ground – fortunately without worse harm to myself than to stun me, leaving me stone deaf for two days to come. But horse and harness were torn to shreds.'

A most puzzling scene ensues. Half-grilled alive in their steel cuirasses, their maned helmets gleaming in the sun as it rises ever higher in the sky, the 2nd Cuirassiers have been standing 'more or less out of range of the roundshot, some of which got as far as to our horses' hoofs'; and since 'another opportunity mightn't present itself' Thirion is curious to see such an artillery battle at close quarters. Accompanied by a comrade, Baffcop by name, 'whose adventurous character I knew', he walks forward until he's in the very midst of one of Sorbier's batteries:

'Reaching this point, I find myself amidst a rain of cannon-balls. Never was I better able to appreciate the dangers run by the artillery, how much valour and what cool heads are needed for this branch of the service! Not only are the Guard batteries, in whose midst I stood, being rapidly bombarded by the artillery in the fortress, they're also being taken in flank by other Russian batteries, set up on an eminence on the other side of the river. How a man or a horse could have escaped from this mass of roundshot coming from two sides and crossing each other in the middle of these batteries, each gun with its six horses and an ammunition wagon, is more than I can conceive.'

And yet here's Murat – strolling to and fro 'with the calm which distinguished him when under fire, smiling at everyone, encouraging the gunners and promising them his wonted success'. This time we know what he was wearing, for he's been seen a few moments earlier by I Corps' paymaster *Duverger* sporting 'a gold-braided pelisse, a pair of flesh-coloured pantaloons that showed off his figure, and a toque on his head, adorned by a tuft of luxurious feathers'. Surprised to see two cuirassier officers standing there, Murat comes up and asks: 'What the devil are you doing here, gentlemen?' Their presence, they explain, is due to a passionate interest in siegecraft. Murat smiles and walks away, leaving Thirion puzzled. Why was the King of Naples, normally surrounded by a numerous staff, alone? 'No ADCs. No escort. What had become of this obligatory accompaniment of a high commander? Had they dispersed, carrying orders?' Or had they all been killed by 'the roundshot which was raining down at this point?'

Evidently he hasn't noticed Belliard, who explains the mystery.

Murat, depressed after the previous evening's conversation, is quite simply trying to get himself killed. When Rossetti had been stunned by the exploding ammunition wagon, Belliard had protested: 'Sire, you'll only get yourself killed – without glory, and to no purpose.' But Murat, mumbling repeatedly 'Moscow, Moscow', tells him irritably to go away. And when Belliard points out that all he'll succeed in doing will be to get his staff killed, bursts out furiously: 'Very well, then, retire! And leave me here alone! Surely you can see your group is giving the enemy a target for his fire?' The officers had scattered – which is why Thirion doesn't see them. But Belliard persists: 'Sire, Your Majesty has decided to get himself killed today. Permit me to do the same at your side.' At this, he says, Murat 'with a gesture of fury and despair, walked quickly away from the spot'.

'Soon we had to admit the operation was impossible. The walls resisted our roundshot. So the breaching project was abandoned, and the Emperor gave orders for them to be mined. But neither could this method, though surer, be implemented, the circumstances being so urgent. So our artillery was employed to enfilade the wall and dismount the enemy guns by firing ricochets. In this way,'

concludes Soltyk, that expert on gunnery and ballistics, 'it sent a great number of shells into the town, causing several fires to break out'.

Meanwhile the infantry assault columns have been massing on the slopes. In the centre, says Captain François of the 36th Line, 'I Corps manoeuvred en masse under the enemy's fire'. But to Dumonceau the forenoon seems to be passing quietly enough. Only when the sun is blazing down from its zenith are the 2nd Guard Lancers ordered to stand to arms. And an ADC leads them forward to the rim of the ravine:

'From there we had a view over the entire enemy army on the plateau opposite us, likewise of the assault columns massing on the slopes opposite the town gates. A crowd of curious persons from the artillery parks and baggage train who'd nothing to do and no need to bestir themselves came running up and lined the valley's rim to watch, as if from the top of an amphitheatre.'

But so far not a single enemy soldier has shown himself in front of the suburbs. And by and by Morand's division forms up

'in a compact column[1] and descends from where we are by the broad Micislaw road. Provisionally leaving one of its brigades in reserve near a bridge at the bottom, it throws out a screen of skirmishers. They're just reaching the crest, when two enemy squadrons, coming up from behind the suburb, draw up on the plain opposite, ready to charge as soon as the line shall appear on the plateau. These skirmishers, still sheltered by the crest of the hill, have no inkling of the danger they are in, though we, from our dominant position, can see it perfectly. Alarmed for the outcome, the crowd of spectators all around us try to ward off Fate by shouts and gesticulations, as if these could be understood at such a distance! But here too our battery comes to the rescue. We can see the cannon-balls ricocheting in front of the enemy squadrons, reaching them and carrying confusion among their ranks, and, after a few instants' hesitation, forcing them to retire. Each of these successes fills our crowd of onlookers with enthusiasm. They applaud noisily, clapping their hands and shouting "Bravo! Bravo!" as if at the theatre. On the skirmishers reaching the crest of the plateau we see them carry out a sudden flank movement at the double, in the direction of a large enclosed area visible at some distance to their right, and which seems to be a cemetery. One by one they get inside it and vanish. To make this movement they've had to pass in front of two long loopholed buildings, or timber outhouses, from which comes a lively fusillade... but so swiftly have they passed in front of it, it only causes them the loss of one man, who's left lying on the ground before our eyes.'

Meanwhile Morand's assault column has been mounting the slope without meeting any resistance. But now

'two enemy guns emerge from the suburb, appear at the head of the incline, and open fire. Whereupon a French battery, sited close beside us on the plateau's edge, crushes them by its superior weight of fire, forcing them to withdraw. Meanwhile the column, moving off the road to the left so as to get more room to manoeuvre, imperturbably goes on climbing the hill. Reaching its brow, it drives before it a confused mass of enemy skirmishers who've been sent out to meet it.'

Now it's within sight of the suburb's first houses,

'which receive it with a sudden rolling fusillade. Marching quickly on these buildings, they turn their extreme right, take them from behind, and thus displace the scene of the fighting to their rear, where it disappears from view. Attacking these houses at the *pas de charge*, the column flows around them and penetrates them at all points, amidst whirling smoke which thereafter hides this engagement going on inside the suburb from our view.'

And now the Red Lancers are themselves being called for. This time it's Friant's division which, together with III Cavalry Corps, is to attack the Roslawl suburb, and they're to support the movement. This assault, too, is followed by some fascinated spectators on a hillock. To the right they see

'Poniatowski's V Polish Corps, deployed in line, marching as if on parade across an open plain, rising imperceptibly toward the Nikolskoïe and Rasaska suburb. A Russian battery, placed out slightly ahead on the slope, unceasingly vomits whirlwinds of smoke and fire, to which the artillery advancing ahead of the Polish line replies. Still further to the right, at the far end of the line, the King of Naples' cavalry seems to be strongly engaged with a cloud of Cossacks.'

Now Dumonceau himself gets some orders. He's to take two troops of lancers and observe the flank of the suburb opposite them, thus guaranteeing the regiment from any surprises on that side. 'Even so, I find I'm being fired on by the skirmishers embuscaded behind garden hedges. In no time two of my men are lightly wounded and a musket-ball rips my mantle, which I'm wearing bandoleer-style, as is the usage when on outpost duty.' Colbert, informed, feels he shouldn't leave the two troops exposed; and orders them to retire.

Only after reiterated efforts – in which Dedem van der Gelder, riding at the head of his infantry brigade, is hit in the chest by a spent musket-ball and has a horse killed under him – does Friant's division penetrate its target. But all Dumonceau can see now is 'a lot of movement, and numerous wounded streaming back out of all the exits. Finally a decisive movement seems to be happening. We see III Cavalry Corps suddenly fling itself in columns of troops into the suburb's broad main street and disappear there, enveloped in a cloud of dust and smoke.' Whereupon Davout flings the entire weight of I Corps at the Malakhofskaia Gate and the strongly pallisaded redoubt covering it. But the Red Lancers have 'no part to play in such engagements. As soon as the suburbs had been captured we returned to our bivouac. None of the Imperial Guard's other units had budged.'

And here – at last – after wandering aimlessly about the countryside is Junot's VIII Corps.

His troops too, are utterly discouraged. 'Depression and weariness with life had spread through the Westphalian army,' says that proud veteran from Wagram, Lance-corporal Wilhelm Heinemann. That morning the Brunswick Chasseurs had just put their cooking pots on to make their soup, and had even sent out marauders to find some bread and flour, when the order had come to get moving again.

'The half-boiled broth had to be thrown away. The meat is tied to our straps – a cruel fate for hungry soldiers! To run for two hours, embarrassed with musket and pack, after already suffering so much from famine, shortages and wearisome marches, is no light matter. Several gave up the ghost and fell exhausted. Others shot themselves in despair. The thunder of the guns is coming closer and closer. We're made to march past Napoleon at the double. How different everthing is from what it had once been at Lobau! Then the French army had been all enthusiasm – one thunderous shout of "Vive l'Empereur!"; and he himself lively as a bird on his dazzling white horse, surrounded by a general staff whose splendour and brilliance seemed better suited to a parade than to serious fighting. Now the Emperor and his entourage were so covered in dust we could hardly make out the colours of their uniforms. Pale and lethargic, his face a sickly hue and his glance sombre, he sat immobile, a bad portrait of himself. Horse and rider were both visibly exhausted.'

As the Westphalians, silent and panting in the dust clouds, double past, a singular detail catches Heinemann's eye: 'On one side the Emperor's underclothes were torn open from knee to hip, baring his leg.' Heinemann thinks it 'shows he isn't sparing himself'.

'On our way', Dumonceau goes on,

'we passed across the front of a handsome regiment of lancers of the Royal Westphalian Guard, formed up in reserve. It was wearing black helmets with a lot of copper ornament, which attracted our attention. We observed one another with curiosity. As they pointed us out we could hear them saying among themselves in German: "Holländer, Holländer". Among them our comrade Captain Bellefroid saw one of his brothers.'

But of Junot himself, the blonde handsome friend of Napoleon's youth, 'whose face, bearing and turnout eight or nine years before had surpassed all the army's officers at the Boulogne Camp,' nothing is left. Secretary Fain is shocked to see him

Armand de Caulaincourt, Master of the Horse and Napoleon's left-hand man. 'Five foot eight inches tall, with a frank and honest appearance... liked and respected by all... an admirable officer, a military man through and through...', he was candidly against the war. Responsible for headquarters transports and the courier service, on campaign he rode immediately to the left of the Emperor's carriage and, upon his exchanging it for one of his Arab greys, held his stirrup as he mounted. By the summer of 1812 this had become more than a ritual gesture.

Above: Three penal regiments – 38,000 deserters – had supplied the Grand Army with the equivalent of a whole infantry division. A political dinner plate, probably from 1814, reminds the diner of a sight all too common during the Empire.

Below: The crossing of the Niemen, 24 June 1812 – engraving by Christian Wilhelm von Faber du Faur, a Württemberg artillery major in Ney's III Corps. 'Full of ardour, lulled by the most beautiful hopes, everyone hastened to reach Russian soil.' The columns crossing the three pontoon bridges are glimpsed in the distance.

Above: Grenadier Pils' watercolour sketch of the sunshade of pine branches erected by Guard sappers for Napoleon on a hillock about 100 yards from the Niemen. The man he's talking to is Marshal Oudinot – "a good fellow, but not much brains" – commander of II Corps.

Below: Philippe de Ségur's *[left]* enthralling history of the disastrous campaign is so full of errors and strokes of the imagination that they were scathingly criticized by his former colleague First Ordnance Officer Gaspard Gourgaud *[right]*. They fought a duel over it. In Russia, Ségur, as Assistant Prefect of the Palace, was in charge of the headquarters mules, which among other things carried Napoleon's gold dinner service.

Below right: The ex-Armenian slave Roustam Raza, Napoleon's bodyguard, slept with drawn scimitar across the door to his bedroom and accompanied him wherever he went, dressed in 'mameluke' costume. – *Portrait attributed to Gros.*

Above: 'The stoutness he acquired during his reign's last years had developed his torso more than the lower part of his body, yielding an impression of a majestic and imposing bust which lacked a base in due proportion,' – Méneval. Girodet de Roucy Triason's portrait sketch of early 1812, too, confirms Castellane's statement that Napoleon had put on a lot of weight.

Above: Marshal Berthier, Prince of Neuchâtel, the army's major-general and head of the General Staff. In 1812 his powers were declining. In reality he was less than handsome, and no little slovenly. Always biting his bleeding fingernails, he would burst into tears when reprimanded by his exacting taskmaster.

Below: Marshal Davout, Prince of Eckmühl, commander of I Corps. A fierce disciplinarian, he had no consideration whatever for his staff. Murat mocked him to his face for wearing spectacles.

Below: Joachim Murat, King of Naples. An incomparable cavalry commander in battle, on the march he took no care whatever of his four huge 'reserve' cavalry corps. He had no taste for the Russian. He wore fantasical uniforms of his own invention.

Above: Faber du Faur's 12-pounders get stuck in a muddy hollow beyond Vilna and have to turn back, temporarily depriving Ney of his reserve artillery as he chases Barclay de Tolly's 1st West Army eastwards. 'Several hundred horses perished there.'

Below: The Italian Guardia d'Onore on the march. The artist, ex-cakemaker Albrecht Adam, had attached to Prince Eugène's staff in search of battle scenes. Long forced marches in burning heat were less to his taste.

Above: The route-march made through impossible terrain by Pino's division of IV Corps to catch up with the advancing columns was not actually witnessed by Albrecht Adam. His touching picture is thus mostly an 'artist's impression'.

Below: Surgeon Heinrich von Roos 'saw enormous cuirassiers riding little Polish horses so small their riders' legs dragged along the ground'. Faber du Faur thought it 'a spectacle at once sad and funny to see carabiniers and cuirassiers, colossi with gigantic limbs, pass our camp at Rudnia on these scraggy horses'. – *Faber du Faur* .

Above: The Napoleonic soldier, in Russia as elsewhere, didn't steal – he 'found'. But the dividing line between authorized marauding and individual pillage could suddenly shift, exposing looters to the firing squad. Grenadiers from III Corps. – *Faber du Faur.*

Below: Only the well-educated Hessian captain Franz Roeder, a stickler for justice, has a good word to say for the Lithuanian Jews. Colonel Bacler d'Albe, Napoleon's topographer-in-chief and closest collaborator, too, found time to draw 'Polish Jews presenting soldiers of the Grand Army with their merchandise'.

Above: Prince Eugène directing the Italian troops' crossing of the Dwina at Beschenkowiczi, 24 July. – *Albrecht Adam.*

Below: 'At least Polotsk looks like a city,' thought Sergeant Bertrand of the 7th Light, reaching it on 24 July. 'It boasts seven or eight church towers and two big monasteries' – one was the seat of the Jesuit order. Polotsk would be the scene of two major battles. – *Faber du Faur*

Above: Napoleon arrives on the scene at the end of the battle of Ostrowno, 26 July. When it was over, Albrecht Adam asked Eugène to sign his sketches, to prove he'd really been in the thick of it. Actually the two-day battle was only a rearguard action, to give Bagration a chance to liaise with Barclay in front of Witebsk. *Albrecht Adam.*

Below: In front of Witebsk, midday 27 July. Surely the decisive battle is at hand? 'The Army of Italy and Murat's cavalry attack the highway supporting the Russian army's left wing.' But Napoleon unexpectedly called off his attack – and next day the Russians had literally vanished. – *Albrecht Adam.*

Above: The Dnieper (the Borysthenes of antiquity) turned out to be "an ordinary little river, so steeply embanked you can hardly see it before you stumble on it". The gigantic concentration described by Dumonceau, and necessary for the flank march on Smolensk. Ney's III Corps crossing at Rossasna, under Napoleon's supervision. – *Faber du Faur.*

Below: Beyond Krasnoi. Murat's fruitless cavalry attacks on the massed square of Neverovski's division as it carries out its fighting withdrawal on to Smolensk get in the way of Ney's guns. – *Faber du Faur.*

Above: The bombardment of Smolensk, 8 August. The ancient town wall proved impermeable to the invaders' roundshot. – *Albrecht Adam.*

Below: Smolensk in flames. Around 'the cathedral cupolas rising above the plain that hid it from our sight, by 10 p.m. we saw rising from the town centre columns of fire, which seemed like a mountain peak. Growing steadily, they formed a jet of fire that turned night into day and lit up the smiling Smolensk countryside.' – *Faber du Faur.*

Above: The heroic Russian NCO who'd died among the shattered willow trees while obstinately sniping at the Württemberg artillery. 'Next day, Aug 9, visiting the spot out of pure curiosity, we found our enemy's body lying face downward among the broken and splintered trees. He'd been killed by one of our roundshot.' – *Faber du Faur.*

Below: Württemberg gunners firing from the walls of Smolensk at the New Town beyond the Dnieper, where the Russian rearguard is still hanging on. 9 Aug. – *Faber du Faur*

Above: Troops moving up to the firing line at Valutina-Gora, 10 August, where the campaign might have been decided if it hadn't been for Junot's ineptitude. The engaving gives a vivid idea of the early autumn landscape. – *Faber du Faur*

Below: The roads in the army's wake were littered with stragglers, wounded, dead and dying men. "Even if I hadn't been able to see the Moscow road, I'd only have had to follow its smell." – *Faber du Faur.*

Above: This early 19th century print gives an authentic idea of the great masses of men crammed together on a Napoleonic battlefield, particularly on 7 September 1812, at Borodino. Also of the rather gloomy weather conditions.

Below: Murat about to take refuge in a square of the 25th Division, having mistaken Russian for Saxon cuirassiers on account of their white jackets. The artist has omitted his heroic Negro servant Narcisse, who risked his own life to alert the square. – *Faber du Faur*.

Above: The 5th Cuirassiers storm the Raevsky Redoubt. 'Overthrowing everything in front of them, they turn the redoubt, entering it by the throat.' But Auguste Caulaincourt, who has guided the movement, lies dead, shot through the heart. His ADC, Lieutenant Wolbert, kneels by his side. – *Early 19th-c. engraving.*

Below: "The whole ploughed up plain, strewn with wreckage and débris and hemmed in by gloomy dark trees, conspired to give the field [of Borodino] a dreadful aspect. Everywhere soldiers were wandering about among the corpses, rifling their dead comrades' packs for food." – *Faber du Faur.*

Above: The wooden noticeboard erected by Marshal Lefebvre on the spot where the popular Montbrun – who in a moment of irritation had told Napoleon to go to the devil – was killed by a howitzer shell. The board was still standing in 1813. In the *background* Borodino church. *Left mid-distance* part of Semenovskaya and one of the flêches. – Lithographic colour-print in J.T. James: *Views of Russia, Sweden and Poland*, London, 1826.

Below: The Grand Army outside Moscow, 14 September. – *Gudin*, one of his idealized engravings *Entrances of the French into Foreign Capitals*.

'come and present himself in a leisurely way at the imperial tent. But Napoleon had gone down into the plain. The general sits down like a man utterly exhausted. He complains of having gone astray on the march. Is afraid he has sunstroke. Asks for something to drink. Wine won't quench his thirst. Offered a carafe of water, he drains it off at a gulp. By and by he becomes more animated. But it's all up with him. His eye no longer lights up at the sight of a battlefield.'[2]

Although his outflanking manoeuvre has failed, there's still a chance of cutting the Moscow road and thus cutting the Russian army off from its line of retreat. But to do this a whole corps will have to cross the Dnieper upstream. And the only one available is Junot's. According to Ségur there was 'a broad and commodious passage only three miles upstream from the town' to the east. So far, for lack of VIII Corps, attempts to find the ford seem to have been half-hearted. But now Belliard, Murat's resourceful chief-of-staff

'orders a few troopers to follow him, and pushing a band of Cossacks into the river upstream of the town, sees on the opposite bank the Smolensk–Moscow road all covered with artillery and marching troops. But the troopers sent to find a ford rode for six miles without finding one and drowned several of their horses.'

Ségur even says Napoleon 'pushed his own horse in that direction, rode several versts, wearied and came back again'. But is the lethargic Junot really capable of crossing the Dnieper and 'with a river at his back, a fortified town, and an enemy army' pinning down so fierce a bulldog as Bagration? Evidently Napoleon is hoping so. For that's what he orders him to do.

In the centre I Corps is fiercely engaged. After 'manoeuvring en masse under the enemy's fire' its other divisions have 'captured the plateau of Mulchowa'. During this operation the 30th Line is ordered by Davout to advance to the attack and 'we lose a lot of men when drawing up under the Russian guns'. To the left the 7th Light certainly aren't being spared:

'In front of us the Russians were waiting for us in a deep ravine covered with shrubs and bushes. We're thrown in by battalions, by companies. The ground is extremely rough, and breaks up our formations; few or none of our officers manage to keep their men with them – except our captain. His name was Moncey,[5] and he'd been one of the Emperor's pages. He's followed by a half-section – I being its fourth man – who are to distribute his orders. At one particular moment I find I've ten Russians in front of me. Having burnt off a cartridge, we're obliged to play with our bayonets, which hardly troubles us. Soon the Russian guns fell silent – in all that scrum and confusion they'd harm their own men as much as us. We're slowly advancing amid this hand-to-hand fighting, when the cry *"En avant!"* is heard. The drums beat the attack. And everyone dashes forward at the double, upwards and out of the ravine, driving everything before him. To our right the bombardment redoubles – and we who by now, without excessive losses, have reached the foot of the walls, have to suffer the fire from the guns up there in the towers and bastions.'

The 'Dromedary of Egypt', too, is in the thick of it. The cemetery's loop-holed walls have been forced, but now graves and mausoleums are providing almost equally good cover for both sides. Captain François' men have broken in only to find themselves exposed to threefold fire: from Russian sharpshooters dodging about among the graves, from enfilading cannon, and from others which are 'vigorously belabouring us from a tower'. Soon Colonel Bouquet has to withdraw François' men

'behind the counterscarp of the ditch surrounding the cemetery. From his higher level the enemy go on throwing roundshot and some kind of triple-vented shells at us. At 2 p.m. one of these falls in front of my company, spewing out flame from its three vents. I run over, pick it up, and drop it into a well a few yards behind me. I burn my hands a little; also the front of my coat. But the superior officers and the whole battalion shout *"Bravo! Vive le Capitaine François!"* If that shell had exploded, it'd have blown up two ammunition wagons to the battalion's left.'

Thereafter the fighting 'became horrible'. Slowly François and his comrades drive back the Russians 'even to the cannon's mouth'. The Russians' resistance astounds everyone. Defying their officers' orders merely to stand firm, the Russian light infantry in the cemetery can only be restrained from counter-attacking by blows with the flats of their officers' swords. 'Major-general Tsilbulski, on horseback in full uniform, told me he couldn't keep his men under control. Over and over again they after exchanging a few shots with the Frenchmen in the cemetery tried to throw them out of it at bayonet point.' A 22-year-old Russian officer who has ridden out of the town to watch the fighting finds

'General Schevitch of the Lifeguard Hussars inspiring the gunners by his presence. One of the town's clergy was personally sighting several of the guns. Letting the Frenchmen get as close as possible, as soon as they were within caseshot range [about 200 yards] the artillery officer, a young man of approximately the same age as myself, flung them down on the ground in enormous heaps. I'd often seen men fall; but never so many knocked over by a single salvo! Only a second earlier the poor victims had been advancing with fixed bayonets and pale faces. Now most of them lay dead or mutilated, lying there armless and legless, drowning in their own blood. Eager to avenge its comrades with a hailstorm of musketry, another column comes on. Many of our gunners are shot down.'[4]

Farther to the left, Ney's corps is no less heavily engaged. Hour after hour Major Faber du Faur's Württemberger battery stands firing a few yards from a little stream where 'a Russian chasseur distinguished himself by his staunchness and courage. He'd taken up position in front of us behind a few willow trees, on the very banks of the stream. Neither by concentrating our fire on him, nor by using a large-calibre gun to bring down all the trees where he was dodging about[5] could we silence him. He went on shooting at us until nightfall.'

Standing 50 paces away from one of Davout's 12-pounder batteries near his bespectacled marshal – he's been attached to his staff – Le Roy too catches sight of a single detached Russian soldier

'walking to and fro, as if guarding something of great importance. Recognizing me despite his extreme near-sightedness, Davout says: "Go and see what that fellow's doing." Without for one moment taking my eyes off the man's movements, against which I've furnished myself with a good pair of pistols, I gallop over and approach him. There seems to be nothing nothing hostile about him, so I assume he must be standing guard over a superior officer, wounded or dead.

The plump major approaches to within six paces. And the Russian

'points with the tip of his bayonet towards a body, apparently seated against a garden hedge. I return at once to make my report to the Marshal, who has already forgotten all about it. Seems surprised, and he remarks: "Our men wouldn't submit to such discipline; and I think they'd be right not to."

Strange words to come from the Iron Marshal. His and the Guard's 12-pounder batteries[5] have cleared the ravine with their enfilading fire. But that's a game at which two can play. As wave after wave of the blue lines roll forward over it, von Suckow, for one, is beginning to feel angry. What's the sense of such massive attacks against troops which at any moment can withdraw behind those towering walls? He sees

'a French staff officer, without even reconnoitering the terrain, lead the Württemberg Light Infantry – in particular its superb Foot Chasseurs – straight up to the high wall, where they're simply mown down. Decimated and furious at being forced to carry out such an absurd mission, they're obliged to beat a retreat, after losing five officers within only a few minutes.'

On the hither side of the ravine the surgeons have their work cut out. Keen to see the battle at close quarters, Paymaster Duverger has made his way forward through a little copse, from whose far end he can clearly see both armies' movements. Just then

'a blast of grapeshot struck a dragoon a few paces away, and gave me notice I'd do well to moderate my curiosity. So I retired towards a dressing station. A gunner had just been brought in, supported by a young officer who was shedding big tears. His arm was shattered. The amputation took place. During it the poor fellow uttered loud cries, begging for someone to kill him. Suddenly a dull rumour announces the Emperor's arrival, and after a moment or two he appears, followed by a brilliant staff. "Sire, I'm wounded, come to me, come to me!" Napoleon hears him, and comes over: "What do you want of me?" – "Sire, three of my brothers have been killed in your service. Look, I'm no longer in a state to serve you any more. I recommend myself to your bounty."

Napoleon tells Berthier to 'make a note of the wounded man's name in his notebook,[6] and he complained no more'. At that moment Duverger also sees Murat gallop up. And after him, Ney, 'but dressed in his uniform of a marshal of France. The Emperor's two lieutenants gave their superior an account of their operations and then, after a few minutes' discussion, both left.'

Again and again observers on the ravine's edge, von Suckow among them, see how

'we gained ground and broke into the suburbs, only to be dislodged by renewed Russian efforts. But then, suddenly, everything succeeds at once, except Ney's attack, which should have been decisive but has been neglected. The enemy is thrown back brusquely behind his walls. Everything which doesn't make haste to follow suit perishes. Even so, our columns, in mounting to this assault, have left behind them a long broad trail of blood, wounded and dead. One platoon of a battalion which had presented its flank to the Russians, we'd noticed, had lost an entire rank from a single cannon-ball – 22 men falling to the same shot. In this way Ney's error of the previous day with one battalion was repeated by the entire army.'

At about nightfall the city goes up in flames. Everywhere the Russians have been driven back to its walls. Nowhere have they been penetrated. At their foot, covered in blood and dust, Captain François and his comrades don't so much see Smolensk burn as hear it. The roar of his guns having at last fallen silent, Major Faber du Faur is noticing how

'The noise and uproar of the stormy day is followed by a profound silence, only broken by the roaring and crackling of flames consuming the houses. By about 10 p.m. the whole of that part of the city which stood on the far side of the river had become a single flame, mirrored in the Dnieper's waters, in the purple glow of the walls, and in the holy city's tartar towers.'

To Dumonceau, looking on from his bivouac in the vicinity of Napoleon's tents, it seems the flames are

'leaping up from behind those sombre walls like an immense furnace and reaching a considerable height under a cloudless sky, splendid with stars. It was a spectacle of marvellous beauty, or anyway, grandeur.'

That night educated men from all over Europe can drink their fill of what they called 'the sublime' – a kind of beauty defined by Edmund Burke[7] as comprising an element of the grandiose and terrible. Another aesthete, who has probably spent the long hot day in perfect safety amid the baggage train or perhaps been one of the idle spectators on the rim of the ravine – Captain Beyle, alias Stendhal, is thinking Smolensk in flames 'an entrancing sight... such a singular spectacle'.[8] The silhouette of its crenellated towers and walls is putting Paul de Bourgoing and his comrades at General Delaborde's headquarters in mind of Homer's description of Troy in flames. While to Major Boulart 'the Russian sharpshooters, posted on the ramparts, like devils in hell or figures in a Chinese shadow play, offered a picturesque spectacle of an entirely novel kind'. In their bivouacs farther away men can only see

'the cathedral cupolas rising above the plain that hid it from our sight. By 10 p.m. we saw rising from the town centre columns of fire, which seemed like a mountain peak. Growing steadily, they formed a jet of fire that turned night into day and lit up the smiling Smolensk countryside.'

But to the Master of the Horse, 'wandering sleeplessly about', this is 'a terrible sight'. He's feeling deeply worried, not to say depressed:

'The conflagration only grew worse as the night wore on. I reflected dismally on what this outcome must infallibly lead to if the Emperor didn't put into effect his good intentions of the previous day. All the time my conversation with him came back to me, and consoled me a little. But the Prince of Neuchâtel's remarks on that subject made themselves felt at least as strongly, and my earlier experiences made me share his opinion and fears.'

Despite the stupendous conflagration the night is turning cold. And at about 2.a.m. Caulaincourt goes up to 'the camp fire burning in front of the Emperor's tent, on the side facing the town' and sits down beside it:

'I was beginning to feel drowsy, when His Majesty came up, with the Prince of Neuchâtel and the Duke of Istria [Bessières]. They gazed at the flaming town. It lit up the whole horizon, which was also sparkling with our camp fires:

"An eruption of Vesuvius!" cried the Emperor, clapping me on the shoulder and rousing me from my torpor. "Isn't that a fine sight, my Master of the Horse?" "Horrible, Sire!"

"Bah!" riposted the Emperor. "Remember, gentlemen, what one of the Roman emperors said: 'an enemy's corpse always smells good!'" We were all shocked by this remark. At once I recalled what the Prince of Neuchâtel had said, and the Emperor's observation long haunted my inmost thoughts.'

Caulaincourt and Berthier exchange 'meaningful glances, as men do who understand each other without need of words'. But Napoleon is sitting 'silent in front of his tent', watching the holocaust.

An hour before midnight, as the fire is beginning to die down, some marauders who've 'made their way into the town through some old breaches the enemy hadn't even bothered to repair' are the first to enter. Venturing up to the foot of the walls, an NCO of the 107th has quietly climbed it. Encouraged by the silence reigning all around him, he's gone into the town, bumped into some of Poniatowski's Poles and 'recognizing their slavonic accents took them for Russians. Fearing himself a prisoner, he fell into a panic'. But gradually others, too, come clambering in over the debris of the town's shattered gates. 'After the powder magazines had been blown up', Rossetti goes on, 'Cossacks had been sent galloping through the streets, telling everyone the Russian army was going to retreat and urging anyone who wanted to go with it to make haste, before the Dnieper bridge was demolished.' Thousands have done so.[9] At 5 a.m. Napoleon is told the place has been evacuated.

It's been the bloodiest storming attempt Surgeon-General Larrey has ever seen:

> 'The approaches to the gates, the breaches, and the main streets were full of dead and dying, almost all Russians. Their losses were immense. It would have been hard to count the huge number of dead we found successively in the town's ditches, the ravines, along the river bank and at the bridgehead.'

That morning the Red Lancers, most exceptionally, are allowed to unsaddle; and Dumonceau decides to go and take a closer look at the ruined suburbs in the direction of the Malakhofskaia Gate, so repeatedly but vainly assaulted by Morand's division:

> 'Everywhere the terrain was ground to dust, encumbered with scattered debris, with twisted or broken weapons, dead men and horses. All were monstrously swollen, something we attributed to decomposition in the extreme heat. Already putrescent, they gave off a foul stench. They'd begun to be buried. Our own wounded had already been taken to the ambulances and disappeared; but the Russians' had been left lying on the ground. We saw them sitting in the shade of houses, their backs to the walls, calm and impassive, resignedly waiting for someone to come and succour them. Some French surgeons were busy giving first aid. Further on, they were being loaded on to ambulance wagons. Elsewhere artillery wagons were busy picking up weapons scattered over the ground. The suburb's houses, too, all of which had been broken into, abandoned and overthrown, were full of corpses and debris.'

At first it had been the Russians who'd suffered worst. But the closer the assailants had come to the town gate, the more thickly the French and Polish dead littered the ground. At first only officers are allowed inside the city. Major Boulart is one of them. 'Inside the town the sights become even more horrible: houses all in flames, houses burnt down, corpses, a population in despair.' 'The enemy corpses,' Dumonceau sees to his horror,

> 'were literally piled up on top of each other. One could hardly take a step without trampling on them. It was the same behind the redoubt in the space separating it from the town gate, where artillery trains had passed over these heaps of human remains, crushing them in a

thick sludge of flesh, broken bones and bleeding wreckage. Beside a wheel I saw the mask of a human face whose posterior had been separated from it and which was lying in the mud like a glove.'

Artillery colonel *Michel Combe* sees how the Russian wounded from earlier engagements too 'lay here in piles, charred, almost without human form, among the smouldering ruins and flaming rafters. The postures of many corpses showed what terrible torments they must have gone through before dying. I trembled with horror at the spectacle, which always haunts my memory.' All this might conceivably have made sense, Dumonceau thought, if the battle could have been called a victory. But 'though the advantage incontestibly lay with us, it didn't seem to offer any decisive result of the kind we'd been hoping for'. Leaving the town, Le Roy, 'choking from the smoke and dust, shaken by what we saw, made haste to get out of the city. I felt I'd left hell behind me.'

Dumonceau is walking down the cobbled main street ('all the rest were tortuous and narrow') when he hears the brash sound of military music. The Italians, beside their idyllic lake, have played no part in the battle.[10] But now 'proud and grim' the Italian Guard is the first unit to enter the charred city

'to the gay strains of our bands. Not once since hostilities had begun had we seen such scenes. We were deeply shaken. I saw a cart filled to the brim with torn off human limbs being carried away for burial far from the bodies they'd belonged to. On the thresholds of surviving houses groups of wounded stood imploring our help. In the streets the only living beings were French and Allied soldiers, straying about in search of something the flames hadn't devoured. The fire, which by now had been put out, had consumed both itself and half the buildings, the market, the houses and most of the dwellings. And it was in the midst of these heaps of cinders and corpses we made ready to spend the night.'

Of the 18,000 souls Smolensk had numbered before the catastrophe, all but one-sixth have left. Its 2,000 timber houses have virtually all been laid in ashes – and the few that haven't are now being 'invaded by the soldiers, leaving the homeless owner and part of his family standing outside his door, weeping over the deaths of his children and the loss of all he'd owned'. Mostly it's the stone or brick buildings that have survived. Prominent among them is the cathedral. Stepping inside, de Laugier sees

'whole families covered in tatters, distraught, shedding tears, exhausted, debilitated, famished, squatting on the paving around the altars. Their eyes, fixed on us, tell us of their agony. All seem to tremble as we approach, are near to crying out in horror at the very sight of us. Turning back to their altars they implore God's help against us. The alarm spreads; a loud outcry breaks out that the French have come to offer them violence. There's a rush towards the high altar. Thunderstruck, the very grenadiers come to a halt. Then the priest raises his voice and manages to obtain silence. Whereupon he utters a long and energetic discourse. To us, who can't understand him, he seems to be giving expression to their fears, which, allayed, give place to a sad, resigned confidence.'

Never in his life has Césare de Laugier heard such fervent prayer. Even Le Roy, convinced deist though he is, is impressed:

'Entering, I see to my amazement the whole temple lit up, as for some grand religious festival. It's full of women, old men and children who've taken refuge in it. Popes, caring little for what was going on on earth were officiating and imploring heaven's assistance. Most of these people have with them their most precious belongings and are lying on them, sure their enemies' rapacity won't go so far as to despoil them even in their very temples. And they were right about that. Just as I, moved, was studying these unfortunates, more than five hundred soldiers came into the church. Surprised and astonished at such a spectacle, they took off their hats as they did so and assumed a diffident and contemplative air, which pleased me.'

But Laugier leaves 'this abode of misery, my heart swollen, firmly resolved not to budge again from our camp'.

Not until 10 a.m. does Napoleon, accompanied by Berthier, Murat, Davout, Ney, Lobau, and of course Caulaincourt, 'mount his horse, reconnoitre the curtain wall to the east, and enter the city through an ancient breach'. Out in front, at the regulation 50-metre interval, Lieutenant *Louis-Joseph Vionnet* is riding at the head of the Horse Grenadiers' duty troop:

'The Emperor visited the battlefield, and I was part of his escort. Halting briefly in front of the great earthwork known as the Citadel, Napoleon contemplated it a moment and seemed to hesitate. Then – to the despair of all present, with the sole exception of the implacable Davout – he declared: "Before the month's out we'll be in Moscow. In six weeks we'll have peace."'

Words, comments the Master of the Horse drily, 'which by no means convinced everyone, at least so far as peace was concerned'. After touring the charred city Napoleon stations himself by the demolished Dnieper bridge to hasten on its repair. A few yards away Colonel Rossetti and the rest of Murat's suite stand respectfully looking on:

'Squatting down on his haunches in front of a hut, he closely examined the position just abandoned to him by the Russians. After a quarter of an hour, no longer able to contain his joy, he declared delightedly: "Poor wretches! Fancy giving up such a position to me! Come on, we'll have to march on Moscow." Immediately a lively discussion arose between the Emperor, the Marshals and high officers of his entourage.'

Should the army cross the Dnieper and pursue the enemy? Or wouldn't it be more prudent to stay in Smolensk?

'As if to put some distance between them and himself, the Emperor walks on ahead a few paces. The King, Berthier, Davout, Ney, Caulaincourt and Lobau go after him, and we stay behind. The discussion between the Emperor and the heads of the army lasted more than an hour. Afterwards we heard that everyone except Davout had opposed the Emperor's project. The upshot of this conference, so utterly important for the destiny of France, was the order to depart on the morrow. The Emperor mounted his horse, and we went back into Smolensk. It was midday. The heat was stunning.'

Acute disappointment always tends to make Murat ill.[11] So now:

'We had him transported to his headquarters, where he was obliged to take to his bed. At about 3 p.m. the Emperor sent for him. Murat sent him his reply: that he had nothing to add to what he'd said that morning – that the Emperor could dispose of his life, but not make him change his mind.'

A refusal which, to Napoleon, certainly means nothing. But Paris and Vilna are another matter. From the governor's palace – one of twenty or so surviving stone buildings – he, in his own hand, as usual, scribbles a letter to Marie-Louise: "*Mon amie*, I've been in Smolensk since this morning. I've taken this city from the Russians, having killed 3,000 of their men and wounded three times that number. My health is good, the heat extreme. My affairs are going well." That would do for Paris. For Maret and the foreign powers' ambassadors at Vilna something more is needed:

"The heat is extreme, there's a lot of dust, and all this is rather tiring. The entire enemy army was here; it was ordered to give battle, but didn't dare to. We've taken Smolensk by frontal assault. It's a very large city, with solid walls and fortifications. We've killed three to four thousand of the enemy's men, their wounded were three times as many. We've found many guns here. Several divisional generals are said to have been killed. The Russian army is retiring toward Moscow, disgruntled and disheartened."

Too exhausted even to sign this hotch-potch of fact and fiction, 'after dictating this letter', the secretary added, 'His Majesty promptly threw himself down on his bed'. According to Fézensac the 'many guns' only amounted to 'a few old iron cannon in bad condition' and a modicum of stores. 'We hadn't taken a single prisoner.'

That afternoon the interpreter Hyde d'Ideville presents a priest (can he have been 'the only one we found in Smolensk' as Ségur claims) to the Emperor. Supposing him to have intentionally burnt down the city,

'the venerable priest firmly reproached him for what he called his acts of sacrilege. The Emperor listened attentively to him: "But your own church," he said at last. "Is it burnt down?" – "No, Sire," replied the priest. "God will be more powerful than you. As I've opened it to all those unfortunates the fire has left without other asylum He will protect it." Moved, Napoleon replied: "You're right. Yes, God will watch over war's innocent victims. He will reward you for your courage." With these words Napoleon sent him back to his temple with an escort.'

It must have been shortly afterwards that the 28-year-old Breton war commissary *Bellot de Kergorre* sees that a posse of Guard grenadiers has been stationed in the cathedral's central aisle, 'to keep order and ensure respect for this asylum'. At first the devotees refuse all help; but after the priest's homily return to their places and accept the meagre rations the French distribute to them.

Back in 1809 Le Roy had been a prisoner of war here, and been billeted on an Italian resident, whose house was next door to the cathedral. Not being the man to let his emotions distract him from practical business, he's making for the Italian's house when he sees that another, which belongs to another person who'd befriended him, the Countess Krapowski, is on fire. But nothing can be done about it, and he assumes that she has 'anyway retired to her estates to avoid contact with the armies. So I walked down the main street and found my Italian in a terrible state of emotion.' His house has been invaded by the soldiery. 'Remembering me at once, he takes me to witness to the value of his services to French prisoners of war.' Le Roy clears the house of its unwelcome guests, and 'the good fellow tells me how during the forenoon some Frenchmen had broken in and robbed him of 40,000 roubles, fruit of twenty years' savings' – a figure which in Le Roy arouses only scepticism:

'While we're quietly chatting, my Italian catches sight of a score of fresh pillagers, who, under pretext of looking for victuals, are paying him a domiciliary visit. Abruptly breaking off our conversation, my man starts tearing his hair and, in an Italian accent that stresses the last syllable of every word, screaming at the top of his voice that they're the very ones who've just robbed him of the 20,000 roubles. My God! Never in all my life had I heard anyone yell like that! Terrified, the marauders promptly evacuate his home. Whereupon seeing them safely outside he comes back to me and calmly resumes our conversation.'

The French, says the Italian, had done wisely not to mount a night assault, because 'more than 60,000 men had been stationed about the town's streets and squares to defend it until all their artillery and baggage had reached the other river bank'. Passing his friend's house again after his visit to the cathedral, Le Roy sees it's 'full of halted soldiers resting there, calmly waiting for the bridges to be re-established. The Guard was lodged in town, and was keeping order and discipline.'

Dumonceau too wants to take a look inside the cathedral. But gets there too late. A sentry, posted outside its door, turns him away. Instead he walks down the steep main street to the Dnieper Bridge, where he gets permission from an infantry major to go up on to the ramparts; but looking out across the river to the New Town sees little sign of the Russian rearguard, which is occupying it.

Otherwise everybody is searching for something to eat. The distinction between legitimate marauding and crude looting enables War Com-missary Kergorre to find shelter with an apothecary,

'out of whose house we evicted some looters. We ourselves, by means of organized marauding, managed to get hold of some victuals: a little butter, flour, a bad cheese, wine made from plums. There was no shortage of butcher's meat. We even got hold of a cow, which we kept with us for the next fortnight.'

One thing of which there is an abundance is roast pork. The Belgian Sergeant *Scheltens*[12] of the 2nd Guard Grenadiers sees how 'the hungry pigs straying about in the ruins found this roast [namely, dead Russians] excellent. We killed these voracious animals, which didn't come amiss in our bivouacs.' But the 5th Tirailleurs aren't so lucky; and have to make do with some 'green apples, still unripened by the northern sun' they've found 'in the pockets of some dead Russian grenadiers, recognizable by the three copper grenades on their very low and concave shakos'. While searching for his dinner Dedem van der Gelder, severely bruised in the chest from that spent musket-ball, comes across the corpse of the governor of Smolensk 'killed by a roundshot'. His supper, when he gets it, consists of 'a large amount of jam, together with two superb pineapples and some peaches. I'd have preferred a nice soup.'

There's the usual incredible wastage. In the lower part of the Old City, largely spared by the flames, Heinrich von Brandt sees 'great stocks of leather and furs being spoiled and lost, something we'd regret the more cruelly later on. I even saw soldiers, not understanding their value, throwing whole armfuls of paper roubles into the fire.'

Captain François has been commended for gallantry by his colonel. But Carabinier-sergeant Bertrand is mourning a friend, shot through the head by a musket-ball. Also the loss of his red pompom another missile has snatched from his shako.

The mood is utterly sombre. On his way back to his unit Césare de Laugier falls in with one of Eugène's ADCs, a Pole. Both try to find a scapegoat for the disaster. Upon de Laugier declaring it's all the fault of the Lithuanians 'for not imitating their compatriots in the Grand Duchy' the Pole ripostes hotly that there's nothing wrong with Lithuanian patriotism – the fault is mostly the officers who, 'instead of busying themselves with food and medicines for their wretched men have filled their wagons with Bordeaux wines and champagne'.

Neither to the Elban nor the Pole does it occur that Lithuanians aren't Poles; but a people who had themselves once had an empire that stretched to the Black Sea.

CHAPTER 16

DEATH IN THE SACRED VALLEY

Von Suckow takes a cold dip – struggle for the northern suburbs – Barclay's danger-ous detour – Ney held up by a feint – where's Junot? – a broken bridge – Valutina – massacre of 65 voltigeurs – Junot's inexplicable reluctance – General Gudin falls – furious assault by the 7th Light – Murat's letter to his daughter – 'Junot's had enough of it' – rewards among scenes of carnage – a dissenter is sent home – St-Cyr gets his marshal's baton – 'Forward, always forward!' – Larrey's heroic feats of surgery – a visit to Ney's headquarters – Davout takes over the van

And still the fighting isn't over. Far from it. The Württembergers had spent the previous evening trying to flush the Russian rearguard out of the northern suburbs – the so-called New Town – and the much reduced 25th Division has had to wade the Dnieper, its waters up to their chests, while being shot at not only by the Russians but also by the brown-coated Portuguese, whose supporting fire from the city walls is falling short and wounding some of von Suckow's troopers. Also stationed on those walls are Faber du Faur's guns. 'Prey to a devouring thirst' his men had forced a terrified Russian girl to bring them water, and between salvos Faber du Faur has had time to sketch one of his guns being served by its crested-helmeted crew – Russian girl, yoke, buckets and all.

But the suburbs prove impenetrable. And at least the rank and file have to take a second dip as they recross the Dnieper. Meanwhile von Suckow is finding it 'a real pleasure' to watch the French pontooneers at work throwing a pontoon bridge:

'Although the water was very cold and they must have had empty stomachs they did their job playfully. It was a veritable bombardment of jokes and quips and witticisms. *Que voulez-vous?* They were true Frenchmen. As for our officers, the pontooneers with typically French courtesy put some boats at our disposal. No sooner are we back in the streets again than one of Ney's orderly officers, a tall per-sonage of astonishing thinness, arrives flat out, shouting at a great distance from his starving nag: "Go back! Go back across the river, it's the Marshal's orders!"'

But the Württembergers have had theirs direct from Napoleon, who has evidently forgotten to inform Ney. Just as they're about to take a third cold bath, von Suckow's colonel turns up and refuses to let them do any such thing – a piece of insubordination loudly supported by the arrival of an imperial ADC. Nevertheless, though soaked through, they're forbid-den to light fires. 'Next morning we had a considerable number of offi-cers and men sick, and to keep warm even they had to spend the chilly night walking briskly to and fro.'

Now, as dawn breaks, Napoleon too is on those northern walls, trying to discern through his spyglass the line of Barclay's retreat. In fact he sees little – except the dense smoke and flames billowing up across the river. Instead of retreating eastwards toward Moscow, Barclay seems to be taking the road northwards, toward Petersburg.[1]

Meanwhile Ney's infantry regiments – Captain Bonnet's 17th Line among them – are making their way through the blazing suburbs:

'Early that morning the Russian rearguard, though few in numbers, had still been there on the other side of the river. But by 4 a.m., when our troops had mounted the high ground on the right bank, they'd disappeared. Having crossed the bridge, we turned to the right and took the new Moscow road.'

Following on with I Corps among the still burning houses, Paymaster Duverger sees how seven to eight thousand Russian wounded

'had all perished, devoured by the fire their compatriots had lit to impede our march. I moved among the debris of these men and among the houses, very much afraid of the pitfalls opened up at each step by cellars and wells, scarcely masked by cinders and charred timbers, and religiously avoiding corpses which the fire had carbonised and reduced to dimensions of infancy.'

Le Roy, too, sees how

'each house, each courtyard – even the gardens – were full of dead and wounded, abandoned without help. The greater number were nothing but semi-incinerated, mutilated and hideous corpses. In the last house I counted 27 who'd already succumbed, plus some others who'd withdrawn into the courtyard. These unfortunates watched us pass without so much as a sigh.'

Amidst all these horrors, once again, the bands are playing, cornets shrilling and drums beating as the leading units march eastward, supported by the Württemberg artillery: 'Soon we'd set up our guns where only a moment ago enemy battalions had been stationed. The debris of their weapons, littered all over the ground, showed how furiously this point had been disputed.'

But suddenly something unexpected happens. 'A cannon-ball smashed into our ranks, ploughing up the plain. Earth and stones flew around us with the rapidity of lightning. The roundshot kept ricocheting from the walls and in the rear of our position.' The roundshot are coming from Faber du Faur's left, which bewilders Ney, who's assuming it's Barclay's rearguard he has ahead of him. Failing to realize that it's only a feint designed to hold him up,[2] and instead of screening off this diversion and by-passing it, wastes a whole hour deploying unit after unit.

Meanwhile Murat, notwithstanding his (probably psychosomatic) temperature of yesterday, is already on horseback and protecting Ney's right flank as his cavalry crosses valley after valley. Still farther to the right, beyond some very rough and wooded terrain, lies the Dnieper. And everyone is taking it for granted that by now Junot must have crossed it near the village of Pruditchino, and is moving in energetically to cut off

Barclay's retreat. But where is he? What's he doing? Why is there no sign of him?

Ney's advance guard, this hot morning, is being led by two companies of the 7th Hussars. Eight miles along the road, descending into a marshy valley, they find the little bridge broken and themselves exposed to grape and roundshot being fired at them by a solitary battery on the far slope. No question, obviously, of crossing the stream! Veering off 'into a wood to our left to place ourselves out of the line of fire', word is sent back to General Jacquinot, who in turn, accompanied by Lieutenant Victor Dupuy, gallops back to inform Ney,

'who seemed annoyed by these news and repeated several times "But are you sure? Have you seen it?" – "No, M. le Maréchal," the general replied, "but I soon shall." And left at once, as fast as his horse could carry him, with me following. As we pass across their front the hussars shout out to us "The bridge is broken. Don't go there!" We halt on the bank of the stream. The enemy battery is keeping up a very lively fire. Roundshot and grape are raining down all round us. "The bridge is broken," I say to the general, "don't let's amuse ourselves counting its planks!" We turned about and left again at the same speed.'

This time Jacquinot has seen the bridge with his own eyes and can assure Ney it really is broken. '"Very well, then!", the marshal said laughing': and orders his leading units to deploy.

Such is the beginning of what will turn out to be the exceedingly bloody battle of Valutina-Gora.

Rushed to the spot by Barclay, more and more Russian infantry are deploying on the opposite slope. For the fate of Russia hangs in the balance. Captain Bonnet can

'see the Russian column very clearly. Gunfire was being exchanged. Finally the 10th Division went up in column a little to our left and briskly drove them off. The regiment then remained in observation on the main road. At 2 p.m. Marshal Ney comes in person to order us to move up. We follow the main road at the tail of the 4th Line, the idea being to surprise the Russian rearguard and tumble it head over heels. The 4th Regiment had found it encamped [*sic*]; but it had put up a vigorous resistance, and the charge had been beaten back. Our regiments veered off from the road to the right, crossing a muddly ditch full of water. We took up our position on the heights opposite the Russian line, which we couldn't see very clearly, as it was screened by big woods and bushes. The 4th battalion was detached and marched off to the right, following the line of the hills. A lancer of the 9th came toward us, saying the Russians could be seen advancing against us.'

Detached with his grenadier company, Bonnet realizes

'almost immediately that the cavalry had mistaken us and our voltigeurs, already out ahead of us, for the enemy. So instead of dispersing my grenadiers in skirmishing order, I wait. Then, noticing the Russians are increasing the numbers of their skirmishers in front of the 1st battalion which we'd left behind us as we'd extended to the right, I face left, deploy into the line of skirmishers and march on. My grenadiers' line is on the slope of the hill, opposite another occupied by the Russians, who're in much greater numbers. We repulse all their attempts to advance, restricting ourselves to this because we'd orders not to press the enemy at this point. It rained musket-balls.'

But now many more of Ney's units are having to be fed in besides the 4th and 18th Line. From a wood in the rear von Suckow and his comrades in the Württemberg cavalry are fascinatedly watching the struggle:

'The valley, called by the Russians – God knows why – the Sacred Valley,[3] offered a singular view. At our feet reigned a veritable chaos, the thunder of the guns interrupting the crackling of musketry, drumrolls, orders in French, in German, Polish, Italian and Portuguese, thousands of vociferating individuals on foot or horseback stumbling over each other, and – enveloping it all – an impenetrable dust!'

One of his officers makes to graze his grey in front of the wood – and promptly brings down a cannonade on to the inactive Württembergers, 'wounding many to no purpose, either by roundshot or branches falling from the trees. Until all the men began shouting at the officer to bring in that white horse!' Faber du Faur has time to sketch the scene as regiment after regiment moves up. Finally Ney has deployed his entire corps – without making the least headway.

'While Ney was making his frontal attack, Murat was flanking him on both sides with his cavalry, but without being able to bring it into action. Some woods to the left and swamps to the right were impeding his movements. Both were awaiting the effect of a flank march by the Westphalians, under Junot.'

But where is he? 'Murat', writes his ADC Colonel Rossetti, 'judging that he should have come up and be engaged but astonished not to hear him attacking, leaves his cavalry, and crosses the wood and the swamps with General Denon and myself'. As it happens the first unit of VIII Corps they come to is Lance-corporal Heinemann's voltigeur company of the Brunswick Chasseurs. They've been posted far out ahead when

'suddenly a little group of horsemen comes galloping toward us. It's the King of Naples and his suite – a massive figure of a man, with brown, strong features and a black beard [sic – perhaps Murat hadn't shaved that morning?]. We recognize him by his magnificent theatrical costume and a square flat cap decorated with innumerable ostrich plumes and diamond brooches. Halting in front of our captain, he shouts: "What are you doing here? Forward! Through those thickets, in line of skirmishers, against the enemy! The army'll come up behind you!"'

Leaving them with this order, Murat rides off in search of Junot's head-quarters. Napoleon too is wondering what's become of him. Earlier in the day he'd ridden out along the Petersburg road to try to fathom Barclay's movements, but hearing of the action at Valutina has finally taken up his command post at a point some five miles – Gourgaud says 'a league' – along the Moscow highway. By that time it must surely be obvious to him that a full-scale battle is developing. Yet at 5 p.m., still ignorant of Junot's movements, or rather lack of them, and after ordering Davout to send in two of his divisions to turn the Russian left, he, 'regarding the day as over' (Gourgaud) goes back to Smolensk, leaving Davout ('who seemed rightly discontented to see these fine corps he'd formed and on whose behalf he'd given himself so much trouble sacrificed to the King of Naples' imprudent valour') to commit Compans' and Gudin's crack divisions to the ever more embittered struggle, while Friant's men stand with shoul-dered arms ready to support them.

Before going back to Smolensk, however, Napoleon has sent Gourgaud to Murat, with

'several officers (among others M. Rohan Chabot, ADC to General Count Narbonne) under his orders, charging him to co-ordinate the movements of Marshal Ney, the King of Naples and the Duke of Abrantès and to send him reports on the affair'.

To their amazement both Murat and Gourgaud find VIII Corps motion-less with piled arms. Galloping up to its commander, Murat yells:

'"What are you doing there? Why aren't you advancing? You're unwor-thy to be the last dragoon in Napoleon's army!" "My cavalry's no use. It's no match for the Russian battalions. Besides I've no definite orders to attack." "Then I'll do it instead! I'll put some fire into these Westphalians of yours!" Galloping up to General Hammerstein's light cavalry brigade and shouting "Follow me, brave Westphalians!", the King of Naples is immediately followed by this allegedly worthless cavalry, who overthrow the screen of Russian sharpshooters and fling them back. Returning to Junot, he says: "Now you can finish it off. Your glory is there, and your marshal's baton."'

And when Junot still shows no sign of budging, Gourgaud asks him what he's to tell the Emperor.

'The Duke of Abrantès was surrounded by his staff, and seemed utterly depressed. He replied angrily: "You'll tell him, Monsieur, that I've taken up my position, because night has fallen.' In vain the ord-nance officer riposted that there were almost four more hours of daylight, that Marshal Ney was suffering badly from the frontal attack he was having to make; all his representations were useless. The Duke of Abrantès wouldn't move.'

No sooner had Murat left them than Heinemann's voltigeur company (of whom 77 of its original 150 'strong young men, wrenched from their dis-tant fatherland' have succumbed to the campaign's rigours') 'as if guessing what was to follow already' have spread out in open order and begun advancing toward the distant enemy:

'Beyond us lay an open field. We waited for our regiments to come up in support. First we caught brief glimpses of groups of Cossacks; then of Russian hussars; and, soon afterwards, whole lines of enemies, swathed in dust clouds. Several units seemed to be moving out to their flank. We look behind us, to see if any of our own are coming up. Not a chance! Not a weapon gleams behind us in the wood. We're all on our own. And at each moment our danger is growing. Innumerable swarms of Cossacks are advancing on us, darkening the air with dust clouds, their forest of lances rolling on like a fog to envelop us.'

If only their captain ('a brave Hessian named Worm') would order the cornet to sound a hasty retreat! But no. His 'inflexible military honour' forbids it. Instead,

'the cornet is calling in our skirmishers, spread out to right and left, and the Cossacks are cutting off our retreat. Realizing we must now become the victims of our own obedience, we stop thinking and obey. Our little force forms a double square, six ranks deep – an insignificant little troop amidst countless enemies! Sabre in hand, our captain steps out boldly from the square, baring his chest to the Cossack skirmishers. He'll be the first to fall, going on ahead to prepare night quarters for 65 comrades in eternity. No little scared, but all our muskets at the ready, we await the enemy. Comes the order: "By platoons, fire!" On the instant all our muskets go off. With thumping heart, swathed in a thick cloud of gunpowder smoke, each of us awaits what the next minute will bring. It must decide whether we're to live or die.'

But it's thumbs down for the brave Brunswickers.

'With a thousandfold hurrah the galloping Cossacks break into our defenceless group from all sides. After a mere couple of minutes our front ranks are lying on the ground, stabbed through by a thousand lances. Our muskets' smoke disperses to reveal a horrible bloodbath. None of us sees the least chance of escaping the slaughter now beginning. The Cossacks are making such easy work of us, our inability to resist seems to stir their blood-lust to madness. Surrender is out of the question. As if driven by some obscure instinct, anyone who's still alive throws himself down on the ground and plays dead. Comes a moment of horrible waiting. Happy he who finds himself lying under heaps of corpses! Even if the blood of those of our comrades who've been stabbed through seeps down over our bodies, if their limbs twitch and jerk on top of ours, if the dying breathe their last sighs into our ears and their corpses press upon us – at least there's still a chance of surviving underneath this terrible rampart. In such lethal need it's every man for himself!

'The lances stab furiously into heaps of dead and living; many a chest or neck is crushed under the horses' hoofs. The Russians' green hussars, avid to join in in this monstrous feast of slaughter, are only prevented from making free use of their sabres by their own densely packed masses as they advance.

'I was one of the few still alive. Blood was seeping through my uniform, soaking me to the skin and glueing my eyelids together. Though still not wounded, I could hear the clash of lances and sabres, mingled with our assassins' dull oaths, muttering between their teeth their terrible *"Pascholl! Sabacki Franzusky!"* [Die, dog of a Frenchman!] as they exerted all their strength to probe the bodies of the dead with their lances and sabres, to see whether beneath them there mightn't be something still alive. Finally my turn comes. A lance-thrust, passing through the chest and back of a comrade who was lying on top of me, strikes my skull a glancing blow and rips open the skin. Yet I feel no pain. Lying there half-conscious, all I long for is an end to the slaughter.'

But now a new danger threatens. The Cossacks have dismounted. Savagely heaving aside the dead, they're trying to find anyone who may still be alive.

'In this terrible moment I can't help opening my eyes to see what's going on. Suddenly I'm aware of a bearded face with white teeth, bending closely down over me, and hear the Cossack's savage scornful laugh as he finds another victim to slaughter. A hundred arms drag me out from amidst the mangled corpses. And above me I see innumerable lances raised, ready to stab me – when, all of a sudden, familiar sounds suddenly ring out. Orders shouted in German! The clash of weapons! Heavenly music... The blue Westphalian hussars are fighting the Cossacks and Russian green hussars hand to hand, and after them come our chasseurs. The Cossacks depart, cursing. Only a few still go on eagerly searching for plunder; then even these gallop off, and all is quiet around our square's burial place.

'Anyone who was still alive and had the strength to do so, stood up. Only the sacred number thirteen were saved, as if by a miracle. Not one unwounded had escaped the butcher's chopping block. We were so dreadfully bloodied and covered in dust no one could recognize anyone else. Not until we'd washed our faces and hands in a stream did many of us recognize some friend.'

Hammerstein's cavalry, too, is done for. Drawn by wildly fleeing Cossacks into an improvised ambush, they're systematically mown down by Russian batteries – batteries Barclay, precisely against this eventuality, has placed along the Moscow road – before they can deploy against a line of Russian élite hussars. Lieutenant Eduard Rüppell, in the thick of it, is finding the Russians' fire 'precise as on a parade ground exercise'.

And that's the end of Junot's *manoeuvre sur les derrières*.

Out on the fiercely contested slopes of the Sacred Valley the fusillade has been going on for three hours, during which time, says Bonnet, 'the Russians were regularly relieved five or six times'. Carabinier-sergeant Bertrand's shako, minus its red pompom, is destined to suffer further mutilations. At the first rumble of gunfire, the 7th Light had been

'ordered to open our cartridge pouches and adjust the shot. A second order, and we're made to advance at the double and enter a wood where Compans' division is at grips with the enemy. This division inclines to the left and mine (Gudin's) replaces it. Hardly has the head of our column debouched from the woods than we're swept by grapeshot. We find we're facing a high steeply edged plateau, at whose foot flows a stream ten to twelve metres wide. The only bridge having been destroyed by the Russians, we must cross this broad ditch under a storm of musketry and roundshot. Our superior officers set the example by jumping into the water. The drums beat the charge. And soon my regiment and the 12th Line, eight battalions in all, are on the other bank. Two battalions of my regiment are sent forward as skirmishers over the entire front of the plateau occupied by the enemy. We encounter some felled trees, which hold us up and oblige us to make a long detour. In the midst of these difficulties our brave General Gudin is just coming toward me when he falls, felled by a roundshot.'

Gudin is one of the army's most popular generals. He has just dismounted and is standing in the middle of the road, about to lead his division into battle, when a 'ricocheting roundshot' tears off one of his legs at the thigh, and the other just below the knee.

Night falls without any abatement in the fighting. And the moon comes out. From his vantage point von Suckow is watching some Illyrians as they descend into the valley,

'to an accompaniment of drums and the sharp screeching sound of fifes.[4] I saw nothing wrong with their using these alleged instruments of music. What astonished me was the tune they were playing: "Let's be happy we're alive!" I couldn't help remarking to a comrade on the bitter irony of leading men to their deaths while offering them such advice! In the moonlight we could very clearly make out the Russian sharpshooters on the crest as they fired. The scene was one of the most interesting. We could see each skirmisher as his shot went off, and clearly made out his green tunic and white trousers.'

At the second assault the Illyrians succeed, but not without heavy losses:

'We were present at a continuous march-past of wounded being carried to the rear. A great number must have succumbed to their wounds, nothing having been arranged to receive them and everything being lacking that would have been needed to organize an ambulance'

The Württember cavalry too is suffering heavily. So heavily that General Marchand 'a man of the *ancien régime*, elegant and chivalrous, the very type of the gentleman and benevolent commander standing there beside his horse toying with his gold snuffbox, had spared us further losses when the Illyrians asked for supports to be thrown in'.

Yet the fighting is only getting still more furious. And up on the far slope Sergeant Bertrand is fighting for his life:

'Either side becomes doubly determined. Feeling a supreme effort is needed, the cry of "En avant!" coming from all voices and the charge being furiously beaten, sweeps us up. Finally, after a terrible scrimmage, we carry the redoubt which is our objective, having turned the battery flanking it. The enemy withdraws by making a stand along the fringe of the wood. Night is just falling on this carnage when we hear our Colonel Rome say "Soldiers of the 7th Light! The Emperor wants to be master of this wood, he wants us to enter it." Immediately, without further orders, the drums again beat the charge. A voice says: "Colonel, we've no cartridges!" "You've got your bayonets," replies our colonel. And into the wood we go, heads down. I'm pursuing an officer when two Russians try to surprise me from behind. "Look out, Bertrand!", shouts one of my comrades, "Stand your ground! I'm coming!" We shake off our two adversaries, I jab at mine with my bayonet so that his eye comes out of its socket.'

This attack seems to have been what was needed to force the Russians to relinquish their grip. And Gourgaud confirms it:

'a considerable column of Russian grenadiers made a bayonet charge against a battalion of the 7th Light and another of the 12th Line. In this mêlée a lieutenant of voltigeurs of the 12th (M. Etienne) flung himself on the Russian general and having hit him twice on the head with his sabre, took him prisoner in the midst of his men.'

'This fighting,' Bertrand ends,

'cost us great losses. From the stream to the crest of the plateau the ground was covered with dead, dying and wounded. The Russians were even more sorely tried than we were. And they were definitely out after my head, because two musket-balls went through my shako.'

According to Bourgoing both the Spaniards, under Count de Bourmont, and the Portuguese fought valiantly: 'The Castilian loyalty and courage didn't gainsay themselves, and the same goes for the Portuguese Legion, both infantry and cavalry, which sustained considerable losses.'

Finally, at about 11 p.m. the firing dies away. And Murat returns to his bivouac, where he pens a sad little letter to his daughter Letitia in faraway Naples:

'Today is my birthday, today the whole family will be gathered and I'm sorry I'm not in your midst, dear children, to receive your best wishes and the beautiful flowers my Letitia would have brought me. I'd have given her a rose in exchange to put in her hair, not that she has any need of it to be pretty... Your letter has made me shed many tears, but my tears have done me a lot of good...'

Incredible numbers of wounded come streaming back through the night. Dr Réné Faure, ordered up from Smolensk with I Cavalry Corps, crosses 'the Dnieper bridge at midnight. The night was sombre and we could hardly make out the road. As day broke we saw many wounded infantrymen coming back to the town. The youngest had lost their martial air. But the officers' features wore quite a different expression. Those who couldn't walk were letting themselves be carried, but were calm. It called for an effort to vanquish the pain. One league from the town we saw a carriage coming toward us, escorted by soldiers with lighted torches. General Gudin, who'd had a thigh carried away in the combat whose firing we'd heard, was being carried to the town with every care brave soldiers could manage.'

The morning of 20 August dawns in a dense mist. After the sun has broken through, the Red Lancers, 'grilled in a furnace-like atmosphere not relieved by a breath of air', are watching a lot of riderless horses galloping about and many wounded fellow-Dutchmen from the 127th Line making for the rear:

'After them appeared a group of soldiers carrying a stretcher covered with a mantle accompanied by a staff officer and a surgeon, from whose afflicted looks we guessed it was some important officer they were carrying. And the officer told us it was the brave and regretted General Gudin who'd had his two legs carried away at the knee by a cannon-ball.'

Gourgaud claims it was he who brought the sad news of Gudin's obviously fatal wound to Napoleon. Also of Junot's ineptitude:

'"Junot's had enough of it," Napoleon said, turning to Berthier. "He didn't want to turn the Russian position. He's caused us this very bloody affair, and of our losing Gudin... I don't want him to command the Westphalians; he'll have to be replaced by Rapp, who speaks German."'

But Caulaincourt hears some of Junot's friends, Berthier among them, intervene on his behalf. So nothing is done about it.

All their lives men will remember with horror the monstrous scene of carnage at Valutina. Early that morning the Württemberg cavalry, descending into the Sacred Valley, had

'no water to give the dying nor bandages for the wounded. We had to cross the frightful scenes of slaughter. It all offered a monstrous sight to the eye, which will never efface itself from my mind,'

von Suckow will write fifty years afterwards.

'At 3 p.m. Napoleon himself appears on the scene, and exclaims: "Ah, that's how I like to see a battlefield, three enemy to each dead Frenchman!" But by then Murat (according to Dedem) has already 'had the corpses of the French dead stripped. He wanted to make His Majesty believe all those he saw were Russians. The Emperor, seemingly not too convinced, reproached his brother-in-law for having sacrificed too many men by a frontal attack on a position which could have been turned,'

- which must also have been Davout's view. 'The corpses were heaped up under the feet of the escort's horses and hindered the regiments' alignment,' Le Roy would tell his grandsons thirty years later. The men of Gudin's division,' writes Ségur – and Rossetti echoes his words,

'were drawn up on top of their companions' and Russian corpses, amidst half-broken trees, on ground ripped up by roundshot, encumbered with the debris of arms, torn clothing, military utensils, overthrown vehicles and scattered limbs. Gudin's battalions were no longer more than platoons. All around was the smell of powder. The Emperor couldn't pass along their front without having to avoid corpses, step over them or push them aside. He was lavish with rewards. The 12th, 21st and 127th Line and the 7th Light received 87 decorations and promotions.'

As for the 7th Light, 'which had suffered particularly', it receives 32 Crosses. One of them goes to Bertrand's young Captain Moncey, the former imperial page who'd performed so valiantly in front of Smolensk. The 127th, however, is a new regiment, and therefore still lacks an eagle. Now it gets one. Brandt is among the onlookers:

'In this setting the ceremony, impressive in itself, took on a truly epic character. The regiment formed square. In the ranks I could make out many a face still blackened with powder, and much equipment still stained with blood. The colonel and his officers were drawn up in a semi-circle around the Emperor. "Soldiers!" he said, "Here's your eagle! It will serve you as a rallying point in moments of danger. Swear to me never to abandon it, to stay always in the path of honour, to defend our country and never to let France, our France, be insulted!"'

What the Dutch conscripts think about being called Frenchmen, Brandt doesn't say:

'But all replied, as a man: "We swear it!" Then the Emperor took the eagle from Marshal Berthier's hands and gave it to the colonel, who in turn handed it to the colour-bearer. At the same instant the square opened, the men formed line, and the colour-bearer, preceded by drums and the band, came to take up his battle station in the centre of the élite platoon. A grenadier sergeant of the same regiment was promoted second lieutenant on the spot. "Have this gallant fellow proclaimed at once," said Napoleon. The colonel pronounced the sacramental words, but abstained from embracing his new officer. "Well, colonel? The accolade! The accolade!" the Emperor said sharply. Nor was it the moment to forget it. Decorations, promotions and monetary awards rained down like hailstones. One could perceive that Napoleon felt an imperative need, both in himself and in others, to react against gloomy thoughts. Coming to the 95th Line, he tells the colonel to give him the names of those who'd distinguished themselves yesterday. As the colonel naturally began with the officers, when he came to the sixth or seventh name, the Emperor interrupted him: "How is it, colonel? Are all your rankers chicken-hearted?" And he personally summoned those NCOs and men who were pointed out to him as worthy of promotion or a decoration to step out from the ranks. Contemplating this scene, I submitted to the irrĕistible fascination Napoleon exercised whenever and wherever he wanted to.'

A few yards from the Emperor staff-captain Girod de l'Ain (he who is forever being balked of his Legion of Honour) is standing chatting with another ADC when his foot strikes against a little box, tied with string. 'We were no little surprised to find inside it two Crosses of the Legion.' Having already been several times recommended, Girod and his friend pocket one apiece -against possible future use. But Colonel Rossetti, that boasted Frenchman, is in ecstasy:

'Never did a field of victory offer a more exalting spectacle! The gift of this well-merited eagle, the pomp of these promotions, the shouts of joy, the glory of these warriors, rewarded on the very spot where they'd gained it, how many good things all at once! But we were deploring the loss of 4,000 brave men.'

Even the critical Labaume concedes that 'all antiquity cannot offer anything more heroic than such a sight amid the dead and dying.'

Next day it's the Italians' turn. Reviewed 'in a vast plain a little below the heights beyond Smolensk where they'd camped' they don their parade uniforms for the second time. And Napoleon, in his most flattering mood, rewards them for their behaviour at Witebsk – and is greeted with acclamations in his native tongue. The cheering, Laugier notes, isn't being

'ordered or incited by the colonels, but comes from the hearts of all these soldiers who, greedy for glory, have grown old in the camps. The Emperor passed brilliantly along the troops' front, spoke to several officers and also to many of the men, asking them whether they were content, whether they'd suffered on the march. More than once he got the reply: "Our only grievance, Sire, is not to have seen the enemy as often as the other corps have." "You'll be seeing them," Napoleon replied. And these were no vain words of flattery. Because flattery is little known to the soldier. These are the whole army's sentiments. The ceremony ended after sunset.'

What Laugier almost certainly doesn't know is why IV Corps' chief-of-staff is suddenly allowed to go back to Paris. Nor, evidently, does Labaume, even though he must have been associating with him daily:

'General Dessoles, disgusted by his services being overlooked, only wanted to enjoy in peace the esteem his talents had brought him.

The army, remembering how he'd shared the glory and disgrace of Moreau, showed its discontent. The Emperor yielded to the requests of this clever general, and granted him an honorable retreat and a pension.'

That's the official version. Actually Dessoles' mail, like so many other people's, has been snapped up by the secret office in the Rue Coq-Héron; and the contents and tenor of his correspondence have unmasked him as an inveterate grumbler and dissident. Packed off back to France, he's replaced by General Guilleminot.

Next day, though the Vistula Legion hasn't taken any part in the fighting, it too is reviewed on the main square. The last time Lieutenant Brandt had paraded before the Emperor had been on the Place du Carousel in Paris; and on that occasion, despite all his arduous service in Spain, Napoleon hadn't regarded him as ripe for promotion. But clearly his photographic memory for faces is no myth:

'I was one of the officers designated. There were fourteen of us who, summoned by the colonel, stepped forward out of the ranks. The Emperor halts, looks at me, draws me towards him by a button of my uniform – as his habit was – and says: "This one should have been promoted captain already, in Paris. Make him captain-adjutant-major." Continuing his tour along the front of the regiment, he notices a sergeant who'd been decorated and is wearing the three stripes that signify twenty years of service. "How is it this man isn't an officer yet?" "Sire, he can't read or write". "It's all one! These poor illiterate fellows no one wants to know about often make the best officers. Make him standard-bearer and second lieutenant of grenadiers. I'm sure he wasn't behindhand at the storming of Saragossa."'

The Russian general (Toutchkoff III) whom Voltigeur-lieutennt Etienne had seized by his collar, turns out to be the brother of his own divisional commander, General Toutchkoff II. And is therefore amiably received. And when, a moment later, a flag of truce arrives to get news of him, Napoleon seizes his opportunity and says that Toutchkoff may by all means write and tell his brother he's well – a letter, however, to be accompanied by another. Dictated to Fain and signed not by Napoleon but by Berthier, it informs the recipient that 'this general has left in good health for Metz:

'On this occasion'[here the Emperor himself takes the pen, and all the rest is in his own semi-illegible handwriting between the lines of his dictated draft) – "on this occasion I renew to Your Excellency the proposal I have made for an exchange of prisoners and for regularizing communications between the two armies; likewise the manner of treating flags of truce. His Majesty is pained to see the evils the country is suffering under. He wishes the Emperor of Russia would leave behind civil governors, to take care of the common people and of property; it is a usage which has been followed in almost all wars. The Emperor, M. le Baron, whom I have informed of the contents of this letter[!], charges me to present his compliments to the Emperor Alexander if he is with the army, or otherwise in your first report to him. Tell him that neither the vicissitudes of war, nor any circumstance, can alter the esteem and friendship he feels for him."

There's nothing, Napoleon tells Toutchkoff, he wants so much "as to conclude peace. We've burnt enough powder and shed enough blood. We must end this some time. But," he adds threateningly: "for Moscow to be occupied would be the equivalent to a girl losing her honour." No more than another letter which Berthier had written from Vilna does this one, though delivered, get an answer.

On the evening of 20 August, 'at the very moment when Napoleon amid incredible scenes of carnage was distributing rewards to the combatants of the previous three days', Lejeune gets back from Polotsk. He has the most welcome news. St-Cyr, taking over from Oudinot who's been seriously wounded,[5] has won the campaign's first signal victory. Hard-pressed by Wittgenstein, on 16 August he'd feigned a withdrawal across the Dnieper, returned under cover of night and in the afternoon of 18 August, too late for any major engagement to be expected, attacked Wittgenstein and routed him.

The news comes at exactly the right moment. And Napoleon sends St-Cyr his marshal's bâton. But Gudin, who'd been generally regarded as next in line for one, has died in agony, despite all Larrey's ministrations. And the artistically minded Lejeune is ordered to arrange a Homeric funeral:

'I guided the procession to the Great Bastion, where I'd had his grave dug and which was to be this illustrious warrior's mausoleum. On the dead man's body I placed a score of muskets, broken in the fighting, arranging them star-wise, so that one day, when Time, which destroys everything, shall uncover a hero's ossuaries, this trophy of arms will draw upon them the same sentiments of attention and respect as we accord to the remains of the valiant Gauls under their antique tumuli.'

Both Bourgoing and Boulart are among the mourners. Bourgoing feels in the air

'a general anxiety. In this grim and religious silence it was easy to see how deeply worried we were for the future. Everyone had had enough of fatigues, chancy affairs and glory for one campaign. No one was keen to go any further. Everyone was frankly avowing his need and wish to halt.'

Quartermaster Anatole de Montesquiou, at headquarters, is finding that 'when we came with orders several of the very generals we'd earlier found so compliant, so confident of success, now received us gruffly with a:

"Well, so it's 'Forwards, forwards, always forwards, is it? Hasn't he had enough yet? Won't he ever?'" And Fézensac:

'The King of Naples never ceased reiterating that the troops were exhausted, that the horses, which only had thatch to eat, could no longer stand up to such fatigues, and that we were risking losing everything by advancing further. His advice didn't prevail. And the order was given to march on.'

Only young officers like Planat de la Faye are in favour: 'we were expecting a great battle which would decide the campaign'.

Never was the old phrase about 'grasping a wolf by the throat' more applicable than to Napoleon at Smolensk. He can neither go forward nor stay where he is. Nor, least of all, retreat.

As for Smolensk itself, it's 'one vast hospital'. Although Larrey and his medical staff find 'some brandy, wines and a few medicines and our reserve ambulances had at last caught up' nothing suffices. The surgeons are working day and night.[6] 'Already during the second night we already lacked anything to bandage the wounded with.' Among the fifteen surviving brick buildings he's using are the Archives:

'In lieu of linen dressings, which had been used up after the first few days, we made use of paper found there. The parchment served for splints and bandages; tow and birch cotton (*setula alba*) served as lint; and the papers also did good service for bedding down the sick. But what difficulties had to be surmounted! What trouble we had to go to! Even so, despite the scanty means at our disposal, all indicated operations had been carried out within the first 24 hours. Myself I amputated eleven arms at the scapulo-humeral articulation,'

i.e., through the shoulder joint.[7] Despite all Larrey's efforts Surgeon *Kerkhove* calls the Smolensk hospitals 'cloaques of misery and infection, where one could observe all the influence of putrid miasmas on causing hospital gangrene by the suppuration of wounds'. Stumbling on such a hospital whose 100 wounded had been completely overlooked, Rapp, says Ségur, 'didn't fail to tell the horrible details to Napoleon, who had his own wine and several pieces of gold distributed to these unfortunates, still clinging to life or sustaining it with revolting foods'.

There are also the dead. On 21 August Berthier, who's having his work cut out to get all the corpses buried, informs Napoleon by letter that though 600 men have been detailed off, 'this operation is still far from finished. To accelerate it, we shall virtually have to employ Russian prisoners. I beg you to let us use 200 of them.'

So badly has III Corps been mauled at Valutina, it can no longer form the advance guard. Granted a 3-day halt to replenish its *matériel* and calculate how much ammunition it has expended, a Württemberg artillery officer finds that 'between July 2 and Aug 2 we'd fired off 214 shells, 433 six-pounder cannon-balls, eleven howitzer shells, and 30 six-pounder caseshot. The loss of horses was very serious and the few which could be replaced by little Russian farm horses were of scant help to us. Time and again the long-indulged hope of getting some captured remounts had been disappointed.'

Paul de Bourgoing has a brother who's one of Ney's ADCs; and gets permission to go and see him. On his way he crosses the battlefield, where he sees the corpses all jumbled up 'the French and Russian infantry having fought face to face, shot at each other point-blank, to the right, to the left, ahead, to the rear, in large and small detachments.' And a mile or two further on reaches Ney's headquarters, a 12ft x 12ft hut of leafy branches. 'An excellent shelter against the sun, but detestable against rain, they in no way resembled those of the other top brass' – Murat's, for instance, comfortably installed in a timber château some five miles further on along the Moscow road. Dedem, who's finding in Ney a great source of malicious gossip about goings on in top circles, regards the redheaded marshal as

'a man of brilliant courage and energy on the field of battle. But outside the theatre of war he was feeble, couldn't make up his mind, and let himself be swayed by his advisers. Basically detesting Napoleon, at odds with the Prince of Neuchâtel, jealous of the other marshals, the only one he was on good terms with was Macdonald. Not very communicative, withdrawn, he rarely saw the generals who served under him.'

And the 28-year-old Intendant *A-D. Pastoret*, who's been left behind at Witebsk to organize that town's supplies declares: 'He wasn't a good-natured man, this Duke of Elchingen; but he was a clever man.' Even more than with his fellow-marshals, war is more than a profession for Ney. It's a religion. And the horrible action at Valutina and its subsequent heroics must have suited him down to the ground. His headquarters, Bourgoing goes on,

'hardly differed from an ordinary officer's. When I got there, Ney was alone. But a few yards away a meal, set for 20 persons, was laid out on the greensward, awaiting his numerous aides. It was served up on a superb dish. Plates, huge bowls, etc., all in silver, symmetrically laid out on the greensward, which served as an oval table around which we sat down, or rather stretched ourselves out in a recumbent position, leaning on our elbows like guests at a sumptuous feast of the great conquerors of Ancient Rome.'

Bourgoing is struck by the great variety of III Corps' uniforms and admires the various regiments' accoutrements. Particularly

'the fine Württemberg cavalry's stood out, having in many cases been arbitrarily chosen by its colonels. The crest of its helmets, instead of being a comb or floating out behind like that of our dra-

goons, was flung forward, half concealing these old warriors' fore-
heads. They were Ney's cavalry escort.'

His visit over, Bourgoing returns to the charred city, only to hear, much to
his disgust, that General Delaborde is to remain behind as governor,
pending Jomini's arrival from Vilna. A couple of days later, after Napoleon has left, he and the rest of Delaborde's staff will move into the
vacated palace. All they find there is a few insignificant scraps of paper,
among them a little list of Napoleon's laundry which Bourgoing pockets
as a souvenir. Also a whole edition, 'several thousand copies' of 'the celebrated Desaugier's drinking songs'. Had they been officially ordered? Or
sent from Paris by mistake? Mediocre both as literature and as poetry –
'surprisingly so, to have come from the author of *Paris à cinq heures du
matin* and many other masterpieces of French *esprit* and frank gaiety' – it
had been tactful, he thought, not to have distributed them to the men
'just now when everyone was being tormented by thirst'.

As for Lejeune and his colleagues on Berthier's staff, all they can
'extract from this brief stay in this deserted town was a few dips in the
Dnieper. These bathes repaired our protracted fatigues and disposed us to
resume our own painful work as invaders...'

CHAPTER 17

STRAGGLERS AND PRISONERS

A loaded musket goes off – hobbling to the rear – 'they weren't the same columns' – a Turk's faith – 'what's all this fuss?' – gangrene – but what a camp! – a miracle – something out of the Arabian Nights – Cossacks and peasants – Heinemann is taken prisoner – a transport – Winzingerode's humanity – 'inhuman cruelty only possible in a land of masters and slaves'

Thousands of wounded, stragglers and looters are swarming on the army's flanks and in its rear. One of them, now, is Lance-corporal Heinemann. After the massacre of their square at Valutina those Brunswick Chasseurs who'd survived – many are suffering from dysentery – feel they've done enough:

'For a moment we hoped to be allowed to return to our fatherland. But in tight spots the ranker is mere cannonfodder. And we'd hardly got our breath back before we had to rejoin our battalion and march, once again, against the enemy.'

Obliged to relieve himself under a tree, Heinemann's sergeant is just propping his loaded musket against its trunk when it goes off; and the ball passes through his foot. No transport to the rear is available. So Wilhelm is detailed off to help him back to the Smolensk hospitals. "Now, comrade," jokes the intrepid sergeant, "we'll see how two men can manage on three legs." "If it's God's will, sergeant, all will be well in the end," says Heinemann, who has his pious moments. "What can't a man do, if he must and will?"

They'll soon find out. 'Up to now we'd been marching in the van with the strongest, who'd no inkling of what a dissolving army looks like.' Hobbling back along the highway, the two men see, for the first time, what things are like in the army's rear:

'These were no longer the same columns. Already they were beaten men, looking only for a spot on this foreign soil to lie down and die. Our comrades went marching past us in open columns. First came the strongest, then the weaker, then others whose strength was almost at an end. And last of all the dying, dragging themselves along at the tail. If any sank down, the thick dust soon covered him, like a pall over a bier. Many went past us, silent and unfeeling. Others joked desperately: "Give my love to mother!" – "If thy foot offend thee, cast it away!" jokes a former candidate for the priesthood. And a junior surgeon offers to amputate it.'

Now and again the two men exchange philosophical reflections. The sergeant, who's a great curser and swearer, sits down for a moment on a dead horse, opining that even if all men are sinners, as Wilhelm has been taught, the story of God's punishment on Adam is disagreeable to a soldier. "So I don't want to hear any more of that stuff! I'm sticking to my good Turk's faith: that everything's pre-ordained. Do what one will, none of us escapes his fate." Heinemann, too little the philosopher to discuss such deep matters, hastily agrees that some such belief is indispensable on campaign. As dusk falls, some vehicles come rolling by, raising the two men's hopes. But no, they belong to the Italian army, and a wounded Westphalian is no concern of theirs. Meanwhile the sergeant's foot is becoming agonizingly painful. Gangrene? Hoping against hope it isn't, the two men struggle on westwards. Realizing they've no mercy to hope for from the exasperated peasants, still less any help, they daren't even seek shelter in any cottage that still may be left standing.

The hot dusty day is followed by an icy foggy night, lethal to a seriously wounded man. Encountering a stray horse, they kill it, cut out its liver and entrails, and dine on horsemeat grilled over a fire of broken wheelspokes, salting it with gunpowder. But this only worsens the sergeant's thirst, which is already becoming terrible, and his swigs at the brandy flask only inflame it still further. To keep warm he spends the night inside the horse's cadaver.

Morning comes. And with it an insight that two men, after all, can't get very far on three legs. "Courage, comrade," Heinemann exhorts. "We've still a long way to go to get to mother's coffeepot!". A reflection at which both men burst into tears.

Now it's the evening of the second day; and by this time Heinemann is virtually carrying his companion. But what's that over there? Five French generals 'nonchalantly wrapped in their greatcoats' are sitting round a brightly burning camp fire for which a cottage's furniture is serving as firewood.

'Their fine-limbed Arab racehorses, little though they can have been used to such fare, were eating the rotted thatch. A little distance away servants in braided livery, their brown black-bearded faces emaciated from hunger and fatigues, were bending over a smaller fire, baking a kind of bread from flour and water on hot stones.'

The two stragglers beg for a share, but are brusquely refused. However, one of the generals, 'whose open greatcoat revealed golden epaulettes adorned with the French eagles', gets up and, coming over, wants to know what the fuss is about. Isn't Heinemann speaking French? Is he a Frenchman? If so, what corps does he belong to? Wasn't it the Westphalian army which had just passed this way? Heinemann salutes, explains proudly how he'd fought under the Emperor at Wagram and Aspern, been demobilized, and had rejoined under the Westphalian flag. It's not on his own behalf he's begging, he says, but for his wounded comrade. The general reprimands his lackeys and the two Westphalian stragglers get some of 'the almost inedible bread'.

But there's a limit to even the greatest courage. By next evening the sergeant knows he's done for. Sitting down beside a cannon 'whose wheels had sunk so deep into the ground that no force had been able to extricate it' and a dead horse which had given up its life while trying to, he declares: 'Here's a resting place worthy of a dying soldier.'

Heinemann protests. He'll nurse his wounded foot. 'For the last time, then,' replies the other. Quite right. Taking off the bandage, what do they see? 'There to our silent horror were the black and dark-red stripes, creeping up from his wound to his leg.' 'So that's it, then,' says the sergeant stoically. 'Even the best of us can be branded like that. It won't be long now until it stops my heartbeats.'

Seeing even less hope for his comrade than for himself, Heinemann reluctantly agrees to leave him there to die. Which he does – but not before the sergeant has told him his own tragic love story and entrusted him with his last wishes, in the unlikely event of his ever getting home to Hildesheim.[1]

And now Heinemann, utterly alone, is wandering at random in the vast stretches of Russian landscape beyond Smolensk.

'Fed up and tired of living, I strayed about on the desolate misty heathlands into the night's deep dusk. By the time I'd reached the forest stretching away toward the horizon to the right of the road it was already pitch dark.'

The forest's silver birches gleam in the murk. Underfoot are the soft mosses, 'and overhead hardly a star. I wondered whether I wasn't myself a shadow, moving in the kingdom of the dead.' Now he hears wolves howling – but in the same instant descries a glimmer of camp fires. Friendly? or Russian? He has no means of knowing. If Russian, do they belong to regular troops, or Cossacks? If the former, perhaps he can save himself by claiming to have deserted the French eagles. If the latter,

'I could be sure of being plundered, beaten with knouts and imprisoned, with a few lance-thrusts into the bargain. If they were refugees from neighbouring villages and the men were away, I could only hope for the women's compassion. The men would have made no bones about killing a *sabacky Franzusky*.'

Well, it's a camp. But what a camp! 'The language I heard being spoken wasn't Russian, but Italian. Yet I knew from of old how the Italians hated the French.' Suddenly he's witness to a drama of jealousy. A lieutenant of the Neapolitan Guard Chasseurs – 'an immense figure of a man, black-bearded and sallow' – has just been assassinated by his rival for smiling at a cantinière. While pretending to embrace the assassin in the dark his *inamorata* stabs him in the back. Deeply shaken, Heinemann joins the crowd round the camp fires.

'They were camp followers, straying about on the army's left flank, searching for food. Here I saw men and women of every race, dressed half in uniform, half in civilian clothes. Almost all the women were past their first youth.'

The only attractive one is she of the dagger – whose charms we shan't waste time describing.

'There were Croats with long moustaches in braided fur jackets, both men and women. Also gypsies, among them pretty but dark-hued beauties, dancing to tambourines, zither and violin. Also a group of Bavarian sutlers... in a word, a real cross-section of those people who made up the baggage train of all the many nations Napoleon's iron will had driven into the icy North.'

With them they have a great variety of wagons, oxen, ponies, mules and donkeys. But also bread. So Wilhelm tenders 'a 5-franc piece as my letter of credence. *"Chè volete, can francese?"* [What do you want, you dog of a Frenchman?] shouts a man with a bloody knife between his teeth, who's busy skinning a hare. *"Matalete il can francese!"* [Kill that French dog!] shouted another.'

The 'French dog', though he hasn't eaten for four days, thinks it the better part of prudence to turn instead to some Bavarians who are roasting potatoes in the ashes. 'If we have any over, *kamerad*,' says a tall sly type, half soldier, half hobo, 'we'll be taking it to the army, where we'll get a hundred francs for a meal, instead of your wretched five!'

So Lance-corporal Heinemann has to grope about in the dark for his dinner among the gardens of a nearby deserted village. He finds a well but lacks any vessel or rope to draw up its sweet-smelling water. And for a moment contemplates throwing himself into it. Finally he drops off to sleep in a barn – with a corpse for bedfellow. In the morning the camp-followers have vanished, leaving only the ashes of their fires.

Once again he's utterly alone – terrified of being found by vengeful peasants and beaten to death, expecting every moment to see a roving Cossack patrol come galloping toward him. Climbing over the fence of the village church, he lies down among the graves under a horse-chestnut tree. Longs only to put an end to himself – but in the same instant realizes that the tree harbours a bees' nest. Thousands of soldiers, he knows, have sickened and died from eating too much of that 'sweet poison'. But now, all hope of salvation gone, he decides that he may as well die of eating honey as any other way. Knocking down the bees' honeycomb, he drives them out of it with gunpowder smoke, 'and with my sabre cut myself a large slice from the comb' – and is promptly stung on the lip for his pains. 'A bee's sting had saved me from suicide.' The reflection throws him into pious thoughts. Entering the shattered church 'plundered even of its icons, filled with a lively sense of the ever-present God' he sinks down in prayer before the altar. But coming out again, sees no sign of the daily bread he has prayed for. 'More inconsolable than ever, I stood in the open place on the far side of the plundered and half-burned village and stared out across the hemp fields towards the grim forest nearby.' He has just primed his musket and is putting its muzzle to his eye – when the miracle occurs: in the shape of a fat pig, which comes galloping towards him from a field! And is shot instead.

'We'll go halves, comrade!' shouts a German voice. And from round the corner of one of the houses a Prussian hussar emerges on a limping horse. After dinner the two men, having loaded it with hams and pork cut-lets, start their search for the army. But everywhere for several versts on each side of its route the countryside has been systematically laid waste. So deciding to push on northwards out of this devastated zone, they by and by come on another deserted village. The only food they can find in it is a heap of grain inside a cottage, which they roast in its stove. They also find a horse, whose owner has fled at their approach, and a cart. So they load it with the rest of the grain. And find a second horse, which makes three. Seeing another, obviously inhabited village below them in the plain, they decide to pretend to be quartermasters, with orders to find lodgings for 500 cavalry and a whole infantry regiment. A Jew who speaks a little German interprets. And in return for some victuals and a night's sleep they offer to divert the approaching regiment elsewhere. And the village elders kiss their hands.

But the peasants aren't all that easily fooled. 'In the morning, meeting only with threatening and suspicious glances', the two men make haste to leave; come off best in a rearguard skirmish with the furious peasants, and go on. By and by they come across an isolated but singularly splendid manor-house. Never in his life has Heinemann seen the likes of its inte-rior décor: 'costliest clocks, immense mirrors reaching up to the ceiling, polished floors of inlaid woods, the finest stucco work and fresco paint-ings, marble, gilt, and curtains, wallcoverings and furniture all clad in thick satin'. It's like something out of the Arabian Nights. A veritable palace. It too has been abandoned by its owner; but not by some of his female servants, by his aged French-speaking superintendent, or by his poultry. Execution is promtly done among the poultry. And in this par-adise the Prussian hussar – his name is Matthias Klarges – promptly strikes up a liaison with a kitchenmaid called Olga. On the other hand, his moral indignation at so much wealth knows no bounds:

'"Know what, brother? The owner of all this couldn't have spent so much on it if he hadn't squeezed it out of his peasants. And such a tyrant deserves to be punished. Don't you think we'd bring down God's blessing on us if we smashed it all up and then set fire to his nest?" And before I could prevent him, he'd drawn his sabre and shattered a mirror and a costly table-top.'

The two stragglers barricade themselves for the night at the top of the stairs with heaps of furniture, light a bonfire to illumine the environs, and lie down booted and spurred to get some sleep amid eiderdown bolsters. But the Prussian has fallen in love with his Olga, and talks the night away about how lovely it would be to become her husband, even if it means marrying her – however many blows of the knout it may entail. And besides 'they can kill us just as easily if we leave as if we stay'. Hearing whis-pers in the night and a shuffling of feet on the gravel, they imagine they're being attacked and discharge their firearms into the dark – and kill the wretched Olga. Tragic moment, highly theatrical. (Did it really happen? Or only nearly? Or not at all?) 'My comrade had flung himself upon her, smothered her in kisses and himself in her blood....' Next morning they find their broadside has also slain the old French superintendent, who lies there expiring in his own blood. So that's that. They leave, the Prussian hussar consoling himself with the soldierly reflection that tears can't revive the dead: 'A soldier must let himself be shot to death, if fate has cast a bullet for him. But the regulations say nothing about dying of grief.'

Next day, coming across 'a fine large village, with a golden cupola in its midst, gleaming in the sunshine like a ball of fire', the Prussian strokes his ginger moustaches and declares he's formed a taste for luxury. Why not take it by storm? Heinemann, more cautious, points out that they've already enough food to keep them alive for many days. At very least his friend, who after all forms their little convoy's cavalry arm, should reconnnoitre before they attack. Which he does. Runs into Cossacks. And, leaving his comrade in the lurch, disappears at a terrified gallop over the horizon. For the second time Heinemann knows his last hour has come:

'Horrified, I saw what the lie of the ground had hidden from my sight. To right and left across the hemp field some Cossacks were racing toward me, long lances lowered; and, straight out of the village, on his magnificent dappled horse, comes a Cossack officer. I give myself up for lost. Climbing down from the cart, I place myself out in the field, and grasping my musket prepare to sell my life dearly. I'm surrounded on all sides.'

But suddenly the Cossacks swerve from their target, and a voice summons him in French:

'"*Pardon, camerade! Abattez vos armes!*" The officer was a slim man, in the flower of his age. His black beard and healthy hue lent his big dark eye and the pure oriental profile an expression of perfect manliness. His clothes, blue and silver, opulent but tasteful, and his whole posture and the resounding tone in which he addressed me in an educated language inspired confidence in his humanity.'

Luckily, Heinemann remembers something. The Russians are said to be reserving their most virulent hatred for the French, but treating their German prisoners less harshly. So, forgetting all about Wagram, etc., he pretends not to understand, and says – in German: "I'm not French, I'm German."

"Throw down your weapons, then!" the officer replies in accented German. For a moment, even if it must mean his own instant death from the Cossacks' lance points, Heinemann feels an impulse to shoot him. But thinks better of it, throws away musket and sabre and falls on his knees.

'"Further away!" Immediately he comes galloping at me, his pistol cocked, sabre dangling from his arm. Also the other Cossacks, with felled lances. I commend my soul to God and my body to the earth, seeming in all my limbs already to feel the pain of the lances' stabs, the bullets piercing my brain. Everything goes black. I can hardly stand upright. I've a first taste of blows from the flats of their sabres, smarting on my shoulders and back.'

In his despair he yells out that a whole squadron of hussars is in the offing. But this only exhilarates the officer: 'Good, the more prisoners the better!' But of course there are no hussars. And his own has fled.

'To begin with he drove me before him at a run, his horse's hoofs at my heels. One of his men was told to keep an eye on me. So far none of the village's peasants had appeared. Soon there came several. So far I hadn't been maltreated. But we halted at a distance from the village and the Cossacks begin visiting me, plundering me in the crude open-hearted way so typical of them. I was their first prisoner. They took all my money, and the one who got it patted me amiably on my cheek, calling me Patruschka, little father. But a second Cossack let me understand that if I didn't produce some more I'd have a taste of the knout. A third greedily grabbed my tchapska, while a fourth went through my wallet, which was inside it, looking for any rouble notes. To me my wallet was endlessly valuable. It contained no money, but everything I held holy, letters from my mother and other personal papers.'

Although his captors try to protect him, the enraged villagers bombard him with stones and dirt, toss him to and fro among themselves and beat him about the head, 'and the women were worst of all. Blood was running down my face. One moment I was lying on the ground, being trampled under their feet; the next, they'd grabbed me up by my clothes and hoisted me high in the air, to rip off my shiny buttons. In this way my uniform was torn to shreds.'

Retrieved and driven away by the Cossacks, Heinemann is amazed to find himself among a lot of other Westphalian prisoners, all from his own regiment. Its voltigeur company had been reconstituted after the massacre at Valutina, but they'd been captured 'not without putting up a fierce resistance, while out on a marauding expedition, the battalion being in dire need of everything'. They're hardly in better case than himself. All have been captured after putting up a valiant resistance in a manor-house, but having to yield to numbers. At first Heinemann has taken his comrades for 'peasants armed with sabres'. Even their valiant Captain Telge, the only officer to have escaped the massacre, is among them. Stripped of his uniform, his only clothing is a Russian nobleman's scarlet nightgown.

Afraid that they are in fact going to be attacked by Prussian cavalry, Cossacks fling their prisoners, most of whom are wounded and some very badly, on to wagons and gallop away with them, into ever more desolate tracts of countryside and swamps, where the Brunswickers, driven on at lance-point, have to jump from one tussock to the next so as not to sink up to their waists in muddy water 'covered with a sort of blueish film that in no way did anything to cheer up the dreary landscape'. Soaked through, starving, at nightfall they're packed into pigstyes where they stand and shiver, although their captors at least heave over some straw on which they can collapse. 'Cossacks and peasants kept watch all around us.'

At midnight they're peremptorily awakened by voices and a freezing north wind. A ferocious-looking long-bearded man with a lantern and a knife is searching about among the wounded.'All I could see was that four Russians were holding down a prisoner on the ground.' Taking it for granted he's their executioner, Heinemann is 'overtaken by a trembling so violent I'd never known its like'. But no. Here's a foot flung aside, there an arm. He's 'one of those kind-hearted Samaritans who are used to cutting off arms and legs by the dozen, like calves' heads. Our wounds are bound up, the bandages a soldier has to carry on him' are put to their proper use.

And now, before dawn, the 'French dogs' are being ordered out, two by two, through the gate. And outside stand two rows of peasants, with arm-fuls of bread:

'A bit was flung to each of us, and we were allowed to drink out of a well used by the cattle. Such was the beginning of a chain of efforts and sufferings no pen can describe.'

One day they reach the headquarters of General Winzingerode, a German aristocrat in the Russian service,[2] who sympathizes with their plight:

'As a native of Germany he took special care of his compatriots. He had soup made for the prisoners, and bought back Captain Telge's uniform for him from a Cossack whose plunder it was. He spoke quite amiably to us and tried to revive our fallen courage, promising us we'd from now on be treated well, would be placed in a proper transport and find a good soup waiting for us at every stopping place. Orders were given that the Germans in particular should be treated kindly since everyone knew they were only serving Napoleon because they were forced to.'

But in Russia promises are one thing; realities another. Their sufferings begin again. Closely herded together like cattle, they're driven on day after day at a brisk trot along foul muddy roads or rotten causeways by peasants armed with clubs:

'Anyone who has ever marched in a column knows how wearisome it is to march close behind the man in front of you. But unable to move on without tramping on his heels, after only an hour's march-ing the strongest man was powerless.'

The Russian peasants' treatment of the prisoners, Heinemann says, 'bore witness to a low bestiality without a trace of humanity in it'. Anyone who collapses is first beaten half to death by the peasants, to try and make him get up; then, when they themselves have to keep up with the column, is left to receive more blows in passing by others following, until

'finally the Cossacks who closed the column reach the point where the man, beaten half to death, lies pale, motionless, covered in filth and no longer even looking like a human being. Now the last attempts are made to revive him with a score or so blows of the knout, and if even these don't have the desired effect, a couple of peasants grab hold of the poor fellow's legs and drag him aside to wait for the wagons which, according to orders, are to pick up the dead and inane. One can imagine that the unwelcome guest isn't received on it without oaths and blows – and the most inhuman cruelty, impossible in any other country than where there are only masters and slaves.'

Few such unfortunates survive. Farther and farther northwards 'towards the measureless interior of Russia our columns of exhausted captives – images of the uttermost human misery – made their way'. Until at last on the Russian Christmas Day (5 January) they reach Archangel, on the White Sea.

Thousands are sharing the same fate.[3]

CHAPTER 18

DUST, HEAT AND THIRST

An uninviting landscape – an impenetrable dust cloud – disappointments at Doroghoboui – news from Moscow – 'I'm going still further away' – Dumonceau sees the army go by – the Cossacks – their appearance – with the vanguard's guns – first signs of autumn – Murat and Davout at loggerheads – the city of fishes – an interrupted funeral – 'the Russians are preparing to give battle' – 'I've a good job, I'm emperor' – 'he made the most comical grimaces'

Now I Corps is in the van, and on the same day that Paul de Bourgoing had dined al fresco at Ney's headquarters the Red Lancers have resumed their scouting. Although all traces indicate a retreat on Moscow, not a soul is to be seen. As for the landscape, it's completely unlike what it had been before Smolensk: 'dreary and desolate, covered only by scrub and conifers'. All the villages lie in ashes. Following on with III Corps and suffering from three bruises sustained at Valutina, Captain Bonnet, 'once again crossed the Dnieper and found on this bank a poverty-stricken landscape, forests and sands, few cultivated fields'.

But gradually it improves. On 21 August Maurice Tascher is amazed to see a long-forgotten sight – 'some peasants busy harvesting their fields. Our men are wrenching the grain out of their hands to feed the horses.' At Prudiche, three days later, some houses are still left standing 'after all the troops had passed through'. The Italians, too, stare at some cattle peacefully grazing in the fields, 'as if at an extraordinary sight'. But are more considerate. Politely asking for some food and permission to rest up, they're given 'food for one day and some horned cattle'. Now Césare de Laugier is finding the landscape 'more attractive and cultivated'. Finding himself amid an abundant supply of necessities, the ranker is 'forgetting his past fatigues'. And on 25 August Tascher's hussars reach the fair-sized town of Janoviczi,

> 'wholly of timber. Some Jews have remained. Our soldiers are busy plundering them. A fine lake. The Cossacks have carried off a great number of our stragglers and marauders. We keep coming upon great holes, filled with linen and other chattels.'

And indeed, on each side of the great Moscow highway, a wave of organized and indescriminate violence is rolling into Old Russia:

> 'In each company were certain men, excellent marchers, who were clever at going out to search for food. They went to the villages, where they plundered all they could, were guilty of all sorts of excesses, and often, after cutting the old men's throats, raping the women and setting fire to the village, returned to their company with some sacks of flour on a small cart drawn by a nanny-goat, a cow, some supplies, i.e., when these hadn't been taken from them by the Imperial Guard or other units they had to pass through. The offi-

cers congratulated these marauders and held them up as examples to be emulated by their comrades.'

Le Roy tells the same grim story:

'Each unit sent out a detachment, now on one flank, now on the other. To find inhabited villages, deserted at our approach, it had to cross the whole army, sometimes between 12 and 15 miles in extent. All was there for the taking and we carried away everything edible. Next day it all had to be done over again. The enemy frequently carried off these detachments, who were immediately put to death by peasant insurgents, excited against us by their popes.'

An 'inconvenient' thing about such ruthless marauding, in Le Roy's eyes, is that it's 'accustoming the rank and file to make a profession of it. Almost always it was the same men who asked to go off à la picorée, to be free and, though running the greatest dangers, avoid the shooting.'

And day after day the hot Russian sun is scorching down.

On 23 August, now 60 miles east of Smolensk, Ney's vanguard comes within sight of Doroghoboui, a largish town lying in a sloping amphitheatre, which offers 'a superb defensive position'. Le Roy jumps to the conclusion that it's here the Russians are at last going to stand and fight. So does Murat. And sends off an ADC to Smolensk. His arrival precipitates IHQ's departure after midnight on the 24th. After travelling along the Moscow highway in his closed carriage, Napoleon gets to Doroghoboui to find it's been fired by the Cossacks, and his own troops are in occupation. Makes some scathing remarks to Murat. Establishes his headquarters. And the advance goes on.

Estafettes (couriers), meanwhile, have brought worrying news. Marching northwards with the Army of Moldavia, Tormasoff has broken into the southern theatre of war, thus threatening the advancing army's right rear. Rapp and his colleagues discuss the army's remoteness from its lines of communication:

'Probably Napoleon had overheard us. Coming in to us, he talked at length about the precautions he'd taken to keep his back free, the corps forming our wings, and the chain of posts from the Niemen that linked us up to the places where we now were. "Tormassoff", he told us, "has put the wind up old and young alike in Warsaw, who've fancied him already master of Prague. But he's had to pull out quicker than he came."'

With these words Napoleon goes back into his office and 'in an indifferent tone of voice, but loud enough for each one of us to hear' begins dictating instructions to Marshal Victor to bring up X Corps to Vilna.[1] He is also given command of all the troops in Lithuania and in Witebsk and Smolensk provinces: "Dombrowski's division, seven to eight thousand strong, is manoeuvring between Molihew, Minsk and Bobruisk. Four battalions of Illyrians, the two battalions and cannon of the 129th Regiment, two battalions of the 33rd Light must go to Smolensk..." After calling in and re-organizing all these widely scattered units, Victor is to "reopen communications between Smolensk and headquarters, should they be cut, and, if need be, come to the army's rescue."'

That day (26 August) the Italians, following a separate road out to the left of the main column, are having a spot of trouble. A little river called the Wop, whose waters are 'flowing calmly and peacefully between rather steep banks' and aren't very deep, is barring their path. The artillery and carriages, Laugier writes irritably in his diary, 'have only with some difficulty got across.'² Otherwise the roads are getting better.

Not a drop of rain has fallen for a whole month. And Bonnet, when his battalion forces the pace to catch up with III Corps some fifteen miles east of Doroghoboui, finds that he's marching through a dense cloud of white dust:

'the entire army in a single mass, marching along a fine highroad in four columns, two of infantry on either side of the road, the artillery on the road itself. You can't see ten paces ahead of you.'

Oddly, on each side of the double avenues of silver birches, the infantry divisions are extended in battle order, and flanked by long lines of cavalry. Perhaps Dumonceau sees Bonnet go by. Called in from their scoutings, the Red Lancers have a long wait by the roadside. They're particularly impressed by the appearance of the 48th Line (I),

'four handsome battalions marching in closed formation, as if on parade. It enjoyed the unique privilege of wearing its number in copper figures on its pouches. Behind it came a brown-clad Portuguese regiment, wearing English-style shakos. After them³ came Ney's corps, among which we noticed a fine Württemberg regiment and a Spanish one, whose uniforms rather closely resembled that of the Portuguese. These troops were marching over the open fields in columns of platoons, on either side of the road, leaving it free for the artillery and baggage which in its enormous confusion presented the most bizarre sight – a weird muddle, made up of every thinkable kind of vehicle; teams of horses, individuals' riding horses, vivandières riding on their nags like a desert Arab on his dromedary, all amidst a mass of pack mules and infantrymen, knapsacks on their backs and muskets hanging bandoleer-fashion as they rode along on little Russian cobs whose legs were shorter than their riders. And amidst all this mass of people the funniest sights: men struggling with the most refractory animals, etc. For two hours, without for a moment feeling bored to see this motley pass along our front, we stood there resting while waiting for the Imperial Guard.'

Boulart's Guard batteries are among those taking the crown of the road. And he isn't the only man to be 'suffering worse from heat and thirst during these ten days than perhaps I've ever done in my life'. So is Girod de l'Ain:

'the heat was excessive: I'd never known it worse even in Spain. But there's a difference: in Russia it doesn't last long. The main Moscow road is sandy, and the army, marching abreast in several serried columns, raised such dust clouds we couldn't see one another two yards off. Our eyes, ears and nostrils were full of it and our faces caked with it. This heat and dust made us extremely thirsty, as can well be imagined, and water was hard to come by. Will you believe men when I say that I saw men lying on their bellies to drink horses' urine in the ditch! On this march and in a rift in the dust cloud, i.e, after a halt long enough for it to settle, I at least had the pleasure of seeing the heavy cavalry division, composed of carabiniers and cuirassiers, fourteen regiments in all. Their cuirasses and helmets, glinting in the sun, made a splendid sight.'

Riding along in their midst, Thirion can't 'make out the trooper ahead. Often we lost sight of our own horses' ears, and had to trust to instinct and these poor horses' acute vision, their eyes not being like human ones.' Caulaincourt explains the heavy cavalry regiments' advanced position as necessary to support the advance guard at a moment's notice. The steel-clad men are having to sit their saddles from 3 a.m. until late in the evening. 'Is there a soldier in the world today who could do the same?'

Von Brandt's Polish veterans, too, are making comparisons with Spain. 'The whirling gusts of wind raised such thick clouds of dust we often couldn't even see the big trees lining the road.' Many try to protect their eyes with

'little bits of windowpane. Others marched with their shakos under one arm and their head swathed in a handkerchief, only leaving in it an opening big enough to let themselves be led and to breathe through. Others made themselves leafy garlands.'

Beyond the flanking cavalry lines swarm great swarms of Cossacks. On 27 August Dumonceau, for the first but by no means last time, sees them *en masse*,

'dressed in every thinkable fashion, with every kind of head-dress. Lacking the least uniformity of appearance, dirty-looking and clad in rags, riding on nasty thin little horses with long necks, low heads, a long mane and guided only by a simple rein, and armed with a long simple whip with a kind of nail at the end, they wheeled in confused and apparently enormous disorder, and to me seemed like swarming insects.'

But Colbert, taking his meerschaum out of his mouth, tells him:

'They're admirable as light cavalry. At the outposts, for reconnaissances, they leave nothing to be desired. But they'll never really attack you as long as you stand firm and don't let yourself be distracted by their deafening shouts. The artillery only has to show up, and they'll vanish in a jiffy. Threaten them with a pistol or any kind of firearm, and they'll avoid you. They never risk a man-to-man combat unless they're several against one. Their traps and ambushes are always cleverly thought out. Nor are they cruel, though less inclined to kill you than to take you prisoner.'

And indeed only yesterday evening (26 August) the 'savages' have snapped up one of Prince Eugène's ADC. Sent across to the main column to get Murat's orders for IV Corps 'he hasn't come back,' Laugier had written in his diary, 'so we've understood what's happened to him'. But Le Roy as usual, though 'dead-beat and dusty as could be' has managed to come by his dinner. His battalion has just bivouacked

'between two woods, where there's a small lake. To freshen up, I take a dip and (remembering my youthful days) amuse myself by search-ing among the rushes. Am sure there must be fish there. In the end I manage to fill my handkerchief with three little fishes, which, boiled in salt water, were relished by the adjutant's mess.'

Above all it's the young Polish officers, Chlapolwsky says, who are happy to be emulating their 17th-century ancestors by advancing into Old Russia. Like the Italians to its left, Poniatowski's V Corps is flanking the main column to the right. Sent to it on some mission, Labaume is impressed by the Poles' appearance, which he unjustly ascribes to 'the Polish army having passed through a less devastated landscape than had fallen to our lot. Since it hadn't suffered at all,[4] it was still superb.' Other Polish units, in Latour Maubourg's IV Cavalry Corps, following on at a considerable distance to the rear, are reminded that day of the brevity of the northern summer. Allowed to rest up at Mscicslaw, the doyen or 'mar-shal' of the local nobility proposes to take General *Boris Turno*[5] and his officers on a tour of the town:

'Dusk was casting an uncertain light over our bivouacs and the lonely landscape, and the sky was covered in grey cold mists. Yet at various points on the horizon something was beginning to stir, at the same time as a kind of mute but incessant trembling sound was heard. The air seemed to be populated; far off in the mist some white objects appeared. It was swans leaving, making a clapping sound with their beaks.'

"Yes, it's the swans leaving this countryside and Russia, to seek a milder cli-mate,' their guide tells them. 'Don't think it's an empty or unsure por-tent. It's terror of the ice that changes these creatures' habits. They've an intimation of what's to come." Undeterred by this portent, General Roz-nicki, approaching Czerepowo two days later,

'orders the Polish troops to halt, forms us up in square and reminds us that we're standing at the limit of the Jagellons' and Batory's one-time empire. After painting for us the heroic aspects of our nation's glorious past he invites all present to dismount and pick up a little dust so as to be able to remind our descendants of this glori-ous event which has brought us back to Poland's former limits.'

From Doroghoboui IHQ has moved on to 'a big house or manor on a hillock beside the River Ouja, at Slavkowo. 'There we found a little corn, the more valuable for the enemy having left us nothing at Smolensk.'

Here several units – Guard units, one supposes – at last get some bread. And Napoleon some news from Moscow. At Smolensk he'd heard that on 24 July the Tsar had entered his 'old' capital. Now d'Ideville reads to him news of 'how Alexander had assembled the nobility and the more prosperous class and, without hiding from them the state's situation, asked them to obtain help from all district governments'.

The evening being warm, IHQ is entertained to a concert and Faber du Faur's gunners, too, as they pass along the broad highway, hear 'music, floating out of a handsome manor-house to the left of the road'.

From Slavkowo Napoleon sends detailed instructions to his outlying corps commanders:

"I am going even further away. The day after tomorrow I shall be at Viazma, five days' march from Moscow. Probably there will be a battle which will open the city gates to me. Act above all in such a manner that any Russians confronting you shall not march against me."

St-Cyr, Napoleon thinks, has more than enough troops to inspire Wittgenstein's respect.[6] As if aware he'll shortly be needing fresh armies, he sends off a decree to Paris for the immediate implementation of the 1813 call-up. As for Smolensk, he remarks to Fain, he's "going to put in a superior commander, one who if need be can take over and act according to circumstances. The city is to be the central point in our communications." It will be Marshal Victor, coming forward with IX Corps, made up of Frenchmen, Germans and Poles.

These scorching days Lejeune is doing a lot of cantering to and fro along the dusty highway between Murat's and Berthier's headquarters; and can't help noticing how the Russians are still

'withdrawing in admirably good order and evidently wishing to defend all positions that offer any advantage. In this way our advancing cavalry had to keep forming columns of attack supported by the artillery, and which only conquered a little ground after exchanging many discharges of grape and attacks with the sabre. This meant a lot of time was being consumed in making but little progress – and still we were over 300 miles from Moscow! By day we sat our horses amid cannonfire. At nights we sat by our camp fires without the slightest scent of any roast beef hanging from pothooks to console our exhausted stomachs.'

Many days Murat, who's still forcing the pace, is covering

'thirty to thirty-six miles. The men were in the saddle from 3 a.m. to 10 p.m. By the end of the day our horses were so wearied that a mere skirmish could cost us several brave fellows, their horses not being able to keep pace.'

Of the 7th Hussars' 1,500 men and horses who'd galloped so gaily into Vilna hardly 1,000 are left; of the 11th Hussars only 300. And Victor Dupuy's existence has become utterly trying:

'Each day from 5 a.m. onwards we were skirmishing with the Cossacks, and sometimes this went on until as late as 10 or 11 p.m. They were carrying off everything they could from the villages and driving away the inhabitants, who fled into the forests. After which they set fire to the village. If we made some bold manoeuvre or brisk attack and didn't give them time to, their artillery fired incendiary shells and produced the same effect by setting alight the thatched roofs – a way of waging war we experienced as greatly to our disadvantage. After days almost totally given up to combats and physical effort we could hardly find enough to eat, and often we'd nothing to give the horses, whose numbers were daily dwindling in an alarming fashion.'

The further the army advances, Lejeune is noticing, 'the worse the devastation. Everything had been burnt and the horses didn't even find any straw on the roofs to live off. Everything lay in ashes.'

Worst off of all are the advance guard's gunners. Immense efforts are being required of Colonel *Séruzier*'s twelve companies, manhandling and serving the 72 light 6-pounders and 24lb howitzers attached to Montbrun's leading cavalry corps:

'My horse artillery and the divisions of light cavalry escorting them fought serious combats with the Russians. We were having to bombard each other for two or three hours at a time, before the enemy were so kind as to leave us a position where we could pass the night. At each withdrawal he blocked the roads and destroyed the bridges. I was every bit as busy rebuilding them. Each evening I saw my men drop from weakness and exhaustion. I went into the water up to my waist and planted the first piquet. Despite their exhaustion, my behaviour gave my men back a little energy. They got up, forced me to retire, and without saying a word got busy repairing the passage.'

Afterwards Boulart won't be able distinctly to recall all these places,

'so uniform is their appearance: largely featureless terrain, offering nothing clear-cut; rather fine harvests; plenty of forests, where the silver birch woods seemed commonest; broad unpaved roads, indicated on either side only by a row or two of magnificent trees.'

The horde of camp-followers the army is dragging along in its wake is being swelled by ever more numerous sick and stragglers. Though very young and vigorous men, lieutenants Vossler (Prince Louis' Hussars), and Dutheillet (57th Line), both suffering grievously from 'dysentery', are at each moment afraid to see their regiments fade away ahead into the advancing dustcloud. Which is exactly what happens to Dutheillet:

'I'd become so weak, and my stomach so oversensitive it couldn't even stand the weight of my swordbelt. I'd attached everything to my horse, together with my haversack and portemanteau. Obliged to dismount to obey a call of nature, I didn't even have time to tether my horse or hold him by bridle. While I'm thus occupied, a regiment of cuirassiers passes by at a trot. My horse, excited, jumps the hedge between us and runs off, carrying with him all my possessions. I try to run after him and demand him back, but haven't the strength. Unable to go a step further I come to a halt, there on the road. What upset me most, apart from the loss of my possessions, was that I could hear gunfire. Knowing my regiment was one of the leading units, I was afraid it might be engaging the enemy, and that my absence would be noticed. This idea was more than I could stand.'

But here's the 111th Line, in I Corps' 3rd brigade, passing by. Dutheillet recognizes a mounted officer, tells him of his misadventure and begs for the loan of his horse to rejoin the 57th. Gets it, and that evening sends it back by his servant. Vossler, too, who has lost all the horses he'd crossed the Niemen with and is riding a 'scruffy Cossack pony', is feeling so weak he can hardly stay on its back without help. Prince Louis' hussars are trying to catch up:

'Apart from some objects too heavy to carry away, such as great hogsheads of spirits, etc., we were finding no supplies or provisions of any kind. All along the highway from Doroghoboui we came across nothing but desolation. The towns had been taken over by the French administration, who stretched themselves out comfortably in such houses as were still standing and in the many and sometimes beautiful monasteries and churches. After Doroghoboui we'd come across many soldiers, sometimes enormously many, who out of sheer exhaustion had collapsed by the roadside, and for lack of all help were dying where they lay. The sight did much to increase our anxieties for the condition of the Grand Army's cavalry and artillery.'

Yet another officer who's feeling very ill and is straggling is Major *Friedrich Wilhelm von Lossberg*,[7] one of Junot's Westphalians. Remarkably, his wife will get his letter at Detmold:

'Feeling ill this morning I had to take medicine from the regiment's doctor, so I couldn't mount my horse until several hours after the army corps had left. This has given me a chance to observe, at close quarters, the miseries and disorder it's leaving in its wake. What masses of carriages haven't I come upon, "kikbitkas" [closed sledges on wheels], whole hordes of cattle with their drovers of all nationalities, either isolated or in big groups! Many were moribund, and most rode wretched konyas. Even if I hadn't been able to see the Moscow road, I'd only have had to follow its smell. At every hundred yards, at least, I was near to tumbling over some horse which had collapsed, or a bullock that had been slaughtered and whose guts lay across the road. In each village or isolated house I came across unburied soldiers, our own and the enemy's. To take a little rest in the shade and drink a little coffee – my servant had everything with him to prepare it – I dismounted beside a building. But it turned out to be in such bad shape, so utterly filthy, and so full of stragglers from every corps, I sat down on the grass a little way off, beside a naked corpse. So feelingless had I become, only one thought absorbed me: "What luck this fellow hasn't had time to putrefy! Otherwise I'd have had to drink my coffee out in the hot sun!"'

Von Lossberg confesses that this day's experiences have convinced him that 'Napoleon doesn't give a damn how many of his soldiers collapse by the roadside, or whether human strength suffices to pursue and if possible attack and destroy the Russian army.' During the twelve days since leaving Smolensk Lieutenant Hubert Lyautey, that lover of military music, is noticing that 'almost a tenth of the army' has melted away from dysentery and desertion'.

Worse, but hardly a matter for surprise, Caulaincourt is noticing that discipline is beginning to break down. On 28 August, as the advance guard is approaching the important town of Viazma and IHQ is following on 'a few leagues behind', Murat's ADC Colonel Rossetti realizes that 'the army, thirsty from marching, heat and dust', has no water: 'Fights were breaking out over muddy wells, which soon got stirred up and fouled. The Emperor himself had to be content with liquid mud.'

As for Davout and Murat, they're becoming more and more exasperated with each other. And at the crossing of the Osma on 27 August – another day of which we have exceptionally many and vivid glimpses – one of Davout's battery commanders refuses to obey Murat's orders to fire, Davout having forbidden it – doubtless to save ammunition.

And now the van is approaching Viazma, 'a small town, but for Russian conditions a very large one'. Or, as Larrey puts it,

'a rather considerable town, well adapted to serve as a storage point for trade between the two parts of Russia. It contained enormous stocks of oil, brandy, soap, sugar, coffee, leather and furs.'

Surrounded by the serpentine Viazma River,[8] it dominates both the plain and, on the Smolensk road, the entrance to a big defile. To eyes inflamed by white dust and the glaring sun its green onion spires hover like a veritable mirage, so that to Dedem it seems 'brand-new'; and to Maurice Tascher 'a superb town, which at a distance appears to be a forest of church towers' – Césare de Laugier, who's heard that Viazma's 1,900 houses are normally occupied by 13,000 inhabitants, thinks he can count 32 spires. No one on the Italian staff has 'seen anything so beautiful or inviting since Witebsk. But Captain Chlapowsky of the 1st Guard Lancers is a patriotic Pole and denigrates everything after Smolensk, the last place where the population had 'at least understood' Polish. To him Viazma is 'just a dozen brick houses around the main marketplace'.

As the army approaches the town 'a mass of cavalry debouches from all sides and camps in the environs'. Entering it in the van with Grouchy's corps, Pierre Aubry finds its streets 'paved with logs, its perimeter vast and its streets irregular'. Alas, its immense stocks of flour and grain are already on fire. To save what he can, Murat orders 'a regiment of carabiniers' to cross the bridge. Unfortunately Davout has already allotted the bridge to the 57th as part of a general well-planned attack, and they've already begun crossing it. Instantly there's a blazing row:

'The Prince of Eckmühl was near the bridge. The carabiniers' colonel went up to him, saying he'd come on behalf of the King of Naples to ask to be allowed to pass. "You're not going to," the Marshal tells him. "If the King of Naples needs cavalry, I need infantry, and this bridge has been allotted me by the Emperor." Upon the colonel insisting, the Marshal orders Colonel Charrière: "Fire on that regiment if it takes another step." The carabinier colonel turns on the Marshal: "I'm retiring – at your orders, and am going to tell the King." "Go on, then, tell him it's Marshal Davout who's forbidden you to cross by this bridge." Seeing the Marshal near the bridge and the Emperor there too, the King of Naples, furious, comes up and reproaches him in the harshest terms with having held up the cavalry.'

Worse, Murat seizes his chance to reproach Davout for having made the 33rd Light, at Minsk, march past with reversed arms:

'"When one wears bifocal spectacles, M. le Maréchal, one should give up campaigning. I tell you this, not because I'm your king. Even if I were your equal I'd say the same thing." Furious, the Marshal replies that Murat isn't his king, and never will be. The Emperor put an end to this loss of tempers by ordering the Marshal to carry a battery of guns that was firing grape at us; which we did, at the double.'

Beside himself with rage, Murat sends off Belliard to tell Napoleon that under such circumstances he, the King of Naples, can no longer command the advance guard. Doubtless Napoleon, after Murat's headlong imbecilities at Krasnoië, realizes only too well that it's Davout who's in the right. But the ranks and dignities of Napoleonic society must be upheld, even in the face of commonsense. And he resolves the problem by ordering Berthier to place Compans' division temporarily under Murat's command. Whereupon an exasperated Davout tells Berthier:

'That man acts like a lunatic! He engages his cavalry without even first reconnoitring the ground, he has his men massacred in totally pointless attacks to obtain results which could equally well be obtained by means of simple demonstrations that wouldn't cost the life of a single man!'

Evidently someone passes on these words to Murat; who wants to challenge Davout to a duel. And when Belliard restrains him – bursts into tears.

All the long way since Smolensk great curtains of smoke have been lying over a horizon in flames. Yet no one at IHQ seems to have tumbled to the implications:

'Some of us had thought this way in which the cities and market towns were always going up in flames as we entered them was as much due to confusion in our vanguard as to the Cossack rearguard, who cared very little for Russia's weal or woe. At first, I admit, I'd shared the same view, nor had I been able to understand what the Russians' intention could be in destroying all their public buildings and even their private houses – little use could they be to us.'

But now, at Viazma, it isn't only the loyal Caulaincourt or the querulous Pion des Loches who's wondering why none of its houses contain a single Russian civilian:

'As we approached the outskirts of Viazma it dawned on me that they were intentionally luring us far inland, to take us by surprise later on, or wear us down with hunger and cold. It wasn't only along the army's path fires were burning, but in other directions, far and near. At night the entire horizon was aglow.'

And now at last even Napoleon, Caulaincourt sees, is beginning to understand the implications of this scorched earth policy:

'He ordered my brother to take a strong Guard detachment next day and follow close on the enemy's heels, so as to enter the city at the same time as his rearguard, and find out for certain what was really going on, and whether the Russians were really setting fire to Viazma. The order was carried out to the letter. Though the enemy rearguard put up a defence, my brother, after a hot fight, entered Viazma at top speed, together with some skirmishers. Already the city was in flames in various places. He saw the Cossacks were setting fire to it with inflammable materials. He found some of these lying about in spots where the fire had broken out before they'd abandoned the town. From some inhabitants who'd stayed behind in their houses and, in particular, from a very intelligent baker, he heard how, long before we'd got there, a detachment of the Cossack rearguard had completed its preparations. The same moment we'd come into sight the town had been set fire to.'

Everyone at IHQ feels bewildered, 'the Emperor as much as those around him, though he pretended to poke fun at this way of waging war. In a joking tone of voice he spoke to me about "people who burn down their houses so we shouldn't be able to pass the night in them".' But the Master of the Horse is 'struck by serious reflections to which this terrible measure gave rise, and on the consequences and duration of a war where the enemy, from the very outset, had made such terrible sacrifices'.

Even while Murat's cavalry is making its attack, Le Roy, who's been fighting on some high ground fourteen kilometres away, has seen 'whirlwinds of fire and smoke devouring the town'. Now, entering it, he finds this

'superb town hadn't a single inhabitant left. To hold up our artillery's advance through the ashes the Russians had set fire to and destroyed 125 palaces [sic]. Locks, weights and other debris bore witness to the householders' former occupations. Only the cross still rose triumphant amidst so many ruins – as on Doomsday,' a strange reflection for a convinced deist. Although the Russian rear-guard, Fain says, had paid particular attention to burning down bridges and the bazaar, two battalions are ordered to fight the conflagration and manage to save two-thirds of the city, which are immediately plundered. Particularly of course by the Guard – e.g., by Boulart's gunners. He's particularly impressed to see houses 'better built than most. Since only part of the town had had time to fall a prey to the flames it could offer more resources.' These Caulaincourt appreciates the more as

'in Poland we'd lacked for everything. At Witebsk, with endless trouble, we'd been able to eat sparingly. At Smolensk, by ransacking the whole countryside, we'd found cornfields, grain, flour, cattle and even fodder, but neither brandy nor wine. After Doroghoboui everything had been in flames. But Viazma's shops and cellars were well-supplied, even opulent. Soon we found that the houses had their hiding-places, where we found an abundance of everything. The men went marauding and since no rations were distributed, nor could be, for lack of transport, no one could stop them.'

Although Lieutenant Lyautey is amazed to see 'chickens and goose feathers at each bivouac', the Master of the Horse notices

'some of the officers going without. Not having entered the houses until they'd been plundered, they couldn't share the spoils. In this way it could happen that beside the men's camp fire where chickens and sheep were being grilled and hams frizzled amidst hundreds of eggs a general or other superior officer sat eating black bread.'

Fish, too, is in plentiful supply. So much so that Sergeant Bertrand's comrades baptize Viazma 'the town of fishes'. Amidst such a cornucopea marauding, however, is a high-risk business. Looking out of a window of the house occupied by IHQ, 'a big one, on the right as you come in', Fain sees

'a sutler go by, arrested by the police while plundering a house. Taken before a court-martial, he'd been condemned to death. His legs would hardly carry him. As the picket taking him to the place of execution was passing in front of the house the Emperor asked what all the noise was about, and ordered us to tell the condemned man he'd pardoned him. The wretched sutler, already half-dead, was overwhelmed by such strong feelings that he dropped dead in terrible convulsions.'

Evidently Fain has a moment's respite from the endless dictations. For he goes on:

'Behind the house's courtyard, at the far end of a garden laid out in the English style, there's a little rotunda, an elegant copy of a Greek temple, supported by six pillars.'

A nearby building arouses his and his companions' curiosity:

'Crossing the street, we find it's a church. Its great door is closed. We walk round it. The side doors, too, are closed. We knock, knock again. No one replies. We call out several times. Finally a Russian of rather furtive aspect puts in an appearance, sees no sign of soldiers, and risks approaching us. He's the sacristan or bell-ringer. We use our few words of Russian to reassure him and, to prove we've not come to take anything away, give him something. Our religious demeanour as we follow him in under the sacred vaultings finally restores his confidence.'

But what a scene! In front of the high altar, on an open bier, lies the corpse of a venerable old man with a long white beard, a mitre on his head, his body swathed in the most superb pontificals.

'Around the catafalque, candles and all the funeral arrangements – this is what the sacristan shows us. We're dumbfounded. Our guide, no longer afraid to speak, says a lot of things we can't understand.'

Finally, they grasp what he's telling them. Just as the church's pontiff, probably the bishop of Viazma,

'had come down the altar steps he'd succumbed to terror at the tumult which had preceded our advance guard. His face at his last hour still preserved the serenity of the just.'

His clergy had just begun chanting the Office for the Dead when the Cossacks had ordered everyone to leave. 'Populace and clergy had fled, all except this unfortunate fellow who'd just opened up to us, and who'd stayed behind to keep watch over the dead man as long as possible.'

Deeply moved, Fain and his colleagues tell Napoleon. Who orders them to take a detachment and complete the old man's funeral. 'The aged pontiff is to be placed in the crypt prepared for him by the clergy.'

From the advance guard's reports as they come in it's becoming obvious, at least to Fain, that the Russians – at last – are preparing to give battle in a prepared position 'at Tsarewo-Zaimitche, near the Vlichewo post-house, between Viazma and Ghjat',[9] i.e., only a day's march ahead.

Among the many orders to Berthier Fain has had to take down in his self-invented shorthand is a letter destined for Vilna. That city's two governors (Maret has written) are hopelessly at loggerheads. Hogendorp and Jomini can't see eye to eye about the least thing. Obedient to Napoleon's orders, a 1,000-man detachment has been sent out under a Major Hell to occupy the Drissa Camp – and has been lost. The detachment had been about to set out when an entire Russian corps had been reported in the vicinity; whereupon Jomini had sensibly postponed Major Hell's departure:

'HOGENDORP: "You're to obey the Emperor's orders!"

JOMINI: "The Emperor certainly wouldn't have ordered a thousand men to engage a whole army corps!"

HOGENDORP: "The battalion will leave."

JOMINI: "Then I must have the order in writing."'

Getting it, he'd refused to endorse it; and to avert, if possible, the impending catastrophe, had given the wretched Major Hell some cavalry to reconnoitre with and advised him to exercise all possible caution and, if his task turned out impossible, not persist in it. But the inevitable happened. Overwhelmed by Russian cavalry, Hell and half his men had been killed. QED. Another major, a Pole, on the Vilna civil authorities refusing him a billet, had flown into a rage and smashed some windows. Jomini supports the major. Hogendorp orders Jomini to place him under arrest. Jomini refuses to obey. Appeals to his friend, Foreign Minister Maret, and at the ball given to celebrate the Emperor's birthday appears in his company. 'Go home!' shouts Hogendorp, 'or I'll send you to prison under an escort of grenadiers!.'

And now a perplexed Maret is asking for instructions.

Fortunately Smolensk needs a governor – Delaborde's Young Guard division is needed for the approaching battle, and it'll be some little time before Marshal Victor can get there. Napoleon cuts the Gordian knot by ordering Berthier to appoint Jomini, adding: 'Speak firmly to General Hogendorp to moderate his enthusiasm and give no further cause for complaint.' (A reprimand addressed, according to Hogendorp, to Jomini.)

One unit which partakes neither of fish nor fowl that evening in Viazma is the 16th Chasseurs. One of its officers 'commanding an advanced post of a hundred horses on the evening of the Viazma affair' becomes a victim of the cavalry's overweening command structure so deprecated by Thirion:

'I was left at my post until midday the following day without anyone relieving me, and under strict orders not to unbridle. Yet the horses' had been harnessed since 6 a.m. the previous day. During the night, having nothing for my outpost, nor even any water close to hand, I sent an officer to tell the general of my plight, asking for some bread and above all some hay. He replied that his business was to make us fight, not to feed us. This meant our horses went for thirty hours without drinking. When I returned with my outpost we were just about to move on. I was given an hour to refresh my detachment, after which I had to rejoin the column at a trot, and was obliged to leave behind a dozen men whose horses could no longer walk. The King of Naples and the generals in his wake were much more occupied with their own affairs than with the troops.'

Only Lejeune's aesthetic appreciation of the bivouac scenes compensates for lack of a proper dinner:

'Life at the advance guard wasn't without its charms. I particularly noted the night of 28/9 August. A beautiful château, seen from afar, seemed to promise King Murat a thoroughly royal residence where he could spend the night. But at close quarters the traces of the fire revealed only smoking ruins, and we had to set up our bivouac at the foot of this château in the prettiest silver birch wood I've ever seen. These trees with their alabaster-white barks were mingled with pines and spruces, whose slender and hardy forms offered delightful arbours. The Polish lancers, bivouacked around us on undulating ground, had planted their lances under these birches' garlands, and the breeze agitated the thousand floating tricolour pennons which adorned their iron points. The flames of our bivouacs, the smoke of our kitchens where enormous braziers were deceptively keeping us waiting – the activity – the gaiety – even the appetite of all these young men who, greedy for glory, were laughingly tightening their belts, hole by hole, after insufficient meals – all this produced a charming effect. Nor was I the only to find it agreeable.'

Von Suckow, too, is experiencing 'superb autumn days, only saddened toward evening by the prospect of the meal awaiting us at the bivouac. Its composition was always the same: a soup of greasy water with fat, seasoned with gunpowder pretending to be salt.' Unlike the French, this is a condiment, Dr von Roos notices, that his Germans, 'absolutely had to have, with a bit of emaciated cow or horse. Apart from this detail of our fare, a very important one, it's true, we'd no reason to complain at all of our fate.'

Honey, on the other hand, is to be had in abundance; but can have disastrous effects:

'Russia is a country peopled with bees. Near even the most wretched hut there were always beehives. One even found them in the woods. These industrious insects, who'd confided the delicious fruits of their labours to the hollows of old trees, hadn't at all expected the Grand Army's troopers, passing nearby, to annex their precious hoards. Our men's swollen faces when they came back from such razzias were sufficient proof of the vigour with which these little animals had defended their property.'

Nor is this the whole of the bees' vengeance. The Württembergers boil the honeycombs, and make themselves ill.

'Every morning the Emperor mounted his horse and passed rapidly from one headquarters to the next, through the midst of the masses following the main Moscow road. As he came abreast of the various units they halted and formed up in line of battle. The drums beat a salute, the eagles of the Grand Army dipped before the great man. Prolonged acclamations were heard. Joy shone on all the soldiers' faces; in his person they seemed to have concentrated all their desires, all their hopes. Only the Guard was forbidden to receive the Emperor with vivats, since they always surrounded his person. If too frequent the shout would so to speak have become banal.'

Soltyk is still seeing things through the rose-coloured spectacles of his Polish patriotism:

'One evening after we'd left Viazma behind us, IHQ was set up in a beautiful meadow. Here and there the foliage of immemorial oaks spread their exquisite shade, which was most enjoyable – it was one of those red hot days which are rather usual at that time of year. In these northern climes the nights can begin to feel rather chilly even while the sun's rays are still blazing hot at midday. Having taken his usual lunch, Napoleon was walking to and fro in the shade of these century-old trees. Not far from him were standing a number of generals and other officers of his household, among them myself. We came very close to him and could clearly hear everything he said. Sometimes he even directed his words to some of his generals. He spoke at length and in the most lively fashion, with the strong conviction which was the hallmark of his eloquence.'

Soltyk says he's sorry he can't give a verbatim transcript of Napoleon's 'impassioned improvisation'. On the other hand he's not going to commit the 'unforgivable error of putting a single thought into my hero's mouth, or even a turn of speech he didn't use'. He'll repeat only what he, immediately on his return to the topographical staff's bivouac, has jotted down:

'First he spoke of Alexander, Hannibal and Caesar, and discussed the special merits now of one, now of another, characterizing each with a few remarkable words. Then, turning his thoughts back to the present circumstances, he said: "True greatness doesn't consist in wearing a purple coat or a grey one. It consists in raising oneself above one's condition. Take me, for example. I've a good job. I'm emperor. I could live in the midst of all the delights of a great capital, let myself be swallowed up by life's pleasures and indolence. Well, I'm waging war for the glory of France, for mankind's happiness, for the future. Here I am, in your midst, at the bivouac. I can be hit by a roundshot in some battle, just like anyone else. I'm raising myself above my condition. Everyone in his own sphere should do the same. There we have real greatness."'

Unfortunately the imperial monologue is interrupted by a despatch. Few prisoners, says Caulaincourt,

'had been taken at Valutina, and in the great pursuit we'd made none at all – not so much as a cart had been seized! Like everyone else the Emperor was amazed at this retreat of an army of 100,000 men, who didn't leave a single straggler or a solitary wagon behind. Not even a horse to mount a guide was to be found within a radius of 30 miles. Often we couldn't find anyone to serve the Emperor as a guide. Often the same man led us for three or four days on end through a countryside he knew no better than we did. The vanguard was in the same plight.'

But now, about six miles from the little town of Ghjat, Murat has at last caught two prisoners. One is a Cossack, whose horse had been killed just as he was making his escape from a village he'd been plundering. The other, captured shortly afterwards, is a Negro who claims to be cook to General Platow, the Cossacks' Hetman.

Napoleon, in his peremptory manner, plies them both with questions. Their replies strike Caulaincourt as 'so odd they're worth noting'. The Negro, for his part, refuses to believe it's Napoleon he's talking to – how can he be so close to the French van? He keeps asking who it is, and

'at the same time making the most comical grimaces and contor-
tions. When again told it really was Napoleon he was speaking to, he
bowed, prostrated himself several times, and then began to dance,
sing and make every imaginable contortion,'
and claims to have eavesdropped the Russian commanders' talk while
waiting on Platow at table. But though he gossips about the various generals' rivalries it's clear he knows nothing about the Russian army's movements. The Cossack, brought in next, is

'a man between 30 and 35, dark, five foot tall, with an open and
intelligent face, a serious air, with quick eyes, and was particularly
troubled at having lost his horse, his money, and what he called his
little package, i.e., the effects he'd taken or stolen, which he carried
on his saddle and used for padding out his seat. The Emperor told
me to give him some gold pieces, and lent him a horse from the stables.'

This loosens the prisoner's tongue.' "If Napoleon had had Cossacks in his
army", he says,

"he'd have been Emperor of China long ago. If the Russian generals
were in the van with the Cossacks, or even with the Russian troops,
the French wouldn't now be at the gates of Ghjat, for there are many
more Russians and Cossacks than there are Frenchmen, and the
Cossacks aren't afraid of the French."'

The Cossacks, he says, like Murat for the fine show he makes. He's a brave
fellow, always first under fire. Word has gone round that he's not to be
killed, "but they'd like to capture him". Everyone, he says, is expecting a
big battle in front of Moscow:

'news which to the Emperor seemed highly probable, afforded him
the greatest pleasure, and which he repeated to everyone: "This plan
of theirs will give me Moscow. But a good battle would finish the war
off sooner and lead us to peace. And that's where we're bound to
end up."'

CHAPTER 19

THE GATHERING STORM

Retire to Smolensk? – a pretty little town – two days' rest – a glut of officers – Le Roy serves carp for dinner – Dumonceau is nearly run over – a yellow carriage gets singed – 'we could make out the Russian lines' – desperate struggle for the Schevardino redoubt – 'The Emperor's temperament was eminently nervous' – his bad cold – noises in the night

Suddenly it's autumn. For two days on end (29 and 30 August) its first cold rains come lashing down. Icy torrents are making the going impossible. Dumonceau isn't the only one who's getting

'stuck in the mud at every step. In the evening, overwhelmed by fatigue, soaked to the bone and filthy, we halted in a wretched bivouac that offered no shelter and where the suffering caused by the cold stormy night was added to those from all kinds of privations.'

Lejeune, as he rides to and fro with orders from Berthier's headquarters, is alarmed to notice how 'discouragement seemed to be overwhelming the army'. And even says that

'Berthier, though very timid about proffering his advice, made so bold as to counsel the Emperor to retreat. Napoleon took this proposal very much amiss, and told him he could clear out if he was tired, but promised to retire if the rains persisted.'

The coolness between them, Lejeune will notice, lasts 'several days, though without interrupting their continuing working relations'. "It's already autumn here, no longer summer," Napoleon writes to Marie-Louise. And indeed the first day of September brings a stupendous thunderstorm, killing with its lightning a trooper of the 2nd Carabiniers and injuring several others. As at the Niemen, the cold rain is causing 'both men and horses to sicken'. On the other hand Dumonceau is wondering whether it isn't preventing the Cossacks from setting fire to the villages, so that only the towns and manor-houses are now going up in flames. Others think it must be due to their being pressed so hard by the advance guard.

The hard-marched 85th has spent its last August night camped in gardens surrounding a manor-house with 'a superb stretch of water. The whole staff lodged in the house.' Suspecting the presence of finny friends in its pond, Le Roy had undressed, got into the water, and begun searching in the rushes:

'Quite right. Soon I feel an enormous carp who has half buried himself in the mud, and as the water is noticeably running away, we soon see his golden back. Pressing it hard, we grab him and finally, not without great efforts, manage to tumble him up on to the bank. We carry him to the château, where he gets the welcome he deserves. The kitchen is perfectly appointed – much better, in fact, than the

247

cellar, where all we find is some bad beer which, thirsty as we are, we nevertheless find delicious.'

But now, on 3 September, just as everyone's in despair, the sun comes out again; and there's no more talk of retiring on Smolensk. 'The sky turned blue,' writes Labaume, 'and I was sent to King Murat to urge him to continue his advance.' From 4 to 6 September Le Roy and the 85th march 'with great circumspection, being sure they were waiting for us at Borodino, on the Kolotchka, only five miles ahead'. Between I Corps and the Russians lies only the 'pretty little town of Ghjat,[1] the most important one on the Smolensk-Moscow road, bisected by the little river of the same name'.

This time, though Ghjat is 'surrounded by streams flowing through small lakes', measures are taken to enter it at a rush, before it can be put to the torch. Through heavy fire from a Russian battery, Murat and Eugène ride in slowly at a slow walk, each trying to look less concerned than the other, 'even though they calmly see several of their entourage fall under the enemy shots'. Despite the steady downpour – it's raining again – the river is so low that IV Corps, following in the wake of I Corps, can cross it on foot.

Le Roy is relieved to find that only the town's eastern side has been fired – 'unfortunately the side with the bazaar and merchants'.

Although the Red Lancers are advancing across country, Colbert seems to be urging them forward at a considerable rate, perhaps in hopes of some brilliant feat of arms 'like the one at Somosierra'.[2] But the extreme congestion at the entrance to Gjhat forces the regiment to bivouac. To get some food and forage they send out a marauding party to a 'village some soldiers said was well-provided'. But hardly has the party gone out than they have to move on again. Just then Dumonceau has no particular duties to perform and, anxious for his possessions, lingers with the regiment's baggage until the marauders shall return. But when they have, trying to catch up again, his sabre gets caught in a wheel of a wagon. This throws him from his horse and he's very nearly run over in the crush. And by the time he's mounted again – the regiment has vanished! Wandering about looking for it in fields beyond the town, he and his horse have to pass the night in a remote barn. 'Luckily it was full of hay.' To judge by her whinnyings, his Liesje seems to be as anxious as her rider. But though Dumonceau tries to stay awake and on the *qui vive*, he drops off into so deep a sleep that he doesn't wake up again until long after daybreak:

'Behind me, on the heights to the right of Ghjat, was a sizeable cavalry bivouac, dominated by lance pennons like ours, agitated by the wind, and at the bottom of the slope some red-uniformed troopers were watering their horses at a nearby lake.'

Hastening to rejoin them, he finds everyone has been so worried by his absence that Jean, his servant, who has feared him lost, greets him with tears in his eyes. Even Colbert has enquired after him several times. And now he's back 'restricted himself to reproaching me with the risks I'd exposed myself to by not sticking with the regiment. Everything was ready to receive me, and soon I was restored by a good breakfast, which I badly needed.'

Evidently the Italians have been following in the wake of Murat's cavalry; for by the time Laugier enters Ghjat's log-paved main street Napoleon, entering at 2 p.m., has already reconnoitred the great plateau dominating the town, 'the hospital, which was by the town gate and not been set fire to, and was hastening on the bridges' reconstruction and the troops crossing them'. Although even fewer inhabitants have stayed behind than at Viazma, Caulaincourt is delighted to see that all the stone houses along the main street and riverside are full of every kind of provisions -'flour, eggs and butter, everything we'd so long gone without'. Those inhabitants who've stayed behind report that the Russian army has just been reinforced by Miladorovitch's 50,000 Cossacks and a lot of artillery.[3] They also confirm that Barclay has been replaced by the one-eyed Kutusov. Since Kutusov is known to the French – quite unjustly – as 'the general who'd run away at Austerlitz', everyone is delighted. And Napoleon orders two days' rest. To Berthier, Ghjat, 2 September 1812:

"*Mon cousin*, give the King of Naples, the Prince of Eckmühl, the Viceroy, Prince Poniatowski orders to rest today, rally their troops, and at 3 p.m. to hold a roll-call and let me know definitely the number of men who will be present at the battle; to have all weapons, cartridge pouches, the artillery and the ambulances inspected; to let the men know that we are approaching the moment of a general engagement, and that they must prepare for it. Further, you must let me know the number of unshod horses which will be present and how much time would be needed to reshoe the cavalry and put it in shape for battle.'

An order which is passed on to the various corps commanders in a circular couched in the flowery language of old French chivalry. General Romeau (Davout's chief-of-staff) to Dedem:

"Sept 2. I have the honour to inform you that it is Monseigneur Marshal the Prince of Eckmühl's intention that the troops be forewarned that we are approaching the moment of a general battle, and that they should prepare for it."

'Each man in I Corps', writes Dedem, 'was issued with five packets of cartridges. Weapons were cleaned. All able-bodied men were withdrawn from the baggage train and came back into the ranks.' At 3 p.m. the review is duly held, and returns made. How grand, by now, is the Grand Army?

Evidently word soon gets round as to the figures for total effectives, for Laugier records them in his diary: 103,000 infantry, 30,000 cavalry, 587 guns. But many units have dwindled terribly. The 25th Division, originally consisting of four 4-battalion Line regiments (Württembergers, Illyrians, Poles, Portuguese) plus four more of light infantry, now has 'companies which hardly could put seven or eight muskets in a row'. Of Nansouty's light cavalry division which crossed the Niemen 7,500 horsemen strong, Victor Dupuy finds less than 1,000 are left, 'and certainly it wasn't enemy fire which had made this immense breach!' Despite the reinforcements which reached the Red Lancers at Witebsk, only 700 of the original 1,200 are still with the pennons. Above all there are altogether too many officers:

'At least they'd been able to afford to buy a little food, even if at fantastically inflated prices. An officer doesn't have to carry a heavy haversack, and he rides a horse. Finally, we had the moral factor on our side.'

The result is an extraordinary imbalance between them and other ranks – hardly an officer is missing from Ney's twelve Württemberger battalions. Since they now number in all no more than a mere 1,450 men they're reformed as only three:

'The entire officer corps formed up in a single rank in a meadow a few yards from our bivouac. Accompanied by his chief surgeon, our divisional general passed along in front of it, stopping in front of each of us in turn, and asking after our state of health. In accordance with the doctor's assessment, he either orders us to one of the battalions, or else puts us on the non-active list; which means following in the army's tracks at a distance of one or two days' march.'

Von Suckow himself, found hale, is one of those sent to a battalion.

The story is doubtless much the same in the other corps, the Old Guard excepted.

Enjoying his two-day repose on the plateau beyond the town, Le Roy pays a courtesy visit to his old regiment, the 108th. One of its sous-lieutenants gives him a fine Polish pony, with 'a strong back, a hanging mane, a lively eye and in other respects well proportioned'. He can no longer afford to feed both it and himself.[4] Le Roy passes the pony on to his faithful servant Guillaume, to carry their larder and the precious iron cookpot which so nearly hadn't even got across the Niemen.

Just as it's about to march, IV Corps is rejoined by Preyssing's Bavarian cavalry. Laugier and Labaume, reaching first one then a second 'pretty little manor-house', find to their distress it's been thoroughly wrecked. At Pokrow,

'a well laid out park, beautiful long alleys, newly built pavilions evincing the owner's good taste, agreeable life-style and luxurious furniture, precious crystals, fine porcelain vases – all is scattered or in fragments. Extremely costly books are lying on the ground.'

Labaume too notes how Pokrow's 'freshly decorated pavilion only offered an image of the most horrible devastation. Everywhere we saw only shattered furniture, bits of precious porcelain strewn about the garden, and expensive engravings ripped out of their frames and scattered to the winds.' No matter. The main thing is that it has plenteous stocks of corn and forage. Stolidly setting up his headquarters amidst all this cultural wreckage, Prince Eugène gives IV Corps, too, an extra day's rest 'for isolated men to catch up. The order about men serving as coachmen has been repeated, so we can be at full strength on the day of battle.'

Of all the army's units except the artillery the baggage train alone hasn't dwindled en route. And many commanders 'out of insouciance, weakness, weariness or compassion' aren't bothering to obey the order to send their carriages to the rear.

"Ghjat, Sept 2, 1812. *Mon Cousin*. The headquarters staff are of no help to me, nor is the provost-general of military police, nor yet the baggage-master; no one is doing his duty as he should. You have received my orders about the baggage; take care the first baggage I'll order to be burnt isn't that of the general staff. If you've no baggage-master, nominate one, so that all the baggage marches under one command. It's impossible to see a worse order than the one prevailing."

All these hundreds of officers' carriages, rolling placidly along behind their units, are getting badly on Napoleon's nerves:

"Ghjat, Sept 3, 1812. *Mon Cousin*, write to the corps commanders that we are losing a lot of men every day because of their disorderly way of searching for food; that it's urgent that they shall concert with the various unit commanders on measures to be taken to put an end a state of affairs which is threatening the army with destruction; that the number of prisoners taken by the enemy daily amounts to several hundreds; that the soldiers must be prevented under the severest penalties from leaving their units and be sent out to get food in the same way as forage; that a general or other superior officer shall command all maraudings."

Strange orders to be issued so late in the day and, on the eve of battle, scarcely capable of being enforced? Perhaps it's because he's angry with himself for even momentarily considering a retreat on Smolensk that Napoleon's fury now falls on Berthier. Neither that day nor for four to come will they eat at the same table. And when Napoleon, overtaking the marching columns at a gallop on 4 September, sees some carriages still intermingled with the artillery trains, it's the last straw. Among them is a fine yellow carriage. Jumping down from 'Moscow'[5] – the charger Caulaincourt has allotted him today – he orders a squad of the escort chasseurs to halt and set fire to the obnoxious carriage – which as it happens belongs to Narbonne:

'M. de Narbonne pointed out that it might mean some officer who'd lose a leg on the morrow being stranded. "It'll cost me even more tomorrow if I've no artillery!" the Emperor rejoined. And, turning to Berthier: "I only wish it had been yours. It'd make an even greater impression. I keep on coming across it all the time." "Behind Your Majesty's own carriage," Berthier replied. "It's all Caulaincourt's fault! However that may be, I've promised to burn it if I come across it. And you needn't sulk over my threat, either – I won't spare my own carriage more than anyone else's. I'm commander-in-chief and must set an example."

Girod de l'Ain, Castellane and other staff officers watch the chasseurs fetch straw and firewood and 'several flaming brands from the bivouac we'd just abandoned; and the Emperor waited until the carriage has caught alight before riding on again'. A calèche and a light trap following behind it are to suffer the same fate. 'No sooner had the fire caught', says Caulaincourt, 'than the Emperor galloped off, and the coachmen, I believe, rescued their slightly singed vehicles.' As Girod de l'Ain confirms: 'Hardly had he ridden a hundred metres than people made haste to quench the flames, after which the carriage rejoined the column as before.' Castellane says Narbonne 'gave the soldiers ten louis for putting out the fire they'd themselves lit'. And Villemain, Narbonne's secretary, adds a characteristic PS:

'Regretting his impulsiveness, but anyway wishing to make good the loss to a man he was fond of, Napoleon suggested to Duroc that he send 1,000 napoleons to M. de Narbonne, "who isn't rich". Duroc, always cultivated and meticulous, after a moment's hesitation as to the proper way of doing this, at the first halt went to the trouble of putting some gold coins in an elegant case adorned with the imperial arms, placed it underneath some exquisitely selected books, and had it all taken to the general. M. de Narbonne opened the case and studied the volumes with pleasure. As for the gold, he sent it immediately with a friendly word to the colonel of a regiment whose young soldiers he'd been tormented to see so harassed that day, and whose ranks were already anxiously thinned. He asked him to distribute the gift among the men of his unit. Next day, before setting out, when everyone was in his proper place, the Emperor said to him gently:

"Well, Narbonne, the damage to the baggage has been made good. You've been reimbursed."

"Yes, Sire, and am grateful. But in a fashion Your Majesty unquestionably would permit I've only kept the letter and of the case's contents only some books, among them, Seneca's two essays: De beneficiis, and De Patientia. They're good to have about one on campaign."'

Napoleon, says Villemain, perfectly understood both the allusion and the Latin titles, and said nothing. But the tale gets round. 'By way of making an example,' Laugier notes in his diary, 'Napoleon has had a carriage belonging to his ADC Narbonne burnt in his presence by some grenadiers of the Guard.'

During the moonlit night of 3/4 September Dumonceau is on duty, his special task being to make sure the horses are watered. So brilliant is the moonlight and so translucent the air he's able to make out objects five kilometres away. And is amazed to see 'all these thousands of men lying resting in the night's silence, like so many graves in a gigantic necropolis'.

By now everyone knows the Russians are waiting for them only a couple of hours' march further on. And that evening (4 September) Séruzier's horse artillery, arriving outside the village of Gridnowo, is more than usually severely rebuffed before it can throw out the Russian rearguard:

'Elsewhere the usual ill-prepared attacks had, as usual, been thrown back, albeit with unusual violence; and estafettes had been sent galloping back to say the entire Russian army was dug in along the slopes beyond a little stream.'

The devastation along the route, too, is becoming steadily more thorough. Everyone notices it.

'Not a blade of grass, not a tree. We never come to a village which hasn't been plundered from top to bottom. Impossible to find the least nourishment for our horses, to renew our larder, or even light a camp fire for the night.'

The Russians have 'laid waste the entire plain we were obliged to camp on. They'd mown the long grass, felled the woods, burnt down the villages. In a word, had left us nothing to eat, nothing to keep our horses alive, nothing to shelter us.'

And the weather is miserable.

The morning of 5 September dawns chill and foggy, with drizzling rain. Only when the mist lifts can Dumonceau look out over 'an open slightly undulating plain where we see our immense column stretching away as far as the eye could reach'. Between the leading units and strong Russian rearguards there are ever more embittered engagements. The 11th Hussars, in particular, catch a bad cold.

So does the Italian light cavalry, marching as usual to the left of the main column. Isn't that the sound of gunfire, away to its right?

'Over there we even see great clouds of smoke rising to the sky, and draw the conclusion that we can't be far from the Moscow post-road which the main column is marching along. [It can only be Séruzier's guns, again at grips with the enemy.] By and by we see, far away, the Russian cavalry gathering, with obvious intent to bar our way. The Viceroy orders the 3rd Italian Chasseurs to attack.'

As usual, it's a trap. Just as the chasseurs are about to reach the Russians 'a great mass of enemies come rushing out at us from a wood, with their usual hurrahs. A terrible scrum ensues.' Finally the Russians withdraw under the protection of infantry and artillery firing at the Italians out of the forest. And IV Corps again joins up with Murat's cavalry divisions.

Now it's 2 p.m. and 'only the advance guard is making some slow progress. The army has halted and formed columns of battalions at several points where there's rising ground.' Looking away across the vast plain to his right, Césare de Laugier sees an immense building, surrounded by white walls. 'The coloured tiles of its roofs gleam in the sunbeams through the dense dust being raised by our enormous masses of cavalry, and stress the savage and grim aspect of the countryside all about.' Although it has the appearance of a town, it is in fact Kolotskoië Abbey, which 'built in the days of the Goths, has often served as a citadel during civil wars, and is still surrounded by trenches'. A mile and a half beyond it a stream winds its placid way eastwards toward the enemy positions.

The Italian light cavalry snatches the manor-house of Woroniemo before the Cossacks can set fire to it. But no sooner have Eugène's aides installed themselves in it and the Viceroy himself has just taken a couple of turns on its terrace, than Napoleon turns up. Von Muraldt, who's there with Eugène's Bavarian cavalry, sees them

> 'gallop flat out across our regiments' front, the imperial entourage dashing with loosened reins at a distance behind them. At this sight all IV Corps' eight cavalry regiments raise such a cheer of *"Vive l'Empereur!"* that the domestics and orderlies, who've been out watering the lead horses, take it for a Cossack "hurrah", and come rushing back in panic. You can imagine how we laughed.'

After which Napoleon goes back 'to the unit he's marching with' and Eugène sets his troops in motion again. The unit in question is the Red Lancers:

> 'Advancing swiftly behind the Emperor, who'd just broken into a gallop, we overtook the various army corps, and almost simultaneously with the advance guard came within view of Borodino, and toward midday halted about three-quarters of a league from that place. Beyond a last undulation of the terrain, straight in front of us, it showed a group of five globular towers at the base of a long line of sheer and wooded heights which, crossing our front, stretched out far on either hand. It was on these heights the enemy army was at long last awaiting us.'

The battlefield Kutusov (or rather one of his aides) has chosen for his great stand is a gently rising plain, flanked by sparse woods, between the old and new Moscow roads. For the great numbers of men who are going to be involved it's no little cramped. The easily fordable Kolotchka stream runs diagonally across it NE-SW. And a tributary, the Semenovskaya, fronts and – in its higher reaches, out of sight of the French – intersects the Russian position. Assuming for some reason that Napoleon will focus his onslaught on the village of Borodino, Kutusov has arranged his two armies quite eccentrically. While Barclay de Tolly's extreme right, where Borodino village, standing above the Kolotchka's west bank, forms a hardly tenable salient, is confronting almost no enemy at all, Bagration's left, facing the French centre, can fairly easily be outflanked. The Kolotchka, easily fordable at most points, separates the two armies 'by turning sharp left at the foot of the heights and some distance further on flowing into the River Moskowa. But to Dumonceau's right front, at a point before this bend, 'the escarpments of its right bank disappeared, flattening out into a low, unbroken and open plain that rose gradually, first towards the two villages of Schevardino and Borodino, ranged on a line parallel to the stream's course, then, beyond, to big woods of high brushwood, lining the horizon a mile and a half away.'

Among the hundreds of new arrivals closely studying this frightening field of battle which is going to offer the Russian guns maximum fire power and the invaders almost no cover at all, is a Saxon dragoon officer, named *von Lessnig*.[6] As far as his inquisitive spyglass can see,

'the whole ground to the left and right and straight ahead was covered with a growth of hazel bushes, juniper and other brushwood which rose to at least a man's height. To the left centre, about a thousand paces distant, stood a village and a nice Byzantine church, which rose from a gentle tree-covered slope and had a pretty tower plated in green copper. To our right was a ridge, covered along almost all its length with masses of Russian infantry and artillery. On some of the highest points, as I could see clearly through my telescope, the Russians had thrown up earthworks with notches cut in them that seemed to be embrasures for the artillery. Obliquely to the right of our regiment rose the towers of Mojaisk and the nearby monastery. Though they were an hour's march away, they lent a touch of beauty to the brooding gloom of this wild and barren neighbourhood.'

From IV Corps' camp von Muraldt through his spyglass can 'clearly make out the mouths of the redoubt's heavy calibre guns and in general everything else going on in the Russian camp'. The Mojaisk church tower, beyond the line of woods, is in fact about eight miles off. But to the right, much closer, projecting and detached from the Russian front, are two villages. Between them Dumonceau sees,

'a broad, tall hillock, like a truncated cone, which we took for a redoubt. Some individuals were visible on its summit, probably put there to observe; and at its base and behind its flanks we could make out two black masses, which could only be the heads of columns intended to support it.'

Although 'prevented from seeing the enemy position clearly by the smoke from the villages he was setting fire to', Lejeune and his colleagues are able to make out that it is 'armed with 12 to 20 guns'. Clearly, before anything else can happen, this outspur or salient, threatening the French right, will have to be nipped off. 'The Emperor', Lejeune goes on, 'immediately ordered it to be attacked by Compans' division,' supported by Nansouty's and Montbrun's cavalry corps. And an order is sent off to Poniatowski, who is marching along the 'old' Moscow road, to the army's right, that his Poles are to advance through the woods and take this advanced enemy position in flank and rear. Colonel Griois, looking on with the rest of the army at Compans' division as it peels off to the right, thinks it 'wonderful to see our troops' keenness. The beauty of the scene was enhanced by the splendid sky and the setting sun, reflected on the muskets and sabres. They were proud to have been chosen as the first to get to grips with the enemy.'

The enemy, Labaume[7] sees, are

'sending considerable forces to defend the redoubt's approaches. First, General Compans bombarded it with all the artillery he had to hand, as far as possible to overthrow the entrenchment, embankment and the palisades. As soon as he thought them in a state to receive the assault, he launched Colonel Charrier at the head of the 57th.'

This is at about 5 p.m. Gourgaud, who is also certainly watching, takes up the tale:

'Between Compans' right and the wood, some of the King of Naples' cavalry advanced, but was contained by the enemy artillery and cavalry. General Compans, at the head of the 57th and the 61st, aimed toward the right of the hillock. At the same time he made General Dupelain march to its left with the 25th, on the Schevardino side. He had the 111th placed still farther to the left, in order to turn the Russians' right. While carrying out his movement Compans was attacked by masses of cavalry,'

and is personally hit in the left arm.

'But he took clever advantage of the lie of the land and of some wattle fencing that enabled him to go on, despite these cavalry masses, and even to repulse them with great loss. Soon a most murderous fusillade started up on this side, between Compans' two regiments and the Russian infantry supporting the redoubt's left flank. Only separated by a couple of dozen yards, the troops on either side of the wattle fences were protected from each other up to chest level. Thus this sanguinary fusillade lasted three-quarters of an hour; its vivacity and noise made it impossible to hear the general's order to advance with the bayonet, a manoeuvre which would have cost us a lot of men.'

Although the Russians are suffering even more heavily from this almost point-blank fusillade, Gourgaud says they can't get their men to attack either. Several voltigeur companies, ordered up by Compans on to a neighbouring mound only 120 yards away, direct a murderous fire into the redoubt. But though night is now falling neither side seems to be gaining the upper hand:

'Wanting at all costs to extricate himself from this terrible situation, Compans took a battalion of the 57th and, having opened up the fences on his right, made it advance in close column of divisions, covering four guns charged with grape that marched behind it. He led this battalion against the extreme right of the Russians flanking the redoubt. When he was 100 yards away, he unmasked his battery, whose grapeshot ravaged the enemy terribly. Profiting from the dis-

order he saw in their ranks, his battalion charged with its bayonets,'
and the Russians give way. Compans, his wound treated, orders a second
assault. This too being repulsed, 'Compans, irritated by these obstacles
and impatient of success, threw in a lively attack at the redoubt's rear' –
the one just described by Gourgaud – 'himself marching in at Charrier's
side at the head of the 57th'. When, simultaneously, the 61st come sweeping into the redoubt, they find, Gourgaud says, 'gunners, horses, every living thing had been been destroyed by our voltigeurs' fire'.

Unfortunately this isn't the end of the matter. Recaptured by Russian
grenadiers, the shattered redoubt has to be stormed a second time, this
time by Morand's and Friant's crack divisions, supported by Nansouty's
cavalry corps. More and more Russian troops too are being fed into this
crepuscular struggle, which in the gathering dusk is developing into a
wholly undesirable encounter battle. Napoleon sends off an aide to
Poniatowski, urging him to make haste. 'For two hours night had been
shedding its shadows on the combatants, whose determination seemed to
grow with the difficulties, and we were getting worried.' But at just the
right moment Poniatowski's Poles emerge from the woods. And Heinrich
von Brandt, watching at a distance, realizes it's all over: 'Suddenly a huge
shout reached us, brought by a violent gust of wind.'

Napoleon orders the victorious troops to remain in position, the
infantry in squares. A wise precaution. For hardly has darkness fallen than
Thirion sees 'a line of cavalry deploying into line of battle in front of a
wood behind the captured redoubt'. Advancing rapidly and taking the
111th by suprise, it breaks into its square, kills a lot of men and seizes its
guns. But the other regiments stand their ground in a darkness

'which though not so dark we couldn't make out this movement, was
dark enough to prevent us from seeing which arm it was composed
of. General Nansouty orders the Red Lancers of Hamburg[8] to charge
the Russian cavalry and throw it back. This regiment flew to the
attack, delivered its charge and fell on the enemy with felled lances,
aimed at the body. The Russian cavalry received the shock without
budging, and in the same moment as the French [*sic*] lance-heads
touched the enemy's chests the regiment about-faced and came back
towards us as if it in its turn had been charged. We, the 2nd and 3rd
Cuirassiers, thought this a poor show, and moved briskly forward to
support them and repulse the enemy cavalry.'

But at the cuirassiers' approach the Russian cavalry calmly withdraw into
the woods. As for the Hamburg Lancers, nothing can induce them to
launch a second attack. What their lances had struck against in the murk
had been the black breastplates of the Cuirassiers of the Russian Imperial
Guard, iron on iron. 'Which only goes to show', Thirion concludes, 'what
an effect one arm can have on another.'

At about midnight, the entire Russian force begins to draw off, abandoning the costly and, in fact, wholly superfluous bastion. This preliminary struggle has cost Compans the lives of 500 of his crack infantrymen,

and 1,000 wounded. The intrepid Colonel Charrier is promptly promoted general, but his 'handsome regiment' too has lost any amount of men. 'The 61st had lost a whole battalion there.' 'Battlefield thick with enemy dead,' Caulaincourt jots down in his notebook, late at night.

An order is issued for all wounded to be taken to the Kolotskoïe Abbey. Is anyone complying? All Dr von Roos, 'while waiting to be ordered into the battle line and after passing ditches filled with arms and legs and corpses', finds when he gets to the immense abbey buildings at a late hour, are 'some persons from Napoleon's suite and the personnel of the imperial printing press'. Soltyk, ordered to interrogate Russian wounded, can't

> 'get any important information out of them. They all wore such an exasperated air, they wouldn't utter a single word. So these proud Moscovites, my country's oppressors, now had to feel in their turn the terrible effects of a foreign invasion!'

Oddly, von Roos' troopers have suddenly been issued with their arrears of pay. Von Roos himself would 'gladly have dispensed with the 3 thalers because of their weight, and because it was impossible to find anything to buy.' Not merely is there nothing to buy – or steal; there are no civilians about, Rapp realizes, to give any information: 'Women, children, old men, cattle, everything, had vanished.'

Meanwhile, as division after division has been turning up, 'an immense crowd had been establishing itself' in the open fields. One such regiment, hastening up from the rear 'almost always through flames from burning barns and houses', is Maurice de Tascher's chasseurs. Passing through Ghjat they'd found it a 'charming little town'; and when the 18th Line had left it on 4 September, Bonnet had written in his diary 'Ghjat was intact; only one or two houses burnt'. But then, a couple of hours later, Tascher is sent back to it and by then 'nothing remained'. A conflagration, caused, according to Faber du Faur, by 'wounded men's stupidity and inexperience in lighting fires in timber houses' and aggravated by a violent west wind, had 'laid the greater part of the town in ashes, among it the main street of stone houses'.

While the battle for the Schevardino salient had been going on 'the Palace' had been installed under canvas near Walomiewo, 'only about a mile and a quarter from the enemy's position. The Emperor's tent was placed in the midst of the Guard' – a little below and very close to the position occupied by Boulart's guns, drawn up there in battery:

> 'There wasn't the least dwelling or barn in the surroundings and the whole Imperial Guard, Young and Old, was concentrated there around the Emperor's tents, five army corps and cavalry crammed together to a depth of three miles and then, to the rear, the crowded assemblage of the central mass of parks and convoys. All afternoon the Emperor had stayed with us, walking to and fro on the edge of

the ravine, his hands behind his back, now and then observing what was going on through his spyglass.'

As for the Russians, they are

'encamped as it were on an amphitheatre. They lit many fires, whose resplendent, almost symmetrical clarity gave this hill an enchanting appearance, in sharp contrast to our bivouacs where the soldier, lacking firewood, was reposing amid shadows, hearing all around him only the groans of the unfortunate wounded.'

Eugène, for his part, has pitched his tent amidst the Italian Guard Cavalry. But everyone else, says Labaume, who's thinking the the Russian position has been much weakened by the loss of the Schevardino redoubt,

'lay down amidst the bushes and slept profoundly, despite the vehement wind and an excessively cold rain. We were in a sandpit, with a long curtain of osiers and foliage hiding Walweiewo, where the Emperor had established his headquarters.'

Always Dumonceau has an eye to the welfare and sufferings of the horses:

'Their misery was great. Apart from a slender ration of oats brought up from Ghjat, they'd nothing to eat but a few bits of straw or grass, everywhere disputed on all sides, and to find which our men had to wander about during part of the night.'

Others are wandering about in search of other things. A Württemberg artillery officer, sent to the rear with four wagons to replenish his unit's ammunition, is having a peculiarly difficult time:

'Everywhere I met with refusal. The divisional reserve was unwilling to issue any ammunition because they said they needed it for the impending battle, and the large corps reserve was still far to the rear, some of it back in Smolensk. Eventually I came on a reserve park whose commander explained that he'd give me as much ammunition as I required provided I brought him a note from the Intendant-General of Artillery, General Lariboisière, who was usually in the Emperor's suite.'

Riding quickly off, he finds Napoleon amidst his staff in the courtyard of Kolotskoïe Abbey,

'pacing up and down and indulging in the innocent pleasure of whacking his boot with a riding-whip. Several officers from whom I inquired the whereabouts of General Lariboisière, replied curtly "I've no idea." But the Emperor, who must have noticed me stumbling about repeating my question, called out to me: "What are you looking for?" "Sire," I replied, "I'm looking for General Lariboisière, to get him to give me a voucher for some ammunition." "Which unit are you from?" "I belong to General Beurmann's light battery. Yesterday and this morning we've burnt up all our powder, and I don't think I'll get the ammunition we're short of without a written note from General Lariboisière." 'The Emperor turned to his suite and shouted "General Lariboisière!" Everybody set about finding the general, and when he turned up the Emperor said to him "Give this officer what he needs." I made the Emperor a deep and cheerful bow, and got everything I needed. At 6 p.m. that evening, with two full ammunition wagons, I rejoined the battery, which for lack of ammunition had remained close to where we'd fought in the morning.'

Labaume, for his part, is busy making a sketch map of the environs. And at about midnight IV Corps' new chief-of-staff comes and tells him the Emperor needs it. Perhaps it's from having studied it that Caulaincourt makes his night reconnaissance: 'visited bivouacs, inspected the captured redoubt and several times rode up and down the line to judge the Russian position with my own eyes'.

But Napoleon, in his tent, is feeling rotten. The Emperor's constitution', writes Yvan, his surgeon, 'was eminently nervous. He was subject to psychosomatic influences and usually the spasm would distribute itself between the stomach and the bladder.'

And now he has caught a very bad cold. 'He was tormented', Yvan goes on,

'by the equinoctial winds, by the mists, the rain and the bivouac. He was utterly susceptible to the atmosphere. If he were to maintain his equilibrium, his skin had to carry out all its functions. As soon as his tissue became constricted, whether the cause was psychological or atmospheric, the irritable apparatus [sic] had a more or less serious effect on him; and from that followed a violent cough, accompanied by ischuria. All these effects passed over as soon as the dermal functions were re-established. When the irritation went to the stomach, he would suffer from nervous coughings which exhausted his moral and physical strength to the point where his intelligence was no longer the same.[10] Usually the bladder, too, was involved in the spasm; and then he was under the influence of an annoying and tiring situation. Horse-riding added to his sufferings. All these accidents together fell upon him at the moment of the battle.'

Summoned to his tent, Dr Mestivier is greeted with the words:

'"Well, doctor, you see I'm growing old, my legs swell, I urinate with difficulty, doubtless it's the humidity of these bivouacs, because I live only through my skin."' Mestivier notes

'a continual dry cough, breathing difficult and spasmodic, urine only coming out drop by drop and with pain... muddy [sic] and full of sediment; the lower part of the legs and feet extremely oedmatose; the pulse feverish and intermittent around the twelfth beat.[11] All these grave symptoms gave cause for justifiable fears of a chest hydropsy.'

Since his patient has 'a high temperature' Chief-pharmacist Sureau is sent for to prepare a potion. Unfortunately its ingredients are 'with the heavy baggage an hour away'. Ségur says that General Lauriston, 'who told me this himself', helped him to place cataplasms on his stomach.

CHAPTER 20

THE MOUTHS OF THE GUNS

An early reconnaissance – outflank the Russians? – effectives – 'in a lugubrious silence... the mouths of the guns' – nothing to eat – Kutusov's 'tomfoolery' – 'a masterpiece' – 'an officer of furtive appearance' – Capt. François gets a nasty leg wound – premonitions – 'like wandering shades' – muddles in the night – 'like the atmosphere before a storm' – 'parade uniforms as if for a holiday' – 'better a horrific end than a horror without end' – 'a profound silence reigned everywhere' – Napoleon's command post

Although 6 September dawns grey, cold and chilly, 'at the first glimmer of daylight [6 a.m.]' Napoleon is on horseback, 'together with Berthier, Eugène, two officers and myself', says Lejeune.

'Without any other suite, he began to traverse the enemy's front. Nowhere were our outposts more than a pistol shot from the enemy's, and neither were firing at the other. The Emperor profited from this circumstance to acquaint himself with the means of getting close to the Russians, in greater detail and closer quarters. Since he was riding on ahead, he found himself face to face with a patrol of 20 Cossacks, four paces away from us – I was a bit worried to see him thus expose himself to the risk of being carried off by a few men who might be hiding behind a bend in the ravine. But it was they who fancied themselves taken by surprise. They were just turning their horses' heads when, seeing our little group put our horses to the gallop to get away from them, they came after us for several hundred paces. Before returning from this reconnaissance, which promised him a major battle for the morrow, the Emperor ordered me to go along the line again and make him a pencil drawing of its topography and also bring him some views of the terrain.'[1]

In this, the first reconnaissance of three, he notes particularly that the Russians have thrown up three earthworks. The largest and most formidable of these, somewhat to the French left but in the centre of their lopsidedly arranged position, crowns a height. Provided with wolftraps and bristling with outward sloping stakes, its eighteen[2] heavy-calibre guns not only sweep the gentle plain sloping away NNW toward Borodino village, whose green church towers are clearly visible, but also the entire French centre. Through their glasses the French can see that this formidable obstacle, unlike the other two fieldworks – shallow, obtuse-angled redans or flèches – is also closed at the rear, but not at its 'gorges', i.e., its ends. If only Napoleon were able to get a still closer view, or the thick mist were not obscuring his field of vision, he'd be able to detect, somewhat to the left rear of the other two flèches, between them and the Grand Redoubt and somewhat retired, yet a third flèche of the same sort. But it lies just out of sight. All three of the visible fieldworks seem to stand on the same ridge. He can't see what lies beyond. Only that the Russians, on the rim of the plateau beyond the high-banked Semenovskaya stream, are busy dismantling Semenovskaya village.

Their entire position is packed with two, perhaps three, lines of densely massed troops. Obviously a frontal assault is going to be extremely costly to both sides. And the whole position is deceptively strong.

Can it be turned? Away to his right, towards the village of Utitza and the old Moscow post-road, along which Poniatowski's Poles performed so well yesterday evening, there's a prehistoric tumulus. But the whole of this part of the battlefield is screened off by woods and thickets. Probes in that direction show that resistance there is unlikely to be what it could be. Perhaps he should combine an all-out onslaught on the Russian centre with a strategic outflanking movement? Attack them also in the rear, roll up the whole Russian army and fling it into the River Moscowa – as at Friedland? But here numbers are of the essence. If his effectives were even nearly what they'd been at Witebsk, there'd be no question of the outcome. And the manoeuvre would be perfectly possible. But they aren't.

To Kutusov's 90,000 infantry, 24,000 cavalry (7,000 of them Cossacks, of little or no use in a pitched battle) and 640 guns, Napoleon has nearly 90,000 infantry, 29,500 cavalry and 587 guns. Only 130,000 against 125,000 – too slight an advantage. For an outflanking force to succeed it must consist of V Corps and at least part of I Corps. And this would gravely weaken his main striking power. Further, any such movement will depend on surprise, and have to be carried out by night. It can go adrift, turn up late, or prove impossible to co-ordinate. And though Russian armies aren't regarded as being as sensitive as others to what goes on in their rear,[3] Kutusov might only have to get the least wind of such a move to decamp again – the very last thing Napoleon or anyone else wants.

His slight superiority in numbers, furthermore, is outweighed by the fact, revealed by his spyglass, that many more of the Russian guns are real battery pieces: 'bone crushers' as the men call them. And the Russian horses are in infinitely better trim. As to the morale factor, it's about equally balanced. Although the Russian masses are totally exposed to artillery, they're notorious not only for their prowess with the bayonet but also for their extreme stolidity under fire. On the French side, on the other hand, there's not a man who isn't grimly aware of the absolute need for victory. A defeat will be a rout. Only half a cannonshot away from the Russian guns' muzzles Le Roy and his 'cold-blooded' fellow veterans of the 85th are having

> 'gloomy reflections on the outcome of a battle fought 2,400 miles
> from France, and about what would become of oneself if wounded.
> As for death, we didn't give it a thought. As to who'd win the battle,
> we were so vain as to believe it would be to our advantage.'

Seeing the Emperor pass his telescope along the Russian lines, Dedem, his brigade fronting I Corps, hears him mutter: 'a big battle ... lots of people ... many, many dead'; but then, turning to Berthier, 'the battle is ours'.

Words, no doubt, he hopes will be passed on to the rest of the staff and thence to the army.

But his cold is getting worse. Several times his uraemia forces him to dismount, and Ségur sees him 'pausing a long while, his forehead pressed against the wheel of one of our guns'.

At 11 a.m. he sends Rapp out on a new reconnaissance, with orders to get as close as he can to the enemy lines. 'I removed my white plumes, put on a soldier's shako, and examined everything with greatest precision. Only a single chasseur of the Guard accompanied me. At several points I was so close I was inside their outposts.' Upon his approaching too close to Borodino village, 'separated from our outposts by a deep and narrow hollow way, they fired a few grapeshot at me and I drew back'. Reporting back to Napoleon, he finds him with Murat and Berthier. All are agreed that, if they don't attack, the Russians will. Now Berthier, too, orders up his horse and himself emulates Rapp's reconnaissance in detail. 'He was given the same reception as I'd had, canister forced him to retire.' Eugène, too, is keen to get a no less maximally detailed idea of the battle-field. And orders Labaume to correct the map he'd made yesterday

'by traversing the entire line and trying to approach the enemy as closely as possible to disclose the accidents of the ground he was encamped on, and above all make sure there weren't any masked batteries, or ravines we didn't know about'.

But neither does Labaume spot Bagration's third, northernmost flèche; nor does he realize that the Russian position is bisected by the upper reaches of the Semenovskaya. It'll be his map Eugène will use next day.[4]

All day the sun shines down out of a clear autumn sky. The compact ranks, division after division, are almost a mile deep.[5] Although the centre, 85,000 men, or two-thirds of the entire army, packs a stupendous punch, yet veterans of all ranks, scanning the equally dense green-clad masses on the opposing heights, are thinking very serious thoughts. For several days now Ségur has been noticing how

'the troops had been strangely quiet, the kind of silence you associate with a state of great expectation or tension, like the atmosphere before a storm, or the feeling in a crowd where people are suddenly plunged into a situation of great danger'.

'A strange thing, modern battles,' soliloquizes Thirion: 'Two armies gradually turn up on a piece of ground, place themselves symmetrically facing each other, their artillery 100 metres to the front. All these preliminaries are carried out with calm barrack-square precision. From one army to the other are heard the commanders' sonorous voices. In a lugubrious silence you see being turned on you the mouths of the guns which are going to send you death.'

Fézensac, at headquarters, is finding

'something sad and imposing in the appearance of these two armies preparing to cut each other's throats. All the regiments had been given orders to put on their parade uniforms, as if for a holiday. The Imperial Guard, above all, seemed rather to be disposing itself for a parade than a fight. Nothing was more striking than these old soldiers' sang-froid. On their faces one read neither disquiet nor enthusiasm. In their eyes a new battle was only one more victory, and it was enough to look at them to share this noble confidence.'

But one of them at least, Boulart, spends the day deep in serious reflections:

'What if we're beaten at 750 to 800 leagues from France, what terrible risks we'll run! Can even one of us hope to see his own country again? If we're the victors, will peace follow at once? That's hardly likely in the Russian nation's unequivocal state of exasperation!'

Yet morale is high. Letters written home that day[6] show how eager the officers, at least, are to rejoin in time for the battle. One who does so that evening is Lieutenant Vossler. Riding into camp he finds the army in

'good and sanguine spirits. We were congratulated on all sides upon our timely arrival. If one discounted our men's pale worn faces, the whole army seemed alive with a cheerful bustle. Most of the troops were busy polishing and preparing weapons for the morrow, and the order reached us to make an early night of it, so as to be ready for the morning's work. Many a soldier stretched himself out carefree and contented, little thinking that this would be his last night on earth. But the thought was common to us all: things couldn't go on much longer as they were. Though the army's numerical strength had shrunk alarmingly, the very considerable forces that remained consisted of the strongest and most experienced troops, and the bold and fiery eyes peering out from haggard faces promised certain victory.'

Girod de l'Ain, Dessaix's ADC, is one of the many who are

'able to make private observations on the points I had within view in front of me, and to judge which would be more and which less nasty to carry. For the rest, throughout the whole of the 6th, I believe, not a single musket shot was fired. All rejoiced to find themselves on the eve of this longed for battle which, we convinced ourselves, was going to decide things. For my part, after quite a long promenade reconnoitring the two armies' respective positions, I came back to our bivouac, where I whiled away my time taking my first lesson in chess from Commandant Fanfette, who was crazy about this game and always carried on him a little cardboard chessboard folding into eight pieces and most ingeniously fashioned by himself.'

Alas, almost no one has anything much to eat. Vossler dines on

'a miserable plateful of bread soup boiled with the stump of a tallow candle. But in my famished condition even this revolting dish

seemed quite appetizing. I lay down and slept as peacefully as if the coming day was to have resembled its fellow as one egg does another.'
In the Young Guard some of Sergeant Bourgogne's comrades of the Fusiliers-Grenadiers are

'cleaning muskets and other weapons; others were making bandages for the wounded, some made their wills, and others again sang or slept in perfect indifference. The whole of the Imperial Guard received orders to appear in full uniform.'

Ordered to attach all the Württemberg, Bavarian and Polish horse artillery to his own batteries, Colonel Séruzier, contemplating the packed green lines ahead of them, realizes only too well what an effort is going to be required. His 108 guns have been split into three major divisions, arranged in such a way that his French batteries have odd numbers, and the Allied equal 'so that each allied battery found itself in line between two French'. Stretched out in an undulating line they occupy nearly three miles of terrain! At 10 a.m. one of his subordinates, General Beurmann, the Saxon who'd found it so hard to replenish his ammunition, had

'summoned all the officers and made a speech in broken German, in which he informed us that the great battle would begin at 2 p.m. that very afternoon. He stressed that under no circumstances, even if enemy shells tore down whole rows of us, even if the Cossacks attacked in flank and from behind, were we to lose our presence of mind. He expressly forbade the evacuation of the wounded during the battle, it would take too many men out of the firing-line. The wounded would be taken care of after the battle. He closed by saying "I shall load you with decorations, because such brave men as you are can never be adequately rewarded."'

Is Napoleon really intending to attack that day? Evidently Beurmann has thought so. But

'at 1 p.m. he returned and told us that on account of the thick mist, which had only lifted at noon, the Emperor hadn't completed his reconnaissance, so the battle wouldn't begin until dawn next day. On receiving this news we spent the whole afternoon cooking and eating, so that whatever happened we shouldn't have to make the journey into the next world on an empty stomach.'

Shortly afterwards comes a false alarm. Murat fancies he can see the Russians retiring, and sends in a report to that effect. But Napoleon, grabbing his spyglass, is relieved to see long columns of artillery wagons still being fed into the Russian lines. And something else. At that moment the invaders are entertained to a curious spectacle:

'Knowing how pious and superstitious his men were, Kutusov didn't fail to have the image of a saintly Russian bishop [sic] pass along the front.'

Actually it's the venerated Black Virgin, rescued from the flames of Smolensk, whom Lejeune and everyone else sees being borne in procession across the Russian lines. 'It excited enthusiasm in all ranks and we could hear the joyful hurrahs of 160,000 Russians applauding as it passed them.' Rapp sees Napoleon's features light up. 'He looked with greatest pleasure on Kutusov's procession. "Good," he said to me. "They're occupying themselves with tomfoolery and won't escape us any longer."' Neither is Rapp impressed:

'St Michael's sword is undoubtedly a terrible sword; but cheerful soldiers are even better. So Kutusov wasn't stingy with the liquor, which did much to enliven the Cossacks' enthusiasm. We had neither preachers nor prophets, nor even any food to eat. But we'd a long and honourable heritage to defend. We were going to decide whether we or the Tartars were going to give laws to the world.'

Although the French haven't a single chaplain in their enlightened ranks,[7] at about midday luck has provided them, too, with a totem. Just arrived from St-Cloud the obese prefect of the palace, de Bausset, has brought with him a letter from Marie Louise and a large portrait, newly painted by Gérard, of the infant King of Rome. It shows the little boy in his cradle, playing cup-and-ball with the globe and an imperial sceptre.[8] On his return from a second reconnaissance, begun at about 2 p.m., the proud father, finding the painting already hung in his tent 'as a surprise', immediately declares it 'a masterpiece', and has it taken down and set up on an easel outside, to be admired by all. And there, at about 3 p.m., it's seen by Heinrich von Brandt who's been 'ordered to carry a message to general headquarters. The soldiers, and above all the veterans, were strongly moved. The officers became all the more concerned for the campaign's outcome.' Vernissage over, Napoleon orders the painting packed up again:

"Take him away, he's too young to see a field of battle," Gourgaud quotes him as saying.

But Brandt also hears about, and sees, another arrival, of more sinister portent. An acquaintance on the staff points out to him

'an officer of furtive appearance who seemed utterly worn out. It was Colonel Fabvier, Marmont's ADC. He'd just ridden flat out from the depths of Spain to tell the Emperor of the disaster where Wellington had decisively beaten Marmont. There under seal of secrecy I heard this bit of bad news, of which many officers, even of high rank, would know nothing until they got back from the campaign.'

Fabvier had been wounded at Salamanca, where Marmont had sacrificed his army to try and save his loot. It has taken him 32 days to cross Europe, including a brief stop in Paris. To Ségur it seems that Napoleon receives him indulgently, perhaps because of the impending crisis of his own campaign. Gourgaud gets quite the opposite impression: 'When the Emperor heard how Marmont had compromised the French army to satisfy a purely personal ambition he gave vent to the sharpest dissatisfaction.' But though the Master of the Horse sees that 'the affairs of Russia were just then too serious for the Emperor to pay much attention to the Duke of Ragusa's reverses in the Peninsula,' Fézensac, doubtless coming and going with messages from Berthier's tent, notices how all that evening Napoleon 'despite his preoccupations', keeps Fabvier with him.[9]

Just as he's surveying the scene one last time from the high ground behind Borodino, Davout comes riding up. Give him 40,000 men, his own and Poniatowski's, he offers, and he'll outflank the weak Russian left and so 'finish off the battle, the campaign, and the whole war'. Napoleon listens intently. Reflects. But declares the gambit too risky: "No! The movement would be far too great. It'd take me away from my objective and lose me too much time!" And when Davout wants to argue the toss, he's told to shut up; and rides off muttering.[10]

So the day has passed in a mood of grim expectation, but also of resolve. Evidently it's difficult to suppress all interchanges with the enemy. Although

'all engagement was carefully avoided that day, Morand's division's tirailleurs had begun to press the Russian sharpshooters and the Prince of Eckmühl ordered me to ride flat out and stop the firing all down the line.'

Evidently Dedem doesn't ride fast enough; at least not fast enough to save Captain François from a nasty leg wound:

'Having rejoined my regiment I give orders for roll-call. I've lost 23 men. Then I have myself dressed by the surgeon major of the 30th, who probes my wound, passing his probe in through the opening made by the ball. Then I hobble back to my company, and spend the rest of the night with them.'

This will be by no means the only wound that the Dromedary of Egypt will sustain. Nor has the 30th's skirmish been the only clash that evening. The 111th Line, having tangled with some Russian cavalry, Dedem orders Colonel Tschüdy to extricate it. And Tschüdy promptly arranges a kind of ambush. Forming up his remaining 400 Spaniards in square near Semenovskaya's flaming timber cottages, he sends forward his voltigeurs with orders to take pot-shots at the troopers and then, when they come to drive them off, to run back toward the square. Dazzled by the flames, their pursuers are mown down by compact fire from 400 Spanish muskets. At Lariboisière's headquarters, meanwhile, Planat de la Faye and his six staff captains are even busier than usual:

'The Emperor wanted to know exactly how many musket rounds there were, and what munitions in the reserve packs. To get all this information one had to run after units on the march, and turn to officers loth to give them, having other things to see to. However, in the name of the Emperor everything became possible. By the end of the day General Lariboisière gave him an exact report on the army's supplies of artillery rounds and infantry cartridges.'

As evening falls the sky clouds over, and a drizzling rain sweeps across the bivouacs. Under cover of it Napoleon makes a last reconnaissance. And when he gets back tells Fain how 'as he'd passed across the front of

Borodino some discharges of grapeshot had forced him to make a detour'.

Towards evening, in the same driving rain, the Guard artillery moves over and takes up position near the captured redoubt. Boulart's, attached as always, to the Chasseur brigade, is lined up between the redoubt and a little copse.

Many men are having presentiments, real or imaginary, of their fate next day. Sent by Pajol to obtain orders from II Cavalry Corps' commander, Biot finds the handsome, well-liked Montbrun

'leaning over his map, deep in thought. When I was announced, he began by asking me if I'd dined. I replied in the negative; whereupon he added "In that case you shall dine with us." Soon afterwards his manservant came in and announced that a certain Verchère, an orderly officer on the general's staff, had returned from accompanying Mme. Montbrun as far as Warsaw. "Bring him in," said the general. The officer in question handed him a letter and a packet, and as he took the latter Montbrun exclaimed, "I know what this is. You left my wife in good health, did you not? As for her letter, we'll read it after the battle."

For some obscure reason Colonel Désirad, commanding his 2nd Brigade, has no such illusions. Biot hears him remark to several of his old friends in the Dragoons of the Guard: 'I think this will be my last battle.'

Not until 8 p.m. does General Dessaix, and therefore presumably also the other divisional generals, get his orders. 'We read them by the light of the camp fire we were crouched around, half asleep. But this reading was much too interesting to us not to pay it the greatest attention.' His division's orders, Girod de l'Ain sees, are

'to get under way at daybreak and in closed columns and at short distance follow the Compans Division's march and support it in its attack on the enemy redoubts [i.e. flèches] it had to carry.'

By no means everyone dines as well as Biot that evening. Brandt's Poles of Claparède's corps are

'cruelly feeling the lack of food. We dined on grilled corn and horsemeat. The night was cold and rainy. Many officers and soldiers, drenched through and perhaps obesssed by sad presentiments, tried in vain to sleep. They got up and like wandering shades walked to and fro in front of the camp fires.'

Colonel Combe's ears are 'ceaselessly assaulted by the endless and confused noise of moving artillery and cavalry columns'. And indeed in the darkness there are all sorts of muddles. At about midnight Pion des Loches' reserve battery, ordered to leave the Young Guard's artillery and move up into the line with the Guard Foot Artillery, is just doing so when suddenly Napoleon appears:

'"What's that artillery there? What are you doing here?"'

Pion explains that an ordnance officer, i.e., one of Gourgaud's subordinates, has given him the order. "'He's a bloody fool. I've already got too much artillery here. Go back to your corps.'"

'That was an order doubtless easily given. But where is this army corps [*sic*] I'd left at midnight? No point in asking. First gun left and left again, and my battery formed in column to retire. After marching for half an hour I see Marshal Mortier and gallop up to him.'

Pion des Loches explains he's been sent back by the Emperor himself. "'Who gave you the order to move?'"

"An ordnance officer, speaking in the Emperor's name." "Those f—fools are always speaking in the Emperor's name. Has anyone ever heard of a corps being deprived of its reserve artillery on the eve of a battle?'" Mortier tells him he's not to obey anyone but himself, and even if orders come from the Emperor he's not to execute them before he, Mortier, has confirmed them.

'Next I run into General Lallemand. "Haven't you seen General Desvaux's batteries?" asks Lariboisière's chief-of staff. "No." "If you see him anywhere, tell him I'm looking for him, and that he's to take two batteries to General Sorbier." "And where's General Sorbier?" But Lallemand had gone on and was no longer listening.'

Such muddles are by no means confined to the artillery. The 23rd Dragoons are one of the regiments transferred to IV Corps to strengthen the left flank. 'Marching and countermarching all night in the enemy's presence,' they're experiencing

'a terrible cold. A number of horses got stuck in the mud as we crossed several ravines where there were running streams. Our misery was at its worst since 3 September. I wasn't able to cook any meat, and during the little time when we got any rest that night we were forbidden to light a fire, leave our horses' bridles, or even speak. It was in this terrible position we waited for day to break.'

A Westphalian captain, *Linsingen*[11] by name, can't

'escape a feeling of something immense, destructive, hanging over us all. This mood led me to look at my men. There they were, sleeping all around me on the cold hard soil. I knew them all very well, and knew that many of these brave troops couldn't survive until tomorrow evening, but would be lying torn and bloody on the battlefield. For a moment it was all too easy to wish the Russians would just steal away again during the night. But then I remembered our sufferings of the past weeks. Better a horrific end than a horror without end! Our only salvation lay in a battle we must win!'

And all the time, as night deepens, Napoleon is feeling less and less well. General Lauriston, Caulaincourt's successor in the Petersburg embassy, is one of the duty ADCs, and helps place some 'emollient poultices' on his stomach. Another, Rapp, though trying to snatch some sleep 'in the room separated off by a canvas partition and reserved for the duty ADC' is all the time aware that his chief is worrying whether there's any sign of the enemy slipping away again. 'The Emperor slept very little. I woke him several times to give him reports from the outposts. All proved the Russians were expecting an attack.' At 3 a.m. he calls for a glass of hot punch and summons Rapp:

'"Well, Rapp. today we're to have to do with that Kutusov fellow, the man, you remember, who was commandant of Braunau during the Austerlitz campaign. He stayed in its fortress for three months without even budging from his room. Didn't even mount his horse to inspect the fortifications."'[12]

Ségur, who can hardly have had any business in the imperial tent that night, reports another, less probable but perhaps not quite impossible soliloquy:

'"What is war? A barbarous profession, whose whole art consists in being stronger at a given point!" He goes on to complain about the fickleness of Fortune which he says he's beginning to experience. A nervous fever, a dry cough, extreme poorliness are consuming him! During the rest of the night he tries in vain to quench a burning thirst.'

By and by he gets up and works for a while with Berthier. His proclamation to the army has already been dictated and sent to the imperial printing works in the Kolotskoïe monastery to be set, printed off, and distributed to the colonels:

'Soldiers! Here is the battle you have so ardently desired. Now victory depends on you: we need one. Victory will give us any amount of supplies, good winter quarters and a prompt return to our native land. Fight as you did at Austerlitz, Friedland, Witebsk and Smolensk, and posterity will proudly remember your conduct on this great day. May it be said of each one of us: "He fought in the great battle under the walls of Moscow!"'

At 4 a.m. he gives some last-minute instructions to the corps commanders. And at 5 a.m. one of Ney's staff officers comes to tell him the Russians are still in position: 'The army is awaiting Your Majesty's order to attack.'

Forbidden like everyone else to light fires, the Italian Royal Guard have spent the night lying on the damp ground. And just before dawn Eugène, finding his regiments unnecessarily exposed, withdraws them behind a fold in the ground. While doing so he's dismayed to find his batteries, drawn up 1,750 yards from the Russians, are 600 yards out of effective range! As they're being hauled forward Césare de Laugier is at every moment expecting the enemy

'to oppose this, but they didn't. It was a question who'd first break the terrifying silence. 5.30 a.m.: 'the sun is dissipating the mist. Immediately ADCs are being sent out in all directions by the Emperor, doubtless to make sure his orders given during the night have been carried out. A luminous burst of light, appearing on the horizon, is the signal for a solemn flourish, beaten or sounded at the same instant in the army corps.'

The proclamation has arrived from the monastery:

'The drum beats, and each colonel has it read out to his regiment, in parade uniform. We of the Italian Guard, formed up in close columns of companies without intervals between our battalions, listen to it on the reverse slope of the hill where the Italian battery is. Everyone admires the frankness, the simplicity, the imposing force of this proclamation, so well suited to our circumstances.'

To the Italians' right, next to Broussier's division, de Laugier sees in the dawn light Morand's division is massed in echelons; beyond it – both have been temporarily detached from I Corps and placed under Eugène – is Gérard's. And beyond and behind them is Grouchy's cavalry corps. 'So we were in the first line! To our left, along the Woina stream, in two lines, near Borodino, was Delzon's division, and, on the banks of the Kolotchka, the light cavalry under Ornano.' The Royal Guard itself is standing massed immediately behind Broussier's division. As for Ornano's eight light cavalry regiments, whose business it is to protect the army's left flank, they're 'so squeezed in between a little wood and some batteries' that the 1st, 2nd, 3rd and 4th Bavarian Chevauxlegers have no room to manoeuvre: 'Behind us stood two heavy cavalry regiments and, further off, the Italian Guard and an infantry brigade belonging to our corps. In front of us a Bavarian battery of horse artillery that throughout the campaign had been assigned to Preyssing's brigade was moving up.' Incomprehensibly, no one has thought of placing some light infantry in the wood to Ornano's left – an oversight they'll by and by become only too acutely conscious of. If Laugier were able to see beyond Nansouty's, Montbrun's and Latour-Maubourg's enormous cavalry masses, away to his right, and, beyond them, Ney's III and Davout's I Corps, supported in turn by Junot's VIII and the Imperial Guard, he'd see that, far out on the army's extreme right, beyond low but thick woods, Poniatowski's Poles are already moving forward to probe the weak and over-exposed Russian left.

At that moment – 5.30 a.m. – while the whole army is 'waiting for the first glimmer of dawn and Poniatowski's first musket shots' – Napoleon summons his aides, and leaves his tent, exclaiming as he does so (according to Ségur):

'"We have them at last! It's a trifle cold, but the sun's bright. It's the sun of Austerlitz! March on! We'll break open the gates of Moscow!"'

After which, as Caulaincourt holds his stirrup, he mounts his horse and followed by him and Berthier, rides slowly over towards his command post in front of the ruined Schevardino redoubt and 'to the fringe of the wood in front' – passing as they do so close to Boulart's battery, stationed between it and the redoubt. In the 'cold, misty and calm weather' the Red Lancers, too, have been

'led in silence, followed by the whole Guard, towards the Schevardino Redoubt. Beyond it we turned at a right angle to the left, and there drew up in closed column, less than a mile from an open space about 600 metres wide, between the woods on either hand and protected by two long entrenchments dug the previous day by Marshal Davout's troops to secure this position. Behind the latter the Old Guard infantry came and deployed by battalions, at considerable intervals, having behind them all the reserve artillery; on their right were the three divisions of the Young Guard and, to their left, the five cavalry regiments. The first line was made up of the Chasseurs, Lancers and Dragoons, the second of the Grenadiers and the élite company [of Gendarmes]. A profound silence reigned everywhere, not a shot had been exchanged.'

Dumonceau sees the Emperor

'come and take up his position to our right, in front of the centre of his Old Guard, whence he could see all the movements as they developed in front of us. He dismounted, and someone brought him a chair, which he sat down on astraddle, his arms resting on its back, his spyglass in his hand, paying close attention to what was going on under his eyes. Berthier and Bessières stood a few paces from him and the rest of his suite a bit further behind.'

Among them, a few yards no doubt behind Berthier, Lejeune too sees him 'sit down on the steep bank of the outer slope, where he followed all the movements, spyglass in hand. The Guard was placed behind him, as in an amphitheatre. The appearance of all these crack troops, beautiful to behold in their impatience to go into action and secure a victory, made a most imposing spectacle.'

And there, all eye-witnesses agree, he'll stay until well into the afternoon.

CHAPTER 21

HOLOCAUST AT BORODINO

'Like an earthquake' – disaster for the 106th – Dutheillet storms a flèche – an unprecedented stream of wounded generals – Morand's attack – two sorts of wound – a gap in the Russian centre – 'send in the Guard!' – 'why doesn't he retire to the Tuileries?' – Ney's picnic – Ouvarov's diversion – the dying cavalry – Montbrun is killed – storming the Great Redoubt – 'take this fool away' – Thirion comforts a doomed recruit – cavalry struggles – 'won't this battle ever end?' – thousands of dead and dying men

The first shot is fired at 6 a.m. Once again Lariboisière and his staff have
'gone to the I Corps' 12-pounder battery, which was to open the firing. At this signal all the batteries along the whole line opened up;
and the enemy wasn't slow to reply.[1] At that moment General
Lariboisière, throwing a glance at the officers who were with him,
caught sight of his son Honoré, who'd been seconded for such service. He reprimanded him severely and ordered him to withdraw,
but it was easy to see he was more filled with a tender concern for
him than for the rules of the service. Only half-obeying his father's
orders, poor Honoré, a trifle confused, retired and stood a few paces
away, behind a little silver birch wood to our right. Then we went on
to III Corps' battery, where General Fouchier was.'
That first shot had been followed by a second. Then – after a horrible
silence – the guns on both sides explode, in a whirlwind of shot and shell
the like of which no one has ever seen. Soltyk, watching from a few paces
behind Napoleon, has
'never heard anything like it. At moments the uproar was so terrible
it was more like broadsides discharged from warships than a land
artillery engagement.'
Others think it's 'like an earthquake'. To Dr von Roos, busy moving his
dressing-station forward to 'a gully in places thick with bushes and through
which flowed a small, easily jumpable stream' [the Semenovskaya] it's 'as
if all Europe's voices were making themselves heard, in all its languages'.
The losses on the long march have compelled Napoleon to pack his
centre, not with infantry, but with Murat's four cavalry corps. And that's
where General Pajol has drawn up his light cavalry division, brigade
behind brigade. At the second discharge Captain Biot, sitting his horse
beside him, sees
'a horse running along our front, its rider thrown on to its cruppers.
I recognized poor Colonel Désirad. A Russian roundshot had taken
off his cranium. From then on we were uninterruptedly assailed by
roundshot and grape. Everything that fell beyond the second line
went on to strike the third; not a shot was lost.'

As usual, the Russian gunners are aiming too high. And roundshot at the very limit of their trajectory come bouncing along the grass at Napoleon's command post. Boulart, standing there with his batteries not a hundred paces away, even sees some pass over the Emperor's head: 'Captain Pantinier, commanding a battery of Friedrich's division, was killed near to and even behind us, before his division came into line.'

But already the first move is being made. Borodino village, a kind of salient on the hither side of the stream, is held by a crack division of Jägers of the Russian Imperial Guard. Only a narrow plank bridge over the Kolotchka links it with its supports.[2] And at 6.30 Delzon's division, headed by the 106th Line in column of platoons, is seen moving to the attack 'with unbelievable speed'. Already the leading Italian battalions have only 200 yards to go. Clearly the salient is completely untenable. And the Jägers are ordered to set fire to the village and evacuate it. Although 'the limit of the 106th's orders' is to capture the village, nothing can restrain it from chasing the Jägers as they, annihilated by the Italian guns, are retreating helter-skelter over the bridge. On the slope beyond, leading gently upwards to the distant Great Redoubt, three other Russian regiments are arrayed. But the 92nd Line, coming up in support and 'listening only to the voice of the guns, advances at the double, crosses the bridges and attacks the three hostile regiments.'[3] Hurrying over the bridge to recall them, General Plauzonne, their brigade commander, is killed. And in the same instant the impetuous 92nd are shattered by a massive counter-attack. After which the remains of Delzons' two regiments withdraw into the burning village, which the Russians don't bother to try and recapture.

Each side has taken a pawn.

Simultaneously with this tactical move on the left an all-out frontal assault is being delivered by I Corps on the right. Its objective is the two southernmost flèches. Lejeune, standing only a few yards to the rear of Napoleon's command post, sees how Compans, preceded by a barrage from 108 guns whose sudden torrent of shells causes

'the peaceful plain and silent slopes to erupt in swirls of fire and smoke, followed almost at once by countless explosions and the howling of cannon shot ripping through the air in every direction, has the honour of being the first to cross his infantry's fire with the Russians. Directing it at their centre to the left of the Passarevo wood, it was his task to mount the heights and carry the flèches barring his passage.'

In no time at all his heads of columns

'have disappeared into a cloud of dust infused by a reddish glow by the radiant sun. The deafening sound of our cannonade was interspersed with a sound that seemed like a distant echo, and came from the batteries on the left around Borodino [and] from beyond the woods to our right', where Poniatowski is advancing towards the village of Utitza.[4]

'The guns's roar and thunder, the crackling and crashing of musketry, the whining and soughing of roundshot large and small, the screams of the wounded and dying, oaths in every language during cavalry and bayonet attacks, the words of command, the cornet signals, the fifes and drums and thereto the masses' wave-like motion backwards and forwards in a smoke of gunpowder, shrouding friend and enemy alike in an obscurity so deep it was often only from the rows of flashing flames one could make out the enemy regiments' positions or their batteries as they came riding up – the impression of all this went through the marrow of one's bones. Anyone who claims to go into enemy fire without an oppressive feeling is a poltroon.'

This being in high degree a *journée*, Lejeune and his colleagues, too, are doubtless wearing their white fox-trimmed sky-blue pélisses, their tight-fitting double gold-striped scarlet trousers, and their gold-chevroned and white ostrich-plumed hussar helmets. From Napoleon's command post he sees the 57th enter the right-hand flèche at the *pas de charge*. And soon it seems to Sous-lieutenant Dutheillet, who's in the thick of it, that his men (6th Coy, 6th Bn) aren't merely fighting but actually winning the battle single-handed:

'The Russians had made a few abbatis which were charged and carried by our last three battalions, while the two first turned them to the right. To our left we'd a redoubt [flèche] which was firing murderously at us. Being at the regiment's left and one of the closest to the redoubt, I began shouting: "at the redoubt, let's march against the redoubt!" And together with some of our battalion's officers and two or three hundred men I flung myself at it. The Russians, seeing our resolution, retired. We entered the redoubt, pursuing them for more than 200 paces beyond our conquest. Meanwhile our colonel has been told of our success and he sends the regiment's fat major Liègre (or Liégue) to command the men who've taken the redoubt. I can say without fear of contradiction that I was one of the first, and was following the Russians, ready to receive the reinforcements behind them, when Major Liègre, a brave old soldier, seeing we weren't by any means numerous enough to repulse the enemy, massed with their cavalry in the ravines, sent us the order to come back into the redoubt to defend and keep it. For a while longer we resisted his orders, wanting to pursue the enemy, and telling the officer he'd sent to us: "Have us supported by other troops." But Major Liègre hadn't any.'

For the rest of the 57th, busy with the wood to its right, is feeling ill-supported. Dutheillet's company, attacked by artillery and fresh Russian troops, repeatedly beats them off. But Major Liègre falls dead at his feet, killed by grapeshot. 'General Teste's ADC suffered the same fate; and by this time I was so short of footwear I stripped the unfortunate ADC, still not cold, of the boots he had on his feet to put them on my own!' The Russians 'like the brave soldiers they were' renew their attacks on the flèche:

> 'A brave officer of that nation, seeing his men about to fall back, placed himself across the entrance to the redoubt and did everything he could to prevent them leaving it, but was shot through the body. Our men rushing forward with the bayonet, I ran towards this officer to protect him if he was still alive; but he died shortly after. I took his belt as a souvenir of his courage, and the men shared the rest of his equipment.'

The flèche so brilliantly captured by the 57th and then lost again to the Russian 7th Combined Grenadier Division is the southernmost. But soon all the terrain the 5th Division has gained is lost, as three Russian cavalry regiments sweep Compans' men on to his supports, Dessaix's 4th. As this happens Compans, already wounded in the left arm two days ago, is hit again, this time in the shoulder by a musket-ball. This second wound is serious, and Dessaix has to take over both divisions:

> 'To follow Compans' division's movement we'd had to descend rather a steep slope from the plateau, through dense thickets. Hardly had we emerged from the wood than General Dessaix receives orders to take command of Compans' division. Accompanied only by Captain de Bourget, Lieutenant Magnan and myself, he galloped to its head. We got there just as the first redoubts had been taken by storm. They were nothing but redans – i.e., chevron-shaped campaign works not closed at their throat, in such a way that the enemy's second line swept their interior with the sharpest musketry and grape. So it was a lot harder to gain a foothold and stay there than to have stormed them. Also, the 5th Division's troops had been massed behind these works and in folds of the ground, as far as possible to shelter from fire while waiting until fresh attacks were made. General Dessaix, whose great personal courage one had to recognize, remained a few instants totally exposed beside one of these redoubts, examining the Russian units' position and movement. And I was near him, contemplating the same view, when a mustket-ball came and smashed a bottle of brandy he'd taken care to provide himself with in one of his saddle's pistol holsters. It was more than he could do not to exclaim angrily, turning to me: "I owe that to your damned white horse!"

And indeed, Girod de l'Ain concedes, his horse was of a brilliant whiteness and a target for enemy skirmishers:

> 'During the few moments we'd halted there Captain du Bourget, for better shelter, had pushed his horse into the ditch of the redoubt. Having seen us dash off ahead at a gallop, he'd tried to follow us. But hardly had he emerged from the ditch than he was hit by a roundshot and fell dead.'

By now Compans' plan for a two-pronged attack seems to have been forgotten. Napoleon sends Rapp to take over his ravaged division, and Dessaix returns to his own, which by now has moved up into the first line. But almost immediately Rapp too is hit

'several times within the space of an hour; first slightly, by two musket-balls, then in the left arm by a roundshot which carried away parts of my coat and shirtsleeve, leaving my bare arm showing. At that moment I was at the head of the 61st Regiment, whose acquaintance I'd first made in Egypt. Soon I received my wound: it was a shot in my left thigh, which threw me off my horse. This was the twenty-second time I'd been wounded during my campaigns. I felt obliged to leave the field, and informed Marshal Ney to that effect, whose troops were mingled with mine. General Dessaix, the only general of this division who hadn't been wounded, took my place.'

But soon it'll be Dessaix's turn. Girod de l'Ain goes on:

'We'd advanced a certain distance and were standing in column on the edge of a wood stretching away to to our right, when we saw a charge of Russian cuirassiers coming at us like a tempest. They weren't exactly aiming at us, but at a battery of 30 of our guns which, under cover of our advance, had come and taken up position a little to our left rear. Although this charge suffered from our fire as it passed us, it didn't slow it down, no more than the discharges of grape from our battery, which it overthrew out of the cuirassiers' reach sabring those gunners who weren't able to throw themselves down between the wheels of the guns and ammunition wagons. But soon, thrown back in disorder by some French squadrons, they again passed across our column's flank and again suffered under our fire and the bayonet thrusts of a crowd of our soldiers who, leaving the ranks, ran out in front of them to cut off their retreat.'

To the French it seems there are about 1,500 cuirassiers, of whom

'scarcely 200 got back to their lines. All the rest, men and horses, remained on the ground. I don't recall our taking a single prisoner. They only wore breastplates, and these, like their helmets, were painted black. Hardly had the cuirassiers disappeared than, a little way off, we caught sight of a mass of infantry which had advanced under shelter of their charge. Left exposed and isolated after the cuirassiers' retreat, it had halted. And in the same instant we saw it as it were swirling around itself and then retiring in some disorder. As it did so, however, it, in turn, unmasked a battery, which sent us several volleys of grape, causing us considerable losses. It was also at this moment that General Dessaix had his right forearm shattered by a roundshot. Lieutenant Morgan and I took him to the rear until we were out of range of the enemy's fire.'

Le Roy, on Davout's staff, is following him about the left centre of the French front. And at 8 a.m. or thereabouts Davout's horse is killed under him, badly bruising and stunning its rider. In no time a rumour reaches headquarters that not merely his horse but the unpopular marshal himself has been killed. But Davout comes to; refuses, though badly bruised, to relinquish his command; and sends Le Roy back to IHQ to give the lie to the rumour:

'I went to tell the General Staff, which I found close to the famous redoubt we'd taken yesterday. The Emperor was seated on the reverse slope of a ditch, his left elbow resting on it. With his right hand he was observing the enemy's movements through his telescope. I heard him tell an ADC: "Hurry up and tell Ney to advance."

Le Roy is surprised to notice that a whole Guard grenadier regiment with plaqueless bearskins and red plumes is clad in white; and assumes, wrongly, they're the Westphalian Royal Guard.[5] Then he returns to the scrum. It's at the very moment he gets there that Dessaix's arm is shattered by a musket-ball. And he is immediately replaced by General Gérard, 'a man of sense and merit, who by his sang-froid and his ability consoled us for the loss we'd sustained'.

And in fact an unprecedented stream of wounded high-ups is flowing back towards Larrey's dressing-station, established in the rear of the Imperial Guard. Accompanying their wounded general, Girod de l'Ain and his other ADCs encounter

'several surgeons coming forward to attend to the wounded, among others the King of Naples' chief surgeon, who gave our general first aid. After examining his wound he strongly advised him to allow his forearm to be amputated. Larrey, who followed immediately after, was of the same opinion, insisting even more strongly that the general should resign himself to it. For the rest, it was Larrey's system on campaign – a system he applied for excellent reasons – to amputate any gravely fractured limb. So he told the general: "Doubtless we might have some chance of success if we tried to save your arm. But for that you'd need a long period of quite special care and resources you can't reasonably count on on campaign and in a country like this, a thousand leagues away from your own. Numberless fatigues and privations still await you and you're running the risk of fateful accidents, whilst within a fortnight you can be sure of your amputation wound forming a perfect scar."'

But Dessaix remains 'deaf to these exhortations and unshakeable in his determination to keep his arm.'[6] The wounded Rapp is there too:

'I had my wound bandaged by Napoleon's surgeon, and that prince [sic] himself came and visited me: "How are things going? You never get off unscathed!" "Sire, I think it'll be necessary to unleash your Guard." "I'll take care not to; I've no desire to see it destroyed. Furthermore it isn't needed. I'm sure to win the battle anyway."'[7]

That Rapp should make such a suggestion so early in the day shows how impressed he is by the Russian resistance.

Knowing that Dessaix's two brothers, one a doctor, the other a commandant, will soon be with him, Girod de l'Ain leaves him in a place of safety with the lieutenant, and returns to the firing line. There he places himself at the disposition of General Friederich, who's taken over;

'In rejoining the division I found Colonel Achard of the 108th[8] a little to the rear of the position it had occupied. With him he only had a handful of men and his eagle. "That's all that's left of my regiment," he told me sadly.'

Nor has the 4th division gained any more ground. 'Nothing important had happened in my absence.' Friant's division, too, has been standing massed in support. But now he, too, is hit; and has to hand it over to General Dufour, his senior brigadier.

Up at the front the slaughter is horrible. Voltigeur-corporal Dumont of the 61st Line is hit in the upper arm by a musket-ball. 'Soon afterwards my wound began to pain me, and I went to the ambulance to have the ball extracted.' He hasn't gone many paces before he meets the regiment's pretty Spanish cantinière Florencia:

'She was in tears. Some men had told her that nearly all the regiment's drummers were killed or wounded. She said she wanted to see them, to help them if she could. So in spite of the pain I was suffering from my wound I made up my mind to accompany her. We were walking amidst wounded men. Some moved painfully and only with difficulty, others were being carried on litters.'

Suddenly, as they pass near to one of the flèches,[9] Florencia starts to utter heart-rending cries:

'But when she caught sight of all the drums of the regiment strewn on the ground she became like a madwoman. "Here, my friend, here!" she screamed. "They're here!" And so they were, lying with broken limbs, their bodies torn by grapeshot. Mad with grief, she went from one to the other, speaking softly to them. But none of them heard. Some, however, still gave signs of life, among them the drum-major she called her father. Stopping by him and falling on her knees she raised his head and poured a few drops of brandy between his lips.'

But at that moment the Russians try to retake the flèche,

'and the firing and cannonade began again. Suddenly the Spanish woman cried out with pain. She'd been stricken by a ball in her left hand, which crushed her thumb and entered the shoulder of the dying man she was holding. She fell unconscious.'

Dumont, with his one good arm, tries to carry her to back to the baggage and ambulance; but it's more than he can do. Fortunately,

'a dismounted cuirassier came by, close to us. He didn't have to be asked. Only said: "Quick! we must hurry, this isn't a nice place to be." In fact the bullets were whistling around us. Without more ado he lifted up the young Spaniard and carried her like a child. She was still unconscious. After walking for ten minutes we got to a little wood where there was an ambulance of the Guard artillery. Here

Florencia came to her senses. M. Larrey, the Emperor's surgeon, amputated her thumb, and extracted the ball from my arm very cleverly.'

By now about two or three hours have passed. And still no significant progress is being made, either in the centre or on either wing. After the 92nd's and the 106th's destruction in front of Borodino village, Eugène, 'whose skirmishers had just dislodged the Russian chasseurs from among the bushes in front of the main battery and along the banks of the Kolotchka', had been ordered to mount a full-scale attack on the Great Redoubt. And the Italian Royal Guard is standing in reserve 'on the left of the Kalotchka, so as to be able to move to right or left in case its presence becomes necessary." Its adjutant-major can't resist the temptation to go and have a look at what's going on:

'Still too young to have been present at one of these famous battles, and hitherto only in a position to have seen combats, certainly sanguinary ones but where no such great masses had figured, only partial actions, sieges, engagements of 10,000 to 18,000 men, how often I've longed to be witness to and be an actor in so gigantic a conflict!'

So he and two other officers get Colonel Moroni's permission to mount the ridge in front of them, where the Italian guns are firing:

'Never in my life shall I forget the sublime impression yielded by the view of this long and vast carnage. No viewpoint could have been more favourable than ours. At a glance we embrace the sinuosities of the terrain, the folds of the ground, the positions of the various arms, the actions engaged on all hands. A marvellous panorama! Far off I see a very thick wood that makes me think of Tasso's and Ariosto's beautiful descriptions. Out of it spurt at each instant great jets of flame accompanied by terrible detonations. Then, under cover of these whirlwinds of fire and smoke, deep masses are deploying to advance under cover of no less terrible a fire. The sun flashes on the arms and cuirasses of infantry and cavalry marching to meet each other. At this moment the 30th Regiment, led by General Bonamy, goes to the attack.'

And of course the 'Dromedary of Egypt', despite his leg wound of the previous evening, is at his post:

'We draw up our battle line at a level ten feet below the plain, which is masked by the ravine's ridge; and General Morand orders us to march against the enemy's great battery [i.e., the Great Redoubt]. Passing along the line to encourage the men and coming in front of my company, he sees I've been seriously wounded: "Captain," he says to me, "you won't be able to keep up, retire to the colour-guard." I answer him: "General, this day holds too much attractions for me not to share the glory this regiment is going to win." "I see you for the man you are," replies the general, taking me by the hand. And

passes on along the battle line amid the roundshot falling from all
quarters.'

As for Laugier, who can 'see it all as a spectator at a circus might make out
what's going on in the ring below him', he's seized with an 'indescribable
anxiety. I can't take my eyes off this group of heroes. The men's turnout is
admirable.' François' regiment

'gets the order to advance. Arrived on the ridge of the ravine, at
half-range from the Russian battery, we're crushed by its grapeshot
and by the fire of others taking us in flank. But nothing checks us.
Like my voltigeurs and despite my wounded leg I skip and jump
about to let the iron balls go their way as they come rolling into our
ranks. Whole files and half-platoons are falling under the enemy's
fire, leaving broad gaps.'

Now Césare de Laugier's aesthetic ecstasy

'suddenly gives place to a feeling of pity. This unhappy regiment
which I've just been admiring is letting itself be massacred, and fresh
Russian batteries have just been placed to reply to the Italian ones on
the heights where I am.'

Captain François, skipping about among the roundshot, goes on:

'General Bonamy, who's at the head of the 30th, orders us to halt in
the midst of the grapeshot. He rallies, and on we go, at the *pas de
charge*. A Russian line tries to stop us. We fire a regimental volley at
thirty paces and pass over it. We rush toward the redoubt and try to
get in through the embrasures. I enter just as one gun has fired. The
Russian gunners receive us with blows of their handspikes and ram-
rods. We fight them man to man and find them to be formidable
adversaries. A great number of Frenchmen fall into the wolfpits pell-
mell with Russians who're in them already. Once inside the redoubt I
defend myself against the gunners with my sabre and slash down
more than one.'

Looking on from the vantage point of the Bavarian Chasseurs, massed
with the rest of Ornano's cavalry behind Borodino village, von Muraldt
sees even Eugène, normally so stolid and unemotional, carried away with
enthusiasm. He 'waved his hat in the air and cried "The battle's won!"'

All Colonel Griois, waiting with his guns in a dip in the ground with
Grouchy's cavalry, can see is immense quantities of smoke rising over the
enemy position; but he hears all the more. And he too assumes that the
great fieldwork has been taken:

'A grenadier who'd been wounded in this attack came back, covered
in blood and drunk on glory, to confirm for us this happy success
which, by opening the enemy centre and separating his two wings,
seemed to decide the victory for us.'

Such indeed is the 30th's impetuosity that François and his men have

'overrun the redoubt by more than 50 paces. But not being followed
by our division's other regiments – with the exception of a battalion
of the 13th Light, who're supporting us, they too are at grips with

the Russians – we're forced to beat a retreat, recrossing the redoubt, the Russian line – which has sprung to its feet again – and the wolf-pits. In this way our regiment is shattered. We rally behind the redoubt, always under enemy grapeshot, and attempt a second charge. But not being supported we're too few to succeed. And with only eleven officers and 55 men we retire. All the rest have been killed or wounded. The brave General Bonamy, who'd never quit his post at the head of the regiment, has been left inside the redoubt.'

Suffering from no fewer than fifteen wounds, bleeding and helpless, Bonamy has only saved his own life by shouting out "I'm the King of Naples!" Believing him, they take him to Kutusov's headquarters, three miles behind the battleline, where the Russian commander-in-chief, completely out of touch with the stupendous conflict, is spending the day lunching and chatting with his handsome young staff officers. Kutusov calls for a surgeon, but otherwise pays him no special attention.

'I'd been through more than one campaign,' François, back on the slope in front of the Grand Redoubt, goes on,

'but never had I found myself in such a bloody mêlée or up against such tenacious soldiers as the Russians. I was in a deplorable state, my shako had been carried away by grapeshot and the tails of my coat had remained in their hands. I was bruised all over, and the wound in my left leg was hurting dreadfully. After a few minutes' rest on a plateau where we'd rallied, I fainted from loss of blood. Some voltigeurs brought me round and carried me to General Morand who'd been wounded in the chin by grapeshot. He recognized me, gave me his hand and when he'd been bandaged signed to a surgeon to attend to me.'

Realizing the triumph has been premature, it seems to Griois that the 30th have failed for lack of adequate support:

'At about the same time a mass of Russian cuirassiers charged on our right, and from where we were we could see it was causing a certain amount of disorder.'

And in fact Eugène has to send Gérard's division to support Morand's right, which is being briskly counter-attacked by two Russian dragoon regiments. As they chase the remnant of the 30th down the slope and lunge at its reserves Césare de Laugier admires the way the 7th Light (Sergeant Bertrand's regiment)

'instantly forms square, lets the dragoons advance and then opens a well-nourished fire by files, which in the twinkling of an eye covers the terrain with men and horses, dead or wounded, forming a new barrier around these brave battalions.'[10]

Griois too sees this mass of cavalry promptly driven back and overthrown, leaving

'the whole esplanade in front of the entrenchment covered by its dead. Half an hour later even sharper firing and hurrahs told us the Russians were still in the works.'

Hearing the Italian Royal Guard ordered to stand to arms, its adjutant-major, still casting lingering glances over his shoulder, goes back to his post.

In the little ravine of the Semenovka whose waters are flowing red with blood, surgeon Roos, with cannon-balls flying overhead and plunging deep into its reverse slope or else rolling towards him down the forward one, is tending his Saxon, Westphalian and Württemberger wounded, 'and even Russians'. He's noticing how deep wounds caused by flying shell fragments, even though they often tear whole chunks out of limbs, etc., bleed very little; whereas cutting wounds do so profusely:

'A cuirassier of the Saxon bodyguard, an extraordinarily big man, presented such a wound in his left buttock. The muscles, torn away, revealed the bared femur from the knee to the big trochanter. The wound wasn't bleeding. The Saxon showed himself full of energy. He said: "My wound is terrible, but I'll cure quickly because I'm healthy and have pure blood!" A very young officer of the same regiment seemed less confident. He wasn't robust, like the other. He was fine and delicate. A musket-ball had passed through the deltoid. It wasn't the pain that made him complain, but the fear of being crippled, the certainty of not being able to count on anyone helping him, and the distance he was at from his own country. I felt full of compassion for him and if we'd been in Dresden, instead of at Borodino, I'd have been only too glad to have placed him in his mother's care.'

This morning all Roos has had to eat has been a mouthful of bread, given him by another surgeon who's borrowing his instruments, washed down with a gulp of cold water from the stream:

'The numbers of wounded turning up were enormous. Other surgeons had joined us. Thanks to their collaboration we were able to give more active help. Many of these unfortunates died on the spot. Ambulances were evacuating those who'd been given first aid. The doctors hadn't been told in advance which point they should evacuate their wounded to, as in other campaigns.'

It's at just such a dressing-station that Captain François is having his wound attended to:

'The doctor comes over to me and examines my wound. Thrusting his little finger into the hole made by the musket-ball, he seizes his lancet, makes the usual cross on each hole, and puts his probe right through my leg between its two bones. "Lucky wound, this," he says, pulling out some splinters. Then he gives me first aid and tells me to go to the army's ambulance at Kolotskoïe,'

where the wounded can already be counted 'in thousands'.

In the centre, meanwhile, a third battle is raging around the flaming embers of Semenovskaya village. Against it – together with the Great Redoubt it's the key to the whole Russian position – III Corps is being thrown in, in wave after wave.[11] Evidently its attacks are overlapping those of I Corps, for Captain Bonnet, too, sees as his objective 'three redoubts' – which can only be the Bagration flèches:

'By a movement to our right we fling ourselves across some bushes and come close to the first redoubt, which is carried by our leading troops. Whereon the regiment marches on the second, its four battalions in line one behind another. Half-way between the first and the second redoubt Commandant Fournier is wounded, and I take command of the battalion – reform it in column, the right on the ditch of the redoubt we've already taken. I've got the flag. I'm awaiting the moment to act. The colonel comes up to me on foot and I ask his permission to send the flag back to that part of the corps which was close to the first redoubt and on the fringe of the copse from which we're emerging. It was done.'

But unfortunately after five minutes Russian sharpshooters

'arrive in good order a little to the left, and a dense column to our right. I deploy my battalion and, without firing, march straight at the column. It recoils. When carrying out this movement we were so exposed to grapeshot from the guns in the village that I saw my battalion falling and being breached like a crenellated wall. But still we went on.'

Reaching the edge of the ravine that separates the village from the crest of the ravine, the 18th Line runs headlong into another column

'which is marching gravely and without hurry. All that's left on its legs of the 4th Battalion makes a half turn, and we withdraw slowly, firing on this column, and re-enter the redoubt. But the place, being open on their side, isn't tenable. I'm the last to jump up on to its parapet, just as a Russian's about to grab my greatcoat. In one leap I jump the ditch. They must have fired 20 shots at me, almost point-blank, without hitting anything except my shako. We withdrew as far as to the bushes near the first redoubt.'

No sooner have the 18th taken refuge in the bushes than they're repeatedly charged by Russian cuirassiers. And it isn't until about midday that the Russians finally evacuate the ruins of what, a few hours before, was the village of Semenovskaya.

A sore throat, a bad cold, migraine and an agonizingly overfull bladder are no friends of a commander-in-chief at the crisis of his fortunes. Soltyk, only about 30 or 40 paces away from Napoleon, is observing him closely. Not paying the least attention to the Russian shells which now and then explode nearby,

'now he'd sit down on the ground; now walk to and fro quietly humming a tune, sometimes mechanically putting his hand in his waistcoat pocket to take out some pills he'd been prescribed against his cold. His face simultaneously expressed preoccupation and impassibility. He also addressed a few brief words to members of his suite, telling them to take his orders to the battlefield.'

At one moment the Polish General Kossakowski 'having picked up a Russian grape cartridge with old rusty brown iron, whose wounds are said to be the most dangerous', and holding it up

'as evidence of Muscovite foul play, went up to him and showed it to him, adding that all means were fair against such enemies. The Emperor replied vivaciously: "Oh, I don't give a damn for them!" Then added immediately: "But that stuff won't carry far."'

How much can he see of the vast conflict going on at his feet? Only Ney's corps and 'almost all the cavalry assembled under Murat', thinks Chlapowsky, who's standing not far away with his squadron of the 1st Polish Lancers. He too thinks the Emperor is ill: 'now walking up and down, now sitting on his folding chair. At no moment did he mount his horse.' Lejeune, making comparisons with Wagram, Essling, Eylau and Friedland, is astonished not to see him 'deploy the activity which produces success.' The rumour that the Emperor isn't well also reaches Dr Flize, medical officer in one of the Guard regiments:

'Not once did Napoleon mount his horse during the whole battle.[12] He walked on foot with his suite of officers, passing ceaselessly to and fro. A steady stream of adjutants took his orders and rode away.'

One of them is Lejeune:

'Returning from all my missions I always found him there sitting in the same posture, following all the movements through his pocket spyglass and giving his orders with imperturbable calm. But we weren't so happy as to see him, as formerly, going to galvanise with his presence the points where too vigorous a resistance made success doubtful. Each of us was astonished not to find the active man of Marengo, Austerlitz, etc. We didn't know Napoleon was ill and that it was this that was making it impossible for him to act in the great struggles taking place under his eyes, exclusively in the interests of his glory. We weren't very satisfied; our judgements were severe.'

Boulart, standing among his guns, horses and ammunition wagons a few yards in front of his command post, sees the Emperor himself, 'his arms crossed on his chest, walking agitatedly to and fro in a small space in the very centre of my own battery. Farther off, groups of officers and generals were standing spyglass in hand. In previous battles the Emperor had produced spectacular effects by one of his characteristic masterstrokes. Now we were living in hope of seeing his face light up with the same exultation as it used to do in his heyday. But on this occasion we waited in vain. At one moment he moved a little further down the slope and, telescope still in hand, lay in a reclining posture on a bearskin rug. Sometimes he'd walk to and fro, his hands behind his back. Mostly he sat on his folding chair peering through his fieldglass or with a gesture summoning Berthier and exchanging a word or two with him.'

Boulart's querulous and pessimistic colleague Captain Pion des Loches says he can even

> 'guarantee that from the beginning of the action until 4 p.m. he didn't budge, because all the time I had my eyes fixed on him. More than 100 staff officers arrived one after another; he listened to their reports, then dismissed them with a gesture of his hand, almost always without uttering a word.'

But the scene just behind him is so much the more impressive. Victor Dupuy, on his way back from fetching himself a fresh mount in the rear from among the 7th Hussars' lead-horses, his own being winded, passes close by and sees how

> 'the Guard was placed behind him, as in an amphitheatre. Massed in columns of battalions, it presented an imposing, magnificent spectacle. The men were all in parade uniforms, as if to march past on the Place du Carousel.'

Dr Flize too will afterwards above all remember 'its bearskins and red plumes'. And Séruzier records that 'despite its privations since Vilna its turnout was as brilliant as in Paris'. Thirion, looking over his shoulder from his place amidst the dense masses of cavalry in the French centre, sees the whole hillock as

> 'a pyramid of men and bayonets, whose summit was the Emperor. A magnificent and imposing coup d'oeil. At its foot the whole Guard cavalry was drawn up in two lines: the first made up of the Chasseurs, Lancers and Dragoons, the second of the Grenadiers and élite company.'

Immediately below and in front are the three regiments of the Legion of the Vistula. Meanwhile, says Dr Flize,

> 'the regimental bands were playing military marches, reminiscent of the first marches of the Revolution, when we'd been fighting for Freedom: Allons, les enfants de la patrie.[13] Here the same strains didn't inspire the military; and some of the older officers laughed when they compared the two epochs.'

Earlier Chlapowski has noted how the 'light infantry clarions were choosing the prettiest pieces in the repertoire, because music makes a great impression on hearts before a battle'. – 'I moved a little closer to the Emperor,' Flize goes on,

> 'who'd not ceased peering at the battlefield through his spyglass. He was wearing his grey uniform and spoke little. Sometimes a cannonball came rolling towards his feet, but he merely stepped aside, as we did who were standing behind him.'

Bausset, who at 10 a.m. serves him a glass of punch, says 'he calmly kicked them aside, as one kicks a stone when taking a walk'.[14] A little farther off Dumonceau is seeing how

> 'every instant trophies captured from the enemy were being brought to us. Among these some presented the most handsome types you could possibly see, both of men and horses. One of the latter, a

superb black courser, was ceded to our Commander Cotti for a 20 fr. piece: then the cuirassier who'd brought it went resolutely back to the scrum.'

At about 11 a.m. everyone notices a kind of lull. It's as if both sides are already showing signs of exhaustion. And Murat sends one of his ADCs, a Colonel Morelli, to Napoleon, urging him to send in the Guard. Arriving at the Schevardino redoubt he hears voices muttering: 'Forward the Guard!' But Napoleon tells him: "And what if there's another battle tomorrow, what shall I fight it with?" Yet goes so far as to give an order for the Young Guard to advance – only immediately to cancel it. And when its commanders, even so, on pretext of straightening its lines, are seen to be 'shuffling' their units in the direction of the firing, sharply orders them to desist. Instead of sending in the Young Guard, and after a renewed attack by Latour-Maubourg's cavalry corps, he orders forward Friant's division. On Dedem's men 'demanding to be sent into the fighting, Napoleon (who he says had 'come up') had replied: "Regiments like this only go into action to decide the victory."

'A moment we remained in column, exposed to roundshot. My two ADCs, General Friant's son and several staff officers were all wounded. Soon we were made to march towards the centre to cover the burnt village of Semenovskaya, several times taken and retaken, and against which the Russians were directing their 20,000-strong reserve.'

Friant, who finds Murat 'all smiles' under furious fire from 100 Russian guns, seizes the burnt-out village; and in the same instant is himself severely wounded.

'Seeing a regiment beginning to give way, Murat runs up to its colonel and seizes him by the collar: "What are you doing?" The colonel, pointing to his hundreds of dead and wounded: "Surely you see we can't hold on here?" Murat: "Well, I'm staying put!" The colonel stares at him: "Quite right, Sire! Let's go and get ourselves killed!"'

Whereupon the remains of Friant's division form two squares, Murat commanding one, and General Gallichet, Friant's chief-of-staff, the other. And under their crossed fire the Russian attack withers away.

At the same time the need for some decisive intervention is clearly growing. Napoleon turns to Lejeune:

'"Go and find Sorbier and tell him to take all the artillery of my Guard to the position occupied by General Friant,[15] and lead him there yourself. He's to deploy 60 pieces at right angles to the enemy line, to crush his flank, and Murat is to support him. *Allez!*"

'I gallop over to the fiery General Sorbier. Guessing my message, he hardly gives me time to explain it, but replies impatiently: "We ought to have done it an hour ago", and gives the order to follow him at a trot. And at once this imposing mass of "thunderers", drawn by 2,000 horses, gets rolling with a clanking of chains and thudding of horse-hoofs and goes off down the hillside; crosses the valley; mounts the easy slope the enemy has covered with trenches, and then breaks into a gallop to gain the necessary space to deploy on his left flank.'

Boulart, left behind with his battery, is watching his colleagues' fate from afar:

'For quite a while my gaze followed the three Guard batteries under a well-nourished fire and covered with a hail of roundshot whose falls one could only see by the dust they were raising. I thought they were lost, or at least half so. Happily, the Russians aimed badly, or too high.'

But Lejeune is accompanying Sorbier into the thick of it:

'In the distance, ahead of me, I see King Murat cavorting in the midst of the horse skirmishers, surrounded by far fewer of his own troops and much less occupied with his own cavalry than with numerous Cossacks. These have recognized him by his panache, his gallantry and courage, also by his little Cossack mantle of long goat's hair which he, like they, is wearing. Happy as on a holiday they'd surrounded him and, hoping to seize him, were shouting "Houra! houra! Murat!" But even at a lance's length none of them dared attack this man whose sabre, swift as lightning, adeptly evaded every danger and struck death into the heart of even the boldest. I gallop up to warn him of what's going to happen [i.e., that the three Guard artillery batteries are going to open fire from his flank], and Murat, leaving the line of sharpshooters, comes and gives his orders to make sure Sorbier is supported. Taking his movement for a flight or a retreat, the Cossacks pursue us. My horse, not so light as Murat's – he's riding a beautiful tawny Arab – gets all four feet entangled and is overthrown by the lashings of a cannon as it makes a 90-degree turn at the gallop. The furious animal, though hurt by the shock of its fall, gets up without throwing me, and takes me over to Sorbier in the centre of the terrible battery which is just firing its first salvo of grape, shells and roundshot, raking the enemy line throughout its whole length, every discharge taking effect. In vain the enemy's cavalry tries to destroy this line of guns. Murat's cavalry is giving it too much to think about; but though it's making brilliant charges, it can't debouch on to the second line occupied by the Russians on the plateau, where we're still separated [from it] by a little gentle slope. We remained the masters of their fortified position. I went back to the Emperor and gave him these details.'

Now no fewer than 400 guns are bombarding the Russian centre, which 300 others are defending. Ney and Davout mount assault after assault. Neither Dumonceau, still in reserve, nor anyone else has ever heard anything like it:

'To the stunning uproar of the cannonade close at hand was mingled like a distant echo that of the batteries to our left around

Borodino, and on the right, beyond the woods where Prince Poniatowski was fighting. Then the sonorous vibrations of the atmosphere, like groans, the sharp soughing of roundshot passing through the air produced the effect of someone ripping up pieces of cloth, the cracklings of an intermittent fusillade, sometimes re-animated by lively and prolonged explosions – all these various noises, mixed with clamour of all kinds, formed an infernal din such as the one at Smolensk had only given us a feeble idea of.'

The slaughter on both sides is inconceivable. For two hours Ségur watches the Russians

'advancing in dense masses, into which our roundshot ploughed wide and deep holes. They kept coming on until the French batteries, redoubling their fire, crushed them with canister. Whole platoons fell at once, and we could see the soldiers trying to restore their ranks under this horrible fire.'

'The roundshot and shells rained down like hail,' Planat goes on,

'and there was so much smoke we could only make out the enemy at rare intervals. The Westphalian Corps was massed in close column in front of the [Schevardino] redoubt, and from time to time received shells which, as they burst, sent shakos and bayonets flying up in the air. At each such blow these poor soldiers flung themselves down flat on their stomachs, and not all got up again.'

Planat himself, as he follows Lariboisière about the battlefield, 'not wanting either to quit my post or dismount', is suffering from

'the worst kind of agony one can imagine – from diarrhoea. I daren't describe just how I managed to dispose of what was tormenting me; but in the process I lost two handkerchiefs, which I, as we passed it, threw as discreetly as I could into the trench of the fortification. A serious loss in a country devoid of washerwomen.'[16]

But up there on the plateau Ney is 'animating everybody with his gestures and his fiery manners'. His Württembergers, too, slowly advancing (Suckow supposes as a feint), are being mown down by the Russian cannon when 'Major de Mangold, of the Württemberg staff, arrives flat out at the head of our column and in a loud voice asks for mounted lieutenants who speak French'. Suckow and another present themselves; and are detailed off. But how to stick with 'Ney's too numerous suite'? The two lieutenants'

'wretched little Russian horses have a thousand difficulties in following the Marshal, who was as active as he was mobile. We saw him giving orders at all points, taking his dispositions, and again and again even leading us to within the enemy's musket range. Very frequently he galloped to the hillock on whose summit Napoleon had placed himself. Probably he was reporting to the Emperor or asking for fresh orders.'

On one such occasion Suckow too hears Napoleon, on foot, ask Ney from a distance: 'Well then, Marshal?' But doesn't hear Ney's answer – only sees

'Napoleon very violently lash the air with the riding whip he was holding in one hand.'

Wave after wave, division upon division, is thrown in. The massed green ranks, exposed on their slight forward slope, are mincemeat for the French guns. Soltyk, who is also dashing about on mission, finds Davout, too, directing his troops' movement in the very storm centre of the fighting:

'I told him I was going to return to the Emperor, and asked for orders. He replied: "Since you're going back to the Emperor, tell him there's been a bit of a scrum, as you've just seen; but that just now everything's going all right."'

At the crisis of the struggle, and just as the Russians seem on the point of yielding, Bagration, commanding the Russian left, is badly wounded in the leg. The Russians waver. And 'the French remain masters of the flèches'.[17]

Which however have been designed to be, and still are, open at the rear to Russian counter-attacks. But this time 'the Prince of Eckmühl went on defending the redoubts he'd taken and from which the enemy were trying to dislodge him'. Now Lejeune is sent to him with

'the unpleasant news that Prince Poniatowski, manoeuvring on his right in the very dense or swampy woods, had run into obstacles which were preventing him from bringing the Polish corps on to the Russian rear and doing them enough harm to make a powerful diversion in favour of I Corps. The Marshal's position was at that moment critical, almost untenable. Though he'd been wounded [*sic*] in the arm, he remained in command. The Marshal, very much annoyed at having to take frontally a position which in his view ought to have been attacked from three sides at once, told me angrily: "He [Napoleon] must have the devil in him, wanting me to seize the bull by the horns!"'

At that moment Davout's chief-of-staff, General Romoef, is hit by a round-shot and, gravely wounded, has to be taken to the rear. But Lejeune hurries

'to King Murat, to explain to him what a critical position Davout was in; and he instantly assembled several masses of his cavalry to support General Friant, to whom I took his order to carry Semenovskaya. An instant later I saw the whole plain covered by innumerable cavalry, Russian, Cossacks, French or Allied, involved in the most obstinate mêlées.'

By now it's getting on for midday; and Le Roy, who's been sent to replace the 85th's Second Major, thinks the fighting on the right flank is slackening. No doubt it's during this lull – but such a vast number of things are of course happening simultaneously as to bewilder all exact chronology – that von Suckow, tagging along on his konya after Ney's splendidly mounted staff, in a moment when they're out of range of the enemy's fire, is amazed when Ney turns to one of his domestics and says: 'Luncheon!' The more so as he's long been living on horseflesh or a bit of black rye bread:

'In the twinkling of an eye the table was laid – it consisted of a big linen tablecloth spread out on the ground, and charged with such appetizing and comforting dishes as butter, cheese, bread, etc. There were even liqueurs in abundance. With a curt "help yourselves, gentlemen!" the Marshal invited us to amply fall to on the delicious things spread out at our feet, and whose very names, so to speak, we'd forgotten.'

Alas, all too little time is allowed for them to do justice to the repast. 'After only a few minutes there was a shout of "To horse, gentlemen!" There was no appealing against it. And again we had to take our places in the scrum.' Everyone, including Ney, has taken fresh horses. Only the two Württemberg lieutenants will have to go on making do with their little konyas. When they point this out to Ney's chief-of-staff they're curtly dismissed and – without having carried a single order.

It's also 'at midday' – i.e., during the same lull – that de Bausset makes so bold as 'officiously' to ask Napoleon whether he'd like to take lunch?

'He signed to me "No." Whereupon I was so unwise as to tell him there was no reason in the world to prevent him from having lunch whenever he wanted to. He dismissed me in a pretty brusque fashion. Later he ate a slice of bread and drank a glass of Chambertin, without diluting it with water.'

But for the two Württemberger officers, only too happy to have at least snatched at so fine a lunch, it's 'no easy matter, dragging our exhausted ponies along behind us, to find our few hundred Württembergers'. And when in the end they do, their comrades are inside one of the flèches, being cannonaded by a battery of 20 Russian guns.

Now a Saxon cuirassier division is thrown in. Climbing up the steep slope of the Semenovskaya, cuirassier lieutenant *von Meerheimb*[18] finds it 'so steep that some of our riders, not realizing it would be better to climb it obliquely, tumbled over backwards and were trampled by the horses coming on behind'. The village on its crest is by this time a mere mass of glowing logs. Beyond it a Russian infantry regiment, caught in the act of forming square, is ridden over; but two others repulse the disorganized cuirassiers with well-disciplined volleys, felling any number of men and horses. Finally a second assault by Friant's division seizes the ground the Russian centre has been holding.

And a gap – at last – opens up in the Russian line.

Through it both Murat and Ney can 'see clearly as far as Mojaisk'. They even make out parts of the Russian baggage train moving off into the woods.

It's the crucial moment.

The moment for the knockout blow.

And this time Murat sends – not an ADC – but his chief-of-staff, to beg Napoleon to send in the Imperial Guard. Belliard rides up, doffs his hat, explains. Napoleon meditates a moment. But temporizes: 'Before I commit by reserves I must be able to see more clearly on my chessboard.' And it's a disappointed Belliard who rides away. Ney too has asked for the Guard. And when it's refused him, exclaims angrily: 'If he's tired, why doesn't he retire to the Tuileries and leave the fighting to the real generals?'

When he gets back to Murat, Belliard is alarmed to see him being pursued by Russian cuirassiers. And where's his suite? All that's left of it, so it seems, 'as extravagantly dressed as himself', is his mameluke Amédé. To escape some Cossacks who're also after him Murat has hastily to take refuge in a square of the Württembergers' 25th division.[19] But Amédé gets left outside:

'The Prince Constantine's cuirassiers's uniform was very similar to that of the Saxon cuirassiers – white tunic and black turnbacks – and their sudden appearance in great numbers had thrown everything into confusion. The Württembergers took them for Saxons and held their fire. But the Negro [*sic*], who hasn't lost his head, keeps shouting: "Fire! Fire!" Placed as he was between the Russians and ourselves, that was magnificent! That "Fire!" could have been the end of him.'

The perilous moment over, Murat remounts, gallops over to Nansouty, and unleashes a new charge; which is also repulsed.

But by now the Russians have plugged the gap in their centre.

And the critical moment has been lost.

There's been a good reason for Napoleon's reluctance to throw in the Guard. A little while before Belliard comes galloping up, begging him to do so, something else has happened.

On the extreme left Ornano's Bavarian Chasseurs have been stolidly suffering under frontal fire from the Russian guns beyond the Kolotchka:

'Packed together, we formed a sure target for the Russian artillery, which had ridden up towards us. As usual the Russian gunners were aiming too high and a lot of their cannonfire passed overhead, so fewer of us in the first line were wounded than might have been expected. But the second line, a brigade of Italian horse chasseurs, were worse off; and the officers were having their hands full getting their men to stay put. Roundshot were falling to right and left, hitting horses and riders. Such a fate struck my sergeant-major Moncrif, a native Frenchman. Our line had become confused, and he'd just ridden along our front to straighten it and had halted in front of my horse to say something to me, when a roundshot suddenly threw him out of his saddle. A few steps away from me lay now only a mutilated corpse, and for the moment we couldn't dismount to drag it aside.'

This has been going on for two hours and the sun is

'high in the sky, when we saw a movement among the numerous
Russian cavalry in front of us; and soon it became clear that a considerable mass of it was moving off toward our left wing.'

It is now that Ornano's, or rather Eugène's, negligence in not taking the
obvious precaution of placing light infantry in the sparse woods to their
left becomes obvious. For it's in this direction, with the overt intention of
occupying them, that the Russian cavalry are now moving. Abruptly aware
of the oversight, Ornano sends an urgent message to Eugène, who hastily,
to make it good, sends him two companies of voltigeurs. But of course
they'll take some time to get there. And meanwhile, von Muraldt contin-
ues,

'the enemy cavalry, consisting of Guard Cossacks, is implementing its
plan. By the time the voltigeurs reach us the wood is already in
enemy hands. And hardly have the voltigeurs drawn up to our left,
within range of it, than individual sharpshooters from the Guard
Cossacks [easily recognizable by their scarlet baggy uniforms] are
already visible on its fringe. As soon as the enemy facing us sees
we've been outflanked he crosses the Kolotchka, everywhere shallow
and easily forded, and, protected by his artillery, attacks our front.
Every moment we're waiting for the order to advance against him;
but whether our general's attention is mainly directed toward the
attack threatening our flank or for some other reasons, no such
order comes; and we can only await the enemy, who are coming at us
flat out. Not until the Russians are 200 paces away does the order
come: "Carbines up! Fire!" And hardly have we fired our carbines –
mostly without effect (as is usual with cavalry) – than we're attacked
and overthrown by two hussar regiments.'

Disaster threatens. The whole left wing is in instant danger of being driven in:

'At the same time the Guard Cossacks are advancing out of the
wood, overriding both our voltigeur companies, and striking into
our flank. Attacked from in front and in flank, and on such utterly
unfavourable terrain, the whole lot of us take to our heels. For a
moment generals, officers and rankers swirl around in a single confused mass. Everyone is spurring his horse to get out of this jam as
quick as ever he can.'

Cursing himself no doubt for his oversight in not investing the Lachariska
wood with light infantry, Eugène sends off an ADC to Napoleon to notify
him of the dangerous irruption. And himself gallops over to the trouble-
spot 'the better to assess the enemy's movement'. Getting there just as the
Russians launch their attack, he's

'swept away in this flight and seeks salvation in his horse's swiftness.
The best mounted of the enemy follow us with loosened reins and
lowered lances.'

The Italian Guard too has been under heavy pressure. Standing there in
support of Gérard's and Morand's divisions, 'impassively suffering the

losses caused by the guns, powerless to avenge itself and trembling at its own inaction' and sure it's this affray that's going to decide the whole battle, they've been demanding to be allowed to join in. 'Shouting with joy', they've just formed an assault column 'of platoons by the right' – the vélites at the head, then the grenadiers, the chasseurs and the dragoons – and 'joy, pride and hope are shining in all our faces amidst falling shells and grenades and to the incessant whistling of iron and lead', they're just about to attack – when Ornano's staff officer comes galloping up

'to warn the Viceroy, in all haste, that numerous Russian cavalry are debouching from the Lachariski wood to outflank and turn our left. The last adjutant to arrive tells us that Delzons and Ornano have already been crushed and forced to retire on to the Italian batteries, Borodino, the Woina and the baggage.'

About turn! Back across the Kolotchka! 'Annoyed to have our movement interrupted but hoping to be compensated in some other way, we retrace our steps, the tail of our columns leading, and hasten to the threatened point.'

By now the intruders, emerging from the wood, are becoming 'at each moment more numerous'; and already half the Italian guns are having to be turned against them. Colonel Achouard of the artillery is killed and two of his cannon have been taken, when Eugène, arriving on the scene at a gallop and 'promising us that the Guard will be here any moment, has no other recourse but to take refuge inside a square of the 84th, which is instantly charged'. 'At that very moment,' Laugier goes on,

'we're [re]fording the Kolotchka, and, while preserving the greatest calm, are hastening our steps, the more ardent for a rumour that the Prince himself is in danger. Meanwhile the Russian cavalry, all the time growing more numerous, renew their charges against the squares of the Croats' 8th Light, of the 84th and the 92nd. Formed in squares, we advance in échelon to meet the Russians, who by now have reached the Italian batteries, extinguished their fire, and overthrown Delzons' regiments.'

Von Muraldt and his fleeing chasseurs have taken refuge behind the crossed bayonets of the Royal Guard:

'A little way from our infantry, which had formed square behind us, Lieutenant Münch and I were among the first who with our shouts and arguments managed to halt our people and bring some order into them again. Others followed our example. Now the Russians too become aware of our distant infantry square and begin to cease their pursuit,'

driven off 'flat out', says Laugier, by the squares' heavy musketry. And, Muraldt goes on:

'A beginning had been made, and soon we throw the Russians back so violently that they've no time to take away the battery to our front which had fallen into their hands when we'd fled.'

Ornano's light cavalry has regrouped and is thirsting for revenge. Seconded by Italian Guard dragoons and the Guardia d'Onore, it 'flings itself again at the Russians, who hastily recross the Woina and the Kolotchka, and don't dare return' – leaving behind them the two captured Italian guns:

'It's about three o'clock. But the order having come to form up again in our previous positions, we didn't pursue them any further. During this episode, which lasted no longer than ten minutes, many of our people had been wounded with sabre cuts and lance-thrusts, but comparatively few had been killed. After this interesting intermezzo, though all the time fired on by the Russian guns, we didn't budge from the spot.'

Part of Uvarov's improvised, badly carried through, but, as it will one day turn out, decisive intervention[20] – has even caused panic in the baggage train. And the Guard's rearmost units, even though it's only been a question of Cossacks, have momentarily had to about-face to receive them.

But Uvarov's real achievement has been to reduce the French impact in the centre – at the critical moment.

What Napoleon has been thinking about it we don't know. But in the hut behind the Imperial Guard which Larrey is using as his dressing-station for the army's top brass, the wounded generals *Teste* and Compans (doubtless also Dessaix and Rapp) have heard the noise of the fighting coming closer to the left, then dying away again; and that 'panic and confusion' have broken out in the rear.

At about 2 p.m. Girod de l'Ain, in the centre, finds Ney

'more or less alone in command of the whole line. Anyway the firing had begun to slacken on both sides and one would have said the battle was about to end for lack of combatants, so huge had both armies' losses been during the forenoon. Only the batteries, at rather long range, went on replying to each other with frequent discharges. On my way to get to Marshal Ney I found myself following the base of a little earthwork with the sound of roundshot going over my head in either direction. Their whistling and – apparently – the emotions of the forenoon had made such an impression on my poor horse that, though hitherto always a model of docility, he chose this moment to become so extremely restive I had to dismount and lead him by his bridle. And the strange thing is, it wasn't the sound of the guns which set him trembling in every limb, but the whistling of the shot, so well did he understand that it was there the danger lay, not in the guns' detonations.'

Ney has sent Girod de l'Ain to tell General Friedrichs to advance and likewise

'the Duke of Abrantès, who was with the Westphalian Corps on our right. Friedrichs obeyed, taking up a position where he could see the Westphalians behind him, and always in touch with Prince Poniatow-

sky's Polish Corps, to his right. As for Junot, I found him in a clearing in the wood, dismounted, making his troops pile arms and
apparently nowise disposed to budge. Nor did he take any account of
what I'd come to tell him: and went on doing, there, what he'd been
accused of at Valutina.'

Le Roy, too, who has left Davout's staff to replace the 85th's Second Major,
feels that the fighting on the right flank is slackening after the flèches
have been turned. Yet no sooner does the 85th, emerging from one of
them at about 3 p.m., try to advance across the great plateau, than the
storm of grape and roundshot starts up again, as intense as ever.

Nor its chief target is Murat's cavalry masses which, for almost nine
hours, have been forming the centre of the French battle line. Hour after
horrific hour has passed, as they sit their horses there, immobile under
the Russian guns, above all from the 'Raevsky'[21] Redoubt's eighteen heavy
pieces. Lejeune sees clearly that, if the Italian artillery had been placed
too far from the enemy, Grouchy's, Latour-Maubourg's and Montbrun's
three cavalry corps have from the outset been stationed unnecessarily
close:

'Out of vanity, or rather, not to give grounds for a false interpreta-
tion, they were loth to retire a few hundred paces and take up a less
exposed position to the rear. In this way thousands of brave troopers
and excellent horses we'd every reason to preserve fell without any
profit to the army.'

As the endless minutes pass, then the hours, Colonel *Roth von Schreckenstein,*[22] commanding the Saxon Life Guard Cuirassiers is finding that

'for strong healthy well-mounted men a cavalry battle is nothing
compared with what Napoleon made his cavalry put up with at
Borodino. To hold out inactively under fire must be one of the most
unpleasant things cavalry can be called upon to do. There can
scarcely have been a man whose neighbour didn't crash to earth with
his horse or die from terrible wounds, screaming for help.'

Captain Aubry sees his colonel's two thighs carried away and two captains
and the regimental paymaster killed, apparently by one and the same
roundshot:

'The sergeant-major on the squadron's right flank was carried off by
a cannon-ball just as I was laying my sabre on his chest to align the
front rank, and I was all spattered by his blood. The farrier, who
replaced him, suffered the same fate. The brigadier, his neighbour,
had three horses killed under him. My turn came soon afterwards. I
was hit by a ricocheting cannon-ball or by an exploding shell fragment on the flat of my spur. The blow was so violent that my boot
burst open like a sheet of paper torn up by children for their amuse-
ment. All that was left was the lining. Fortunately the projectile
passed on the side of my instep instead of by the heel – if it hadn't,
my leg would have been carried away. I got off with losing all my
nails and the flesh of my toes.'

Victor Dupuy had earlier been riding at his general's side

'when a roundshot passed so close to my face I felt its heat. Making an involuntary movement with my body, I gave my horse's bridle a sharp tug. He jerked in the opposite direction and we came apart. Stunned by my fall I lay motionless on the ground. The column halted. General Jacquinot, Colonel Gobrecht of the 9th Lancers and some officers came and stood around me. I heard them saying: "This poor Dupuy has been killed!" A few are already dismounting to give me what help they can, when I suddenly come to myself again, get lightly to my feet, shake my head, and saying "there's nothing wrong with me!", remount my horse. For a few moments this accident, which, most happily for me, was only comic, cheered us all up.'

As the nightmarish hours wear on and on, the 7th Hussars, too, are melting away. Two Russian batteries, one in the redoubt, the other taking them in flank, are slowly decimating their ranks. Dupuy's squadron-leader, Brousselier, comes riding up to him:

'He asked me if I'd anything to give him to drink. I proffered him my flask with a little rum in it. Having taken a swig he said: "Let's go! I'll go back. If I must be killed, it shall be at my post!" Hardly had he got these words out than a roundshot hit him in the chest. He died on the spot. If he'd stayed with me only one minute longer this untoward roundshot wouldn't have been for him.'

All around him, cuirassier Captain Bréaut des Marlots, a man of stoic philosophy if ever there was one, sees only

'dead or dying men. Twice during the battle I went to review the faces of the cuirassiers of my company to see which were the brave ones. I told them so on the spot. Just as I was going up to a young officer, M. de Gramont, to felicitate him on keeping a good countenance and he was telling me he had no complaints to make but would like a glass of water, a cannon-ball comes and cuts him in two. I turn to another officer and tell him how much I regret poor M. de Gramont. Before he can reply his horse is hit and killed by a roundshot. I give my horse to be held for half a minute – the cuirassier who's holding it is knocked over and killed. But though I'm covered with earth the shells are throwing up at me, I don't suffer the least scratch.'

In such dire circumstances he's finding a clear conscience is a soldier's best friend:

'And here's what gave me the calm I needed: "It's a lottery. Even if you get out of this, you'll have to die some day. Do you prefer to live dishonoured or die with honour?" When you're sabring each other you're in motion. The fire which animates you takes away all kind of reflection. But to see virtually certain death, or to put it better, to wait for it, to be surrounded only by dead and dying, this is often beyond human strength, and only philosophy, I do believe, has the power to raise us by showing us the nothingness of our being. The bad man is never a good soldier, remorse stifles his courage. He's only good for some desperate enterprise, charges, etc., and I've often seen this proven. All this proves that all men have a more or less tender conscience, and that no one can wholly stifle it. At the sight of a great danger it's reborn. It's the voice of God, it's the greatest proof of His existence.'

Some people – perhaps their consciences aren't quite so good – are wondering whether it's really necessary to be quite so exposed:

'Shortly afterwards, General Bruyère's horse hurting him in its fall, General Jacquinot, who'd at once withdrawn the 7th Hussars to a less exposed position behind a wood, takes over the light cavalry division.'

Maurice Tascher too will write in his diary: 'Remained for nine hours under cannon and grape.' He's wondering how the many novices 'who could hardly sit a horse' and have fallen by the wayside, would have stood up to this?

For it mustn't be imagined that no one, novice or not, runs away. Vossler sees 'a regiment of Polish lancers break under the fire, passing through us before it could be halted'. There are even general officers who're glad of a pretext, however slim, to quit. General Burot, of the 1st Light Cavalry Brigade (5th and 9th Hussars), known for his cowardice,

'was advancing at the head of his brigade when a roundshot carried away the corner of his hat. As he was retiring he met Marshal Ney, to whom he recounted his mishap. "Are you wounded?" "No, M. le Maréchal, I don't think so." "In that case," the Duke of Elchingen replied ironically, "go back to your brigade, and after the battle you'll have no difficulty in finding something else to put on your head!"'[23]

To the left of this great mass and advanced beyond a deep ravine in front of the Great Redoubt, Griois' guns are firing back at 'the artillery in the redoubts [i.e., flèches] on our right and left, and against the masses of cavalry and infantry facing us':

'All the cavalry reserves have united on this point and formed up in several lines to the right of my batteries. Musket-balls, shells and grape, raining down on us from all sides, were blasting great holes in our cavalry, which stood there for several hours without budging. The plain was covered with wounded men making for the ambulances and horses without riders galloping about in disorder. Close to me I noticed a regiment of Württemberg cuirassiers whom the roundshot seemed to be striking by preference; in all its ranks helmets and cuirasses were flying in pieces. The French Carabiniers, too, placed farther ahead, were also suffering a lot, above all from the musketry, whose balls were ringing out on their armour. My artillery was sorely tried, and soon I'd two guns dismounted and a great number of men and horses dead.'

A shell blows up under Colonel Séruzier's horse and stuns him. 'Just as I was about to mount again, the brave General Montbrun, who'd seen me fall, comes up to me and asks whether I'm not wounded. I thanked him, telling him I'd got off with a mere bruise.' Colonels and generals falling like ninepins. And now it's Montbrun's turn. Riding up to his divisional general Pajol, he

'asks him how he feels, and whether he couldn't move over into a dip in the ground to his left. "But that's where the Vistula Legion are, so I can't. I've already sent someone to look." "Who?" "Biot." "Oh well," Montbrun replies, "let's go and have a look anyway." And there we were, passing along the front of our line. General Montbrun was to our right, flanking us toward the enemy, General Pajol in the middle, and to his left, on a front of three. Behind us came his escort, but none of his ADCs was at his side. Suddenly I hear a dull thud. "Someone's been wounded," I exclaimed. At the same instant General Montbrun rolls off his horse. A 3-pounder had hit him in his left side and remained in his body.'

Roos, working at his surgery only thirty yards away, sees him fall:

'Suddenly I saw General Montbrun turn pale and fall from his horse. I ran to help him. Two French doctors, who were closer than I was, got there first. The wound wasn't bleeding very much. He'd very quickly turned pale and yellow. His very lively look had been extinguished and we saw his strength gradually fail.'

Summoned to the spot, Larrey finds the roundshot has

'passed through the region of his kidneys from side to side. There was little to be done. Death was certain and not far off. I applied a dressing, and had him carried to a little village nearby. I'd run the greatest danger while attending to his wound, a cannon-ball having killed some horses behind us.'

From the dying Montbrun he goes to his colleague General Nansouty, who has 'a musket-ball in his knee'. But the handsome popular Montbrun won't even live long enough to open his wife's letter.

But the hardest nut of all to crack, key to the entire Russian position, is the Great Redoubt. To Dumonceau, waiting by his horse to see what role the lancer brigade is going to play in this murderous symphony, it looks like a 'volcano crowned with vapours, engaged in a violent artillery battle while a compact mob swarms round its base'. Now and then Marshal Bessières, walking to and fro in front of the Schevardino redoubt, comes and asks Pion des Loches whether he can't see a lot of movement there:

'I replied that I saw nothing, didn't even know where what he called the Great Redoubt lay; and His Excellency, I imagine, knew as little about it as I did, because if he had known he wouldn't have failed to indicate which direction it lay in. Each time he withdrew, muttering between his teeth: "We're going to have a lot of trouble to take that big redoubt!"'

Yet now it must be taken.

Although they're immobilizing him physically, neither Napoleon's thudding migraine nor his excruciating dysuria are evidently clouding his mind. For as soon as the threat to the left wing has been staved off he decides on a bold, unconventional stroke.

Its embrasures reduced (as Captain François had found out) to rubble under the crossfire of 170 guns, the Great Redoubt, unlike the flèches, is closed at the rear and in front by great walls of pointed stakes. Also, in front, by a deep ditch and wolfpits. But perhaps it can be carried through its 'throats', left open at each end, by a mass onslaught of heavy cavalry?

It's nearly 3 p.m. And an all-out effort is to be launched.

Caulaincourt's brother Auguste having just returned from a mission to the right side of the field, Napoleon, hearing that Montbrun has fallen,[24] summons him and explains his idea.

While the whole of IV Corps, reinforced by Morand's and Gérard's divisions and under cover of maximum bombardment, mount a frontal assault, Latour-Maubourg's IV Cavalry Corps,[25] supported by Montbrun's II Cavalry Corps, are to feign an attack on the infantry masses which are supporting the redoubt on each of its sides. But at the last moment, Auguste Caulaincourt, animating and guiding the cuirassiers' movement, is to swing in at a right angle and try to force a way in through the redoubt's two open 'throats'. A highly unusual, if not unique, way of capturing a fieldwork!

Napoleon tells him: 'Go and do as you did at Arzobispo!'[26] And Belliard tells him to

'seize the moment when he'll see Gérard's infantry column beginning to mount the hill toward the redoubt. Forming a column of four regiments of cuirassiers and two of carabiniers, he's to lead it at a trot toward his right, leaving the redoubt somewhat to one side, as if about to attack the Russian cavalry corps in the plain to his right. Having given the infantry time to mount the slope, he's to turn swiftly to his left and, at the moment when he sees Gérard's troops are ready to storm the parapets, enter the redoubt at a gallop by the gorge, thus taking the enemy between two fires.'

Caulaincourt:

'The Prince of Neuchâtel sent him a written order for the divisional generals to see. My brother seized my hand, saying, "Things have become so hot that I don't suppose I'll see you again. We'll win, or I'll get myself killed."'

At this 'ominous farewell' the Master of the Horse is seized with a dreadful foreboding. But down in the plain[27] Griois, who so far hasn't seen any high-up except Eugène, is relieved to see Murat appear

'with his numerous and brilliant entourage. We were quite sure he'd put an end to a murderous cannonade which was leading to nothing and even slowing down for lack of ammunition, and that he'd dispose of enough troops at one and the same point to make a fresh and decisive attack. And in fact, having examined the situation and ridden over the terrain where, for several hours now, our cavalry was being crushed, he notices that the parapets of the central big redoubt have almost been wiped out by our gunnery.'

Biot has just dismounted to have the dying Montbrun carried to the rear, and Pajol has taken over his command, when one of Murat's ADCs comes galloping up. And gives the order to charge:

'"Let's go," said Pajol, "but someone'll have to make room for me to do so." The king, says the officer, has placed all the cavalry in front of him under Pajol's orders. In the front line, sheltered by a little hill, were the 12th Hussars, a Dutch regiment (Colonel Liegeard) and another chasseur regiment, whose number I don't remember.'

At 3 p.m. 'preparations for a charge,' Tascher notes in his diary. 'La Bourdonnais, etc., etc., wounded'. And Vossler:

'We were on the point of charging, but the enemy recoiled without waiting for the impact, leaving grapeshot from one side and solid cannon-balls from the other to tear through our ranks. In front of us a ravine had been taken by our troops. We followed quickly in their tracks, finding at the bottom of it some brief respite from the murderous fire. But upon breasting the other side we were hit at even closer range and with even greater intensity. For half an hour we were exposed to this murderous fire.'

The Vistula Legion, to the right, is to support the movement. General Claparède is standing in front of the grenadiers of its 1st Regiment in the dip in the ground that Pajol had envied, when an imperial ordnance officer gallops up and orders him forward. Crossing 'a thin rivulet of water [the Kolotchka] that ran across a great part of the battlefield' Brandt sees to his right 'immense struggles going on'; and, to his left, the 'huge mass of halted cavalry files where the enemy fire is making great breaches'. Everywhere the terrain is encumbered by many dead men 'but above all by killed and mutilated horses'. Farther away to his left Brandt glimpses the cupola of Borodino church, the sun flashing on its green tiles. But then the Poles halt again, deafened from all sides by a roar of musketry and artillery fire, and can see nothing.

Now Colbert's brigade, too, which all morning has been in reserve, is moving forward, also to support the movement; and the Red Lancers are beginning 'to be exposed to stray roundshot'. As they cross the Kolotchka they're allowed a moment to water their horses. The Vistula Legion, advancing again, crosses the Semenovskaya:

'Reaching the opposite height we saw an incredible dust. An immense clamour accompanied by an intense cannonade was shattering the air. The roundshot was passing over us and through our columns.'

And now, at last, the vast mass of heavy cavalry, the sun glittering on its plumed and horsetailed helmets and gleaming cuirasses, gets under way. Von Muraldt's men of the 4th Bavarian Lancers, watching from in front of

Borodino, 'can hardly believe their eyes'. In the van, charging up the highway from the village, are the two glamorous Carabinier regiments. After Semenovskaya had fallen Lariboisière and the artillery staff had retired behind Borodino; and as an infantry column comes by – presumably one of Gérard's – Lariboisière's son Ferdinand comes and shakes his hand, saying "we're going to charge". And a few moments later does so.[28]

In front of the village Labaume and the rest of Eugène's staff, too, are watching the mass onslaught. Von Muraldt notices that at this moment the sun breaks through, flashing on the mass of steel cuirasses:

'The whole eminence overhanging us appeared in an instant a mass of moving iron: the glitter of arms, the sun's rays reflected in the dragoons' helmets and on cuirasses mingled with the guns' flashes vomiting forth death from all sides made it seem like a volcano in the midst of an army.'

Lejeune, too, watching from Napoleon's command post, somewhat farther away, is reminded of a volcano:

'I couldn't be a spectator of these beautiful actions without also seeing it with a painter's eye, admiring the effect of these whirlwinds of dust and silvery smoke. A shell having set fire to a barrel of the resin the Russians use to grease their artillery's axles with, instantly purplish flames, coiling along the ground like the threshings of an irritated snake, rose to join the clouds, projecting broad zones of darkness across the sun. If I live to be a hundred, this moving picture [sic] will never efface itself from my thoughts.'[29]

Immediately, says Griois,

'everything opens up. The numerous cavalry forms up in columns, the II Corps' cuirassiers (they were, as far as I can recall, the 5th Cuirassiers) at their head, start to gallop. Overthrowing everything in front of them, they turn the redoubt, entering it by the throat [sic] and by the place where the earth that had rolled down into the ditches made it easier of access. At the same time the Viceroy, with his infantry, attacks the redoubt from the left.'

As the cavalry assault develops, Eugène's three infantry divisions, led by Gérard's, begins struggling up the slope against a gale of enemy grape. Sergeant Bertrand's 4th Carabinier Company of the 7th Light is

'suffering horribly. A roundshot took my captain's head off, killing or mortally wounding four men in the first rank. The lieutenant takes the captain's place; scarcely is he at his post than he's himself stricken by a piece of grape which shatters his thigh. In the same instant the sous-lieutenant's foot is shattered by another shell fragment. The officers hors de combat, the sergeant-major absent, I, as senior sergeant, take command of the company. We're at the foot of the redoubt, two of the regiment's battalions seem to be retiring by échelons, and the two others making an oblique movement. The colonel orders me not to budge. The reasons for his order are beyond me, but I'm proud to be commanding an élite company. My

musket on my shoulder, facing the redoubt and under grapeshot, I'm speaking to my comrades when suddenly a platoon of Russian dragoons emerges from it with a hurrah.'
Bertrand orders his company to form a circle around him,

'which is done in a flash. Without waiting for further orders my comrades open a rolling fire which costs the horsemen, already almost on our bayonets, dear. They vanish, and thanks to my comrades' presence of mind and courage help reached us. The [Russian cavalry] regiment returned toward the redoubt, but again we were forced to retire.'

But just as the leading division (Wathier's cuirassiers) are about to burst in through the northern throat, they're checked by a devastating volley from a Russian infantry formation, 60 yards to its rear. And Auguste Caulaincourt, at the head of the 5th Cuirassiers,[30] falls from his horse, dead, with a musket-ball just beneath the heart. Simultaneously IV Cavalry Corps, led by Zastrow's cuirassier squadrons, are either forcing their way in through the southern throat or else – like the 5th Cuirassiers – which 'because of their position found themselves facing the redoubt' -

'are crossing the ditch, mounting the gentle embankment and crushing the Russian infantry under the weight of its horses and sabring others, then riding against the supporting infantry beyond.'

Colonel von Meerheimb, in Lorge's cuirassier division, makes for the crumbled breastwork, scrambles in, through, and over the shattered embrasures and finds

'the cramped area inside filled with murderous cavalry and Russian infantry[31] thrown together pellmell and doing their best to throttle and mangle each other'.

In the event the leading files of Eugène's infantry, too, are able to scramble in over the shattered embrasures in the cavalry's wake:

'Major Del Fante, on the Viceroy's staff, at the head of the 9th and the 35th Line, turns the redoubt to its left and despite a valorous defence by the Russians, who are fighting desperately, penetrates it; but since the besieged won't surrender, there's the most terrible carnage. Del Fante himself, recognizing a Russian general – General Likatcheff – in the scrum – throws himself at him, disarms him, snatches him from the fury of the men and, in spite of him, saves his life,'

an exploit for which Eugène commends and promotes Dal Fante on the spot – 'a worthy reward', comments Césare de Laugier, 'that honoured at once the prince and the soldier.'

Looking through his telescope, Berthier declares: 'The redoubt's taken! The Saxons are inside!'

Prince Eugène, watching from his vantage point, is heard to exclaim 'The battle's won!' And the whole Italian army cheers. The Grand Redoubt is taken – but which unit has actually captured it? According to Colonel von Schreckenstein (who, being in the struggle himself, must have heard it from some member of the staff) Napoleon takes 'the same telescope' from Berthier and looking through it declares: 'You're wrong. They're wearing blue, and must be *my* cuirassiers!' apparently forgetting that Laforge's Saxon and Polish cuirassiers also wear blue.

(And so, to the Saxons' and Poles' mortification, the imperial bulletin will determine the matter.)

Still in reserve, the Vistula Legion has halted again. But now it reaches the scene of action. And after the dust has abated somewhat Brandt too sees 'the French had taken the Great Redoubt, and the cavalry were fighting beyond it'. Moving forward in support, Brandt finds scenes around the redoubt that defy description:

> 'Men and horses, alive, mutilated, dead but lying by sixes and eights heaped on top of each other covered the approaches all round, filled the ditch and the work's interior. While we were advancing they were carrying away General Caulaincourt. He passed in front of us, carried by several cuirassiers on a white cuirassier mantle covered with great bloodstains.'

One of the officers who had brought the news of the redoubt's capture and of Auguste Caulaincourt's death is his ADC, Lieutenant Wolbert 'who'd not quitted his side'. Wolbert, says Castellane, 'came up sobbing'. His chief had been laid low, he tells an impassive Napoleon and a distraught Master of the Horse, 'just as he was coming out of the redoubt to pursue the enemy, who'd rallied at some distance and were rallying to retake it'. Ségur sees how Caulaincourt, is

> 'at first overcome, but soon steeled himself, and except for the tears that rolled silently down his cheeks, he appeared impassive. The Emperor said "You've heard the news; would you like to retire?" [or Castellane: "go to my tent"] accompanying these words with a gesture of sympathy. But at that moment we were going towards the enemy. The Master of the Horse merely lifted his hat slightly as a token of his gratitude and refusal.'

'He has died as a brave man should,' Caulaincourt will afterwards remember Napoleon as saying, 'and that is, in deciding the battle. France loses one of her best officers.'

But though the success is spectacular, it has a sinister feature. Almost no prisoners have been taken – 'at most a few Russian cavalrymen during our various charges, but I don't recall seeing a single officer taken prisoner,' a Saxon cuirassier will later recall.

Immediately sending several aides to check up on this worrying fact, Napoleon observes to Berthier: 'These Russians let themselves be killed like automata. There's no taking them alive. This doesn't help us at all. These citadels must be demolished by cannon.' But now, says Ségur,

> 'after the capture of the Great Redoubt he thought he ought to go and see for himself what to do next. I saw him mount his horse

slowly and painfully. It was at that moment the old General Likatcheff, the redoubt's defender, was brought to him.'

Del Fante, his rescuer and captor, has brought him in person, 'together with fifteen other prisoners':

'The officer in charge of them [i.e., Del Fante] told the Emperor that they'd put up a gallant defence. The Emperor received the general well. Seeing his prisoner without his sword, Napoleon regretted that he'd been disarmed: "I respect the courage of the unfortunate too much, monsieur", he said, "not to give myself the pleasure of returning his arms to a brave man."'

Dedem – certainly no eye-witness – says that Likatcheff, 'though in his cups, replied with dignity'. But then something goes wrong. Turning to Del Fante, Napoleon asks for Likatcheff's sword – but is given his ADC's instead. 'He took it in his hand, and holding it out to him said: "Here's your sword."' But according to Soltyk, who's there to interpret,

'The Muscovite replied in a dry tone of voice, shaking his head: *"Niet, niet"*, and persisted in refusing it from the Emperor's hands. A cloud passed over Napoleon's face, and turning to me: "What's he saying?" Having in my turn asked Likatcheff to explain his queer behaviour, he replied that it wasn't his sword, but his ADC's, who'd been captured with him; which I hastened to repeat to the Emperor. But already Napoleon's face had resumed its serenity. He smiled disdainfully, handed the sword back to the French [*sic*] ADC who'd brought him in, and with a gesture ordered the Russian general to be taken away. All this happened in a matter of moments. Only afterwards did I hear Likatcheff had a sword of honour, and didn't want to exchange it for his ADC's.'

In 'a weak and languishing voice' Napoleon tells Ségur

'to take care of him, listen to what he had to say, and then come and report it to him. After which, walking slowly away, he went on, doubtless in the same manner; for ten minutes later I rejoined him at no great distance. All I'd been able to get out of Likatcheff, deeply upset by his defeat, were the following words: "Ah, Monsieur le Général, what a disaster! Do you think your Emperor will let us go on being Russians?" When I repeated these words to the Emperor they made little impression on him, for all their singularity. It's true he'd just heard of the deaths of Caulaincourt and of Canouville, the one the brother of the Master of the Horse, the other of his quartermaster, the former killed by a musket-ball, the other by a piece of grapeshot in the forehead.'

Second-lieutenant *Mailly Nesle*,[32] a 20-year-old aristocrat in the 2nd Carabiniers – being an ADC to General Durosnel (since Witebsk aide-major-général of the cavalry), he hadn't charged with his regiment – is sent by him to General Jeannin, the commander of the Gendarmerie d'Elite, to tell him to get the Surgeon-major to embalm Auguste Caulaincourt's heart.

Although six of the redoubt's heavy pieces, incredibly, had been whipped out of it at the very last moment, not one of the Russian gunners has survived. They'd fought to the death. Not one had abandoned his guns. Inside the redoubt, amidst an incredible wreckage of men, guns and gun carriages,[33] Eugène's ADC Labaume finds

'the body of a Russian gunner decorated with three Crosses. In one hand he held a broken sword, and with the other was convulsively grasping the carriage of the gun he'd so valiantly fought with.'

Heinrich von Brandt, too, notices him – or is it another?

'By the entrance an elderly staff officer was leaning against one of the guns with a gaping head wound. Dead and mutilated men and horses lay six or eight deep. Their corpses covered the whole area at the gorges, filled the ditch and were heaped up inside. Most of the dead along the front of the redoubt were infantrymen. To the right and inside lay the bodies of cuirassiers in white and blue uniforms – Saxon Bodyguards, Zastrow Cuirassiers in yellow and black uniforms, and men from the 5th and, if I'm not mistaken, also the 8th Cuirassier regiments.'

Although the 2nd Cuirassiers, too, have been in the attack, they're one of the regiments which, by-passing the redoubt to its right, have galloped towards 'a line of Russian guns, supported only 60 or 80 metres away by a line of Russian cuirassiers and dragoons'. Sergeant-major Thirion is just wondering why this cavalry doesn't 'move to the front of its artillery to protect it' when his regiment's leading ranks almost come to grief – by tumbling headlong into a deep ravine:

'Typical of the terrain, it prevented us from getting at them. But we gave them proof of our desire to see them at close quarters by going down into the ravine to cross it; but the bottom was so swampy the first horses got stuck in the mud. So we had to get ourselves out again and draw up facing the enemy,'

whose guns are spewing a rolling fire of grape and caseshot at them.

'Rarely, I declare, have I found myself in so hot a spot. Immobile in front of the Russian guns, we see them loading the projectiles they're going to fire at us, can even make out the eye of the pointer who's aiming them at us, and we need a certain dose of sang-froid to stay put. Happily, they aim too high.'

For quite a while Thirion and his steel-clad comrades wait patiently for some infantry to turn up and open a path:

'Finally a Westphalian division puts itself behind us. Separated from the Russians by our two ranks of horses, it imagines itself under cover. But when we, by moving off by platoons to the right, open up a gateway for them to move ahead of us between each platoon, these poor Westphalians, partly recruits, surprised to find themselves so close to thundering guns and to see us making to move off, begin shouting: *"Wir bleiben nicht hier!"* [we're not staying here!], and try to follow our withdrawal, which obliges us to retrace our footsteps to support, or rather comfort, this infantry, at whose heels our horses were marching.'

This pushes the Westphalians down into the ravine,

'where the men's heads are more or less at a level with the terrain in front of them, and thus sheltered from the Russian guns, which can't aim so low. Immediately this infantry opens fire on the artillery and its supporting cavalry. And these troops, 60 metres away from the muskets, have no choice but to make a prompt retreat and are replaced by infantry which skirmish with these Westphalians of ours.'

The 2nd Cuirassiers have just formed up again among the copses when, somewhere behind him, Thirion hears someone plaintively calling out; and together with his adventurous friend Baffcop rides over to see what it can be:

'At the foot of an oak tree we find a young sergeant-major of light infantry who's lost his leg from above the knee and which is only attached to its calf by a little sliver of flesh. This courageous young man tells us he has several times tried to get up and walk, but can't because his foot is so heavy and dragging too painfully at the bit of flesh still attaching his foreleg to his thigh. He insists we shall rid him of this now more than useless limb.'

And so they do, making the best tourniquet they can with handkerchiefs taken from Thirion's knapsack. After fixing the fracture and

'helping the poor fellow to get up, we provided him with two muskets of which he made two crutches and left for the ambulance, saying, "Now I shan't want for courage. I'm saved."'

But Thirion fears he's losing too much blood for lack of a real tourniquet and will never make it. All this is in sad contrast to another death. While the regiment is drawn up there amid the copses, a young conscript falls into a panic and begs Thirion to let him retire,

'assuring me he'd be killed if I didn't. I try to reassure him by placing myself close to him, and more or less succeed. At that moment, exhausted and hungry – I'd eaten nothing since the previous day – I ask one of my comrades for a bit of bread, knowing he still has a little bit on him. He makes haste to share it with me. Just as I'm holding out my arm to take my share, a roundshot takes off my young cuirassier's head: the same shot has hit my left elbow and the bit of bread has fallen to the ground.'

Although his arm hurts dreadfully, Thirion inspects it and finds it's intact. Since it was lower than the poor conscript's head, the flying cannon-ball had passed just above it, and his elbow can only only have been hurt by a bit of his shattered helmet:

'Not wanting to lose my bit of bread, I picked it up on the point of my sword and, finding it soiled by a bit of the dead man's brains, had to remove the wet bit.'

Thirion has often heard of men having presentiments of their own death in battle, but this is the first and only time he'll ever hear a soldier beg to leave his post because he's sure he's going to be killed, and 'if it hadn't been my duty to keep the men in their ranks and encourage the young soldiers I'd have granted this poor young man's prayer'.

Meanwhile a furious artillery duel has begun over the captured redoubt. And very soon what's left of its rear parapet is being carried away 'like a breach'. Not many yards away Claparède's Poles are falling by dozens under the bursting shells and screaming roundshot. Dead and dying alike are being blown to pieces. By and by, though his officers 'naturally awaited death standing', Claparède orders his men to lie down. A grenadier who gets up to help a comrade immediately has his head blown off, spattering brains and blood on Brandt's tunic.[34]

> 'The battery closest to us had lost all its older officers. A very young
> one was commanding it and seemed delighted with his task.'

Oddly enough – very oddly, in view of their having lost so many gunners, dead or dying – not one of the French batteries has been silenced by enemy fire. And all, whenever they can distinguish friend from foe, are firing busily into a vast mass of struggling men, gradually melting away into folds in the terrain. All Brandt can see now is an unsupported line of guns 'stretching away as far as the eye could see'. No wonder Sorbier will afterwards remember the battle as a series of more or less unimpeded leaps forward by his artillery.

Each time that Ney or Murat have begged Napoleon to send in the Guard he has refused: 'I'm not going to have my Guard destroyed. When you're eight hundred leagues from France you don't wreck your last reserve.' But now, after stupendous efforts, the Great Redoubt has been captured; and things on the extreme right aren't going too badly either. Soltyk, in his suite, has seen

> 'a young officer, a Polish artillery lieutenant called Rostworowski,
> coming towards us. He was pale and his coat was covered in blood.
> He could hardly keep his horse. Sent by Poniatowski to Napoleon to
> tell him the village of Utitza had been occupied, one of this brave
> officer's arms had been broken by a musket-ball on the way, and he
> was losing a lot of blood. Yet he'd had the courage to carry out his
> mission. Scarcely had he arrived at the ambulance to have his wound
> attended to than he fainted.'

Various small trophies have also been brought in:

> 'A detachment of Polish cuirassiers brought a gun their regiment
> had captured. But these events were of secondary importance and
> had in no way drawn the great man's attention.'

What absorbs him now – Pion des Loches sets the time at 'about 4 p.m.' – is the state of affairs in the centre. And Napoleon mounts his third horse to ride forward and study the situation on the spot. After the Likatcheff incident von Roos sees him and his entourage as they approach from the rear and slowly cross the ravine where he has his first-aid station:

'This seemed to us to indicate that he was calm and satisfied. As yet we hadn't learnt to read those severe features which in all circumstances, no matter what, would always seem to us calm and cold.'

While on his way to a dressing-station – perhaps the same, perhaps not – Vossler, too, after having been hit by a ricochet on his 'helmet's brass chinscale and knocked unconscious', sees him, 'somewhat cold and aloof'.

Meanwhile, on the plateau beyond Semenovskaya, a new and final struggle has started up – a huge and confused cavalry battle. At one moment the Saxon Life Guards go dashing after some Russian dragoons and past scattered Russian infantry who are taking pot-shots at them: and Lieutenant Roth von Schreckenstein, in the thick of it, sees how their colonel can't restrain them:

'I'd almost reached that part of the Saxon Life Guard regiment which was gradually giving up its pursuit of the Russian cavalry when my horse fell back, pierced by several case-shot bullets, fired from somewhere to my left. I looked around for another horse, but the ones nearest me had been wounded. One Russian horse which I did mount refused to move, even when I clapped spurs to it; so I was on the point of moving off on foot, pistol in hand, without really knowing which way to flee. I saw enemies on all sides, either because of an illusion due to fear or because they were really there.'

But again and again the cavalry divisions, with musket-balls 'screeching like rockets around their ears' find themselves up against unshakeable Russian squares. In ever-thickening dust clouds 'and hordes of riderless horses neighing with terror and with streaming manes among the dead and wounded' the struggle goes on and on. Inconclusively. For two more hours.

And still, unknown to the French, the Russians have a large, as yet unemployed artillery reserve. Its commander having been killed, it still hasn't fired a shot.

Neither do the cavalry's attacks and counter-attacks seem to be getting anywhere. At about 5 p.m. Captain Henri Beyle (Stendhal), no doubt well in the rear, out of cannon-shot and amid the baggage train, hears a certain Count Corner, 'a goodhearted man, twice decorated by Napoleon', say: 'Isn't this damnable battle ever going to end?'

But in fact it's dying away of its own accord. 'Only the guns kept firing.' By 6.30 or so a kind of stunned stupor seems to have fallen on both armies.

To straighten their front line, badly mauled but forming an exposed salient on its left, the Russians fall back some 1,500 metres, on to their second. Although 'His Majesty immediately set off at a gallop in front of the [Guard] cavalry to join the King of Naples in following up this success,' the French are in reality too utterly exhausted to pursue:

'The Emperor flattered himself that the Russians were going to hasten their retreat. In order to make out their movements he went with the sharpshooters. Balls whistled around him; but he'd ordered his escort to stay behind. "It's over," [he tells Caulaincourt. And adds considerately:] "Go and wait for me at headquarters." I thanked him, but remained with him. The Emperor was certainly running a great risk, as the fusillade became so lively that the King of Naples and several generals came hurrying up to urge him to retire.'

Although he wants to make a final effort to take the last remaining (third) Russian flèche and a fieldwork commanding the Moscow road, Berthier and Murat try to dissuade him. Besides it's too late in the day. Too many commanding officers have been killed. The Russians,

'though certainly retreating, were doing so in good order and showing an inclination to dispute every inch of the ground, irrespective of how much havoc our guns were wreaking in their ranks.'

Berthier and Murat also stress that

'the only chance of success would be to use the Old Guard, and that in the present circumstances success at such a price would really be a check, whilst failure would be a reverse that would counterbalance the entire success of the battle. The Emperor hesitated; then went forward once more to observe the enemy's movements for himself.'[34]

Caulaincourt, impressed by the 'determined mien of the freshly massing Russians', sees

'the Emperor come to a decision. He suspended the order to attack and contented himself with sending up supports, in case the enemy should attempt something fresh, unlikely as it was; for their losses too were immense. Nightfall put an end to the fighting. Both sides were so tired that in several places the firing ceased without any orders being given.'[35]

As dusk falls, Murat, afraid that his remaining cavalry won't even be up to resuming the battle, has recourse to a *ruse de guerre*. The shattered divisions – Thirion's is one of them – are ordered

'to mount, with a loud din of its trumpets, and when he passed along our front the cries of "Vive l'Empereur!" were to be as loud and strong as if it had been Napoleon himself who was in front of us. Never was real enthusiasm noisier! The aim: to make the enemy believe it was the Emperor who was there with the main body. Afraid we were going to attack them tomorrow, they wouldn't think of attacking.'

By now it's quite dark. A cold damp north wind is blowing over the wreckage of two shattered armies, the thousands of dead and dying. Shocked and shaken in a way they've never been before, the survivors know in their bones that the sacrifice has been in vain. The battle has been neither won nor lost. Which, 3,000 miles from France, is almost as bad as a defeat: 'This victory, instead of arousing any general rejoicing, filled us with grim forebodings.' Half of Vossler's 180 Prussian hussars have been killed or wounded. And he's only one of the many who realize that 'the Russians had withdrawn defeated, but by no means routed'.

During the battle von Muraldt's servant has found him a cow and prepared him a good dinner. But he finds he can't enjoy it. Even the normally sanguine Le Roy is 'so depressed' he can't 'swallow my dram of aquavit' – whether of the French or Russian variety, he doesn't say; but the flèches are strewn with Russian corpses, which Biot sees the French infantrymen 'disembarrassing of the bad brandy in their water-bottles.' Trying some 'of this terrible beverage' himself, he finds 'the pepper and vitriol tore your mouth off'.

Even the bloodsoaked acres that have been gained at such terrible expense are so thickly strewn with dead and wounded men and horses, debris and roundshot, it's virtually impossible to bivouac on them. And many units – for instance the Red Lancers, who haven't come under fire – are retiring behind the Kolotchka. Particularly shocking to Dumonceau as he rides back in the gloaming are the huge numbers of dead and dying horses:

'Some were complaining dolorously or, with no more than a breath of life left in them, giving their death-rattles, every now and again twisting themselves under some convulsive impression. One saw some which, though horribly disembowelled or mutilated, yet kept their legs, motionless, with hanging heads, drenching the ground with their blood, or else, straying painfully about in search of some grazing, dragging beneath them strips of shattered harness, intestines or a broken limb; or else lying stretched out at full length on the ground, now and then lifting their heads to look at their gaping wounds.'

The whole atmosphere is

'in tune with these lugubrious scenes. Sombre clouds spread a melancholy shadow over the plain which that morning had been so filled with uproar, so animated, but was now grim and silent. A few rare cannon-shots were still being exchanged in the distance, but these were only feeble partial engagements, among the dead, strewn all over the battlefield as far as the eye could see.'

The Belgian lancer captain's attention is specially captured by

'a Spanish or Portuguese sergeant, on account of his fine martial air. He seemed to have been shot in the middle of an access of hilarity and his features still bore the impression of it.'

On the fringe of the wood beyond the Schevardino redoubt Dumonceau's servant Jean, too, has as usual prepared him his dinner. Also 'a good bed of moss and leaves with its back comfortably against a tree trunk facing a great flaming fire'. Seen from here

'the army, like the enemy, seemed to have disappeared over the horizon. All we could see now were a few cavalry units on patrol to our right and, at the limit of the plain, facing us, a vast stretch of forest.'

Nearby, the Imperial Guard, bivouacked around its camp fires, is massed around the Emperor's tents. Lejeune sees all five of them have been raised

'at the foot of the field of battle. No doubt this was a token of victory. But the Russian army was still only a musket-shot away from us, and all our superior officers should have been taking measures to be able to begin again. Soon the night became very black, and little by little we saw too many fires being lit on either side not to give us serious preoccupations about another day's fighting on the morrow.'

Having replenished his ammunition and promoted new NCOs, Colonel Griois takes a walk over the battlefield. Most of all he's struck by the numbers of dead Russian cuirassiers:

'The resources of our ambulances, considerable as these were, didn't suffice, and the French wounded had to be given preference. Such wounded Russians as I saw, overcome by their sufferings and by the cold of the night, made no complaint. Nearly every wounded soldier was clasping a medallion or image of St Nicholas, which they kissed eagerly and this helped them to forget their pain.'

Every house still standing is packed with wounded, French and Allied. Labaume sees 'Borodino church, which stood alone and where everyone wanted to camp, filled with wounded whose limbs the surgeons had amputated'. Here as elsewhere wounded highs-ups and other privileged persons are getting priority treatment. And in the darkness Girod de l'Ain – luckily, though he's been as much in the thick of it as Ney himself, he hasn't suffered a scratch,[36] – finds his way back to General Dessaix's bivouac:

'In the midst of his own people and patiently supporting the pains from his wound, he immediately ordered me to draw up the report he had to send in to Davout, and signed it with his left hand.'

Although the spent roundshot which had stricken Davout's chief-of-staff in the lumbar region has left 'no exterior trace', inside, General Romoef – he whose style when writing to divisional generals on the eve of battle was so chivalrous and elegant – is a horrible mess. Larrey realizes the muscles are 'torn and reduced to a mush, the coxal bone and the corresponding lumbar vertebrae broken'. As he attends to him and other top brass he's thinking 'it's impossible to show more valour and courage than these honorable victims'.

At 10 p.m. Planet comes back to a 'tent the gunners had most artistically made of planks for Lariboisière' behind Borodino village. Inside he's horrified to find young Ferdinand lying there groaning. A few moments after he'd come and shaken his father's hand,

'he'd been hit by a mustket-ball while charging down the main Smolensk–Moscow road. After passing through his cuirass and whole body it had lodged itself between his flanks above the kidney.'

Ferdinand has had to wait before being picked up and brought here. Yvan, the Emperor's surgeon, has extracted the missile; but the pain of the operation was and is agonizing. And now he's running a dangerously high temperature.

Yet he's privileged, even so. Where the rank and file are concerned, Lejeune sees

'the wretched wounded dragging themselves toward Kolotskoië, where Baron Larrey had set up his ambulance. Those for whom there were means of being picked up were being carried there. In no time there was an immense number. But everything was lacking at once.'

Captain Francois, among the thousands being taken there – always on the principle 'officers first' – finds himself in the company of

'27 officers from our regiment, five of them amputated, lying on straw or on the floor, lacking absolutely everything. Every room was full of wounded,'

– altogether more than 10,000, he thinks. As for the rest of the 30th's casualties 'they're up there in the redoubt'. In the 7th Light, Sergeant Bertrand's carabiniers have come and presented him with a 'certificate, declaring what I'd done during the battle'. Unlike so many comrades he's counting himself lucky to have got off with a light musket wound in his shoulder 'thanks to the buckle of my pack', when suddenly, though the fighting is over, a musket-ball out of the dark knocks off his shako and kills 'a sergeant, my compatriot, dead. We weren't slow to discover the assassins, hidden in a big hole in the middle of a little ravine. We did justice on them with two balls and our bayonets.'

Lieutenant Maurice Tascher, also miraculously untouched, is spending the night carrying water to the wounded. At one moment he's startled to see a half-buried Russian getting out of his grave. All sorts of gruesome things are happening in the cold wet windy night. Other Russians are roaming about in the darkness. When Colonel von Meerheimb, of the Saxon Guard, who'd been surrounded and knocked unconscious at the storming of the Great Redoubt, comes to, he realizes he's being plundered by some of his Russian colleagues. Fortunately, a French-speaking officer and an elderly grey-haired Russian cuirassier intervene and drive them away:

'The old man bound up my head with a cloth, lifted me on to a second horse, took it by the bridle, and led me carefully and patiently through a birch copse. Whenever he met any of the armed peasants who constituted a reserve militia for transporting, escorting and guarding prisoners, he always made a detour, explaining that it was dangerous to fall into their hands. I became very weak and could barely keep myself up in the saddle. But he kept telling me not to lose heart and frequently called out *Hauptquartieru nie daleku!* which meant, as I later discovered, that headquarters wasn't very far away. He seemed to take special pleasure in my helmet, which he'd taken as booty. The good man probably believed it was made of gold and would ensure him a carefree existence in old age.'

Taken to a Russian field ambulance, Meerheimb is cared for by a Swiss surgeon named Bernhardt, together with many wounded Russian officers.

In the middle of the night Brandt's Poles, too, are attacked, this time by some Cossacks. But they're on the *qui vive* and give them a hot reception. Later still Cuirassier-captain Bréaut des Marlots speaks for about two hours with a Russian flag of truce:

'We asked each other what we thought about the war. "We know as well as you do we're going to be beaten," he said. "All we're hoping for is salvation in the winter which will amplify your troubles. Winter and hunger will be the arms against which your courage will give in. Believe me, I know my country's climate, I hope it won't have any malignant effect on you personally."'

As for the Great Redoubt, a Cossack patrol probing about in the darkness is surprised to find it's been abandoned.[37]

At 11 p.m. Napoleon calls for an orderly officer. It's Lejeune's turn. He finds that everyone at IHQ is in 'a heavy sleep. Three hours before daybreak he sent for me and said: "Go and find the Viceroy. Reconnoitre the Russian line to his front with him and come back at once and tell me what's going on."'

It's 8 September.

CHAPTER 22

THE BUTCHER'S BILL

'This theatre of carnage' – Dutheillet misses his Cross – 'Honour his ashes' – an obstinate rearguard – 'The Emperor was very thoughtful and worried' – Dedem distributes brandy – 'Only the Emperor's pen and mallet make themselves heard' – Lejeune's unwelcome promotion – miseries of the wounded – Planat tots up figures – 'he was hardly eighteen years old' – one barrel of flour for 26 wounded generals

Next morning 'under a leaden sky and a cold rain driven by a violent wind' Napoleon rides out over the battlefield. Ségur is in his suite. Slowly they ride over the terrain. It's so thickly strewn with corpses[1] that

'it was impossible, no matter how careful one was, always to walk one's horse on the ground. The Emperor, I saw, was still ill, and the only animated gesture I saw him make was of irritation. One of our horses, striking one of these victims, had drawn a groan from him, alas it was I who'd caused it. Upon one of us remarking that the dying man was a Russian, the Emperor retorted: "There are no enemies after a victory!" and immediately had Roustam pick the man up and give him to drink from his own brandy flask which the mameluke always carried on him.'

Passing at the charred ruins of Semenovskaya, they see how

'the whole ploughed up plain, strewn with wreckage and debris and hemmed in by gloomy dark trees, conspired to give the field a dreadful aspect. Everywhere soldiers were wandering about among the corpses, rifling their dead comrades' packs for food. Russian musketballs were bigger than ours so the wounds of the fallen were terrible. The Russian wounded sat stoically clutching their St Nicholas' crosses as they'd done at Smolensk, or else tried to hobble away in the wake of the Russian army. The Emperor carefully examined every bit of the battlefield, each corps' positions, their movements, the difficulties they'd had to surmount. At each point he asked for minute details of everything that had happened. Arriving at the second flèche, he noticed some 60 or 80 men, with four or five officers. Astonished to find these men still standing there when the rest of the troops had gone on ahead, he asked the officer in charge, an old campaigner, why he was there.

"I've been ordered to stay here," was the answer. "Rejoin your regiment," said the Emperor.

"It's here," replied the officer, pointing to the redoubt's approaches and ditches. Not understanding what he meant, the Emperor asked again:

"I want to know where your regiment is. You must join up with it."

"It's here!" the officer replied, pointing to the same spots, and betraying his own annoyance at the Emperor's failure to comprehend him.'

Only when a young subaltern explains does he understand. The battalions, unable to hold the redoubt they'd stormed so impetuously, had been wiped out. Labaume too is inspecting the battlefield. Everywhere he sees
> 'mounds of wounded, and the little spaces where there weren't any were covered with debris of arms, lances, helmets or cuirasses, or by cannon-balls as numerous as hailstones after a violent storm.'[2]

But the most terrible sight of all is the interior of the ravines. The wounded who have crawled there to avoid further exposure are
> 'piled up on top of each other, lacking all succour and swimming in their own blood, groaning terribly. Begging to be allowed to die, they asked us to put a term to their horrible sacrifice. There weren't enough ambulances. There was nothing anyone could do for them.'

As Napoleon enters the Great Redoubt, Bausset notices how 'two of our party, yielding to a very natural grief, aren't following him. 'Tears in their eyes, M. de Caulaincourt and M. de Canouville turned away from the spot that contained the glorious remains of their brothers.' For quite a while Lieutenant Brandt, who's still standing nearby, can observe the Emperor, 'his eyes fixed on this theatre of carnage', at close quarters. On his calling over one of his suite and saying something to him,
> 'this officer at once went into the redoubt with some chasseurs, whom he arranged in a square, so as to circumscribe a little area within which they counted the dead. The same manoeuvre was repeated at various points; and I realized that by this sort of mathematical operation they were trying to get an approximate idea of the number of victims. During this time the Emperor's face remained impassive, only he was very pale.'

The butcher's bill is horrendous. In a letter to his *belle amie* in Paris – a letter the Cossacks will capture – the 25th Line's clothing officer, a certain Lieutenant Paradis, writes with pardonable exaggeration: 'I've counted 20 Russians dead for each Frenchman. The battles of Austerlitz, Iéna, Eckmühl and Wagram didn't come up to this.' The Russian army has certainly lost a third of its effectives. And on the French side some 30,000 men haven't survived to tell their grandchildren they've been at the great battle 'under the walls of Moscow'.

Never have so many generals been killed in a battle. Inspector of Reviews Deniée, totting up the losses, finds among the casualties no fewer than 49 generals – fourteen generals of division, 33 generals of brigade, 37 colonels,[3] 37 staff officers and 86 ADCs.

The cavalry's losses are especially disastrous. In Maurice Tascher's chasseur regiment 280 men had mounted their horses at dawn yesterday. But after standing motionless for eight hours being slaughtered by cannon-fire it has lost ten officers and 87 troopers killed, wounded or dismounted. Heinrich von Roos sees Vossler's regiment ride by – reduced to three officers and 20 men. As Vossler confirms:

'Of the 180 men the regiment had been able to muster that morning half were either dead or wounded. The general commanding our division, General Waltier, and the brigadier of our brigade, as well as their seconds-in-command, had all been wounded and another senior divisional staff officer killed.'

Losses in the infantry regiments are no less appalling. The 7th Light's carabinier company reports 37 men killed, wounded or missing. Many units are all but wiped out. Dutheillet's heroic 57th has lost

'almost 1,400 men, 600 already having been put out of action on 5 September. More than 50 of its officers had been killed or wounded; the colonel had had two horses killed under him.'

Of all the army corps Junot's Westphalians are among the worst hit. Initially 17,000 men and 3,500 horses strong at the Niemen, by nightfall, having lost 59 NCOs and soldiers killed, 580 wounded, five more officers killed – including the officer commanding its infantry, 'a magnificent soldier, a benevolent commander and a gentleman in the real sense of the word' – it has dwindled to a mere 1,300 combatants.

Montbrun's death seems in some way to strike everyone as quite specially ominous – perhaps because it doesn't even figure in the imperial bulletin? Instead it's Auguste Caulaincourt who's been singled out to be the hero of the occasion. Whether to console his grief-stricken brother or because he meant it, Napoleon told him the previous evening: 'He was my best cavalry officer. He had a quick eye and he was brave. By the end of the campaign he'd have replaced Murat.' Once again it's Lejeune who has to arrange the funeral:

'When I climbed up the Great Redoubt to check up on the state of the position which had so occupied us the day before, I found our men working on the burial of their numerous comrades and officers. Caulaincourt was placed in the middle of their entrenchment and I placed the brave Vasserot beside him. All one side of his face had been carried away without destroying or even changing the animated expression on the other part, which still seemed to be ordering his men to fire: "Friends, follow me! We'll be victorious!" I had these two bodies covered with a great number of pieces of the wreckage of armaments, muskets, cuirasses, as I'd already done for General Gudin.'

But Montbrun has many personal friends. And one of them, old Marshal Lefèbvre, commanding the Guard infantry, has a wooden noticeboard erected to honour this man whom Vossler describes as his

'dear and gracious general, a man as kind and considerate to his subordinates as he'd been brave in war, and who, though he'd won all his decorations in battle, had yet miraculously escaped being wounded until the day of his death.'

The noticeboard, 'a rough board, erected on a staff, bore a monumental inscription in his honour, written in ink, after the hurry of the day was over':[4]

HERE LIES GEN MONTBRUN
PASSER-BY OF WHATEVER NATION,
HONOUR HIS ASHES.
THEY ARE THE REMAINS OF
ONE OF THE BRAVEST OF THE BRAVE,
OF GENERAL MONTBRUN.
THE DUKE OF DANZIG
MARSHAL OF FRANCE
HAS ERECTED THIS MODEST MONUMENT IN HIS HONOUR.
HIS MEMORY WILL LIVE FOR EVER IN THE HEARTS
OF THE GRAND ARMY.

Other survivors are interring less illustrious, if not less well-liked comrades. Von Muraldt and his fellow-Bavarians, despite the Russian gunners having aimed too high, have suffered such losses and their 'officers are so exhausted' that they find they're being commanded by the brigade sergeant-major (von Muraldt himself is astounded to hear he's one of six in his regiment who've been recommended for the Cross, 'a distinction the more flattering as I was its youngest subaltern'). It is dreadful for them to have to bury

'the mangled remains of our sergeant-major, whom we'd all been so fond of. At dawn we dug a hole and laid his mangled corpse in it, which we after some difficulty had found on the battlefield – an honour admittedly not accorded to many of the innumerable dead lying scattered in this area.'

Although certainly no necrophile, Boulart too takes a look over the terrible field:

'The ground was piled high, it was hard to move without stepping on corpses, the ground was so thick with them. Between the redoubts, the lines of battle, whole squares were traced by the dead or wounded left there.'

The dead at least are at rest. For the thousands of wounded there's only suffering. An anonymous officer is appalled to see how there's

'virtually no sanitary service or activity. All the villages and houses close to the Moscow road were packed full with wounded in an utterly helpless state. The villages were destroyed by endless fires which ravaged the regions occupied or traversed by the French army. Those wounded who managed to save themselves from the flames crawled in their thousands along the high road, seeking some way to prolong their pitiful existence.'

Dr Réné Bourgeois is horrified to see that there is

'no real ambulance equipment, no pharmacy where one could obtain the means of preparing the wounded for their operations or assure their success. On the battlefield the surgeons had to rip up the wounded men's own clothes for bandages to give them first aid, after which they remained all jumbled up and heaped together with several thousand others.'

'Nothing was sadder than other aspects of this battlefield,' Lejeune concludes,

'covered with groups busy picking up 20,000 wounded and taking from the dead such little food as might be left in their knapsacks. The wretched wounded were dragging themselves toward Kolotskoië, where Baron Larrey had set up his ambulance. Those for whom there were means of being picked up were being carried there. In no time there was an immense number. But everything was lacking at once, and they perished, victims of hunger, regretting they hadn't suffered the same fate as those whom death had carried off immediately.'

After Larrey has checked up on the condition of his top-brass patients in the Schevardino Redoubt, Compans and Teste want to get away from there as fast as ever they can – somewhat naturally, since of the 'fourteen of us closely packed in this little redoubt the previous evening, next morning after M. Larrey had been ordered by the Emperor to visit wounded generals, we found ourselves surrounded by twelve corpses.'

Once again everyone is astounded at the enemy's orderly retreat. While realizing that the Russians have 'had no option but to leave many wounded on the battlefield' Colonel Roth von Schreckenstein is 'of the opinion any other army would have left twice as many'. 'A very small number of stragglers had been rounded up; the enemy hadn't abandoned so much as a cart. The enemy had taken with them most of their wounded and we had only a few prisoners, twelve guns from the redoubt plus three or four other pieces taken during our troops' initial assault. The Russians had shown the utmost tenacity. Their ranks hadn't broken. Never had ground been attacked with greater fury or skill, or more stubbornly defended.'

And still, six miles away to the east, can be heard the obstinate rumble of Russian guns.

After completing his survey of the battlefield, Napoleon, with Caulaincourt as usual at his heels, 'galloped off to the advance guard'. Consisting of two cuirassier divisions, several light cavalry regiments and – as always – what had been Friant's infantry, it's advancing slowly through the big forest between Borodino and Mojaisk. On the 'cold windswept battlefield', meanwhile, Colonel Boulart has has taken refuge from this 'first attack of the bad season under my wagon, or rather, in my tent'. There he's sharing a meagre breakfast with d'Hautpoul ('who, though accustomed to a much better one, adapted to it very well') and he's just giving Berthier's ADC some scraps of useful information when the two of them have 'a moment of emotion'. Away to the right a Cossack 'Hurrah!' is heard.

Colbert's combined lancer brigade, 'diagonally traversing the battle-field, which was like a desert' and where 'only a few ambulance wagons were busy picking up the wounded and others were being used to carry away a vast quantity of weapons which had been collected', also hear a rumour that a *coup de main* has been attempted against imperial head-quarters, causing the Guard to spring to arms. Alarm over, the Dutch and Polish Lancers resume their way onwards through the 'cold foggy weather' toward Mojaisk, crossing as they do so the scene of Poniatowski's action. 'Not very many dead,' Dumonceau notes, 'and they much scat-tered, compared with what I'd seen on the main part of the battlefield'.[5]

To judge from the distant rumbling of the guns the Russian rearguard is putting up a stiffer resistance than anyone has thought possible.

Friant's division, now shrunk to only two brigades, is still under Murat's orders. Friant himself being *hors de combat* his command has temporarily passed to General Dufour. They've set out in the early hours. And I Corps' other units are following on behind.

Never a man to stay long in the dumps, Le Roy is finding the cool night air is helping him forget his 'sad reflections on the ambition and vanity of conquerors'. At the same time Dutheillet is surprised to find that the excitement of battle, combined with his superiors' praises and his com-rades' esteem, is curing him of his 'dysentery'. Best of all he's been rec-ommended for a full lieutenancy and the Cross. By 10 a.m. the 57th, too, are under arms:

> 'Each of us is expecting the Emperor, when an adjutant comes to tell our general we're to gulp down our soup and follow the army's movement. So we pocket our ambition until the next opportunity and follow on as cheerfully as may be.'

As usual the 7th Hussars are in the van. The Russian rearguard's sharp-shooters, Victor Dupuy notices, are gradually reducing their fire when

> 'a musket-ball, striking the boss of Colonel Gobrecht's horse, rico-cheted and struck me on the tip of my right elbow. I felt a very sharp pain, but it was nothing, the skin was hardly broken. But my right arm turned completely black.'

At first Griois, emerging from the 'broad and well-maintained road through the vast forest of pines and birches' which it's taking III Cavalry Corps almost two hours to cross, assumes that Mojaisk, lying on the River Moskova in the centre of a vast 'pronouncedly sloping plain, criss-crossed by ravines', will be a walkover. A view evidently shared by Murat. For with-out properly reconnoitring the terrain, but supporting his gravely dimin-ished squadrons with Griois' gunfire, he throws them forward – only to have them brought up short by some ravines, which force them to retrace their steps under almost point-blank Russian grapeshot:

> 'The cavalry lost a lot of men in this affair. That of III [Cavalry] Corps, though only in the second line, suffered from the artillery fire it was constantly exposed to.'[6]

But orders are orders. And Mojaisk is to be occupied before nightfall 'because the Emperor wishes to establish himself there'. And now Boulart's guns, too, are moving up, with orders to 'to go and take up position a mile and a half away, toward Mojaisk'. But Mojaisk is proving surprisingly hard to take. Although Dedem's two regiments manage to lodge four voltigeur companies in its suburbs, the Russians are clinging on stubbornly while they evacuate as many as possible of their wounded.

But now night is falling, and Boulart is told to wait until 'daybreak to attack the heights beyond the town'. And Ségur, sent forward no doubt to set up 'the Palace' in the little town, is returning, mission not accomplished, when he narrowly misses being hit by a bouncing roundshot. He's just exchanging some words with Marshal Mortier when he sees

'a solitary person, on foot, in a grey overcoat, on the other side of the road. Head down, he was walking painfully toward Mojaisk. Crossing the road and placing myself in front of him, I observed that it was on fire. Slowly raising his head, he replied: "So the Russians are still holding out in Mojaisk?" Daylight was just coming to an end, and I pointed out to him the camp fires of some 40,000 men, behind the town and dominating it. The Emperor, in a voice as languishing as his whole posture, swung round heavily, as it were all in one piece, and said to me: "If that's the way of it, let's wait until tomorrow!"'[7]

With the same tired dejected air ['abattement de démarche'] Napoleon goes back to spend the night in a ruined village called Ukarino, on the forest fringe, 'at the point where the plain opens out in front of Mojaisk'. But when the Guard turns up, it finds Ukarino (or is Deniée right in thinking its name is Starokowno?) already occupied by the 23rd Dragoons who have spent the dreary day 'picking up leaves and cutting pine branches' to give their horses something to eat. After leaving the battlefield at 4 p.m. they're just settling down for the night in the village when the Guard 'which so far hadn't fired a shot' comes and ejects them. 'We were irritated with them and they had to resort to force to make us leave the village; not that they'd profit from it very long,' Auvray adds with relish, 'because it caught fire on all sides'.

Meanwhile a 'hurricane of snow' has suddenly begun to fall. And when Colbert's lancers, too, reach their appointed bivouac they refuses to share their 'sad camp fires' with a regiment of Saxon cuirassiers, even though it was they who'd stormed the Great Redoubt.

At IHQ, with the first light snow whirling around Ukarino's log dwellings, everyone is noticing the Emperor is

'very thoughtful and worried. Yet he kept saying "Peace lies in Moscow. When the great nobles see us master of their capital they'll think twice before fighting on. The battle will open my brother Alexander's eyes, and the capture of Moscow will open his nobles'."'

At the same time he's sure yesterday's battle, unparalleled in his or anyone else's experience, won't

'have any result beyond allowing him to gain further ground. The prospect of entering Moscow still enticed him; but even that wouldn't be conclusive as long as the Russian army remained intact.'
And that's the hard fact of the matter, which won't go away. Though he and Berthier have hardly been on speaking terms since their tiff, five days ago, over Narbonne's carriage, since the battle he's spoken to no one else:
'From what the Prince told me, he kept repeating that a large number of men had been killed to no real purpose. No prisoners, no booty – that was what chiefly vexed him and formed the constant burden of his complaints. The state of affairs in Spain, too, was weighing him down just when those in Russia were so far from satisfactory, and he was deeply preoccupied. The condition of the various corps he'd seen was deplorable. All were sadly reduced in strength. His victory had cost him dear. One moment he was imagining signing a peace on the spot, which would give some indication of his victory. The next he wanted to go on to Moscow, stay there a week, then retire on Smolensk.'
But Caulaincourt and Berthier, once again, are agreed: the only thing to do is to quit Moscow 48 hours after entering it and go back to Witebsk.

Although the cold night is marked by 'some sustained firing', Dedem, in the outskirts of Mojaisk, is waiting for dawn to carry out his mission. 'As soon as daylight revealed our bivouacs, a masked battery opened fire from the cemetery'. Hearing Dedem's musketry at first glimmer of daylight (7 a.m.) Boulart's gunners, too, run to their pieces – though as yet they can only see 300 or 400 metres ahead of them, 'only the town, no enemy'. Only to find the Russians have
'retired during the night; their rearguard was still visible on the high ground beyond the town, being followed by our scouts'.
After what Fain calls 'quite a sharp action', Dufour's division advances in two columns, which join up and occupy the town. Part of it is in flames. But not all. And Dedem is happy to find the fire hasn't yet reached 'a big store of brandy' which, despite 'a swarm of Cossacks caracoling about the place', he promptly distributes
'to the advance guard's various units, even though some of Berthier's aides, as usual, had come to order it to be reserved for the Imperial Guard'.
After enjoying their share in the Mojaisk ravine his division debouches on to the plateau beyond the town, and after a mile and a half's march finds itself faced with an 'enemy rearguard in line of battle', whose guns are shelling the burning town to give the Russian baggage train time to draw off. Even so, they're having to abandon 'large numbers of their wounded, both from the battle and from this new action', to perish in the flames in Mojaisk's streets and gardens.
One of the first staff officers to enter Mojaisk with the light cavalry patrols is Planat de la Faye. He has an urgent errand. Not merely to find a

house where the artillery staff can do its paperwork – always immense after a battle – but which can also provide shelter for poor young Ferdinand:

> 'We'd brought him with us, carried in a litter by four gunners. Just as I was writing up General Lariboisière's name on the door of a house in Mojaisk's first side street on the right a shell fell close to me. I just had time to fling myself inside the house – and the shell exploded, but hurt no one.'

What it has done, however, is scatter his competitors, who are

> 'snatching lodgings from each other. Many ADCs were getting so violent towards one another that anywhere else it'd have ended in duels. The house was very small and rather dirty. But to us, compared with the places we'd lain down in these last few days, and above all with our cold bivouacs at Borodino, it seemed a palace. Ferdinand was given a little room to himself and confided to the cares of our surgeon, a man called Gudolle – quite a good sort of a fellow, but a terrible chatterbox who, I fancy, knew very little.'[8]

Surgeon Trastour, too, working heroically for his wounded, has arrived with Compans, in his carriage, and Teste in his calèche, and manages to find them quarters in a house where Friant, Dessaix and many other wounded generals have already installed themselves.

In the main square, on the left-hand side, is 'a new house, not quite completed, which the palace quartermaster had noticed on reaching the square. It hadn't any doors, but the windows could be closed'. But it has stoves that can be lit. And this, in view of Napoleon's ever-worsening cold, decides the matter. Occupying the upper storey at noon, 'no sooner has he settled into this lodging than he wants to resume the office work, suspended for the past five days'. But here's a contretemps:

> 'He'd lost his voice completely. In this embarrassing situation he had recourse to his pen. Resigning himself to it, he sat down and began covering sheets of paper with all the orders teeming in his head. His secretaries, Méneval and Fain, the office vassals, d'Albe, Mounier and Ponthon[9] copy at top speed.'

Even Daru and Berthier have to lend a hand,

> 'but at every line we're held up by some difficulty of decipherment. Yet the Emperor, who minute by minute is finishing one order after another, bangs unceasingly on the table for us to come and take the drafts that are piling upon it.'

Whatever Dr Yvan may say about the usual effects of his bladder complaint, it's obvious that neither his energy nor his clarity of mind are suffering:

> '"Reconnoitre the town and trace out a redoubt to cover the defile" – "Have two bridges built over the Moskova river" – "Write to Eugène, ordering him to go to Rouza and build bridges at Sergiewo" – "Collect plenty of cattle and victuals" – "Tell Ney to come here

tomorrow with his corps" – "Leave the Duke of Abrantès to guard the battlefield.'"

Fain scribbles and scribbles. Even the French bishops aren't forgotten. They're to

'have Te Deums sung for the victory! The whole day passes in these silent labours, where only Napoleon's pen and mallet make themselves heard.'

As always after a great battle numberless promotions have to be approved, at all levels. His chief-of-staff Ramoef having died under the surgeon's knife, Davout has asked for Lejeune to succeed him,

'news which would have flattered anyone else but which I found utterly distasteful. I insisted the Major-General shouldn't follow up this request. But that same evening the Emperor had the commission given to me, signed by himself, and I could only obey. I found the Marshal in his tent on the Moscow road.'

But before Lejeune can take up his new and, as he rightly fears, onerous duties, he has some other writing to do. And goes up into a house

'whose street and courtyard were choc-a-bloc with wounded horses which, though still alive, couldn't get to their feet. When I came down an hour later I was astonished to find all these horses had been dismembered, and their flesh in great part removed. It was the first time we'd seen the men eating horse flesh'

– men from the 23rd Dragoons perhaps, who're beginning to be 'without clothes, without shoes, and without food. Those days we were reduced to eating uncooked cabbages and horse.' But Lejeune goes off to join Davout's headquarters on the Moscow road. One of his colleagues on Berthier's staff has also been promoted. Among the many colonels either dead or *hors de combat* is Colonel Massy, of the 4th Line. Berthier, Fézensac says, was always good to his ADCs.

Up in his first-storey room overlooking the main square, where the Old Guard infantry is bivouacked, Napoleon – however inadequately – is first and foremost occupied with making arrangements for the wounded. A Colonel Bourmont is to remain behind to see to it that they're all picked up. Bourmont will have to search for food for fifteen miles around. And it'll take Dr Réné Bourgeois a whole week and more to help him collect them all,

'both French and Russian, for whom there was, even so, no ambulance equipment and no pharmacy where one could obtain the means of preparing the wounded for their operations or assuring their success.'

There's also a grave shortage of surgical instruments: 'these instruments existed and could have been used, had their transportation and care not been exclusively deputed to individuals wholly foreign to this art'. And in the little house off the main street where Planat and his clerk Cailly are busily totting up

'the all too many items used up, lost or deteriorated after a great battle, putting the matériel into condition again and hastening up the
ammunition, replacing killed officers and preparing the work of rec-
ompenses and promotions,'
poor young Ferdinand Lariboisière, in the other room, is sinking in agony
to imminent death:
'Although I'd known him but slightly, I'd taken a great liking to him.
There was something gay, chivalrous and generous about him, which
pleased everybody. A charming young man, as frank and loyal as
could be. Truly born to the military estate, he'd just come from the
pages. I believe he was hardly eighteen years old.'
And when in the afternoon of 12 September IHQ moves on,
'having got certain knowledge of the exact figure of the losses suffered by both armies, the enemy's movements, the quality of the victuals, the state of the administration, of the imminent arrival of the
route battalions and Smolensk squadrons, and made quite sure the
ammunition consumed was already replaced,'
Lariboisière, together with his chief-of-staff General Charbonnel, lingers
for a few hours 'waiting for his son to yield up his last breath'. Obliged at
last to tear himself away, he asks Planat to stay
'until his last moment. About 4 p.m. the poor young fellow, who'd
been groaning from his wound ever since morning, began to rattle
and suffer convulsive spasms that heralded his end. Ferdinand then
opened his eyes a moment, put one arm around my neck and, a
moment afterwards, died.'
Almost suffocated with grief, the sensitive Planat informs the father. 'The
general squeezed my hand and a few moments later left to rejoin the
Emperor.' Entrusted with the boy's funeral, that night Planat receives a
note written in the handwriting of his friend and fellow-ADC, Honoré
Lariboisière. His brother's heart is to be taken out and preserved:
'After allowing twenty-four hours to pass, Gudolle opened up the
corpse and, in my presence, extracted the heart, for me a very terrible and dolorous spectacle. This heart was placed in a little beaker of
spirits of wine,'
and the corpse itself in a rough-and-ready coffin,
'nailed together by the workmen of the Engineer Corps. In it I
enclosed a scroll of strong paper, on which I'd written these words:
"The body of Ferdinand Gaston de Lariboisière, lieutenant of
Carabiniers, killed at the Battle of the Moscowa, Sept. 1812. His
father recommends his remains to the public piety." The funeral
took place at nightfall, without any religious ceremony, we having no
priest with us.[10] A detachment of 25 gunners commanded by a lieutenant escorted the coffin. To secure it from any profanation we'd
dug a ditch in the old town wall, of Tartar construction, which was in
ruins. Enormous stone blocks had been displaced and were afterwards put back again on top of the coffin, with such care it was

impossible to see what had been done. Yet if I were to visit Mojaisk I could still point to the spot where Ferdinand is buried.'

IHQ having moved on, Planat sends a lock of Ferdinand's hair to his brother, together with his heart and his belongings.

Mojaisk is indeed full of dead, wounded and dying men, both Russians evacuated from the battle and also an ever-growing number of Frenchmen, notably senior officers. Arriving there on 10 September, the Flemish war commissary Bellot de Kergorre had settled in at first as best he could in the Guard's bivouac on the main square; but has immediately had been detailed off to feed all these sufferers:

'Bandaged with hay and groaning dreadfully, they lived for the first few days on the few grains they could find in the straw they were lying on and the little flour I was able to give them. When soup was made it had to be taken to them, but we'd nothing to put it in! Providentially I came upon a fair number of little bowls intended for lamps, so we were able to give our patients some water. The lack of candles was a terrible privation.'

After distributing a little food that evening by the smoky light of a flaming pine torch, Kergorre is horrified to find he has lost

'some men who, hidden in the straw, had been overlooked. A shocking thing was the impossibility of removing the dead from among the living. I'd neither medical orderlies nor stretchers. Not only the hospital but also the streets and houses were full of corpses.'

One of these wounded is Captain Aubry of the 12th Chasseurs. His boot has been ripped off his leg by the roundshot which has also deprived him of his toes. Little consolation to hear that his wound is unique and that the surgeon at the field hospital has "never seen one like it!" Lying there in the straw in Mojaisk

'I'd quite enough to do driving off people who came too close. The stirring of the least blade of straw around me caused me atrocious pain. The famous Dr Larrey and his surgeons had made so many amputations at Mojaisk that there was a heap of legs and arms so big a large room couldn't have contained them'.[11]

Several days pass before Kergorre can even get hold of some little carts to remove the dead from the improvised hospital: 'I personally took away 128 who'd had been serving as pillows for the sick and were several days old.' As for 600 wounded Russians, abandoned where they'd fallen in the town's gardens, 'they were living on cauliflower stalks and human flesh. Of this at least there was no shortage!'

In blatant contrast to this charnel-house, the wounded Teste sees how the inept and grossly self-indulgent Junot, whose corps is to protect the town, has 'grabbed everything. Junot had occupied the governor's palace with his brilliant staff. There everything was found in abundance and those gentlemen's orgies were in striking contrast to the sufferings and distress of so many wounded.'

Not very far away, at the ruined and deserted village of Elmia, von Suckow, too, has been detailed off to supervise the treatment of 40 wounded Württemberg officers and 500 men. Among them is Lieutenant Vossler, who together with eight others finds himself 'bedded on the floor, which was covered with thatch. Medical supplies were practically non-existent.' Upon the village catching fire and being partly laid in ashes, the survivors are moved to the nearby château of Selso-Karazhin. An hour's march to the rear, it's

'a vast building whose interior offered great comfort. The occupants had fled – precipitously, to judge by the disorder prevailing every-where, perhaps only a few minutes before we'd got there. In an ele-gantly furnished room was a fine piano which they hadn't troubled themselves to close. A volume of music was on the desk. What had become of the lady who a minute earlier, perhaps, had been extract-ing harmonious sounds from this instrument?'

But at least the château abounds in food. 'The sick could be separated from the wounded, and the latter be quartered in lighter and more cheer-ful surroundings,' though after midnight the cold night air blowing in through the broken windowpanes prevents the patients from getting any sleep. As for the days,

'we spent them either sitting in front of the stove and keeping the fire going or visiting other wounded who were confined to their beds. We spent many cheerful hours with Lieut. von H., who'd lost a foot but none of his gaiety and wit. I whiled away much of my time bringing my diary up to date, though my room mate's garrulous dis-position made this something of an effort. The food was as a rule totally inadequate.'

Many of these wounded, too, are dying; some because, like General Dessaix, they've refused to be operated upon. One colonel, 'relying too much on his military authority' tries to counter the pain from his leg by saying over and over again: "Leg, I order you to stop hurting me!"

'We deposited them in the middle of the fields, entrusting the disap-pearance of their remains to the air and worms, for we'd long lost the habit of burying our corpses.'

For Intendant-General Dumas, it has been a

'painful duty to have to follow on with IHQ and leave behind between four and five thousand wounded in the environs of the bat-tlefield, with so little of what was needed for their relief. Our field hospitals were nearly exhausted, and yet we had to anticipate the results of another battle and be sparing of the scanty means which we still had left to provide for them.'

But Kergorre and his immediate superior, a man called Trussot, move into a little house occupied by a temporary assistant named Ligerot, freshly arrived from Paris. All Dumas has been able to leave him for his 3,000 patients 'in two stone houses, the only ones in town', is 'one barrel of flour, which we distributed to the generals, 4 or 5 pounds apiece. There were twelve divisional generals and 14 brigadiers. As for the other wounded, they were excluded from this issue.'

The scenes at the Kolotskoië monastery are, if possible, even worse. 'They were daily appealing to us for help. Fortunately,' says Kergorre,

'nature, amidst so many horrors, furthered the cause of medicine. I had very few feverish cases and apart from two or three hundred deaths during the first few days I saved all my patients.'

At first he has heated debates with Superintendent Trussot, who's

'been expressly forbidden to touch the convoys destined for headquarters and ordered to live off the country. But I told him I'd take full responsibility for levying a tithe on the convoys, preferring to be court-martialled for feeding the wounded entrusted to my care than to let them die of hunger.'[12]

He also has to feed 'some *ingénieurs géographes*, among them M. Labaume, busy drawing up his plan of the battle'. He also defies his orders by giving the odd loaf to officers passing through en route for the army; among them the former French consul at St Petersburg, de Lesseps, he who'd been deprived of his job and his expense account for reporting unpalatable facts. He'd been

'on his way home to Paris with his wife and eight children when a courier had caught up with him as he was disembarking at Danzig, and handed him imperative orders to proceed at once to IHQ, then at the gates of Moscow',

whose civil governor he, willy-nilly, is to be. 'He had nothing at all to eat.'

CHAPTER 23

THE LAST LAP

*Fézensac takes over the 4th Line – 'even the officer seemed worried' – an unneces-
sary engagement -Cossacks and peasants – 'our camp looked like a market' – IV
Corps loots Rouza – the splendours of Zvenigorod Abbey*

'The road to Moscow is a masterpiece,' thinks cuirassier captain Bréaut
des Marlots,

'you can march along it ten vehicles abreast. On either side are two
rows of very tall trees and between them a path for pedestrians.
These trees look very much like weeping willows. In summer their
hospitable shade preserves you from the fierce heats and in winter
they serve as a guide when the snows fill up the frequent precipices,
blending sky with the surface of the ground.'

Riding on from a Mojaisk in flames Le Roy had seen 'our cavalry at grips
with the enemy in a superb plain. It was a pleasure to see the way they
manoeuvred.' And on 9 September Tascher notes in his diary that his hussars have launched three successive attacks, only for the Russians to retire
as soon as [Séruzier's] guns had opened up on them:

'In the evening, a charge by the Prussians. Pajol wounded. Sept 10:
Same circus as yesterday. But at least at 4 p.m. they halt and stand
firm. We get lost and trot until 9 p.m. Bivouac in a wood, without
water, or bread, or forage. Ate horsemeat, extreme misery. The regiment reduced to six troops. The Russians are burning everything,
even the villages with their wounded in them. My spyglass stolen. Did
twelve miles.'

And so on, day after day. Although the Russian is all the time retreating
Le Roy sees him

'at each position turning about and sacrificing some men to prevent
a rout which would have become unavoidable if he'd let himself be
pressed too hard. For my part I was surprised to see the discipline,
the good order reigning in a beaten army. Being myself in the
advance guard, I can affirm that I never once saw a single cart, not a
horse, in a word not one single Russian soldier abandoned or straggling.'

For three days Dedem's men go on 'advancing in line, the cavalry occupying the intervals between the infantry'. All the time Colonel Tschudi's
Spaniards are

'only having skirmishes. We in the advance guard were making thirty
to thirty-five miles a day, and in the evening we lay down regularly in
square, having two ranks alternatingly on their feet and one sitting
down.'

On 11 September the left wing of Dufour's division is marching in square
close to some woods when

'three regiments of Russian cavalry charged the 33rd Line's 2nd battalion, its extreme left. No more than 176 men were still present. For a moment the King of Naples thought this little unit had been driven in, and sent me to its assistance. As I approached, the hostile cavalry had surrounded the battalion and were shouting to the French to surrender. But as I appeared they showed signs of retreating. Then a salvo by our infantry at almost point-blank range dismounted more than 76 Cossacks and killed 33 men.'

Murat afterwards asks Napoleon to promote all the dwindled little unit's officers, 'a sergeant-major who'd particularly distinguished himself and the Cross for Captain Callier, commanding the 2nd battalion after the death of its major'.

Now it's Ney who's marching in Murat's wake. Leaving Mojaisk on the morning of 12 September, the newly fledged *Colonel* Fézensac reaches his headquarters in the evening at a village near Koubinoskoië, which he finds surrounded by III corps' bivouacs. It's there he's to take over his regiment. The 4th Line is one of those which had been

'formed in the first years of the Revolution and been through all the German campaigns and it counted Joseph Bonaparte among its colonels. Next day I was received by General d'Henin, the brigade commander. From the very first day I was struck by the troops' exhaustion and their numerical weakness. At IHQ only results counted, without a thought to the the cost; and people had no idea of the state of the army. But when I assumed command of the regiment I had to go into all the details about which I knew nothing and to learn how deep the trouble went. Out of the 2,000 men who'd crossed the Rhine the 4th Regiment was reduced to 900.'

Its original four battalions have shrunk to only two, and each company has a double cadre of officers and NCOs.

'All parts of its clothing and above all its boots were in a bad state. Though we still had enough flour and some herds of bullocks and flocks of sheep, it wouldn't be long before these resources were exhausted. Since twenty-four hours sufficed for us to ravage the country we were passing through we had to keep on the move to replenish them.'

All of which, Fézensac says, was also true of III Corps as a whole,

'and especially of the Württemberg Division, which was almost destroyed. I can assure you there were no more than 8,000 men left of an army corps of 25,000. I noticed the absence of many officers wounded in the last affair, among others, of the 46th, 72nd and 73rd Line. Never had we suffered such heavy losses. Never had the army's morale been in such a sorry state. I no longer found the soldiers gay as they'd used to be. The songs and funny stories which formerly had helped them forget the fatigue of the long marches had given way to a gloomy silence. Even the officers seemed worried, and were only serving out of a sense of duty and honour.'

A general's death, demotion or incapacitation could strip his staff of their privileges.[1] Grouchy being among the many top brass wounded at Borodino, Colonel Griois too finds his situation has changed for the worse. Command of III Cavalry Corps has passed to General Lahoussaye who, if not quite as obtuse as old General St-Germain (he of the rotten bales of hay), is 'far from enjoying our confidence and daily proving how little he merited it'. Although still in command of III Corps' artillery, Griois now finds himself

'without victuals, without provisions, without any distribution at all. I lacked for everything, as did those around me, and we're only too happy when the gunners shared with us the fruits of their maraudings, organized, for the rest, with the best possible order!'

This miserable state of personal indigence he's sharing with his friend Colonel Jumilhac who 'no longer having any troops under his immediate orders, was even worse off'. A scion of the *ancien régime* – Jumilhac is an authentic duke – Griois' friend is

'an arrogant man, violent and choleric towards his inferiors, but amiable, witty and excellent towards his comrades, and we mutually helped each other to put up with our privations and our detestable bivouacs. We were also quite close with Colonel Caumont de la Force, chief-of-staff of the dragoon division – a bon vivant, very gay, altogether original, loving wine and women and seizing every opportunity to get them, without too much care for the quality.'

A few days after leaving Mojaisk, however, III Cavalry Corps is ordered to leave the Moscow highway and follow the Army of Italy as it makes for Rouza.

Just while Fézensac is being received by Ney, Murat is again at grips with the Russians. This time the bone of contention is the charming little château of Fominskoië, 'with a little green dome, and which His Majesty coveted'. Follows what Dedem's men will afterwards call

'the war of the château. We weren't at all pleased about it. With reason – because the King's and his staff's good pleasure were frequently costing the lives of 30 to 80 brave soldiers. I never saw a headquarters that troubled itself so little about its men as that one.'

The Russians, who know the ground, are clinging to their position in front of the château, which has the only stream in the neighbourhood. But Murat, who's in a hurry to get into it to spend the night, takes personal command of the cavalry and orders Dufour to outflank the Russian right, leaving his divisional artillery on the road. Whereupon

'part of the Russian cavalry turned the wood we were to debouch by, fell on a battalion of the 48th and our extreme left and, before it even had time to form up, cut it to pieces at the exit from the forest.'

The French right, meanwhile, is on the highway, and Dedem's two weak infantry battalions, one from the 33rd, the other Tschudi's Spaniards, are being ravaged by enemy grapeshot. Almost the whole Spanish battalion is thrown to the ground and loses all its officers. Tschudi himself has two horses killed under him and his clothes are peppered with musket-balls. In the centre matters are hardly less desperate:

'Not even giving the 15th Light time to form up, His Majesty had the charge beaten, and the soldiers ran at the enemy like so many skirmishers. Having no unit to support them they were cut up by the enemy cavalry, who did real butchery among them. Nothing was saved of this fine regiment except some companies which had got mingled up with the 33rd when crossing the copses and which I'd kept behind me. Upon the 33rd debouching simultaneously with the 15th Light, the King's ADCs had wanted to engage it, too, with the cavalry. But defying these gentlemen's loud-voiced complaints I formed up my battalions before advancing: partly so as to gain time and partly to enable the wreckage of the 48th and 15th to make good its retreat. The King, seeing the outcome of his crazy enterprise, sent generals Déri and Excelmans to me, one after the other, ordering me not to engage. But there was no longer any question of that! The affair was already only too thoroughly engaged. And though the enemy opposed me with three times my remaining forces, I thought it my duty to sustain the combat to give other troops time to turn up and save our retreat from turning into a rout. My skirmishers held the enemy in check; but his artillery, placed in a grove of tall trees, was doing me a lot of damage. All I had to oppose him with was infantry fire.'

Finally the French withdraw, in fairly good order, to 'the position the Russians had allocated to us that morning'. The action has cost the remains of what had once been Friant's crack division the cream of its surviving officers. The admirable Swiss colonel Tschudi has lost one of his two Spanish battalions. And Dedem's ADC Beaucourt, 'an educated officer of great bravery' already wounded at Borodino, has received a musket-ball in his thigh. When it's all over, Dedem annoys Murat by handing in an exact account of the butcher's bill. Worse, he and his officers go to Davout next day and implore him to take them back under his command. Whereupon there's another blazing row between Murat and Davout in front of Napoleon:

'The Marshal could not but be pained to see his army corps' finest divisions being destroyed to no purpose, and a man who he knew was his enemy and who possessed no other military virtue than ebullient courage and great audacity being allowed to commit stupidities with impunity, just because he was the Emperor's brother-in-law. A corporal would have managed the affair better.'

Napoleon, meanwhile, is wholly in the dark, not merely as to Kutusov's intentions, but even his very whereabouts:

'On the 13th, when the whole army was again on the move, the Emperor halted all the columns. Our cavalry were so exhausted they couldn't push their reconnaissance to any distance, and just then we knew so little of the enemy's movements that the Emperor, doubtful as to the direction taken by Kutusov, of whom there was no news, judged it advisable to pause. He hadn't received any reports from Prince Poniatowski on our right and for a moment was uneasy about him, feeling the Russians might have taken advantage of our rest to throw themselves to that side and threaten our flank and rear, in hope of stopping, or at least delaying, our entry into Moscow until they'd had replies from Petersburg,'

i.e., to whatever report Kutusov must have sent to his government after the battle. Perhaps he's even withdrawing, not on Moscow, but on Kaluga, away to the south? Anyway, Colbert is ordered to cut the Kaluga road. Probing in that direction, the lancer brigade finds no trace of the enemy. Sometimes the peasants are even taking his men for Russian Uhlans:

'There were plenty of provisions and forage in these villages, and since our men's discipline was excellent the inhabitants, so far from fleeing, gave us a good reception. Some complained of their own government. Several times these same peasants warned us of the appearance of Cossacks in the surroundings.'

But by no means always. Approaching stealthily, Cossacks nevertheless (again) carry off the Dutch regiment's outpost picket. And again 'only one man escaped flat out at a gallop and brought the news to our camp. Even an hour and a half's pursuit couldn't catch up with the Cossacks.' Mortified by this second surprise of the campaign, Colbert doubles the 2nd Regiment's outposts; and, to make assurance doubly sure, mingles the Dutchmen with his warier, more experienced Poles. And beyond Kijow they capture a mailcoach, one of whose occupants turns out to be one of the Tsar's ministers, a Count Gouriew, whom Colbert sends to Napoleon, no doubt with a request for further orders. Once again he's feeling very much out on a limb: 'Although he had an important cavalry command,' Captain Zalusky of the Polish Lancers is noticing, 'he's not getting any orders, and it even seems his reports aren't reaching the general staff.'

Which is strange. For Caulaincourt is noticing that it's precisely from that quarter Napoleon is all the time expecting Kutusov to attack him. That is, if he doesn't sue for peace. Which he's sure he will, while at the same time offering another battle, for form's sake:

'Officers were sent out one after another in all directions. The King of Naples was ordered to push forward a strong reconnaissance along the Kaluga road. At last the Emperor was reassured, and the army resumed its march. Nevertheless he couldn't explain this movement of the whole [Russian] army on Moscow, as it didn't offer battle.'

Upon Murat reporting that the Russians are neither showing any signs of resistance nor have made any proposals for an armistice, Napoleon is 'amazed. From it he inferred, and he repeated it more than once, that the Russian army had lost far more heavily at the Moscova than had been supposed. He seemed to be in continual anxiety.'

Also probing the countryside over a 12–15 mile front to the right is a strong detachment of Dessaix's division, now taken over by General Friedrichs. Ever since 11 September Le Roy, in command of one of its units, has been 'marching, with no other guide than a bad map that hardly even gave any distances'. Next day – i.e., the day of the Fominskoïë affair – his men, without encountering any opposition, enter the pleasant little town of Vereia. But find neither the military stores nor the garrison they've expected. Since all its inhabitants have fled, however, provisions are plentiful:

'An hour later our camp looked like a market: wines, liqueurs, brandy, carboys of crystallized fruits, dragées, hams, sausages, bread, meat, etc., etc. From direst poverty we'd passed abruptly to the greatest abundance. Imagine to yourself a line of 2,000 men, camped in a semi-circle, sitting on the ground, surrounded by bottles, drinking out of them and regaling themselves like millionaires. After the victuals arrived the furs, cloths, silverware, jewels and all the wealth the inhabitants, taken by surprise, hadn't been able to carry off or hide. Terrified to see us coming, they'd only saved their families and some food, retiring into nearby forests, where they were waiting for the storm to pass over.'

And soon everyone, except Le Roy, always alive to his duties, is sleeping off the unwonted feast. The staff having moved into Vereia itself, Le Roy, finding himself in command of the camp, takes care to inspect the outposts before finally returning to sit down to take part in the general jollification, close to the majors and adjutants-major. 'Finally day broke, and revealed to our sight more than half the troops in no state to depart.' Leaving at 6 p.m. the detachment

'destroyed everything they couldn't carry off. It was odd to see the ranker embarrassed to know what to choose as between drink and food. He'd have been only too glad to leave his weapons behind to load himself with provisions.'

Thereafter all the 85th find is a deserted countryside, abandoned villages. Life is less agreeable for the Italians out on the left flank. There too the peasants are fleeing. From a Colonel Asselin, whom Eugène has sent to reconnoitre in the direction of Rouza, Labaume hears how some of them have put up a fight, before being quickly routed by his dozen Bavarian chasseurs – all but the lord of the manor who'd organized this resistance. Despite Asselin's entreaties this nobleman had fought to the death with his dagger, shouting "how can I survive my country's dishonour?" and ended his life on the chasseurs' bayonets.

Beyond Rouza, 'a little town built on a height', the peasants, with their valuables piled on carts, are in full flight – the first time, Labaume says, 'we'd seen such a sight'. The cavalry, of course, easily catch up with them, 'and a very touching spectacle it was to see these carts laden with children and aged invalids. One's heart was ravaged with sorrow at the thought of how our men would share these carts and horses among themselves, laying waste these families' entire fortune.'

Every house in Rouza is pillaged,

'without heed to their owners' cries or a mother's tears as she showed the victors the child in her lap. Wringing their hands, these innocents only begged us to spare their lives.'

Even Labaume exonerates those among the Italians and Bavarians

'who were dying of hunger and only trying to get some food. For them this ardour for pillage was legitimate. Many others under its pretext sacked everything, stripping both women and children, even to the rags they were covered with.'

But then, in a twinkling, everything changes. Some Bavarian lancers come galloping back into town, announcing that whole squadrons of Cossacks are advancing against them. And instantly the pillagers' contentment turns into acute alarm:

'What have we here to oppose them with? Nothing. Only a few wretched soldiers, come to pillage the peasants. Yet it's our only recourse. Immediately they're assembled in the square, hardly 60 of them, half without their weapons.'

Yet when Eugène and his staff ride out to repel this redoubtable foe, they're amazed to see only 'a dozen or so horsemen, so far away they could hardly be made out'. Summoning up two battalions to secure the town, the Italian staff go back to their dinner 'with exquisite wines'.

The pillage of Rouza causes all the 'newly armed' peasants to flee into the forests, having set on fire their villages and the harvest. At the village of Apalchtchouina the Italians find

'the houses abandoned, the château deserted, the furniture smashed, and the provisions wasted, everywhere a picture of terrible desolation. All these ravages showed us what lengths a people can go to if it's sufficiently great to prefer its independence to its riches.'

Just as IV Corps is leaving again, III Cavalry Corps arrives. Although the town strikes Griois as 'rather pretty, it no longer had any inhabitants. Everything was in disorder.' After spending the night there another and different experience is in store for him:

'We came to a vast abbey, a veritable fortress surrounded by high crenellated walls and drawbridges. Only a few leagues from Moscow, I think it's called Zvenigorod. There were still some monks there, whose haggard faces, hidden by a thick beard, expressed hatred and despair. Enormous blue drapes disguised all their figures and gave them the air of veritable phantoms. Seeing us, they withdrew into the most secret recesses of their monastery; and when they couldn't escape us, all we could get out of them was an absolute silence and or a negative sign to all our questions.'

Much of the immense, almost unfurnished abbey, has already been devastated, presumably after IV Corps' visitation:

'but taken as a whole it still looked splendid and magnificent. One hall was wholly embellished with portraits of the ancient dukes of Muscovy, some of them not without merit. Their clothes and their hairstyles, varied as the centuries they lived in, rivalled each other in opulence and singularity, and the long beards enhancing all these faces gave several of them a truly extraordinary expression.'

There's also a small but splendid church, whose many tombs

'of a bizarre and recherché architecture, loaded with inscriptions in Russian lettering and thus illegible to me, were almost all covered in a gilded metal which seemed to me to be silver gilt. The men of IV Corps, who'd got to Zvenigorod before us, had forced their way into the church and taking these plaques of silver or perhaps copper gilt for pure gold, had ripped off part of it. They'd even opened or smashed some tombs in hopes of finding in them precious ornaments or jewels. The disorder in this temple which a whole people had venerated for centuries presented a spectacle as painful to see as to think about.'

Now everyone is noticing how, the closer the army is coming to Moscow, the more opulent is the countryside and its dwellings. Dutheillet, still on the main highway, sees

'châteaux of Asiatic luxury, magnificently furnished with expensive furniture, orangeries and shrubberies of all kinds, splendid stables and, alongside these superb dwellings devastated by both armies' marauders, miserable peasant shacks, built of loam and covered with thatch'.

Still probing towards the Kaluga road under Colbert, the Polish Guard Lancers are 'coming upon all kinds of objects we found extraordinary: palaces housing libraries, greenhouses, gardens'. Squadron-leader Chlapowsky, Soltyk's friend, invites Captain Zalusky to 'a meal so exceptional I could no longer recall a similar abundance'. Between Fominskoië and Vereia a patrol comes across a large sugar-beet factory, whose store Dumonceau draws on to cure his men's dysentery:

'One night we were surprised to see a great number of little vehicles turn up, loaded with lumps of sugar. From this moment I too began using little britchkas; with my lieutenants I'd two of them, and, behind, two milch cows, a supply of sugar and various victuals.'

Zalusky will afterwards date the final catastrophe from the moment he, too, adopted that bad habit.

CHAPTER 24

'MOSCOW! MOSCOW!'

Another battle? – 'We gazed at the immense city' – 'no chimney smoked' – a parley – von Muraldt's mission – 'all the streets were empty' – amateur heroes – 'Never had I seen him so depressed' – 'I was frozen with terror' – 'to find some humane person' – 'the Tsar won't make peace' – Murat crosses Moscow – 'swans were swimming peacefully' – two dinner parties – 'Fire!, fire!'

Not knowing what's going on to his right, but sure he must at long last be approaching Moscow, Prince Eugène on 14 September

'mounted a hill to our right, and for a long while tried to see if the city of Moscow were visible. Several hills still veiled it from our sight and all we saw were whirlwinds of dust which, parallel to our route, showed the way the Grand Army was marching. From a few cannon-shots fired afar off and at long intervals we concluded that our troops were nearing Moscow without meeting much resistance.'

To get more news of the main column Eugène sends off von Muraldt, the Bavarian Chasseurs' youngest but only French-speaking officer, to Murat. Providing him with a small escort, he urges him not to fall into the hands of Cossacks. It's a brilliantly sunny day. After an anxious half-hour during which his escort kept seeing Cossacks everywhere, Muraldt reaches the Moscow-Mojaisk road, along which he finds 'the Imperial Guard's infantry and artillery advancing rapidly in columns'. Hurrying forward to catch up with Murat, he sees

'only cheerful faces. As the road was very broad, artillery and infantry were marching side by side, and everyone was hurrying on with winged footsteps. Here and there, especially in the Young Guard, the cry "Vive l'Empereur!" was heard. But the old bearskins were quieter and more serious.'

At long last, the Grand Army is nearing its goal. But must it fight another battle before entering it? Napoleon is still sure Kutusov will 'offer battle once again before giving up the capital, but this time with a sword in one hand and peace proposals in the other'. Determined to sign the peace in Moscow, he wants 'to stay there a week and then retire on Smolensk:

"Swords have been crossed. In the eyes of the world honour is satis-fied. And the Russians have suffered so much harm there's no other satisfaction I can ask of them. They'll be no more anxious for me to pay them a second visit than I shall be to come back to Borodino."'

As for himself and Berthier, Caulaincourt goes on, 'we agreed there was no way of finishing this war except by quitting Moscow forty-eight hours after entering it, and returning to Witebsk.' Nor are Griois and his com-rades

'in any way afraid of a new battle. Indeed we wanted one, to put an end to things; but not at Moscow or under its walls, because it was easy to foresee that if we won it, as none of us doubted we would, the town would be put to the sack and perhaps burnt before being handed over to us, and all our hopes were placed in the resources we counted on finding there.'

And indeed that day (14 September) Dedem van der Gelder, advancing along the tree-lined highway behind Murat's cavalry, hears that the advance guard has heard from a deserter that the Russians are fortifying 'a position much more formidable than the one at Borodino'. That morning too the Fusiliers-Grenadiers of the Young Guard enter the last big forest pass 'near a ravine where the Russians had begun to make redoubts for defence'. Emerging from the woods, Dedem sees 'trees cut down, a redoubt, and a line of cavalry crowning the heights'. But just then the light cavalry advance guard – among them Lieutenant Count von Wedel, of the 9th Polish Lancers – reaches a crest of a hill. And there, only a couple of miles away, lies... Moscow:

'"Moscow!, Moscow!" the shout rose from the ranks. We gazed at the huge town, with its golden spires, its red and black painted roofs, its palaces and more modest houses, and the large green parks inside the city, which bears no resemblance to our towns and has a wholly oriental character.'

One only has to peer at the fantastic spectacle through one's telecope to see at a glance that Moscow, the most distant and exotic of all Europe's capitals,[1] is an open city. Only a shallow ditch fronts its suburbs. Otherwise there are no fortifications. Nor is the Russian army deployed in front of it.

But then von Wedel sees something else. And it strikes him as far more sinister:

'On the far side of the city we, through our spyglasses, made out masses of people on foot, on horseback, or in vehicles. They were leaving the town. No chimney smoked. Could the inhabitants have fled? Surely they couldn't be abandoning their homes just as a few hundred people leave a village?'

For three hours the advance guard, ordered onwards down from the Sparrow Hills, is held up by the Russian rearguard. It has rallied 'in little trenches thrown up in front of the town at various distances from each other'. And Murat orders his cavalry and light field artillery

'to deploy in line. The Russians fired three or four rounds. But soon the firing ceased, and the rumour spread that negotiations were being held.'

And in fact Séruzier has seen a Russian general coming towards him, accompanied by an escort. He's been sent by Miloradowitch, commander of the rearguard. Setting his staff at a distance 'in a stentorian voice', Murat rides forward and listens to what he has to propose:

'We should pass through Moscow without halting and go as far as six miles along the Kasan road, our advance guard being preceded at a distance of 200 yards by a squadron of Cossacks.'

If this isn't agreed to, says the spokesman, the city will be set on fire. What to do? After some hestitation Murat replies that he'll have to go and ask the Emperor. Whereupon his interlocutor turns away and begins to go back to the city – but has only gone fifty yards when Murat calls him back and says he'll take it upon himself to agree. Sends off an ADC to tell Napoleon. Dismounts. And is immediately surrounded by admiring Cossacks 'with inverted lances'.

Ever since Tilsit they've remembered him as a giver of lavish gifts. So also now. Lieutenant Tascher sees them clustering around him. Having no other such kingly trifles to give them, Murat, much to that fiery-tempered officer's annoyance, purloins Gourgaud's treasured watch – 'a very fine piece of jewellery' which Gourgaud himself had 'received from an illustrious hand. No one seemed to be making any difficulties. Evidently they'd already decided to surrender the town to us.'

IHQ has passed the previous night at a superb manor-house owned by the immensely rich Prince Galitzin. Lying beside a lake, it was 'the first really fine château we'd seen in Russia. The soldiers of the advance guard,' Castellane had been sorry to see, had 'damaged it somewhat, as was their custom, by slashing the upholstery' of its 'very elegant furniture'. It's also remarkable for 'some very charming sculptures, some of them really good', which Captain Bonnet – at the same time finding its position 'a bit dreary, surrounded by woods pierced on one side by avenues, with a little stream and with lakes, frozen for eight months in the year, and formed with the help of dikes' – will relish, bivouacking there by and by with with Razout's division (III). At 8 a.m. Napoleon has left the château in his carriage for Malo-Wiazma, seven versts from Moscow. And it's there Murat's ADC tells him what's happening. His first words, according to Ségur, are:

"Well then, there's this famous city. And about time too!" His marshals, who'd been discontented since the great battle and held themselves apart from him, now forgot their complaints. We saw them pressing around the Emperor, rendering homage to his fortune and already tempted to ascribe to the foresight of his genius the lack of care he'd taken on Sept 7 to complete his victory.'[2]

Narbonne, a reasonably pacific personage, is sent to Murat to confirm the truce. He's to order him to

'follow the Russians step by step, enter the city, but as far as possible circumvent it, and press them as far as possible as soon as they're outside the barriers. Also to send the Emperor a deputation of the municipal authorities,'

who are to meet him at the city gate. Overtaking Dedem's sorely tried infantry, Narbonne tells him: "And that's the end of it. The Russians are abandoning Moscow and entrusting it to French generosity."

'Soon afterwards the Emperor passed in his carriage, and having called me over to him said: "Get your men on the move. It isn't the end." He seemed worried, I don't know why. Perhaps His Majesty wasn't pleased with the soldiers' outbursts of joy at the idea that we'd be treating for peace, a sentiment they manifested only too clearly as they saluted the Emperor when he went by them to approach the city.'

Following close on his carriage and entourage – much to I and III Corps' annoyance – is the Imperial Guard. Nor do all the troops break out into cheers, anyway not the 57th Line. 'A few shouts of *"Vive l'Empereur!,* there's the holy city!" were heard, but without much enthusiasm.' It's a 'beautiful summer's day'. Marching swiftly, the Guard infantry is headed by the Fusiliers-Grenadiers. And at *their* head, commanding a posse of fifteen men, marches Vélite-sergeant Bourgogne:

'In my charge I had several officers taken prisoner in the great battle, some of whom spoke French. One of them was a pope, probably a regimental chaplain. He too spoke good French, but seemed much sadder and more preoccupied than his companions in misfortune.'

By and by they, too, halt on the Sparrow Hills:

'The sun was reflected on all the domes, the spires and gilded palaces. The many capitals I'd seen – such as Paris, Berlin, Warsaw, Vienna and Madrid – had only produced an ordinary impression on me. But this was quite different! On me as on everyone else the effect was magical.'

Bourgogne notices how all his prisoners

'bowed and crossed themselves several times. I went up to the priest and asked him why. "Monsieur," he said, "this hill is called the Hill of Salvation, and every good Muscovite must bow and cross himself on seeing the holy city." Soon afterwards we descended the hill.'

Suddenly, much to Lieutenant von Wedel's annoyance,

'one of the Emperor's orderly officers galloped past, and immediately afterwards the order rang out: "Column, halt!" Then the Imperial Guard, in full dress uniforms, went by, as if to a parade. "There's the Guard, who haven't fought once throughout the campaign! They're going to show off in Moscow. As for us riff-raff, we shan't even be allowed to stick our noses inside! It's a disgrace! a scandal!" With suppressed rage we watched this splendid, envied, favoured Guard go past, and already our fine fancies began to evaporate.'

Finally, after a quarter of an hour, Bourgogne reaches the city gate. 'The Emperor was already there with his staff. We halted. And to our left I noticed an immense cemetery.' Soon Boulart arrives and parks there with his guns; 'Everyone was extraordinarily excited.' He and his gunners are dying to make their 'triumphal entry. We were consumed with a curiosity incomparably more devouring than our appetite.'

'At noon the Emperor reached the barrier at the moat and dismounted. His impatience increased with every moment. Every instant he kept sending out fresh orders, continually asking whether the deputation or any notables were on their way.'

He tells Caulaincourt to write to Maret, at Vilna, and to the Arch-Chancellor, Cambacérès, in Paris 'informing them we were in Moscow, and dating my letter from that city'. Shortly afterwards he orders General Durosnel, whom he has appointed military governor, to enter Moscow 'with as many military police as he can muster'. He's to establish order, take possession of the public buildings, guard the Kremlin and keep him supplied with information. But no one else is to go inside the city. Pickets are to be placed 'to prevent any soldier from entering, but there were so many gaps in the walls the precaution was of little avail'.

At the entrance to the suburbs there's a timber bridge. And at 2 p.m. Murat, preceded by the 1st Squadron of the 1st Polish Hussars and followed by Séruzier's guns,[3] crosses it at the head of the 4th Light Cavalry Division and the 2nd and 4th Cuirassier Divisions. Just as he's about to ride into the suburb one of his officers announces a messenger from Prince Eugène. It's von Muraldt:

'I found the King of Naples surrounded by a brilliant and numerous suite and by Cossacks and generals who were flattering him on his bravery. One of the hetmans said: "I've known you a long while now, Sire. You're the King of Naples. The difference between you and me is that I've seen you every day since the Niemen, always the first man at the head of your army. Whilst I, for three months now, have constantly been the last man in ours.'

Like everyone else who sees him for the first time, the Bavarian lieutenant is struck by Murat's theatrical costume:

'It consisted of a short coatee of dark-red sammet with slashed arms. A short straight sword hung from a richly embroidered belt. His boots were of red morocco leather, and on his head he wore a big three-cornered hat, embroidered with gold borders and with a long plume, which he'd put on back to front. His long brown hair hung down in curls on to his shoulders,'

- all no doubt in striking contrast to the ragged and in many cases barefooted appearance of his troops. A few hundred yards away the Cossacks are already withdrawing into the town. Murat tells the Bavarian officer to go back to Eugène and tell him the city is being evacuated under a truce.

But Muraldt has no intention of doing any such thing. Not until he has seen something of 'this remarkable capital. It was even closer to my heart to take some food back with me.' So mingling with Murat's staff he rides on with them; amazed to see that

'all the streets we rode through were empty, the houses barred and bolted. Not a face appeared at any window. And all shops were shut. This deathly silence and desertedness struck me as rather worrying, as it certainly did many others.'

Pajol's light cavalry division is in the van. Ahead of Surgeon von Roos' 3rd Württemberger Chasseurs are the 10th Polish Hussars and a regiment of Prussian lancers 'commanded by a Major de Werther'; behind them come the 'four regiments of French hussars [5th and 9th] and chasseurs [11th and 12th] which made up our division, and some horse artillery':

'Each of us was feeling more or less deeply the pride of a conqueror. And for any one who wasn't there was no lack of officers and old soldiers to point out, with grave words, the importance of what was happening. It was forbidden, on pain of death, to get off one's horse or leave the ranks, on no matter what pretext. This order applied equally to us doctors, and we submitted. We followed the road as far as to the Moscova without encountering a single inhabitant. The bridge had been destroyed. We forded the river. The water came up to the axles of the guns and our horses' knees. On the far side we saw a few individuals behind their doors and windows. Their curiosity didn't seem very great. There were some gentlemen and ladies on the balconies of pretty stone and wooden houses. Our officers saluted them amiably, and they replied in the same fashion. However, we saw very few inhabitants. By and by we came up with some exhausted Russian soldiers, men straggling on foot on horseback, or in abandoned baggage vehicles, butchers' beef on the hoof, etc. We let them all pass.'

Amazed at so many superb palaces set in gardens, at 'the profusion of churches with their queer architecture and elaborately ornamented towers', Pajol's division debouches into a market place. All its wooden shops are open

'their merchandise scattered in disorder and thrown on the ground, as if pillagers had passed by. We were riding slowly, often halting, and this enabled our men to notice that Russians asleep in the streets had brandy in their water-bottles. It being forbidden to dismount, they got the ingenious idea of using the points of their sabres to cut the cords and so snatched them up.'

Murat, is 'everywhere, supervising everything, and kept passing and repassing our ranks'. After they've ridden for half an hour, the Kremlin comes into view. Hardly is Murat's entourage

'forty or fifty paces from it than a mob of drunken soldiers and peasants comes rushing out from its entrance and from a church opposite, and some shots are fired at us. There were also some officers in the crowd.'

One of these, obviously drunk, rushes at von Muraldt's horse,

'holding a drawn sabre in one hand and a bottle in the other. I receive him with a blow on his shako, which fells him to the ground.'

Now, 'between two rows of ancient buildings', the great Arsenal, a vast neo-classical building, comes into sight. Von Roos sees its doors are

'wide open, and men of all kinds, above all men who seemed to be peasants, were coming out of it with weapons. Inside, others were swarming and jostling. The road and the square where we were were littered with various weapons, most of them new. Underneath the Arsenal gateway some sharp words were being exchanged between the king's ADCs and the men who were carrying off the weapons. Some even pushed their way into the Arsenal on horseback and the quarrel became venemous. Meanwhile the populace had massed in the square. It became impatient and noisy.'

Muraldt goes on: 'Furious at this breach of the terms of the capitulation, the King of Naples orders forward two pieces of horse artillery.' And Colonel Séruzier, who has ridden out ahead, is within an inch of being

'killed by bullets fired from all the Arsenal's windows.[4] Hearing this fusillade I put my artillery to the gallop, surround the arsenal, and send forward a trumpeter with an officer to parley with these sharp-shooters, whom I took to be inhabitants of the town, reduced to despair. My trumpet sounds for a truce, but all we get for a reply is a discharge of musketry. One of my captains, the one accompanying the trumpeter, one of my adjutants and the trumpeter himself have been dangerously wounded. Immediately I give the order to fire – I'd placed my two guns under each of the vaultings serving as an entrance to the Arsenal – and pitilessly rain grape on this troop, who come and fall on their knees in front of my guns, begging for mercy.'

Three salvoes suffice to disperse the crowd, most of which Muraldt sees 'taking to their heels in all directions'. It's then Séruzier realizes who it is he has to do with:

'Not the inhabitants of Moscow, nor soldiers trying to defend the Arsenal and the Kremlin in the teeth of the convention. It was the dregs of society, criminals let out of prison. They'd been promised a pardon and their freedom on condition they revolted against these "dogs" of Frenchmen. I seized part of this scum – galley slaves, there were several thousand of them – and handed them over to our infantry.'

The whole episode has 'only lasted a couple of minutes'. Meanwhile Roos has snapped up a souvenir, suited to the occasion:

'Under the very feet of my horse were various weapons. One of them, a handsome sabre, drew my attention. There was no one there to hand it up to me. And I couldn't use the method invented by our men to get hold of water-bottles. Flouting the ban on dismounting, I quickly got off my horse and in a flash was up again.'

Immediately after Murat had crossed the barrier Napoleon has also sent in several staff officers to find out what's really going on, and above all why no deputation has come out to present him with the keys of the city and implore his clemency. Roman Soltyk is one of them. And he too is alarmed to find the town deserted:

'All doors and windows being closed, I came to believe all the inhabitants had taken refuge in the side streets, and turned off in search of them.'

There the only sign of life he comes across is a group of rich Polish hostages from White Russia – the very ones, perhaps, who'd been carried off from Witebsk? They're guarded, if that's the right word, by 30 Russian stragglers, all very drunk. These are pillaging nearby shops and breaking into brandy stores. Welcomed by his compatriots, Soltyk, despite his Polish uniform, quite simply takes command of their warders:

'It didn't even occur to them to grab up their muskets, propped against the walls of the ground-floor rooms. Instead, seeing my epaulettes and true to the respect Russian troops always have for rank, they doff their forage caps and do their best to scramble to their feet. Their own officer couldn't have been received more respectfully!'

Disarming them, Soltyk loses no time in taking both guards and hostages back to the Dorogomilov Gate, where he finds Napoleon

'at the entrance to the Smolensk district. He was standing on the left of the road. A very large-scale map of Moscow was laid out on the grass in front of him. He was studying it closely and then questioning the people who were being brought to him from the town centre. Obliged to wait for a favourable moment to speak to him, I was present at everything that took place. All reports agreed. Most of the inhabitants had fled.'

At that moment Gourgaud, too, comes back. With him he has '40 fully armed Cossacks he, with the help of a single lancer officer he'd had with him, had captured inside the very Kremlin'.

And now the moment has come for some Guard units to enter. Just as Sergeant Bourgogne has reached the bridge he has seen a third officer – Marshal Duroc – come out through the gate and present 'several of the inhabitants who could speak French. The Emperor questioned them.' 'Most of the people brought to him,' Soltyk goes on,

'were foreigners. One of these, a Frenchman by origin, and director of the Museum of Natural History whose status had given him connections in the highest classes of society, gave the most complete elucidation of the present situation. He assured Napoleon that all the authorities had quit Moscow, or at least abandoned their posts. This seemed to affect the Emperor vividly, and he remained plunged in deep reflections.'

What Soltyk has to report, on the other hand, interests Napoleon as little as his Cossack prisoners,

'nor did I see the cloud that had settled on his brow grow lighter. Doubtless having from this moment a presentiment of the fateful consequences of the system of warfare adoped by the Russians, he didn't even wish to interrogate the Polish hostages I'd brought him. Never had a great capital been delivered into a conqueror's hands in a more extraordinary fashion! How different to his entries into Vienna and Berlin!'

Caulaincourt, too, is observing him narrowly:

'At last reports came in from the King and General Durosnel. Far from having found any of the civic authorities, they hadn't discovered so much as a single prominent inhabitant. All had fled. Moscow was a deserted city, where no one could be found but a few wretches of the lowest classes. His face, normally so impassive, showed instantly and unmistakeably the mark of his bitter disappointment. Never have I seen him so deeply impressed. Already greatly disturbed and impatient at having to wait two hours outside the city gate, this report undoubtedly plunged him into the gravest reflections.'

Mortified he certainly is. But perhaps not quite so surprised as he'd been outside Witebsk. Telling him about the Kremlin episode, Duroc says '"Those wretches are all drunk and can't listen to reason." "Break down the doors with cannon", the Emperor replied, "and drive out all you can find behind them."' Which of course has already been done. But now the Guard's drums begin to roll, and Sergeant Bourgogne gets the order

'*Garde à vous!*, the signal for entering the city. It was 3 p.m., and we made our entrance in compact columns, the bands playing out in front. I was in the advance guard of 30 men, commanded by M. Césarisse, our company's lieutenant. Hardly had we entered the suburbs than we met several of the miserable creatures expelled from the Kremlin. They had horrible faces, and were armed with muskets, staves and pitchforks. As we were crossing the [stone] bridge leading from the suburbs to the town itself, a man crept out from under the bridge and placed himself athwart the regiment. He was muffled up in a sheepskin cape, long grey hair fell down on to his shoulders, and a thick white beard came down to his waist. He carried a three-pronged fork and looked like Neptune rising from the sea. Thus accoutred, he walked up to the drum-major and, taking him on account of his smart uniform and lace for the general, aimed a blow at him with his pitchfork. Snatching the wretch's weapon from him, the drum-major seized him by the shoulders; then giving him a kick from behind, he launched him over the bridge into the water he'd just left. But he didn't get out again. Swept away by the current, we only saw him come up at intervals. Finally he disappeared for ever.'

So much for an amateur hero. And they meet others, some of whom 'only had wooden flintlocks to their muskets. Since they didn't wound anyone we contented ourselves with taking their weapons from them and breaking them. And if they came back for more, got rid of them by blows in their backs with our musket butts. After crossing the bridge we marched along a broad and handsome street. We were astonished not to see anyone come out, not even a lady, to listen to our band playing *La victoire est à nous*. We couldn't understand this total silence, and imagined the inhabitants, not daring to show themselves, were peeping out at us from behind their shutters. Here and there we saw a few servants in livery and some Russian soldiers.'

Pion des Loches' is the first Guard battery to enter:

'At 6 p.m., the Emperor still hadn't made his entry, and he watched us cross the bridge. He was surrounded by generals, but nowhere near him did I see a single Russian. I passed down immense streets in the wake of the infantry. I looked up to the houses' windows to see if I could see any inhabitants behind them. I didn't see a living soul. I was frozen with terror. Sometimes cavalry regiments, galloping hither and thither without meeting anyone, crossed our path. I said aloud the city had been abandoned; and I still laugh at the sententious tone of a Captain Lefrançois as he replied: "No one abandons a great city. These people seem to have hid. We'll find them all right, we'll see them at our knees!"'

Lacking further orders, Boulart forms up his regiment in a square on the road leading to the Kremlin,

'beside the Petrovski family's town palace. On one side was a long straight promenade, planted with trees. On the other a nunnery. I formed my park in square, the guns in battery at the corners, the men and horses in the middle. I forbade the men to absent themselves. Then, having dismounted, I sent my lieutenants with a few gunners to the nearby streets to get some food. Everywhere they found the doors closed and barricaded. So we had to force them. In a trice everything was being pillaged, and doubtless it was the same throughout the city. Afraid of being taken by surprise, I ordered everyone to come back at the sound of a musket-shot.'

Although the Fusilier-Grenadiers, too, have been forbidden to absent themselves, after an hour their bivouac is

'filled with everything we could want, and an enormous quantity of sweet cakes and flour; but no bread. We went into the houses on the square, to ask for food and drink. But as we found no one there, we helped ourselves.'

Outside the Dorogomilov gate the conqueror of Europe is still waiting. Finally, says Ségur, when no deputation appears, an officer

'either anxious to please or else convinced that everything the Emperor desired had to take place, went into the city, caught five or six vagrants, and pushing them before his horse, brought them into the Emperor's presence. From these unfortunates' very first reply Napoleon saw he'd only a few wretched workmen in front of him. Only then did he cease to doubt that Moscow had been evacuated. Shrugging his shoulders he exclaimed with that scornful air with which he crushed everything that opposed his wishes: "Ah! The Russians still don't realize what effect the capture of their capital will produce on them!"'

It had been about midday when Eugène and his staff had sighted the city. And the Italians have nothing of the Germans' phlegm. Up there on the hilltop 'faces light up with joy. The men are transformed. We all embrace each other, we raise our hands to heaven in gestures of gratitude. Many shed tears of joy, and everywhere one hears people repeating "At last! at last! there's Moscow!" We were carried away with amazement at seeing so beautiful a sight, all the more seductive because of all the dreary ones we'd been witnessing. No one could contain his joy, on a spontaneous impulse we all shouted "Moscow! Moscow!". At this name, so long desired, everyone ran up on to the hill en masse. All were struck by the superb picture offered by this great city.'[5]

Césare de Laugier, like so many educated officers, half-consciously re-enacting all sorts of classical paradigms and literary allusions and scribbling it all down in his diary, calls to mind the moment when Tasso's crusaders first caught sight of Jerusalem:

> 'Ali ha ciascuno al cuore ed ali al piede
> Né del suo ratto andar pero s'accorge.
> Ma quanto il sol gli aridi campi fiede
> con raggi assai ferventi, e in alto sorge,
> Ecco apparir Gerusalemmme si vede...', etc.[6]

But to Labaume, Fantin des Odoarts and many others the scene is like something out of the *Arabian Nights*. As Griois' battery reaches the foot of the hill where IV Corps has halted, he joins the Viceroy on top of it,

'together with several of III Cavalry Corps' generals and superior officers. It seems impossible to describe the sensation I felt when, at the summit of this hill, which I was told was called the Sacred Mountain, I heard all mouths repeating the name of Moscow and saw all eyes fixed in the same direction, all spyglasses turned on this city. Sitting down at the crest I contemplated at my leisure, about six miles away, this immense town.'

Although all he gets at such a distance is an overall impression,

'its innumerable bell towers, each of which consists of several cupolas of different sizes and heights and are almost all clad in gilded metal or coloured tiles, glittered most vividly in the sun's rays. In no way did it resemble any cities I'd seen in Europe. As yet nothing was known about what was going on inside it, but the most contradictory rumours were going the rounds.'

The Italians are standing there lost in imagination when, across the intervening plain, they see a solitary figure coming towards them. It turns out to be a ruined merchant who, flouting the government's order to leave, has come out here 'to find some humane person who'll protect his family'. Count Rostopchin, he assures them, the city's governor, has ordered it to be burnt to the ground – 'at which everyone exclaimed it was impossible'. Bursting into tears, the fugitive begs them to prevent such a catastrophe.

347

Where the Italians cross it, too, the Moscova is only a few feet deep and they don't even wait for their pontooneers to throw a bridge, but fording it skirt the city 'at about half an hour's distance', and leave it to their right. And it's there von Muraldt, back from his mission, finds them, bivouacked on either side of the Petersburg road – and tells them Moscow has been abandoned. He too has quite a tale to tell. Determined to find something to eat, he'd hammered on the closed door of a big house where a German-speaking servant had finally come and opened. Taken upstairs, he'd found a German professor of Moscow University dining with some French ladies, and had been regaled with the best the house could offer; likewise, downstairs, his two chasseurs. His host had told him frankly he didn't think Alexander would ever make peace,

'"even if his second capital should fall to the enemy. He doesn't lack resources. And winter, which is approaching, will force the French to retreat. Anyone who thinks the Russians will immediately submit doesn't know them."'

Wined and dined and laden with provisions for his comrades, he'd set out again. Crossing the Dorogmilov bridge he'd seen

'the Emperor, wearing his chasseur uniform, with the usual four chasseurs posted in a square around him, strolling to and fro with his hands clasped behind his back and talking to the Prince of Neuchâtel. Our strange helmets made us instantly recognizable, and the Emperor waved to an officer and spoke a couple of words to him,'

to go over and ask these Bavarian chasseurs what they're doing there. Explaining, von Muraldt is sent on his way. What he has to tell them arouses in his listeners 'many grim forebodings. Not even the most happy-go-lucky saw the future in rosy tints'.

And in fact, no sooner have the Italians bivouacked than they're attacked by Cossacks, 'who set up their outposts under the very noses of ours'. Not far off to their left is a long straight road, 'lined, almost uninterruptedly, by country houses, most of no great size, but all more or less elegant and well decorated' – all of them abandoned by their owners, 'like those in all the other parts of the country we've passed through. Some of us won't even believe it, and laugh at our comrades who're telling them about it.' As for the road to their left, it leads out to a 'curious turretted Gothic-style building in red brick.'[7] It's the Petrovski Palace, where the Tsars reside on the eve of their coronations. Griois and his aristocratic friend Colonel Jumilhac install themselves in one, where they find – oh delight of delights! – even beds. 'For the first time since leaving Prussia I was able to undress and lie down comfortably.'

Since 'the town's surroundings were cultivated in garden plots that offered our men an abundance of those vegetables they'd so long been deprived of, notably enormous cabbages,' all the Germans have immediately begun making sauerkraut – the more welcome as that morning Heinrich von Roos and his men have been reduced to 'devouring juniper berries while our horses ate shrubs'. To its captors Moscow is above all something they're going to eat.

For the third time since leaving Germany the Italians, eagerly awaiting the return of Eugène's adjutant with orders to march in, don their parade uniforms. But alas, Lieutenant Wedel's assessment of Napoleonic priorities turns out to be perfectly correct:

'Stirred by a variety of emotions, we're gazing at Moscow, when a strong force of Cossacks appears away to our left. Good-bye Moscow! The Cossacks ride through the Moscova, we follow them across the river, and soon they're out of sight. We set up our bivouac close to one of the suburbs, on a hill by the main Petersburg road. This time our camp had a peculiar animation. Everyone was excited by the nearness of the town, by hopes of peace, by annoyance over the supposed slight inflicted on us by the Guard, whom we regarded as mere parade ground troops.'

Even the Italian Royal Guard has to cool its heels until the morrow.

Meanwhile Murat's cavalry, preceded at 300 paces by the Cossack rearguard, are crossing the city in the direction of the Kazan Gate. Riding slowly onwards down endless streets of single-storey timber houses interspersed with superb stone palaces, Victor Dupuy and his hussars hardly have time to glimpse the Kremlin's moats and gateways. Even in the remoter parts of the city houses and palaces are all shut up, silent. Claparède's Poles, too, are making very slow progress:

'It took us six hours to do about eight versts [8,800 yards]. During all this time we only met with one inhabitant – a Russian of gigantic stature, who, just as we were passing, came abruptly out of a house so as to cross over to another opposite. In doing so he bumped up roughly against some of the men, and even against an officer, who threatened him with his sword. Immediately this man, who seemed very much lit up, rips open his kaftan and shouts: "Plunge your iron into this Russian bosom!" As we'd been told to treat the inhabitants with the greatest consideration we let the fellow go. "If they're all like that," a sergeant said to me, "we aren't at the end of our troubles."

Brandt has been mysteriously warned by several French residents of 'a fateful plan'. But no more than Maurice Tascher does he see any fires or hear any explosions. But Séruzier, very much on the *qui vive*, has ordered his horse gunners to drag their guns by their bindings, ready for instant action. 'It was the first time I'd passed through a town with my guns on their bindings.' And what a town! Surgeon Roos, still riding on slowly, a little way ahead of them, is realizing that Moscow is

'certainly the biggest city I'd ever seen. Mingled with ourselves, Russians kept passing us on horseback, making for the same gate as we were. We let all that lot pass. Only one Russian officer's orderly, despite his objections, was obliged to decend from his admirable steed.'

Finally, after three hours, the advance guard reaches the Kazan Gate. And there's a small but bloody affray:

'Reaching the gate we were to pass through, we found two Cossacks on horseback who at all costs were determined to bar our way.'

One Russian officer who's lingered behind in hopes of reassuring his relatives that all is well with him, gets a nasty head wound, which Roos has to bind up for him. Otherwise, both sides seem to be joyfully anticipating an end to hostilities:

'Leaving the town, we found several regiments of Russian dragoons, some in line, others riding slowly onwards. We approached each other with the friendliest intentions, which they responded to. Officers and men went up to each other, shook hands, lent each other their water-bottles filled with brandy, and chatted as best they could.'

But then

'a Russian officer of the highest rank, accompanied by his ADC, turned up and very severely put an end to these conversations. But at least we'd had time to notice that peace would be as welcome to them as to ourselves. Their horses were no less exhausted than ours. When they had to jump a ditch many of them fell and only with difficulty got up again. Despite our extreme fatigue, everything was contributing to make us happy, and our camp was unusually animated. No one gave a thought to sleep.'

On the 10,000-acre plain fringed with silver birch woods to the west of the city I and III Corps' bivouacs are spreading out. Strictly forbidden to enter the city, Fézensac's 4th Line, for instance, have been ordered to stay at a distance of three miles. That afternoon Dedem and the Cossacks share

'a numerous herd of magnificent cattle which my soldiers, God knows how, had got their hands on. The Cossacks told us they were theirs, that they'd have nothing for supper if we didn't give some of them back. They weren't worried about the next day and 15 cattle would suffice for them. I had 22 given back to them, and they seemed most content. A secret joy stood painted on their faces, and a malignant smile indicated the hope they already had of punishing us for having got as far as Moscow.'

Delaborde's Young Guard division, which had been left behind at Smolensk, has just caught up, and out of some empty soap boxes 'found in a factory' Paul de Bourgoing and his comrades on Delaborde's staff are making themselves a kind of roofless barrack.

But at the Dorogomilov Gate Napoleon – largely at Durosnel's suggestion – has put off his official entry until tomorrow.

'After pacing up and down in front of the gate for some while, he mounted his charger, rejoined the Prince of Eckmühl a little distance away, and we all went with him to the village near the town,'
where he also reconnoitres the surroundings to a considerable distance. Then, coming back, he passes through the suburb, and goes
'as far as the partly demolished [stone] bridge. The river was only a couple of feet deep, and we were able to ford it. The Emperor went as far as the street on the opposite bank, then turned in his tracks to hasten the repairs to the bridge so that the ammunition could cross it.'

Meanwhile Count Daru and his staff have been sent into town at the heels of Murat's advance guard 'to ascertain the state of affairs and make a report the following day'. Penetrating the city's
'vast and magnificent solitude we passed the Kremlin, the square of the Bazaar, and the street leading to the square in front of the governor's palace. The night was fine; the moon's unclouded beams illumined those fine edifices, those vast palaces, those deserted streets, in which reigned the silence of the tomb.'
By and by they too fall in with a professor – whether Muraldt's host or another? – and some French residents
'who'd gone into hiding and couldn't comprehend this sudden disappearance of a population of 300,000 souls'.
And in fact many foreign residents, some of them of many years' standing, fearing or not being allowed to leave with the rest of the population, have remained behind, in terror of being 'massacred by moujiks' – i.e., the common people. Two such are *Madame Louise Fusil* and her friend, both of them actresses in Moscow's French theatre. Earlier that day 'the police had come knocking on every door to urge the occupants to leave, as the city was going to be set on fire and the fire-pumps had been taken away'. But the two Frenchwomen have stayed. Terrified when someone else comes knocking at their door, they're both relieved and amazed when he turns out to be a compatriot, who tells them the French are already in the city. Meanwhile Soltyk and his companions have been entering various palaces:
'All the doors were open. I took up my abode in a palace I was told belonged to the Countess Mackanow, at one of the corners of the square. In its underground kitchens I found two serfs who showed me the apartments. Everything was in as good order as if we'd been expected. In the drawing-room, which had two others opening out from it, there was a round table, on which the ladies' embroidery-work was still lying. Not even the most trifling piece of furniture wasn't in its place. In a very handsome bedchamber the keys were still in the drawers. Afterwards I heard all the linen and most valuable effects had been deposited in a cellar. Among them were two busts of the emperor and empress, concealed in casks of honey. I

took the keys of this cellar into my own keeping, so that nothing should be taken away. Five or six new carriages, all in very fine condition, were in the coach-houses.'

Soltyk too, has been sent back into the deserted town. His chief, General Sokolnicki, wants him to find the topographical department some suitable lodgings near the Kremlin, which the Emperor, deputation or no deputation, intends to occupy tomorrow:

'So I re-entered Moscow around 5 p.m., followed only by one muleteer leading a lead-horse. I made for the centre of town. The streets were deserted, and the inhabitants still shut up inside their houses.'

Despite his strong Polish and therefore anti-Russian sympathies, Soltyk can't help being impressed by the architecture of the houses around the Kremlin and their owners' good taste:

'Pushkin's, particularly, struck me by its magnificence. Built in the Italian style and surmounted by a golden cupola from which you could see the whole of Moscow and its environs, it was quite enormous. In the middle of its courtyard was a jet of clear water and a basin where some swans were swimming peaceably. I could even choose from a hundred houses where to spend the night, each wealthier and more magnificent than the next. What a contrast for a man who'd spent several months in bivouacs and the most miserable dwellings! For me they were the enchanted palaces of the Arabian Nights.'

After examining the whole street, Soltyk selects a moderate-sized one,

'yet more than ample to lodge the general and his suite. I was astonished to see a dozen of the Countess Maszenpuszkin's servants hastening to meet me. At their head walked a valet or major-domo, elegantly dessed and in silk stockings. In quite good French he asks me what I want, adding that, when leaving, the Countess had given orders to receive us properly, and has left enough servants in the house to wait on us.'

Her palace is exquisitely furnished, 'marquetry parquet floors, the furniture in walnut or ebony. A little mistress in Paris couldn't have desired anything better.' After an hour a sumptuous dinner is served up, with various wines, even champagne. Still better, the major-domo asks Soltyk whether he'd like to share his dinner with two French ladies whose patriotism has kept them from leaving Moscow until their compatriots arrive,

'the one being the Countess' governess, the other her companion. I conducted them to the dining-room where dinner had been served. And soon there I was, sitting at table between two amiable women whose conversation I found most attractive.'

Elsewhere, Pion des Loches and his fellow artillery officers, too, are at dinner, in the house of a French resident. There the menu is 'vermicelli soup, a whole side of beef, macaroni, some excellent bottles of Bordeaux – perhaps I've never had a better meal in my whole life'.

'But soon gloomy presentiments came to mingle with our pleasant meal,' Soltyk goes on:

'Dinner still wasn't over and daylight was still fading when suddenly one of these ladies, seated facing a window from which much of Moscow could be seen, gets up, runs over to the window and exclaims agitatedly: "There's the fire!" I follow her, and in the distance see a flame of no great size, but clear, rising from the top of a building they tell me is the Bazaar and contains an immense amount of merchandise.'

It's nothing, Soltyk assures them. Just the soldiers' negligence. It'll soon be put out. But the ladies aren't so sure. The feelings of the Muscovite nobles, they tell him, are 'violently aroused against us, and we must expect some great misfortune'.

Misfortune?

They tell him about Rostopchin's project of setting fire to the city (that vague, madcap and apparently self-authorized scheme which Louise Fusil, too, has heard about and now feels ominously confirmed as she hears an explosion, and running over to *her* window sees in the sky something that looks like a 'sword of flame'). But Soltyk gives little credence to

'these scraps of information, based merely on some vague words that had escaped the great lords of the country and been uttered in the intimacy of their homes. Mostly I ascribed them to the timidity of their sex.'

Pion des Loches' amiable host, too, is just saying 'there are so many palaces here, you'll each be able to have one apiece', when they hear that the Stock Exchange is on fire: "Stock Exchange? What's the Stock Exchange?" "A building bigger than the Palais Royal [in Paris]. It's stuffed with works of jewellery, the world's richest artefacts. This night's losses will be incalculable."

'I went outside and saw how the whole horizon really was on fire. I murmured into the ear of one of my lieutenants: "We're lost, the Russians are going to burn Moscow. Let's get back to our park."'

If the Stock Exchange fire, alarming though it is, isn't spreading, it's partly due to the efforts of Major Vionnet of the Fusiliers-Tirailleurs of the Young Guard:

'To prevent it spreading, we brought up 100 men and put the rest of the battalion under arms. Although I'd done this very quickly, on my return I found a house all on fire. Seeing I'm searching for fire pumps, an inhabitant tells me in Italian they've all been taken out of the city at the governor's orders. Worse, the fires have been started intentionally.'

Aided by eighteen Muscovites, however, Vionnet and his men get busy pulling down an adjacent house to contain the conflagration:

'After four hours of wearisome efforts, the little house was demolished. Hardly able to stand on my feet, I returned to my lodging. I'd slept for about an hour and a half when I was awakened to be told

the fire had caught another part of the Stock Exchange, in a building exposed to the wind.'

So he turns out again. And by about midnight this fire, too, has been mas-
tered. 'We were dead with fatigue.'

Soltyk and his hosts are relieved to see that no further fires have broken
out anywhere else[8] but 'these ladies, even so, remained silent and sad, and
our dinner ended less gaily than it had begun'.

As for the always prescient Pion des Loches, he's instantly sure the army
will have to retreat. And at his orders his gunners begin getting in some
flour, liquor and warm clothes:

'I myself had the doors of a magazine forced and a good number of
sacks of flour taken out – not without difficulty – by my gunners, who
preferred to go further and search for gold. These sacks once safely
in the middle of the park, I went back to my host's house and there
spent the night on a chair, clothed and armed.'

After which he installs his men in a magnificent empty palace, without furniture but 'with plenty of rooms where I without loss of time proposed to
bake plenty of bread'; installing himself meanwhile in a neighbouring
palace which, though fully furnished, has

'no other provisions except some fowl, plenty of oats and an opulent
cellar. On forcing the door, I found the prince's servants had spent
the night there drinking, the floor being covered with empty bottles
and spilt wine. Apart from an enormous, more than 400-bottle tun,
all the wine was in bottles laid out on the sand. Glass in hand we
identified the most exquisite vintages: Bordeaux, Frontignan,
malaga, dry madeira, as well as liqueurs and syrups. Without exaggerating, this cellar was worth more than 10,000 crowns. Still struck
with the idea that we'd soon be having to put up with great privations, I then had a barrel placed in my wagon, which was filled with
bottles of madeira, some sacks of flour and some salted fish. My gunners too tried to furnish themselves, but without using their intelligence. From a confectionery store they brought me baskets full of
dragées, macaroons and grilled almonds. I'd all the trouble in the
world getting them to give them up and carry off tuns of excellent
porter found in an ice cellar, and a freshly slaughtered ox, hung up
in a butcher's shop.'

Dedem, for his part, has just posted sentries in the Kremlin, when he's
been recognized by

'the valet of a princess, who'd seen me in Italy. Coming up to me, he
begs me to save her house. His mistress has left only an hour ago. I
authorize him to break into the writing-desk which he says contains
some papers, and promise him a safeguard.'[9]

At first the Dutchman too has thought all these servants' talk of the city
being set on fire really only means they're afraid the French will do it.
'But then they explained to me that more than a thousand persons had

been left behind as incendiaries, and that M.le Comte de Rostopchin had had all the pumps removed from Moscow.'

Since the Guard are beginning to pillage on their own account, this is a serious matter. And at about 11 p.m. Soltyk, trying to get a night's real rest in his 'good bed', hears someone knock violently at his door:

'It was the two French ladies. They'd come to tell me the house was being invaded by soldiers who were threatening to loot it; that they'd already broken into the wine cellars and right now were busy draining off one bottle after another. The servants didn't dare resist them. I dressed promptly, attached my sabre to my belt, and made haste to go down and repress these disorders. At the entrance to the cellar I found ten or twelve grenadiers of the Old Guard, armed with muskets. Most were completely drunk.'

Luckily Soltyk, as we know, speaks fluent French:

'I reprimanded them sharply and ordered them to get out, shouting at them that they were in the lodging of a general who belonged to the Emperor's household. One of the grenadiers came at me, menacing me with his fist. Several others followed to back him up. Drawing my sabre, I aimed such a blow at the plaque of the bearskin of the soldier who'd threatened me, that I knocked him down to the floor. This demonstration momentarily checked the grenadiers. The ones who were least drunk remonstrated with their comrades, reminding them of the respect they owed to rank and their obligation to observe military subordination. Despite this, after a moment's hesitation, two or three of them flung themselves at me with levelled bayonets. I parried the blows and, remounting the staircase, went back into my room, locking its door and shouting to my pursuers that the first man to try and force the door would get a ball from my pistols in him, because they were loaded.'

At that moment a Russian servant intervenes. And Soltyk's adventure ends peacefully. A moment later the house is 'evacuated by the marauders, who left, taking with them a goodly number of bottles to their bivouac. And the rest of the night passed calmly.'

Earlier, during the afternoon – at 5 p.m., says Fain,

'Napoleon had passed the barrier, gone some yards forward, and taken up his provisional quarters in a big inn on the right-hand side',

an inn Caulaincourt will afterwards remember as 'a mean tavern, built of wood, at the entrance to the suburb', but at the time notes down as 'a little timber house', But which to Bausset, the obese prefect of this temporary palace, seems to be 'a fine wooden house'. Repeated assurances are coming in from Murat that

'numerous stragglers are being caught, that they're all saying the [Russian] army is being disbanded, that the Cossacks are declaring openly they'll fight no more. He confirmed the information we'd obtained inside the city: that Kutusov, until only yesterday, hadn't said a word about having lost the battle or retreating on Moscow. Not until forty-eight hours before we'd entered Moscow had the governor, Rostopchin, even heard that the battle had been lost. The King of Naples was confidently expecting to seize part of the enemy's convoys and was sure he'd be able to break up their rearguard, so utterly disheartened did he believe the Russians to be.' All these details, Caulaincourt sees, 'delighted the Emperor and restored his good cheer'.

Although both Mortier and Durosnel have been sent there, no importance is being attributed to the fire in the Stock Exchange, which they, for lack of fire pumps, aren't able to do much about. Two smaller fires are attributed to the Guard's carelessness in lighting its camp fires. All this in spite of a catch made by interpreter Lelorgne d'Ideville while he'd been in town, trying to rustle up a deputation,

'a police officer, a simpleton, who knew everything that was afoot, and was very candid in all his avowals. At first he became so terrified he seemed to be slightly deranged. Such at least was the impression given by his statements, and no heed was paid to him. Seeing the first small fire break out, he'd declared that before long there'd be many more. Orders had been given to burn down the whole city. His revelations seemed to be delusions of a lunatic. This unfortunate fellow kicked his heels for some time in the guardhouse, where he was left when we had no more use for him.'

Eighty-two days have passed since the Grand Army crossed the Niemen. In that time it has marched some 825 miles, fought two major battles – one of them, the bloodiest in modern times, neither won, lost nor drawn – and several minor ones. Only two-thirds of its effectives are still with its eagles; of the cavalry scarcely half.[10] Yet Napoleon isn't an inch nearer to his objective – to force Russia back into his Continental System – than he was when he'd set out from Paris.

And tomorrow he'll get the shock of his life – as Moscow, as if by spontaneous combustion, bursts into flame.

Fiery prelude to a terrible retreat.

NOTES

Preface

1. All temperatures are in Réaumur. Since water boils at 80° Réaumur, centigrade (Celsius) temperatures will be proportionately higher – or lower.

Chapter 1. Overture to 1812

1 See bibliography under Villemain. Bibliographical references are given for all names italicized when first mentioned in the text.

2. Odenleben writes: 'With incomparable energy and efficiency he provided everything Napoleon needed. Chief among his virtues was an enterprise that knew no limits. He had an ability to say everything in a few words. After passing the night working together with Napoleon, he was the first at his post at dawn, almost always on horseback and constantly present at the Emperor's carriage door. He saw to it that strict economy was observed in all respects.' 'My notes', Caulaincourt himself tells us, 'were made everywhere, at my desk and in camp, every day and at all times of day; they are the work of every moment. I have touched up nothing.' There were moments when he was afraid his master might get to see them. Of this faithful and unusually candid man Napoleon would afterwards say at St Helena: 'He was an excellent Master of the Horse, but couldn't write.' An absurd judgement. Of Caulaincourt's memoirs it has been said that if all others from the period were lost, they alone would suffice to give us an accurate idea of it. Discovered in a locked tin box amid the ruins of the family château after the First World War, there is some evidence that they may have been tampered with; but not in what concerns the Russian campaign. There is no evidence that Caulaincourt's emphatic claims of having been against the war from the outset are an *ex post facto* rationalization. They'll accompany us at highest and most initiated level all the way to Moscow and back to Paris.

3. Since we hear no more of his being in poor health we canonly conclude that it was a pretext.

4. In her *Mes Dix Années d'Exil*, Germaine de Staël, who had sat at dinner with him when he was First Consul, notes that 'his eyes didn't smile'.

5. Like so many others, Constant would quit Napoleon's service at Fontainebleau in 1814, having either been (according to Napoleon) summarily dismissed, or perhaps (according to Constant himself) resigning, in connection with an attempted theft of (or perhaps misunderstanding about) a sum of 100,000 francs. In later years he'd spend his time fishing. After witnessing the Return of the Ashes, he'd say in tears to General Thiébault: 'I don't know how that devil of a man managed it, but he bewitched us all.' Of no man is the saying less true than that of Napoleon's that, 'no man is a hero to his valet'. Although Constant's memoirs, based on his anecdotes, are mainly the work of other pens, the portrait that transpires of a man who, if naturally exigent, was the best and most considerate of masters, is exactly the same as that given by his successor, the transparently honest Marchand, who accompanied Napoleon to St Helena and was rewarded by being made a count. No little melodramatic, the incident seems in its circumstantiality to have the hallmark of truth about it, and as far as I know has never been challenged.

6. Le Roy (or Leroy) says he wrote his memoirs as guidance for his two grandsons who were going in for the military profession. Hence – quite apart from his Lucullan temperament – the circumstantiality with which he describes how he got his dinner each day, sometimes under the most trying circumstances. Although he had a son who was a sergeant in another

battalion of the 85th, he had only one friend, his irrepressible adjutant-major Lieutenant Nicolas Jacquet, to whom he gave 'all my confidence and the little friendship I'm capable of. I've been so often deceived and the dupe of my good faith that I regard friendship as something impossible, above all on reaching the age of discretion, leaving aside those childishnesses which, in some people, even so, last longer than the liaisons of their maturity.'

7. Among other things she had recorded in it a visit by Davout: 'and weary work it was, trying to enliven him, for nothing more stolid and uncommunicative can be imagined than this thoroughly unpleasant man. Though neither malicious nor intellectual, his face betrays that he can be very curt and brutal. His aides-de-camp were every bit as disagreeable.'

8. The Coburgers were assigned to the 4th Regiment of the Confederation of the Rhine. They wore a French shako with brass rhomboid plate bearing a hunting horn, white cords, company pompom (grenadiers had bearskins) red cords and plumes, red epaulettes), on a dark-green Prussian-style coat, with two rows of white buttons on the chest, dark-green cuff flaps, yellow collar and cuffs, red turnbacks, three white lace buttonholes on the square cuff flaps, light-blue Hungarian breeches with yellow thigh and side lacing, short black gaiters with a point at the front, white belts.

9. Heinrich von Roos relates that when asked what the imperial 'N's on his men's saddlecloths stood for, they'd reply: 'Noch nur norden!' (anywhere except northwards!).

10. By 1812 the price of such a substitute – many were professionals, who sold themselves over and over again and then disappeared – had risen to the astronomical sum of 4,000 francs, and few but the very well-off could any longer afford it. This partly explains Caulaincourt's observation to Napoleon, on the banks of the Niemen, that this new war was not regarded as 'national' – i.e., in the inter-

ests of the French middle class ('la nation'). It was one thing to draft the sons of the people (le peuple) to be slaughtered in their hundreds of thousands; quite another for one's own more or less well-educated son to have to go.

11. Brandt was from that part of East Prussia which Napoleon had sliced off and incorporated in the Grand Duchy of Warsaw.

12. Guitard's proudest boast was that he'd captured 6,000 British troops near Bilbao in 1810.

13. He would serve during the Russian campaign as Assistant Prefect of the Palace, his particular task being to supervise the headquarters mules that carried among other things Napoleon's gold field service.

14. Quoted from Lagerbielke's report to the Swedish Foreign Office.

15. Captain Ross of HMS *Northumberland*, who didn't like Napoleon, describes the ex-Emperor's gait as 'something between a strut and a waddle', partly no doubt because of his having put on so much weight and partly because of the ship's movement.

16. See under Barre de Nanteuil in bibliography.

17. Yet it was this amiable monarch whose ultra-reactionary ideas – or lack of ideas – would most of all be responsible for the massive oppression that would fall on Europe after 1815.

18. Like his assessments of his policies, Méneval's striking portrait of Napoleon's personality, which introduces the third volume of his memoirs – unfortunately skimpy in what concerns 1812 – is wholly positive, yet unquestionably sincere.

19. It would be captured by Cossacks at Krasnoië during the retreat, together with his marshal's baton.

Chapter 2. The Rape of Poland

1. He had found the gross deceit and official perfidy employed to ruin an honest German merchant particularly scandalous. Like Captain Franz Roeder of the Hessians, he was shocked by the reduced straits of the Mecklenburg fishermen consequent on the Continental Blockade and the ubiquity of Napoleon's customs officers.

2. Heinemann had served in a French line regiment at Wagram, a fact of which he was inordinately proud. This hadn't prevented him from trying to desert while the Brunswick Chasseurs, part of Vandamme's VIII Corps, marched through Germany.

3. Brandt says that in his company, which had been serving in Spain, there wasn't one man who hadn't been wounded since 1809. And when the regiment, en route for Russia, had been been reviewed by Napoleon on the Place du Carousel, expectations had run high: 'One needs to have lived and served in that epoch to understand the importance of such a miliary fete, and what emotions set the heart of the boldest beating at the approach and aspect of this extraordinary man. The upshot of the review, however, didn't come up to everyone's expectations. We were counting on a rain of promotions, decorations, gratifications! In all there were only some 30 for this 2nd Vistula Regiment, which for four years had been living, or rather dying, in an atmosphere thick with musket-balls and grapeshot.'

4. After the Dresden event Marie-Louise had accompanied her father and – violently jealous – stepmother on a visit to Prague.

5. Butkevicius says, most improbably, that Napoleon was 'driving a wagon' – certainly an error in translation.

Chapter 3. Midsummer at the Niemen

1. It seems to have been by no means unusual for Napoleon to disguise himself at the outposts. Corporal Heinemann, then serving in a French Line regiment, was on outpost duty on the Isle of Lobau in the Danube in 1810, when suddenly Napoleon had turned up, borrowed a light infantryman's grey overcoat and shako and, thus attired, had done sentry duty on the river bank to examine the Austrian positions at close quarters. Heinemann relates proudly how his comrades 'elected the Emperor a voltigeur in our company'.

2. The Russian high command at Vilna were still unaware of his proximity, and had no idea of the real size of his effectives. Their latest figures, filched back in February by a Russian officer who'd bribed a French war ministry official in Paris – he'd been arrested and guillotined – were hopelessly out of date. Even the amplest Russian estimates didn't come up to half the Grand Army's real numbers.

3. The only tears this unemotional young man would shed during a campaign that would cause so many would be when Liesje died of exhaustion in a snowdrift, not far from where he was now.

4. Pils was not only a gifted although untrained water-colour artist. He also kept a *journal de marche*, in which he recorded his marshal's – but not his own – doings. Since Oudinot was forever being wounded, Pils always dogged his footsteps with a first-aid box. His son, Isidor Pils, one of France's most famous painters of his day, held his father's oil paintings, based on water-colour sketches made in Russia, in very high esteem. But no amount of research on my part has been able to track them down. What has become of these paintings which, artistic merit apart, must possess first-class documentary value? For example, the one, particularly admired by his son, of the fatal burning of the Berezina bridge during the retreat? – Oudinot's 32 wounds, of which he only considered nineteen to have been grave enough to be worth mentioning in his *états de service*, were by no means untypical. General Houchard had been wounded 48 times, General Achard 28, Rapp 26, Grouchy 25, Junot 18 – and

at the Battle of Heilsberg, Commandant Chipault of the 4th Cuirassiers had received 56 sabre cuts – and recovered perfectly! The account of Oudinot's wedding in his young wife Eugénie de Coussy's memoirs is well worth reading on its own account. See also my short study in Chandler's *Napoleon's Marshals,* Macmillan NY and Weidenfeldt & Nicholson, London 1987.

5. Roustam, an Armenian slave who had entered Napoleon's service in Cairo and on whom he lavished benefits, would also abandon him at Fontainebleau at the time of his first abdication. Hortense Beauharnais painted his portrait.

6. Lejeune had designed his romantic uniform for himself and Berthier's other aides in Spain, where he had been captured by guerrillas and shot; survived; been taken prisoner by the British and taken to England. From there, breaking his parole, he had got back to France thanks to the services of Romney Marsh smugglers, who at one point, however, contemplated cutting his throat. Back in Paris he had immediately reported for duty to Napoleon. Many of his elegant battle paintings are to be seen at Versailles.

7. Thirion, who had joined up in 1805 and been twice wounded, had been in Spain with the 22nd Dragoons. He had once been fined 3 francs by Napoleon for having lost his bayonet. 'I've always thought he wasn't annoyed to be able to show he knew the price of a bayonet.' Thirion died aged 82, in 1869, at Metz.

8. Increasingly faithful to Napoleon as his star waned, Planat de la Faye would volunteer to go with him to St Helena, but was outmanoeuvred aboard HMS *Bellepheron* by Gourgaud. Napoleon's last years might have been very different if Planat, instead of the hyper-emotional Gourgaud, had been in attendance at Longwood. He might even have proved a match for the sinister playboy Montholon. See Forshuvud, Sten: *Who Killed Napoleon?* and Hapgood: *The Murder of Napoleon,* New York, 1981.

9. Berthier's senior ADC had been one of Pauline Bonaparte's lovers. She had given him some priceless diamonds, a gift from Napoleon – who, however, instantly recognized them, sewn into this officer's pélisse, and taken umbrage. Whereupon they'd had to be returned.

10. Gourgaud had two obsessive ambitions: to rise in Napoleon's estimation, and to get married. In the end he succeeded in neither. Gourgaud's father had been a violonist at Versailles and his mother had been the Bourbon Duc de Berry's wet-nurse. In 1815, having betrayed his oath to the Bourbons by weeping, raging and sulking himself back into Napoleon's entourage – at one moment he'd even locked himself up in an attic of the Tuileries and refused to come out until taken back into the Emperor's good graces – he'd escape the firing squad by going with him to St Helena, where his violent jealousy, e.g., of Montholon who while fixing the best accommodation for himself and his wife arranged for Gourgaud to live in a tent in the garden, would finally become the bane of the ex-emperor's existence. Falling violently ill – Forshuvud thinks as a result of Montholon's expertise with arsenic – his mind seems to have become temporarily unhinged and his pathological jealousy made him more and more of a nuisance, so that he finally had to leave. After betraying Napoleon's secrets first to Sir Hudson Lowe, then to Lord Bathurst in London (with the result that Napoleon's confinement was made even more miserable), he would return to Belgium, where he'd pose as the ex-emperor's best friend and finally reinstate himself as a Bonapartist hero of St Helena.

11. Although exceedingly readable, Marbot is always the hero of his own occasion and his memoirs must at times be taken with a fistful of salt. Throughout the campaign he would be the 23rd Chasseurs' acting colonel, its commander Colonel Nougarède being too gouty to sit a horse, 'and this was no way to command a regiment of light cavalry on campaign'. Since the regiment, brigaded with the 24th Chasseurs, formed part of Oudinot's II

Corps, we shall not rejoin it until the Berezina, during the retreat.

12. In the evening of 20 May Coignet had driven his little two-wagon convoy into the Place Vendôme, near the Tuileries cellars, and loaded them with small barrels, each holding 28,000 gold francs. Two others were filled with officers' trunks. Catching up with his regiment at Metz he, at his own suggestion, had gone on ahead to pick up the regimental mail at postes restantes in Germany. On one memorable occasion, when Napoleon, who only measured 5 feet 2 inches, had wished to impress the diplomatic corps and had personally ordered both grenadier regiments' drill movements on the Place du Carousel, little Coignet had had to repeat his orders, making a half-turn and saluting each time as he did so.

13. Throughout the Empire period there were complaints of a shortage of carriages in Paris, the more so as the city only had three cab stands!

14. Unfortunately Stendhal's diary for the 1812 campaign was lost in the retreat. All we have is a few of his letters.

15. Attempts to ignore this regulation could come abruptly to grief. At Elbing, where the 2nd Swiss had bivouacked in a plain outside the town, one of voltigeur *Jean-Marc Bussy*'s comrades, Pillonnel by name, had been detailed off to be batman to that master of the theory if not the practice of warfare, the Swiss General *Henri de Jomini*. The said Pillonel had been cheerfully on his way into town, when 'an officer, looking out of the window of his lodgings, sees him passing with all his equipment. And calls out: "Swiss, where are you off to?" Pillonel answers: "I'm going to General Jomini." – "Well then, you go straight back to your battalion, and don't leave it again!" It was Napoleon himself, playing the military policeman.'

16. Despite his unsteady seat he had a habit of galloping headlong down ravines so steep his suite hardly dared follow. On one occasion he had ridden from Valladolid to Burgos, a distance of 96 miles, in 36 hours, and none of his staff had been able to keep up with him. Yet the only person who is known to have thought him the 'finest horseman in the world' would be the teenager Fanny Balcombe, for whom he made Admiral Cockburn's horse wheel about on the lawn at The Briars, on St Helena. It was Jardin, the First Groom's, duty to 'throw dogs and pigs between the legs of his Arab greys to accustom them to all kinds of sounds and sights'. Had Jardin neglected his duties, or was Friedland affected by its rider's mood?

17. Caulaincourt's claim that he was always frank with his master is confirmed by a Prussian officer who saw a lot of them in 1813: 'While fully recognizing Caulaincourt's qualities and abilities I think Bonaparte was less reserved with Duroc. The former was no less devoted to his master, but he was too cold and reserved, too bound by etiquette, whereas Duroc knew when to forget formality. On the other hand Caulaincourt spoke frankly to Napoleon and openly discussed matters which others dared not mention for fear of falling into disgrace.' For a striking, and indeed moving short biography of Caulaincourt, see Jean Hannoteau's introduction to the Memoirs.

18. When Philippe de Ségur's – from a literary point of view enthralling – *La Campagne de Russie* appeared in 1823 it made an immense impression, not least on fervent Bonapartists who accused it of a reactionary tendency. Gourgaud was particularly furious. His scathing – and in points undoubtedly correct – critique led to a duel between the two ex-officers of the Imperial Household. Stendhal too accuses Ségur of currying favour with the Bourbons. Ségur's classical models make him present Napoleon (a) as a victim of hubris, and (b) as suffering from ill-health. While Gourgaud doggedly maintains that he was in the best of health. There is doubtless something in both points of view.

19. But in Stockholm, a couple of hundred miles from Kovno as the crow flies,

Bernadotte, with unusual perspicacity, was writing to the Tsar that Napoleon by invading Russia was 'committing suicide'. Historians have not generally recognized Bernadotte's potentially critical role in 1812. Had he sided with Napoleon and simultaneously attacked Finland and marched on Petersburg, thereby tying down Wittgenstein's corps and so releasing Oudinot's corps, it is just possible that the Russian withdrawal from Vilnius might not have been so successful, and the whole outcome would have been different? This is why Napoleon himself said on St Helena that in 1812 the world's destinies lay in the hands of 'a Frenchman', i.e., Bernadotte. Naturally the remark was also part of his general self-exculpation.

Chapter 4. 'Get into Vilna!'

1. This according to Dr *Heinrich von Roos* of the Württemberg cavalry, III Corps.

2. 'It was only with difficulty that the French could persuade us Poles to take service on their staffs, to replace or supplement "dumb" Frenchmen...' When Napoleon had written to Prince Poniatowski, commanding V Corps, asking for six Polish officers of good family who 'spoke Polish, French, German and (if possible) Russian' to be seconded to imperial headquarters, no one, according to Grabowski, had been very keen. Doubtless, though he doesn't say so, Soltyk had been co-opted as a result of the reconnaissance on the morning of 24 June.

3. In the French army a white plume was the distinguishing mark of a colonel. No regiment, as far as I know – except the 2nd Guard Lancers, which were a new unit – wore them.

4. Cuirassier-captain *Jean Bréaut des Marlots* in a letter home to his sister.

5. He was a brother-in-law of Marshal Lannes. The scene is the one caricatured by Tolstoy in *War and Peace*, obviously on the basis of Ségur's melodramatic account. According to Ségur, Napoleon 'ordered a squadron of Poles to throw themselves into the river. Unhesitatingly these élite troops do so. At first they ride in good order, and when they can no longer touch bottom they redouble their efforts. Swimming, they soon reach midstream. But the current, which is at its swiftest there, scatters them. Their horses panic. Their loss is certain, but it's their own country that lies ahead, their devotion is to the liberator! About to be engulfed, they renounce their efforts, and turning their heads towards Napoleon, shout *"Vive l'Empereur!"* as they drown.' Which sounds dubious, to say, the least of it. As it happens, we've a third account. Marbot says his 23rd Chasseurs, heading II Corps, turned up at the same moment. And certainly he isn't the man to spoil a good yarn. Yet all he saw was *one* man drown: 'I took the man's name. It was Tzsinski.' Gourgaud, too, pours scorn on Ségur's mock-heroics. A Captain *Joseph Zalusky*, he says, commanding the first squadron of the Polish Lancers of the Guard, 'having abandoned his horse, was in danger of drowning. He was saved by some sapper-workmen and light infantrymen' – luckily for us, as he'll have a lot to relate.

6. Blaze explains that in the eyes of the Napoleonic soldier everyone who wasn't a military man was either a 'peasant' or a 'bourgeois'. One didn't steal their property. One simply 'found' and 'took' it: 'No one who hasn't been to war can ever imagine the evils it entails. We officers lived off what our men "found". How could we have done otherwise? Our supplies, even when we had any, couldn't possibly keep up with our rapid marches. In rich countries we would carry into camp twenty times more provisions than we could possibly consume; the rest was wasted. The soldier lives for today. Yesterday he lacked everything. Today he's in abundance. An army's marauders always have this excuse: "I'm hungry, I'm looking for bread." There's no answer to this. The cavalry troopers have a double excuse: they're searching for forage for their horses.'

7. The French armies were unique in having a more or less reliable postal service,

through which anyone could write home to his family or friends. In 1812 the Russians would capture quite a lot of such letters and afterwards publish them.

8. The word 'dysentery' was used indifferently in those days to include diarrhoea.

9. Roeder is absolutely an acquaintance worth making. I am grateful to Miss Helen Roeder, his descendant, for permission to quote from her book, one of the most vivid and personal of all the accounts.

10. Fivaz was Jomini's brother-in-law, and would shortly become his ADC. See: *Soldats Suisses au Service de la France.*

11. It is almost impossible to identify the traditional place-names, spelt differently by various participants in the campaign, on a modern map of Lithuania. Lithuanian place names seem to be as different from the traditional Polish ones as Finnish place-names are from Swedish ones in Finland. Evê is presumably Vievis, Novo-Troki is Trakai, etc.

12. It's Davout who, in Tolstoy's *War and Peace*, orders Pierre Bezhukov to be shot, after he's betrayed his educated status by correctly addressing him as Monseigneur.

13. A privilege Jerome Bonaparte liked to usurp. Sometimes Berthier would be mistaken for his master on account of his hat. Three years later it would be partly for lack of Berthier's routines that Napoleon would be definitively beaten at Waterloo. 'Berthier would have posted an ordnance officer at the Charleroi bridge...'

14. The formerly beautiful Madame Visconti was the passion of Berthier's life. During the earlier campaigns he'd installed a veritable shrine to her in his tent, and the whole army had laughed at him for doing so. The lady had a withered arm. After Napoleon, forbidding him to marry her, had married him off to a German princess, all three lived in a harmonious *ménage à trois* in Paris and at the superb château of Grosbois, whenever Berthier had leisure to be there. Formerly owned by the guillotined Duke of Orleans ('Philippe Egalité'), brother of Louis XVI, Grosbois had been given to Berthier in his capacity of Master of the Hunt. It was currently occupied by the kidnapped Spanish royal family.

15. Staël, Germaine de: *Mes Dix Années d'Exil.* On 14 July, after escaping from the isolation of her Swiss estate to which Napoleon had condemned her, the most famous novelist and critic of his regime in Europe was also to 'invade' Russia; getting to Moscow before him and leaving for Petersburg before the Grand Army's arrival. Going on to Stockholm to hobnob with and flatter Bernadotte, she would play an important part in stimulating the rising against Napoleon's regime in 1813-14 – and live to regret his fall.

16. According to Dedem it would be his compatriots the Dutch who would be 'least able to stand the privations. Their morale would be quickly affected. We were content with their bravery and their officers' education. But above all the younger men were attacked by depression, becoming discouraged at the idea of being taken so far from their country. They regretted their methodical habits and, for the most part at least, were neither imbued with the spirit of conquest and domination nor with the gaiety characteristic of the French.'

17. The episode is paraphrased from Thomas: *Les Grands Cavaliers du Premier Empire* (nd).

18. Ségur, Philippe de: *Du Rhin à Fontainebleau*, Edn. Nelson, Paris. In his – often very inaccurate – campaign history he writes in the grand heroic style, modelled on classical writers, and makes no mention of his personal actions or feelings. But here, in his personal memoirs, he writes with accents of personal suffering.

19. The Jagellon dynasty (1386-1499) extended the borders of Lithuania to include the whole of Poland.

Chapter 5. Bagration gives Davout the Slip

1. A 'division', in this sense, consisted of two companies.

2. His name was Amédé, and his features are described as 'cherubic'. Napoleon's stepdaughter, ex-Queen Hortense of Holland, who was quite a good artist as well as being perhaps the only really admirable person in the imperial family, had painted his portrait.

3. 'One of the two officers who malingered, Lieutenant Lesueur, who held the Legion of Honour, had to command the laggers and next day got a severe dressing-down from Bessières. Temporarily attached to the Horse Chasseurs of the Guard, they didn't rejoin until later.' – Dumonceau.

4. Allegedly the change was made at the advice of Berthier, his mortal enemy, though it seems unlikely that Napoleon would have taken so important a step at the advice of a man of whose intelligence he had so low an opinion. The three detached divisions were commanded by Count Lobau.

5. In five months' time Smorgoni would become famous as the place where Napoleon, after signing his last bulletin announcing the Grand Army's complete destruction, would quit its last relics to hasten back to Paris.

6. Published in a journal, I have taken this brief résumé from Tarle's more extensive one in *Napoleon's Invasion of Russia, 1812*, London, 1942. At St Helena Napoleon wouldn't even be able to recall the envoy's name: 'Alexander sent someone to tell me that if I'd evacuate the invaded territory and go back to the Niemen he'd treat for peace. But I in turn took it for a ruse. I was swollen with success. I'd caught the Russian army on the hop, had thrown everything into disorder. I'd cut off Bagration. I'd high hopes of destroying him. So I thought Alexander was only hoping to gain time, elude me and rally his forces. No question but that if I'd been convinced of Alexander's good faith I'd have retired to the Niemen, and we wouldn't have come further than the Dwina. Vilna would have been neutralized; and we'd both have gone there, each with a few battalions of our guards, and treated in person. How many combinations I'd have introduced! He'd only have had to choose. And we'd have parted as good friends.' Napoleon's words, uttered in the presence of Caulaincourt, Duroc and Bessières, gives this retrospective daydream the lie.

7. One of the merits of Curtis Cate's admirable book *The War of the Two Emperors* is that he makes it perfectly plain that it was impossible for Jerome to arrive on time in the theatre of war.

8. Jerome liked to preempt Berthier's privilege, unique in the army, of wearing a Swiss-style civilian hat, of the kind Napoleon had made so famous. A certain colonel Latouche, a Frenchman from the Illyrian provinces, who bore a striking resemblance to Napoleon, was doing so too. According to what Colonel Jumilhac told his friend Colonel Griois, Latouche had been up to his tricks in Warsaw, where he'd pretended to be Napoleon incognito and promised he'd promote Jumilhac to general's rank, which of course he couldn't do. On 25 June, Dessolles, IV Corps' chief-of-staff, had sent Latouche back to France because 'he affects to play on his resemblance to the Emperor and provoke ridiculous misunderstandings, he has been arrested and sent to headquarters'.

9. If Vandamme, instead of the by now sick and supine Junot, had been in charge of VIII Corps at Valutina the Russian army would certainly not have escaped total destruction.

10. Metternich, Napoleon's arch-enemy, would say of Fain: 'Baron Fain is a man of probity, conscientious, who always relates facts as they happened or as they have been presented to him in accounts he feels he should believe. He's a good historian and an honest man.' This, despite the fact that Fain's view of Napoleon is always positive.

11. Alexander had absolutely no illusions as to Napoleon's 'personal friendship' for him. He would write to his sister Catherine in September: 'This spring, before my departure for Vilna, I had been informed on good authority that the constant work of Napoleon's secret agents... if I was with the army, to put all the reverses that might happen down to my account and to represent me as having sacrificed my personal pride by preventing more experienced generals than myself from obtaining successes over the enemy; and, on the other hand, if I was not with the army, to impute it to a lack of courage on my part.'

12. A verst is 1,100 yards.

13. 'Formerly I could keep four or five secretaries busy, but then I was Napoleon. Now it's an effort even to open my eyelids.' – Napoleon in his last sickness, to Dr Antommarchi in November 1820.

14. This could have been as a result of an order from Napoleon to send the gendarmerie to deal with the 33rd Regiment, which was busy pillaging at Voronovo. He'd been told some of Davout's men were making for Lida, on pretext of joining I Corps, but 'really to pillage this valley, which is superb'.

15. Ordered by Barclay to march for Minsk, Bagration had then received another from Alexander himself, countermanding it and ordering him to march north-eastwards for the Drissa Camp, i.e., right across the path of the advancing Grand Army. It had been while trying to cross the Vilna-Minsk road, at Ochmiana, that his advance guard had bumped into Pajol's cavalry. Not knowing that Davout, deprived of Friant's, Gudin's and Morand's divisions, was now at less than half-strength, he'd supposed himself to have to do with 60,000 crack troops – nearly twice his own 35,000. Veering back, he'd made tracks south-eastwards for Slutsk, on the edge of the Pripet Marshes (a vast trackless area dividing the northern from the southern theatres of war). After a 9-day forced march, he'd rested his troops at Slutsk, and was now head-ing eastwards for Borissow, on the Berezina.

16. One wonders what had become of a certain voltigeur whom Napoleon, when the regiment had paraded in front of him at the Tuileries, had singled out on account of his 'embonpoint, excessive in a voltigeur'; and, turning to General Krasinski, had said: 'Ask that fellow where he's put on so much fat!' And upon the man's replying that it was in France, rejoined smiling: 'Tell him to put himself on a diet, because soon they may well have to fast.'

17. Davout, who in his youth had been a devotee of Montaigne, was nevertheless a convinced atheist.

18. Other eye-witnesses' memories seem inexact. One says it was the 111th Regiment, made up of Piedmontese, that suffered; another, more vaguely, 'a German regiment who'd lost a great many men en route, some of whom had been pillaging and causing disorders'. But that they marched past with dignity, even so.

Chapter 5. Problems at Vilna

1. The Drissa Camp, brain-child of a certain Colonel von Pfull, the Tsar's military adviser, was a system of earthworks on the River Dwina. The idea was that 50,000 men should shut themselves up in it, lure Napoleon to besiege them, and then attack him in flank and rear. Never having been properly completed, it was already being abandoned.

2. 'He understood me in his own way and carried out his task independently,' Napoleon would say of Bacler d'Albe at St Helena. Unfortunately d'Albe's *Souvenirs Pittoresques*, with their admirable engravings of important battlefields, lack a commentary. His son was ADC to Philippe de Ségur. In the rout after Waterloo the valet Marchand would see 'poor little M. d'Albe walking along looking dazed. He'd lost his box of coloured pins.'

3.The day Castellane made his irritated diary entry, Planat had to implement the following:

'Vilna, July 7: I must inform you, *M. le Général*, that General Eblé is being given orders undelayedly to organize a bridging train of thirty-two boats, with two companies of pontooneers and one company of marines, which he will place under the command of General Kirgener [commanding the Guards Engineers], who will take with him one company of the Marines of the Guard, the company of Sappers of the Guard, that of the Grand Duchy of Berg, the three companies of sappers attached to the Guard, two companies of workmen from the Danube Battalion with their vehicles, two companies of miners and two of sappers from the General Engineer Park. This train will march for Widzoni (Vidzeme), where it will be under the King of Naples' orders. However, since the bridging train may retard these troops on the march, the Emperor orders that the pontooneers and one company of sappers be left behind to escort it. General Kirgener will march ahead with the rest of his troops to have all the bridges on the route put back into proper shape. The Emperor demands a detailed report on the bridges.'

Next day comes another letter, no less exhaustive, ordering the bridging trains' successive departures for Sventsiany on 9, 10 and 11 July, each of 30 vehicles. The rigging teams – vital for throwing pontoon bridges across rivers – left behind at Kovno are to be brought up by oxen 'two to each vehicle'. The Intendant-General is to supply Eblé with barley and 200 pairs of oxen.

'The Guard is leaving behind far too many of its guns. Since we have men, and all that is lacking is horses, oxen must be used, these being very suitable for the reserve parks. The Emperor's intention is that you recommend the same method to III, II and I Corps. Since the oxen do not need barley they will infallibly arrive, even if later, but always in time to bring the divisions their replacements.'

Alas, neither oxen, nor goads, nor barley, nor qualified drivers are just now to be

had. This doesn't alter the fact that several major rivers lie ahead; and 12 July brings the wretched overworked Planat two more orders anent the bridging teams: 'Everything must gradually arrive, whether drawn by horses or oxen, but tomorrow it's imperative that the entire personnel shall leave, because without pontoons His Majesty will have to use skiffs and trestles...' Later the same day comes another:

'*M. le Général.* The Emperor orders you to bring 5,000 muskets up to Vilna and as many again to Kovno, and sabres in proportion, to arm the French infantry... Likewise the King of Saxony's 30,900 muskets, which are at Bromberg; the 5,000 new musketoons and 8,000 sabres to arm the insurrection...', etc., etc.

Next day come three more letters. One informs Lariboisière that the siege train has been ordered (apparently over his head) to march for Tilsit, where it's to be embarked to help Macdonald's X Corps invest Riga. Relays of vehicles are to be set up every fifteen miles 'and consist of at least 150 to 200 vehicles'. Two companies, one of naval workmen and one of sappers, are being left at Kovno to rebuild the Niemen and Vilia bridges:

'Construct a redoubt on the high ground on the Niemen's left bank, to defend the bridge. Establish the projected fort on the high ground (right bank of the Niemen, and at the Vilia bridgehead). Each of these works is to have twelve guns. The commandant there will furnish six hundred soldiers to be employed on these works, and twelve hundred peasants...'

(It will be with these guns that Ney with his last rearguard of Bavarians will fire the last shots of the campaign in December.) Gen. Eblé's pontoon bridges 'which are very good' are to be re-utilized at various points along the Vilia as soon as the regular Niemen bridges have been rebuilt.

3. Later, as the summer grew hotter and drier, the whole scheme, so carefully worked out in Paris, would have to be dropped and supplies brought into the town on carts by commercial contract with local Jews.

4. There are vivid accounts of this minor battle by Marbot – who as usual declares himself its hero – by 'grenadier' Pils, and by the Piedmontese *maréchal-des-logis Jean Calosso*. It is in Calosso's account, which in certain points convincingly contradicts Marbot's more vainglorious and self-centred one, that we find the source of the famous incident of the soldier who, having lost his arm in the battle, went back to find it and cut off a finger to recover his treasured ring!

5. Maret had his own secret police, headed by the enigmatic Sémonville, Montholon's stepfather. So did Fouché, and so did Napoleon – all three organizations were busy spying on one another. One of Maret's more ingenious devices was to have his wife, knowing all mail was opened by Napoleon's secret police, insert fictitious bits of gossip into her letters about how devoted her husband was to His Majesty.

6. His violently critical book, in which Pradt writes that 'Bonaparte made himself an imaginary Poland', would be echoed by Sir Hudson Lowe at St Helena: 'Now he's inventing an imaginary St Helena.'

7. Hogendorp had been Governor of Java and Dutch Ambassador to Petersburg. He would end his life in Brazil.

8. It had been Jomini's ambition to write a scientific analysis of General Bonaparte's early campaigns. And Napoleon had personally given orders that he should have access to the War Archives. But the project had been systematically scotched by Berthier, who in this Swiss no doubt sensed a potential rival, and by Salomon, his near relative and chief assistant. Access to all the crucial documents, so necessary to Jomini's great work, had been denied him. It is by no means certain that here Napoleon wasn't playing a double game. Did Napoleon, whose whole empire was in crucial respects dependent on myth-making, really want to have Jomini studying original documents in the War Archives?

9. An idea not altogether unfamiliar to Zalusky. Like many educated Poles he was well up in the history of Charles XII of Sweden, who'd been treated in exactly this manner. In his boyhood he'd also heard an 'Irish doctor Hasselqvist' (certainly a Swede, possibly from Finland) tell his grandmother that if ever the Russians were attacked by a French army this was exactly what they'd do. Brandt, too, had heard his colonel, 'an educated and sensible man', say how afraid he was that

'the Emperor is making the same mistakes. Look how he's forcing his way into the heart of Russia, leaving behind him a disorganized Poland and a Lithuania that's been put to the sack! In this situation the least setback can't fail to have the same consequences. The whole of Germany will revolt and things'll turn out just like they have in Spain, but on quite a different scale. The kings who are just now attached to the Emperor's chariot will hasten to break his yoke.'
Of course such memories, wise after the event, can in some degree be filtered through hindsight. But not, one feels, entirely.

10. In a word, exactly the same insouciance that Marbot accuses Oudinot of showing at Wilkomir.

Chapter 7. With the Advancing Columns

1. That is, if he wasn't travelling even more lightly in the calèche which Fain says served to transport him 'from one army corps to another, or to cover in a few hours a road for which the troops needed a whole day. In this way of advancing by leaps and bounds two Chasseurs à Cheval rode a couple of paces ahead of the calèche, with two ordnance officers. At the right door rode the duty stable officer, at the left the Guard general commanding the escort. Around the carriage and behind it pressed the Emperor's ADCs – mostly generals, twelve at most – and the pages; and lastly the escort piquet

of some 24 Chasseurs. Sometimes a second calèche followed, for Grand Marshal of the Palace Duroc, the Master of the Horse, and the duty ADC.' In either case Caulaincourt's office would have placed out 'brigades' of riding horses.

2. The deserters were from the 2nd and 3rd Battalions of the Joseph Napoleon Regiment, commanded by the extremely experienced Swiss colonel Tschudy. Its 1st and 4th Battalions were serving in II Corps and are not recorded as giving any trouble.

3. Jerome had even threatened to abdicate, as his brother Louis had done in Holland. Now he wrote to his wife that he wouldn't submit to such degradation, and hoped to be home within 45 days. When his letter reached his wife on 29 July it would cause her to write in her diary: 'I'm more dead than alive. What will be the results of this action? However unjust the Emperor may be towards the King, he should have bowed to circumstance. Nothing is to be gained by standing up to the Emperor.' Taking the waters at Neudorf, Jerome afterwards tried to make good his blunder by raising a new route-regiment, 800-man strong, infantry, cavalry, guns and train horses, to send off to Russia. Twelve new cannon were to be cast. 'Before 1 Jan, I'll have a small division of 6,000 men: a regiment of the Queen's infantry, a regiment of cavalry, and a battalion of light infantry.'

4 When Rossetti told Napoleon he'd never served against France he wasn't telling the truth. He had in fact served in the Piedmontese army.

5. All quotations from Heinemann's memoirs are translated from an old Swedish translation. Although probably ghost-written and in parts romanticized, the authenticity of most passages is obvious.

6. Madame de Staël, who had been through Austria earlier in the summer when fleeing from Switzerland to Russia – her book *Sur l'Allemagne* (*On Germany*) had given the most profound offence – says the introduction of paper money in

that ruined state had demoralized the population.

On 18 July, the day Napoleon had left Vilna, she had crossed the frontier into Galicia, her goal being Petersburg, which she could now only reach via Moscow. 'Do you imagine, Madame,' Napoleon's Minister of Police had said, 'we've been waging war in Germany for eighteen years in order that so celebrated a person as yourself should publish a book without saying a word about us? This book must be destroyed, and we ought to have put its author in Vincennes!' Published originally only in London, after the Russian débâcle, her book would become a powerful factor in rousing all Germany against the oppressor. On this talkative, talented, plain-looking Swiss woman with a Parisian soul, Napoleon projected all his misogyny and detestation of female emancipation. Hadn't it been an important factor in the *ancien régime*'s undoing? And wasn't this new one directed towards the re-establishment of 'order', after ten chaotic years of Revolution which had finally brought France to a state of complete ruin and threatened civilization itself? And hadn't the Revolution been inspired from first to last by 'ideologists?' of exactly her kind? Their hatred was mutual. Madame de Stael's view of Napoleon was simplicity itself: 'Man is not hindered on his evil course unless by insuperable obstacles or by prick of conscience. Napoleon has not run into the former, and has easily liberated himself from the latter. He stands at the head of a million soldiers, has a hundred millions in income, disposes of all the prisons in Europe and uses its kings as gaolers, a man who uses the printing press when he himself wishes to speak, whilst the oppressed hardly dare confide their reply to the silence of the most intimate friendship.' (If one thinks this an exaggeration, even by the standards of our own time's dictatorships, we should read what Dutheillet has to say about his own childhood in working-class Paris, where 'during the Empire people always spoke of public affairs in hushed voices'.) Madame de Staël goes on: 'In other despotic states there are customs, laws and a religion which the ruler never violates, no matter how sovereign he may be. But in France everything is new, just as France herself is something new in Europe. The limited number of free nations can have no idea of the state of insecurity prevailing there; a state of affairs which has become habitual under Napoleon's sabre. For fifty leagues from the Swiss frontier France is stuffed with lookout towers, prisons and fortresses serving as prisons, and everywhere one sees nothing but private individuals under durance from one person's will or unfortunates held by force in distraint far from the places where they want to live.'

7. Back at the first manor, Legler has just freed the cook – who all this time has had his hands tied behind his back – when 'a beautiful woman, holding two children by the hand and her hair all loose, came rushing toward us and flung herself down on the knees, begging us to help her. During our absence several other units had come to the house and ruthlessly taken away all their animals, 300 in all. "Now I've no food left for my children," she said. "Take pity on us, give us a cow so my children can go on living." "Madame, choose not one, but six, and hide them deep in the forest. I'll stay with you til you've done it." The 'baron', his wife, his cook and two of his servants take the six cows – and six calves into the bargain. Also, 'since I had a rich booty', the 12 sacks of grain and three big loaves. 'I thought to myself, a Christian's duty is to live and let live.' Our memoirists' pages are full of such tales. For another, see Brett-James' (op. cit.) account of Lieutenant Houdart's account of his mission; and, in Helen Roeder's book the very funny story of Lieutenant Grandeville's marauding mission, both omitted here for reasons of space.

8. Labaume, who must also have been present, glosses over the incident, merely saying the Italian Royal Guard co-operated in jealously guarding the biscuit stores against any surprise attack by Cossacks.

9. Even so, Laugier's diary insists, 'these calamities are less keenly felt in the Army of Italy, and least of all in the Royal Guard. Worthy of the name it bears, it wishes above all to distinguish itself by its unremitting discipline, turnout, resignation and firmness of will.'

10. Of all the top brass, says Marbot, St-Cyr was 'the one who best knew how to use his troops on the battlefield; but also incontestibly the one who paid least attention to their welfare. He never asked whether his men had victuals, clothes, shoes, or enquired after the state of their weapons. He never reviewed them, never visited hospitals, or even asked whether any existed! According to him, his generals had to see to all that.' Was this why his Bavarians had arrived at Glubokoïe in such a shocking state? Nor would it get any better, as we shall see.

11. He would soon be able to gauge it and find it shallow. On 22 July Marmont would lose the Battle of Salamanca (which the French called Arapiles) against Wellington. St-Cyr says Napoleon's judgements 'at the head of 500,000 men and seeing the Russians fleeing in all directions' were very different from what he'd later have to say about himself and his colleagues at St Helena.

12. – 'only to be dashed afterwards when I saw Napoleon doing exactly the opposite of what he'd so sagaciously worked out'.

Chapter 8. First Clashes

1. Polotsk was the seat of the Jesuit Order, suppressed by the Pope in 1773 and only surviving in Russia. It was here it had its general, its printing works, 44 priests, 46 novices and 29 assistants. 'These religious', comments Dedem van der Gelder sourly, 'lived up to their reputation by promising us a lot and leaving us in the lurch as soon as we depended on them.'

2. Maurice Tascher was one of three brothers. His diary would be saved by his brother Ferdinand after he'd died in his arms in a Berlin hospital on 27 January 1813.

3. *'Faire la diane'*. The practice dated officially from an order issued at Schoenbrunn on 14 November 1805: 'Before dawn generals and colonels must inspect their outposts, and the line must stand to arms until the reconnaissance patrols have returned. It must always be assumed that the enemy has been manoeuvring during the night in order to attack at dawn.'

4. Of all our eye-witnesses only Dedem has a good word to say for Davout: 'If ever I have to make war again, it's under Marshal Davout I'd wish to do so. The Prince of Eckmühl is the man who best knows how to obey, and thereby has learnt to command. There was never a chief more severe in point of discipline, juster, or who occupied himself more with the welfare of the ranker, his instruction and his needs; and no sovereign ever had a more faithful or devoted servant.'

6. The current year's and the following year's call ups. Napoleon had already ordered the call up for 1813.

7. The Russians had tried the same psychological warfare against Charles XII's Swedes in 1708.

8. D'Hautpoul's instructions are an oft-quoted example of what could be expected of a headquarters ADC on mission. He was to

'go to Beschenkowiczi, where he'll stay until the three bridges have been thrown across and the bridgehead marked out. He'll ensure six ovens are built at those points where they can be erected most swiftly. As there are relay posts between Beschenkowiczi and Kamen, he'll write to me two or three times a day. He'll find out on the spot the whereabouts of Friant's, Gudin's and Nansouty's divisions, Montbrun's cuirassiers and those of Nansouty, and, finally, whether there's any news of the King of Naples. He'll send me all information thus collected. On his way to Beschenkowiczi d'Hautpoul will write me a first letter

from Koszikowa, to inform me of the state of the bridge, the population and that place's resources.'

Chapter 9. Battle at Ostrowno

1. The order to Oudinot, still in the Polotsk area, is that he shall attack Wittgenstein, who is unsupported since Barclay's withdrawal to Witebsk; and the one to St-Cyr is that his VI Corps shall remain at Ouchat to secure the army's communications and go to II Corps' assistance if it's attacked. Having reinforced Wittgenstein with 25,000 of his own troops, Barclay is now left with only 75,000 and therefore more than ever desperately in need of Bagration's forces if he's to be able to give battle at Witebsk.

2. Confirming Marbot on this point. At Wilkomir on 28 June his splendid 23rd Chasseurs, riding on at the head of Oudinot's corps, had all but fallen into the same trap: 'Doubtless you'll be astonished that [Wittgenstein's 25,000 to 30,000 men] had neither major nor minor outposts, nor scouts placed out in front of them; but such is the Russian habit when they're resolved to defend a good position, to let their enemy approach as close as possible without their sharpshooters' fire warning him of the resistance he's going to run into, and it's only when his masses are at close range that they smash into them with their artillery and musketry, astounding and shaking their adversary's men!'

Chapter 10. Fézensac on Mission

1. Van Zuylen would return from captivity but his billiards partner would die, a prisoner, on 17 January 1813.

2. Only a month earlier, on the eve of the invasion, this swashbuckling but effete grandee had been desperately urging his brother to make peace at all costs. During the retreat he'd gratify a dying French officer's last wish by personally cutting his head off.

3. It had been the campaign's second serious battle – depending of course what one means by a battle, as distinct from a mere engagement, '*combat*' or '*affaire*'. The usual definition of a battle was that a whole corps was involved. On the Grand Army's northern and southern flanks Macdonald, Schwarzenberg and Oudinot had all had serious fights with the retreating Russians which, however, cannot be included within the scope of this book.

4. Faced with the threat of French invasion, a whole series of fortresses were to have been established. Borissow was to have been one of them.

5. Girod de l'Ain also reflects on the difference between Russian and French military psychologies: 'The Russian soldier stands up admirably under fire, and it's easier to demolish him than force him to retreat. But this comes above all of excessive discipline, i.e., a habitual blind obedience to his officers. Usually it's not he who'll lead his comrades, either forwards by his dash or backwards by his flight. He stays where he's been put, or else where he's run into too lively a resistance. This passive and unintelligent obedience is also habitual in officers of all grades. A unit unhappily placed where a battery can enfilade it will remain there, needlessly and profitlessly exposed, as long as the officer commanding it receives no order from his superior to change its position.' All in contrast with the typical behaviour of a French officer, who 'depend upon it, will never hesitate to dispose his unit where it'll suffer as little as possible from enemy fire, and, in order to shelter it, will profit by such facilities as the least bit of space, the least fold in the ground, can offer him, without waiting for orders from above, but always taking care, when changing position, to offer the enemy no advantage.'

6. According to Schuerman's *Itinéraire Général de Napoléon1er*, the imperial tents were pitched near a burnt mill, not far from the Luchiesa stream, a little to the left of the main road. Constant describes the layout of Napoleon's own: 'It was separated into three rooms by curtains. The Emperor slept in one of them, the office was in the second, his ADCs and duty officers were in the third. Usually this room served the Emperor to take his meals in, which were prepared outside. I alone slept in the bedroom. Roustam, who accompanied His Majesty on horseback when he went out, slept in the passages of the tent, not to have his sleep disturbed, necessary as it was to him. The secretaries slept in the passages. The grand officers and duty officers ate wherever and however they could. Like simple soldiers, they did not scruple to eat with their hands. Prince Berthier [*sic*] had his tent close to the Emperor's. He always lunched and dined with him. The meals were served on campaign by M. Collin, the food-taster, and by Roustam or one of the valets.'

Chapter 11. An Army Vanishes

1. My account is essentially made up of Caulaincourt's, Labaume's, Laugier's, Dedem's and Bonnet's.

2. Despite all Gourgaud's urgings at St Helena, Napoleon would never write his own account of the 1812 campaign; so we, too, can only speculate.

3. Straying about for a whole week searching for his own division, Biot had already discovered that in Russia's sandy soil 'footprints of men and horses leave a very feeble mark, and vanish totally at the least breath of wind'.

4. Napoleon could be amazingly quick on the uptake. Others too would notice that the Witebsk people, 'though Polish, no longer cared for the Polish cause'. Soltyk says they had no confidence in a French victory.

5. Lefèbvre-Desnouëttes had been taken prisoner when his Chasseurs of the Guard had been routed in Spain. Like Lejeune, he'd broken his parole (at Cheltenham) and got back to France.

6. Schwarzenberg, in command of the 30,000-strong Austrian contingent, was

defending the Grand Army's extreme right flank in Galicia and Volhynia. See next chapter, when another of his officers arrives.

Chapter 12. Worries at Witebsk

1. After its setback at Babinowiczi Dumonceau's troop had encountered some French chasseurs escorting an officer bearing orders to Davout to rejoin at Witebsk. Just as his regiment was entering the town he'd met with an acquaintance who'd had his arm shattered at Ostrovno, and whose days as a hussar were over. He was looking for another friend, Captain Monceau ('son of the Marshal') to get him a post back in France. This can only be the Captain Monceau of the 7th Light who, Sergeant Bertrand says, had 'just come from the Imperial pages' and would distinguish himself at Smolensk and Valutina.

2. Delaborde's folding campaign desk is to be seen in the museum at Antibes. Whether it's the one he used in Russia I don't know.

3. Only the Guard had a real medical service; otherwise there were only the regimental surgeons, a body of often thinly experienced but intrepid men who tended to be cold-shouldered by their fellow-officers until their services were suddenly needed. Over and over again Napoleon had turned a deaf ear to Larrey's remonstrances and petitions. Back in January an order had been issued that each regiment should bring with it 'eight medical officers, ten mattresses, twelve litters, a box of amputation instruments, 100 kilos of lint, 125 kilos of bandages and a box of medicines weighing at least five kilos' – a risible supply for between 1,000 and 2,500 men, especially as, for every man killed in battle, eight others afterwards succumbed to gangrene – sometimes tetanus, from rusty saws – or typhus. Whatever Gourgaud may say – he can't understand why if the artillery parks could keep up the pace the ambulances couldn't – Ségur is certainly right in regarding the shortage of medical equip-

ment as Napoleon's own fault. After Waterloo Larrey, captured by the Prussians, would be placed in front of a firing squad and only saved in the nick of time by a British officer.

4. Chambray was an artillery officer. He would be the campaign's first objective historian.

5. In 1813 Dedem would serve as *de facto* divisional general under Ney, who would ask for his formal promotion to that rank. But Napoleon had a long memory, and recalling Dedem's critical attitudes in Russia refused it.

6. 'Not Voltaire's,' says Fain, 'which he regarded as unreliable, but Adlerbeth's'. The Voltaire was a little volume bound in green morocco, as we know from Mailly-Nesle who would borrow it during the retreat.

7. His letters to Marie-Louise are the only ones he wrote in his own hand. There is no question of his uxorious devotion to this 20-year-old Austrian princess, niece of Marie-Antoinette's, who after his exile to Elba would capriciously abandon him for the one-eyed Austrian Count Neipperg.

8. Napoleon seems to have had a pathological – but also perhaps justifiable – antipathy to taking medicine of any kind. And indeed, according to the Swedish researcher Sten Forshuvud, it would be through Montholon's 'medicine' he would finally be assassinated. See *The Murder of Napoleon*, by Ben Weider and David Hapgood, Congdon & Lattès Inc., NY, 1982.

9. Napoleon said he took more pleasure in this book, bound in red leather and kept up to date by Hyde d'Ideville, 'than a girl in a novel'. During the retreat it would be captured by the Russians, who were so impressed by its detailed accuracy that they reproached the French with having stolen its contents.

10. This according to Labaume, who however isn't trustworthy in matters he didn't personally witness, and who can only have

been told about this by Eugène. Indeed it's hard to see why Napoleon should have rejoiced at Alexander's rumoured asassination, since he was counting on his own former ascendancy over him to make peace after his 'good battle'.

11. Begos' book, which is also found in *Soldats Suisses au Service Etranger*, Geneva, 1909, was inspired by a need to stress the part played by the Swiss, which he felt Thiers had overlooked.

12. Gourgaud calls him so, and scorns Flahaut's 'pirouettes' at Malmaison in 1815, after Waterloo, when he not merely deserted Napoleon but indulged in sarcastic remarks about the paucity of those who weren't doing so. Flahaut, said to be an illegitimate son of Talleyrand, had an affair with Napoleon's step-daughter, the ill-used Queen Hortense, and is believed to have been the father of her son Napoleon III.

13. A week of exhausting forced marches across endless swamps on roads built on piles or 'here and there crude hides, impracticable either for men or horses' had brought Schwarzenberg's Austrians into Volhynia. On 26 July General Kleingel's advance guard had bumped into Tormassoff's, coming up from the south, and been overwhelmed. After nine hours' bitter fighting, while he'd waited in vain for Reynier to come to his support, Kleingel's 2,500 Saxons, driven back into a convent, had surrendered, together with eight guns. Whereupon Reynier had had to beat a hasty retreat to Slonim and call on Schwarzenberg to come to his support. It was in this predicament that Schwarzenberg had sought orders. Grüber says he saw Napoleon at Minsk. But since Napoleon was never anywhere near that city, he can only mean Witebsk.

Chapter 13. The Great Manoeuvre

1. Since forests in those days were not the object of modern silviculture they were usually impenetrable. Hundred-year-old pines and spruces lay entangled criss-cross and only foresters' and – in ironmaking

districts – charcoal-burners' paths gave uncertain and unmapped access to their depths.

2. Tascher would worry endlessly about the fate of Sergeant-major Lelerc who was 'suffering on his behalf', nor did he cease trying to find out what had become of him. But though he sent a flag of truce and 25 golden louis he never heard from him again.

3. Barclay even seems to have been bewildered by it, marching and countermarching his troops to no purpose until, suddenly he is informed that the Tsar, yielding to popular opinion – which regards his sage withdrawals as mere cowardice, if not treachery – has relieved him of the supreme command of both armies. Naturally this doesn't improve the collaboration with Bagration, who scornfully refers to him as 'the Minister' [i.e., of War, which he also was] and is openly declaring him a traitor.

4. It was by no means an illiterate army. In the 33rd Line, Dedem had found 500 privates worthy of non-commissioned rank, and 'more than 700 who understood the decimal system, the first three rules of arithmetic, the basic elements of campaign fortification; and 300 could have been placed as secretaries in a ministry of state'. Many of the officers were classically educated. Paul de Bourgoing came from a literary family and had a markedly literary sensibility. Captain Faré of the Foot Grenadiers had brought with him La Bruyères' *Charactères*, Fénélon's *Télémaque*, Lafontaine's *Fables* and 'above all' Horace, and was promising himself he'd relearn Latin as soon as he had time, to enjoy him in the original. Napoleon himself had a field-library of a hundred books, among them Voltaire's *Life of Charles XII of Sweden*, a 'little volume bound in green calf leather'. Having carefully perused it, together with a lot of other books about Russia, both old and new – not to mention two as yet unpublished works on the Russian army – he'd declared to more than one listener that he certainly wasn't going to make the same mistake as the Swedish military

hero, whose march on Moscow in 1708 had proved so utterly disastrous and marked the beginning of the end of the Swedish empire.

5. This defile, with steep unscalable sides, was approached by a bridge over a deep ravine, at the foot of a steep slope. Frozen, it would cause the loss of innumerable vehicles and guns during the retreat (15-17 November, the second Battle of Krasnoïe).

6. It would be Dombrowski's division, turned out of Minsk head over heels by Tchitchakoff in November, which would fail to secure the Berezina bridge at Borissow. Dombrowski had served with the French armies since 1796.

7. This suggests that up to 15 August he'd been keeping the exact purpose of his manoeuvre secret, even from his top commanders; which is not impossible.

8. Hastening up to Vilna to nurse her wounded husband at the turn of the month, Oudinot's heroic young duchess will in fact meet Hogendorp's equally young wife at Kovno, on her way back to Germany. She was very ill, and died soon after.

Chapter 14. The Walls of Smolensk

1. Most still stand, despite heavy fighting during the Second World War.

2. Here we can take our choice from other accounts of his costume on other occasions. Was it perhaps a 'hat with turned up brim, garnished with plumes and ostrich feathers'? Or did a 'Polish cap surmounted by an enormous panache' set off a 'goatskin waistcoat *à la chevalière*, with crimson trousers and yellow bootees'? Or perhaps over his shoulders a 'short gold-embroidered green velvet mantle, or an elegant fur, decked out with gold braidings and bullion, thrown over his shoulders'? Griois doesn't say.

3. It was in fact Bagration's Second West Army. Terrified that Barclay, 'to the ever-lasting disgrace of the 'Russian army', would tamely abandon Smolensk, and no longer being his subordinate, Bagration was marching at top speed to prevent the French from cutting the Moscow road.

4. It was actually Neverovski's division, being withdrawn while fresh troops poured into the city to relieve them.

Chapter 15. Smolensk – The First Shock

1. Probably the divisions or perhaps companies forming the column's width had been closed up to two paces from one another. A compact mass, it had little firepower but great weight.

2. Junot's health had been destroyed partly by excessive eating and drinking – he'd swallow 2 dozen oysters before dinner – but also by a sabre cut to his head, a wound, his wife says in her fascinating memoirs, which never quite healed. Junot would in fact become insane and commit suicide in the following year.

3. The nephew of Marshal Moncey's, referred to above.

4. He goes on: 'A mere spectator with no desire to get myself killed to no purpose, I crouch down behind a rampart where the musket-balls go whining over my head. Then ride back into Smolensk. The town seemed to have died. A few drunken or wounded men were staggering about in its abandoned streets. The suburbs were in flames. The military stores and some houses had been looted. Outside, the great battle thundered on. The bloodbath I'd just seen upset me intensely. I felt utterly abandoned. Suddenly I was overwhelmed by a fear so terrible I'd gladly have hid in a mousehole. Every loud explosion made me tremble.'

5. According to G.F. Nafziger's tables, these must have come from the 1st and 2nd Old Guard Foot Artillery (six guns + two howitzers, and the 1st Foot Artillery (six guns + two howitzers). No other corps had more than six 12-pounders. There

were no larger calibre guns, and most of the batteries consisted mainly of 6-pounders.

6. In fact it was a green notebook. M. Dufresne, the First Auditor, had an assistant whose sole business it was to implement all the Emperor's promotions and awards of medals and pensions, etc.

7. Edmund Burke: *On the Sublime and the Beautiful*, 1756.

8. In a letter written a couple of days later to a Parisian friend.

9. Scenes from that terrible night would brand themselves forever on the memory of a certain Ivan Maslow: 'The burning suburbs, the dense and variously coloured smoke, the red glow, the crash of exploding shells, the thunder of cannon, the crackling musketry, the beating drums, the moans and groans of old men, women and children, a whole population falling on its knees, arms upstretched to the skies... Crowds of inhabitants running from the flames without knowing whither... Russian regiments running into the flames, some to save lives, some to sacrifice their own... A long line of carts rolling slowly on, carrying away the wounded. As the twilight deepened, the Holy Mother of God, icon of Smolensk, was carried out of the city, while the dismal tolling of bells merged with the crash of falling houses and the din of battle.'

10. Césare de Laugier had described the scene in his diary: 'From time to time a stir passes through our camp: it's an ADC who's arrived from the battle being delivered under the walls of Smolensk. Eager for news, everyone surrounds the newcomer. Meanwhile the gunfire never ceases making itself heard. All of a sudden we're told a brigade of Italian light cavalry we've long been separated from after leaving it behind at Surash has turned up. Immediately the whole camp is thrown into commotion. Running up to our comrades we all throw ourselves into their arms, embracing them as if we hadn't seen each other for years. Everyone's terribly impatient to get into the battle and earn his share of distinctions. Pleased as Punch, the newly arrived chasseurs happily accept their comrades' praises, proudly showing off their scars and decorations. They give us some bread, meat and brandy, which we've so long lacked. The evening is all fireworks and bonfires, whose costs are defrayed by the wood where we're encamped.'

11. When, for instance, he'd heard from Napoleon in Madrid that he was offered the choice, not of the Spanish crown as he'd hoped, but between those of Portugal and Naples, he'd fallen ill and taken to his bed.

12. I have been unable to obtain a copy of this very rare book, and I am quoting from a quote.

Chapter 16. Death in the Sacred Valley

1. Barclay's evacuation of Smolensk had been no simple matter. Without so much as a by-your-leave, Bagration, furious to have to abandon the city, had made off along the Moscow highway; and Barclay, to avoid congestion and not expose his columns to possible French gunfire from the southern hills bordering the Dnieper, had therefore opted for a circuitous retreat route. His five divisions were to follow the Petersburg road northwards, then two parallel side roads which would enable them to debouch some ten miles along the Moscow road, the first at Lubino, the second – left-hand column – at Prouditchi. But the scheme had gone agley. Not only had his artillery got stuck in the ravines and bottomless lanes which had proved much less practicable than he'd expected: even his own coachman had gone astray. So that, waking up at dawn, he'd found himself within earshot of French clarions and drums. Not only his carriage, but an entire division had gone round in a circle!

2. Realizing that his entire army was in grave danger of being taken in flank and annihilated, Barclay had ordered young Prince Eugen of Württemberg to stage a diversion so as at all costs to hold up

Ney's advancing column long enough for the Russian van to reach the Lubino crossroads. It was Eugène's fire that was 'ploughing up the plain' near Faber du Faur.

3. It was here that the Russians had withstood the Poles in the 16th and 17th centuries.

4. '...which they'd probably inherited from the Austrians whose subjects they so long have been' von Suckow adds.

5. Oudinot was always getting wounded, more or less seriously. This time a fragment of grapeshot had shattered his shoulder. Of the campaign's premonitions and strange coincidences, the one experienced by his young duchess, whom he'd married just before setting out for Russia, was among the strangest and best authenticated. A bust of her husband, commissioned from a Berlin sculptor, was being unpacked when it fell to the floor and its shoulder had shattered. Shortly afterwards the news came that this was exactly what had happened to the living original! Defying the imperial ban on any woman crossing the Niemen, the intrepid young Duchess of Reggio had immediately set out for Vilna to tend her husband. – Despite numerous first-hand accounts it's impossible for reasons of space to describe in detail the First Battle of Polotsk. Both Colonel St-Chamans and Colonel Sebastien-Joseph de Comeau, the Bavarians' chief-of-staff, were wounded.

6. One of them, newly arrived from Vilna, was Surgeon Déchy, whom Napoleon had reprimanded for bringing his 13-year-old son with him to the wars. After the town's storming, writes Déchy, 'my father and I and other senior officers went and took possession of a superb house, recently abandoned, and which distinguished itself by its sumptuous furniture. Three days after we'd installed ourselves, a large and beautiful lady appeared,' the proprietress. All his life his son would remember her with affection and respect for the kindnesses she showered on him. When his father was ordered back to typhus-ridden Vilna she provided lavishly for their

journey. Was she perhaps the same countess who had befriended Le Roy in 1807?

7. Nine of these patients, Larrey adds proudly, would have completely recovered by the time he got back to Smolensk in November. The two others had died of dysentery. Among the more remarkable wounds 'was one inflicted on a corporal of the 13th Line. A large-calibre roundshot had smashed the head of the left humerus, the clavicle and whole of the shoulder-blade and neck muscles. The bone fragments had been flung on to the back, with the soft parts torn. A wound of terrifying appearance! This soldier, in a state of unbearable suffering, was demanding at the top of his voice that we rid him of the rest of his arm and a mass of bone splinters. Despite the little hope we could hold out for this unfortunate man, I attempted the following operation. Having removed the arm, which clung by a mere few shreds of flesh, and having tied the main artery, I extracted all the detached pieces of bone from the muscles and their periostea. I cut off the the main disorganized shreds. I brought together the frayed edges of this enormous wound and fixed them in place by using a few fascines where the blood had clotted and a large piece of linen soaked in a solution of sodium sulphate, with muriate of soda, some fine cotton pads and the scapular bandage completed the dressing. After the operation was over this wounded man became completely calm. I confided him to M. Sponville, one of the surgeons-major of the flying ambulances.' On the thirty-fifth day the patient would be evacuated from Smolensk back to Poland, 'and was on a good way to being cured. Since then I've had no more news of him, but there's every reason to believe this soldier's life was saved, unless he fell sick in some other way.'

Chapter 17. Stragglers and Prisoners

1. But in fact the sergeant was picked up by an ambulance, his leg was amputated in time, and the first person Heinemann, after his terrible experiences as a Russian prisoner of war, would see when he got

home was the sergeant calmly sitting on his doorstep, having married his girlfriend at Hildesheim.

2. Winzingerode would himself be taken prisoner, having ventured prematurely into Moscow as the French rearguard was abandoning it. Taken to Napoleon, he would be furiously berated and threatened as a 'traitor' since his domains lay within the French Empire. Sent under escort to France, he would be rescued by Cossacks before reaching Minsk.

3. The account of Heinemann's and his comrades' captivity is too awful, too long, and too circumstantial to print. 'Soon our column consisted of a variegated mixture of Spaniards, Frenchmen, Germans from the countries of the Federation of the Rhine, Prussians and Austrians, Hungarians, Croats, Italians and Poles, at nights huddled together in shacks and fighting one another with their fists – for lack of knives'. Particularly painful to the Spaniards and Italians (Heinemann says nothing about any Portuguese) was that the Russian peasants who'd been told they'd come to Russia

'to smash up all images of saints and didn't believe in any God, were real Antichrists. Already we'd burnt down Smolensk and now were going to do the same to Moscow. Curious to see such atheists, the peasants were attracted in droves from far and wide. Also the neighbourhood's superior Russians turned up. For them a kind of gallery of planks had been built for them to contemplate us prisoners from all nations who, beneath them, were lying or standing as best we could on the barn floor. Over our heads we could see broad bearded peasant faces, stupid and curious, peering down through the cracks in the roof. The well-to-do Russians had brought baskets filled with bread and turnips that excited our appetite. But when the hungry prisoners held up their hands and implored to be given some, the Russians were so embittered they couldn't bring themselves to give us any. "Franzus fse propall" ("Frenchmen all kaput"), they

mocked us and spat on us. "They aren't Christians," said others, and only rarely did anyone throw us down a bit of bread.'

And though some of the French, Italians and Spaniards make the sign of the cross in the Catholic fashion, to show what they are, the Russians shout back "Frenchmen not Christians – Frenchmen dogs!" Until a red-headed Protestant Westphalian forces his way forward and crosses himself in Orthodox fashion, 'whereupon they threw him all the bread and turnips he could possibly eat.'

Chapter 18. Dust, Hear and Thirst

1. '*M. le Duc.* You have received orders to leave Kovno and proceed to Vilna. You should march in four columns. At Kovno have ten pounds of rice taken out per man, which the ranker shall carry in his knapsack, and you must see to it that he does not consume more than one ounce a day. You will draw biscuit for six days, irrespective of how much you will be able to have transported behind you in light wagons. At Vilna you will draw food sufficient to reach Minsk, and at Minsk for as far as to Borissow, and at Borissow to Orsha. From Orsha to Smolensk your army corps must march by divisions, so as to arrive within three days: the cavalry shall march first. Exploit your presence to prepare a maximum of supplies along the road from Vilna to Minsk and Orsha. Since the Emperor is directing his march on Moscow, your corps cannot arrive too soon at Smolensk, in order to maintain our communications and form our reserve.'

2. He'd have been still more troubled had he known that it would be here, one frozen November evening amid scenes of horror and despair, that the Army of Italy would lose almost its last guns and the whole of its loot-swollen baggage train.

3. Evidently III Corps was led by the 1st or 2nd Portuguese Regiment. The 3rd was serving with II Corps. The Württembergers would have been part of Marchand's 25th Division. But the Spaniards must

have been those in I Corps, under Colonel Tschudi. Evidently Dumonceau's memory is confused as to the order in which they passed by.

4. This wasn't true. The Poles had suffered heavily, both during their attempts to catch Bagration and at Smolensk, where several generals had been wounded. Zalusky, of the 1st Guard Lancers writes: 'We greatly regretted that the Polish army hadn't been called to form the Army's right wing in Volhynia and Podonia' [instead of Schwartzenberg's Austrians]. 'We couldn't forgive Prince Joseph Poniatowski for having been so soft with Bagration.'

5. Turno's memoir is a particularly important source of information on the campaign, seen from the Polish point of view.

6. 'You have five cavalry depots: Kovno, Merecz, Minsk, Glubokoië, Lepel. You are to establish march squadrons.'

7. Lossberg's letter is in a collection of letters home.

8. The Viazma, a tributary of the Dnieper, was a river port, with a big barge-building industry.

9. The position had been selected by one of Kutusov's aides, but on closer inspection was found to be unsatisfactory.

Chapter 19. The Gathering Storm

1. Ghjat has been renamed Gagarin, after the first man in space, whose native town it evidently was.

2. Montbrun and Auguste Caulaincourt, leading the Polish Lancers of the Guard, had carried the heavily gunned pass of Somosierra, an exploit which had made the regiment's name.

3. This was a gross exaggeration. Napoleon estimated the true figure at 30,000. In fact it was only 15,000.

4. Although he didn't know it, the *konya* would save his life in the tightest of all spots, at the Berezina.

5. Caulaincourt's daily record, in which he among other things notes the various horses ridden by Napoleon from day to day, is in the *Archives de l'Itinéraire du Général Caulaincourt.*

6. Quoted at third hand from Christopher Duffy's *Borodino, and the War of 1812,* which in turn quotes from P. Holzhausen's *Die Deutschen in Russland,* Berlin, 1912.

7. It is possible that the action may have been screened from IV Corps by a fold in the ground. Laugier makes no mention of it. The idea of fortifying and defending the mound, originally intended only as an observation point, had been Bennigsen's. 'He'd chosen the position and didn't want to lose face. Consequently on 5 September he sacrificed six or seven thousand brave men and three guns.' See Christopher Duffy: *Borodino and the War of 1812,*1972. I have followed the order of his account of Borodino throughout.

8. Not to be confused with the 2nd Guard Lancers.

9. An anonymous German general calls it so.

10. A contestible statement, as will be seen at Mojaisk on 8/9 September, where Napoleon's mental activity, though he was still suffering acutely from all these symptoms, clearly remained undiminished. Probably it wasn't his cognitive but his conative faculties, his energy, which suffered at Borodino and may well have affected the outcome, or so various generals, including St-Cyr, would afterwards think.

11. Napoleon's heartbeat was extraordinarily slow, only 50. On St Helena he'd tell Gourgaud that he had never felt his own heart beating.

Chapter 20. The Mouths of the Guns

1. 'I spent the rest of this day at this honorable task,' Lejeune goes on, 'which made me make a more exact study of the locality. The Emperor received my sketches, recognized the places he'd seen and seemed satisfied. On his return he'd ordered Bacler d'Albe to demand a similar work to mine from the topographical engineers; and before evening fell an elevation drawing had been made of the Russian positions.' Cf., what Labaume has to say, below.

2. Some writers say 18, others 24 guns, all of heavy calibre.

3. According to Elzéar Blaze, less so than Western European armies.

4. This meticulously revised version is the basis of the earliest known map of the Battle of Borodino, the one Labaume would print in his book two years later.

5. From right to left: Poniatowski (V), Davout (I) supported by Nansouty's, Montbrun's and Latour-Maubourg's cavalry corps, Ney (III), Junot (VIII) (headed by Morand's division and backed up by the Guard artillery, its cavalry, the Young Guard, and Old Guard), and, north of the Kolotchka behind and beyond Borodino, Eugène (IV), supported by Gérard's and Morand's divisions and Grouchy's Cavalry Corps and with extra light cavalry (Otnano's Bavarians and Italians) to guard the army's left.

6. Captured by Cossacks, they are to be read in Holzhausen. See bibliography.

7. The chaplain of the French colony in Moscow, Adrien Suffugé, would be horrified to find that the French army didn't have a single chaplain to show for itself. This single detail, like so many others, seems to show that the Napoleonic military cult should be regarded as a kind of proto-totalitarian religion in itself, forerunner of our modern ones.

8. Gérard's painting wasn't the only portrait of the King of Rome to reach Napoleon in Russia. At Smolensk an auditor of state had brought him a miniature of the little boy seated on a sheep, by Mademoiselle Aimée Thibault. Hung in Napoleon's room in the Kremlin, Gérard's large portrait would be lost during the retreat. Luckily the artist had made several copies.

9. Next day the army would see the bringer of bad tidings 'fighting on foot as a volunteer, to demonstrate that the Army of Spain, despite its resounding defeat, was worthy of the Army of Russia'.

10. At St. Helena, on Saturday, 27 April 1817, Napoleon would tell Gourgaud he'd made a mistake: 'At the battle of the Moscowa I was wrong to attack the Russians' entrenched positions. The fact was, I was thirsting for a great battle, for an army which has plenty of good cavalry and which can manouevre behind a system of good redoubts should never be attacked. One should manoeuvre him out of his position.'

11. Quoted at second hand from Curtis Cate's *The War of the Two Emperors*.

12. Fain, who was passing the night in the company of Caulaincourt's brother, declares explicitly that Rapp's memoirs err.

Chapter 21. Holocaust at Borodino

1. 'The first roundshot he sent in our direction hit Marshal Davout's horse,' Planat goes on. 'It fell at once, dragging under it its rider, whom we thought was seriously wounded. But the marshal got up laughing and had another horse brought to him.' If this is true and Planat's memory isn't confusing the incident of two hours later, then Davout must have lost two horses shot under him at Borodino, a detail no other writer mentions. See Le Roy's account of what happened at 8 a.m.

2. The Jäger regiment had been placed there in the teeth of Barclay's wishes. Césare de Laugier, who was looking on, says there were several bridges. But no

one else mentions more than one in front of the Italians. There were others to their right, constructed during the night.

3. '...delivers the 106th,' Laugier goes on, 'and, obedient to orders, returns in triumph to Borodino'. But as yet Laugier isn't watching, and his account of the outcome differs from all others.

4. Actually V Corps had got off to a slow start. It wouldn't begin seriously to attack the Russian left until about 8 a.m. For events in that sector see Duffy, *op. cit.*, whose lucid account of the battle I shall in the main be following. I've taken the description of what it felt like to be in such an assault column of infantry from Heinemann, *op. cit.* Heinemann, of course, wasn't at Borodino – with his fellow-prisoners he was still being herded on by Cossacks to a camp in the far north. But he describes how the novices in Compans'columns must have felt.

5. Actually it was the 3rd (Dutch) Grenadiers. They would be virtually wiped out during the retreat.

6. 'The outcome justified him,' Girod de l'Ain goes on, 'but it was thanks to a combination of circumstances as happy as fortuitous, and above all improbable. Even so, he was condemned to suffer all his life from his wound, from which splinters kept coming out even ten years later.'

7. How far away was Larrey's dressing-station? No one else makes any mention of Napoleon's leaving his post to visit Rapp there.

8. It was Colonel Achard, it will be remembered, who at Salta-Novka had had to turn Davout round to see how close the Russians were.

9. When Dumont tells this story to Sergeant Bourgogne, just before reaching Moscow, he calls it the 'great redoubt'. Perhaps he in fact thought afterwards that it was the Great Redoubt the 61st had attacked. In fact it can only have been one of the flèches. Florencia of course is the same Spanish cantinière Bourgogne

had met at Witebsk, and the dead drummers the ones who'd entertained him to supper there.

10. General Kutaisoff, leading them, was one of those who fell.

11. Standing on an emplacement 'measuring about 1 square verst' [135,000 sq yds] Prince Nicholas Boris Galitzin, too, was thinking the gunfire
'unexampled in the annals of murderous battles. The fire of our pieces doesn't hold up the French. Scorning danger, they keep closing their ranks as the grapeshot carries them off, and marching to almost certain death they continue to advance at a steady pace, with sloped arms and a remarkable impassivity. Though they can only advance by trampling on their comrades' bodies, they're already on the point of reaching our guns. At this critical moment, at a signal from Bagration, the whole Russian line, headed by its commander-in-chief, advances. Bayonet is crossed with bayonet and a hand-to-hand fight of extermination begins. The cavalry, hastening up from either side into this horrible mêlée, finally climaxes the confusion; and soon infantrymen, troopers, gunners, Russian and French, form only a single confused mass, with everyone dealing out death to whomever falls under his hand.' – Galitzin, Prince Niocolas Boris: La Bataille de Borodino, par un témoin oculaire, St. Petersburg, 1840.

12. This may be rhetorically true, but not factually. Caulaincourt's *Itinéraire* records that the Emperor that day rode three of his horses: Lüzelberg, Emir and Courtois. Pion des Loches even says he 'didn't give a single order', which is certainly absurd and therefore casts doubt on the accuracy of everything else he says. An anonymous eye-witness says about 100 ADCs came and went for orders during the battle. Dedem says he was sitting 300 paces ahead of the redoubt, all the while holding his miniature of his son 'which the Empress had sent him by M. de Bausset. He toyed with it, and often repeated: "he

must see what he'll have to at 25". This sounds apocryphal. Dedem, presumably at the head of his brigade in Friant's division, can hardly have been so close an eye-witness.

13. As far as I know this is the only historical evidence to justify Tchaikowsky's introduction of the Marseillaise into his overture. Otherwise this highly revolutionary and anti-authoritarian ditty was forbidden throughout the Empire period, and Rouget de l'Isle, who in a flash of inspiration had composed both words and music to sing at a salon in Strasburg (not Marseilles!) had remained an obscure and unrewarded infantry captain. Only as an old man did he become famous, but even then hardly outside the confines of his own district.

14. A most dangerous thing to do, if he really did it. One could easily misjudge the force left in a spent roundshot and lose one's foot.

15. This must have been after Friant's division had been flung in, see below.

16. It is a – for us – curious but persistent complaint among our officer eye-witnesses that they had no one to do their laundering for them. To have to wash even one's own handkerchiefs was clearly about the most humiliating thing they could experience!

17. Though Bagration 'at first tries to hide his condition, he's overcome by pain and his wound betrayed by the blood dripping from his boot; and is helped from his horse and laid out on the greensward. Finally he has to retire, his glance still turning back to the battlefield.' – Prince Galitzin's account, quoted in Brett-James, *op. cit.*

18. Von Meerheimb's account is to be found in Holzhausen's collection of memoirs of the campaign.

19. '... by no means unsteady soldiers (as Ségur falsely says),' writes Faber du Faur indignantly; 'for it was these Württembergers who'd taken the flèche after a bloody fight and would defend it until the end of the battle'.

20. Ouvarov was severely reprimanded for making such a mess of his diversion. It was only years afterwards that he and his fellow Russian generals realized that he had saved Russia from the disaster which would have overtaken its army had Napoleon, in his usual manner, thrown in the Imperial Guard through the hole that, between 11 and 1 o'clock, had been blasted in the Russian centre. Only the Prussians' timely arrival at Waterloo would save Wellington from exactly the same catastrophe.

21. So-called by the Russians, after General Raevsky, who had had it thrown up. He fell in the battle.

22. Duffy calls Schreckenstein's memoir 'probably the most useful account by a survivor of the battle'. He was in Latour-Maubourg's IV Cavalry Corps.

23. There was also M. de St-P***, squadron-leader in the 5th Hussars 'whose colonel had even undertaken in General Montbrun's presence to issue him with a certificate of officerly cowardice any day he asked for it. Several times he'd let his men charge without accompanying them. At Inkowo he'd even slid from his horse and surrendered!' There were also many other strange and idiosyncratic characters, like the one described by Blaze who, being quite exceptionally hirsute, stripped to the waist and at whose furious charge the enemy, as if seeing a bear, as often as not would flee the field. Another regimental officer who admitted to everyone that he was terrified at the sight of the enemy, used to charge them *sitting back to front* on his horse.

24. Dedem says Montbrun had 'just come to ask for the Emperor's orders, and died charging at the head of his cavalry'. The first statement may be true, the second certainly isn't. Indeed much of what Dedem has to relate about the battle seem to be based on ill-founded hearsay. Similarly, Séruzier says Montbrun was 'hit

in the chest and dropped dead at my feet'. And Vossler that he was killed by a howitzer. But Biot's account is the most circumstantial, and anyway Montbrun didn't die until the evening.

25. It was made up of the Saxon Zastrow Cuirassiers, a Polish lancer division, a Westphalian brigade and a Saxon and Polish regiment. The Zastrow Cuirassiers, writes Roth von Schreckenstein, 'wore very heavy, bullet-proof, black iron cuirasses, though only the breast. At that time it was still not considered fitting for a cuirassier to ride a chestnut, or a grey, or a piebald, though the officers rode horses of all colours. The Cuirassiers of the Saxon Guard and the Zastrow Cuirassiers had much smaller, though sturdy horses, either black or very dark-bown, supplied by dealers as Mecklenburgers.'

26. A reference to the occasion three years before when he'd taken some dragoons and forced the Tagus.

27. Only a few paces away from the spot where Montbrun had fallen, Lejeune admiringly saw Ney 'standing there on the parapet of one of the flèches, directing the combatants swarming at his feet, who only lost him from sight when he was enveloped in swirling smoke!' Seeing Grouchy and his staff standing on the edge of the ravine behind Griois' guns, Ney sends for him:
'Hardly am I beside him than the enemy begins firing on our group and a few moments afterwards several ordnance officers and staff officers are killed or wounded by the grapeshot. General Grouchy's horse, stricken in the chest by a roundshot, falls on top of his master, whom we take for dead, but who gets off with a bad bruise.'

28. From Planat's brief account it's not quite clear that the 2nd Carabiniers' charge was part of the assault on the Great Redoubt. But Lejeune has placed the stricken Ferdinand pathetically in his elegant painting, and no doubt for a good reason. Lejeune's painting of the capture of the Raevsky Redoubt is more iconographic than realistic. In the *foreground*

Ferdinand is receiving first aid (which Planat says didn't happen until in the evening after the fighting was over) while a much-slimmer-than-in-reality Napoleon hands back (an equally idealized) General Likhatcheff his sword. Meanwhile in the *background* the Great Redoubt, its height considerably exaggerated, is still being stormed! Although great care has been lavished on details of uniforms, etc., the whole is reminiscent of an ancient Egyptian battle painting, where successive events are shown simultaneously.

29. Griois writes 'at about 2 or 3 p.m.'. We who are used to modern communications and transport can find it hard to realize how much time it took to organize and carry out troop movements in those days.

30. Some historians have questioned whether Auguste Caulaincourt's role in the storming of the Great Redoubt has not been exaggerated, all too naturally, by his brother.

31. In fact they must have been gunners. But there also seem to have been some Russian infantry placed along the front of the redoubt, outside it.

32. Mailly-Nesle was related to, but not a direct descendant of, the illustrious Marshal de Mailly. This kind of preferential treatment of scions of the old nobility with illustrious names (wounded at Tarutino, Mailly-Nesle would spend a large part of the retreat in a comfortable carriage with some ladies and two doctors!) seems to have been a feature of Napoleon's declared policy of integrating the old aristocracy in his regime. But Fézensac, who belonged to it, tells us that behind his back and among themselves such privileged officers used to refer to the Emperor as 'M. Bonaparte'. And almost all would desert him in 1814.

33. On the Russian side Prince Galitzin, too, could
'compare nothing to the picture offered by this scene of carnage, whose theatre was the redoubt, at the moment which decided its fate. You'd

have thought it was a volcano vomiting flames and smoke from every point in its circumference. This burning mountain, attacked on all sides, thunders, explodes, pours torrents of fire. Then, suddenly, all this uproar is followed by a lugubrious silence. The cavalryman sabring, the infantryman striking out and defending himself by blows of his butt or bayonet, the clashing of weapons, the sun reflected on the steel, the helmets, the cuirasses, the yells coming out of this horrible mêlée – all this made of this terrible scene a picture worthy of the ablest painter's brush. Without fear of contradiction one can say it was one of the most magnificent horrors ever met with in war.'

34. Afterwards whenever he tidied it up and beat it 'the place where the brains had been flung appeared in the shape of a greasy spot like a *memento mori*'.

35. Caulaincourt's account of the battle's closing stages seems rather blurred, no doubt because of the shock of his brother's death. But his testimony concerning Berthier's and, this time, Murat's dissuading Napoleon from sending in the Guard, and of Napoleon's 'hesitation' is of course as crucial as it is reliable.

36. But his 'intelligent horse' has. Along its neck the hair had been shaved as by a razor, without touching the skin, and it had had another such close shave above one hoof.

37. On Kutusov's declaring he'd resume the battle next day, Barclay had even ordered it to be retaken at dawn. After spending the day drinking and eating with sycophantic young officers several miles from the battlefield, Kutusov had sent off the news of his great victory to Petersburg. Later that night, after a council-of-war, he would change his mind and order a general withdrawal. For glimpses of the battle as seen from the Russian side, see Duffy, *op. cit.*

Chapter 22. The Butcher's Bill

1. Next year the peasants would have to bury a total of 58,521 corpses and the carcasses of 35,478 horses.

2. 'Passing behind the Grand Redoubt we saw its broad interior sloping sharply down towards us, all encumbered with corpses and dead horses jumbled up with overturned cannon, cuirasses, helmets and all sorts of scattered wreckage in an indescribable confusion and disorder.' – Dumonceau. Moving forward a month later to a village recently evacuated by a light cavalry unit, Vossler would see how 'the first corpses lay singly, then in heaps. Often my horse couldn't find a way through them and I had to ride over the bodies, the horror of the scene mounting as I passed. Soon I reached the Raevsky Redoubt. Here the corpses lay piled higher and higher. The ditches were filled to the brim with bodies. I found bodies by the hundred in the Württemberg uniform. The top of these fortifications provided a comprehensive view of almost the entire field of battle. Sword and shot had raged terribly everywhere. Men and horses had been gashed and mashed in every conceivable way, and on the faces of the fallen Frenchmen you could still discern the various emotions in which death had overtaken them: courage, desperation, defiance, cold unbearable pain and, among the Russians, passionate fury, apathy and stupor.'

3. One of the colonels killed was the man who'd shattered Robespierre's jaw with a pistol shot.

4. Quoted from J.T. James: *Views of Russia, Sweden and Poland*, London, 1826.

5. For V Corps' contribution to the battle see Duffy, op. cit. Dumonceau may not have been impressed by the Poles' losses, but they'd made a vital contribution by drawing off major forces to the Russian left wing which would have been badly needed in the centre.

6. Among those who were wounded was 'the youthful Colonel Sopransi of the 7th Dragoons, a young Italian, son of Mme. Visconti' – Berthier's adorata. Griois says he was wounded in the ankle, Castellane in the knee.

7. The episode is not to be found in Ségur's impersonally and rhetorically written history but in his autobiography *Du Rhin à Fontainebleau*. Is this one of Ségur's flights of fancy? Why was Napoleon alone? Why on foot? The whole incident seems strange – yet at the same time strangely convincing. A similarly surprising encounter would happen to Dedem outside Smolensk during the retreat.

8. 'But in those huge armies', Planat goes on, 'one didn't enquire too closely into such matters. When twelve or fifteen hundred surgeons have to be appointed one takes what one can find.' Blaze, too, describes these tyros' immense incompetence, how they used rusty saws for amputations, etc., with the result that the ratio of those who died after a battle to those killed during it was usually 8:1. This does not mean there weren't also many well-trained and dedicated men, like Déchy's father.

9. Colonel Ponthon, it will be remembered, was the engineer officer who, brought back to Paris from St Petersburg to join Napoleon's war cabinet, had (according to Caulaincourt) gone down on his knees to beg him not to invade Russia.

10. Planat's categorical statement confirms at first hand the Moscow chaplain Adrien Suffugé's statement. Probably it applies first and foremost to the French units. But I have not found any mention of military chaplains in any of the German accounts either. Nor does Laugier refer to one among the Italians. Almost certainly the Poles must have had chaplains.

11. Refusing to be sent back to Vilna, Aubry would finally reach Moscow thanks to his *cantinière*, who, 'in tears', lent him 400 francs, and to a voltigeur who'd shot a hare. Upon his offering his benefactress a portion she reprimanded the voltigeur for 'paying attention to such useless targets'.

12. Kergorre would afterwards be so fortunate as to have his conduct approved.

Chapter 23. The Last Lap

1. While at the Kremlin, Caulaincourt would have to ask Napoleon to do something for his brother Auguste's ADCs. Strangely, Napoleon had never shown the least interest in their fate after Auguste Caulaincourt's heroic death at Borodino.

Chapter 24. 'Moscow! Moscow!'

1. In the early 19th century very few westerners knew anything about the interior of Russia. It was only after 1812 that such travel books as J. T. James's *Journal* and R. Johnston's *Travels through the Russian Empire and country of Poland* (1815), R. Ackermann's *Sketches of Russia* (1814) and Edouard de Montulé's *Voyage en Angleterre et en Russie* (1825) began to appear. Indeed the first map of Siberia had been made only a century earlier by a Swedish prisoner of war from Charles XII's army.

2. This kind of passage is typical of Ségur, whose vivid account under close examination often tends to fall to pieces. Which marshals? It could only be Davout and Ney; and such an about-face, not to say such adulation, is utterly unlike either of these two men's ways of thinking. On the other hand Ségur may well have been present. Perhaps the wrong word is 'marshals'? From Fain we know that a great deal of flattery and adulation went on from 'courtiers' at IHQ. – Caulaincourt would afterwards remember him as having been 'on the last height overlooking Moscow, called Sparrow Hills' when he got the news. This seems to be an instance of two memories fusing together.

3. According to Roos the first units to enter Moscow were the 10th Polish

Hussars, followed by Prussian Uhlans and the Württemberger Chasseurs.

4. The Arsenal was a large modern building in neo-Classical style. It was found to contain huge stores of British muskets.

5. I have merged Laugier's and Labaume's descriptions.

6. 'All hearts, all feet have wings / How light has now the march become! / How brightly shines the sun on arid fields / and in the zenith stands when now appears / Jerusalem, it's reached, ah yes / Jerusalem, it's there, acclaimed / in unison of voices thousandfold, / Jerusalem!' – Tasso: *Gerusalemme Liberata*.

7. It would remind Soltyk of Hampton Court.

8. The outbreak of fire in the Bazaar – or as others called it the Stock Exchange – on the evening of the 14th remains a mystery. Was it caused by pillaging soldiers of the Guard? Or by civilian looters? Or had one of the incendiaries, drunk perhaps, not waited for the agreed signal at 9 p.m. on the evening of the 15th and jumped the gun? Afterwards, too, many of our eye-witnesses seem very naturally to have confused their memories of the events of the night of 14/15 September with those of the much more terrible night of 15/16th. I have disentangled them as best I can.

9. '...and in fact I sent one. But it couldn't find the palace and for several days went astray in the immense deserted city'.

10. Of Murat's 42,000 horsemen only 18,000 had reached Moscow. Davout's magnificently trained I Corps, originally 79,000, strong, was down to 29,000. Ney's III Corps, once 44,000 strong, was down to a mere 11,000. And of the 50,000 men of IV Corps who had paraded so brilliantly at Glogau in May there were only 24,000 infantry and 1,600 cavalry. (Of Pino's once magnificent 15th Division's 13,000 men, only 4,000.) And of the 39,000 Poles of Poniatowski's V Corps, only 4,844 infantry and a mere 868 cavalry. In worst case of all was Junot's VIII Corps, back at Mojaisk.

Even the Imperial Guard, taken as a whole, had suffered terrible losses, even though, its artillery apart, it hadn't fired a shot. Of an original 50,000 men, 17,871 infantry and foot artillery, 4,609 cavalry and horse artillery had reached Moscow. Although Chambray's figures refer to effectives shortly before leaving Moscow in mid-October, give or take a little they must be approximately valid for arrival there. The campaign's first serious historian seems to have gone to much trouble to check the figures.

BIBLIOGRAPHY

Adam, Albrecht. *Aus dem Leben eines Schlachtenmalers. Selbstbiographie nebst einem Anhange herausgegeben von Dr. H. Holland.* Stuttgart, 1886

Aubry, Capitaine Thomas-Joseph. *Souvenirs du 12ème de Chasseurs, 1799-1815.* Paris, 1889

Augusta, Duchess. *In Napoleonic Days. Extracts from the private diary of Augusta, Duchess of Saxe-Coburg-Saalfeld, Queen Victoria's maternal grandmother, 1806-1821.* Selected and translated by HRH the Princess Beatrice. London, 1941

Bacler d'Albe, Baron Louis-Albert-Guislain. *Souvenirs Pittoresques.* 2 vols., Paris, 1898-92

Barre de Nanteuil. *Le Comte Daru, ou l'Administration Militaire sous la Révolution et l'Empire.* J. Peyronnet & Cie, Paris, 1966

Bausset Joseph, Baron de. *Mémoires anecdotiques sur l'intérieur du palais...* 2 vols., Baudoin, Paris, 1827-9

Beauharnais, Eugène de. *Mémoires et correspondance politique et militaire du prince Eugène, annotés et mis en ordre par A. Du Casse.* 10 vols., Lévy, Paris, 1858-60

Beaulieu, Drujon de. *Souvenirs d'un militaire pendant quelques années du règne de Napoléon Bonaparte.* Paris, 1831

Begos, Louis. *Souvenirs de campagnes du lieutenant-général Louis Begos, ancien capitaine adjudant-major au 2ᵉ régiment suisse au service de la France.* Delafontaine, Lausanne, 1859, and in *Soldats suisses au service étranger.* Geneva, 1909

Belliard, Augustin-Daniel. *Mémoires du comte Belliard, lieutenant-général, pair de France, écrits par lui-même, recueillis et mis en ordre par M. Vinet, l'un de ses aides-de-camp.* Paris, 1842

Berthezène, General Baron Pierre. *Souvenirs Militaires de la République et de l'Empire.* 2 vols., Paris, 1855

Bertin, Georges. *La Campagne de 1812 d'après des témoins oculaires.* Flammarion, Paris, 1895

Bertrand, Vincent. *Mémoires du capitaine Vincent Bertrand, recueillis et publiés par le colonel Chaland de la Guillanche.* Siraudeau, Angers, 1909

Beulay, Honoré. *Mémoires d'un grenadier de la Grande Armée (18 avril 1808 - 18 octobre 1815).* Préface du commandant Driant, Champion, Paris, 1907

Biot, Hubert-François. *Souvenirs anecdotiques et militaires du Colonel Biot, aide de camp du Général Pajol, avec une introduction et des notes par le comte Fleury.* Vivien, Paris, 1901

Blaze, Elzéar. *La Vie Militaire sous l'Empire,* Garnier Freres, Paris, 1837. English editions: 'Recollections of Military Life' in Sir Charles Napier (ed.), *Lights and Shades of Military Life,* Henry Colburn, London, 1850; and *Recollections of an Officer in Napoleon's Army.* Meras, New York, 1911

Bonaparte, Napoleon. *Correspondance de Napoléon 1ᵉʳ, publiée par ordre de l'Empereur Napoléon III.* 32 vols., Imprimerie impériale, Paris, 1858-70

Borcke, Johann von. *Kriegerleben des Johann von Borcke, weiland kgl. preuss. Obersteleutnants, 1806-1815, nach dessen Aufzeichnungen bearbeitet von V. Leszynski.* Mittler, Berlin, 1888

Boulart, Jean-François. *Mémoires Militaires du Général Baron Boulart sur les Guerres de la République et l'Empire.* Librairie Illustrée, Paris, 1892.

Bourgeois, Réné. *Tableau de la campagne de 1812, par Bourgeois témoin oculaire.* Dentu, Paris, 1814

Bourgogne, Adrien-Jean-Baptiste-François. *Mémoires publiés d'après le manuscrit original, par Paul Cottin.* Paris, 1898. *The Memoirs of Sergeant Bourgogne, 1812-1813,* Heinemann, London and Doubleday, New York, 1899; and Peter Davies, 1926. Reprinted with a foreword by David G. Chandler. Arms & Armour Press, London, and Hippocrene Books, Inc, New York, 1979

Bourgoing, Baron Paul-Charles-Amable de. *Souvenirs d'histoire contemporaine. Épisodes militaires et politiques.* Paris, 1864; and *Souvenirs militaires du Baron de Bourgoing (1791-1815), publiés par le Baron Pierre de Bourgoing.* Plon-Nourrit, Paris, 1897

Boyen, L.H.C. von. *Erinnerungen aus dem Leben des General-Feldmarschalls Hermann von Boyen.* 3 vols., Hirzel, Leipzig, 1889

Brandt, Heinrich von. *Souvenirs d'un officier polonais. Scènes de ma vie militaire en Espagne et en Russie (1808-1812).* Ed. Baron Ernouf, Charpentier, Paris, 1877

Bréaut des Marlots, Jean. *Lettre d'un capitaine de cuirassiers sur la campagne de Russie, publiée par Leher.* Chez tous les librairies, Paris, 1885

Brett-James, Antony. *1812; Eye-witness accounts of Napoleon's Defeat in Russia.* Macmillan, London, and St. Martins, New York, 1966

Bro, Louis. *Mémoires du Général Bro (1796-1844), publiés par son petit-fils le Baron Henry Bro de Comères.* Paris, 1914

Bussy, Marc. in *Soldats Suisses au service de la France.* Geneva, 1909

Calosso, Jean. *Mémoires d'un Vieux Soldat.* Gianini, Turin, 1857

Castellane, Victor-Elisabeth Boniface, comte de. *Journal du maréchal de Castellane (1804-1862).* 5 vols., Plon-Nourrit, Paris, 1895-7

Cate, Curtis. *The War of the Two Emperors.* Random House, New York and Weidenfeld, London, 1989

Caulaincourt, Armand de. *Mémoires du Général de Caulaincourt, Duc de Vizence, Grand Ecuyer de l'Empereur.* Introduction and notes by Jean Hanoteau. 3 vols., Plon-Nourrit, Paris, 1933. English translation in 2 vols.; vol.1 *Memoirs of General de Caulaincourt,* Cassell, London, 1935 and *With Napoleon in Russia,* Morrow, New York, 1935; vol.2 *No Peace With Napoleon,* Morrow, New York and Cassell, London, 1936

Chambray, Marquis de. *Histoire de l'Expedition de Russie.* Paris, 1825

Chandler, David. *The Campaigns of Napoleon.* Macmillan, New York, 1966, and Weidenfeld, London, 1966. *Dictionary of the Napoleonic Wars.* Macmillan, New York, 1979, and Arms and Armour Press, London,

1979; also Simon and Schuster, New York and Greenhill Books, London, 1993. *The Illustrated Napoleon.* Henry Holt, New York and Greenhill Books, London, 1990

Chevalier, Jean-Michel. *Souvenirs des guerres napoléoniennes, publiés d'après le manuscrit original par Jean Mistler et Hélène Michaud.* Paris, 1970

Chlapowsky, Désiré. *Mémoires sur les guerres de Napoléon (1806-1813), publiés par ses fils. Traduits par Jan Celminskiet Malibran.* Plon-Nourrit, Paris, 1908

Clausewitz, Karl von. *La Campagne de 1812 en Russie, traduit de l'allemand par Loredan Larchey, d'après le manuscrit original.* Paris, 1883. Translated from the original 'Feldzug 1812 in Russland' in *Hinterlassene Werke über Krieg und Kriegfuhrung* (1832-1837). Dummler, Berlin. English edition *The Campaign of 1812 in Russia.* 1843; and Greenhill Books, London, 1992

Coignet, Capitaine Jean-Roch. *Cahiers.* Hachette, Paris, 1883. *The Notebooks of Captain Coignet,* Davies, London, 1928; reprinted Greenhill Books, London, 1986.

Combe, Michel. *Mémoires du colonel Combe sur les campagnes de Russie (1812), de Saxe (1813), de France (1814 et 1815).* Blot, Paris, 1853

Comeau de Charry, Sébastien-Joseph, Baron de. *Souvenirs des Guerres d'Allemagne pendant la Révolution et l'Empire.* Plon-Nourrit, Paris, 1900

Compans, Jean-Dominique. *Le Général Compans (1769-1845), d'après ses notes de campagne et sa correspondance de 1812 à 1813, par son petit-fils M. Ternaux-Compans.* Plon-Nourrit, Paris, 1912

Constant, *see* Wairy

Curely, Jean-Nicolas. *Le général Curely. Itinéraire d'un cavalier léger de la Grande Armée (1793-1815), publié d'après un manuscrit authentique par le général Thoumais.* Berger-Levrault, Paris, 1887

Davout, Maréchal Louis-Nicolas, Prince d'Eckmühl. *Correspondance du Maréchal Davout, 1801-1815, avec introduction et note par Ch. de Mazade.* 5 vols., Paris, 1885

Déchy, Edouard. *Souvenirs d'un garde du corps du roi de la compagnie de Noailles, suivis de souvenirs d'Allemagne et de Russie.* Paris, 1869

Dellard, Baron Jean-Pierre. *Mémoires Militaires du général Baron Dellard sur les guerres de la Révolution et de l'Empire.* Paris, 1892

(Dedem) van der Gelder, Baron Antoine-Baudoin-Gisbert. *Mémoires publiés d'après le manuscrit original par Jean Puraye.* 3 vols., Brussels, 1958-63

Denniée, P.P. *Itinéraire de l'Empereur Napoléon.* Paris, 1842

Duffy, Christopher. *Borodino, and the War of 1812.* Seeley, Service, London, 1972. Scribner, New York, 1993.

Dumas, Mathieu. *Souvenirs de Lieutenant-Général Comte Mathieu Dumas de 1770 à 1836, publiés par son fils.* 3 vols., Paris, 1839

Dumonceau, François. *Mémoires du Général Comte François Dumonceau, publiés d'après le manuscrit original par Jean Puraye.* 3 vols., Brepols, Brussels, 1958-63

Dupuy, Victor. *Souvenirs Militaires, 1794-1816.* Calmann-Lévy, Paris, 1892

Dutheillet de La mothe, Aubin. *Mémoires du Lieut-colonel Aubin Dutheillet de la Mothe.* Brussels, 1899

Duverger, P.T. *Mes Aventures dans la Campagne de Russie.* Paris, nd

Faber du Faur, G. de. *La Campagne de Russie (1812), d'après le journal illustré d'un témoin oculaire. Texte explicatif, par F. de Kausler, Introduction par A. Dayot.* Flammarion, Paris, 1895

Fabry, Lieutenant G. *Campagne de Russie (1812). Publié sous la Direction de la Section Historique de l'Etat-major de l'Armée.* 5 vols., Lucien Gougy, Paris, 1901-3

Fain, Baron Agathon-Jean-François. *Manuscrit de Mil-Huit Cent Douze, contentant le précis des événements de cette année, pour servir à l'histoire de l'Empereur Napoléon; par le Baron Fain, son Secrétaire-Archiviste à cette époque.* 2 vols., Delannay, Paris, 1827 and *Mémoires du Baron Fain, Premier Secrétaire du Cabinet de l'Empereur, publiés par ses arrière-petits-fils.* Plon-Nourrit, Paris, 1908

Fantin des Odoards, Louis-Florimond. *Journal du général Fantin des Odoards. Etapes d'un officier de la Grande Armée, 1800-1830.* 4 vols., Plon-Nourrit, Paris, 1895

Faré, Charles-Armand. *Lettres d'un jeune officier à sa mère, 1803 à 1814.* Delagrave Paris, 1863

Faure, Raymond. *Souvenirs du Nord ou la guerre, la Russie et les Russes ou l'esclavage.* Paris, 1821

Fézensac, M. le Duc de. *Souvenirs militaires de 1804 à 1814.* Dumaine, Paris, 1863. *A Journal of the Russian Campaigns of 1812,* London 1852; Trotman, Cambridge 1988.

François, Charles. *Journal du Capitaine François (dit le Dromadaire d'Egypte), 1793-1830.* 2 vols., Carrington, Paris, 1903-4

Fusil, Louise. *Souvenirs d'une Femme sur la retraite de Russie.* 2 vols., Dumont, Paris, 1841. New edn. 1910

Förster, Friedrich. *Preussen und Deutschland unter der Fremherrschaft, 1807-1813.* Berlin, nd. *Napoleons I Russischer Feldzung 1812.* G. Hempel, Berlin, 1856

Giesse, Friedrich. *Kassel-Moskau-Kustrin Tagebuch während des russischen Feldzuges.* Dyk, Leipzig, 1912

Girod de l'Ain, Général Baron. *Dix ans de mes Souvenirs militaires (de 1805 à 1815).* Dumaine, Paris, 1873

Gourgaud, Gaspard. *Napoléon et la Grande Armée en Russie. Examen critique de l'oeuvre de M. de Ségur.* Bossange, Paris, 1825

Gouvion St-Cyr, Laurent de. *Mémoires pour servir à l'histoire militaire sous le Directoire, le Consulat et l'Empire.* 4 vols., Anselin, Paris, 1831

Grabowski, Jozef. *Mémoires Militaires.* Plon-Nourrit, Paris, 1907

Griois, Lubin. *Mémoires du Général Griois, 1792-1822.* 2 vols., Plon-Nourrit, Paris, 1909

Grüber, Carl-Johann Ritter von. *Souvenirs du chevalier Grüber, publiés par son neveu. Traduits de l'allemand avec des notes par Maleissye.* Paris, 1909

Guitard, Joseph-Esprit-Florentin. *Souvenirs militaires du Premier Empire. Mémoires d'un grenadier de la Garde, publiés pour la première fois par E.H.Guitard.* Paris, 1934

Heinemann, Wilhelm. *Bilder från mina Krigs- och Vandringsår, af Wilhelm Heinemann, enligt hans muntliga berättelser, bearbetade och meddelade af H.E.R. Belani.* Trans. from the German. Stockholm, 1835

Henckens, Lieutenant J.L. *Mémoires se rapportant à son service militaire au 6ème Régiment de Chasseurs à cheval français de février 1803 à août 1816. Publiés par son fils E.F.C.Henckens.* Nijhoff, The Hague, 1910

Herzen, A. *Erinnerungen von Alexander Herzen, aus dem Russischen übertragen, herausgegeben und eingeleitet von Dr. Otto Buck.* 2 vols., Wiegandt und Grieben, Berlin, 1907

Hochberg, Wilhelm, Graf von. *La Campagne de 1812. Mémoires du Margrave de Bade. Traduction, Introduction et Notes par Arthur Chuquet.* Paris, 1912

Hogendorp, Dirk van. *Mémoires du général Dirk van Hogendorp, comte de l'Empire, publiés par son petit-fils.* Nijhoff, The Hague, 1887

Holzhausen, Paul. *Die Deutschen in Russland, 1812. Leben und Leiden auf der Moskauer Heerfahrt.* Morawe und Scheffelt, Berlin, 1912

Jacquemot, Porphyre. 'Carnet de route d'un officier d'artillerie (1812-1813)' in *Souvenirs et Mémoires,* pp. 97-121, 1899

Jomini, Baron Henri de. *Précis de l'Art de Guerre.* Paris, 1838, augmented with appendix, 1855. *The Art of War.* J.B. Lippincott & Co., Philadelphia, 1862, and Greenhill Books, London, 1992

Kergorre, Alexandre Bellot de. *Un commissaire des guerres pendant le premier empire. Journal de Bellot de Kergorre, publié par le vicomte de Grouchy.* Paris, 1899

Kerkhove de. *Histoire des maladies observées à la Grande Armée pendant les campagnes de Russie en 1812 et en Allemagne en 1813.* Anvers, 1836

Kügelgen, Wilhelm von. *Jugenderinnerungen eines alten Mannes.* Ebenhausen bei München, new edn. 1907

Kurz, Hauptmann von. *Der Feldzug von 1812. Denkwüdigkeiten eines württembergischen Offiziers.* ed. Horst Kohl. Esslingen, 1838; new edn. Leipzig, nd

Labaume, Eugène. *Rélation circonstanciée de la campagne de Russie.* Panckoucke, Paris, 1814. *A circumstantial narrative of the Campaign in Russia.* London, 1814. Also translated as *The Crime of 1812 and its Retribution.* Andrew Melrose, London, 1912.

Lagneau, L. A-A, Comte de. *Journal d'un Chirugien de la Grande Armée, 1803-1815.* Ed. Eugène Tattet, Emile-Paul, Paris, 1913

Langeron, L. A-A-, Comte de. *Mémoires de Langeron, Général d'infanterie dans l'armée russe. Campagnes de 1812, 1813, 1814. Publiés d'après le manuscrit original pour la Société d'histoire contemporaine, par L.-G. F.* Picard, Paris, 1902

Larrey, Dominique-Jean. *Mémoires de chirurgie militaire et campagnes.* J. Smith, Paris, 1812-17

Laugier, Césare de. *La Grande Armée: Récits de Césare de Laugier.* Ed. M. Henry Lyonnet. Fayard, Paris, 1910

Le Roy, C.F.M. *Souvenirs de Leroy, major d'infanterie, vétéran des armées de la République et de l'Empire.* Dijon, 1908

Lecointe de Laveau, G. *Moscou avant et après l'Incendie, par G.L.D., témoin oculaire.* Paris, 1814

Legler, Thomas. *Beresina.* Bern, 1942

Lejeune, Louis-François. *Mémoires du Général Lejeune,* publiés par M. Germain Bapst, 2 vols., Firmin-Didot, Paris, 1895-6

Lettres interceptées par les Russes durant la campagne de 1812, publiées d'après les pièces communiquées par S.E.M. Gorainow, Directeur des Archives de l'Etat et des Affairs étrangères de Russie et annotées par Léon Hennet et le Commandant E. Martin. Paris, 1913

Lignières, Marie-Henry, Comte de. *Souvenirs de la Grande Armée et de la Vieille Garde Impériale.* Pierre Roger, Paris, 1933

Lossberg, General Leutenant Friedrich Wilhelm von. *Briefe in die Heimath geschrieben während des Feldzuges 1812 in Russland.* Cassel, 1844

Mailly(-Nesle), Adrien-Augustin-Amalric, Comte de. *Mon journal pendant la campagne de Russie écrit de mémoire après mon retour à Paris.* Paris, 1841

Marbot, Antoine-Marcellin. *Mémoires du Général Baron de Marbot.* 3 vols., Plon-Nourrit, , Paris, 1891. *The Memoirs of Baron de Marbot.* 2 vols., Longmans Green & Co., London, 1892, and Greenhill Books, London, 1988

Maret, Hugues Bernard, duc de Bassano. *Souvenirs intimes de la Révolution et de l'Empire, recueillis et publiés par Mme Ch. de Sor.* 2 vols., Brussels, 1843

Martens, Carl von. *Dänkwürdigkeiten aus dem Leben eines alten Offiziers. Ein Beitrag zur Geschichte der letzten vierzig Jahre.* Arnold, Dresden and Leipzig, 1848

Martens, Christian Septimus von. *Vor fünfzig Jahren. Tagebuch meines Feldzuges in Russland, 1812.* Schaber, Stuttgart and Oehringen, 1862

Mayer, Louis. *Soldats Suisses au service de la France.* Geneva, 1909

Meerheimb, Franz Ludwig August von. *Erlebnisse eines Veteranen der grossen Armee während des Feldzuges in Russland, 1812, herausgegeben von dessen Sohn Richard von Meerheimb.* Arnold, Dresden, 1860

Méneval, Baron Claude-François de. *Mémoires pour servir à l'histoire de Napoléon I depuis 1802 jusqu' à 1815.* Paris, 1894. English edn., London, 1894

Montesquiou, Ambroise Anatole Augustin, Comte de. *Souvenirs de la Révolution, l'Empire, la Restauration, et le règne de Louis-Philippe.* Ed. Robert Barnaud, Paris, 1961

Murat, Joachim. *Lettres et documents pour servir à l'histoire de la France, 1761-1815, publiés par le Prince Murat, avec une introduction et des notes par Paul de Brethona.* Paris, nd

Nafziger, George F. *Napoleon's Invasion of Russia,* with a foreword by David Chandler. Presidio Press, Novato, 1988.

Noël, Colonel Jean-Nicholas-Auguste. *Souvenirs militaires d'un Officier du Premier Empire, 1795-1832.* Berger-Lerrault, Paris, 1895

Oginski, Michel. *Mémoires de Michel Oginski sur la Pologne et les Polonais, depuis 1788 jusqu' à la fin de 1815.* 4 vols., Ponthieu, Paris, 1826-27

Olivier, Daira. *L'incendie de Moscow.* Laffont, Paris, 1964. *The Burning of Moscow.* Allen & Unwin, London, 1966

Oudinot, Marie Charlotte. Récits de guerre et de Foyer. Paris, 1894. Also *see* Stiegler

Paixhans, General Henri-Joseph de. *Retraite de Moscou, Notes écrites au Quartier-Général de l'Empereur.* Metz, 1868

Pelleport, Pierre Vicomte de. *Souvenirs militaires et intimes du général vicomte de Pelleport de 1793 à 1853, publiés par son fils sur manuscrits originaux, lettres notes et documents officiels laissés par l'auteur.* 2 vols., Paris, 1857.

Peyrusse, Guillaume. *Lettres inédites du Baron Guillaume Peyrusse, écrites à son frère André pendant les Campagnes de l'Empire de 1809 à 1814.* Perrin, Paris, 1894

Pils, François. *Journal de marche du Grenadier Pils, (1804-1814), recueilli et annoté par M. Raoul de Cisternes. Illustrations d'après des dessins originaux de PILS.* Ollendorff, Paris, 1895

Pion des Loches, Antoine-Augustin. *Mes Campagnes (1792-1815). Notes et correspondance du colonel d'artillerie Pion des Loches, mises en ordre et publiées par Maurice Chipon et Léonce Pingaud.* Paris, 1889

Planat de la Faye, Nicolas Louis. *Vie de Planat de la Faye, aide-de-camp des généraux Lariboisière et Drouot, officier d'ordonnance de Napoléon 1ᵉʳ. Souvenirs, Lettres, dictés et annotés par sa veuve.* Ollendorff, Paris, 1895

Potocka, Anna. *Mémoires de la Comtessse Potocka, 1794-1820, publiés par Casimir Stryienski.* Plon-Nourrit, Paris, 1897

Pradt, Dominique-Georges-Frédéric de Fourt de. *Histoire de l'Ambassade dans le Grand Duché de Varsovie en 1812.* Paris, 1815

Puybusque, L.-G. de: *Souvenirs d'un invalide pendant le dernier demi-siècle.* 2 vols., Paris, 1840

Rambuteau, Claude Philibert Barthelot, *Mémoires du Comte de Rambuteau, publiés par son petit-fils.* Lévy, Paris, 1905

Rapp, Jean. *Mémoires écrits par lui-même et publiés par sa famille.* Bossange, Paris, 1823. *Memoirs of General Count Rapp.* Henry Colburn, 1823 and Trotman, Cambridge, 1985

Reggio, Duchesse de. *See* Stiegler

Rellstab, Ludwig. *Aus meinem Leben.* 2 vols., Berlin, 1861

Richter, Adrian Ludwig. *Lebenserinnerungen eines deutschen Mahlers, ausgegeben von Heinrich Richter.* Frankfurt-am-Main, 1885

Roch-Godart. *Mémoires du général-baron, Roch Godart, 1792-1815, publiés par J.B. Antoine.* Paris, 1895. New edn Flammarion, nd

Rochechouart, Louis-Victor-Léon, Général Comte de. *Souvenirs sur la Révolution, l'Empire et la Restauration, publiés par son fils.* Plon-Nourrit, Paris, 1889

Roeder, Helen. *The Ordeal of Captain Roeder, from the Diary of an Officer of the First Battalion of Hessian Lifeguards during the Moscow Campaign of 1812-13, translated and edited from the original manuscript.* Methuen, London, 1960. Original German edition is: Röder, Franz. *Der Kriegszug Napoleons gegen Russland im Jahre 1812. Nach den besten Quellen und seinen eigenen Tagebüchern dargestellt nach der Zitfolge der Begebenheaiten* Leipzig, 1848

Roguet, François. *Mémoires militaires du lieutenant-général comte Roguet, colonel en second des grenadiers à pied de la Vieille Garde.* Dumaine, Paris, 1862-5

Roos, Heinrich von. *Avec Napoléon en Russie. Souvenirs de la campagne de 1812, traduits par le lieutenant-colonel Buat. Introduction et notes par P. Holzhausen.* Chapelot, Paris, 1913. And *Souvenirs d'un médecin de la Grande Armée, traduits d'après l'édition originale de 1832 par Mme Lamotte.* Perrin, Paris, 1913. These are translated from the original *Ein Jahr aus meinem Leben oder Reise von den westlichen Ufern der Donau an die Nara, südlich von Moskva, und zurück an die Beresina, mit der grossen Armee Napoleons, im Jahre 1812.* St. Petersburg, 1832

Rosselet, Abraham. *Souvenirs de Abraham Rosselet, lieutenant-colonel en retraite au service de la France. Publiés par R. de Steiger.* Attinger, Neuchâtel, 1857

Rotenhan. *Dänkwürdigkeiten eines württembergischen Offiziers aus den Feldzuge im Jahre 1812. Veröffentlicht durch Freiherrn von Rotenhan.* Berlin, 1892. 3rd edn., Finsterlin, Munich, 1900

Roustam Raza. *Souvenirs de Roustam, mameluck de Napoléon. Introduction et notes de Paul Cottin. Préface de Frédéric Masson.* Paris, 1821

Ruppel, Eduard. *Kriegsgefangene im Herzen Russlands, 1812-1814.* Paetel, Berlin, 1912

St-Chamans, Alfred-Armand-Robert. *Mémoires du Général Comte de Saint-Chamans, ancien aide-de-camp du Maréchal Soult, 1802-1832.* Plon-Nourrit, Paris, 1896

Sauvage, N.J. *Rélation de la Campagne de Russie.* Paris, nd

Scheltens. *Souvenirs d'un vieux soldat belge de la garde impériale.* Brussels, 1880

Schlosser, Ludwig Wilhelm Gottlob. *Erlebnisse eines sachsischen Landpredigers in den Kriegsjahren von 1806 bis 1815.* Leipzig, 1846

Schrafel, Joseph. *Merkwürdige Schicksale des ehemaligen Feldwebels im köngl. bayer. 5te Linien-Infanterie-Regiment, Joseph Schrafel, vorzüglich im russischen Feldzuge und in der Gefangenschaft, in den Jahren 1812 bis 1814, von ihm selbstbeschrieben.* Nuremberg, 1834

Schreckenstein, Roth von. *Die Kavallerie in der Schlacht ander Moskwa.* Schendorff, Münster, 1858

Schuerman, Albert. *Itinéraire Général de Napoléon 1er.* 2nd edn., Paris, 1911

Ségur, Philippe, Comte de. *Histoire de Napoléon et la Grande Armée en 1812.* Paris, 1824. Also: *Du Rhin à Fontainebleau. Mémoires du Général Comte de Ségur (aide-de-camp de Napoléon).* Edn. Nelson, 1910. *History of Napoleon's Expedition to Russia*, 2 vols., London, 1825s. *Napoleon's Russian Campaign*, Joseph, London, 1959

Sérang. *Les prisonniers français en Russie. Mémoires et souvenirs de M. le marquis de Sérang, recuellis et publiés par M. de Puybusque.* 2 vols., Paris, 1837

Séruzier, Théodore-Jean-Joseph, Baron. *Mémoires militaires du baron Séruzier, colonel d'artillerie légère, mis en ordre et rédigés par son ami M. Le Mière de Corvey.* Paris, 1824.

Soltyk, Comte Roman. *Napoléon en 1812. Mémoires Historiques et militaires sur la Campagne de Russie.* Bertrand, Paris, 1836

Staël, Germaine de. *Mémoires de Dix Années d'Exil.* Paris, 1848. *Ten Years Exile.* London, 1821

Stendhal, M. de. *Journal de Stendhal (1801-1814), publié par Casimir Stryienski et François de Nion.* Paris, 1888. *The Private Diaries of Stendhal.* London, Gollancz, 1955. And *Vie de Henri Brulard, nouvelle édition établie et commentée par Henri Martineau.* Le Divan, Paris, 1953

Stiegler, Gaston. *Le Maréchal Oudinot, Duc de Reggio, d'après les souvenirs inédits de la Maréchale.* 2nd edn., Plon-Nourrit, Paris, 1894. *Memoirs of Marshal Oudinot compiled from the hitherto unpublished Souvenirs of the Duchesse of Reggio by G. Stiegler.* Henry, London, 1896

Suckow, Karl von. *Aus meinem Soldatenleben.* Stuttgart, 1862; French translation: *D'Iéna à Moscou, fragments de ma vie.* Paris, 1902

Surugué, l'Abbé Adrien. *Lettre sur l'Incendie de Moscou en 1812.* Paris, 1821; and *Un Témoin de la Campagne de Russie,* par Léon Mirot. Paris, 1914

Szymanowski, Général Joseph. *Mémoires, 1806-1814. Traduits du polonais par Bodhane Osckinczye.* Lavauzelle, Paris, 1900

Tarle, Eugene. *Napoleon's Invasion of Russia, 1812.* London and New York, 1942. Original edition Moscow, 1938

Tascher, Maurice de. *Notes de Campagne (1806-1813).* Chateauroux, 1938

Thirion, Auguste (de Metz). *Souvenirs Militaires, 1807-1818.* Paris, 1892

Tulard, Jean. *Bibliographie des Mémoires sur le Consulat et l'Empire, écrites ou traduites en français.* Librairie Droz, Genève-Paris, 1971

Van der Gelder, *see* (Dedem) van der Gelder

Vaudoncourt, Frédéric-Guillaume de. *Mémoires pour servir à la guerre entre la France et la Russie en 1812, par un officier de l'état-major française.* 2 vols., Deboffe, London, 1815

Villemain, Abel François. *Souvenirs contemporains d'histoire et de littérature.* 2 vols., Paris, 1854

Vionnet, Lieutenant-Général Louis-Joseph, Vicomte de Marignoné. *Campagnes de Russie et de Saxe, 1812-1813.* Also *Souvenirs d'un ex-commandant des Grenadiers de la Vieille Garde, avec une préface de Rodolf Vagnair.* Paris, 1899

Vossler, Heinrich August. *With Napoleon in Russia, the Diary of a Lieutenant of the Grand Army 1812-13.* The Folio Society, London, 1969

Wairy, Louis Constant. *Mémoires de Constant, premier valet de chambre de Napoléon Ier, avec une introduction et des notes par Arnould Halopin.* Paris, nd. *Memoirs of Constant.* Nichols, London, 1896

Walter, Jakob. *The Diary of a Napoleonic Foot Soldier,* edited and with an introduction by Marc Raeff, Windrush Press, Gloucestershire, and Doubleday, New York, 1991

Wedel, Carl Anton Wilhelm, Graf von. *Geschichte eines Offiziers im Kriege gegen Russland, 1812, in russischer Gefangenschaft 1813 bis 1814, im Feldzuge gegen Napoleon 1815, Lebenserinnerungen.* Asher, Berlin, 1897

Weider, Ben & David Hapgood. *The Murder of Napoleon,* Congdon & Lattès, New York, 1982

Wesemann, J.H.C. *Kanonier des Kaisers. Kriegstagenbuch der Heinrich Wesemann, 1808-14.* Ed: Ho. Wesemann. Verlag Wissenschaft und Politik, Cologne, 1971

Wilson, Sir Robert. *Narrative of Events during the Invasion of Russia by Napoleon Bonaparte, and the Retreat of the French Army, 1812.* Edited by his nephew and son-in-law, the Revd. Herbert Randoph. Murray, London, 1860. Also: *Private Diary of Travels, Personal Services, and Public Events, during Mission and Employment with the European Armies in the Campaigns of 1812, 1813, 1814, from the Invasion of Russia to the Capture of Paris.* Edited by the Revd. Herbert Randolph. 2 vols., J. Murray, London, 1861. Also: *General Wilson's Journal, 1812-1814,* ed. Antony Brett-James. Kimber, London, 1964

Ysarn de Villefort, François d'. *Relation du Séjour des Français à Moscou et de l'Incendie de cette Ville en 1812, par un habitant de Moscou.* Gadárnel, Brussels, 1871

Articles

Auvray, Pierre. 'Souvenirs militaires de Pierre Auvray, sous-lieutenant au 23ème régiment de dragons (1797-1815)' in *Carnet de la Sabretache,* 1919

Bonnet, Guillaume. 'Journal du Capitaine Bonnet du 18ème de ligne' in *Carnet de la Sabretache,* 1912

Butkevicius. 'Napoléon en Lithuanie 1812, d'après des documents inédits', trans. René Martel, in *La Revue de Paris,* 15 August 1932

Everts, Henri-Pierre. 'Campagne et captivité en Russie' in *Carnet de la Sabretache,* Paris, 1901

Kalckreuth, von. 'Erinnerungen' in *Zeitschrift für Kunst, Wissenschaft und Geschichte des Krieges.* Vol. V, 1835

Lyautey, Hubert. 'Lettres d'un Lieutenant de la Grande Armée' published by Pierre Lyautey in *La Revue des Deux Mondes,* 12 December 1962

Pastoret, Amédée-David, Marquis de. 'De Witebsk à la Bérézina' in *Revue de Paris,* April, 1902

Rambaud, Alfred Nicholas. 'La Grande Armée à Moscou. Récits de témoins oculaires russes. D'après l'ouvrage publié par T. Tolytchef' in *Revue des Deux Mondes.* Paris, 1 July 1873

Rossetti, Marie-Joseph-Thomas. 'Journal inédit' published by R. Recouty in *Revue de France,* Sept-Dec 1931, Jan-April 1932

Skalkowski, A. 'Les Mémoires du Général Turno' in *Revue des Etudes Napoléoniennes,* vol.II, pp. 99-116, 129-45, Paris, 1931

Turno, Boris. *See* Skalkowski, A

Zalusky, Joseph-Henri. 'Souvenirs du général comte Zalusky. Les chevaulégers de la garde dans la campagne de 1812' in *Carnet de la Sabretache*, 1897

MAPS

The campaign of 1812 dramatically illustrated in a graph drawn by Charles Joseph Minard (1781–1870) in 1861. The width of the line shows the strength of the army at each location. One can follow the invasion (tinted line) from left to right – Poland to Moscow – and the retreat (solid line) back to the left (west). The latter is linked to the temperature scale below, the temperatures indicated being in degrees Réaumur (in which 80° = 100°C = 212°F).

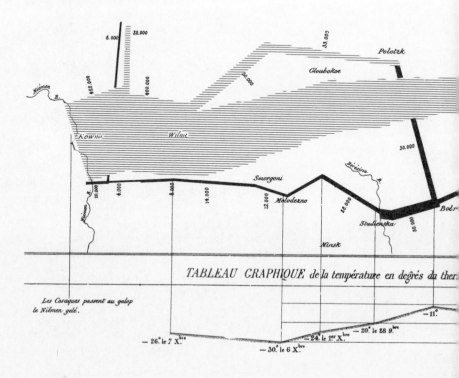

398

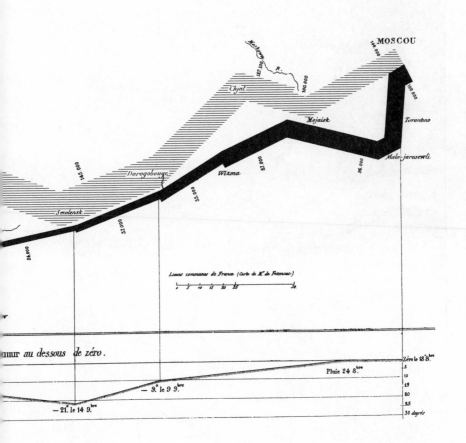

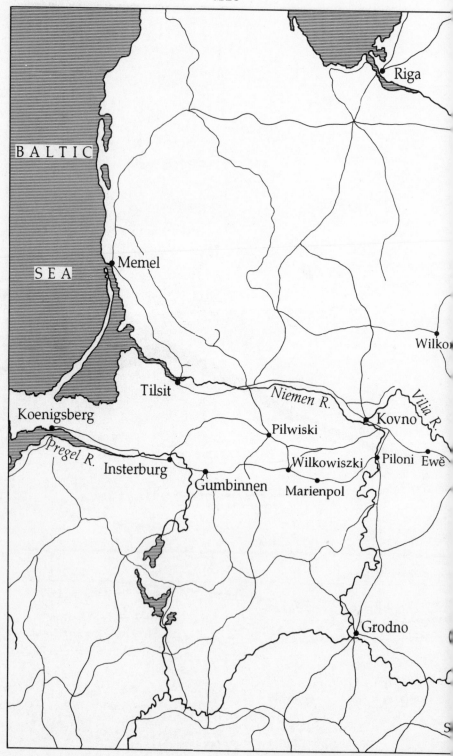

borg

Dwina R.

Drissa

Druï

Newel

Polotsk

Surash

Ostrowno

ntsiany

Glubokoïe

Witebsk

Beschenkowiczi

Liozna

Kamen

Babinowiczi

Berezina

Smoliany

Senne

Orsha

Czereia

iednicky

Pleschenkowiczi

Baranni

Toloczin

Dnieper R.

miana

Smorgoni

Studianka

Weselowo

Bobr

Borissow

Velejin

Minsk

Molihew

Salta-Novka

Niemen R.

Berezina R.

Mir

Slutsk

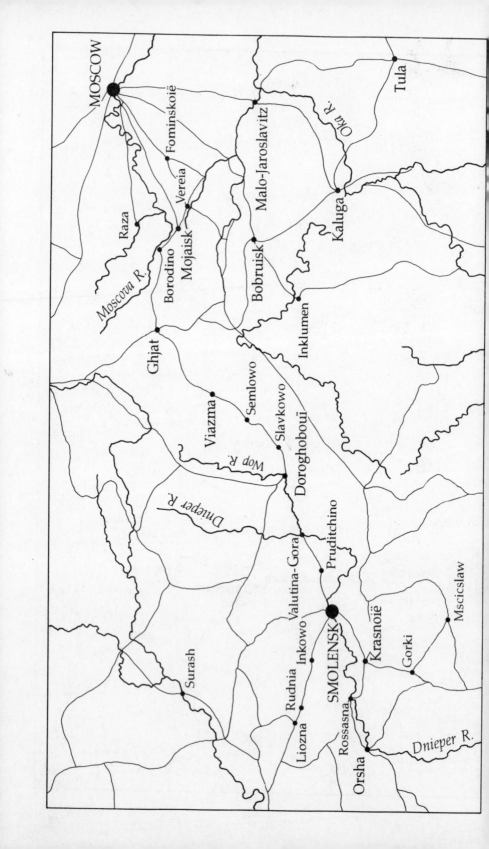

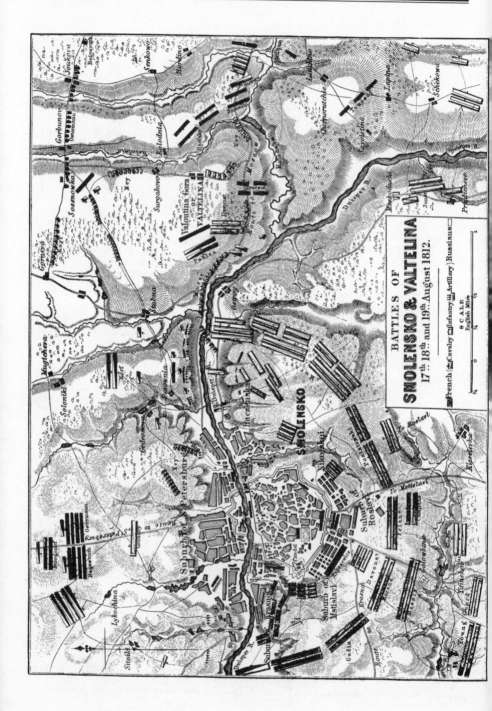

BATTLES OF
SMOLENSKO & VALTELINA
17th. 18th. and 19th. August 1812.

SCALE
English Miles

French ▬ Cavalry ▬ Infantry ▦ Artillery Russians ☐

INDEX